Multinationals in North America

THIS VOLUME MARKS the transition from the former Investment Canada Research Series to the Industry Canada Research Series. This Research Series, together with a Working Paper Series and an Occasional Paper Series, are part of the Industry Canada Publications Program. This program sponsors and produces applied public policy papers intended to contribute to informed debate over issues relating to the department, especially micro-economic policy and analysis.

The views expressed in all the papers in this volume are the responsibility of the individual authors: they do not necessarily reflect the opinions or policies of Industry Canada or the Government of Canada.

GENERAL EDITOR: LORRAINE EDEN

Multinationals in North America

The Industry Canada Research Series

The University of Calgary Press

© Minister of Supply and Services Canada 1994

ISBN 1-895176-47-6
ISSN 1188-0988

Reprinted 1996

University of Calgary Press
2500 University Dr. N.W.
Calgary, Alberta, Canada T2N 1N4

Canadian Cataloguing in Publication Data
  Main entry under title:
  Multinationals in North America

    (Industry Canada research series, ISSN 1188-0988 ; v.3)
    Issued also in French under title: Multinationales en Amérique du Nord.
    Includes bibliographical references.
    ISBN 1-895176-47-6

    1. International business enterprises—North America. 2. Free trade—North
America. 3. North America—Industries—Location. I. Eden, Lorraine, 1948- II. Series.
HD2755.5.M84 1993   338.8'887   C94-910067-6

This book was produced by Industry Canada with the assistance of the Centre for Trade
Policy and Law at Carleton University and the University of Ottawa.
The University of Calgary Press appreciates the assistance of the Alberta Foundation for
the Arts (a beneficiary of Alberta Lotteries) for its 1994 publishing program.

EDITORIAL & PUBLISHING CO-ORDINATION: Ampersand Communications Inc.
COVER & INTERIOR DESIGN: Brant Cowie/ArtPlus Limited

Printed and bound in Canada

⊗ This book is printed on acid-free paper.

Table of Contents

PART III   POLICY

PART IV LESSONS AND NEW DIRECTIONS

Preface

THIS INDUSTRY CANADA RESEARCH VOLUME was inspired by the rapidly changing economic landscape in North America. The Canada-U.S. Free Trade Agreement (FTA) and the North American Free Trade Agreement (NAFTA) are associated with falling trade and investment barriers in North America. At the same time, new technological products and processes are making it easier for firms to keep in touch with distant affiliates, raising the costs of new discoveries while product cycles are shortening, and increasing the need for firms to be close to their major markets and suppliers. Governments and multinational enterprises (MNEs) in North America are affected by these changes, but they also have a role in responding to the changes.

The focus of this volume is on the actions of multinational enterprises in North America and on the policies of the three national governments — Canada, the United States and Mexico. Numerous economic analyses have emphasized the special role that large firms can play in transferring technology, management and distribution expertise to smaller suppliers and customers through so-called "spillovers". Given the economic importance of MNEs and their contribution to economic growth and efficiency, it is important to understand how MNEs are responding to recent changes in technology, trade and investment policies. Many studies on the NAFTA and on regional integration have focused on international trade aspects, not on the reactions of MNEs. This volume is unique in its focus on the investment, production and trade strategies of MNEs and on their implications for policy making in the North American free trade area.

On May 20 and 21, 1993 distinguished academics from Canada, Europe, Mexico and the United States presented papers on issues relating to North American multinational enterprises at a conference in Ottawa. Incorporating comments received from discussants and participants at the conference, the authors revised their papers for publication in this volume. Under the direction of Lorraine Eden, who presided over the conference and served as General Editor for the volume, the revised papers and rapporteurs' comments now comprise the third volume in the Industry Canada Research Series.

Earlier volumes in the series emphasized issues linked to globalization and investment: *Corporate Globalization through Mergers and Acquisitions*, edited by Leonard Waverman; and *Foreign Investment, Technology and Economic Growth*, edited by Don McFetridge. The present volume, *Multinationals in North America*, serves to mark the transition from the former Investment Canada Research Series to the publications program of Industry Canada. The Industry Canada publications program, which also includes a Working Paper series and an Occasional Paper series, provides a forum for informed debate on a wide range of issues related to the work of Industry Canada. This new department is involved in micro-economic policy and analysis and thus the publication program is designed to allow the department to contribute to the policy-making debate in this area.

The research assembled in this volume is mostly the product of work undertaken outside the department by academic researchers from Canada, the United States, Mexico and England. Industry Canada staff, however, sponsored and managed the project, and offered comments on each of the papers. Nonetheless, the papers ultimately remain the sole responsibility of each author, and do not necessarily reflect the policies or opinions of Industry Canada or the Government of Canada.

I would like to take this opportunity to thank all of the authors for their work, particularly Lorraine Eden in her capacity as both author and General Editor. I know that this volume will be of interest to the policy-making community as well as to the wider public interested in economic issues here in Canada and abroad.

JOHN MANLEY
MINISTER OF INDUSTRY

Lorraine Eden
Professor
The Norman Paterson School of International Affairs
Carleton University

1

Multinationals in North America: An Introduction to the Issues

INTRODUCTION

MULTINATIONALS IN NORTH AMERICA examines the policy choices and actions of the largest business corporations and the three national governments in North America (defined as Canada, the United States and Mexico) as they respond to the enormous changes in technology and trade policies that began in the early 1980s and have continued into the 1990s. The volume focuses on MNEs and nation states in North America in the context of regional free trade (the Canada-U.S. Free Trade Agreement or FTA, and the proposed North American Free Trade Agreement or NAFTA) and technological change, as the underlying technology paradigm shifts from mass production to lean or flexible production. The core idea is that multinationals and nation states are actors faced by change and, at the same time, are agents of change. In this volume, we examine the strategic options and interactions of MNEs and nation states as they attempt to manage their activities in a globalized world economy.

The largest firms in each country are best placed to anticipate and to take advantage of on-going changes in trade policies and technology. How these firms make strategic decisions in the North American environment can act as a bellwether for medium-sized and small multinationals. Large multinationals are in the forefront of the movement towards a free trade area uniting Canada, the United States and Mexico. MNE crossborder flows of investment, technology, goods and services are hampered by international barriers; hence large firms have an interest in reducing barriers to trade and investment.

Multinationals are already heavily involved in the three economies. Over 50 percent of all Canada-U.S. trade and over 30 percent of Mexico-U.S. trade occurs among related affiliates. Approximately 25 percent of the non-financial capital stock in Canada (45 percent in manufacturing) is owned/controlled by foreigners, 9 percent in the United States and less than 10 percent in Mexico. The United States is the heaviest investor, controlling US$ 68 billion or 70 percent of the stock of foreign direct investment (FDI) in Canada and US$ 17 billion or 63 percent in Mexico in 1989. Japanese and

European multinationals are also large investors in all three North American countries.

Policy-makers are also actively involved in the creation of a North American free trade area. The Canada-U.S. Free Trade Agreement (FTA), which came into force in January 1989, will eliminate tariff barriers between the two countries over a ten-year period. Nontariff barriers are similarly being eliminated, reduced or harmonized. The FTA is much broader than a traditional free trade agreement because it also includes investment provisions and some liberalization of movement of professional workers. In addition, the three governments have negotiated a North American Free Trade Agreement (NAFTA), which is currently before the U.S. Congress for ratification. If, as proposed, the NAFTA comes into effect on January 1, 1994, an understanding of its likely effects on the organizational and locational decisions of MNEs is crucial for policy-makers. Even if a deal is not signed, the impetus for reduction of intra-North American trade barriers is likely to continue.

Investment policies among the three countries have already changed substantially since the 1980s. Canada and Mexico have both significantly relaxed their regulations on inward FDI; Mexico through investment and sectoral decrees, Canada through the 1985 restructuring of the Foreign Investment Review Agency (FIRA) into Investment Canada (now Industry Canada) and the investment chapter (e.g. national treatment) in the FTA. The United States, on the other hand, has increased its regulations on inward FDI in the past few years, partly due to the enormous increase in inflows over the 1980s. In 1988 the Exon-Florio amendment was passed, giving the President authority to disallow foreign takeovers on national security grounds. A screening process was set up under the Committee on Foreign Investment in the United States (CFIUS). In addition, the U.S. government has imposed new disclosure and taxation requirements on foreign firms. Thus, while all three countries have a relatively open attitude toward FDI, informal barriers remain and, in the case of the United States, formal barriers are increasing.

While trade and investment policies are more closely linking the three economies, there are on-going changes in process and product technologies — characterized in the terms "lean production", "flexible specialization" or "post-Fordism" — that are also influencing MNE organizational and locational choices. Firms are adopting less labour- and resource-intensive production methods, developing tighter linkages with suppliers and buyers, and adopting the new Japanese managerial methods such as just-in-time production and delivery and quality circles. Canadian businesses are being forced by globalized markets to downsize and grow leaner as they face increasing competition for shares of the world market.

Understanding how multinationals are responding to trade and technology in terms of investment, production and trade strategies changes is of critical importance to our understanding of the political economy of a NAFTA. Studies that focus on general equilibrium econometric modelling of regional trading blocs assume the firms that are trading are unrelated to one another, a clearly unrealistic assumption. Given the importance of MNEs in all three economies, it is therefore crucial that international trade studies of North American economic integration are accompanied by studies of the reactions of multinational enterprises to this integration. To date, most published works on the NAFTA have focused on its international trade aspects; this volume is different because it focuses closely on the strategic management of MNEs (i.e., their international production and investment decisions) and their implications for policy making in an evolving North American free trade area.

STRUCTURE OF THE BOOK

M*ULTINATIONALS IN NORTH AMERICA* contains 18 chapters on different aspects of MNEs and governments in North America written by leading experts in the field. The first versions of the papers were presented at an Ottawa conference organized and funded by Investment Canada (now Industry Canada), with the assistance of the Centre for Trade Policy and Law, in May 1993. My own paper, and the one prepared by Knubley, Legault & Rao of Industry Canada, were used as background papers to the conference. Also included in the volume is a revised version of the opening address to the conference given by C. Fred Bergsten, Director, Institute for International Economics, with comments by Sylvia Ostry, Director, Centre for International Studies, University of Toronto. Following two full days of sessions consisting of presentations by the authors, comments by invited discussants, roundtable discussions, and a concluding session with three Rapporteurs, the papers were revised for inclusion in this volume.

The volume is divided into four parts: *Theory, Evidence, Policy,* and *Lessons and New Directions.*

Part I, *Theory,* contains chapters by Vernon on the roles of MNEs and nation states in NAFTA; Eaton, Lipsey & Safarian in two chapters, the first on the theory of plant location in a free trade area, and the second on agglomeration and disagglomeration effects, both with application to the NAFTA; Rugman & D'Cruz on business networks as a new business organizational structure in North America; and Kogut on the importance of history and institutions as factors affecting MNE reactions to NAFTA.

Part II, *Evidence,* consists of seven chapters. The first, by Knubley, Legault & Rao, looks at multinationals in North America from a macro perspective (foreign direct investment patterns) and a micro perspective (activities of the largest 1,000 MNEs). The second chapter is my own study, which focuses on the location strategies of the veterans (the U.S. multinationals) while the third chapter by Westney looks at the immigrants (Japanese MNEs) in North America. The fourth (Dunning) and fifth (Encarnation) chapters contrast MNE trade and investment strategies in North America and the European Community. The last two chapters, by Unger and Niosi, examine FDI patterns since 1980 in Mexico and Canada respectively, and speculate about the impact of the NAFTA on these patterns.

In Part III, *Policy*, the studies center on government initiatives and responses regarding MNEs in North America. The first chapter, by Bergsten, with comment by Ostry, examines the need at the multilateral level for a new approach to regulating multinational investment. Kudrle provides an overview of national and sectoral regulation of MNEs in North America. The next three papers focus on particular policy areas: Frost & Graham on national security issues, Graham & Warner on competition policy, and Mayer on labour and environmental policies.

Part IV, *Lessons and New Directions*, draws together the lessons and new directions from the other chapters, as seen by the three Rapporteurs at the conference: Christopher Maule, Murray Smith and Alan Nymark.

Main Themes

THREE THEMES RUN THROUGH *Multinationals in North America*.

- How multinationals in North America, both domestic and foreign, have been, are and will be reorganizing themselves — in terms of both locational choices and organizational structures — as trade barriers fall within North America and as technological changes such as lean production alter the most efficient ways of doing business. This includes topics such as decisions on plant location and function, ownership, strategic alliances, clustering of firms, in- and out-sourcing of parts, whether low wages and polluting activities will shift to Mexico, whether R&D activities will be decentralized, how Japanese MNEs will respond to NAFTA, and so on. These issues are addressed primarily by the authors in Parts I and II of the volume, and in the Rapporteurs' comments.

- How nation states in North America are changing the policy environment that affects MNEs. Here the general issue of regulating MNEs *per se* — both domestic and foreign — is important, together with policy issues where MNEs are important influences on the outcome, areas such as competition, labour and environmental issues, taxation, national security, sovereignty, and so on. Will MNEs create pressures for deeper integration of the three countries? How are the three countries likely to respond? What are the sensitive policy issues with respect to regulating MNEs likely to be? What should governments be doing? These issues are addressed primarily in Parts I, III and IV.

- The changing nature of MNE-state relations in North America. Both MNEs and nation states are key actors in NAFTA. How are their relationships changing, and likely to change, after NAFTA? Will policy stances towards MNEs be more or less confrontational in the future? What does this mean for the role of U.S. MNEs and the U.S. government within North America? How do the two small countries, Canada and Mexico, fit within MNE locational and organizational choices? What policy options are available to their governments? What are the likely contentious issues and how should they be resolved? What is the emerging policy agenda? These issues are addressed throughout the volume.

BRIEF SUMMARIES OF THE CHAPTERS

MULTINATIONALS AND GOVERNMENTS: KEY ACTORS IN THE NAFTA

IN THIS, THE FIRST CHAPTER IN PART I, *Theory*, Raymond Vernon argues that two groups will play dominant roles in determining the consequences of the NAFTA: the three signatory governments and the multinational enterprises operating in the area.

Looking first at MNEs, the NAFTA should reduce risks for business firms, with short-run and long-run effects on MNE location decisions. In the short run, U.S. multinationals (which comprise the bulk of the MNEs within North America) will engage in "locational shufflings" of plant functions among the three countries. Where unexploited economies of scale or agglomeration economies exist within the U.S. parent's operations, there will be a short-run tendency to close out smaller plants in Canada and Mexico and shift production to the larger U.S. facilities. This reshuffling is likely to be reinforced by the declines in truck transport costs the NAFTA will also bring. Activities of Canadian and Mexican MNEs, and of MNEs from outside North America, may also be drawn to the United States in the short run. In addition, the new technologies of production require suppliers to locate close to their downstream customers; lean production therefore provides another reason for increased agglomeration of investment activity within the United States as a short-run response to the NAFTA. Vernon argues that long-run adjustments are likely to work in the opposite direction, causing investments to disperse to Canada and Mexico, as economies of scale are exhausted and congestion increases.

With respect to MNE-state relations, Vernon asserts that the tendency for progressive integration of MNE activities within the free trade area will exacerbate some old problems and create new ones. In this chapter, he focuses on two difficult issues: the regional allocation of taxable MNE profits, and the regional content of MNE products. How are governments likely to respond? Vernon notes first that ambitious international agreements generally come from great political changes affecting all the member countries. Such was not the case with the NAFTA, nor with the FTA. As a result, he argues that the NAFTA lacks centralized institutions so that its effectiveness will depend on its interpretation by national officials, each with their own parochial interests. Vernon compares the institutional political structures within the three countries and finds the probability for inconsistent and uncoordinated government policies in administering the NAFTA to be quite high, especially in the United States.

Therefore, since the NAFTA does not directly acknowledge and deal with the existence of multinational enterprises and the difficult issues raised by their integrative behaviour, Vernon — even though he supports passage of the NAFTA — concludes that it may face a troubled future once ratified. He recommends that the NAFTA be modified to focus more attention on MNE-related issues and to develop a stronger institutional, supra-national framework.

THE THEORY OF MULTINATIONAL PLANT LOCATION IN A REGIONAL TRADING AREA

THIS, THE FIRST OF TWO CHAPTERS by Curtis Eaton, Richard Lipsey and Edward Safarian, explores two issues: the determinants of investment decisions, and the effects of the policy framework on foreign direct investment flows.

The authors first review the literature on the impact of free trade agreements on investment flows, finding that these agreements tend to generate increased intra-industry FDI. As a result, adjustment effects (e.g. on employment) are smaller because adjustment takes place within industries rather than between industries. The key to investment decisions under the FTA and the NAFTA is the reduction in policy risk due to increased security of market access. The FTA and the NAFTA eliminate tariffs among member countries, but only reduce nontariff barriers. Therefore security of market access is improved by the elimination of tariffs, but may be more apparent than real for nontariff barriers, depending on the probability of firms in one country being harassed by nontariff barriers erected by the other member country. Comparing the welfare ranking of alternatives for Canada, the authors find that Canada's order of preference is: 1) the FTA only, 2) the NAFTA only, 3) the FTA plus a Mexico-U.S. FTA, 4) no bilateral FTAs, 5) a Mexico-U.S. FTA and no FTA. The authors argue that NAFTA is unlikely to create a North American trading block because both the FTA and the NAFTA lack the essential ingredient of a trading block, that is, a common commercial policy facing nonmember countries.

THE THEORY OF MULTINATIONAL PLANT LOCATION: AGGLOMERATIONS AND DISAGGLOMERATIONS

THIS CHAPTER BY EATON, LIPSEY AND SAFARIAN is a companion piece examining the economic geography of (dis)agglomerations of investment. It focuses in particular on the geographic location of R&D in multinational networks.

The authors develop a theory of agglomeration which explains geographic concentration of business activity as the outcome of two opposing forces: economies of scale at the plant level (encouraging concentration) and transportation and communication costs (discouraging concentration). Restrictive trade policies can encourage agglomeration; the reverse, however, does not necessarily follow. The authors conclude that the probable effects of the FTA and the NAFTA on agglomeration are unclear since scale economies and asset specificity discourage quick dissolutions, and thus have opposite effects to falling trade barriers. In addition, the new technologies of production have both reduced the importance of labour and transport and communications costs and increased the need for supplier firms to locate proximate to their downstream customers. As a result, lean production may lead to increased diversity in patterns of industrial location. In terms of the location of research and development activities in MNE networks, there are strong forces favouring the centralization of R&D at the parent firm's head-quarters. However, significant decentralization of R&D has occurred for some countries and industries over the past 10 years as the knowledge base becomes more geographically dispersed. If free trade areas encourage rationalization of firm activities and reduce the autonomy of foreign manufacturing subsidiaries, the authors conclude that the production of local R&D by subsidiaries may also be reduced.

A THEORY OF BUSINESS NETWORKS

THIS CHAPTER BY ALAN RUGMAN AND JOE R. D'CRUZ argues that business networks are a hybrid form of business organization between markets and hierarchies. Global competition means that firms cannot excel in all business areas. As a result, successful North American multinationals are specializing in parts of the "value chain" where they have core competence, and are then linking with other entities to create business networks which can compete globally in many business areas.

Rugman and D'Cruz hypothesize that a business network consists of five partners. The network is led by a multinational enterprise, called a "flagship firm", which competes in global markets. The flagship firm has four partners: suppliers, customers, competitors, and the non-business infrastructure; the last includes the government sector. Strategic management of the network comes from the flagship firm while the five partners share in successful operations; thus the relationship between the MNE and its partners is asymmetric. The authors describe two examples of business networks: Benetton, the retail clothing MNE, and the Bell/Stentor telecommunications network.

The authors outline three implications of business networks for Canadian public policy. First, since the relationship among the partners is asymmetric, governments can only play a supporting, not a leadership, role in business networks; second, the implications for competition policy are unclear;

and third, government regulations can have (and have had) substantial effects on the formation and structure of business networks.

AN EVOLUTIONARY PERSPECTIVE ON THE NAFTA

IN THIS, THE FINAL CHAPTER IN PART I, *Theory*, Bruce Kogut draws together several of the key points in the earlier chapters, and provides an important bridge to the chapters in Part II, *Evidence*. Kogut argues that countries have different historical industrial structures and processes. MNEs tend to reflect the national organizing principles of their home countries (a type of country-specific advantage). These organizing principles diffuse more easily between firms than between countries, and even more easily between affiliates of a multinational enterprise. Therefore foreign direct investment is the means by which MNEs act as agents of change or "investment bridges" in transferring home country organizing principles to host countries. Incumbent or veteran firms in the host country will vary in the speed at which they adopt new technologies. Generally, there will be resistance to adopting new technologies due to inertia, lack of information, and the costs of switching. As time passes, however, these technological changes diffuse and firm-specific advantages play a more important role in determining competitiveness.

Kogut argues that the current decade is witnessing a period of enormous technological change as a new set of organizing principles, lean production, transforms firm strategies and structures. For Kogut, Japanese MNEs are the current investment bridges, diffusing lean production techniques throughout North America and Europe. In the case of lean production, a highly trained workforce is a critical country-specific advantage influencing the rate of adoption of these new work practices. Faced with the threat of Japanese competition, U.S. firms can respond by hiring high-skilled labour and adopting lean production techniques, or by continuing to employ low-skilled labour and mass production techniques. He concludes that firms may be reluctant to switch, at least in the short run, and are thus trapped in low-wage strategies.

When governments move to introduce the NAFTA, a free trade area encompassing both rich and poor countries, at the same time as rapid technological change is taking place, incumbent MNEs are faced with a decision: either keep their historical practices or shift to new ones that may or may not succeed. Kogut suggests that some firms will respond by searching for low wage sites (e.g. move to the southern United States, to Mexico, or offshore), others will cluster their investments in core industrial districts in the United States. Kogut concludes that the NAFTA should be seen as nested within a period of enormous technological change and severe international competition for North American industry. Whatever is done, he believes the "decisions made at this time will have, due to the particular juncture of history, long-lasting and irreversible consequences". If the behaviour of North American firms appears to be driven by short-run considerations, there may be a role for governments, if the NAFTA passes, in facilitating the transition to the new technological paradigm.

MULTINATIONALS AND FOREIGN DIRECT INVESTMENT IN NORTH AMERICA

THIS FIRST CHAPTER IN PART II, *Evidence*, by John Knubley, Marc Legault and Someshwar Rao is divided into two parts: first, a macroeconomic analysis of foreign direct investment and trade patterns in North America since 1980, and, second, a microeconomic study of the structure, performance and characteristics of the top 1,000 multinationals in North America.

In the macroeconomics part, the authors focus first on world trends in trade and FDI, and then analyze trade and FDI linkages among Canada, the United States and Mexico, and their commercial relations with Japan and the European Community. Using 1991 data, the authors document the "hub-and-spoke" nature of this trade and investment; examine inward and outward FDI in Canada over the period 1980 to 1992; and conclude with an analysis of the industrial composition of U.S. trade and investment with Canada, and with Mexico.

In the microeconomics part, the authors created a data base of the top 1,008 firms in North America, based on sales in 1991. The sample includes 823 U.S.-based, 158 Canadian and 27 Mexican companies. Of the 158 located in Canada, 39 are foreign-controlled; in addition, most of the Mexican firms are U.S. subsidiaries. The authors determine which industries the firms are in, calculate national indexes of revealed comparative advantage, and investigate the productivity, growth and R&D performance of these top firms. Finally, data on the average size and outward orientation of the firms are provided.

The authors present five main findings.

1) Both inward and outward FDI in Canada have diversified away from the United States and into Europe.

2) Canadian MNEs have a revealed comparative advantage in resources and resource-intensive manufacturing and financial services; U.S. MNEs in technology-intensive manufacturing and commercial services; and Mexican MNEs in resources, and in the low-skill parts of resource-intensive and technology-intensive manufacturing.

3) The labour productivity of Canadian MNEs is high, relative to firms in the United States, for foreign-controlled firms and for Canadian-controlled firms in the construction, utilities, trade and financial sectors, but low for Canadian-controlled manufacturing

firms. Labour productivity is significantly lower in the Mexican top firms.

4) On average, R&D-to-sales ratios in Canada are considerably below U.S. levels; but Canadian levels are higher in mining and labour-intensive manufacturing.

5) The top U.S. firms, on average, are twice the size of, but are less outward oriented than, the top Canadian firms; Mexican firms are smaller and less outward oriented.

The authors conclude that increased economic integration within North America should cause the largest firms, and the three countries, to increase further their specialization along the lines of their revealed comparative advantage, generating pressures on Canadian firms to rationalize and restructure their operations.

WHO DOES WHAT AFTER NAFTA? LOCATION STRATEGIES OF U.S. MULTINATIONALS

THIS CHAPTER BY LORRAINE EDEN asks: Will there be massive job losses and plant closures as U.S. multinationals shift their operations to Mexico to take advantage of cheaper labour costs? Based on analysis of the NAFTA and theory of MNE plant location strategies, together with a statistical analysis of the majority owned foreign affiliates (MOFAs) of U.S. multinationals, the paper concludes that there is both a simple answer and a complex one to this question.

The simple answer is "no", the NAFTA will not cause a massive exodus of plants from Canada and the United States to Mexico. An examination of U.S. MOFAs shows that wide differentials exist in average employee compensation between MOFAs in the same industry but in different countries. However, unit labour costs are much more homogeneous, reflecting the fact that highly productive workers are paid better; in some industries unit labour costs for U.S. MOFAs were higher in Mexico than in Canada. Therefore widespread closures of U.S. branch plants in Canada, in order to move to Mexico, are unlikely.

The complex answer to the question, according to Eden, is that there will be major plant reorganizations throughout North America. These are likely to be much greater than econometric trade models predict because the NAFTA is much broader than a simple tariff-removal exercise. As regulatory and trade barriers fall, liberalization will lead to reorganization and rationalization of MNE activities within each country and between countries. U.S. MNEs are the firms best placed to take advantage of the falling tariff and nontariff barriers that the FTA and the NAFTA will bring because they are already located in all three countries. These veteran MNEs can be expected to locate, close and/or expand their plants with the whole North American market in mind. This should lead to reduced numbers of product lines in various plants and increased horizontal trade among plants. MNEs are also likely to segment their production process among plants so that more vertical intra-firm trade takes place. As a result there should be more cross-border vertical and horizontal intra-firm trade flows. Eden concludes that low wages, for most U.S. MNEs, are a minor consideration in these location decisions. Rationalization of plant functions, to accommodate horizontal specialization in particular product lines and vertical specialization in particular processes, is much more likely than plant flight to Mexico.

JAPANESE MULTINATIONALS IN NORTH AMERICA

THIS CHAPTER BY ELEANOR WESTNEY focuses on the new multinationals — the Japanese transplants — in North America. Westney argues that the influx of Japanese MNEs in the 1980s was largely for defensive reasons, to protect exports threatened by U.S. protectionism and the rising value of the yen. The rapidity of the growth in Japanese FDI in North America, however, has caused both a general backlash by the public and a growing debate among academic scholars as to whether Japanese MNEs are different from Western MNEs and, if so, what explains this difference.

Westney first examines macroeconomic patterns of Japanese FDI in North America from 1980 to 1992, documenting its "extraordinary compression"; two-thirds of the FDI occurred between 1986 and 1989. Since 1990, Japanese FDI has fallen rapidly and she concludes that this slowdown is not a temporary phenomenon as Japanese MNEs appear to be shifting their FDI activities from North America to Asia. Westney concludes that the Canada-U.S. FTA had no discernable effect on Japanese FDI in Canada and, similarly, there is no apparent interest by Japanese MNEs in the NAFTA.

Turning to the question of whether Japanese MNEs are different from Western MNEs, Westney notes that Japanese transplants in North America: 1) employ a high proportion of home country managers in key positions; 2) depend more heavily on the parent firm for decision making and support activities; 3) tend to re-create the home-country organization set (the *kieretsu* structure of a small, core firm in a network structure with a pyramid of subsidiaries) in the host country; 4) earn relatively low profits; and 5) are more likely to create multiple subsidiaries within major markets, for example, setting up independent R&D subsidiaries, rather than the single "country subsidiary" organizational structure preferred by Western MNEs.

Westney reviews the challenges facing Japanese transplants in North America in the 1990s as Japanese firms face the effects of their internationalization. These challenges are: 1) coping with the rising yen-dollar exchange rate; 2) political and social pressures from host countries to become "insiders"; and 3) pressures to open up the *kieretsu* structure in Japan.

She suggests that Japanese MNEs are moving towards a three-region, rather than a multi-country, organizational structure, with regional, semi-autonomous headquarters in Asia, Europe and North America. This structure may create conflicts between the goals of the parent firms for interdependent units and the desire of host countries for locally autonomous transplants.

In Canada, Westney notes that the regional strategy of the transplants has really been a one-country strategy centered on the United States. She concludes that Canada needs to articulate a clear role for itself in a North American regional strategy in order to attract new investments from Japan.

MNE ACTIVITY: COMPARING THE NAFTA AND THE EUROPEAN COMMUNITY

IN THIS CHAPTER JOHN DUNNING looks at the strategic responses of multinationals to regional integration in North America and in the European Community, pre- and post-1992. He first outlines the similarities and differences between the proposed North American Free Trade Agreement and the current level of economic integration in the European Community. Dunning then theorizes about the likely effects of regional integration on foreign direct investment, distinguishing between the initial effects of integration (on the costs of supplying goods and services from various locations) and the secondary effects (from restructuring of production and markets, new opportunities for insider firms, and incentives to innovation and technological change). He argues that the effects will be industry- and country-specific.

Dunning then addresses the effects of MNEs on regional integration, distinguishing between intra-regional FDI and extra-regional FDI. He argues that there are four main kinds of MNE activity: market-seeking, resource-seeking, efficiency-seeking, and strategic-asset-seeking, and that the effects of regional integration on each activity differ. Firms inside the region see benefits from lower intra-regional barriers and will rationalize product lines (horizontal integration) and/or production processes (vertical integration) to better exploit economies of scale and scope. Firms outside the region may be induced to become insiders.

Dunning argues that the EC's regulatory framework affecting intra-regional and extra-regional FDI has increasingly become more liberal, which should cause an increase in efficiency- and strategic-asset-seeking FDI in the future. After reviewing the literature on the effects of Mark I integration (1958-70) with Mark II integration (EC 1992) on FDI, he compares both forms of integration with the NAFTA and concludes there are similarities and differences. Tariff removal has similar effects in all three cases, but the failure to establish a common external tariff under the

NAFTA has distinctive consequences. Differences also arise in the case of EC 1992 where the removal of intra-regional non-tariff barriers is more extensive and thus the effects on efficiency- and strategic-asset-seeking FDI are likely to be greater.

Intra-firm Trade in North America and the European Community

IN THIS CHAPTER DENNIS ENCARNATION compares and contrasts the trade and FDI patterns of multinationals in North America and the European Community as these MNEs seek to secure market access through FDI. The paper examines: 1) the impact of majority versus minority affiliates on intra-firm trade patterns; 2) the MNE's choice of supplying overseas markets through foreign investment or international trade; 3) the relative importance of domestic versus export markets; 4) whether foreign subsidiaries are primarily engaged in offshore production or distribution; 5) the importance of intra-firm versus arm's length trade for the MNE; and 6) the implications for public policy.

Encarnation argues that MNEs see wholly-owned affiliates as the preferred method for gaining and maintaining market access. Where FDI is new, or host country regulation constrains ownership, the levels of minority ownership are higher. For the United States, overseas sales of U.S. MNEs have exceeded U.S. exports for several decades; in other countries where MNEs are of more recent origin, the ratio of overseas sales to exports is smaller but still generally greater than one. Once established, foreign subsidiaries tend to sell primarily in the host market, with smaller amounts of exports to the parent network. Regional integration, however, leads to tighter integration of the MNE family and greater intra-firm trade flows in both directions. The choice between production and distribution appears to vary considerably by country of origin of the MNE, with wholesaling activities being very important for Japanese MNEs, for example, but less important for U.S. and European MNEs. Intra-firm trade dominates MNE trade flows, particularly in the auto industry. Finally, Encarnation argues that the NAFTA will encourage the development of regional integration strategies by MNEs in North America. He predicts the NAFTA will cause firms in Canada to increase their exports, FDI and local sales in the United States; a similar deepening of economic linkages should happen with U.S. MNEs. This deepening should be seen as a positive contribution to economic growth and national welfare.

Foreign Direct Investment in Mexico

IN THIS CHAPTER KURT UNGER examines the changing role of Mexico as host country for foreign direct investment, particularly since the 1982 debt crisis, focusing on macroeconomic and sectoral changes in FDI. The Unger chapter first presents a statistical portrait of inward FDI for 1980-92, documenting the difference between FDI approvals and actual investments, the recent rise in FDI in services and the stock market, and the importance of the United States as the key investor. He then chronicles the shift in Mexico's balance of payments from a surplus in 1982-88 to a growing deficit in 1989-92, showing that trade is concentrated in a few products and a few firms, and that the import propensity of foreign firms has risen as the Mexican government has relaxed its trade balancing restrictions. Examining the nature of maquiladora operations, he finds that maquila exports have grown more rapidly than exports of manufactured goods or total Mexican exports, but that the basic function of the maquilas — as assemblers of imported inputs — has not changed.

Based on his analysis, Unger argues that new FDI in Mexico has been more limited than the official numbers suggest; that new FDI has gone mostly into the stock market and services rather than into manufacturing; and that the new FDI is encouraging imports into Mexico from U.S. plants with excess capacity. He suggests that regional integration under the NAFTA will lead to a rationalization of the activities of multinational firms on a continental basis. Since many U.S. firms have excess capacity and Mexican manufacturing firms are producing close to their capacity limits, he expects new growth in the Mexican market to be supplied from imports of finished goods rather than from new investment in Mexico. The MNE activities located in Mexico that will survive international competition are mature products or segments of industries reliant on imported inputs; as a result, more of the Mexican economy may become like the maquiladora firms, assembling imported, intra-firm parts and components for domestic or foreign sale. Thus the deficit on the balance of trade should grow, while FDI growth in existing MNE-dominated sectors such as autos will stagnate; the combination will worsen Mexico's balance of payments and constrain Mexican growth rates. In a separate Appendix, Unger reviews recent legal and institutional changes in Mexico's FDI policy regime.

FOREIGN DIRECT INVESTMENT IN CANADA

IN THIS LAST CHAPTER IN PART II, Jorge Niosi examines the changing role of Canada as a host and home country for foreign direct investment since the early 1980s. He documents the country composition of the inward stock of FDI for Canada from 1950 to 1991, showing the declining share of U.S., and the rising share of EC, FDI in total FDI, and in manufacturing FDI. The same pattern is apparent for U.S. inward FDI, both total FDI and in manufacturing; that is, Canada's share declines and the EC share rises. Niosi then looks at Canada's foreign technical alliances in 1990-91 and finds that Canadian firms concluded more alliances with European partners than with U.S. partners. His general conclusion, based on these statistics, is that Canada and the United States are investing less heavily in one another.

Most of the economic forecasts of the effects of the FTA, and of the NAFTA, have argued that intra-industry and cross-border FDI flows should increase between Canada and the United States, as both are developed market economies with similar economic structures. However, each country's share in the other's FDI stock — that is, cross-investment — has continued to decline over the past ten years in spite of the FTA and possible NAFTA. What can explain the difference between the theoretical predictions and the data?

There are several possibilities. Some reasons focus on the responses of Canadian and U.S. MNEs to North American pressures.

- The removal of tariffs together with unexploited economies of scale have led to rationalization of activities on a continental scale by existing U.S. and Canadian MNEs, and thus to plant closures and the replacement of FDI by exports from the remaining plants.

- Intense competition in their domestic market from foreign transplants has forced U.S. MNEs to consolidate their domestic operations, close Canadian plants and serve the Canadian market from exports.

- Canada may be a less attractive environment for U.S. investment due to the recession, higher costs, less developed infrastructure, currency risks, and political uncertainties.

Other factors stress the attraction of extra-North American locations.

- EC 1992 has attracted new U.S. and Canadian FDI to shift from North America to Europe.

- Canadian MNEs have a large stock of FDI in the United States already and thus are diversifying into new markets such as Europe, while U.S. MNEs are diversifying into Europe and Asia.

Other arguments focus on the behaviour of foreign investors.

- The FTA and NAFTA have attracted offensive, export-substituting investments by EC and Asian firms and this has diversified investment partners for Canada and the United States.

- Canada has liberalized its inward FDI stance while the United States is adopting more protectionist policies, thus providing an additional motivation for North American investments to go to the United States rather than to Canada.

Having demonstrated the paradox and outlined some explanations, Niosi leaves it up to other researchers to investigate which of these explanations best fits the facts. He does believe that the relative decline in Canada-U.S. cross-investment is likely to continue for the foreseeable future.

NEW RULES FOR INTERNATIONAL INVESTMENT

IN THIS FIRST CHAPTER IN PART III, *Policy*, Fred Bergsten discusses the changing international climate for regulating foreign direct investment, arguing that there has been substantial unilateral liberalization of investment rules. At the same time, trade and investment have become inextricably linked, illustrated by the impact of the *kieretsu* structure on trade imbalances between Japan and the United States. The prospects for an international investment regime depend on what happens to the Uruguay Round and the views of the Clinton administration on managed trade. Bergsten believes the NAFTA will pass the U.S. Congress and be beneficial to the three countries. However, the NAFTA is widely disliked by the Pacific Rim countries because it is seen as the first move toward "Fortress North America". He concludes that the world trading system is characterized by even more uncertainty than usual; if the Uruguay Round concludes successfully, investment issues will move to the center of the multilateral agenda.

Sylvia Ostry's comment on Bergsten's paper focuses on the problems in setting rules for international investment. She sees the Uruguay Round as too much, too late; it deals with issues of the 1970s, such as TRIMs (trade-related investment measures) rather than issues of the 1980s and 1990s. Since the early 1980s, trade policy has been used as investment policy so IRTMs (investment-related trade measures) should be on the agenda. In addition, investment-related industrial policy measures (IRIPs) have emerged to link FDI and industrial policy in the high-tech area. For example, national security has been used to justify the exclusion of foreign MNEs from high-tech consortia. IRIPs are also not on the Uruguay Round agenda. Another system friction is the asymmetry of market access through FDI between Japan and the other OECD countries. All of these new issues are being discussed bilaterally by Japanese and U.S. officials. The United States therefore appears to have rejected the multilateral, rules-based route to creating an international investment regime. Ostry argues that this is a mistake since bilateral negotiations among the super powers tend to favour the powerful countries at the expense of the non-powerful ones. A multilateral approach to setting investment rules would be better for Canada and other small and middle-sized countries.

REGULATING MULTINATIONAL ENTERPRISES IN NORTH AMERICA

IN THIS CHAPTER ROBERT KUDRLE provides a detailed examination of North American policies towards multinational enterprises, focusing on general policies and sectoral restrictions.

The chapter first reviews the history of restrictions on MNE activity and inward FDI in the United States, Canada and Mexico. While the United States has no general restrictions against inward FDI, both Canada and Mexico do. Kudrle reviews the Foreign Investment Review Agency (later Investment Canada) in Canada and the Comision Nacional de Inversion Extranjera (CNIE) in Mexico, and the effect of the NAFTA on these institutions. He then turns to a discussion of sectoral restrictions in each country, looking at finance, culture, telecommunications, energy, and transportation sectors, and the impact of the NAFTA on these regulations.

Kudrle argues that Canada and Mexico have both substantially liberalized their regulation of MNE activity and inward FDI since 1980 in order to encourage closer economic linkages with the U.S. economy. Such linkages were seen as the only way for small, open economies to ensure their competitiveness, prosperity and long-run growth potential. Security motivations do not appear to have been a factor in their policy shift. Autonomy considerations have, however, been a factor in the continued closure of certain sectors (e.g. culture in Canada, petroleum in Mexico).

Kudrle then compares MNE policy in the three countries in terms of openness, discrimination and asymmetry, finding that: 1) even after the NAFTA is fully phased in, Mexico will be less open than its partners; 2) the NAFTA does contain features discriminating in favour of member country investors; and 3) asymmetry at the sectoral level in terms of openness remains a continuing feature of North American economic relations.

Assessing the prospects for further liberalization after the NAFTA, he finds possibilities for unilateral liberalization based on interest-group demands and for co-operative liberalization in the area of competition policy.

Finally, Kudrle discusses North American regulation of MNEs in a global context, situating the NAFTA within the multilateral GATT negotiations on TRIMs and TRIPs and "system friction" issues such as competition, R&D and FDI policies. He concludes with an analysis of the prospects for the NAFTA's passage within the United States, stressing the important role domestic politics plays in U.S. attitudes towards MNEs and inward FDI.

MULTINATIONALS AND NORTH AMERICAN SECURITY

IN THEIR CHAPTER ELLEN FROST AND EDWARD M. GRAHAM investigate the linkages between national security, multinational enterprises and government policy in North America. The authors argue that national security concerns, especially in the United States, are becoming economic security concerns, interpreted either as certain activities must be carried out at home rather than offshore or that certain sectors are closed to foreign investment. Competition from European defense and high-tech MNEs is seen by U.S. officials as unfairly subsidized; increasing import penetration of leading edge technologies is also of great concern. As a result, U.S.

policy-makers are widening the definition of national security to focus on economic issues.

Frost and Graham then look at national security legislation in North America. All G7 countries except Canada have the authority to block or limit FDI inflows on national security grounds. In the United States, certain sectors (e.g. coastal shipping, air transport, broadcasting) that are seen as vital to national security are closed to FDI; in addition, the Exon-Florio amendment allows the U.S. President to block an acquisition or takeover of a U.S. firm on national security grounds. In Canada, the *Investment Canada Act* allows Canada to screen inward FDI; this screening power will be reduced for U.S. and Mexican investments under the NAFTA. However, Canada cannot block acquisitions on national security grounds. Mexico has recently announced that it will create an authority with powers to block inward FDI on national security grounds. The authors argue that Canada should have the authority to do so, similar to the Exon-Florio amendment, and suggest how this national security function might be established.

MULTINATIONALS AND COMPETITION POLICY IN NORTH AMERICA

IN THIS CHAPTER EDWARD M. GRAHAM AND MARK WARNER examine the external dimensions of competition policy, linking it to trade and FDI in North America. Competition policy includes the regulation of market monopolization (antitrust policy) and state aids to industry (state aids policy). In North America, each of the three governments has its own antitrust policy but not a formal state-aids policy. In the European Community, on the other hand, competition policy covers both types of regulation. The NAFTA does not create a trilateral competition policy, rather it requires each country to have its own competition laws and the countries to co-operate in enforcement of domestic laws. The authors ask two questions: Should the NAFTA explicitly contain competition policy provisions? Is the case for such provisions strengthened by the presence of multinational enterprises? They answer both questions in the affirmative.

Why should the NAFTA have its own trilateral competition policy? The authors provide five reasons.

1) At present, private barriers to trade can offset the gains from the NAFTA.

2) Some competition policy issues have a North American dimension, in particular, intra-North American mergers and acquisitions; national policies, however, may be parochial and ignore this North American dimension.

3) Competition laws in the three countries are not fully harmonized so there are potential conflicts between the regulations. A supranational authority is not necessary or sufficient for harmonization but may play a catalytic role.

4) A trilateral competition policy would logically replace trade remedy laws, especially anti-dumping duties, countervailing duties and safeguard measures. These less-than-fair-value (LTFV) measures can turn into disguised backdoor protectionism for domestic firms. A trilateral competition policy would remove the pro-business bias of these LTFV policies.

5) A trilateral competition policy could be used to regulate governments, (including sub-federal) in terms of state aid to firms.

The authors then provide a detailed discussion of what a trilateral North American Competition Commission (NACC) should look like and what its functions should be. Two detailed Appendices conclude the chapter, one on merger review rules in the three countries, and a second on predation/price discrimination laws.

THE NAFTA, MULTINATIONALS AND SOCIAL POLICY

IN HIS CHAPTER FREDERICK MAYER examines the changing interrelationships between MNEs and labour and environmental standards in North America. Mayer looks at two issues. First, have MNEs adjusted their location decisions to take advantage of differences in social regulation in North America? Second, how are governments responding to these perceived adjustments and thus changing the playing field for the MNEs in North America?

Mayer finds that differences in social policies have had some effect on business location decisions but that, with a few exceptions, the effects are small. Mexico's social regulatory environment has traditionally been more lax and much FDI has flown into Mexico in previous years, but the two events are not necessarily connected; that is, the primary motivation for FDI does not appear to have been differences in regulatory costs.

The perception of Mexico as a social-hazard haven, however, mobilized interest groups in Canada and the United States. Mayer examines the domestic political responses to the NAFTA negotiations and categorizes them as either reactive, strategic or symbolic. Labour and environmental groups believed their interests were threatened by the NAFTA and thus reacted by seeking ways to either block its passage or modify its effects. However, the responses were more than simply reaction. Mayer argues that interest groups, particularly the environmentalists, behaved opportunistically, attempting to hold the NAFTA hostage for ransom to be paid in terms of their own issues. Labour unions lobbied less strategically and, as a result, were less successful than the environmental groups in having their demands met. The side accord on the environment is widely seen as being broader and more restrictive than that on labour standards. Mayer also argues that the NAFTA was treated by some detractors as a political symbol of "big business against the people". Mayer concludes, somewhat ironically, that the NAFTA was a catalyst for the political response in the United States. As a result of that response, the long-run impact of the NAFTA may be exactly the reverse of its opponents' charges. That is, the NAFTA may lead to increased regulatory co-operation among the three countries, raising the social regulatory standards of Mexico, and initiating a recapture of power by nation states, albeit at the regional rather than the national level.

LESSONS AND NEW DIRECTIONS

PART IV, *LESSONS AND NEW DIRECTIONS*, presents three reviews by the Rapporteurs at the conference. Christopher Maule assesses the contribution of the papers to the theory of multinationals and industrial organization; Murray Smith looks at lessons and new directions at the multilateral level, and Alan Nymark assesses their policy implications for Canada.

THANKS

FINALLY, I WANT TO THANK some of the many people who have worked with me on this project. First, the staff at Industry Canada have put in long hours on their own chapter (prepared by John Knubley and his staff), organizing and running the conference, and working on the volume; in particular, I would like to thank the people with whom I worked most closely: Trudy Dickie, John Knubley, Geoff Nimmo, Alan Nymark, Ross Preston, Emmy Verdun, Christopher Wilkie, and Don Wilson. The contract was administered through the Centre for Trade Policy and Law, and Murray Smith, Melanie Burston and Cindy Murray were heavily involved in all stages of the project. Alan Rugman, Murray Smith, Christopher Maule, Chuck Hermann, Raymond Vernon and Maureen Molot provided helpful advice and good listening posts. Ed Matheson and Eunice Thorne at Ampersand were a pleasure to work with on the copy editing.

Different stages of the project were completed, first while I was at Carleton University, then on sabbatical on a Canada-U.S. Fulbright at Harvard University and The Ohio State University, and finally back at Carleton; I would like to thank these institutions for their support. My special thanks to all the participants at the conference — authors, discussants and Industry Canada staff — and all those involved in the development of the book itself for their cooperation and good humour throughout the project.

Lorraine Eden
Ottawa
November, 1993

ENDNOTE

1 Statistics are from *The Opportunities and Challenges of North American Free Trade: A Canadian Perspective* (Investment Canada Working Paper #7, April 1991).

Part I   Theory

Raymond Vernon
Professor of International Affairs Emeritus and
Professor of International Business Management Emeritus
Harvard University

2

Multinationals and Governments: Key Actors in the NAFTA

TWO KEY GROUPS PROMISE to play dominant roles in determining the consequences of the NAFTA: the signatory governments themselves and the multinational enterprises that operate in the area. Other institutions, including labour unions and environmental organizations, are also sure to exert some influence. But the influence of the multinational enterprises (MNEs) and of governments is likely to be dominant, and the interactions between them are likely to determine much of the agenda pursued under the agreement.

One cannot say, of course, just what the goals of these institutions will be in the NAFTA. Few economists and policy makers will be content to accept the proposition that scholars so commonly offer when they confront issues of this sort, such as, "Let us assume that the multinational enterprises are profit maximizers and that the governments are realists" because they know that almost any kind of behaviour on the part of multinational enterprises and governments can be explained in these terms. My task in this study, then, is to move beyond such unsatisfying generalizations and to speculate on the behaviour of multinational enterprises and of the signatory governments, drawing on what we already know and on what others have had to say about the motives and behavioral patterns of these key institutions.

THE MULTINATIONALS

FIRST PRINCIPLES REVISITED

NO ONE DOUBTS THAT multinational enterprises are usually profit maximizers, pursuing their goals through a network of units related through a common parent and dispersed over a number of different countries. (The term "network" is sometimes used to describe other organizational structures.) The units that make up a multinational enterprise typically respond to a common strategy and draw on a common pool of technical, financial, or human resources. Presumably, too, all the units in the network have survived the internalization test; that is, each is performing functions that the managers of the network believe are best performed by an affiliated unit rather than by an independent outside party. Still, the various units are also in a sense specialized in their contributions to the network's overall strategy, with each such specialty being closely related to its geographical location.

Nevertheless, as other authors emphasize, the functions of some units are explained largely by inertial historical forces. The location of the parent unit of a multinational enterprise, for instance, is usually determined by the nationality of the entrepreneurs and by the fact that their initial concentration was on the home market; and many headquarters functions are likely to remain at that location long after a *de novo* decision would have placed them somewhere else. The locations of most units of a multinational network, however, are reasonably compatible with their functions. Some are located as a result of straightforward least-cost calculations, aimed at minimizing the delivered cost of a product or service to a given market or the cost and quality of after-sale service in that market. In other cases, a subsidiary may be established in a particular location in order to take advantage of low-cost inputs such as labour or raw materials or unique inputs such as technology, for the benefit of the network as a whole.

The location of many subsidiaries, however, cannot be readily explained without considering various forms of perceived risk.[1] Some subsidiaries are committed to reducing random risk through diversification, whether through the penetration of new markets or the production of required inputs from additional sources. Others are committed to reducing more specific risks, such as the possibility that a government might block imports to a specific market.

Some of the units of multinational networks, however, are located with an eye to reducing the risks created by the manoeuverings of competitors, such as the perceived risk that rivals might attempt to preempt markets or sources of supply. The classic response to that kind of threat in an oligopoly is a follow-the-leader strategy; for in tight oligopolies, where barriers to entry are high, the participants need not worry whether they have chosen the most efficient solution so long as none of them has stolen a lead on the others.[2] Sudden surges in the expansion of Japan-based multinational networks in Mexico, the United States, the United Kingdom, and Germany during the 1980s and 1990s, for example, suggest that follow-the-leader patterns continue to be important.

Another set of distinctions also helps to explain locational responses. As Kogut, Encarnation, and Westney emphasize elsewhere in this volume, multinationals with headquarters in the NAFTA area can be usefully distinguished from those headquartered in relatively distant locations, such as Europe, Japan or Brazil. Among those headquartered outside of the NAFTA area, those with facilities already in place in Mexico, the United States, or Canada at the time of the NAFTA's establishment are likely to respond differently from those without such facilities in place. Finally, one must not overlook the responses of firms inside the NAFTA area that are currently located in only one of the three member countries, such as a beer producer in Mexico or a bank in Canada.

In an unsullied neoclassical view of the world, any emphasis on the national origins of the multinational enterprise is difficult to justify. But as Kogut points out, it has long been known that the behaviour of multinational enterprises is deeply influenced by their national origins.[3] Nationality *does* shape the bundle of technological, financial, and managerial resources that a headquarters unit acquires in response to earlier challenges, thereby influencing its strategy at later stages. Moreover, national origins affect the way in which a headquarters unit scans the world: how sensitive it is to foreign environments compared with the home environment, and what parts of the world it is prepared to scan most readily.[4] Historically, for instance, U.S.-based firms have been characteristically slow to scan foreign environments. The usual pattern was for them to set up their first foreign subsidiaries in Canada, then to enter Mexico with more alacrity than more distant parts of Latin America. Japan-based firms, by contrast, have been extremely sensitive to conditions in foreign markets, yet have found it easier to establish their earliest foreign facilities in south and southeast Asia than in the western hemisphere.

All told, then, experience suggests the desirability of considering the effects of a NAFTA using a two-dimensional matrix. One side of the grid distinguishes among the units of the multinational networks according to the functional factors that influence their location, such as cost reduction or risk reduction; the other side distinguishes among them according to their national origins and their presence in the NAFTA area.[5] Because U.S.-based firms figure so overwhelmingly in the NAFTA area and because many of the boxes in any such grid will prove inconsequential, there is no need to develop this approach in any detail. Nonetheless, the concept does serve to reduce the risk that in the studies that follow some major force generated by the adoption of the NAFTA may be overlooked.

ADJUSTING TO THE NAFTA

IF THE NAFTA IS TO HAVE ANY EFFECT on the locational decisions of multinational enterprises, it will be to reduce the perception among MNEs that the risks affecting trade and investment because of future governmental measures are high. Although risks from non-governmental sources will continue to influence locational decisions, the perceived decline of risk attributable to governmental action should encourage managers to add more weight to straightforward considerations of cost. Changes of this sort will have a variety of effects on the locational decisions of multinational enterprises — some sooner than others.[6]

Short-run Adjustments

The sheer dominance of U.S.-based multinational enterprises within the NAFTA area suggests that the reactions of this group will be critical in determining the NAFTA's short-term effects. In both Mexico and Canada, the subsidiaries of U.S.-based enterprises account for about two thirds of the country's foreign direct investment (FDI).[7] The history of the spread of U.S.-based enterprises into Canada and Mexico is filled with references to the importance of import barriers in explaining the initial decision.[8] In any event, the original function of the majority of U.S.-owned subsidiaries in Mexico and Canada was to serve the local market. Over time, it is true, some of these subsidiaries began to acquire other functions, including exports to the United States and to other countries.[9] But even as late as 1989, those Mexican subsidiaries of U.S.-based firms engaged in manufacturing were selling about two thirds of their output in the local market, with an almost identical ratio for Canadian subsidiaries.[10]

The folklore of multinational enterprises is rich with illustrations supporting the proposition that foreign subsidiaries created to serve a local market in the face of existing or prospective import restrictions are often inefficient. Established to serve relatively small markets, many have either employed obsolete technology or operated at less than optimal levels of output. With the introduction of the NAFTA, therefore, many U.S.-based multi-nationals can be expected to consider whether to alter the existing functions of a Canadian or Mexican subsidiary, either by abandoning the production of some product lines in the subsidiary or by expanding its output at the expense of other production units in the network.[11] In the case of Canadian subsidiaries, some of this adjustment will already have taken place, partly in reaction to the decades-old free trade arrangement with the United States in automobiles, and partly in reaction to the free trade agreement (FTA) entered into in 1989. Subsidiaries in Mexico, too, have been undergoing change since 1986, responding to the country's adherence to the General Agreement on Tariffs and Trade (GATT) and to the prospective existence of a free trade area; but many of Mexico's adjustments are still in the making.

Not all multinationals, however, will move to consolidate their production facilities into technically efficient units. In this respect, the NAFTA falls far short of creating a common market among its members, since it fails to deal with many major impediments to the easy movement of goods and services among its members. Some of the remaining impediments are the result of public policies, such as provisions for consumer protection, environmental control, and patent grants. Others stem from separate currencies, which generate an added set of risks for exporters and importers. Moreover, local service requirements, local product adaptations, and transport costs may argue for the continued existence of separate production units.

Despite these caveats, however, there is strong evidence to support the argument that multinationals with producing units already in Canada, the United States and Mexico will use the introduction of the NAFTA to consider whether or not to modify the function of these units. The most obvious tendency will be to consider concentrating production in one of the three areas in order to exploit hitherto underexploited economies of scale. That tendency will be reinforced by the fact that, under the terms of the treaty, the obstacles to unimpeded truck transport across the borders promise to be substantially reduced.

Such locational reshufflings may well provide the most evident reactions to the NAFTA in the short run. Yet it is still unclear which countries will be the winners and which the losers from that source. In some cases, a U.S.-based enterprise may decide to close out production in Canada or Mexico that was originally established in order to overcome a governmental barrier to imports; firms that stand to gain from economies of scale or agglomeration are particularly likely to make such adjustments.

The propensity of U.S.-based firms to close out smaller facilities in Canada and Mexico in favour of enlarging a major facility in the United States will be particularly strong for firms that place a heavy emphasis on minimizing their short-term costs of disruption in responding to the NAFTA. Some firms, on the other hand, can be expected to shape their responses to the NAFTA more rationally — by taking into account the expected stream of all present and future costs associated with different locations, notably including labour costs, transport costs, communication costs, and taxes. On that basis, lower labour costs in Mexico or lower material costs in Canada could produce a movement out of the United States in some industries, as firms choose to consolidate their production activities in Mexico and Canada.

The locational reconsideration by multinationals generated by the introduction of the NAFTA will affect firms headquartered in Canada and Mexico as well as U.S.-based firms. Those few Mexico-based and Canada-based multinationals with a substantial stake in the U.S. market, such as Canada's Northern Telecom and Mexico's Cervecería Modelo, can also be expected to undertake such a review. Although this category is of no great consequence in aggregate terms, any significant move on the part of such firms to serve their home markets from facilities in the United States would prove particularly delicate in political terms.

In any event, whatever the dominant reactions to the introduction of the NAFTA may be, the overall tendency is likely to be amplified by a follow-the-leader phenomenon. The power of follow-the-leader behaviour in the short and medium term can easily be underestimated. The example of the waves of new entrants that established their presence as maquiladoras in the northern free zones of Mexico during the latter 1980s suggests that the follow-the-leader factor could prove to be particularly strong in the short run. In some cases, as in clothing and consumer electronics (as Westney notes) the drive may come from a compelling need to match the cost structure of competitors; in other cases, as in automobile transplants, the drive may come from the fear of losing market share to competitors inside the NAFTA area.

The urge to follow-the-leader may prove especially powerful among firms headquartered outside the NAFTA area that are considering whether to establish a production facility within the area for the first time. If such firms are unfamiliar with the advantages and drawbacks of alternative locations in the NAFTA, they may opt for a follow-the-leader solution on the assumption that those already in the area are operating on the basis of superior knowledge and experience.

Another factor that could prove significant in determining the responses of the multinationals is the movement of suppliers, especially in light of the value-added requirements imposed by the treaty. With a follow-the-leader tendency resulting in a cluster of rival firms in a common location, the cluster, in turn, could attract a ring of suppliers that would otherwise choose another location. Indeed, as Maureen Molot pointed out, the increasing emphasis on just-in-time production in some industries may well increase these agglomerative tendencies, thereby amplifying the effects of the locational decisions of the producers being served.[12]

Understandably, there are political and business leaders in each of the three countries who are afraid that the adjustments of the sorts described above made by multinational enterprises could prove adverse to their interests. With the possibilities of locational shifts running in so many different directions, none of the three countries is immune from threat. One can expect, therefore, to see a certain amount of tension in all three countries as individual cases of adjustment emerge. Such initial adjustments, however, are unlikely to be reliable guides to the longer-run effects of the NAFTA arrangements.

Longer-term Adjustments

Over the longer term, adjustments could take a different turn from the initial responses. For any given technology related to a product or service, the advantages derived from clustering among producing units and from scale advantages inside each unit are decidedly limited. So far, the characteristic history of industrial location has recorded a gradual dispersion of producing units from their early clusters. Within most national markets, it has been common for new industries to record their first surge of growth in a concentrated geographical area — such as New England in the United States or Sao Paolo in Brazil — then to develop outward in a more dispersed pattern of growth. Also, similar patterns have been common between countries. Indeed, automobiles, chemicals, electronics and machinery, all industries heavily populated by multinational enterprises, amply illustrate the trend. Until the 1960s, production in these industries outside North America and Europe was quite limited; but thereafter many new countries joined the list of producers.

Of course, there is nothing inevitable in such a tendency, inasmuch as it is the result of a complex interplay among scale advantages, factor prices, transport costs, scanning capabilities, risk perception, and inertia. But the long-term tendency toward dispersion does offer promise that the long-term adjustments to the NAFTA could be quite different from those that appear at the outset. It seems reasonable to suppose that over the longer term, the various provisions of the NAFTA designed to reassure foreign direct investors regarding the safety of their undertakings will increasingly influence the distribution of such investments. As the perceived risks of foreign direct investment decline, the importance of differences in costs will grow. Moreover, the advantages associated with existing agglomerations will in many cases turn into disadvantages associated with congestion. Accordingly, the propensity of firms in any country to look favorably on locations with lower costs, is likely to increase. In the longer term, such a tendency, can be expected to lead some firms to areas that were passed over in the earlier periods of response to the NAFTA's existence.[13]

How these disparate trends will play out in aggregate terms is unclear. Any well-founded estimate will require exhaustive analysis of a kind that, so far, has not been undertaken. Presumably, if the NAFTA is adopted, all three countries will boost their efficiency a little by virtue of a decline in existing restrictions and in perceived risks; so all three may gain in the end. However, if the media concentrate on cases of apparent loss while overlooking the diffuse gains, reality could prove to be quite different from perception. And as time moves forward and economic circumstances change, it will be increasingly difficult to guess what would have occurred if the NAFTA had *not* been adopted.

Recurrent Issues

Multinational enterprises already account for a considerable proportion of the traffic in goods and services crossing national borders among the NAFTA signatories. In 1989, the units of multinational networks located in the United States accounted for 69 percent of total exports from the United States to Canada; and of these network exports to Canada, 65 percent were shipped to affiliates of the network exporter. For exports to Mexico, the analogous figures were 46 percent and 52 percent.[14] All told, therefore, intra-affiliate exports from the United States accounted for a considerable proportion of aggregate exports from the U.S. to Canada and Mexico. If my expectations are realized, the relative importance of multinational enterprises in those international flows will increase, perhaps even substantially. In that case, some familiar problems associated with the international operations of multinational enterprises will also grow significantly, challenging the signatory countries to find more effective solutions.

The cross-border transactions that occur among the affiliated units of a multinational enterprise differ in one fundamental respect from the transactions consummated across borders among independent parties. In the case of international transactions between independent parties, the objective functions of both parties shape the terms of the transaction. In the case of transactions undertaken by the units of a multinational enterprise, however, the aim of the parties is, in principle, to satisfy only one basic objective, namely, the global interests of the network.

Of course the implications of that salient fact differ from one enterprise to the next. In some multinational networks, the individual units are permitted to operate almost as independent free-standing businesses, while in others the operations of each unit are intimately linked to those of the other units. However, as communications costs decline along with the sense of risk from governmental sources through agreements such as the NAFTA, the tendency of multinational networks to integrate their operations across international borders will continue to grow.[15]

The progressive integration in the activities of multinational enterprises spurred on by the NAFTA will exacerbate some existing problems and create some new ones. Some problems, such as those created by the increasing role of foreign-owned subsidiaries in the political life of host countries, are likely to prove extremely complex; others are relatively simple, at least in concept if not in actual detail. Two areas have been selected for consideration; while conceptually simple, they are at the same time likely to figure substantially in future relations between the NAFTA parties. One is that of determining the taxable profits of any multinational network in each of the taxing jurisdictions in the NAFTA; the second is that of determining the regional content of products as proof of their right to duty-free treatment inside the free trade area.

The Taxable Profits Issue

The NAFTA agreement does not deal directly with the many questions of taxation in which the three signatory governments have mutual or conflicting interests. Nevertheless, as the operations of multinational enterprises expand and become more deeply integrated across national borders, the agreement promises to complicate and exacerbate these questions substantially.

When reviewing the terms of international transactions among the units of a multinational enterprise, national authorities usually begin with the assumption that they can distinguish between terms that are "right" and those that are "wrong" by applying objective standards. According to widely accepted international norms, the prime standard is the price that would figure in a transaction between independent parties, that is, the "arm's length price".

Where standardized products like copper ore or crude oil are involved, no serious problems exist in using market prices to determine a plausible value. With many of the products and services that characteristically pass between the units of a multinational network, however, there is little or no hope of obtaining independent guidance from a relevant market created by independent parties. Adding to this problem is the fact that the nature of some of the goods and services exchanged among the members of a multinational network are often highly technical, proprietary and ephemeral. Such non-tangible resources include access to a unique pool of technology and to some specialized managerial skills intimately linked to the firm's existing assets, the use of a specific trade name, or a parental guarantee that clears the way for the subsidiary's assumption of local debt.[16] Because the parent does not relinquish control of any of the intangibles when transferring them to a subsidiary, and because the problems of asymmetrical information are not involved in the transfer, the prices associated with similar transfers in the open market (assuming any can be found) are of no relevance. Even the concept of a transfer price in this case is obscure.

Where intermediate products are being transferred between units, the tangible character of the product may seem to provide a more solid base for estimating its arm's length price. Although the product may be unique in many respects and unavailable in the open market, the tax collector may still attempt to set a value on it by estimating its contribution to the price of the product in which it is incorporated or by estimating its production cost. Anyone who is familiar with the problems of costing such products is uncomfortably aware of the overwhelmingly arbitrary character of the process. Where joint costs and overheads are a large part of total cost, value estimates are made largely at the discretion of the estimator, and challenges to those estimates are no less arbitrary.

Managers of multinational enterprises have, of course, been acutely aware of the vulnerability of the various alternatives they have been offered for determining the appropriate transfer prices among their affiliated units. For understandable reasons, their discomfort has been particularly acute in cases of the transfer of intangibles, such as the right to use a trade name or a patent bestowed by a parent on a subsidiary. Offered a series of alternative standards by U.S. tax authorities in the pricing of such transfers, the majority of taxpayers have elected the so-called "fourth option", an option that invites them to apply their own *ad hoc* methods for fixing such prices, subject to subsequent IRS approval.[17]

Another substantial problem in the calculation of the net profit of a unit in a multinational network — commonly overlooked in discussions of this sort — is that of determining which unit of a multinational enterprise should be credited with a given sale to an outside buyer. The answer to that question determines which taxing jurisdiction has the benefit of the income generated. This problem arises in various contexts. For instance, in the sale of big-ticket products, such as a pre-packaged plant or a supercomputer, various units of a multinational enterprise may be involved, creating ambiguity as to the locus of the transaction. With the sale of intangibles (such as the services of an international bank, an international management consultant firm, or an international advertising agency) to a multinational network, assigning a specific locus to the transaction can prove even more arbitrary.

To finesse problems of this sort, policymakers have sometimes turned in frustration to the possibility of inferring the level of profit from the level of assets employed by the taxpaying unit.[18] But the definition of assets contains as many problems of arbitrary assignment as the definition of profits. The critical elements in the package of assets employed by any subsidiary include the same intangibles that create such difficulties in the estimation of profits: access to the data, skills, and guarantees of the rest of the multinational network, licenses to use existing trademarks and patents, and so on.

To make matters even more difficult, the value of a unit to the multinational network as a whole is often not reflected in its profit and loss statement. If each unit of the network were nothing more than a portfolio investment of the parent, a profit-and-loss statement might be highly informative as to the value of the unit. Seen from the viewpoint of the network, however, the principal function of a given unit may be to acquire information and experience in the local environment to be shared with others in the network, or to reduce the rent that a global rival might otherwise capture through its sales in the local market.

The tax problems described above are not created by the NAFTA; they have existed as long as governments have taxed the units of multinational networks. When they have arisen in the past, they have been disposed of by lawyers and accountants wrestling with national tax collectors and national courts. Bilateral tax treaties have taken the edges off incipient conflicts between rival national collectors, but the unilateral power of the state, largely through the pretense that it can determine an objectively defensible measure of profit, has been the principal force determining the outcome.

It remains to be seen whether the efforts of tax collectors to capture the profits of the multinational network can be contained in the heightened intimacy among the parties that the NAFTA is expected to create. Recent signs are not reassuring.[19] Between 1980 and 1987, the U.S. Internal Revenue Service increased its staff of international examiners from 200 to 500, and between 1984 and 1991 its related staff of economists grew from 20 to 80. During this period, IRS progressively elaborated and extended its regulations regarding transfer pricing,[20] while Congress moved to place increasing burdens and penalties on taxpayers in connection with the allocation process.[21] Not surprisingly, therefore, litigation arising out of the allocations made by multinational enterprises increased considerably in numbers and amounts, while pending cases faced interminable delays.[22]

To be sure, the U.S. Treasury Department has struggled to find new ways to address the allocations issue, including the possibility of giving advance approval to taxpayers on the methods they propose to use. From early indications, it appears that large enterprises that can foresee substantial shipments of well-defined products and services across borders inside the NAFTA area may well be able to reduce their fiscal uncertainties through these advance pricing agreements; indeed, in terms of tax dollars at stake, such agreements may dispose of a large part of the problem. But indications so far are that the costs of developing such agreements to both taxpayer and government will prove so forbidding as to represent a continuing barrier to entry for all but the largest taxpayers.[23]

Measuring Regional Content

More immediate problems, however, will be created by the requirements in the NAFTA treaty limiting free trade privileges for some products to those with specified minimum regional content. As other studies in this volume note, the criteria for determining regional content as prescribed by the NAFTA vary from product to product and service to service. Most of these provisions are carefully designed to ensure that suppliers from outside countries will be denied any of the indirect benefits of the free trade agreement, such as having their goods and services incorporated in products that move freely inside the free trade area.

In order to qualify a shipment for duty-free treatment inside the NAFTA, the units of multinational enterprises that are shipping their products across borders inside the area will commonly be obliged to demonstrate that the regional content of a shipment exceeds a prescribed standard, ordinarily 50 percent of its value. When calculating the regional content, the enterprise will be required to subtract from the total value of the shipment any components acquired from outside the region, as well as various expenditures inside the area that ordinarily would be regarded as a business cost, such as advertising and after-sale services. In the case of automobiles and parts, however, the taxpayer will actually have to delete not only the components imported from outside the region but also the imported subcomponents for components assembled in the region. To respond to such requirements, multinational networks will have to make at least three kinds of allocations: distributing the expenditures of the network among its various affiliated units; distributing the expenses of any unit among the products it produces; and distributing the expenses for any product between those remaining in the originating country and those shipped across a border in the NAFTA region. In this never-never land of accounting practice, the incentive of the taxpayer to make such allocations in the first instance along lines that favour its interests should prove irresistible.

As with taxes, the provisions of the treaty will be interpreted in the first instance by national authorities, leading to national decisions whether to extend the free trade privilege to any given shipment. A disconcerting preview of what such determinations will entail is provided by the U.S. Treasury's interminable deliberations over the regulations required to implement the relevant provisions of the FTA. And a glimpse of the unending campaigns likely to be launched over such issues is afforded by experiences under the FTA, such as the efforts of U.S. interests to demonstrate that the Honda Civic, assembled in Canada, is not a North American car. In this case, the authorities who investigated this question in the United States and in Canada produced flatly different results.[24] It takes no great leap of the imagination to visualize the cases piling up for adjudication and arbitration, as lawyers, accountants and customs officials debate the application of the treaty's uncertain standards in ways that best serve their respective interests.

THE GOVERNMENTS

THE NAFTA SIGNATORIES will not find it simple to accommodate the cross-border links among the units of multinational enterprises in the agreements governing their economic relations, including those relating to taxation and the measurement of regional content in the free trade area. In the heightened economic intimacy among the three parties sought by the NAFTA, there will no doubt be other difficult issues (addressed elsewhere in this volume) involving these multinational networks, such as the application of antitrust policy (Graham & Warner), security policy (Frost & Graham), and social policy (Mayer). Under the anticipated rules of the game, therefore, the occasions for mutual irritation among the signatory states are likely to increase in number. What is more, experience indicates that issues that seem limited and parochial to the United States may be seen as major threats by Mexico and Canada, commanding the attention of heads of state and altering the atmosphere in which the foreign relations of all three countries are conducted.[25]

That prospect raises the question of the future behaviour of the member governments as these irritations materialize. Will institutions and attitudes evolve and adapt in response to a learning process? Or will the irritations rise to a destructive level threatening neighbourly relations? The answers to these questions are anyone's guess, but some general observations regarding the political processes involved should help to narrow the guesswork.

SETTING THE STAGE

AMONG INDUSTRIALIZED DEMOCRATIC countries projects as ambitious as the North American Free Trade Agreement, aimed at recasting international economic relationships, are relatively rare. Usually, when such projects are launched they are linked to some major international development that temporarily reduces the veto power of powerful groups inside the participating countries. In the aftermath of the Second World War, for instance, interest group pressures were relatively restrained as governments negotiated agreements on the Bretton Woods institutions, on trade liberalization measures under the General Agreement on Tariffs and Trade, and on a succession of projects culminating in the creation of the European Economic Community. The altered economic map these measures produced in Europe led European states outside the Community to huddle together under the European Free Trade Agreement. And, precipitated by the dissolution of the Soviet Union and the end of the Cold War, a wave of radical international proposals emerged from Europe that could not have been seriously entertained in less perilous times.

The North American Free Trade Agreement, on the other hand, is not the obvious product of great political changes affecting all its member countries. Of the three countries, during the 1980s, only Mexico was wrestling with the kind of challenge that is usually associated with major changes in international economic relations. This was the period during which Mexicans were just beginning to recover from the traumatic experiences of a debt default and a sudden plunge in living standards. Canada, too, was suffering from major political stresses at the time; but these were largely internal, involving its neighbouring countries only peripherally. In the United States, as usual, the western hemisphere occupied a back seat to relations with Europe, Asia and the Soviet bloc.

In retrospect, the formulation of the North American Free Trade Agreement was the result of two political initiatives, neither of which came from its key member, the United States. The first of these initiatives, from Canada, produced the Free Trade Agreement. And the second, from Mexico City, led to the negotiation of the NAFTA. In both instances, the negotiations commanded front-page attention in the home newspapers of the initiating country, while being almost entirely disregarded in the U.S. media.

In the case of negotiations between Canada and the United States over the FTA, the first few years were an exercise in acute frustration for the Canadian side.[26] To begin with, the U.S. Congress had to consider whether to endow the president with so-called fast track authority, a step needed to ensure that Congress would take up any negotiated agreement for approval in timely fashion and without the option of amendment. In the event, the negotiations were almost stillborn. As the project became entangled with a trade dispute over the importation of softwood lumber from Canada, a critical congressional committee almost quashed the idea of authorizing the president to undertake the negotiations.

Once the authorization was received, U.S. responses to Canadian initiatives represented a study in slow motion. And when the Canadians put forward proposals representing a radical departure from past practices — such as provisions that would substantially restrain both countries from applying import restrictions to offset subsidies and dumping — the proposals were referred to officials at relatively low levels of the U.S. government, who realistically saw themselves as lacking any mandate for significant change.

As the negotiators approached the end of the period in which the president could exercise fast-track powers,U.S. procrastination eventually led to a crisis. On the Canadian side, the issue had long been seen as one of paramount importance, engaging the full-time attention of its prime minister. On the U.S. side, the threat of a collapse in negotiations finally elevated the issue to cabinet level, commanding the attention of James A. Baker, then President Reagan's Secretary of the Treasury. The compromises that were hurriedly crafted in the face of imminent deadlines engaged no more than a handful of officials. Some of those proposals, such as that for a binational court to deal with certain disputes, were highly imaginative and full of promise, but on the whole they did not reflect anything deeper on the U.S. side than the cleverness of a few officials in an emergency.

The negotiations among Mexico, the United States and Canada over a NAFTA, which followed a few years later, were launched on the initiative of Mexico alone. Canada entered into the negotiations (according to Maureen Molot) largely to protect itself from a dilution of the preferential advantages in the U.S. market it had previously acquired under the FTA. The positive response of the United States to the Mexican initiative was due largely to a perception in the Bush administration that the negotiations might generate some short-run tactical advantages for the United States. Chief among those advantages, it was thought, would be the influence of the negotiations on the outcome of concurrent negotiations in the so-called Uruguay round, a global effort under the sponsorship of the GATT to reduce existing barriers to trade in goods and services. Accordingly, U.S. proposals in the NAFTA negotiations were framed in part with an eye to the content of the GATT negotiations. One U.S. objective was to secure the adoption under the NAFTA of provisions on which the United States feared it might be rebuffed in the GATT negotiations, such as strengthening intellectual property laws and restraining governments from imposing performance requirements on foreign-owned firms. The NAFTA negotiations were also useful from the U.S. standpoint in signalling Europe and Japan that the United States might have an effective counteraction if the rest of the world were to organize itself in exclusionary trading blocs.

In the United States, however, issues such as these are not the stuff of high politics. Although in Mexico and Canada the negotiations may have been seen as entailing fateful choices affecting the basic structure of their international relations, in the United States they were seen largely as a technical exercise of limited consequence, to be judged by their marginal effects on the environment, employment, Mexican emigration, and similar limited criteria.

Other studies in this volume note with some satisfaction (as rightly they should) the extent of the commitments to free trade and investment among its signatories.[27] Yet, one must not overlook the fact that the agreement skirts all the hard issues of sovereignty that the European Community treaty tackles head on. The NAFTA represents a set of explicit agreements to be interpreted and enforced in the first instance by national officials, not a blueprint for a set of institutions that would develop and oversee the operation of a free trade area. The NAFTA is much more akin to the familiar bilateral treaties among governments that in the past have sought to introduce some semblance of predictability into the treatment of foreign investments by governments[28] and its interpretation is left to future negotiation and arbitration among the parties rather than to any autonomous institutions endowed with that power. Many of the investment provisions of the NAFTA are modeled on similar provisions found in such treaties, and the lists of exceptions from the treaty's principles that each government has declared are typical of such treaties.

Lacking central institutions, the effectiveness of such treaties depends overwhelmingly on the history, values and institutions of its signatories, a subject addressed below. I can confidently offer certain generalizations about U.S. history, values and institutions bearing on its likely behaviour under the NAFTA, including questions relating to the issues surrounding multinational enterprises. I am also prepared to take the risk and accept the responsibility for some observations with regard to Mexico. Writing for a Canadian audience on Canadian territory, however, I cannot summon the courage to make any but the most qualified observations about Canada, leaving an extension of my observations on that score to the Canadian authors in this volume.

THE UNITED STATES

ONE OF THE BASIC CHARACTERISTICS of the political process in the United States is its persistent pursuit of two objectives that seem close to irreconcilable: efficiency in the execution of public programs, and the development of a system of checks and balances that diffuses public authority and restrains any office from controlling the decisionmaking process. Any democratic society, of course, is bound to exhibit some interest in both of these objectives; but the emphasis on the diffusion of authority reflected in institutions and values in the United States is unmatched among the industrialized democracies.

Observers outside the United States have some difficulty reconciling that generalization with the picture of the United States as the one remaining superpower, alone able to mobilize and employ the resources for a Gulf War. It is true that in matters of high politics, where the issue is that of confronting an external adversary, the U.S. president exerts unusual power in his dual roles as commander-in-chief and head of state. However, there is a stark contrast in the president's power between facing an enemy without and apportioning economic costs and benefits within the economy.

The underlying reasons for the pronounced dispersion of power in the U.S. federal structure are of only passing interest here, although they merit some brief comment because they hint broadly at a pattern of poorly co-ordinated and inconsistent behaviour, which is unlikely to maintain strong national support over the long run.[29]

The most obvious reason for the dispersion is the three-branch structure of the U.S. government, a structure that allows the courts and the Congress to stop the executive in its tracks on many issues. Reflecting that division, one sees within the executive branch a marked degree of autonomy among the various agencies and departments, with each such unit cultivating links to related congressional committees and special interest organizations that might prove useful in the protection of that autonomy.

Another reason for the dispersion of power within the executive branch of the U.S. government derives from the staffing of some 3,000 top positions in the executive branch—positions classified as exempt from civil service hiring requirements. Such positions, as the Clinton administration's experience amply demonstrates, bring together a team of great diversity—diverse in background and experience, in educational attainment, in geographical origin, and in personal values. As a result, the possibility of co-ordination among bureaus and departments on any issue of common interest faces special obstacles.

Moreover, most members of the team have no intention of making a career in the executive branch of government; indeed, experience tells us that on the average they are likely to hold their jobs for less than three years. Many see themselves as policy entrepreneurs, charged with selling a given set of policies in the shortest possible time. Such officials usually feel obliged to move fast, avoiding wherever they can the time-consuming processes of building coalitions and framing a wide consensus in support of any issue. As a result, many members of these teams exhibit a heavy preference for building a direct route to the White House, hoping to bypass the formal structures of inter-agency committees and subcommittees that each administration erects in an effort to improve its internal coordination processes. To be sure, such committees often struggle with heavy agendas, especially in the processing of decisions such as the details of trade agreements and of export control measures that have been relegated by their political masters to the permanent civil service. But the processing of substantial policy changes within the executive branch commonly bypasses the formal co-ordinating structures, to be settled by the president or those immediately surrounding him.

These shortcircuiting manoeuvers sometimes allow the executive branch to take positions with relative alacrity and flexibility, a capability that accounts in part for the relative activism of U.S. representatives in international negotiations. These same manoeuvers also substantially increase the risk of producing results that are unco-ordinated and inconsistent and are incapable of garnering national support in the long run.

The problems of co-ordination and consensus-building in the U.S. political process are not helped by the fact that the Congress has developed a structure over the past few decades in which effective co-ordination is especially difficult. Hundreds of subcommittees exert their influence on obscure provisions of increasingly lengthy statutes. The principal co-ordination among government agencies often comes from interest groups that have a special interest in some specific provision, rather than from the leadership in Congress or in the executive branch. The content of statutes is frequently shaped, therefore, by little-ventilated provisions that emerge from arcane struggles among interest groups.

This thumbnail sketch of the decision-making processes in the United States does offer a few hints as to the role the U.S. is likely to play in the evolution of the NAFTA. As I observed earlier, the 1,500 pages of the NAFTA text touch the interests of many departments and agencies of the executive branch, and committees of the legislative branch of the U.S. government. Moreover, it bears repeating that the interpretation and application of these NAFTA provisions will lie in the first instance with national officials drawn from these departments and agencies, and accountable in part to these legislative committees. These circumstances suggest the possibility of reactions and initiatives from a number of sources. Furthermore, if my generalizations are accurate, these reactions and initiatives will not likely be responsive to any overarching public policy. In the NAFTA context, for example, those who expect some degree of co-ordination between the customs authorities and the tax authorities, both housed in the Treasury Department, will find that a thicket of legal and bureaucratic restraints places draconian limits on such co-ordination.

The implications are especially disconcerting for issues likely to involve multinational enterprises, including not only issues of income allocation and regional content, but also issues of national security, antitrust, and technology transfer. The guidelines of the NAFTA, detailed though they may be, still leave ample room for interpretation, offering assiduous national officials and interest groups in the United States numerous opportunities to use the agreement for self-serving initiatives against foreign interests. The pressures from litigious domestic groups, targeted at congressional committees and government agencies, could also produce a pattern of responses on the part of the United States that are so self-serving and parochial as to put its partners in the agreement constantly on the defensive. The risk, therefore, is that U.S. reactions to the provisions of the NAFTA may in the end undermine the agreement, through a process that the Chinese describe as "death by a thousand cuts". The question then would be whether the fragile dispute-resolution machinery of the NAFTA is capable of bearing the burden.

MEXICO

THE HISTORY, INSTITUTIONS AND VALUES of Mexico that have a bearing on its behaviour under the NAFTA have little in common with those of the United States, and suggest a very different set of outcomes.[30]

Mexico is a country caught up in a process of extremely rapid change. That change is most apparent in the economic sphere, where a decade of disastrous performance under Presidents Echeverria and Lopez Portillo has been followed by one of recovery and growth under de la Madrid and Salinas de Gortari. Meanwhile, the social structure of Mexico has also been changing in ways that are consistent with that of a rapidly industrializing country. An urban middle class has been growing rapidly. It includes a substantial contingent of entrepreneurs, technicians and skilled workers whose economic roots are in the private sector to a far greater degree than in the past.[31]

The apparatus of government, especially in its topmost echelons, has become increasingly capable and efficient; indeed, when measured by their technical credentials, the cabinet-level officials of the Mexican government outshine their counterparts in most governments in the world, not excluding their neighbours to the north. Corruption and inefficiency remain an endemic problem, pervading the lower ranks of the bureaucracy and sometimes involving their superiors, but despite the vigorous measures taken to deal with such issues, such problems will likely persist; and, inasmuch as the NAFTA relies upon national officials at relatively low levels to apply its many complex provisions, it is reasonable to anticipate that Mexico's application of those provisions will not be free of such problems.

Projecting the political evolution of Mexico poses more difficult questions. Until very recently, the Mexican political process persistently exhibited some of the characteristic patterns of the hispanic political culture from which it had sprung. In nearly two centuries of the country's existence, the concept of a loyal opposition was almost unknown. Accordingly, any organized dissent was seen as carrying the seeds of potential armed rebellion. The autonomous power of the office of the presidency far exceeded anything to be found elsewhere in North America. The right of ministers and their agents to dispense privileges and punishments selectively was rarely challenged. There was little recourse for an aggrieved citizenry.

However, as the Unger study suggests elsewhere in this volume, some substantial shifts in Mexico's political processes have been apparent over the past decade. The Salinas administration has formally supported the idea of ending the monopoly of power that its party, the Partido Revolucionario Institucional, has exercised. Opposition parties have been much less inhibited in their expressions of dissent, and the government has been much more responsive to allegations of electoral fraud. Whether these are early signs of a major shift in Mexican politics, presaging genuinely contested national elections for the presidency, is unclear. If major changes are in the wind, however, the changes introduce a new uncertainty in assessing Mexico's future commitment to the NAFTA.

On the whole, Mexico's formal adherence to the NAFTA is probably less in question than that of its partners. With public opinion and the judicial process in a relatively weak position to compel policy changes from the executive, Mexico's president is more likely to have the determining role in setting the country's policies toward the NAFTA. One could picture a future president renouncing its commitment to the NAFTA in an uninhibited exercise of power akin to President Cardenas' 1938 nationalization of foreign oil properties. But, given the likely advantages for Mexico implicit in the NAFTA, a more plausible projection is that of Mexico's continued adherence, even in an atmosphere of acrimonious exchanges with its partners.

If Mexico's adherence to the provisions of the NAFTA proves grossly incomplete in any respect, it is likely to be due to the inadequacy of its bureaucratic resources, the corruption of some of its officials, and the lack of independence of its courts. For some functions, such as the levying of duties, corruption or incompetence are unlikely to threaten relations among the NAFTA partners very seriously. In other areas, however, such as the curbing of pollution and the enforcement of labour laws, allegations of corruption or incompetence could prove more serious. Issues such as these, however, are more likely to constitute a threat to the continued adherence of the United States to the treaty, as they are pressed by special interest groups, than to that of Mexico.

One added factor that should be considered in the present context is whether the central role of multinational enterprises under the NAFTA arrangements will affect Mexico's reactions to the treaty. Until the 1980s, Mexico's ambivalence toward U.S.-based multinational enterprises provided a major ingredient for its foreign economic policies. On the one hand, most Mexican governments assiduously sought to persuade such enterprises to set up units on Mexican soil. On the other, Mexican law excluded such enterprises from substantial segments of the Mexican economy such as the oil industry, and demanded joint ventures with selected Mexican interests for most of those admitted. And once admitted, Mexican ministries did not hesitate to squeeze major concessions from such units wherever they thought their demands would not drive the unit out of the country.

One of the most dramatic changes in Mexican policy embodied in the NAFTA, as Unger emphasizes, is the lifting of many of the restraints on foreign direct investment heretofore in effect. It is widely taken for granted that this shift represents a widespread change in Mexican attitudes, unlikely to be reversed. My judgment is much more reserved. Having observed the equivocal reaction of U.S. interests to the increase in Japanese investment in the United States, I have no difficulty in imagining a swing of the pendulum in Mexico that could put foreign investors in that country once more on the defensive, thereby straining some of the agreements incorporated in the NAFTA. But, unless the U.S. government adopts an extraordinarily aggressive role in protecting and defending the Mexican units of U.S.-based multinational networks, it seems unlikely that Mexican adherence to the agreement will be threatened from this quarter.

CANADA

THE STUDIES OF SOME of my Canadian colleagues in this volume cover some of the same territory for Canada that my remarks on the United States and Mexico have sought to cover. To this outsider, however, Canada's behaviour under the NAFTA seems to pose a more difficult problem in projection than does the behaviour of the United States or Mexico. Canada has a long history of trying to maintain its political and cultural distinctiveness against the powerful centripetal pull of its southern neighbor.

Understandably, Canada has often reacted with the strongest reservations to any proposal that seemed to pool the sovereign power of Canada with that of the United States, seeing such proposals as the pitting of a mouse against an elephant. In supporting a free trade agreement with the United States, therefore, some Canadians have seen their choice as the lesser of two evils, that is, as a means for avoiding the even greater harm that the uninhibited unilateral trade measures of the United States might otherwise inflict.

With that background, as Maureen Molot has pointed out to me, some Canadians can be expected to resist the harmonization of national rules and practices among the three member countries, fearful that U.S. practices may dominate. A *fortiori*, there will be considerable resistance to the creation of supranational institutions in which the United States participates unless numerous other countries are included in the arrangement.[32]

Another factor to be taken into account in speculating over the behaviour of Canada in the NAFTA is the parliamentary form of its national government. Once the NAFTA is in force, continued adherence to the treaty is likely to be treated as a major issue of great consequence, to be fought out on the political battlefield. Within any administration, therefore, one might expect a relatively high degree of predictability and control in the country's policies toward the NAFTA, especially in those cases in which one party holds a majority in the national parliament. But the likelihood of shifts in party control from time to time does seem to introduce an element of uncertainty not to be found in the United States or Mexico.

The question I find myself puzzling over, then, is how a country with Canada's unique characteristics is likely to behave over the long run. Will the strength of its provincial governments serve to punch holes in the fabric of the agreement? Will its periodic crises over Quebec affect the country's position? Will the east-west division of the country, reflecting very different relationships with the United States, play a role? From my uninstructed vantage point, the problems of prediction seem formidable.

CONCLUSIONS

THE NAFTA IS A PRODUCT OF ITS TIMES. It reflects some of the resignation of political leaders in its three member countries to the fact that no nation is an island, and that the intertwining of economic destinies is an inescapable trend. It reflects, too, a pervasive uncertainty among policymakers whether that process is best achieved through small regional groupings or through global efforts such as those in the GATT. One cannot assume, therefore, that its adoption or rejection will greatly influence the future shape of events over the long term.

Nevertheless, the rejection of the NAFTA or the egregious malfunctioning of the treaty could easily help to generate a long detour in international economic relations as sectoral and regional interests in each of the member countries turn inward in a vain search for security and growth. As usual, therefore, the stakes in the NAFTA lie more in the risk of losses than in the hope of significant gains.

As I have previously observed, the provisions of the NAFTA suffer from a touch of unreality in their failure directly to acknowledge the existence of multinational enterprises and to deal realistically with some of the issues associated with such structures. That omission is likely to be revealed in time, creating very substantial difficulties in the application of the agreement. I doubt, however, that the omission will prove so fateful as to lead to the denunciation of the agreement once it has been ratified. Nevertheless, once ratified, the NAFTA faces a troubled future. The fact that the agreement has not arisen out of some compelling political threat recognized by all its members constitutes an endemic source of weakness. That problem is exacerbated by the fact that its application lies so completely in the hands of national authorities; when coupled with the internal structure of the federal government in the United States, the probability of inconsistent and unco-ordinated U.S. responses seems distressingly high. So too does the probability that those responses will have been initiated in the first instance by special interests unconcerned with the overall impact of the treaty on their respective economies.

On the other hand, the treaty brings manifest advantages to some major economic sectors in each of the three member countries. Some of its provisions for the freeing of trade in goods and services and for the treatment of foreign investment, for instance, break altogether new ground. This could mean that the NAFTA will eventually create its own supporting constituencies, such as border communities, service industries, and multinational enterprises. With such support, the NAFTA could come to represent the first stage in a learning process that produces successive modifications as experience accumulates.

In that case, what modifications should Canada be seeking once the agreement is in force? In exploring this question, much will depend on whether Canadians decide that their best strategy toward the United States is to hold it at arm's length or to hug it more closely to their national bosom. If Canadians regard any closer contact with the U.S. economy as a dangerous move, it is difficult to see how the manifest weaknesses of the NAFTA can be reduced. If, on the other hand, Canadians decide that Canada's influence on the United States will grow with the strengthening of its economic ties, a number of approaches seem possible.

In that case, a major objective for Canada should be to reduce the scope and importance of the regional content requirements of the treaty, which in their present form constitute a threat to its effective operation. The NAFTA already provides for a common level in national duties on computers, thereby obviating the need for calculating regional content on that item. One possibility, therefore, would be to provide for the phased expansion of a list of products which the NAFTA members would use to bring their national duties to a common level.

Another objective should be to reduce the issue of transfer prices in tax matters to more manageable proportions. A start on that objective could be made if multinational enterprises with North American operations that are fairly autonomous from the rest of their global networks were given the option of allocating their North American income to national tax authorities on the basis of a unitary allocation formula.

Still another objective, more general and more ambitious in nature, should be to abandon antisubsidy, antidumping, and other restrictions on "unfair" trade imposed at national borders in favour of a common competition policy applicable to the NAFTA area, an approach championed in the Graham-Warner study in this volume. That pioneering step has already been taken by Australia and New Zealand in trade between them, and it is of course an integral part of the arrangements within the European Community.

Finally, any measures to strengthen the NAFTA agreements, whether taken in the directions suggested above or in other respects, will require an institutional framework far stronger than that contained within the present treaty. Lacking executive or legislative powers, relying almost entirely on arbitration and consultation as a means of reducing its anticipated dossier of conflicts, the NAFTA is threatened from birth with an inability to respond to the lessons learned. Remedying that defect should be a high priority for any Canadian government which believes that on balance the NAFTA serves its national interests.

ENDNOTES

1   For an elaboration of these themes, see my study, "Organizational and Institutional Responses to International Risk" in Richard J. Herring (ed.), *Managing International Risk*, (New York: Cambridge University Press, 1983) pp. 191-216.

2   A classic study demonstrating the existence of the follow-the-leader phenomenon among U.S.-based firms and exploring the motivations behind it is Frederick T. Knickerbocker, *Oligopolistic Reaction and Multinational Enterprise*, (Boston: Harvard Business School, 1973). See also C.J. Yu and K. Ito, "Oligopolistic Reaction and Foreign Direct Investment," *Journal of International Business Studies*, 19, 3, (Fall 1988):449-60. In a subsequent unpublished study, Knickerbocker reported finding similar patterns of behaviour among European-based enterprises. The behaviour of Japan-based enterprises in the United States, Mexico, and Europe suggests a similar pattern; but careful econometric work will be required before one can dispose of alternative explanations.

3   For an extensive contemporary treatment of the point see Michael Porter, *Competitive Advantage of Nations*, (New York: Free Press, 1990). The influence of national origin was probably even more pronounced in earlier years. See for instance Michael Y. Yoshino, *Japan's Multinational Enterprises*, (Cambridge: Harvard University Press, 1976) pp. 61-77; Lawrence G. Franko, *The European Multinationals*, (New York: Harper, 1976) pp. 24-44; and Raymond Vernon, "Influence of National Origins on the Strategy of Multinational Enterprise," *Revue Economique*, xxiii, 5, (July 1972): 547-62.

4   In a number of unpublished memoranda produced in the 1970s, James W. Vaupel confirmed the fact that multinational enterprises had been following characteristic patterns in the geographic sequences by which they established foreign subsidiaries. Such patterns differed according to the home of the parent unit in the multinational enterprise, with cultural and geographical distances apparently playing a major role in the sequencing. For a presentation of some of his results for U.S.-based multinational enterprises, see Raymond Vernon and William Davidson, "Foreign Production of Technology-Intensive Products by U.S.-based Multinational Enterprises," Report to the National Science Foundation, no. PB 80 148638, January 1979.

5   Lorraine Eden suggested this approach, while reacting to an earlier paper of mine on a related subject.

6   In an exemplary study sponsored by the U.N. Department of Economic and Social Development, directed by John H. Dunning and Karl Sauvant and "finalized" by Michelle Gittelman, the reactions of multinational enterprises are carefully explored in the context of the European Community's initiation of its Single Market program in 1987. The analysis

addresses many of the points raised here. See *From the Common Market to EC 92: Regional Economic Integration in the European Community and Transnational Corporations*, (New York: United Nations, 1993).

7 Fact Sheet IV-5-1, December 30, 1992, Investment Canada, Ottawa.

8   An excellent source for Canada until 1970 is Mira Wilkins, *The Maturing of Multinational Enterprises: American Business Abroad from 1914 to 1970*, (Cambridge: Harvard University Press, 1974) esp. p. 143. For Mexico until 1970 see Fernando Fajnzylber and Trinidad Martínez Tarragó, *Las Empresas Transnacionales*, (Mexico, D.F.: Fondo de Cultura Economica, 1976) esp. pp. 285-317.

9   Sales in their local markets by the foreign manufacturing subsidiaries of U.S.-based enterprises fell from 84 percent of their total sales in 1957 to 61 percent in 1987, accompanied by a corresponding increase in their exports. *From the Common Market to EC 92*, Table IV.1, p. 62, based on various reports of the U.S. Department of Commerce.

10 *U.S. Direct Investment Abroad: 1991 Benchmark Survey*, U.S. Department of Commerce, October 1991, various tables.

11 The subsidiaries of U.S.-based multinational networks in the European Community apparently responded to the Community's adoption of its Single Market program in 1985 with a wave of consolidations and adjustments. See *From the Common Market to EC 92*, p. 51.

12 For analyses of past patterns, see for instance Anthony Blackbourn, "The Spatial Behaviour of American Firms in Western Europe," F. F. Ian Hamilton (ed.), *Spatial Perspectives on Industrial Organization and Decision Making*, (London: Wiley, 1974) pp. 245-64; also Cletus C. Cockburn et al., "State Characteristics and the Location of Foreign Direct Investment within the United States," *Review of Economics and Statistics*, xiii, 4, (Nov. 1991):675-83.

13 The experience of the southeast United States as a location for the subsidiaries of foreign manufacturing firms is highly relevant. See for instance "Why German Firms Choose the Carolinas to Build U.S. Plants," *The Wall Street Journal*, May 4, 1993, p. 1.

14 The data were compiled by Subi Rangan from *U.S. Direct Investment Abroad: 1989 Benchmark Survey*, Preliminary Results, U.S. Dept. of Commerce, 1991, Table 86; *Foreign Direct Investment in the United States*, U.S. Dept. of Commerce, 1991, Table G-2; and *Statistical Abstract of the United States*, U.S. Dept. of Commerce. 1991, Table 1404.

15 See Michael Gould, "Strategic Control in the Decentralized Firm," *Sloan Management Review*, 32, 2, (Winter 1991):69; also Anant R. Neganghi, "External and Internal Functioning of American, German, and Japanese Multinational Corporations: Decisionmaking and Policy Issues," in Mark Casson, (ed.), *Multinational Corporations*, (Brookfield, Vermont: Edward Elgar, 1990) pp. 557-78.

16 A hint of the limited relevance of financial resources from the parent in the setting up of foreign subsidiaries is provided in Table C-1, *Foreign Direct*

Investment in the United States: Operations of U.S. Affiliates of Foreign Companies, preliminary 1989 estimates, U.S. Department of Commerce, August 1991, Washington, DC, which shows that, even after excluding retained earnings, 73 percent of the financing of these units came from U.S. sources.

17 The results of five surveys are reported in *A Study of Intercompany Pricing*, U.S. Dept. of Treasury, Washington DC, 1988, Table 6.4.

18 Proposals were made in the course of the 1992 presidential campaign to estimate the taxable income of foreign-owned subsidiaries in the United States by assuming the same return on investment as that recorded by domestically owned firms. These were eventually abandoned in favour of proposals to tighten up existing transfer price regulations; for the latter, see *Summary of the President's Revenue Proposals*, Joint Committee on Taxation, JCS 4-93, USGPO, Washington, DC, 1993, pp. 48-51.

19 For similar opinions, see Dale W. Wickman and Charles J. Kerster, "New Directions Needed for Solution of the International Transfer Pricing Tax Puzzle: Internationally Agreed Rules or Tax Warfare?" *Tax Notes, July 20, 1992*, 56, 3, (July 20, 1992): 349 *passim*, and Gary C. Hufbauer and Joanna van Rooij, "The Coming Global Tax War," *The International Economy*, (Jan./Feb. 1993): 20.

20 For details at various stages in the process, see *A Study of Intercompany Pricing*, Doc. 88-8504, U.S. Treasury Department, Washington, DC; George Carlson, "The Proposed Transfer Pricing Rules: New Wine in an Old Bottle?" *Tax Notes*, (February 10, 1992): 691-716; Elizabeth King, "The Section 482 White Paper and the Proposed Regulations: A Comparison of Key Provisions," *Tax Notes International*, (February 17, 1992): 331-42; and John E. O'Grady, "An Overview of the New Temporary Transfer Pricing Regulations," *Tax Notes International*, (January 25, 1993): 211-23.

21 For an analysis of relevant provisions in the 1990 Omnibus Budget Reconciliation Act, see Dale W. Wickman, "The New U.S. Transfer Pricing Tax Penalty," *The International Tax Journal*, 18, 1, (Winter 1991):1-45.

22 See John Turro, "U.S. Congressional Committee Blasts Foreign Firms for Tax Dodging," *Tax Notes International*, 2, 8, (August [n.d.] 1990): 799; and John E. O'Grady, "Apple and IRS Enter into First Transfer-Pricing Arbitration Under U.S. Tax Court Rule," *Tax Notes International*, 4, 11, (March 16, 1992): 519.

23 See Gerald C. Shea, "APAs May Effectively Address Income and Expense Allocation Problems Faced by Global Trading Businesses," *Tax Notes International*, 4, 20, (May 18, 1992): 1022-24.

24 For background, see Paul Magnusson, "Honda: Is It an American Car?" *Business Week*, 3240, (Nov. 18, 1991): 109; and Lindsay Chappell, "Customs Slaps Honda with Bill for Duty," *Automotive News*, 5433, (Feb. 17, 1992): 1.

25 Experiences under the FTA point in that direction. See for instance, Nancy Wood, "Estranged Partners: Trade Disputes Threaten the FTA," *Macleans*, March 16, 1992, p. 34.

26 For a detailed account of the negotiation as seen through U.S. eyes, see Raymond Vernon, Debora L. Spar, and Glenn Tobin, *Iron Triangles and Revolving Doors: Cases in U.S. Foreign Economic Policymaking*, (New York: Praeger Publishers, 1991) pp. 21-53.

27 For a useful summary and evaluation, see Gary C. Hufbauer and Jeffrey J. Schott, *NAFTA: An Assessment*, (Washington, DC: Institute for International Economics, 1993).

28 See *Bilateral Investment Treaties, 1959-1991*, UN Centre on Transnational Corporations, United Nations, New York, 1992.

29 Among the many sources describing the U.S. decisionmaking process on foreign economic issues are: I.M. Destler, *American Trade Politics*, 2nd edition, (Washington, DC: Institute for International Economics, 1992); Stephen D. Cohen, *The Making of United States International Economic Policy*, (New York: Praeger, 1989); and Raymond Vernon, *et al.*, *Iron Triangles and Revolving Doors*, (New York: Praeger, 1991).

30 See for instance Roberto Newell G. and Luis Rubio F., *Mexico's Dilemma: The Political Origins of Economic Crisis*, (Boulder, Colorado: Westview Press, 1984); Wayne A. Cornelius and Ann L. Craig, *The Mexican Political System in Transition*, (San Diego: University of California, 1991); and Van R. Whiting, Jr., *The Political Economy of Foreign Investment in Mexico*, (Baltimore: Johns Hopkins Press, 1992).

31 See Sylvia Maxfield and Ricardo Anzaldúa Montonoya (eds.) *Government and Private Sector in Contemporary Mexico*, (San Diego: University of California, 1987); and Nora Lustig, *Mexico: the Remaking of an Economy*, (Washington DC: Brookings Institution, 1992).

32 It is worth noting that France's decision to join the European Economic Community despite its strong supranational character was partly motivated by the opposite assumption, namely, by the assumption that France would be able to exercise influence over Germany more effectively in a supranational organization than by intergovernmental agreements.

ACKNOWLEDGEMENT

I WISH TO THANK Katherine Comerford for her indispensable support, especially in her detailed review of U.S. practices relating to taxes and regional content.

BIBLIOGRAPHY

Blackbourn, Anthony. "The Spatial Behaviour of American Firms in Western Europe." In *Spatial Perspectives on Industrial Organization and Decision Making*. Edited by F. E. Ian Hamilton. London: Wiley, 1974, pp. 245-64.

Carlson, George. "The Proposed Transfer Pricing Rules: New Wine in an Old Bottle?" *Tax Notes*, February 10, 1992, pp. 691-716.

Chappell, Lindsay. "Customs Slaps Honda with Bill for Duty." *Automotive News*, February 17, 1992, No. 5433, p. 1.

Cockburn, Cletus C. et al. "State Characteristics and the Location of Foreign Direct Investment within the United States." *Review of Economics and Statistics*, 63, 4 (November 1991): 675-83.

Cohen, Stephen D. *The Making of United States International Economic Policy*. New York: Praeger, 1989.

Cornelius, Wayne A. and Ann L. Craig. *The Mexican Political System in Transition*. San Diego: University of California, 1991.

Destler, I. M. *American Trade Politics*, 2nd edition. Washington, DC: Institute for International Economics, 1992.

Fernando Fajnzylber and Trinidad Martínez Tarragó. *Las Empresas Transnacionales*. Mexico, D.F.: Fondo de Cultura Economica, 1976, pp. 285-317.

Franko, Lawrence G. *The European Multinationals*. New York: Harper, 1976, pp. 24-44.

Gould, Michael. "Strategic Control in the Decentralized Firm." *Sloan Management Review*, 32, 2, (Winter 1991): 69.

Hufbauer, Gary C. and Jeffrey J. Schott. *NAFTA: An Assessment*. Washington, D.C.: Institute for International Economics, 1993.

Hufbauer, Gary C. and Joanna M. van Rooij. "The Coming Global Tax War." *The International Economy*. (January/February 1993): 20.

Investment Canada. Fact Sheet 4-5-1. Ottawa, December 30, 1992.

Joint Committee on Taxation. *Summary of the President's Revenue Proposals*. JCS 4-93. Washington, DC: U.S. Government Printing Office, 1993, pp. 48-51.

King, Elizabeth. "The Section 482 White Paper and the Proposed Regulations: A Comparison of Key Provisions." *Tax Notes International*. February 17, 1992, pp. 331-42.

Knickerbocker, Frederick T. *Oligopolistic Reaction and Multinational Enterprise*. Boston: Harvard Business School, 1973.

Lustig, Nora. *Mexico: The Remaking of an Economy*. Washington, DC: The Brookings Institution, 1992.

Magnusson, Paul. "Honda: Is It an American Car?" *Business Week*, 3240, (November 18, 1991): 109.

Maxfield, Sylvia and Ricardo Anzaldúa Montonoya (eds). *Government and Private Sector in Contemporary Mexico*. San Diego: University of California, 1987.

Neganghi, Anant R. "External and Internal Functioning of American, German, and Japanese Multinational Corporations: Decisionmaking and Policy Issues." In *Multinational Corporations*. Edited by Mark Casson. Brookfield, Vermont: Edward Elgar, 1990, pp. 557-78.

Newell, Roberto G. and Luis Rubio F. *Mexico's Dilemma: The Political Origins of Economic Crisis*. Boulder, Colorado: Westview Press, 1984.

O'Grady, John E. "An Overview of the New Temporary Transfer Pricing Regulations." *Tax Notes International*. (January 25, 1993): 211-23.

_____. "Apple and IRS Enter into First Transfer-Pricing Arbitration Under U.S. Tax Court Rule." *Tax Notes International*, 4, 11, (March 16, 1992): 519.

Porter, Michael. *Competitive Advantage of Nations*. New York: Free Press, 1990.

Shea, Gerald C. "APAs May Effectively Address Income and Expense Allocation Problems Faced by Global Trading Businesses." *Tax Notes International*, 4, 20, (May 18, 1992): 1022-24.

Turro, John. "U.S. Congressional Committee Blasts Foreign Firms for Tax Dodging." *Tax Notes International*, 2, 8, (August (n.d.) 1990): 799.

U.S. Department of Commerce. *Foreign Direct Investment in the United States: Operations of U.S. Affiliates of Foreign Companies*, Preliminary 1989 Estimates. Washington, DC: August 1991, Table C-1.

_____. *Foreign Direct Investment in the United States*. Washington, DC: 1991, Table G-2.

_____. *Statistical Abstract of the United States*. Washington, DC: 1991, Table 1404.

_____. *U.S. Direct Investment Abroad: 1989 Benchmark Survey*, Preliminary Results, 1989, Table 86, and *passim*.

U.S. Treasury Department. *A Study of Intercompany Pricing*. Document 88-8504. Washington, DC: 1988, Table 6.4.

United Nations Centre on Transnational Corporations. *Bilateral Investment Treaties, 1959-1991*. New York: United Nations, 1992.

United Nations. *From the Common Market to EC 92: Regional Economic Integration in the European Community and Transnational Corporations*. New York: 1993, p. 51 and Table 4.1, p. 62.

Vernon, Raymond. "Influence of National Origins on the Strategy of Multinational Enterprise." *Revue Economique*, 23, 5, (July 1972): 547-62.

_____. "Organizational and Institutional Responses to International Risk." In *Managing International Risk*. Edited by Richard J. Herring. New York: Cambridge University Press, 1983, pp. 191-216.

Vernon, Raymond and William Davidson. "Foreign Production of Technology-Intensive Products by U.S.-based Multinational Enterprises." Report to the National Science Foundation, No. PB 80 148638, (January 1979).

Vernon, Raymond et al. *Iron Triangles and Revolving Doors: Cases in U.S. Foreign Economic Policymaking*. New York: Praeger Publishers, 1991, pp. 21-53.

Whiting, Van R. Jr. *The Political Economy of Foreign Investment in Mexico*. Baltimore: Johns Hopkins Press, 1992.

Wickman, Dale W. "The New U.S. Transfer Pricing Tax Penalty." *The International Tax Journal*, 18, 1, (Winter 1991): pp. 1-45.

Wickman, Dale W. and Charles J. Kerster. "New Directions Needed for Solution of the International Transfer Pricing Tax Puzzle: Internationally Agreed Rules or Tax Warfare?" *Tax Notes*, 56, 3, (July 20, 1992): 349 and *passim*.

Wilkins, Mira. *The Maturing of Multinational Enterprises: American Business Abroad from 1914 to 1970*. Cambridge: Harvard University Press, 1974, esp. p. 143.

Wood, Nancy. "Estranged Partners: Trade Disputes Threaten the FTA." *Macleans*, (March 16, 1992): 34.

Yoshino, Michael Y. *Japan's Multinational Enterprises*. Cambridge: Harvard University Press, 1976, pp. 61-77.

Yu, C. J. and K. Ito. "Oligopolistic Reaction and Foreign Direct Investment." *Journal of International Business Studies*, 19, 3, (Fall 1988): 449-60.

B. Curtis Eaton, Richard G. Lipsey & A. Edward Safarian
Economic Growth and Policy Program
Canadian Institute for Advanced Research

3

The Theory of Multinational Plant Location in a Regional Trading Area

INTRODUCTION

THE TASK SET FOR THE AUTHORS of this (and the following) paper was formidable. We were asked to "consider theories of MNE plant location within a regional trading bloc, focusing on how trade and investment policies and technologies are creating tighter economic linkages within North America, and their effects on MNE investment and production decisions". The range of possible sub-topics covers much that is being examined by other authors presenting papers at this Conference.

In deciding which issues to explore, we were guided by several key ideas. First, the investment decisions of interest to the policy makers are not simply those affecting new investment; decisions affecting the existing operations of multinational enterprises (MNEs) are also of interest. Dunning (1993, Ch.3) and others have noted that in earlier periods MNEs passed through an internationalization phase where investments were located in response to local markets and supplies. More recently, MNEs have been going through a globalization phase where the emphasis in investment and divestment is on rationalizing existing operations to secure efficient networks, often under strong competitive pressures. Second, we are interested in changes of so-called headquarters functions as well as in changes of production facilities. Third, although we have manufacturing investment primarily in mind, much of what we say applies, *mutatis mutandis*, to investment in service industries. Finally, both papers are exploratory; they ask more questions than they answer. We hope our preliminary analysis identifies some interesting issues which we can follow up with more detailed work.

The issues we explore in this paper and the one that follows can be grouped under three broad headings. The first is the determinants of investment decisions by MNEs. Second, we consider how the policy framework, particularly regional trading arrangements, affects flows of FDI. Finally, (in the second paper) we examine the effects of such arrangements on the existing concentrations or agglomerations of investment.

The first section of this paper is an overview of the literature on MNE plant location and its application to North America; it is brief in view of Eden's substantial contribution to this topic elsewhere in this volume. A theory of MNE investment should cover three issues: in what form (markets, firms, or alliances) do firms choose to exploit their firm-specific assets; which aspects of a country's advantages attract or retain investment; and how does business strategy more generally affect investment decisions? Most studies suggest that a regional trading arrangement should increase both the inward and outward bound FDI of member countries. If technological change is endogenous, gains would be larger than those often predicted. Moreover, the adjustment effect of an FTA should be relatively small, since so much of it is intra-industry.

The second section explores at some length the effects of the policy framework. Probably the most important influence of free trade areas on FDI comes through alteration of the amount, and security, of access to a set of national markets that can be obtained by locating production facilities in one country. Under both of the North American trading arrangements, however, the effects of non-tariff barriers are merely reduced, and possibilities for trade protection — while reduced — remain. We also explore in some depth various investment effects of the FTA and the NAFTA, such as whether small countries gain more from security of access and just how significant will be the trade and investment diversion implicit in regional trading arrangements.

DETERMINANTS OF MNE INVESTMENT DECISIONS

THERE IS NO AGREED *general* theory of MNE investment, but its elements might be expressed by combining transactional, locational and (other) strategic approaches.[1] The transactional approach notes that a firm has a set of ownership-specific assets or skills, both tangible and intangible, covering production technology, marketing and other skills. The decision to use a controlled subsidiary when going abroad, rather than exports (markets) or licenses and other forms of alliance (contracts), reflects a view that the subsidiary can more fully realize the returns on firm-specific assets, at least up to the point where the costs of such internalization outweigh benefits. The subsidiary form allows opportunistic behaviour by the MNE (e.g., transfer pricing) and limits such behaviour by others (e.g., rapid imitation). It also permits real economies in the sense of more efficient use or transfer of firm-specific assets where markets for these are imperfect. Newer and more advanced technologies, for example, are often more difficult to transfer through market mechanisms (Teece, 1977; Davidson and McFetridge, 1984). Clearly, the precise mode of transfer utilized by MNEs in exploiting their firm-specific advantages abroad has significant consequences for the international location of production. It is of interest, too, that alliance strategies have spread in the 1980s, a topic addressed by Rugman and D'Cruz elsewhere in this volume.

Changes in the location of production have been ascribed generally to four broad sets of factors (McFetridge, 1989, ch. 2): changes in production and distribution technologies; changes in the relative prices of the factors of production; changes in local production costs that are not fully offset by changes in the exchange rate; and, finally, a range of public policies, such as those relating to trade and investment. In addition to these factors, several studies have also tested the important ways in which the size, growth and composition of markets, as well as supply and socio-political parameters, have influenced FDI (Dunning, 1993, Ch. 6). Table 15 in Eden's overview paper elsewhere in this volume, summarizes many of these influences on the location of production by detailing various country-specific advantages and disadvantages for Canada, the United States and Mexico for the 1990s, using a Porter-type classification.

Writers specializing in the study of MNEs have long emphasized such locational issues, which are explicit, for example, in the product cycle model developed by Vernon (1967, 1979). This model describes a sequence in which innovations lead to exports which, in turn, lead to foreign production through FDI. As the product becomes standardized over time and production costs become the major determinant of plant location, the good is frequently exported back to the innovating country. Over the past decade, particularly, trade theory has incorporated MNEs into its predictions on trade and investment by emphasizing imperfect competition and increasing returns. The link to the transactions cost approach is the existence of some inputs (such as research and other firm-specific assets noted earlier) which can serve product lines abroad without being located there. The recognition of such economies of multi-plant operation yield further insights into the location decisions of MNEs, as Scherer et al. (1975) have noted in some detail. Another important recent development is based on Romer's research (1986, 1990) in which technological change is endogenous and human capital is more fully integrated into models of growth. Grossman and Helpman (1990) develop the implications of this at the international level. Their distinction between efficiency in production and efficiency in R&D is brought out further in the concluding section of the next paper. It may be noted that countries must deal with such technological changes regardless of the nature of trading arrangements. Their interaction with MNEs and trade liberalization are complex. We deal with them briefly at several points in this paper.

We suggest that business strategy be treated as a third determinant of MNE investment patterns along with transactional and locational determinants. Typically, the degree of interdependence among MNEs is high. In light of this, questions of location of production also encompass the element of business strategy, which is developed in relation to the firm's competitive environment. This involves a broad spectrum of choices well beyond simple considerations of price and production, including the nature and timing of investment in R&D, the organizational structure of the MNE, and the basic decision as to whether to locate in a particular country.

It may seem odd at first to break out industry structure from firm-specific assets (transactional factors) and country-specific assets (location factors), particularly the former. After all, the industrial organization literature has explored strategic issues in depth, thanks in part to Caves' (1971) extension of Hymers' analysis, while the literature on business strategy continues to provide valuable additional research (for example, Porter 1986, 1990 and Morrison, 1990). We emphasize the fact that the firm's management must make long-term commitments under conditions of substantial uncertainty — driven both by factors outside the control of the industry and by the presumed or actual reactions of competitors.[2]

As Graham (1991) has noted, the topic of strategy keeps moving in and out of the economics literature, whereas it deserves a central place. In support of this contention, one can cite the example that the gains a country derives from trade liberalization depend to a considerable degree on the precise nature of the oligopolistic — strategic — responses which occur, a point brought out later in this paper. Another example is that international mergers and acquisitions, as distinct from greenfield investment, now dominate the value of inward FDI being made in such countries as the United States, Canada and the United Kingdom, and that these mergers and acquisitions have become relatively more important for these countries and for Europe over time.[3] Both theory and empirical tests suggest that an important strategic response to trade liberalization is to increase FDI in general and international mergers in particular (for example, Graham, 1978, 1991; Mersenier & Schmitt (1992); and Caves & Mehra, 1986).

MNE INVESTMENTS AND NORTH AMERICAN TRADING ARRANGEMENTS: RECENT STUDIES

THE DEVELOPMENT OF regional trading arrangements between Canada and the United States and between those countries and Mexico has spurred a number of studies exploring the effect of these trading arrangements on investment and production in general and those by MNEs in particular. Eden's paper in this volume includes a review of those studies involving Canada and MNE investments. Various other sources include Eden (1991), Safarian (1991), and McFetridge (1989). At the risk of over-simplification, we have summarized these conclusions below to identify some particular issues on which we focus.

First, a major objective for Canada in the FTA negotiations was to preserve trading access to the much larger U.S. market so that investment would remain in, or continue to be attracted to, Canada. Clearly, Canada's posture with respect to investment was defensive — as was its position in deciding to enter the NAFTA. The alternative would likely have been the development of an extensive hub-and-spoke model wherein the United States makes separate bilateral deals with each of several countries, and hence is the only country where investment has freer access to each market. One extreme way to look at this defensive approach is to measure the cost to Canada in terms of short-term job losses resulting from a trade war between the United States and its major trading partners in which both sides sideswipe Canada by putting a 20 percent import surcharge on most manufactured goods. In 1988, the Economic Council of Canada estimated this job loss at close to 450,000 jobs.[4] (Of course, as with tariff changes, the unemployment is only transitory — but the period of good jobs lost to poorer jobs lasts as long as the trade restrictions last.) We consider the issue of policy stability later in the section on Security of Access.

Second, according to conventional trade theory Canada was, with some qualifications, likely to gain significantly from trade liberalization in terms of real income. Moreover, the adjustment involved for most sectors would be relatively swift. The arguments for the real income gains went well beyond the traditional case for more specialization and access to a much larger market. Unrealized scale economies, it was argued, would be significant given the inefficient structure of production in much of the Canadian manufacturing sector (resulting from long-term protection of small markets where oligopoly was common). General equilibrium models with imperfect competition and scale economies pointed to significant gains from reduced protection in both directions (Harris & Cox, 1984). One qualification, however, was that many of the potential gains from scale and specialization had already been realized subsequent to the Kennedy and Tokyo rounds and that the size of the gains depended on the particular assumptions which were made about pricing behaviour and entry barriers (Hazledine, 1990). A further qualification noted by Harris & Cox and in other studies was that, while most of the adjustment would be intra-industry and hence relatively swift, this would not be the case for a number of relatively labour-intensive sectors where adjustment costs were significant.

Third, the effects of protection on direct investment are either weaker or more complex than suggested by some earlier studies. Variables other than trade protection are important to FDI location, as our survey of the determinants of MNE location suggested. MNEs may favour subsidiaries rather than markets or alliances quite apart from whether protection exists. Moreover, the notion that trade and FDI are merely substitutes has long since been challenged convincingly (for example, Lipsey & Weiss 1981, 1984). Clearly, protection is relevant to FDI decisions in some situations. For many firms located in Canada, however, although the protection that existed when they entered the industry decades ago may have been relevant, the protection existing in the 1980s was not necessarily so. The issue then becomes how established firms — both domestically and foreign-owned — will react in response to import pressures and export opportunities offered by freer trade. The concensus appearing in the literature elsewhere (such as the EC) is that economic integration tends to increase FDI within and into the area and, with a lag, it increases outward-bound investment as well. It is true that any decrease in protection should reduce protection-induced FDI. This effect is likely to be outweighed by the reduction in transfer costs, so that MNEs head-quartered both inside and outside the free trade area can co-ordinate production facilities more effectively throughout the larger market (Dunning 1993, 483-4). We have already noted (at the end of the previous section) that an important strategic response to trade liberalization is to increase FDI generally, and FDI related to international mergers particularly.

One set of studies for Canada, based on responses to the trade liberalization, supply shocks and other competitive pressures in the 1970s and early 1980s, was retrospective. The general conclusion appeared to be that both MNEs and domestic firms engage in product specialization in response to trade liberalization, but it is difficult to measure specialization precisely (McFetridge, 1989, pp. 15-16). For example, from a close study of a small number of matched domestic and foreign-owned firms, Daly & MacCharles (1986) concluded that the latter adjusted more slowly to trade changes, while in a detailed statistical analysis over time Baldwin & Gorecki (1983) apparently found little difference in this respect.

Prospective studies used surveys to examine firms' expected responses to future trade liberalization. (For a summary see McFetridge, 1989, 18-19). They emphasize specialization rather than exit. Rugman (1988) in particular points to a relatively easy adjustment by most of the larger U.S.-owned firms that are already competitive or can be made so within the MNE network. By contrast smaller domestic and foreign-owned firms, particularly those geared to the domestic market, are expected to have larger problems, even though many were rationalized before the free trade agreement. More such rationalization appears likely for the affiliates (Crookell & Bishop, 1985). Both foreign and domestic firms will also engage in "niche playing" and developing their existing small-batch, small-market skills. In general, these studies conclude that a wave of plant closures is unlikely to result from freer trade.

The firms on which these studies are based are largely domestic and foreign-owned manufacturers already in Canada. The FTA was expected to precipitate increased investment in Canadian natural resources by both foreign and Canadian MNE's, given that Canada has a comparative advantage in respect of these and the effects that even small, actual or threatened barriers to exports can have in this sector. The removal of such barriers to FDI in services should also increase investment. Overseas investors might increase FDI in Canada to serve the combined market, other things equal, on the grounds that access to the larger market was less likely to be blocked.

Finally, Canada's FDI in the United States would decline insofar as its presence there constituted a response to actual or potential protection, but it would increase insofar as the FDI was complementary to the increased trade that occurs when co-ordination costs are reduced. In general, these considerations point to increases in both inward- and outward-bound FDI as a result of the FTA. In the section on Security of Access, we examine the critical issue of market access that underlies many of these studies.

It is still too early for definitive studies of the actual effects of the FTA (much less the NAFTA), but two observations are in order. The first is that Canadian debate has focused on the magnitude (i.e., the number) of job losses allegedly attributable to the FTA, as distinct from other causes such as recession and an over-valued Canadian dollar. A survey of the five studies that have addressed this issue — tentative as they are — suggests that at most 15 per cent of the current job losses are attributable to the short-term adjustments due to the FTA (Waverman, 1993). Of course, job losses are only the first half of the process of the gains from tariff reduction, which come from the reallocation of labour: i) out of inefficient, mainly import-competing industries (job losses) and ii) into efficient, mainly exporting industries (job gains). The long-term effects of the FTA on increased efficiency, and possibly on overall growth, have not yet been felt. Those longer-term issues are the main focus of this and the paper that follows.

Our second point is that Canada is engaged in a very complex re-organization of its national production, involving a wide range of business elements, including MNEs, and that this re-organization is being driven not just by North American trading arrangements, but by increased trade and investment competition and by technological changes generally. Investment motives differ by type of MNE, as noted earlier but, clearly, some significant restructuring is occurring by way of further specialization and consequent increases in intra-firm trade. This restructuring raises a number of important questions, one of which is the focus for the rest of this paper — namely the extent to which North American trading arrangements offer policy stability for domestic and foreign investment. How far can we actually go in removing barriers to product and factor mobility? In the accompanying paper, we also consider what happens to the agglomerations of economic activity built up in each of the three North American countries when trade is liberalized among them.

FORMAL ANALYSES OF THE EFFECTS OF FDI

THE EFFECTS OF, AND THE GAINS FROM, trade have been fully studied and incorporated into elaborate general equilibrium, theoretical structures such as the Ricardian and the Hecksher-Ohlin models. What is studied in these models is the allocation of resources among industries subject to *constant*, or *exogenously changing*, technology. The effects of, and gains from, international investment flows have attracted less attention from formal theorists, probably because there is not much to add when international investment flows are considered within the confines of the standard, text-book models.

In contrast, a high degree of the *policy-oriented* interest in FDI is related to a world of *endogenous* technological change. Since FDI undoubtedly influences such change, its potential to bring gain is greater and its theoretical analysis is more complex than in the constant-technology model. Much of the study of the effects of FDI on technological change has been in a partial equilibrium setting. Direct gains in the receiving sector have not always been set against possible losses in other sectors caused by the FDI. Such losses may not be discernable outside a general equilibrium setting. For example, even if the greenfield investment financed by FDI is accomplished totally by employing previously unemployed factors, the capital transfer may cause a current account deficit which takes the form of a fall in net exports with an accompanying (offsetting) loss of employment and income.

With these considerations in mind, we ask: Does a nation gain if it attracts FDI? Consider first the text-book world of homogeneous commodities, fixed supplies of homogeneous factors, and perfect competition. If capital is internationally mobile it will move to equate returns world wide. If a country imposes tariffs on a capital intensive industry its production will expand and capital will be drawn in from the rest of the world. The consequences will then depend on a number of the economy's structural parameters. This kind of model bears little relation to what is seen in the world where the great majority of advanced and developing nations are in active competition to attract a limited supply of foreign direct investment. A few of the key differences from the standard models are:

- Unemployment is endemic especially in the EC and many LDCs, where it is sometimes disguised as underemployment on the land.

- FDI often goes to produce new products.

- FDI often brings with it new process technology or new capabilities in such aspects as distribution and marketing.

- FDI often brings with it direct R&D capacity, or channels to tap into foreign-based R&D within the same MNE.

In each of these cases, there may be gains to the receiving country that are not captured by the standard model. Such gains deserve much more careful theoretical attention in a general equilibrium setting than we believe they have so far received. In the meantime, we note that the gains include the following:

- The entire value of the domestic incomes created by the FDI in cases in which previously unemployed factors are put to work (at least over the time period, possibly a decade or more, when the factors would otherwise have remained unemployed). This gain will go partly to the factors that are newly employed and partly to those responsible for their support (directly or through tax payments) during their unemployment.

- The human capital this employment creates in people who would otherwise be unemployed.

- A tariff that attracts FDI may cause an increase in the value of a nation's output as the result of the development of new products or new process technologies, whose effects on output exceed the value of the output sacrificed when factors employed by the FDI move from other employments. These gains are not found in the standard model where the products and processes are given, and tariffs invariably lead to less productive allocations of resources.[5]

- By creating its own R&D or tapping into the R&D done elsewhere, the FDI may raise the host country's growth rate.

There is much unnecessary debate because different models are being used to evaluate the effects of FDI. This includes, first, the textbook, general equilibrium model which tends to underestimate the value of FDI by assuming technology to be exogenous. Second, there is a partial equilibrium approach that stresses the value of FDI in technology transfer and other dynamic effects. This approach, however, may overestimate the value of FDI by neglecting real costs that are imposed on other parts of the economy, but which are easy to overlook without reference to the third approach. The third approach, or model, provides a specifically general equilibrium framework of analysis with endogenous technological change and the possibility of serious unemployment.

SECURITY OF ACCESS

A N FTA INFLUENCES INTERNATIONAL INVESTMENT by altering the amount and security of access to a set of several national markets that can be obtained by locating production facilities in one of these markets.

REMOVAL OF TARIFFS

A SINGLE COUNTRY CAN MAKE ITSELF attractive to foreign investment of a restricted sort by raising tariffs and nontariff barriers. If the domestic market is large enough, a firm will find an output at which its costs can be covered and investment will occur to serve the local market. Companies that are either domestically or foreign-owned may make the required investment. Examples include the tariff factories established under the high tariff of Canada's National Policy established in 1878.

General Effects

An FTA leaves the member countries' external tariffs in place, but, by removing all tariffs among members, it creates a single market for goods within the FTA. There are a number of effects.

1) Investment and disinvestment will be made to accomplish a rationalization of production if a given set of goods were produced in more than one partner country. (This results in trade creation.) As noted earlier, evidence provided by the tariff cuts mandated by the Tokyo and Kennedy rounds of GATT, and the Canada-U.S. auto pact suggests that rationalization with specialization of product lines was a key part of Canada-U.S. adjustment. Similar rationalizations could, therefore, be expected to be a key part of the current adjustment to the FTA and to the NAFTA. The FTA does, however, appear to have caused more interindustry adjustment than did previous Canadian tariff cuts.

2) The location decisions for new investments going to member countries are no longer distorted by tariffs.

3) Investment by tariff-protected industries located within the FTA occurs in order to serve other markets within the FTA that were formerly served by imports from the outside world. (This results in trade diversion.)

4) Investment to produce goods not formerly produced within the FTA occurs if the combined market is large enough to allow a good to cover its costs whereas no single market was large enough prior to the FTA.

The first point is more likely to be important when the FTA includes several large economies, as does the FTA and the NAFTA. The second point applies to all FTAs. The third point is more likely to be relevant when the FTA includes one large country with tariff-protected production and one or more small countries that do not have similar industries. The fourth point is more likely to be important when an FTA includes only relatively small countries, as would some future, fully effective Association of South East Asian Nations (ASEAN) free trade agreement. All apply equally to investment that is home-owned, owned by residents of other FTA members, or owned by non-FTA residents.

The Added Gain for Small Countries

All members of an FTA are likely to gain from becoming more attractive to foreign investment and by having all investment more efficiently allocated within the FTA. For smaller countries, an added gain is commonly alleged. Consider a large country and a small country, such as Canada and the United States, that would naturally comprise a single market were it not for tariffs. Let both countries levy similar tariffs and let a firm intending to serve both markets from a single plant decide in which country to locate its plant. It is commonly argued that in this scenario the larger country has an advantage over the smaller because locating the plant in the larger country allows it to sell tariff-free in the larger part of the total market and tariff-burdened in the smaller part. By contrast, locating in the smaller country implies that the larger part of total sales will be subject to a tariff. The plant will locate in the smaller country only if the margin of all other advantages is sufficient to out-weigh the tariff-created disadvantage. So goes the standard argument. A free trade area, however, confers an added advantage on the small country by removing the disadvantage it suffers when all countries levy tariffs.

The above argument clearly depends not on the relative sizes of the two countries' markets (their relative GDPs) but on *the size of an individual firm's market.* If the degree of competition in the two markets is such that a new entrant expects to have the same sales in both markets, there is no locational advantage for the larger country. If, however, the firm expects to serve some-thing like the same proportion of each market, then its sales will be larger in the large country than in the small one. Assume, for example, that at each given price the firm expects to sell in the smaller country the same proportion of what it sells in the larger country. It is easy to prove that if both countries levy a common rate of tariff, a single firm serving the combined market maximizes its profits by locating in the larger market and exporting to the smaller country.[6] By choosing this location, it makes most of its sales tariff-free in its home market, whereas if it locates in the small country, it makes most of its sales in the tariff-burdened foreign market. If the two countries form an FTA, there is no longer any tariff-related reason to locate in either country and other economic forces will therefore dictate location.[7]

Of course, this argument applies only to goods that meet the rules of origin requirement. Low value-added goods that do not meet the rules of origin required for tariff exemption continue to have an advantage in locating in the member country with the larger market. The advantage is not created by the FTA as such — as some critics imply. It exists under a non-discrimina-tory tariff and merely continues into the FTA; the FTA only removes the large-country advantage from goods that meet the rules of origin. *On this account, FTAs are inferior to customs unions* where all value-added within the member countries passes duty free across their borders.

Reductions of the Impact of Non Tariff Barriers

There are two types of non tariff barrier (NTB). The first constitutes legitimate measures explicitly designed to reduce the volume of "fair trade" such as VERs, or escape clause action against import surges. The second arises from the misuse of measures designed to ensure fair trade by "levelling the playing field", such as countervailing and anti-dumping duties. Both give rise to so-called "contingent protection".

General Effects

Although an FTA removes virtually all tariffs, the impact of NTBs is merely reduced. The opportunity to employ the first type of NTB, such as escape clause actions, is reduced by constraining the circumstances under which they can be used. (For example, the escape clause action against Canadian shakes and shingles, which is still in place, would probably have been disallowed under the FTA.) The opportunity to employ the second type of NTB is also reduced, in this case by controlling the circumstances under which fair trade laws can be applied. Both of these changes reduce the likelihood that a firm will be hit by such "contingent protection", while increasing the probability that an appeal will succeed if it is required. Uncertainty about access remains, but is significantly reduced.

Exposure to the risk of countervail depends on the amount and type of government assistance. Overt subsidies carry high current risk, although any form of government assistance carries a future risk of being deemed countervailable. The exposure to anti-dumping action depends on the structure of the industry in which the firm is operating and on the type of product being sold. The use of anti-dumping duties is becoming more common and the scope of application is increasing steadily. Although Canadians tend to be harassed more by U.S. countervailing duties, anti-dumping duties are much more frequently used world wide. Unfortunately, an FTA provides no protection against changes in anti-dumping legislation; it only helps to ensure that existing laws are more fairly administered.

Effects on Smaller Partners

Because of the existence of NTBs and legitimate trade protection laws, the bias towards locating investment to produce goods that meet the rules of origin in the largest market is only reduced, rather than removed entirely, when an FTA is formed. To gain some idea of the magnitude of this problem, Hufbauer & Schott (1993) estimate that with the NAFTA fully in place 17 percent of all trade among the three countries will still be subject to tariffs of one sort or another. In the extreme, the possibility that markets may still be fully closed on one pretext or another provides a strong advantage to locating within the largest market and exporting to the smaller one.

The Value of NTB Control

Compared to Canada's bargaining objectives of eliminating the use of anti-dumping and countervail as NTBs the provisions of the FTA and the NAFTA are second-best substitutes. Compared to what Canadian exporters suffered before the FTA, the dispute settlement mechanism of the FTA is a distinct gain. (See Horlick and DeBusk for a full description of its very impressive record to date.) Consequently, the present situation with respect to countervail and anti-dumping provides grounds for trying to do better by way of controlling NTBs, but it is not a valid argument for staying out of the NAFTA or abrogating the FTA and hence losing the real advantages of the dispute settlement mechanism.

DEGREE OF COMMITMENT

FIRMS MAKING LONG-TERM INVESTMENT decisions are interested in the degree of government commitment to maintain at least the existing levels of access to their relevant markets. As a device to achieve international commitment, an FTA has strong advantages over both unilateral reductions in trade barriers and international sectoral agreements. The key is that both a series of sectoral agreements and reciprocal cuts in protectionist measures can be abandoned piecemeal. If one country sees advantages in raising trade restrictions on sector X, it can abandon its participation in a sectoral agreement for X, or it can rescind any unilateral reductions in those restrictions (sometimes made with the tacit understanding that other countries will also maintain such reductions). In contrast, an FTA is embodied in a single treaty. It can be abandoned only as a whole, not piecemeal. Once the adjustments to it have been made, a wide set of constituencies will have vested interests in maintaining it. Because abrogating the treaty would meet with strong opposition from all these groups and likely trigger a major event (if not a crisis) in international relations, it is less likely to be politically acceptable.

It seems to us, therefore, that as a device for committing nations to reciprocal freedom of access to each other's markets, in the face of well-known political pressures for piecemeal increases in trade restrictions, an FTA enshrined in a formal treaty has no equal.

EFFECTS ON INVESTMENT

INSOFAR AS AN FTA REDUCES government interference with investment entering the country, and insofar as it makes investments more secure once they are in place, an FTA has desirable effects on investment.

Provisions of the FTA and the NAFTA

In the context of the FTA and the NAFTA some of the most important of these effects are:

- The cornerstone of both agreements is a principle long embodied in the General Agreement on Tariffs and Trade (GATT) called *national treatment*. According to the principle of national treatment, each country can have whatever laws it wishes and these need not be harmonized across the NAFTA countries; *these must, however, apply equally to domestic and to other NAFTA investors.* This critical provision eliminates many sources of discrimination.

- The NAFTA is much more extensive in its coverage than was the FTA, extending to virtually all foreign investment, including equities and debt, profits, business real estate, etc.

- Both agreements increase the attractiveness of the total free trade area for investment owned in member countries. The NAFTA also extends coverage to fourth-party investors expanding from one NAFTA market into another, as long as they have "substantial business activities" in the territory where they were originally established.

- Both agreements reduce national asymmetries in attractiveness due to (primarily) unequal security of access to other member countries' markets.

- The NAFTA introduces an elaborate dispute settlement mechanism (DSM) for investment issues, which can make binding decisions on many important classes of dispute.

- Both agreements guarantee fair and full compensation for expropriated investments.

An important part of any agreement is the body of rules governing retaliation by one country against exemptions from national treatment by another. Under the FTA rules, retaliation was to "equivalent commercial effect". For example, if Canadian cultural restrictions hurt Americans, they could retaliate by inflicting *equal harm* to Canadians. Under the NAFTA rules, retaliation includes the introduction of *equal measures*, thus treating Canadian investors in U.S. cultural industries as *unequally* as Canadians treat U.S.

investors. This tit-for-tat rule greatly increases the stakes in departing from national treatment, especially in a small country whose commercial impact on the large country might be small (equivalent commercial effect) but which could be greatly harmed by measures adopted by the large country of a type equivalent to the original discrimination (equivalent measures). This acts as a further deterrent for foreign investors to invest in one of these industries protected in Canada or Mexico, since tit-for-tat will make it more difficult for them to penetrate the U.S. market.

Against these important liberalizing measures must be set the enormous rag bag of existing detailed "national-treatment-violating" investment provisions grandfathered under the NAFTA. This greatly reduces the liberalizing force of the investment chapter but, unlike the FTA, it is done on a "negative list" basis. Under the FTA, all existing measures were grandfathered, which meant that obscure legislation might be dug up at any time in the future. Under the NAFTA, a list of exceptions rooted in past legislation is to be published and everything *not* on that list is subject to the rules of the NAFTA. This increases transparency and reduces uncertainty.

All three countries also have some quite general measures that allow them to depart from national treatment. Canada is permitted to review all FDI over $150 million. Mexico has restrictions on FDI in six different categories. Some sectors are reserved exclusively for the Mexican state, others have varying restrictions on the amount of foreign ownership permitted — ranging from zero to 49 percent across five categories. The United States has a review process related to national security, which was exempted from all terms of the treaty including the dispute settlement mechanism (DSM). The U.S. legislation, the so-called Exon-Florio amendment, is extremely vague. Also the U.S. "hi-tech consortia", such as Sematech and high definition TV which are open only to domestically owned firms, are ostensibly linked to national security and so they, too, are exempt. Since, in the case of all three countries, the broad exceptions referred to in this paragraph are not subject to any DSM, their power to harass investors will be limited mainly by the good will of each country's administration.

All of the investment provisions that depart from the general principle of national treatment restrict the freedom of investors to invest where they wish. These measures will directly affect the flow of international investment and trade. *Unlike NTBs, however, they do not affect access for goods produced by the investment once the investment is in place.* For example, if the United States subsequently decides to restrict investment in industry X for reasons of national security, this will not influence the ability of a firm already established in Canada or Mexico to sell into the U.S. market. Indeed if, as so often happens, the U.S. restrictions reduce efficiency by reducing domestic competition,[8] investments in Canada and Mexico serving the U.S. market in those areas may be rendered more profitable and hence more attractive.

Investment Diversion   Will every encouragement for investment to locate within an FTA be beneficial, or will some be harmful? In other words, do FTAs carry the potential for *investment diversion* that is separate from the potential loss through *trade diversion*? Here, we consider three cases: the first involves investment diversion between the outside world and the FTA due to removal of tariffs; the second case involves investment diversion due to the removal of NTBs; the third case involves investment diversion with the member countries.

Case 1 cannot be studied within the frameworks of the basic Ricardian or the Hecksher-Ohlin models (in which there are different opportunity costs of producing homogeneous commodities in three countries, and full-employment constraints on output) because the fixed supplies of land, labour and capital are internationally immobile by assumption. There are, however, various ways to alter these models to allow for internationally mobile capital. In all the cases we have studied, the following conclusion holds: *When capital is allocated differently from the way it would be under a uniform world wide rate of tariff, the (sole) effect is a misallocation of resources that can be seen through i) the flows of trade diversion, ii) the resource misallocation of the investment flows, or iii) the stock misallocation of capital. In effect, there are three ways to look at, and measure, one loss.* This result depends on some critical assumptions that do not mirror what is discussed in the applied literature on international investment flows. Two obvious cases involve the assumptions of homogeneous products, and static or exogenously changing technology.

If we assume differentiated products and profit-seeking R&D, which makes technological change endogenous, it may matter to which country a given value of trade and investment is diverted. Depending on whether it goes to A or to B, a variant of the generic product may be produced and/or the diverted production may be in the hands of a different firm. When variants of the same product have different income-generating capacities and different firms have different operating, investment, and R&D behaviours, the specific result matters. In these circumstances, we may need to distinguish the effects of trade diversion from those of investment diversion and accept that the same amount of trade diversion may have different effects depending on the nature of the induced investment.

In Case 2, which is related to NTBs, an actual tariff is paid by all imports when they enter the country, while the NTB operates more as a lottery. A firm's goods may enter uninhibited, or they may be the subject of an anti-dumping suit or an import-surge duty, or they may be countervailed. Each of these operates a little differently. For example, an anti-dumping suit can usually be avoided by raising the price (which is what firms typically do). An escape clause action against an import surge can be avoided (at much higher cost) by a VER. There is little option, however, but to fight a countervail case (other than withdrawing from the market altogether). Another difference is that anti-dumping is product-specific, while countervail is usually firm-specific.

When a firm is considering investing in either country B or C and exporting to A prior to an FTA, it has only a subjective, probabilistic notion of the dangers of NTBs. When B signs an FTA with A, the firm knows that the probability of being hit with an NTB is reduced and that of winning an appeal (through the DSM), is increased in the event that an NTB is levied. In these circumstances, there will be a tendency for some A-market-serving investment that would have gone to C to go to B instead.

The important difference between this and the tariff case is that when investment is diverted from C to B, some real costs are avoided. Document preparation, hearings, appeals, etc., all require effort from within the firms as well as expensive professional assistance from outsiders such as lawyers and accountants. There are in addition other, possibly larger costs associated with uncertainty created by the unpredictable application of NTBs. The net world loss is the lower productivity of capital in B versus C *minus* the gain in freeing resources involved in meeting the harassment costs when the good came from C.[9]

Finally, Case 3 involves the intra-FTA diversion of investment. For example, one of the anti-NAFTA charges most commonly heard in Canada is that investment will be diverted from Canada to Mexico: Canada-based firms will move to Mexico, and new investors, both domestic and foreign, will choose Mexico rather than Canada. We consider this concern *only from the limited perspective of how likely it is that Canada's attraction for footloose FDI will be affected by the arrangement in question.* There are five alternative situations ranked.[10]

First, Canada's attraction for FDI has already strengthened by entering the FTA for the reasons discussed earlier in this section. This includes the possibility of attracting some investment that might otherwise have gone to Mexico.

Second, if Mexico forms an FTA with the United States, Canada loses any differential advantage that it obtained under the Canada-U.S. FTA in diverting investment from Mexico to Canada. This loss occurs whether or not Canada is a party to the Mexico-U.S. FTA.

Third, if Canada were to remain outside the Mexico-U.S. FTA, she would become a spoke country relative to the United States, which would be the hub country, and in the process Canada would also become less attractive to FDI. (In the hub and spoke model, the United States has a series of bilateral FTAs with other partners, making the U.S. hub the most attractive for investment since it in the only country with tariff-free access to all the spokes. In contrast, the spoke countries are less attractive, relative to the United States, since they have tariff-free access only to the U.S. market but not to each other.) So, given that Mexico and the United States decided to form an FTA, Canada would have something to lose and nothing to gain (by way of becoming more attractive to FDI) by staying out of the deal. This establishes the order of preference for Canada: first an FTA only; second a NAFTA only; and third a hub and spoke model.

Next, we must consider whether Canada will lose under the NAFTA relative to its position if there were no FTA among any of the countries. In a case with no FTAs at all, U.S. and Mexican trade restrictions would make Canada less attractive to investment designed to serve the North American market. Canadian trade restrictions, however, make Canada more attractive to investment designed to serve the local market. Given today's globalizing markets, most countries — especially small ones — have concluded that it is more important to be attractive to investment designed to serve an export market (as well as the domestic market) than to be attractive to investment designed to serve a protected domestic market alone. Given this judgement, a case where there are no FTAs between any of the three countries is worse than any of the three alternatives considered above.

Finally, assume that there is no FTA — either because it was never negotiated or because some future Canadian government abrogated both the FTA and the NAFTA and exited from the deal altogether. Would Canada then lose from a Mexico-U.S. FTA? The answer is "yes", because Mexico would then be more attractive than Canada *ceteris paribus* in that a Mexican location would offer tariff-free access to the United States while a Canadian location would not. This establishes that, from the Canadian point of view, a Mexico-U.S. FTA, with Canada having no arrangement with either of these countries, is the worst of all five possible cases.

From the narrow perspective of Canada becoming as attractive as possible to footloose FDI, Canada's order of preference is, therefore, 1) an FTA only, 2) a NAFTA only, 3) an FTA plus a Mexico-U.S. FTA (hub and spoke), 4) no agreements between any of the three countries, and 5) a Mexico-U.S. agreement with no Canada-U.S. FTA.

Assuming that the United States goes ahead with its FTA with Mexico, alternatives 1) and 4) would be ruled out. This leaves 2) as the most preferred option, followed by 3) and then 5). It is amazing how opponents to the NAFTA have been allowed to get away with asserting the opposite. Some opponents argue that Canada will lose foreign investment by entering the NAFTA and so they opt for alternative 3). Others argue that the FTA should be abrogated in order to stop (among other things) the haemorrhage of investment to Mexico and so they opt for alternative 5), which is the worst of all the possible cases.

A REGIONAL TRADING & INVESTMENT BLOCK

THIRD COUNTRIES, particularly those in East Asia, often express the concern that the NAFTA and the European Community (EC) are both trading blocks and, as such, they threaten both to divert substantial amounts of investment and trade into their own areas and to replace the multilateral trading system. This is not really a static argument about existing barriers; it is, rather, a dynamic argument about how the FTA will evolve in response both to its own internal tensions and to its policy negotiations with such outside jurisdictions as the GATT. There are several reasons why we are not inclined to give much credence to these fears.

First, as an FTA rather than a customs union, the NAFTA lacks the supranational administrative body required to develop and administer a common external trade policy. In particular, the NTBs and anti-dumping duties which are so commonly used by the EC and the United States, cannot be levied in common by the NAFTA countries. *By its very constitution, an FTA lacks the essential ingredient of a trading block: the ability to present a common commercial policy to the rest of the world.* Our belief that the NAFTA is best left this way is one of the several reasons why we oppose Vernon's proposal for a supranational NAFTA administrative body. (Another reason is to avoid creating a new layer of government and bureaucracy whenever possible.)

Second, contrary to what some economists have argued, we believe that the NAFTA has little chance in the foreseeable future of evolving into a customs union that would have the above-mentioned essential characteristic of a trading block. Non-U.S. members would adamantly oppose such a customs union because they would regard a common trade policy as being set almost exclusively by the United States. *For the United States, as a super power, trade policy has always been an instrument of foreign policy.* To this end, the United States has at one time or another either prevented or restricted trade with such "unfriendly" countries as Cuba, China, Vietnam and the USSR. It would be unrealistic to expect the United States to give up this power. *For small countries such as Canada, however, foreign policy is an instrument of trade policy:* keeping foreign markets open is critical for our economic prosperity. It is equally unrealistic to expect Canadians to give up the power to act independently of politically oriented, U.S. trade policy. For this reason, Canadians would never form a customs union with the United States. The same considerations apply (with varying amounts of force) to the various Latin American countries whether or not the implications of a union are fully understood.

Third, both Mexico and Canada, countries next to the U.S. colossus, worry about excessive dependence on that country. The facts of life dictate a heavy dependence on the United States; the desire for independence dictates that this dependence be minimized, not maximized. This objective will help to keep the non-U.S. members of any NAFTA or Western Hemisphere Free Trade Area (WHFTA) reluctant to enter a true trading block, which the United States would necessarily dominate.

Fourth, Mexico and Canada see their FTAs with the United States as part of a market-oriented, outward-looking package of reforms. Belonging to an inward-looking fortress North America would be akin to reverting to the old, failed policies — only on a grander scale. It is unlikely that the governments of either Mexico or Canada (or any other Latin American countries that had pursued domestic liberalization far enough to be able to join a WHFTA) would so alter its stance as to take part in the formation of a trading block of any kind that included the United States, let alone a block that was genuinely inward-looking.

Fifth, without a common external commercial policy, the dynamic pressures within the member countries of an FTA are to harmonize tariffs *downward* rather than *upward*. Here are some of our reasons for holding this view.

- When an FTA is formed, there is no bargaining up of tariffs towards the highest member's level, as often occurs when a customs union is formed.

- Because there is no common commercial policy against the rest of the world, it is more difficult to increase tariffs later on a go-it-alone basis. Every increase confers an advantage on the members who do not increase their tariffs.

- Under an FTA in which each country has different tariffs against non-members, there are pressures to reduce tariffs towards the lowest rates of any member. Much modern trade is in intermediate goods. Producers in high-tariff member countries perceive their tariffs as conferring a competitive disadvantage *vis-à-vis* competitors in low-tariff member countries. The solution is simple: lower tariffs to the lowest rates levied by any member. (In Canada there is already under way a serious review of tariffs that do not protect domestic industries and that are higher than those in the United States and/or Mexico.)

- Any country that suffers seriously from trade diversion has the remedy in its own hands: unilaterally lower its external tariff on the good in question. After all, trade diversion only occurs because of the preferential access afforded to other member countries, and the amount of that preference is in the hands of the country to which trade will be diverted. Furthermore, the country that suffers from trade diversion has no protected domestic producers, so there are no producers to oppose the remedy: make sufficient unilateral tariff reduction to eliminate the diversion.

- The computer agreement in the NAFTA provides a way for an FTA to evolve into a partial customs union without the administrative apparatus of a trading block. In this case, the countries agreed to a common external tariff and to the resulting absence of any rules of origin. A future FTA should legalize this by adding the provision that whenever the three countries set common tariffs on any import, the rules of origin tests are suspended.

Against this formidable set of considerations, it has been argued that the common set of rules of origin required of an FTA creates something in the nature of a *de facto* trading block. Domestic content rules can certainly be set high enough to divert trade and investment to the FTA — and this is probably the case with autos under the NAFTA.

It should be noted that the typical rule, which is in the order of 50 percent of total costs being domestic, certainly reduces the effective tariff on many imported parts and components. Under the pre-FTA regime, tariff cascading meant that components imported to one member country could be taxed twice — once when they entered and once when the final good containing the component(s) was exported to another member country. The FTA removes this cascading and makes the tariff rate on the component when it is initially imported into the FTA equal to the effective tariff on that component when it is traded anywhere within the FTA as a part of some final good that meets the rules of origin requirements. Furthermore, rules of origin tend to be set at the inception of an FTA and are rarely, if ever, altered. This means that the FTA members do not present a common front to the rest of the world in any subsequent trade negotiations.

Conclusions

A THEORY OF MNE INVESTMENT must cover three issues. What organizational forms (subsidiaries, markets, alliances) do firms choose in given contexts to exploit their firm-specific assets? Which aspects of a country's advantages attract and retain particular investments? How does business strategy, broadly conceived, affect investment decisions? The third issue cannot be assumed to be included in the other two.

A free trade agreement alters the relative attractiveness of the member countries to international investment. The most important effect of such an agreement is to increase the amount and the security of access to a set of national markets that can be obtained by locating production in any one country. In doing so, it removes the relative disadvantage of small member countries over large member countries due to tariffs on goods that meet a rules-of-origin test; it also reduces the disadvantage that is due to NTBs.

The evidence of other FTAs suggests that as a result of these changes FTAs encourage both outward- and inward-bound foreign direct investment.

An FTA is an effective inter-temporal commitment device for trade-liberalizing measures that attract investment. Compared to other more embracing forms of economic union, FTAs minimize the chances of turning into an active trading block.

The gains from rationalizing investment are probably underestimated in models in which technological change is exogenous compared with models that reflect the fact that technological change is largely endogenous to the system.

ENDNOTES

1 It will be evident that we have collapsed ownership-specific advantages with those related to internalization and added other forms of strategy to Dunning's Ownership-Location-Internalization "eclectic paradigm". We take this to be the most broadly accepted approach to the study of foreign direct investment and MNEs. For extensive comment on this approach, see Dunning, 1993, especially chapter four.

2 Vernon (1974, p. 100) notes that the entry to the United States by Royal Dutch Shell early in the century was a countermove to the earlier entry to Sumatra by Standard Oil. See Dunning, 1993, p. 87 and p. 93 for a statement of what is involved in incorporating strategic issues into theory on MNEs.

3 See Safarian (1993) for data on these trends, and Waverman (ed., 1991) for an analysis of the broader issues involved in international mergers.

4 Economic Council of Canada, *Twenty-Third Annual Review*, (Ottawa: Minister of Supply and Services Canada, 1986, p. 24 and p. 85). Subsequent research using applied game theory suggests that such an agreement is rational even if Canada makes more concessions than it receives, assuming the alternative is a bilateral trade war. In the latter case both countries lose, but Canada's losses are about ten times larger as a percent of GNP. See G. W. Harrison & E. E. Ruström, "Trade Wars, Trade Negotiations and Applied Game Theory," *The Economic Journal*, p. 101, May 1991, p. 420 - 35, especially pp. 430 and 434.

5 Bhagwati and Brecher argue that if the tariff-protected sector is built up through foreign capital and it takes resources from the domestically owned sector, it may redistribute income from domestic to foreign residents. This is simply an illustration of how complex the effect can become once one passes away from traditional simplified models of trade theory.

6 Of course the proposition seems obvious; but what is obvious is not always correct. In this case a formal proof showed that it was correct.

7 A complication arises if elasticities differ in the two countries at common prices and if anti-dumping duties constrain the firm's ability to price discriminate. Assume that the two countries' anti-dumping laws dictate that the price in the foreign market must not be less than the price in the home market. Further, assume that at all common prices demand elasticity is lower in the smaller market than in the larger market. The profit-maximizing firm will wish to charge a higher price in the smaller market than in the larger one. If it locates in the larger country, it can do so; if it locates in the smaller country, it is prevented from doing so by anti-dumping laws. If there is typically more competition in the larger country than in the smaller country, the demand for the firm's product will tend to be more elastic in the larger country, thus providing an added attraction for the larger country. If the elasticities are reversed, there is an attraction

in locating in the smaller market in order to be able to charge a higher price in the other market.

8 This case has been made by such writers as Robert Reich, Nathan Rosenberg and David Mowery.

9 There will also be harassment associated with selling from M to A so the correct statement is the net difference in harassment costs when the good comes from M rather than from S.

10 These alternatives have been studied in more detail in several pieces by Lipsey and by Wonnacott. See, for example, Lipsey (1991) and Wonnacott (1991).

ACKNOWLEDGEMENT

GRATEFUL ACKNOWLEDGEMENT is made of helpful comments received from Rachel McCulloch, Lorraine Eden and Industry Canada staff on an earlier draft.

BIBLIOGRAPHY

Baldwin, J.R. & P.K. Gorecki. "Trade, Tariffs, Product Diversity and Length of Production Run in Canadian Manufacturing Industries: 1970-79." Ottawa: Economic Council of Canada, Discussion Paper 247, 1983.

Bhagwati, J. and R.A. Brecher. "National Welfare in an Open Economy in the Presence of Foreign-owned Factors of Production." *Journal of International Economics*, 10:103-15.

Bishop, P and H. Crookell. "Specialization and Foreign Investment in Canada." In *Canadian Industry in Transition*. Edited by D.G. McFetridge. Toronto: University of Toronto Press, 1985.

Caves R.E. and S. Mehra. "Entry of Foreign Multinationals into US Manufacturing." In *Competition in Global Industries*. Edited by M.E. Porter. Boston: Harvard Business School Press, 1986.

Caves, R.E. "International Corporations: The Industrial Economics of Foreign Investment." *Economica*, 38, (1971):1-27.

Daly, D.J. and D.C. MacCharles. *Canadian Manufactured Exports: Constraints and Opportunities*. Montreal: Institute for Research on Public Policy, 1986.

Davidson, W.H. and D.G. McFetridge. "International Technology Transactions and the Theory of the Firm." *Journal of Industrial Economics*, 3, (1984):253-64.

Dunning, J.H. *Multinational Enterprises and the Global Economy*. New York: Addison-Wesley Publishing Company, 1993, pp. 303-04.

Economic Council of Canada. *Venturing Forth: an Assessment of the Canada-U.S. Free Trade Agreement*. Ottawa: 1988.

Eden, L. "Multinational Responses to Trade and Technology Changes: Implications for Canada." In *Foreign Investment, Technology and Growth*, The Investment Canada Research Series. Edited by McFetridge. Calgary: University of Calgary Press, 1991, pp. 133-72.

Graham, E.M. "Strategic Management and Transnational Firm Behaviour: A Formal Approach." In *The Nature of the Transnational Firm*. Edited by C.N. Pitselis and R. Sugden. London: Rutledge, 1991, pp. 155-67.

Graham, E.M. "Transatlantic Investment by Multinational Firms: a Rivalistic Phenomenon?" *Journal of Post-Keynesian Economics*, 1,1, (1978):82-99.

Grossman, G.M. and E. Helpman. "Comparative Advantage and Long-Run Growth." *American Economic Review*, 80, (1990):796-815.

Harris, R.D. and D. Cox. *Trade, Industrial Policy and Canadian Manufacturing*. Toronto: University of Toronto Press, 1984.

Hazledine, T. "Why do the Free Trade Gain Numbers Differ So Much? The Role of Industrial Organization in General Equilibrium." *Canadian Journal of Economics*, 23, (1990):791-806.

Horlick, G.N. and F.A. DeBusk "The Functioning of the FTA Dispute Resolution Panels." Chapter 1 in *Negotiating and Implementing a North American Free Trade Agreement*. Edited by L. Waverman. Vancouver: The Fraser Institute, 1992.

Hufbauer, G. and J. Schott. "NAFTA: An Assessment." Washington: Institute of International Economics, 1993.

Lipsey, R.E and M.Y. Weiss. "Foreign Production and Exports in Manufacturing Industries." *Review of Economics and Statistics*, 63, (1981):488-94.

_____. "Foreign Production and Exports of Individual Firms." *Review of Economics and Statistics*, 66, (1984):304-8.

McFetridge, D.G. *Trade Liberalization and the Multinationals*. Ottawa: Economic Council of Canada, 1989.

McFetridge, D.G. (ed). *Foreign Investment, Technology and Economic Growth*, The Investment Canada Research Series. Calgary: University of Calgary Press, 1991.

Mersenier, Jean and Nicolas Schmitt. "Sunk Costs, Free Entry Equilibrium and Trade Liberalization in Applied General Equilibrium." Simon Fraser University, Department of Economics, Working Paper 92-16, 1992.

Morrison, A.J. *Strategies in Global Industries, How do US Businesses Compete*. New York: Quorum Books, 1990.

Porter, M.E. (ed.). *Competition in Global Industries*. Boston: Harvard Business School, 1986.

Romer, P.M. "Increasing Returns and Long-Run Growth." *Journal of Political Economy*, 94, (1986):1002-37.

Romer, P.M. "Endogenous Technological Change." *Journal of Political Economy*, 98, (1990):S71-102.

Rugman, A.M. "Trade Liberalization and International Investment." Ottawa: Economic Council of Canada, 1988.

Safarian, A.E. "Have Transnational Mergers or Joint Ventures Increased?" In *Competition Policy in an Interdependent World Economy*. Edited by E. Katzenbach et al. Baden-Baden: Nomos Verlagesellschaft, 1993.

Scherer, F.M. et al. *The Economics of Multiplant Operation: An International Comparison Study*. Cambridge: Harvard University Press, 1975.

Teece, D.J. "Technology Transfer by Multinational Firms: The Resource Cost of Transferring Technological Know How." *Economic Journal* 87, (1977):241-61.

Vernon, R. "International Investment and International Trade in the Product Cycle." *Quarterly Journal of Economics*, 80, (1967):190-207.

Vernon, R. "The Product Cycle Hypothesis in a New International Environment." *Oxford Bulletin of Economics and Statistics*, 41, (1979):255-67.

_____. "The Location of Economic Activity." In *Economic Analysis and Multinational Enterprise*. Edited by J. Dunning. London: Allen and Unwin, 1974.

Waverman, L. "The NAFTA Agreement: A Canadian Perspective." In *Assessing NAFTA: A Transnational Analysis*. Edited by S. Globerman and M. Walker, 1993.

B. Curtis Eaton, Richard G. Lipsey & A. Edward Safarian
Economic Growth and Policy Program
Canadian Institute for Advanced Research

4

The Theory of Multinational Plant Location: Agglomerations and Disagglomerations

INTRODUCTION

THIS CHAPTER, LIKE THE PREVIOUS ONE, is concerned with multinational plant location. The previous chapter considered how the decision to allocate individual investments among countries may be influenced by national differences in incentives to invest. This chapter considers the inter-action among individual investments; interaction which creates tendencies for investments to cluster together in regional and/or national agglomerations. Although each chapter can be read on its own, we urge the reader to obtain some perspective on this one by beginning with the previous chapter.

As Paul Krugman notes in *Geography and Trade*, his charming and brilliant lectures on economic geography, "the most striking feature of the geography of economic activity [is its] concentration" (Krugman, p 5). In this vein, one of the most striking features of Canada is its agglomerations of economic activity.

During the debate over the Canada-U.S. Free Trade Agreement (FTA), some Canadian critics expressed concern that these agglomerations, such as are found in Toronto, throughout Southern Ontario, the industrial part of Quebec and, to a lesser extent, in the lower mainland of British Columbia, around Halifax, and a number of other centres, would be undone by the removal of the tariffs on Canada-U.S. trade. It was alleged that Canadians would revert to being "hewers of wood and drawers of water". Others argued that the broader forces of technological change are also working to dissolve agglomerations of economic activity, particularly in small open economies such as Sweden and Canada.

To address these and a number of related issues we first review the theory of agglomerations. We consider how economies of scale on the one hand, and transportation and communication costs on the other, interact to produce agglomerations. The theory provides no definitive answer to the worrying claim that free trade will unwind all or any Canadian agglomerations; theoretically, the possibility certainly exists, but history suggests the probability is small. Next, we review the new technologies now coming into use. These technologies appear more likely to contribute to a growing diversity in patterns of industrial location than to the rise of a few massive agglomerations. Finally, we review the evidence on R&D conducted by MNEs — evidence which indicates there is substantial continuing concentration in the home countries. There is, however, a clear trend toward decentralization within some industries and in a number of home countries (although the pace is very slow in the case of the United States).

THE THEORY OF AGGLOMERATION

AGGLOMERATIONS ARE DRIVEN BY two potent forces: economies of scale and costs of transportation. Traditional trade theorists consider transport costs mainly in the context of convex technologies. In this context, transport costs do little more than reduce the gains from trade that would occur in a world of costless transportation. The new trade theorists, such as Brander, Grossman, Helpman, Krugman and Spencer have incorporated economies of scale and imperfect competition into trade theory. So far, however, no one — neither traditional nor new trade theorists — appears to have considered the combined forces of scale effects and transportation costs to study agglomerations. Following Krugman's 1991 lead, we turn to economic geography.

To advance the discussion one must have at least a rudimentary understanding of the implications of trade policy for the agglomeration of economic activity in Canada as well as in a world context. To ensure this, we first review what is known about economies of scale, and then look at the way in which those economies interact with transportation and communication costs to produce agglomeration. We then discuss some general features of this interaction and related processes. Finally, we turn to questions raised by trade policy where, regrettably, we can do little more than provide a conceptual framework within which they can be pondered.

ECONOMIES OF SCALE

IN THE FIRST FEW PAGES of The Wealth of Nations, Adam Smith establishes the foundation of our understanding of economies of scale by accounting for them in terms of specialization and the division of labour. According to Smith, specialization facilitates learning by doing; it economizes on human capital; it tends to reduce the inventory of goods in process; and finally, it promotes technical change. All but the last of these work to create static economies of scale: the last works to create what might be described as "dynamic" economies of scale. Today Smith's emphasis on specialization and the division of labour plays an important, even central, role in informal theories of the firm.

Sadly, one important strand of our understanding of economies of scale has all but disappeared in modern economics. It relates to what Eaton

& Lipsey (1993) call real capital theory (i.e., the theory of production for indivisible capital goods). It can be illustrated by Gustav Akerman's (1923) account of the durable axe. He asks: Why do we see durable axes, axes that will provide a flow of service for 25 years or more? He answers: Given a positive rate of interest, and assuming the producers of axes to be cost minimizers, one must conclude that there are economies of scale in the activities embodying the services an axe provides in a durable axe. The very existence of capital goods is evidence of economies of scale in the act of embodying productive services in durable, indivisible capital goods. Since all economic activity involves a variety of capital goods, increasing returns over some initial scale of activity would also seem to be a pervasive fact of economic life. These economies can be seen as yet another aspect of specialization and the division of labour since they involve specialization in the domain of time. Robinson Crusoe first specializes in producing and storing the services of a fishing rod (by producing a durable rod), and subsequently specializes in catching fish with the aid of the rod. Eaton & Lipsey (1993) attempt to reconstruct and reinterpret the important insights provided by Akerman, and buried by neoclassical economists.

In this broad sense then, economies of scale can be attributed to specialization and the division of labour. Moreover, such specialization inevitably involves the acquisition of both human and physical capital and, to some extent, this capital is product-specific. Both the skills and the implements that the workers wielded in Smith's famous pin factory were useful in producing pins but, one imagines, not in other economic activities. The skills constituted pin-specific human capital; the implements were pin-specific capital goods.

To determine whether a particular economic activity will be internal or external to a specific firm, and therefore whether internal or external economies exist, we must understand the basics of the modern theory of the firm. Ronald Coase (1937) provided the key insight on which the modern theory of the firm is built. He began with the simple observation that economic activity can be directly co-ordinated within the firm, or indirectly co-ordinated *via* markets, and that the boundary between the firm and the market is therefore endogenous. This boundary between internal, hands-on co-ordination, and external, arms-length co-ordination is determined by transaction costs, i.e., the costs of direct coordination and control on the one hand, and the costs of arm's length transactions on the other. Oliver Williamson, in *Markets and Hierarchies*, contributed a wealth of detail in support of Coase's research, and two key insights relevant to our purpose here. First, he noted that product- and firm-specific assets, including goods in process, special purpose capital goods, firm-specific human capital and the detailed economic know-how that is necessary to transform a bright idea into a commercially viable product (or process), create co-ordination problems that cannot be solved by arm's-length, market transactions. No supplier will produce components for

General Motors cars in the hope that GM will buy them because, once produced, the components are useful to GM and to no one else. To produce such specific components in the absence of some sort of commitment from GM (formal, as is typical in the United States, or informal, as is typical in Japan) would be folly because it puts the producer in a decidedly disadvantageous bargaining position. In the modern world of differentiated products, specific assets, specific components and specific human capital are nearly universal. In Williamson's view, the firm is an organization designed to manage the difficult co-ordination problems associated with asset specificity.

Williamson's second great contribution was to recognize that these co-ordination problems can be managed in a number of different ways, sometimes within one firm, and sometimes between firms using a variety of means to control the opportunistic behaviour that specific assets invite. As noted earlier, much of the modern theory of the MNE is based on these fundamental insights.

AGGLOMERATION

AT AN ELEMENTARY LEVEL, agglomeration is the result of two opposing forces: *economies of scale* that produce concentration; and *transportation and communication costs* that inhibit concentration. To realize economies of scale at the plant level, supplementary activities involving transportation and communication must occur: inputs (labour and materials) must be transported to the plant; output must be transported from the plant to the market; and the firm must communicate with its suppliers and customers. These supplementary activities are costly, and their cost tends to increase with distance.

To see how these forces interact to produce agglomeration, consider the problems of a planner who must choose the number and locations of plants to produce and market a fixed quantity of a final good while minimizing total costs. In this context, total costs *include* transportation and communication. For simplicity, imagine a setting in which the inputs used to produce the final good, and the demand for the final good, are uniformly distributed over a geographic area. In the solution, the number (and geographic distribution) of plants will be such that the cost savings that would be realized using one plant fewer (simultaneously optimally readjusting the locations of the remaining plants) and operating all the remaining plants a little further down the declining portion of the average cost curve, is counterbalanced by the added cost of transportation and communication entailed by the increased average distance between plants. *In this one product, partial equilibrium setting, the degree of agglomeration is determined jointly by the interaction of economies of scale at the plant level, which work to create agglomeration by encouraging fewer larger plants, and transportation and communication costs, which work to limit agglomeration by encouraging more smaller plants.* Although reality is considerably more complex than this simple example, it nevertheless illustrates one of the fundamental mechanisms of economic geography.

To appreciate the interaction of these forces more fully, consider the above example with two modifications: 1) many manufactured products rather than one, and 2) allow individuals to choose their locations in space. Imagine, then, a one-country world in which the country's population and its natural resources are, initially, uniformly distributed and all economic activity is agricultural. Assume, too, that the geographic distribution of the country's natural resources is fixed while that of its population is endogenous. In this pristine agricultural state, all economic activity is, in effect, hand-to-mouth and perfectly localized — virtually no resources are devoted to transportation and communication.

Now introduce the production of a single manufactured good. Of course, we suppose that there are economies of scale associated with the production of this good, and that the production of the good requires product-specific capital goods, product-specific human capital, and natural resources. Notice that the specific capital, both physical and human, necessarily dictates geographic inhomogeneities in economic activity and therefore require transport of something, and, of course, the need for some sort of communication. Broadly speaking, there are two possibilities. First, the population remains geographically dispersed. This requires that natural resources, goods in process, and final goods (but not agricultural goods) must be transported from specialized worker to specialized worker, and finally to the consumer of the finished good. (This sounds very much like the "putting out" system that prevailed in England prior to the industrial revolution.) Second, the specialized workers in manufacturing themselves, and all stages of the production process become concentrated in "cities". This second possibility eliminates the transportation of goods-in-process and the final goods consumed by the workers who produce them (and live) in the city. It does, however, necessitate the transportation of agricultural goods and natural resources to the city, and some finished goods from the city to consumers in the agricultural sector.

If there is only one (or a few) manufactured good(s), and if the bulk of the population is engaged in agricultural activity, then the population may remain geographically dispersed. If more and more manufactured goods are added, and the proportion of the population engaged in non-agricultural activity increases, agglomeration becomes increasingly plausible from an efficiency standpoint. As in the one good, partial equilibrium model, the model here is also driven by the interaction of economies of scale and the costs of transportation and communication. The important additional force in the many good model concerns economies in transportation and communication that can be had if many goods are produced in the same city. Agglomeration in the same city, of the people who produce different goods, but each of whom consumes many of the goods produced in the city, eliminates the need to transport the final and intermediate goods consumed by the city dwellers. These savings in the resources devoted to transportation and communications are economies of agglomeration across different goods that are external to the individual firms producing them. As more and more goods are produced in the economy, these external agglomeration economies make agglomerations increasingly viable, but because these are external economies, the agglomeration process may be slow to start and the resulting degree and pattern of agglomeration may not be optimal.

However it begins, once begun this geographic concentration tends to feed on and reinforce itself. As each city grows, it will support the production of progressively more products and services. But the production of the additional goods and services itself contributes to yet more concentration of population, permitting yet more products to achieve the economies of scale required to bring them into production. In other words, the process of agglomeration involves positive feedback. This mechanism also involves self-reinforcing growth in both the size of the city and the range of goods produced within it.

Of course there is negative feedback as well. As was stressed at the beginning of this section, the costs of transporting raw materials to cities also tends to limit city size, because as cities get larger and fewer in number, the average distance over which raw materials are transported to the city increases. (In the example here, population is held constant, so increasing average city size entails fewer, more dispersed cities.) Similarly, the average distance manufactured goods must be transported to rural consumers increases as city size increases, which also tends to limit city size. Also, population growth itself produces a variety of all too familiar congestion effects that also tend to limit growth.

PROPERTIES OF MODELS OF URBAN AGGLOMERATION

IN THE PREVIOUS SECTION we sketched a non-linear, dynamic model of agglomeration of economic activity with two sources of non-linearity: economies of scale in the production of individual goods, and economies of agglomeration. This sort of model has recently attracted the attention of economists and researchers in the biological and physical sciences, and therefore much is known about their properties. This section includes a discussion of some of these in the context of our model of agglomeration. For a wide ranging discussion in the context of models of technical change see Silverberg (1990).

Multiple Equilibria

The most important feature of these models is multiple equilibria. Our simple model of agglomeration provides two illustrations. First, given a number of cities in equilibrium, their locations are not unique. If the entire southern Ontario agglomeration is moved east by 10 or even 100 miles, it will tend to stay put. Second, the number and sizes of urban agglomerations are not unique. If we focus on one small region, it is possible for there to be one equilibrium in which the population is very small (no agglomeration of activity) and another in which it is very large. The possibility of multiple equilibria in this sort of model is intuitive. The glue that holds urban areas together is, in essence, a complex web of positive externalities among all the economic actors in the city. The more pervasive these externalities, the stronger the forces that hold an arbitrary agglomeration of economic activity together, and the more equilibria there tend to be.

No Invisible Hand

The corollary to the proposition that multiple equilibria exist, is that there is no force guiding the economy toward some preferred equilibrium. Also, there is no reason to believe that any of the equilibria are Pareto-efficient. In other words, there is no invisible hand guiding the economy to an equilibrium with the optimal number, size(s), and locational configuration of cities. This result is also intuitive. Optimality theorems employed by economists are invariably driven by assumptions of convexity (which rule out economies of scale) and lack of external economies (which rule out economies of agglomeration). Yet, cities and regional economies exhibit pervasive non-convexities and pervasive agglomeration externalities. Clearly, standard optimality theorems have no application in this sort of economy.

Tipping

In this model, small exogenous changes or shocks can have large effects, since small shocks can tip the model from one equilibrium to another. Also, a small change in any exogenous variable, including policy variables, can lead to large changes in the equilibrium values of the endogenous variables.

History or Path Dependence

Another immediate corollary of multiple equilibria is path dependence. If current values for the model's exogenous variables are fixed, many equilibria are possible. The state of equilibrium achieved by the model is, in effect, selected by the past history of those exogenous variables.

Bygones May Last Forever

As was argued earlier, the essential stuff of economies of scale is product-specific human and non-human capital. Some of this capital is, undoubtedly, location-specific as well. For example, the stock of housing and other buildings in cities is largely location-specific, and to the extent that labour is not internationally mobile, human capital is also location-specific. Location-specific capital of this sort is another source of path dependence.

Unravelling

Path dependence has clear implications for unravelling. In our model, a pro-agglomeration policy adopted by a small region early in the process of agglomeration can have irreversible effects that survive the elimination of the policy itself.

TRADE POLICY AND DISAGGLOMERATION

SO FAR, WE HAVE ARGUED that in order to understand the geographic concentration of economic activity that exists in the world today, one must seriously consider external economies of agglomeration. These external economies are pervasive and they imply cumulative causation, the existence of multiple equilibria, and a potential role for policy to influence the process of agglomeration.

Similar results are seen with endogenous technology that creates positive feedback loops with all the potential instabilities these imply (see for example, Silverberg, 1990). These models have some cautionary messages for policy makers, even though they cannot yet be tied closely to data. Where positive feedback loops exist, because of either scale economies or endogenous technological change, small causes can have large effects that are not reversible. Enforcing the wrong policy may cause some agglomeration to unravel. Reversing the policy may not stop, let alone reverse, the unravelling. What is even more worrying, is that the absence of any strong reaction to past doses of a particular policy is no guarantee that there will not be strong reactions to small doses of that policy in future. These threshold effects can be important. For example, firms may put up with a series of small increments in the basic tax rate without responding negatively. At some critical level, however, a few leaders may decide it is time to flee and the loss of their positive external economies may lead to a more general exodus.

RAISING TARIFFS TO CREATE AGGLOMERATIONS

THE EXTENT TO WHICH Sir John A. Macdonald's National Policy of high tariffs helped to create agglomerations of economic activity has long been debated by economic historians. Three points warrant mentioning, however. First, there was a significant amount of agglomeration long before tariffs, suggesting that, although agglomerations may have been encouraged by tariffs, they were not created by them. A key reference is Mackintosh (1967), including the Preface by Dales. Second, by protecting eastern manufacturing industries, the National Policy no doubt changed the nature of the agglomerations to be more goods- and less service-oriented than they otherwise would have been. This may also have contributed to their growth, resulting in larger agglomerations than would otherwise have been the case, at least at the time. Third (and as an offsetting consideration to the second point), long-term protection of oligopolistic industries in a small market can lead to an inefficient industry structure, and hence an industry that is limited in respect of both its international competitiveness and its size. The key reference here is Eastman & Stykolt (1967). When such protected firms are subjected to increased foreign competition, as might occur because of the globalization of markets caused by falling costs of transportation and communication, their inefficiencies, and lack of technological dynamism make it difficult for them to compete. If they lose out, then the agglomerations, of which they are a significant part, will shrink.

LOWERING TARIFFS AND DISAGGLOMERATION

IF RESTRICTIVE TRADE POLICIES create agglomeration, will free trade not lead to disagglomeration? We have no definitive answer, but some theoretical and empirical evidence suggests that unravelling may not be a significant problem.

Theory highlights at least three points. First, because the unilateral introduction and subsequent unilateral removal of trade barriers can shift the economy from a small-agglomeration equilibrium to a high-agglomeration equilibrium, agglomerations created by trade barriers do not necessarily require trade barriers for their support. Second, the sunk costs associated with agglomeration produce an important lock-in effect that works against unravelling — as noted above, bygones may have influences that last forever. Third, and perhaps most importantly, the FTA is bilateral and the NAFTA is multilateral. Although foreign firms gain enhanced access to Canadian markets, Canadian firms gain enhanced access to the markets of other member countries. Hence, the direct effects on agglomeration can go either way, and may very well be neutral.

Empirical evidence also identifies three main points. First, the purpose of infant industry protection is to establish industries *that can stand up to open competition after the requisite human capital, technological know-how and infra-structure are in place*.[1] Such policies appear to have been successful in, for example, the Japanese automobile industry and many industries in the NICs.

Second, the protection provided by the National Policy and subsequent protectionist initiatives reached its peak in 1935 and has since been reduced slowly, first as a result of bilateral treaties with the United States in the 1930s and later by successive rounds of GATT-negotiated tariff reductions starting in the 1950s. The Economic Council of Canada (1983) studied the adjustments to the substantial tariff reductions instituted by the Kennedy round of GATT negotiations and found no tendency for agglomerations of economic activity to break up. The evidence up to the end of the implementation phase of the Tokyo Round cuts in 1984 is reviewed in Lipsey & Smith (1985). No one in the debate surrounding the FTA succeeded in showing good economic reasons why the removal of the final tariffs on U.S.-Canada trade would produce structurally different results from those following the major reductions of tariff protection between 1935 and 1985.

Third, well over half of the tariff cuts called for by the FTA have already been made: some tariffs were removed immediately; some were eliminated by mutual agreement of the industries involved at the end of the first and second years of the FTA; more than 50 percent of those on five- and seven-year schedules have already been removed; and 40 percent of those remaining (those on a ten-year schedule) have been removed. The preliminary evidence from the first adjustments to the FTA is not dissimilar to the evidence for adjustments to earlier tariff cuts — although there appears to be more inter-industry adjustment this time. For example, Schwanen (1993) has shown that the main job losses have been in import-competing industries, and that exports to the United States (but not to the rest of the world) have increased since tariffs began to fall under the FTA. (This includes the period of the world recession in the early 1990s.) This evidence is consistent with the success of the Canadian government's policy objective of strengthening Canadian agglomerations by transferring resources from weak, tariff-protected industries to the stronger exporting industries.

NEW TECHNOLOGIES

IN CONSIDERING THE ISSUE of the profound effect of changes in technology on agglomerations of economic activity currently being experienced throughout the world, we deal first with the rapid globalization which has mainly been caused by lowered transport costs, the greater ease and declining costs of co-ordination, and falling tariffs. We then take a brief look at the production technologies themselves.

TRANSFER COSTS AND TARIFFS

WE USE THE TERM 'TRANSFER COSTS' to mean the costs of transport and co-ordination over distance plus tariffs. All of them contribute to the costs of producing in one region for use in another. Reductions in such costs set up two opposing tendencies related to globalization.

The first tendency has already been covered in the geographic analysis of location discussed above. We determined that economies of scale in production work to increase agglomeration while transfer costs work to limit it. Lowering transfer costs (including trade barriers) has the effect of encouraging the agglomeration of those types of production that are subject to significant scale economies.

The second tendency relates to the production of intermediate goods. To put it into perspective, consider a production method that uses a *centralized assembly plant and a number of decentralized parts producers.* This method of production, still in common use today, was introduced at the end of the 19th century in response to the development and widespread use of electric motors.[2] At the beginning of the 20th century when transport costs were high, all of the parts had to be produced nearby, so a model of fully-integrated production that ignored decentralized parts production was a reasonable approximation at a national level. However, due to reductions in actual shipping costs, co-ordination costs and tariffs, what we here call 'transfer costs', have fallen dramatically over the decades. As a result, parts production has been uncoupled geographically from the assembly operation to the extent that many parts can be produced almost anywhere in the world. Simple parts requiring unskilled labour are now often produced in low-wage LDCs; parts requiring more skilled labour are often made in high-wage advanced countries. This mechanism contributes to the decentralization of economic activity.

It should be noted that there is nothing contradictory in these two forces. One exploits large scale economies in the production of one good and leads to *fewer and larger economic units*, the size of the unit being limited by transport costs. The other exploits factor price differences around the world and leads to the *decentralization* of parts production, the amount of decentralization also being limited by transport and co-ordination costs. So, tariff reductions, which constitute one part of the reduction in transfer costs, set up two opposing forces. First, they lead to decentralization (in response to geographic differences in factor costs) whenever component parts of production (either goods or services) can be separated. Second, they lead to increased agglomeration whenever there are unexploited scale economies.

NEW PRODUCTION METHODS

MODERN TECHNOLOGY AND newly developed production techniques now make it possible for manufacturers to tailor many products to individual specifications. This means that long production runs of standardized product lines are no longer necessary to achieve low costs. Nonetheless, a large overall production volume is still needed to keep a flexible factory busy doing productive work. Scope economies are important even if scale economies related to standardized product lines are becoming less so.

The new manufacturing technology is evolving with enormous speed. In their first generation, computers did what was already being done, except that they did it faster and cheaper. In subsequent generations, computer technology continues to lead to new ways to do things and new ways to conceptualize what we do. According to Goldhar (1989), new computer-integrated production in manufacturing is smaller, faster, more integrated and more flexible than anything we now have in place. It will lead to firms taking control of the market place by "deliberately truncating the product life cycle, proliferating the range and complexity of products, and fragmenting the market". In his view we can, over the next decade, confidently expect to see the development of "manufacturing process technology that reduces the economic advantage of large scale factories and makes possible a greater variety of low volume manufacturing at a single location at low cost". (p. 262)

The new technology is also accomplishing a steady reduction of the percentage of product costs accounted for by direct labour. What will matter in the future is low capital cost, effective product design and process management. This means that the competitive advantage of low-cost labour will all but disappear and (the other side of the same coin) high-cost labour locations will not necessarily be at a competitive disadvantage.

Forces that will tend to stop production from agglomerating in only a few areas include the following: i) high competition among innovating companies with home bases in all three Triad areas; ii) the need to be close to consumers of rapidly evolving products (partly because feedback from end-users to producer is critical); and iii) the localization of markets and customization of products. Flaherty assesses the outcome of these forces as follows:

> ...world-class managers will have to operate in all three major industrial centers of the Triad — Western Europe, North America and Japan and the newly industrialising countries of the Far East. The fundamental reason for this is that in these centers companies with technology and employees of comparable sophistication will simultaneously and independently be generating new products and innovations as byproducts of doing business in their local environments. By combining the three courses for improvement, mangers can almost surely achieve products and operations superior to those of companies accessing only one. Conversely, without access to the new technological directions and products emerging in each location, a company operating in only one or two of the major industrial centers could easily be blindsided when confronted with a mature, version of a technology developed elsewhere. (Flaherty, 1989, 96.)

Considerations such as those given above lead us to expect *growing diversity in patterns of industrial location*, not the rise of a few massive agglomerations with low activity elsewhere. Goldhar supports this expectation in the following words:

> We will see examples of single global scale factories with high levels of scope economies serving fragmented, but global market segments and in other situations networks of specialized focus factories contributing to a single world standard, and very likely businesses with a proliferation of locally integrated factories; all existing together in a complex global business environment. There is no 'standard solution' to the search for the 'best' way to organize manufacturing for the international market. (Goldhar, 1989, 264.)

In the circumstances, any prediction pointing toward, or away from, regional agglomeration as a result of the new technologies would be rash at this time. What is clear, however, is that the *development* of new technologies will continue to be centred in a few highly innovative centres, while the over-all *use* of new technologies in production facilities will be spread over much of the world — with concentration in some being offset by dispersal in others. This is in line with much of what we know about the new technologies: they seem to be leading to increasing concentration in some fields and to "small is beautiful" developments in other fields. (Later in this study we consider a related issue — the pattern of R&D concentration in MNEs.)

The above-noted tendencies suggest that any rational basis that might currently exist for opposing the reduction of tariffs against low wage countries such as Mexico on the grounds of heavy adjustment costs in high wage countries may diminish greatly over the next decade. They also suggest that there is a potential from many countries to take part in the globalization of production. To do so it is important that these countries develop good back-ground policies in order to be attractive to FDI rather than rely on trade restrictions to support import-competing industries.

There is also a political concern. If the rate of change and structural adjustment accelerates, any trade liberalizing agreement that is negotiated is likely to be blamed for these changes just as in Canada the FTA was blamed for the consequences of the world recession in the early 1990s.

THE GEOGRAPHIC LOCATION OF R&D IN MNE NETWORKS

IN THIS SECTION WE CONSIDER the international allocation of R&D and, more broadly, the allocation of technological capabilities within MNEs. One of our concerns is how far this critical input is likely to remain centralized in parent firms, particularly in the aftermath of trade liberalization. Another concern is the related effects of such centralization on agglomerations of economic activity.

RESEARCH AND DEVELOPMENT

BY WAY OF BACKGROUND, we consider why many countries, especially smaller ones, continue to rely on importing technology while simultaneously trying to develop their own technologies. Making firm-specific assets available to their affiliates abroad is seen by some as the key to MNE activity. The related transfer of technology can occur in many ways, which may or may not include capital transfers. To be "transferred" successfully, however, most methods depend on contacts between specific individuals or groups. Such methods include formal research and development, informal technical exchanges involving know-how, skills development of the affiliates' personnel, knowledge embodied in products and services and the accompanying technical specifications. Much of this knowledge is tacit, and is related to continuous improvement in the production and marketing process. Partly for these reasons, and partly for proprietary and strategic reasons, much of this knowledge may not be available at an early stage or fully through markets or alliances.[3] In such instances, its importation through affiliates and the consequent spillover to local firms can cause a significant gain to national welfare.

It is not difficult to understand why national governments seek to develop technological capabilities at the same time. Innovations are centered on firms but, to some extent, they are also specific to locations. Firms draw on universities and public aspects of a country's scientific and technological capabilities. Companies (even rivals) share information at a technical level, and many local influences, such as educational systems and business and labour practices, influence the technological development paths in each location. MNEs utilize such local innovation capacities to broaden and strengthen their home-based capacities (Cantwell, 1991, p. 34).[4] Grossman & Helpman (1990) undertook formal studies of models of trade and growth where productivity gains arise not only from cross-country differences in manufacturing efficiency, but also from differences in R&D efficiency. A country may wish to develop its local technological capabilities first in order to utilize efficiently the stock of world knowledge and, second, to spur innovations that are central to growth. In both cases, developing such capabilities efficiently is recognized as a major policy challenge, particularly when the new forms of production are knowledge-intensive.

Until recently, the evidence has been that MNEs retain their R&D mainly in their home countries. What debate there was centered on the degree to which local affiliates differ from domestic firms in their propensity to undertake R&D, or go beyond simple adaptation of products and processes developed in the parent firm. There was no debate, however, on the fact that such local affiliates were generally far less R&D-intensive than their parents, especially with respect to research (R) and the innovation-related aspects of development (D).

The evidence clearly suggests that MNEs do develop most of their R&D at home, but it also shows that this depends on a variety of factors, such as the size and the technical characteristics of the home and host countries.[5] Unfortunately, analysis of this topic is severely limited by the lack of overall data on the technological and innovative capacity of firms categorized by country of ownership. We have no option but to use data on R&D and patenting, which are likely to be far more concentrated by home country than is technological capacity (as understood in the evolutionary theory of the firm). None of this, incidentally, should be confused with the *use* of technology: sectors that do not produce technology may nonetheless be highly intensive users of technology.

MNEs in two of the three largest home countries, Japan and the United States, concentrate very high degrees of R&D within their national boundaries. Japanese MNEs are believed to have spent less than 5 percent abroad in 1989. In that same year, U.S. multinationals had only 13 per cent of their R&D abroad, a figure which had risen slowly from about 6 percent in 1966. The U.S. figure shows wide variation by country and sector, however. Virtually all of the U.S. spending abroad was in developed countries, notably countries such as Germany and the UK, both of which have a substantial technological base. Also, U.S. R&D located abroad was well above the average in some sectors, such as household appliances and drugs (UN, 1992, p. 137 and Dunning, 1993, pp. 303-304).

MNEs in most other home countries, particularly those in smaller ones, appear to do a larger proportion of their R&D abroad. It has been estimated, for example, that the R&D intensity, measured by the number of R&D workers, was about the same in German affiliates in the developed countries as in domestic German manufacturers (Dörrenbächer and Wortmann, 1991). As an example of a smaller home country, the 15 largest Swiss MNEs had almost 40 percent of their R&D abroad in 1980, (Borner, et al., 1985, p. 3). Moreover, the trend to establish R&D units abroad has been accelerating, judging by a study of 167 of the world's largest industrial firms (Pearce & Singh, 1992). Prior to 1960 these firms established only 17 percent of their new R&D units abroad. This rose to 34 percent between 1960 and 1969 and 66 percent and 63 percent respectively over the next two decades.

Before proceeding further, it is necessary to distinguish between types of R&D and laboratories. We follow Pearce (1990, Ch. 8) in noting the familiar, if imprecise, distinctions between basic, applied and developmental research. He adds a useful distinction between development that is closely related to the *innovation* of a product or process, and development that focuses on the *adaptation* of products or processes to the needs of local markets.

Pearce's studies point to significant differences in the orientation and type of R&D engaged in by subsidiaries. Three types of subsidiary R&D laboratories are identified (see also Hood & Young, 1982, cited p. 310, Dunning, 1993). *Support laboratories* are the most common type, concentrating on adaptive development of the parent's products and processes whether for the local market or for export. *Locally integrated laboratories* focus more on innovation development than on adaptation. *Internationally independent* laboratories play a specialized role within the MNE's centralized R&D program. All three types of laboratory involve communication with, and co-ordination by, the MNE network, but the second type, which implies more independence, may also require more explicit performance. Pearce goes on to note that the support laboratory is most likely to appear where the product line of the subsidiary is either a *miniature replica* of the parent's or is *rationalized* (specialized). The locally integrated laboratory suits the replica subsidiary. It also suits those where the subsidiary has won a *product mandate*. In this case the subsidiary has not only the responsibility to produce a particular line (or lines) on a regional or global basis as in the rationalized subsidiary, it must also carry out a number of headquarters functions related to these lines. The internationally integrated laboratory may have little relationship to the subsidiary's production lines, although such a laboratory often carries a certain prestige from a scientific viewpoint because there is little adaptive research involved.[6]

What determines the division of R&D between a parent company and its subsidiaries? The discussion so far suggests that strong forces favour the centralization of R&D. Those forces begin with the historic development of firm-specific advantages within the home country, followed by the accumulated R&D and know-how that go with this developed in the laboratories, production processes and supporting industries of the home base. Economies of scale and agglomeration, and reduced co-ordination problems contribute to centralization. What promotes decentralization is the need to serve local markets or take advantage of local materials, the need to utilize (or at least to monitor) local technological skills, requirements to meet government incentives or pressures, and a variety of factors related to competitive strategy. If data on know-how rather than R&D were available, the links to local production would likely be more evident. In the Pearce & Singh sample, the responding executives assigned the largest weights to various market needs in explaining the existence of subsidiary R&D units, but the technological capability of the particular country was also an important factor. Other studies have confirmed the role of these and other factors (for example, Hirschey & Caves, 1980; Dunning, 1993:307-11). A strategic factor being noted increasingly is the desire by a number of more globalized firms to locate both production and research in each of the parts of the Triad.

In the process of liberalizing trade, the roles of both local subsidiaries and Canadian-owned MNEs are changing. At present, a critical issue for subsidiaries is how far their roles will be re-defined and the extent to which that redefinition will enable them to maintain or increase their technological capacity. Eden (1991:140) has noted that in manufacturing this largely involves the sub-assembly and final-assembly types of subsidiaries, where the potential for high-level technological production exists. Trade liberalization tends to reduce the role of miniature replica subsidiaries in favour of more specialized production, distribution and servicing activities within the MNE. Along with this, support laboratory functions are also reduced (although not necessarily the capability to monitor R&D). Of course, a subsidiary may also find an enhanced role for itself in niche or small-batch production in foreign markets. The MNE may also bring its entire network to bear from time to time to solve particular problems. Nonetheless, the logic of more specialized production by the subsidiary for global markets strongly suggests that its R&D functions will diminish — unless it can find a role as a lead producer or obtain a regional or world product mandate. It may also have a role to play for historic reasons; with vertical integration or because of a merger, a subsidiary may have a significantly different product line and/or R&D focus from that of its parent and other affiliates. With restructuring pressures, however, it will still have to work hard to retain or to develop its distinction.

The rapid rise of Canadian FDI abroad over the past two decades has presented Canadian-owned MNEs and the Canadian government with a particular challenge. Canada's substantial capacity in the primary resource and processing sector has encouraged investment abroad by Canadian firms with strong marketing and other skills not closely related to R&D as conventionally measured (Niosi, 1985; Rugman, 1987). Canadian FDI in the services sector is also increasing rapidly, in part to take advantage of liberalization of entry under the Canada-U.S. Free Trade Agreement. It is not yet clear, however, whether an increase in production abroad by Canadian manufacturers will lead to further development of R&D abroad, whether through the acquisition of technology-intensive firms or the re-allocation of some Canadian capacity abroad. All of this is happening to some extent, and as Eden (1993:25) notes, some Canadian subsidiaries in the United States may very well come to dominate their Canadian parents in production and perhaps even some headquarters functions.

Similar concerns have been expressed in other home countries, both large and small, from the United States to Sweden. Policy responses, such as limiting outward FDI, run the risk of damaging the competitive power of the firms they are intended to protect. After attempting a variety of restrictions (see Safarian, 1993:194 and 367) the governments of most industrial countries appear to have concluded that the risks are too great. The related point in theory is that the competitive powers of firms and of countries are not identical. Firms draw on the resources of locations other than the home country, even as they try to maintain the characteristics of the latter.

PRODUCT MANDATES

A KEY QUESTION FOR CANADIANS is: how far will MNE restructuring lead to product mandates for Canadian subsidiaries? Given a product mandate, a subsidiary is assigned regional or global responsibility for a product or product line, including all the related R&D and perhaps other functions, such as international marketing, as well. There are, however, important limits to such mandates. The subsidiary remains part of an MNE network. It continues to draw on the knowledge resources of that network, including its research and marketing skills. Also, while it may have a broader base of responsibility than a specialized subsidiary, it is still accountable to the parent for its performance. Indeed, in consideration of the risks to the parent's management in decentralizing central functions (albeit selectively by product line) the subsidiary management is likely to be under considerable pressure to perform well if it is to keep its mandate.

A number of studies have documented the difficulties with which subsidiary managements must deal in moving to such mandates. Many are ill-prepared in terms of the experience and organization necessary for strategic planning. Much depends on having a significant technological or other capacity in the subsidiary or at least the potential for one. There is also the problem of persuading a sometimes sceptical management group in the parent company to follow this course. It has been well documented that local government support has played a role in some of the better-known cases.[7] The technological competence theory provides a pessimistic view of the prospects for the development of product mandates, at least for countries lacking a high degree of technological competence with respect to production (see Cantwell, 1991 and comment by Safarian). The theory contends that MNEs will internalize the research which is central to them in strategic terms, notably in core technologies. Where they locate R&D abroad, it will be in countries that have similar levels of technological competence and with complementary technologies. Thus, technological competence is likely to remain more concentrated than competence in production and assembly.

There are several reasons for considering this view to be overly pessimistic. First, the argument may be more relevant to manufacturing than to other sectors where Canada's comparative advantage is more evident. Second, the view may be too aggregative even for manufacturing, in the sense that a country can have advantages in some sectors that support mandating, while technological opportunities may cluster in a way that benefits such a country (or some of its regions) if its investments in human capital, organization and infrastructure are such as to allow it to take advantage of these opportunities. Third, 'globalization' has been interpreted by some firms as requiring more emphasis on developing international sources of competitive advantage along with joint exploration of such possibilities. In such circumstances there should be scope for regional or global mandates as well as specialization as such.

Some of the factors that determine the scope for product mandates, as distinct from specialization, are brought out in two studies. Etemad & Dulude (1986) used patenting data to study 84 subsidiaries in Ontario and Quebec, each of which had at least one product mandate. These data suggest that subsidiaries with a capability for independent research are more likely to be part of an MNE which itself has a high technological capability. The data also suggest that such subsidiaries are also more likely to be part of a U.S.-controlled firm than one controlled overseas. Such subsidiaries are also more likely to occur when the subsidiaries and the parent firms are large in absolute terms, when the subsidiary is large relative to the parent, and when there are many subsidiaries in the global network..

Roth & Morrison (1992) analyzed these issues in the context of a set of manufacturing industries where a high degree of globalization exists. Using questionnaires involving 125 subsidiaries in six countries, including Canada, they determined that a subsidiary is more likely to have a global mandate: a) when the primary activities in the value chain are located in several countries, but the support activities (such as R&D, information systems, and management of capital) are in one site; b) when the proportion of products similar to those produced elsewhere in the MNE falls; and c) when its management, relative to the management in other subsidiaries, has expertise on issues of strategic flexibility, in contrast with expertise managing various types of interdependencies. Several other determinants often noted in the literature were not supported by their tests. These include the relative size of the subsidiary's R&D and its competency (compared to other subsidiaries), in manufacturing, R&D and marketing. This research is preliminary: finer specifications and further research may resolve some of the apparent contradictions.

There are strong pressures to maintain headquarters-type functions such as R&D in the home country. Trade liberalization and the smaller role for miniature replica subsidiaries will also tend to reduce local support laboratories. This is particularly important for a country like Canada, given the appeal of the United States as a centre for R&D and the exceptionally slow decentralization of research by U.S. multinationals. Nevertheless, the evidence clearly suggests that significant decentralization of R&D has already occurred for a number of other home countries and for some types of industries. While most formal R&D laboratories will continue to be concentrated in home countries, process developments associated with an evolutionary approach to investment still offer scope for significantly increased decentralization. The global corporation is unlikely to overlook the possibility of utilizing a key knowledge resource wherever it is located, particularly in view of the declining costs of coordinating such activities. In these circumstances, there is a role for smaller countries especially in attracting product mandates where their technological and other capabilities are attractive.

Conclusions

The following summarizes the main themes of this paper and our tentative conclusions.

- Theories of agglomeration, generally, are based on the interaction between scale economies in production and transport costs. Models incorporating such forces typically display agglomeration effects, multiple equilibria, path dependency, sensitivity to small disturbances, non-reversibilities, and other characteristics that are currently attracting the attention of economists.

- These characteristics suggest that current agglomerations and comparative advantages may owe as much to past policies as to impersonal economic and physical forces. There is no doubt that policies can have large effects, and that in some countries they have had large effects. What is in doubt is whether we know enough to influence the future in predictable ways by using policies designed to create specific comparative advantages and encourage specific agglomeration.

• The extent to which protectionist policies contributed to the buildup of industrial agglomerations in Canada in the past, as they no doubt did in many of the NICs, is subject to debate. Wrenching readjustments due to such forces as the FTA, globalization and new technologies, are currently being made in the Canadian manufacturing sector. The contribution of the FTA is difficult to disentangle but there is no strong evidence that the agglomerations themselves will disappear. Path dependency, due to accumulated human and physical capital, well-developed institutions and attitudes, and more traditional sources of comparative advantage (such as climate and natural resources) suggest that it would take strong, sustained shocks to undo well-established agglomerations of Canadian industrial activity. Policy makers cannot, however, take shelter behind what is unlikely. The theory is clear in its message that thresholds can be passed, and that beyond those thresholds a cumulative unravelling of agglomerations is possible; if such a process is allowed to begin, it may be impossible to reverse it with marginal policy changes.

• The continued rapid development of the new knowledge-based technologies will have major effects on agglomerations and hence on the location of investment in countries such as Canada. The new technologies are only one of the many forces exerting pressure toward fewer and bigger agglomerations while, at the same time, pushing toward more decentralization (particularly in parts manufacturing). The net effect appears to be preserving, even enhancing, the niches available for smaller countries that have the requisite human capital to participate in the new wave of manufacturing production.

• Trade liberalization is continuing to exert pressures to centralize R&D, particularly as the role of branch plants and subsidiaries is diminished. In contrast, a decentralization of R&D seems to be occurring in some types of industry; the geographic availability of human capital, the specialized demands of local markets, and the need to have development capacity for new products near customers, are all working in this direction — with more or less force, depending on the type of product and the organization of the company producing it.

• These trends do not point to the inevitable economic decline of smaller advanced industrial countries assuming, of course, that those countries can provide good conditions for production and for R&D. Policies that provide for such conditions include those that emphasize human capital, competitive factor prices, favourable tax regimes, and attractive background conditions for international investment. The value of other, more focused, policies is still being debated. Given the strength and complexity of the forces operating, there is much to be said for a policy framework that gets the background conditions right and then lets private decisions determine specific investment and trade flows.

ENDNOTES

1 Modern analysis of the economics of endogenous technological change with costly and difficult diffusion due to such things as the tacitness of much technological knowledge, provides a richer analysis of infant industry tariff protection than does the text-book analysis based on the desire to import given tehcnology where the only barrier is static scale economies.

2 The size of each parts producer is influenced by its scale effects.

3 The word 'may' is used intentionally here to allow for apparent exceptions, such as Japan for a period following the Second World War.

4 These items are developed at length by the evolutionary approach to technological change (for example, see Dosi et al., 1988). Also, a number of authors have challenged Porter (1990), arguing that MNEs draw on much more than their home base for competitive power. See, for example, the 1993 special issue of *Management International Review* devoted to this theme.

5 There is a good overview of the issue in Dunning (1993, Ch. 11). See also McFetridge (ed.) 1991, especially the articles noted on p. xii. Also, two notable recent books are Pearce (1989) and Casson (1991).

6 Pearce notes that an overseas R&D facility can support functions other than those noted here, including a window on local capabilities which may be of use within the MNE group.

7 See, for example, D'Cruz (1986), Bishop & Crookell (1985), Daly & MacCharles (1986), and Rugman (1986).

ACKNOWLEDGEMENT

GRATEFUL ACKNOWLEDGEMENT is made of helpful comments received from Rachel McCulloch, Lorraine Eden and Industry Canada staff on an earlier draft.

BIBLIOGRAPHY

Akerman, Johan Gustev, "Realkapital und Kapitalzing: Hept I." Stockholm: Centraltryckeriet, 1923.

Borner, S. et al. "Global Structural Change and International Competition Among Industrial Firms: the Case of Switzerland." *Kyklos*, 38, (1985):77-103.

Cantwell, J. "The Theory of Technological Competence and its Application to International Production." In *Foreign Investment, Technology and Economic Growth*, The Investment Canada Research Series. Edited by D. McFetridge. Calgary: University of Calgary Press, 1991, pp. 33-67.

Cantwell, J. "A Survey of Theories of International Production." In *The Nature of the Transnational Firm*. Edited by C. N. Pitelis and R. Sugden. London: Rutledge, 1991.

Coase, Ronald. "The Nature of the Firm.", *Economica* 4, (November 1937):386-405.

D'Cruz, J. "Strategic Management of Subsidiaries." In *Managing the International Subsidiary*. Edited by Etemad and Dulude. London: Croom Helm, 1986.

Dörrenbächer, C. and M. Wortmann. "The Internationalization of Corporate Research and Development." *Intereconomics*, 26, 3, (May/June 1991):139-44.

Eastman, H.C. and S. Stykolt. *The Tariff and Competition in Canada*. Toronto: Macmillan, 1967.

Eaton, B. Curtis and Richard G. Lipsey. "Increasing Returns and All That." Discussion Paper, Department of Economics, Simon Fraser University, 1993.

Economic Council of Canada. *The Bottom Line: Technology, Trade and Income Growth*. Ottawa: Supply and Services, 1983, p. 116.

Eden, L. "Multinational Responses to Trade and Technology Changes: Implications for Canada." In *Foreign Investment, Technology and Growth*, The Investment Canada Research Series. Edited by D. McFetridge. Calgary: University of Calgary Press, 1991, pp. 133-72.

_____. "Multinationals in North America: After NAFTA," (First draft), mimeo, March 10, 1993.

Etemad, H., and L.S. Dulude (eds). *Managing the Multinational Subsidiary*. London: Croom Helm, 1986.

Flaherty, T. "International Sourcing: Beyond Catalog Shopping and Franchising." In *Managing International Manufacturing*. Edited by K. Ferdows. Amsterdam: North-Holland, 1989, p. 96.

Goldhar, J.D. "Implications of CIM for International Manufacturing." In *Managing International Manufacturing*. Edited by K. Ferdows. Amsterdam: North-Holland, 1989, p. 262.

Helpman, E. and P.R. Krugman. *Market Structure and Foreign Trade*. Cambridge, Mass: M.I.T. Press, 1985.

Hirschey, R.C. and R.E. Caves. "International Decentralization of Research and Transfer of Technology by Multinational Enterprises." Harvard University Discussion Paper 779, 1980.

Hood N. and S. Young. "U.S. Multinational R and D: Corporate Strategies and Policy Implications in the U.K." *Multinational Business*, 2, (1982):10-23.

Krugman, Paul. *Geography and Trade*. Cambridge, Mass: M.I.T. Press, 1991.

Lipsey, Richard and Murray Smith. *Taking the Initiative: Canada's Trade Options in a Turbulent World*. Toronto: C.D. Howe Institute, 1985.

Mackintosh, W.A. *The Economic Background of Dominion Provincial Relations*. Carleton Library #13. Toronto: McClelland and Stewart, 1967.

McFetridge, D.G. (ed). *Foreign Investment, Technology and Economic Growth*, The Investment Canada Research Series. Calgary: University of Calgary Press, 1991.

Niosi, J. *Canadian Multinationals*. Toronto: Between the Lines, 1985.

Pearce, R.D. and S Singh. "Internationalization of R and D Among the World's Leading Enterprises." In *Technology, Management and International Business*. Edited by O. Grandstrand et al. Chichester: John Wiley and Sons, 1992.

Pearce, R.D. *The Internationalization of Research and Development*. London: Macmillan, 1990.

Roth, K. and A.J. Morrison. "Implementing Global Strategy: Characteristics of Global Subsidiary Mandates." *Journal of International Business Studies*. Fourth Quarter, 23, 4, (1992):715-35.

Rugman, A.M. *Outward Bound: Canadian Direct Investment in the United States*. Toronto and Washington: C.D. Howe Institute and National Planning Association, 1987.

Safarian, A.E. "Direct Investment Strategies and the Canada-United States Free Trade Agreement." In *The Dynamics of North American Trade and Investment*. Edited by W. Reynolds et al. Berkley: Stanford University Press,1991a.

_____. *Multinational Enterprise and Public Policy*. Aldershott: Edward Elgar Publishing, 1993, pp. 194-367.

Schwanen, Daniel "Were the Optimists Wrong on Free Trade?" Toronto: C.D. Howe Institute, Commentary No. 37, 1993.

Silverberg, Gerald. "Modeling Economic Dynamics and Technical Change." In *Technical Change and Economic Theory*. Edited by G. C. Dosi et al. London: Pinter Publishers, 1990.

United Nations. *World Investment Report: Transnational Corporations as Engineers of Growth*. New York: United Nations, 1992.

Vernon, R. "The Location of Economic Activity." In *Economic Analysis and Multinational Enterprise*. Edited by J. Dunning. London: Allen and Unwin, 1974.

Williamson, Oliver E. *Markets and Heirarchies: Analysis and Anti-Trust Implications*. Glencoe, Illinois: Free Press, 1975.

Alan M. Rugman
Professor of International Business
University of Toronto

& Joe R. D'Cruz
Associate Professor of Strategic Management
University of Toronto

5

A Theory of Business Networks

INTRODUCTION

A S THE NATURE OF INTERNATIONAL TRADE and competition changes to reflect an increasingly borderless world, it is apparent that the organization of multinational enterprises and their relationships with all pertinent stakeholders are changing as well. This is occurring due to the predominant role of multinational enterprises as global economic coordinators of production and investment. In fact, the changing organization of the firm in terms of structure, task, and strategy can be viewed as a natural process of evolution which employs and deploys the resources of the firm in the most strategic and economically efficient manner.

A related issue in this process of globalization of the firm is the appropriate role of government and the nature of the nation state in an interdependent and highly integrated global economic system. We shall develop a framework wherein the multinational enterprise is at the centre of a "business network". In this context, a *business network* is defined as a group of suppliers, customers, competitors and members of the non-business infrastructure, all linked together and sharing a common global strategy of a "flagship firm" (a lead multinational enterprise). A multinational enterprise is a "flagship firm", since it provides strategic leadership to all the partners in the business network. Furthermore, the need for the flagship firm to compete globally leads it to adopt and operationalize internationally based benchmarks of competitiveness. In turn, these international benchmarks become the relevant ones for the partners in the business network because they share the global strategy of the flagship firm.

These arguments have been developed in an applied Canadian context by Rugman & D'Cruz (1991) and D'Cruz & Rugman (1992). Here we provide an analytical foundation for our concept of a business network and advance the analysis in a new dimension by addressing the asymmetry in relationships between the flagship firm and its partners, including government.

To summarize, the objectives of this study are:

• To develop the rationale for a business network.

• To demonstrate the asymmetrical nature of strategic management in business networks and to discuss their organizational structures.

• To provide examples of the asymmetrical partnerships of business networks by illustrating the leadership of flagship firms and their linkages with suppliers, customers, competitors and members of the non-business infrastructure.

• To draw out the implications of business networks and their organizational structures for the engineering of the international competitiveness of multinationals and their partners in a North American context.

THE RELATED THEORETICAL LITERATURE

FIRMS IN NORTH AMERICA can no longer operate as isolated, totally independent economic units, free to garner and employ closely held resources for optimal economic gain. Firms oriented in this manner are now finding themselves competing against global businesses that are already benefitting from the coordination of strategies, competencies and resources in some sort of implicit or explicit network structure (for example, the Japanese *kereitsu*-based multinationals, the Korean *chaebols* and the Chinese family firms all use various forms of "network" structure). Few North American firms have the internal resources or, most importantly, the ability to coordinate the resources they do have in order to remain competitive in the long term. In their strategy formulation, therefore, firms are recognizing that they cannot excel in all areas of their business system against global competition. Successful North American firms are beginning to focus on those aspects of the micro business system (value chain) where they have an advantage or special competence, and are linking themselves to other participants in the economy to create a business network.

While competitive strategy considerations are paramount in driving the decisions of a business that result in organizational change, the analysis for restructuring business systems is grounded in an activity's economic efficiency and contribution to the value-added in a product. Coase (1937) had the foresight to argue that firms can and often do perform effectively the functions of markets in terms of economic coordination and organization. Williamson's (1975) contribution was to apply explicit transaction cost analysis to the issue. He argued that a hierarchical structure will replace a market when transaction costs impede the efficient operation of the latter. Williamson worked with four types of transaction costs: bounded rationality, opportunism, uncertainty/complexity, and the small numbers problem.

Ouchi (1980) built on Williamson's transaction cost analysis by incorporating explicit organizational structures. He paired bounded rationality with uncertainty/complexity and opportunism with the small numbers problem to generate three types of organizational structures: markets, bureaucracies and clans. These three systems usually have different information requirements: prices, rules, or traditions. Furthermore a clan will have several normative requirements: reciprocity, legitimate authority, and a common set of values and beliefs. A hierarchy needs only the first two of these, and markets only the first.

Similar ideas have been applied to analyze MNEs. Internalization occurs when the benefits of control through internal markets exceed the governance costs and when environmental factors preclude exporting, licensing, or joint ventures as viable methods of servicing foreign markets (Rugman, 1981). Yet, internalization through the "visible hand" results in the organizational costs of running large integrated, hierarchical internal markets, in which managerial and administrative complexity eventually limit the successful growth of the firm (Rugman, 1986).

The basis of a business network is a form of economic organization found as a hybrid between markets and hierarchies. In a business network, economic transactions can be mediated at lower cost than through market mechanisms or an integrated firm. Jarillo (1988) developed the concept of a "strategic" network as a co-operative type of market structure, adding it to the three organizational modes of Ouchi — markets, bureaucracies and clans. Jarillo also developed the notion of a "hub" firm — which is not exactly the same as the "flagship firm" used in this study. A flagship firm differs from Jarillo's (1988) "hub" firm in that Jarillo uses the term to refer to the hierarchical leader of a strategic network, whereas we use it to refer to leadership of a business network where the other players are partners rather than subordinates. The partners follow the strategic leadership of the flagship firm but are also involved in two-way organizational linkages rather than one-way hierarchical linkages.

The theory of networks in a Japanese context explains networks as alternatives to both markets and hierarchies (Kagono et al., 1985; Westney, 1990). The network concept denies the notion that all economic activities be organized into discrete units that must necessarily be owned by the firm. It also repudiates the idea that maximization of gains is most likely to occur if there is a winner and a loser and if a firm minimizes the sharing of resources (be they people, ideas, information, resources, etc.)

THE BUSINESS NETWORK MODEL

A BUSINESS NETWORK has a flagship firm at its centre and four partners: suppliers, customers, competitors, and the non-business infrastructure. This

FIGURE 1

ELEMENTS OF A BUSINESS NETWORK

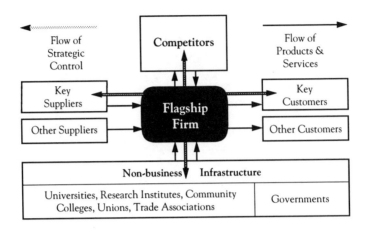

last partner relates to the non-trading service sectors, which include government, education, health care, social services, and cultural industries. The partners can include many small businesses, as well as much larger firms. Indeed, some of the partners may employ more people than the flagship firm itself, as in the case of a major electric utility or all the employees in the health and education sectors of a business network. At the centre of the business network is the flagship firm (a multinational enterprise), which takes on the responsibility of forging the overall strategy and structure of the network. The business network, has a web of organizational linkages that tie the individual members together (Figure 1).

The flagship firm distinguishes its relationships between those customers and suppliers that are very important and those which are necessary but not critical to the firm's success. The inter-organizational relationships with key *suppliers* are characterized by a high degree of harmonization and sharing of information, technology, strategies and responsibilities through formal business linkages. Less critical strategic relationships are kept at the usual arm's length of commercial relationships. These are distinguished by transaction-by-transaction characteristics rather than by the greater stability of a relationship characterized by multiple transactions.

Relationships with key *customers* involve greater sharing of information and more open communication of strategies, and in this respect it is important not to confuse customers with consumers. In a business network customers are intermediaries between the flagship firm and final consumers (end users). In other words, customers are like intermediate producers, and are a part of a business relationship. Customers are often agents or distributors — as with auto producers and food processing firms, for example.

Business network relationships with *competitors* may include technology transfers, supplier development, market sharing agreements, etc., but such relationships will depend more upon close interaction between managers than on contractual arrangements to govern the operational aspects of the relationship. Competitors, like suppliers or customers, can be across national borders. Given the Canada-U.S. Free Trade Agreement, and the proposed NAFTA, it is important to recognize the probable increase in strategic alliances and joint ventures, often dictated by high costs of technological development and related business costs when operating on a global scale. However, strategic alliances and the international business literature related thereto are not our primary concern in this study, so we shall pass it by.

The *non-business infrastructure*, which employs over one-half of the 70 percent of Canadians working in services (often in small business), affects the ability of the exporting sector to remain internationally competitive by virtue of the quality and cost of the services provided to this sector. The traditional arm's length nature of the flagship firm's relationships to the non-business infrastructure is changing and is becoming more collaborative and interdependent. This is the most difficult organizational relationship to develop, since many employees (in the public sector especially) are stuck with an "equity"-based view of government, rather than the efficiency-based view required for a business network to become globally competitive.

The business network developed above is also different from Porter's strategic cluster. As is well-known, Porter's work has always emphasized industry-level determinants of competitive advantage (Porter, 1980, 1985, 1990). In Porter (1990), related and supporting industries in the home-based diamond of competitive advantage interact with industry rivals, industry-level demand conditions, and natural and human resource conditions. Porter's strategic clusters are industry clusters. The organizational relationships of relevance are intra-industry, rather than the inter-industry relationships of concern to us in this analysis of business networks. In Porter (1990) the case studies reported, and the empirical tests of the sixteen strategic clusters, are all at the industry level. The unit of analysis for Porter's (1990) strategic clusters is the same industry level as in Porter (1980): not firm level or even business unit level.

The business network, unlike the strategic cluster, has non-industry partners and asymmetric strategic control within the network. The strategic cluster is not concerned with the identification of a flagship firm because it is simply a descriptive term for an industry grouping which has evolved over time. The business network, indeed, is a new theoretical construct, where firms interact to achieve commonly held strategic and cost objectives.

Asymmetry in the Business Network

THE BASIC STRUCTURE of the business network, as outlined above, is not complicated in design. The challenge lies in making it work. It is the formation and implementation (management of relationships) of the business network that will require an acceptance of new organizational linkages and a willingness to redefine, continually, such managerial and inter-organizational relationships. The strategic management of the business network emanates from the flagship firm. The flagship firm competes globally and its international benchmarks become those of the business network. It outlines what is produced and where it is produced. How it is produced is largely determined by the partners in the business network. The operational management of production and distribution is controlled outside the flagship for those products/services unbundled from the flagship's micro business system. Similarly, the flagship sets the global strategic agenda in the relationships with the non-business infrastructure.

Clearly, the relationships between the flagship firm and the respective business network partners are asymmetric. The flagship firm exercises its bargaining power and, in its relationships with key *suppliers*, requires exclusivity. In return for yielding autonomy in strategic decision making, suppliers receive incentives and rewards. Specifically,

a) due to the flagship's supplier reduction program, the supplier benefits from increased volume and multi-year supply cotracts;

b) through unbundled flagship activities, the supplier benefits from capturing a greater share of the value-added in the business network;

c) due to the multi-year supply contracts (Fama, 1980, indicates uncertainty is reduced for suppliers in multi-year, open-ended contracts) and the assumption of some technology- and capital-expenditure risks by the flagship firm, the supplier benefits from a reduction in its business risk.

The flagship assumes responsibility for the prosperity of *key customers* (again, these customers are part of the business network relationships). It commits to helping customers (intermediate producers) achieve their strategic and business objectives. Strategy development, therefore, begins with an analysis by the flagship firm of the final consumer (end user) the customer will serve.

Relationships with the *non-business infrastructure* will also be characterized by the flagship leading the strategic decision-making process and mobilizing financial resources for this part of the business network (e.g., universities). Building links with governments should follow, not precede, the creation of a network structure with the rest of the infrastructure. If governments are brought into the process too early, their agendas will tend to reflect attention away from competitiveness issues. Given the legacy of unsuccessful, large-scale regional economic development in Canada, it is apparent that new methods of developing infrastructure are needed. By concentrating on networks in geographic strategic clusters first, later government involvement (i.e., in the form of training funds to upgrade the skill base) may prove more beneficial.

Relationships with *competitors*, in the form of joint ventures, market sharing arrangements, etc., are characterized by more collaborative thinking and a reliance upon shared human capital (not just financial). In relationships between a flagship firm and its competitors, there are three benefits of network linkages that derive as part of the global strategy of a multinational:

1) becoming part of a globally competitive team at a time when industry is restructuring into such units;

2) learning the business systems of foreign partners to improve organizational learning at home;

3) participating in specific projects (e.g. new technology development).

The asymmetry in the business network of Figure 1 necessitates the implementation of external benchmarking to measure the process and product of the suppliers. In other words, because the flagship firm needs exclusivity from its key suppliers, those suppliers lose the feedback of the market mechanism to determine if they are remaining competitive in production methods, product innovation, and so forth. Key suppliers will have to re-examine the trade-offs in such a relationship to determine if continued dependence on the flagship is worthwhile. Non-key suppliers will also have an incentive to see if they can make it as key suppliers.

EXAMPLES OF BUSINESS NETWORKS

BENETTON PROVIDES a good example of asymmetry in relationships between closely associated companies and of the management of outsourced company functions (Jarillo & Martinez, 1988; Jarillo & Stevenson, 1991). With over 4,000 stores and worldwide revenues of several billion dollars, Benetton's management of relationships and business activities illustrates how unusual structures can facilitate strategic success. In its relationships with its subcontractors and agents, Benetton's goal, and those of its subcontractors and agents, is to use trust and cooperation to facilitate stable relationships and long-term associations. Stable, long-term relationships are necessary for Benetton's business system to operate effectively because such relationships reduce the risk and transaction costs associated with its outsourced activities.

Benetton subcontracts approximately 95 percent of its activities in manufacturing, distribution and sales; and keeps raw material purchases and the dyeing and cutting operations in-house. As the world's largest purchaser of wool, it achieves huge economies of scale through central buying. Dyeing and cutting are retained due to the high-technology processes used with chemicals and CAD/CAM, respectively. These processes are too expensive and technically sophisticated for the subcontractor to implement in its operations. The company also keeps production planning, technical research, and product development as part of its internal activities.

Through a network of between 350 and 400 subcontractors, Benetton orchestrates production by providing the following services to its subcontractors: production planning, materials requirement planning, raw materials in exact quantities, technical documentation, technical assistance for quality control, machinery purchase advice, and financial aid *via* leasing and factoring subsidiaries. In return, Benetton demands exclusivity from its subcontractors who, while recognizing the risk of having only one client, enjoy a guaranteed

FIGURE 2

THE BENETTON BUSINESS NETWORK

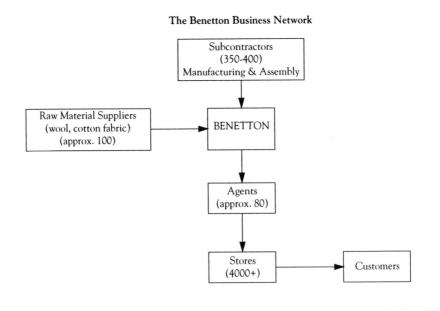

The Benetton Business Network

Source: Adapted from Jarillo, Carlos J. and Jon I. Martinez, Teaching note for "Benetton S.p.A.". Case study N9-389-074. Boston: HBS Case Services, Harvard Business School, 1988.

market and full-capacity utilization. This risk is also accepted for other reasons, including the stability and predictability of sales, the prestige of working for Benetton, the opportunity to operate as small companies (most subcontractors are family-owned units of fewer than 15 people — an arrangement preferred by Benetton in terms of cultural background — and because larger companies face more regulation under Italian law), and the opportunity to establish companies in the region where one's family is located. These relationships are illustrated in Figure 2.

Benetton often recruits less experienced contractors in order to indoctrinate them with the Benetton approach and thereby create loyalty to and dependency on the company. Benetton also encourages its managers to own or be directors of subcontracting firms and to start up new ones. The company also takes equity positions in the large subcontractors. This system of sub-contracting offers both flexibility in production (overtime, reallocation of production on short notice, etc.) and low costs. Because the manufacturing is low-skill and labour-intensive, costs are contained, not by technological break-throughs, but through the "constant effort of hundreds of small entrepreneurs to find ways to cut costs" (Jarillo & Martinez, 1988).

In terms of distribution and sales, Benetton uses 80 independent agents to manage the 4,000-plus investor-owned retail stores. These agents, most of whom have been hired by Luciano Benetton, obtain exclusive rights to a sales territory and are responsible for selecting new store locations, finding new store investors and owners, training store managers, helping the store owners/managers to control their stores, presenting garment collections to the stores, and collecting the orders. The agents also own large numbers of stores themselves. The agents are managed by a small number of area managers, most of whom are Italian. To illustrate the effectiveness of the system, Jarillo & Martinez cite the example of an agent in Northern Italy with 200 stores in his territory; he owns between 35 and 40 of them himself; the remainder are owned by a group of 50 to 60 owner/investors. In ten years, only five or six people have been replaced as store owners. The agent and owner network provides Benetton with high service levels and immediate market knowledge.

Through its promotion of involvement (managers as subcontractors, agents as store owners), Benetton intimately links the marketplace to the company. The company's structure explicitly rewards cooperation and relationship building. Opportunism, such as having subcontractors raise prices in tight capacity situations, is counter-productive because it reduces trust and increases transaction costs. Jarillo and Stevenson suggest that Benetton is intentionally organized to capitalize on the benefits of relationships, where the rational behaviour is to cooperate. Such cooperation fosters trust, and trust reduces costs in several areas: in contract enforcement and negotiation; with supplier opportunism and lack of attention; by protecting company processes (e.g. loss of proprietary technology); and with obtaining market knowledge.

Stentor and the Canadian telecommunications industry is another example of an industry that has created an effective business network structure. Stentor Canadian Network Management, formed by Bell Canada and eight provincial telephone companies, was created to provide "seamless telecommunications service, nationally" with the primary focus on the business/commercial segment. The existence of Stentor effectively implies that the partners believe they can better meet customer needs through this network arrangement than each could alone. Undoubtedly, industry deregulation and the resulting increased competition have changed the dynamics of the industry. As other alliances are also having to face global competitors (e.g. Unitel and AT&T, Bell Canada and Mercury, MCI and British Telecom, Stentor and MCI), it is apparent that the industry's boundaries are changing to reflect service/product requirements of companies and individuals communicating globally. Moreover, the convergence of telecommunications, computers and entertainment is forcing telecommunications companies to change the way they define their businesses.

The Stentor partners believe they can deliver greater value to their customers by coordinating the delivery of telecommunications services to those customers (key customers). The strategic priorities for delivering these services are determined by national account teams whose membership is drawn from the Stentor partner telephone companies (telcos). Any given service or component of a service may be implemented by a single telco, but addressing and meeting customer requirements is viewed as an offering from the alliance as a whole. Service to key customers has been labelled "Signature Service", wherein the specifics of service commitments are negotiated with the customer and a service document is signed by the CEO of the alliance partner which has responsibility for the account.

Stentor has formed two new companies to address explicitly the roles of the alliance. Stentor Resource Centre Inc. was established to strengthen and consolidate the partners' efforts in marketing and development. Stentor Telecom Policy Inc. was formed to act as the alliance's government relations advisory arm. Both organizations are expected to operate as independent units after the initial coordination stages.

Northern Telecom is an internationally competitive developer and manufacturer of telecommunications hardware and is a primary supplier to Bell Canada and the other Stentor partners. Bell Canada is connected closely to Northern Telecom through Bell Canada Enterprises (BCE) (Bell's parent) and BCE's 53 percent ownership in Northern Telecom. Bell Northern Research (BNR) is the research and development arm of both Northern Telecom and Bell Canada (70 percent and 30 percent ownership, respectively) and also effectively acts as a link to other researchers in industry and academia. The relationship between Bell Canada and several of the other Stentor partners is also more formalized because of the ownership positions held in those companies by BCE (MT&T - 34.3 percent, NB Tel - 37 percent,

Newfoundland Tel - 55.3 percent, Northwest Tel - 100 percent, and indirectly through MT & T's 52 percent ownership of Island Telephone).

The business network of the Canadian telecommunications system is shown in Figure 3. It is apparent that with Bell Canada as the flagship firm, the network includes linkages to key suppliers, customers, competitors, and the non-business infrastructure (government and academia).

BUSINESS NETWORKS AND DE-INTEGRATION

FLAGSHIP FIRMS ARE FINDING it necessary to de-integrate some of their business system activities, either for strategic reasons or because the internalization of the activity is now more costly than external costs plus transaction costs. De-integration takes place by transfer of selected activities from the flagship firm to its network partners. Thus, the flagship firms are coming to view themselves as competing within business systems rather than in industries. Indeed, Blois (1990) indicates that de-integration is becoming quite common and widespread in some industries.

FIGURE 3

THE BUSINESS NETWORK OF THE CANADIAN TELECOMMUNICATIONS SYSTEM

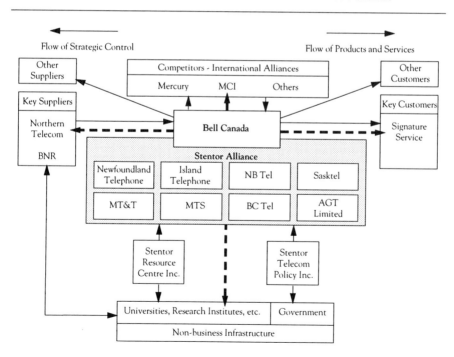

The decision to de-integrate, that is, to have an activity in the business system performed outside the traditional boundaries of the firm, is based on strategic as well as cost factors. Business system activities can be performed better outside the flagship when perceived value by the customer is less than the flagship firm's delivered cost, and when internal costs (including governance costs) are greater than external costs. By not internalizing these activities, the firm can remain focussed on its competitive advantages, allocate resources internally to more effective use, and improve firm performance by not sub-optimizing its own performance through directing effort at low value-creating activities.

The Benetton example illustrates both strategic and cost-related factors in the decision to outsource. It is a particularly incisive example because it shows that a de-integration of business system activities to network partners can accomplish very sophisticated strategic objectives. There is too much of a tendency in the literature to view outsourcing as the abdication or loss of control of activities which are relevant to a firm's business system. The Benetton example demonstrates that de-integration and loss of strategic control are not synonymous. Moreover, strategic control need not be viewed simply in terms of bargaining power. Trust and cooperation can also be used as building blocks to long-lasting relationships.

CONCLUSIONS

WE NEED TO FOCUS more attention on the role of business networks as an organizational form that plays an important role in the growth process of contemporary global industries. This requires a strategic management perspective of the global business strategy of the flagship firm and its partners. A good example of a business network is the current Canadian telecommunications system linking the Stentor alliance with Bell Canada, Northern Telecom, BNR and others (see D'Cruz, 1993). Indeed, the success of Northern Telecom as one of Canada's leading multinational enterprises can be better understood through the use of our business network framework than by employing previous attempts to analyze its firm-specific advantages using internalization theory alone (see Rugman & McIlveen, 1985).

Just as business networks themselves are poorly understood, the implications for Canadian public policy are also unclear. Much research is needed to clarify these issues. Here we make three simple points.

First, we believe that in order to improve Canadian competitiveness it is vital to focus attention on the managerial processes by which Canadian firms can improve their international competencies. We contend that the competitiveness of nations depends upon the business skills of key flagship firms and their related business networks. Government departments and agencies cannot play the flagship role. They can and should form part of business networks, but the flagships must be free to perform the function of strategic management of the network.

Governments should play a supporting role, not a leadership role. This will be difficult for some provincial governments in Canada to accept.

Second, regarding competition policy, it is unclear what the appropriate stance should be toward business networks. Many difficult questions remain unaddressed. Are networks anti-competitive? Porter would have us believe that the enhancement of rivalry between the leading firms in an industry is healthy. His prescriptions urge that competition policy be rigidly enforced to ensure that rivalry is sharp. Yet, business networks are based as much on cooperative behaviour among their members as they rely on competition with members of other networks. How far should Canadian competition policy go in continuing to insist on the maintenance of a competitive environment? Should business networks be treated as a single unit in assessing the competitive structure of an industry? What does one do when competitors join a network?

Third, regulatory policy has had a significant effect on the formation and structure of business networks in the telecommunications industry. The choice of activities to include in the rate base has been a major issue in the regulation of telephone utilities. The effect of Canadian policy has been to encourage Bell Canada and other "telcos" to spin off subsidiaries into a business network-style relationship to avoid having the activities of those subsidiaries included in the rate base. In particular, subsidiaries engaged in high-risk ventures, such as new technology development, were thought to require a higher rate of return on equity than was allowed on the lower-risk public utility aspects of their business. Some would argue that this has been healthy for Canada because it was a major factor behind the establishment of Northern Telecom and its subsequent development into a major competitor in the global switching market.

The remaining research agenda is long. What is the theory, and what hard evidence is there to support the claim that business networks will increase competitiveness rather than inter-firm rivalry and short-term cooperation? The likelihood and practicality of business network formation needs to be examined. Will business network leaders (flagship firms) arise? Is it possible for links that are much more interdependent to develop within the non-business infrastructure? Are business networks stable forms of organization, or will opportunism defeat long-term associations? We have begun to explore some of these issues elsewhere, (D'Cruz, 1993) but great scope remains for both theoretical and case-based empirical research in this area.

ACKNOWLEDGEMENTS

We wish to acknowledge helpful assistance from Michael Scott, Research Associate at the Centre for International Business, University of Toronto. Helpful comments have also been received from Professor Lorraine Eden.

BIBLIOGRAPHY

Blois, Keith J. "Transactions Costs and Networks." *Strategic Management Journal* 11 (1990):493-99.

Coase, Richard H. "The Nature of the Firm." *Economica* 4 (1937): 386-405.

D'Cruz, Joseph R. "Mobilizing Business Networks for Global Competitiveness." *Business Quarterly* (Spring) 1993: 93-98.

D'Cruz, Joseph R., and Alan M. Rugman. *New Compacts for Canadian Competitiveness.* Toronto: Kodak Canada Inc., 1992.

Fama, E. "Agency Problems and the Theory of the Firm." *Journal of Political Economy* 88 (1980): 288-307.

Jarillo, Carlos J. "On Strategic Networks." *Strategic Management Journal* 9 (1988):31-41.

Jarillo, Carlos J. and Jon I. Martinez. "Benetton S.p.A." Case study N9-389-074. Boston: HBS Case Services, Harvard Business School, 1988.

Jarillo, Carlos J. and Howard H. Stevenson. "Co-operative Strategies – the Payoffs and the Pitfalls." *Long Range Planning* 24 (February 1991):64-70.

Kagono, Tadao, et al. *Strategic vs. Evolutionary Management: A U.S.-Japan Comparison of Strategy and Organization.* New York: North-Holland, 1985.

Ouchi, William G. "Markets, Bureaucracies and Clans." *Administrative Science Quarterly* 25 (1980): 129-42.

Porter, Michael E. *Competitive Strategy: Techniques for Analysing Industries and Companies.* New York: Free Press, 1980.

_____. *Competitive Advantage: Creating and Sustaining Superior Performance.* New York: Free Press, 1985.

_____. *The Competitive Advantage of Nations.* New York: Free Press, 1990.

Rugman, Alan M. *Inside the Multinationals: The Economics of Internal Markets.* New York: Columbia University Press, 1981.

_____. "New Theories of the Multinational Enterprise: An Assessment of Internalization Theory." *Bulletin of Economic Research* 38 (1986):101-18.

Rugman, Alan M. and John McIlveen. *Megafirms: Strategies for Canada's Multinationals.* Toronto: Methuen, 1985.

Rugman, Alan M. and Joseph R. D'Cruz. *Fast Forward: Improving Canada's International Competitiveness.* Toronto: Kodak Canada Inc., 1991.

Westney, Eleanor. "Internal and External Linkages in the MNC: the Case of R&D Subsidiaries in Japan." In *Managing the Global Firm.* Edited by Christopher Bartlett et al. London: Routledge, 1990.

Williamson, Oliver. *Markets and Hierarchies: Analysis and Antitrust Implications.* New York: Free Press, 1975.

Bruce Kogut
Professor of Management
Wharton School, University of Pennsylvania

6

An Evolutionary Perspective on the NAFTA

THE CREATION OF A North American free trade area is a classical case of gains to an expansion of commerce. If wage and other factor costs were similar among the United States, Mexico and Canada, then the gains to this expansion could be realized through the impact of a larger market on the economies of scale in research, production, logistics and sales. As factor costs clearly differ between Mexico and the two countries to the north, then additional gains should be expected through the better allocation of resources in each geographical region.

Such gains, moreover, may be augmented by reductions in the numbers of necessary customs agents and trade lobbyists, and the reduction in governmental machinery required to administer commercial policy. Although domestic-content rules will necessitate border guards in the interim, the development of a common third-party policy will eventually eliminate these costs. Thus, for reasons of dynamic gains to scale, an improved allocation of resources, and the elimination of rent-seeking and administrative costs, the NAFTA treaty promises the potential for gains to the three partners.

If we move from the abstract to the NAFTA agreement, there are additional reasons to believe that this is in the common interests of the signatories. By any logic, the opening of the Mexican border to trade should enhance investment flows to Mexico to take advantage of the lower costs of labour. Moreover, contrary to a classical approach of viewing profits as the outcome of investment, the expectations of firms regarding the profitability of investing in the area will themselves induce growth. The effect of this development should stabilize Mexico politically and reduce immigration pressures on the United States. Both political stability and a diminution in emigration must rank as desired policy outcomes for the government of the United States.

Despite these obvious benefits of the NAFTA, the report from the United States government's Office of Technology Assessment (OTA) is decidedly cautious. This report warns that "notwithstanding conventional economic wisdom ... the long-term impact of a NAFTA on U.S. workers and productivity growth could be negative unless government and the private sector take steps to prevent that outcome".[1] These steps, the OTA report explains, would be directed to improve the educational and skill levels of workers, as well as promote "worker participation and worker commitment necessary to compete on a basis other than wages".

It is facile to dismiss these recommendations as a classic example of what March and Olsen (1980) called a "garbage can model of decision making". In their view of how organizations make decisions, problems do not engender solutions; rather, it is the solutions offered by interested parties that seek out problems. The OTA and the consultants to this report are on record as supporting a number of policy *solutions* that are incorporated in the report on the NAFTA.

How can the conclusion that the "long-term impact" will be negative in the absence of government policy be reconciled with the unequivocally positive assessment suggested by an economic analysis? Certainly, it would not be contested that short-run losses, especially for sectors such as textiles, would be realized, as can be expected in any adjustment process. More open borders will result in some re-allocation of capital and workers among sectors; a portion of the efficiency gains of the NAFTA will come at the expense of some textile workers and worker adjustment programs in the efforts to find new work in other sectors of the economy. Yet, in the long run, the attainment of the above gains would seem to justify the short-run adjustment costs, especially in today's environment of low interest rates.

The difficulty in understanding the OTA analysis, despite its being strikingly thorough and well researched, is that we do not have an adequate theoretical framework within which to evaluate the argument. Let us assume, for example, that as a result of the NAFTA the American workers who are uneducated and poorly trained are rendered unemployed or are able to survive only in minimum-wage service jobs which are not import-competing, such as fast-food outlets. This outcome, however distasteful, is not clearly undesirable within an economic analysis, given the likely benefits listed above. In fact, one could argue that the greater wealth, no matter how it is distributed initially, would allow for an enhanced program of income transfer to the needy.

We can go further. For those at the poverty level, any policy that increases the upside of national wealth should be seen as desirable, even if the probability of increased income transfer is small. Moreover, the OTA report notes that the effect of increased exports on the U.S. economy is at worst neutral. The very poor have at least a mildly improved prospect for income transfer, and there is little reason to believe that the number of poor or unemployed would increase.

The concerns of the OTA, one suspects, rest upon three basic premises. The first is Marshall's orthodox view that external economies generate industrial districts that draw upon ideas in a common *atmosphere*. The second is that managers and policy-makers make decisions on the basis of accumulated practices, sometimes called *know-how* and limited information. The third is that the combination of externalities and the *local* knowledge of managerial practices imply that historical events take on a singular importance.

In the following pages, I argue that the establishment of the NAFTA poses a set of critical issues in the context of current historical changes. The argument is "evolutionary" in its approach and owes its point of departure to the work of Vernon (1966), Linder (1961), and Nelson & Winter (1982). However, to be clear, my analysis does not propose the abandonment of the NAFTA. Rather, it endorses the general vision (although not all of the specifics) of the OTA report — i.e., that the elimination of North American tariffs and trade impediments necessitates a program of regional development and worker training. To understand the strategic responses of large corporations to the NAFTA first requires some understanding and consideration of the historical and institutional context surrounding the policy position adopted by the U.S. government.

NATIONAL ORGANIZING PRINCIPLES AND DIRECT INVESTMENT

HISTORY IS IMPORTANT to our understanding of the effect of the NAFTA on the corporate decisions of large and small firms. The creation of a NAFTA would have implied a significantly different set of outcomes if the proposal had been made 30 years ago. Firms in the United States were then still at the frontier of what is now recognized as best practice. The need to make radical changes in the established practices and patterns of behaviour, whether internal to the firm (e.g. techniques of mass production) or related to how firms compete (e.g. radical product innovation), was certainly not compelling.

To understand the effect of the NAFTA on the strategies of firms and the policies of governments also requires some understanding of the particular challenges confronting firms at this critical juncture. There are fundamental and interrelated challenges to large incumbent corporations, which are often expressed in terms of the globalization of markets, especially the penetration of the U.S. market by Japanese and (to a lesser extent) by European firms.

A more telling issue, however, is the impact of foreign competition, which is now so great because the organizing principles underlying the capabilities and strengths of firms are in the process of radical transformation. U.S. firms rose to positions of world dominance during the first two-thirds of this century because of their innovations and early adoption of practices of standardization, interchangeability, and mass production — or what is sometimes grouped under Taylorism and Fordism. The *relative* rise of the United States in the early part of this century eventually led to the dominance of American multinational corporations with subsidiaries dispersed internationally.[2]

Current trends in direct investment flows show an entirely different picture. In 1985, the United States accounted for 22.6 percent of world flows of direct investment and Japan accounted for 11.1 percent. In 1991, the United States and Japan were responsible for 15.0 percent and 16.9 percent, respectively.[3] This wave of Japanese investment, following their pattern of exports, was motivated by a strikingly different set of organizational practices from those characterized by U.S. action. These practices, often called Toyotism, consist of a reliance on a small central parent, on a quasi-integrated supplier and sales network, and on the flexible use of multi-skilled workers who are given relatively large autonomy in decision making.

These new organizing principles account for the historical rise in Japanese investments abroad. Of course there are many motives for direct investment. Yet, the long-term data in direct investment show clear national patterns, with the United Kingdom and the United States dominant at the beginning and middle periods of this century, respectively. To explain these national patterns requires the identification of a factor common to many firms and industries within a country, which leads to direct investment, rather than to portfolio outward investment.

Organizing principles satisfy these concerns because they are not strictly industry-specific; they also require within-firm transfer, i.e., transfer to an affiliate by direct investment. The practice of standardizing tasks, for example, spread across the United States through industries as diverse as armaments and sewing machine manufacturing and from bicycle makers to the auto industry. Time/motion and efficiency studies diffused rapidly to service industries, and were seen in their application to suturing techniques used in Boston hospitals, to Filene's department stores, and to secretarial pools.[4] By 1920, this gradual trajectory beginning in the early 1800s spanned a remarkable accumulation of learning and knowledge that was widely diffused throughout American industry.

This diffusion was both spatially and temporally bounded. In other words, the proximity of innovating firms to adopting firms created distinctive geographic patterns in the process of diffusion. The development of industrial districts is one expression of this spatial characteristic. In early U.S. history, junctions of waterways served as places where new ideas were quickly diffused (Sokoloff, 1988). Currently, there is increasing evidence that technologies based on basic science tend to diffuse more rapidly within an area surrounding the originating university than to other sites (Jaffe, Trachtenberg & Henderson, forthcoming). Generally, national boundaries, because they denote areas characterized by common institutional structures (e.g., educational, labour, cultural), are an important dimension in the speed of diffusion.

In addition to the geographic dimension, there is also a temporal element in the development of new techniques. Historically, a cumulative path of development orders the growth of knowledge in the expansion of these practices (i.e., mass production techniques presume the existence of a factory system). Consequently, there is both a spatial and a temporal ordering, or trajectory, to technological and organizational developments.

Of course such developments are frequently firm-embodied, even if they are initially country-specific. Organizing principles, unlike the scientific foundations of a technology, have an important tacit aspect insofar as they are grounded in the structure, and information and incentive systems of firms. Nelson (1982) rightly noted that the compound of the words "techno" and "logy" implies private and public aspects. Somewhat ironically, the way work is organized is a quintessential example of the former aspect.

For this reason, exploitation of such knowledge tends to proceed by its transfer to foreign sites in the form of direct investment rather than through arm's length sales. *Foreign direct investment is simply the transfer of organizing principles from one country to another.* If we then accept the premise that particular countries at particular junctures in history lead in the innovation of new practices that are bounded both spatially and temporally, it follows that we should expect to see country-specific patterns in the long-term series of direct investment.

CHANGES IN WORK DESIGN AND
JAPANESE DIRECT INVESTMENT

LET US NOW PUT THESE ideas into the context of current changes in organizational practices. For complex reasons, enterprises are currently facing what Piore and Sabel (1982) call a "second industrial divide". A new set of organizing practices, which they label "flexible specialization", is transforming the structures and strategies of enterprises in the more developed countries.[5] Although these principles are often associated with smaller firms, there is a strong case for applying them to large firms as well, evidenced by the broad trends for the 500 largest U.S. corporations over the last decade: sales growth has been flat, their share of employment has fallen dramatically, and asset growth is slower. (The trend for individual firms is even more striking.) This pattern, which emerged in the 1980s, is in contrast to that of the previous decades.[6]

There is a wide consensus that Japanese enterprises have been in the forefront in ushering in a new set of practices over the past 30 to 40 years. It is interesting that these practices, while stemming from traditional roots, represent innovations of rather recent origins. Nishiguchi (1993) argues that the sub-contracting system grew out of the war-time frustration in Japan with the poor quality of aircraft and other transport equipment. Ohno (1978), a principal architect of Toyotism, traces the innovations to the 1950s, although a few experiments were made in the 1930s.

These practices have been described by many authors. Aoki (1988) is an influential analyst who identified the following principal elements (see also Westney in this volume).

- Decentralization of decision making and horizontal communication and cooperation across functions at lower levels of the organization.

- Vertical control structures within the enterprise, with a main bank monitoring the performance of top management.

- Reliance upon suppliers for the production of parts outside the competence of the corporation, with the use of incentive systems to guarantee quality and to reduce costs and inventory levels.

Of the many notable outcomes of these practices, a remarkable feature is that the Japanese corporation is much smaller than its American counterpart. U.S corporations, as shown in the Industry Canada data, are large. For example, in 1987 General Motors had 813,400 employees, compared to Toyota's 64,329; IBM, 389,348 to Hitachi's 76,210; and Du Pont 140,145 to Asahi Chemicals' 15,595 (Fruin, 1992). Canadian corporations, though smaller than their U.S. counterparts, are no less daunting in the context of their national market. According to the Industry Canada study elsewhere in this volume, 158 Canadian firms in the list of the 1000 largest multinational firms in North America account for 52 percent of Canada's gross domestic output and 19 percent of its total employment.

The relatively smaller Japanese corporate units serve as a focal point in a quasi-integrated network of suppliers who tend to be geographically contiguous. One of the most important practices in the coordination of this network is the use of the *just-in-time* (JIT) and *kanban* systems to reduce overall inventory levels.[7] Just-in-time places the burden on the supplier to deliver parts on an "as needed" basis; kanban is manufacturing to market "pull" as opposed to the Fordist mass volume and low cost "push" strategy. The two practices are linked in that by keeping inventory low, the firm avoids being locked into a particular product mix. On the other hand, this system places a burden on the supplier regarding not only inventory levels but also the rapid provision of the required parts. Through these practices, Toyota acts as a focal firm that assembles the components manufactured by geographically contiguous firms.

It is difficult to gauge the degree by which these new practices have diffused within Japan, no less than internationally. However, in the case of JIT, an accessible and reasonable measure is the trend in inventory levels as a proportion of sales over time. Figure 1 gives these trends for the United States and Japan.[8] (The series is not detrended, although dividing by nominal sales provides a natural deflator.) What is interesting here is that Japan's decline (since 1981) is of rather recent origin and that its decline continued to be impressive throughout the 1980s. The American trend also shows a decline, but it begins later and is barely perceptible. The diffusion process of JIT therefore appears to be more rapid inside Japan than outside its borders.

FIGURE 1

TOTAL INVENTORY AS A PROPORTION OF SALES (%)

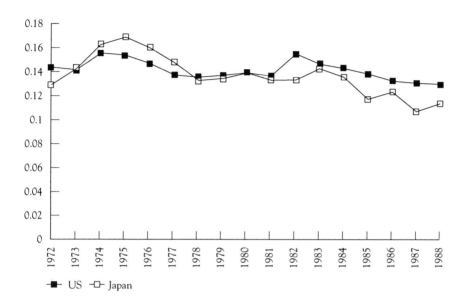

Of course, the fact that Japanese practices are being transferred across its borders is evidenced in the many studies on joint ventures in the auto industry.[9] Yet, the process of diffusion points to two very different modalities: the adoption of practices by non-Japanese firms, and the displacement of foreign firms by Japanese subsidiaries located overseas. To a great extent, there is a race between the abilities of incumbent firms to learn new practices and the speed with which Japanese firms can expand into foreign markets.

The declining relative share of North American firms in their home market shows up in the data on foreign investment in the United States. The share of sales and employment held by foreign affiliates in the United States manufacturing industries rose from 5 percent and 3 percent in 1977 to 12 percent and 9 percent in 1988. Penetration was highest in the chemical and glass industries, with 28.8 percent and 17.5 percent of the U.S. workforce employed by foreign affiliates.[10]

Figure 2 shows the sectoral breakdown for the major countries investing in the United States. Canada is unique with respect to the importance of its agricultural investments in its overall portfolio. Japan is especially dominant in the manufacturing sector, as well as in the "other" category, which consists mainly of wholesale and distribution outlets; Japanese direct investments in distribution channels were three times greater than the corresponding German

FIGURE 2

DISTRIBUTION OF FOREIGN DIRECT INVESTMENT BY SECTOR AND COUNTRY 1974-89

FIGURE 2

DISTRIBUTION OF FOREIGN DIRECT INVESTMENT BY SECTOR AND COUNTRY 1974-89

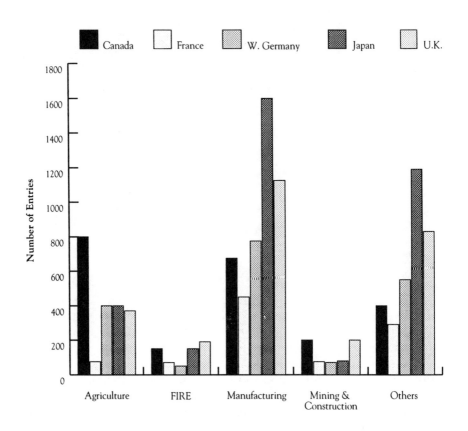

or U.K. totals during the 1980s. However, during the decade Japanese invest-ment shifted from distribution channels (needed to support their exports) to manufacturing.

Of course the motivation for these trends is not restricted to the superiority of organizational practices. Traditional motives, such as the "push" of home rivalry among national firms which spills over into other markets, are consistently found to be an important influence. Moreover, there is increasing evidence that the technological and organizational capabilities of a country "pull" investment. Japanese firms were found, for example, to use joint ventures in industries where the U.S. firms maintained relatively higher expenditures in R&D (Kogut & Chang, 1991). Shan (1993) also found that Japanese firms bought minority stakes in U.S. biotechnology firms with strong patenting histories.

While industry and firm factors are important determinants of direct investment flows, the explanation for the *country* pattern in direct investment requires the additional consideration of national characteristics. As noted above, foreign penetration has proceeded rapidly in the United States — an expression of the decline in the relative advantage of the U.S. firms to defend their markets and the attractiveness of the North American market. Similarly, the share of industrial sales held by foreign affiliates in (West) Germany, France, and the U.K. were 16 percent, 22 percent, and 13 percent for 1988. The corresponding figure for Japan fell from 2 percent in 1977 to 1 percent in 1988 during a period when its share of world direct investment rose from 3.8 percent (1980) to 12.2 percent (1990).[11]

At an historical junction during which new work practices evolve in particular countries, competition among international firms has a strong national character. Organizing principles and technologies develop along a trajectory characterized by the accumulation of learning and its inter-industry diffusion. These principles, rooted in social behavior and institutions, are anchored in and reflect the existing social structure and organization of a country. As a result, their adoption favours firms from the same locality. In other words, the permeability of the borders of a firm is greater than the permeability of the geographic borders of a country.

Eventually, the diffusion of country advantages levels the playing field among firms of different national origins. Competition, then, reverts more to the characteristics of industries and firms (although national effects may still be evident). It is not surprising, therefore, that Kravis and Lipsey found that the share of U.S. multinational corporations around the world has been more stable than the share of U.S. exports. Since the initial investments have been established for decades for many firms, they tend to share in the prosperity of the regional economy. The rise and diffusion of national organizing principles underlie the country cycles in direct investment.

In the current decade, the diffusion of Japanese organizing principles is the distinguishing feature of international competition. In the case of Japanese direct investment, this diffusion takes an initial form in the establishment of an export office and then a manufacturing plant in the foreign country. In the United States, a simple but primary predictor of subsequent investment is whether a Japanese firm has an existing sales office or plant (in the United States) to serve as a platform for expansion (Kogut & Chang, 1993). Yamawaki (1992) has also found that Japanese subsidiaries in Europe and the United States diversify differently, depending upon local market conditions; local opportunities influence the expansion path. When the process of initial investment, expansion and diversification is over, other national firms will have adopted similar, or competitive, practices. By that time, however, the stock of Japanese investment in the world is likely to be much higher, with Japanese affiliates firmly implanted throughout the world economy.

HETEROGENEITY OF PRACTICES AND WAGES

A S IMPLIED ABOVE, new organizing practices are not always Japanese in origin. In fact, depending on the firm, industry and country, the organizing principles that underlie the capabilities by which firms respond flexibly and rapidly to market conditions can differ widely. There is, in other words, a "functional equivalence" across countries: different ways to organize work can produce the identical products and services.

A good example is described in the study by Whittaker (1993) concerning the use of computer numerically-controlled machinery. In Japan, these machines tend to be operated and programmed by the same (usually young) employee; frequently, they are left to operate unmanned at night. In the U.K., the tendency is to give an engineer the task of programming, with operation left to a skilled worker; the machines rarely run unmanned. The explanation for these variations appears to lie in both relative wages and institutional rules. The British system tends to comply *de facto* with a seniority rule; in Japan, the older workers are given other tasks or retired.

However, a "functional equivalence" is not always found. Many firms in Whittaker's British sample simply lagged behind in the use of advanced machinery or did not use the machinery flexibly. Part of the explanation for this, as suggested above, is the resistance of traditional work structures to accommodate new technologies. But an equally probable explanation is the difficulty in understanding the implications of new work designs for exploiting strategies of flexibility and the delivery of high-quality production and services.

Over the past 10 years the British and French governments have introduced a number of important reforms in the education and training of workers to increase their skill levels. The impetus of these reforms has been due as much to a concern with German as with Japanese competition.[12] A highly trained workforce is one of the primary examples of a country-specific factor that influences the capability embodied in firms to adopt and develop new work practices. National institutions, such as labour laws, are often seen as impediments to markets. On the contrary, these institutions are often "enabling" in the sense that they augment the quality of resources available to firms.

The United States, perhaps due to the greater decentralization of its educational institutions, has been slower in introducing new reforms.[13] It is not without importance that studies show American wages falling in real terms relative to Japanese and European levels. More strikingly, those wages are falling dramatically for less skilled workers due to a decrease in demand

(Katz & Loveman, 1993). The U.S. labour market is more polarized today than it was at the beginning of the 1980s.

For many U.S. firms, the polarity in the labour market corresponds to two very different kinds of strategies, as the OTA report discussed. The first strategy consists of drawing upon a highly-skilled labour pool that, at the cost of high wages, is capable of responding to the market quickly with products designed to satisfy customer demand. Examples of this strategy can be found in many industries — from General Motor's Saturn operations, to Hewlett Packard's development of a just-in-time supplier network close to its assembly plants and its customer service outlets.

For many firms, the accessibility of a pool of low-wage workers prolongs the viability of a mass production, standardized product strategy. The heterogeneity of the American work force is far greater than that of the German, and hence some U.S. mass production firms can seek to survive by hiring low-wage and low-skill workers. Given the uncertainty over the efficacy and the costs of adopting new methods, many firms persist in using traditional forms of production. Some of these costs relate to "information" acquisition and derive from identifying and learning these new practices; firms might shift to new practices if they knew what these practices were or how to manage them. Other costs derive from scrapping out-dated capital equipment designed for mass production. There are costs related to learning the techniques — the "how to" of new production methods (e.g., flexible manufacturing).

It is important that firms, especially early adopters, are uncertain over the benefits. For example, the gains, from adopting higher quality programs are rarely quantifiable.[14] As a result, there is a kind of "hysteresis" that characterizes the adoption choice. The costs of switching in a context of uncertainty encourages firms to persist with antiquated work practices beyond what seems to be the optimal switching point; they are not sure of the future benefits and hence delay their adoption choice. If after all the anticipated benefits are not achieved, or if the older technology should improve, then it would be costly to shift back.

Figure 3 illustrates the implications of hysteresis on the choice of new techniques for the case of mass production and craft techniques.[15] As stressed by Chandler (1977), a critical factor in the adoption of mass (volume) production was the increasing speed of production. For example, Frederick Taylor first became known internationally at the turn of this century for his innovation to cut steel at rapid speeds; the adoption of this method in the U.K. was impeded by the failure of craft methods to adapt easily to the new speed of work.

This "co-evolution" of work and technology is depicted in Figure 3. As production speed increases (which is shown as increasing uniformly), the adoption of mass production methods becomes more attractive. Yet, many firms will persist in their old practices beyond the statically "optimal" switching point (shown as the lower dotted line) as long as managers are uncertain about prices and the future evolution of technologies.

FIGURE 3

FIGURE 3

THE IMPLICATIONS OF HYSTERESIS ON THE CHOICE OF NEW TECHNIQUES

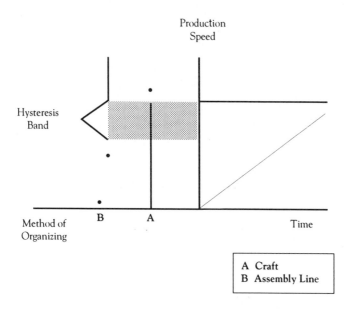

Moreover, the reluctance to switch is increased if we consider a more realistic pattern of firm behavior, which stems from the fact that managerial information regarding these techniques is very limited. However convenient for the purposes of economic explanation, the assumption that forward-looking managers will act on the basis of known parameters (even if probabilistic) contradicts the way we know decisions are made — on the basis of rules and information — inside organizations.[16] These rules, which structure firms and their decision-making process and information systems, constitute the "knowledge" of the firm. A rule that requires organization of operations by function, e.g., R&D, production, and marketing, defines the capability of a firm, that is, *what it can know how to do*. To be faster to the market appears to require adopting new rules, or recipes, by which to organize activities in multi-functional teams.

Hysteresis in the form of the persistence of practices is a powerful description of the process of change because it can be the outcome of economic foresight or myopic behaviour arising out of these rules. Either way, it has important implications because firms, individually and collectively, can easily be trapped with low wage levels and outdated techniques.

CREATION OF FREE TRADE AREAS IN A HYBRID AGE

T HE PERSISTENCE OF old principles is, as described in the previous section, a logical outcome of the relative decline in labour's wage levels, managerial expectations regarding future technological and price (both factor and product) developments, and the existing body of managerial practices and information. A shift in any of these influences the rate of adoption of new practices. For example, the heterogeneity of labour institutions in the United States permits firms to locate in non-union areas in order to apply Fordist methods in low wage rate environments. As long as firms are uncertain over the future evolution of wages, old practices will persist, even if other (new) practices appear to be superior.

Of course, a government can intervene by mandating a higher wage. Indeed, in such a case, by constraining the power of the firm to make decisions (by limiting its freedom to set wages), this policy may induce a shift to newer practices; it can no longer survive by actively reducing its production wage costs relative to foreign competitors. Moreover, if there are externalities affecting the adoption decision, this policy can qualitatively shift the diffusion process, as the decision to adopt by one firm makes it more attractive for another to make a similar decision.

These considerations are not far from the experiences of some countries. For example, the German experience is remarkable in that during the 1970s, the economy was structurally foundering under the shocks of oil price increases. Given the strength of well-organized labour unions, concessions for these increases were readily obtained from employers — resulting in spiralling wage costs. Moreover, the presence of labour on the boards of many German companies influenced the location decisions of German enterprises. In a celebrated incident, the head of VW stepped down over the decision to build plants outside Germany in Pennsylvania due to the protest of "exporting" jobs to the United States. Managerial decision-making is highly constrained. Yet, because workers were highly skilled and an educational system existed by which they could be retrained, German management and labour co-operated in the redesign of work and the introduction of new technologies.[17] The German environment did not allow for a low-wage strategy. Firms and workers were constrained to move along an adjustment path towards a more rapid introduction of new methods and technologies.

Where such institutions are missing, should governments mandate higher wages as a way to constrain firm choice towards the adoption of new work practices? There are two major problems with this policy. First, the decision to adopt radically new organizational practices is not like installing new capital equipment on the factory floor. Consider the three elements suggested by Aoki regarding Japanese practices. A transfer of decision making to lower levels of the firm is a complex problem, ranging from the motivation and training of lower management and workers to internal politics. Creating a financial system in which a main bank plays a dominating role is not only a radical departure from existing practice, it is also not possible in the U.S. context due to restrictions on equity participation of banks in industrial firms. Finally, increased reliance on a network of independent suppliers implies a major divestment and deintegration of supplying units inside large U.S. manufacturing firms.

In other words, new ways of working are part of a coherent system that link the firm and the institutional environment. Adopting any one of these three elements is, consequently, a very costly departure from existing practice. Moreover, it is not clear whether all three elements would have to be adopted. Relations of cause and effect in the context of a "system" of practices are difficult to detect.

The second major problem is that large U.S. corporations are multinational; many of their assets and sales are overseas.[18] Rather than promoting the attractiveness of new methods in the U.S. market, increasing wage rates may only encourage a transfer of more investment overseas.

It is critical to emphasize that pressures to change work practices occur in response to competitive pressures. In simple terms, firms know they should adopt practices which are in their long-run interest. However, when the issue appears to be a question of survival, short-run considerations are likely to dominate. Outsourcing and overseas production are common strategies used in such circumstances to reduce costs rapidly.

The expansion of free trade with Mexico exhibits similarities with a policy of reducing wages at home. On average, Mexican hourly wage rates are less than one-fifth of U.S. costs (unpublished data from the Department of Commerce). There is, however, a great heterogeneity in wages as well as in productivity levels. Given an inferior infrastructure, the distance from the more northern markets in the United States and a less skilled workforce, wage levels are not the only consideration in the location decisions of large firms.

There are still good reasons to believe that the Mexican workforce will attract the migration of some industry. First, the heterogeneity of labour means that multinational corporations can hire the relatively more skilled workers. In fact, studies on productivity of U.S. affiliates in Mexico have estimated that, on average, the Mexican level was 93 percent of the U.S. productivity level and, in several industries, was even superior (Blomstrom & Wolff, forthcoming). However, labour productivity rates for Mexican-owned firms were far lower. This differential suggests that U.S. affiliates were able to tap into a more skilled workforce or that Mexican plants do not have the same level of capital investment and managerial ability. In any case, high productivity is certainly possible in the Mexican environment.

Second, U.S. multinational corporations have had a long history of involvement in Mexico, with Ford and other companies operating plants there since the 1920s. In 1977 U.S. firms employed over 300,000 people in Mexico. This number increased dramatically throughout the 1980s, especially in the maquiladora zone. In 1991, the maquila plants alone employed 450,000 people, and accounted for more than one-third of all exports (OTA, 1991:65).

Finally, the evidence to date already shows a considerable rise in investment in Mexico. U.S. direct investment flows rose to over $2 billion in 1990 and 1991, considerably higher than the $1.5 billion in 1980 (which was the largest annual flow during the 1980s). Mexico, of course, is attractive for reasons other than serving as a platform for production to be exported back to the United States. Part of this investment is directed at producing for a growing domestic market. Nevertheless, as the above figures on the maquila plants suggest, a good deal of the investment is export oriented.

On the other hand, it is interesting to note that total inward direct investment was $5 billion in 1991. The U.S. share, consequently, is only about 40 percent of the total, smaller than at any time during the 1980s. Mexico is pulling in an increasing flow of investment from firms whose origins lie outside North America. In other words, Mexico has become an extension of the geography of international competition between American and non-American firms.

The dynamics of this extension must be seen against the background of the overall pattern of foreign entry into North America. Figure 4 shows the data relevant to the Canada and Latin America. Canadian entries also rose

FIGURE 4

FDI ENTRIES INTO THE UNITED STATES, 1974-89

o Canada

♦ Latin America

o Rest

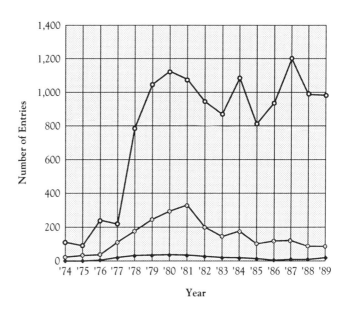

Year

FIGURE 5

FDI ENTRIES INTO THE UNITED STATES FROM CANADA, LATIN AMERICA AND THE NICs, 1974-89

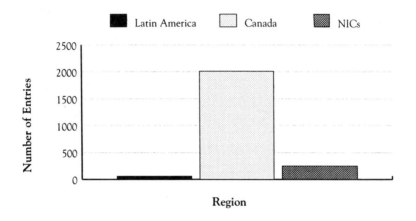

dramatically in the early 1980s, but slowed down over the decade relative to other countries. Mexican entries are barely perceptible, but when coupled with all Latin American entries, a slight rise appeared in the 1980s, primarily in the service, real estate, and oil and extraction industries.

To give some sense of the benchmark by which to measure the presence or absence of Latin American investment in the United States, Figure 5 compares entries from this region with those from the Asian newly industrialized countries (NICs). Despite greater distances, the NICs have almost twice the number of entries, with their sectoral distribution concentrated in distribution channels and some manufacturing.

In short, investment flows into Latin and North America are strongly affected by the wider dynamic of competition among the industrialized countries. Canadian enterprises are by no means minor players in these flows, especially in light of the size of their national economy. The United States remains, as Eden's contribution to this volume shows, the investment and trade hub for Mexico and Canada. Yet, the long-term trend shows a faster growth of non-North American direct investment in the region than of intra-regional flows.

These trends should be compared against the European case to understand their significance. The Japanese entry into Europe is instructive as a clean experiment, as there was little Japanese investment prior to the mid-1980s when discussions relating to the 1992 reforms began (see Dunning, this volume). For example, Yamawaki's (1991) study on Japanese investment in Europe shows a similar polarity. Spain and the U.K., although much richer

than Mexico, attract Japanese investment due to their low wage environments. Germany has been the other major site for Japanese investment,
especially in the areas of residential technological strength, such as electronics
and machine-tools. Thus, Japanese location strategies appear to be split
between the use of export platforms of relatively labour-intensive activities in
lower-wage countries, and the pull of industrial districts where technological
capabilities and final user demand are concentrated.

What is different about the European case, however, is the centripetal
trend in investment. Of 1,804 cases of acquisition or of majority investment
between 1986 and 1990, 899 were by national firms and 640 by firms from
other Economic Community countries; only 264 were by firms from the outside (including neighbouring countries of Sweden, Switzerland and Austria).
In the chemical industry, the number of within-nation to within-EC
acquisitions was 145 to 196; in transport, it was 36 to 34 (Commissariat du
Plan, 1992: 44). Of the mergers in 1990, 44 percent involved a firm size
greater than five billion ECU. The prospect of a NAFTA has not yet led to a
similar predominance of intra-regional direct investment in the overall direct
investment flows in the North American region.

POLICY CONSIDERATIONS FOR THE NAFTA REGION

THE EUROPEAN COMMUNITY is, of course, further along in its integration
than the North American countries. Its members share a fairly common
policy regarding third countries, especially with respect to trade. It is also a
region of greater economic homogeneity in income, wage levels and
environmental standardization. The effect of the 1992 legislation, even if
dampened by the events of German unification, has been to heighten
competition among industrial districts and, at the same time, to regionalize
competition among the major companies. Consequently, the EC shows in
microcosm a world wide trend: localized competition among small- and
medium-size firms, with large firms competing internationally, partly by acting
as investment bridges between these regional districts in order to tap into
markets and technologies or to source materials and labour.

The NAFTA is a much more limited experiment. Yet, since trade barriers
are one of the most important stimulants to the timing of direct investment, their elimination is bound to have important effects on a region. To
the extent that a common policy on third-country domestic content is
maintained, the effects may seem to be limited to investment flows among
the member countries. But, as the above data have suggested, the variations
in national advantage, as well as the impact of freer trade on growth,
strongly influence the magnitude and location of direct investment from
other regions.

The NAFTA is also a confounded experiment in that it is occurring at a
time when there is a structural break in the long-term trajectory of firms and

countries. The stagnation of sales growth in the largest firms, the internationalization of their markets, and their rapidly diminishing share of employment reflect a fundamental break in work practices.[19] What is being observed is not simply the transformation of industries from national to international rivalry; it is also a historical transformation of the capabilities — and the work practices which generate such capabilities — of North American business enterprises.

The lessons of history show that it is critical to understand the direction and nature of this change. The issue of the NAFTA must not be relegated to an abstract plane of analysis. Rather, it must be placed in the context of the historical conditions that now exist. In the absence of policy recommendations, I put forward five considerations which are implied by the above discussion.

1. RE-LOCATION OF ACTIVITIES

A PRIMARY MOTIVE for foreign direct investment, noted in one of the first studies on U.S. direct investment overseas, is the ability to avoid tariff barriers by exporting firms. This motive remains a primary determinant of Japanese investment in the United States (Kogut and Chang, 1991). The elimination of borders means that some activities, previously justified by trade barriers, can now be integrated into headquarter functions.

However, the trimming of the staff of foreign and home operations is also a characteristic of recent changes in corporate organization. The public announcement by IBM that it intends to make drastic reductions in its managerial overhead also noted that a fair proportion of this rationalization will occur in the European and other regional operations. By allowing for more integrated corporate activities, the elimination of trade barriers amplifies the trend toward a reduction of overheads; but this trend is already in force, whether or not a NAFTA exists.

2. NETWORK CONFIGURATIONS OF SUPPLIERS AND CUSTOMERS

RAPID RESPONSE TO MARKETS and the disintegration of the firm by outsourcing critical technologies places a premium on the spatial contiguity of suppliers and the focal assembly firm (Toyota for example). Whereas information technologies permit a greater coordination of dispersed activities, the *prima facie* evidence witnessed in the replication of Japanese domestic auto networks in the United States and Canada suggest that proximity is a powerful driver of location. To a certain extent, the replication of these networks in greenfield sites using workers with little industrial experience underlines the arbitrariness of history. Once a focal firm has located, these regions become increasingly coherent industrial districts.

The data on foreign direct investment in the United States show a country pattern where entries are bunched in particular sectors. For example, German firms are very active in chemicals; Japanese entries are concentrated in auto production and parts supply and, secondarily, in electronics. In part, this pattern is the outcome of trade restrictions and revealed advantage. But in some sectoral cases, such as Japanese investment in autos, it is the outcome of what can be called "network threshold" effects. At a particular critical mass the industrial network of the home market recreates itself, although never exactly (some members are eliminated and some target country suppliers are admitted). The characteristics of this network effect generate strong incentives for regions and nation states to bid for investment by focused firms. They also create an incentive to monitor dominant firms regarding their re-location decisions.[20]

3. Role of technological centers

As noted earlier, some industries have a strong regional characteristic due to their reliance on basic science. Biotechnology companies, for example, tend to locate around universities with frontier research in the underlying science. Some 40 years after the fundamental innovations in the laboratories of Palo Alto, the semiconductor industry is still concentrated in this area.

The role of foreign firms in these regional science networks poses difficult questions regarding the spatial boundaries of diffusion. Since science is often subsidized by governments and since such subsidies frequently underlie other agreements to create important public externalities, national and regional governments have an interest in restricting the appropriability of these benefits to national firms. In one study of inter-firm agreements it was found, for example, that U.S. biotechnology start-up companies are significantly tied to large companies, whether American, Japanese or European.[21] The boundaries of public policy are much more difficult to define in an era of internationalization of industrial networks. Government support for high technology poles would be mistaken unless coupled with the creation of regional programs that encourage the co-location of production and user industries.

4. Training and skill levels

There is increasing convergence in public policies among competing developed countries in the training and skill upgrading of the workforce. Because education is at worst consumption and at best an important invest-ment in human capital formation, it tends to be a "motherhood" issue. The commonly held belief, however, is that a rising skill level is vital to prevent the out-migration of industry.

The German system, which is frequently cited as a model in national government reports, is based on internships and apprenticeships usually sponsored by the large corporations in a district. The program results in a degree which confers a specific professional status recognized in a market. The worker is not always hired by the sponsor firm and, in fact, inter-firm mobility is high, although inter-regional mobility is not. Since the state government bears the cost of this training program, the geographic stability of labour is critical. It is not clear whether a national government, without proximity to the region, could effectively engage the cooperation of enterprises; nor is it clear that regional governments could justify the cost if geographic labour mobility were high. The decentralization of the German administrative and fiscal system may be a necessary ingredient in solving this collective choice problem that might fit the Canadian case. Therefore, coupling local administration with federal fiscal support may also be a viable alternative in the context of the high inter-regional mobility of labour in the United States.

5. FAIR COMPETITION

ONE OBSERVATION MADE on the diffusion of unions is that management often promotes legislation requiring collective bargaining, or its equivalent in other nations. The motivation for management support was to eliminate wages as a source of rivalry in an industry and to reduce the vulnerability of employers to the demands of their workforce. There was, in other words, a notion that competition in the form of wage cutting was not "fair".

This issue is of obvious importance to the creation of a free trade agreement which precedes the harmonization of social and environmental policy. The relocation of industry due to the more lenient and/or more weakly enforced environmental policies of a particular region may not be seen as fair or desirable. The hiring of a young workforce in a country where health insurance is part of the cost of the compensation package offered to workers is a stimulus for shifting corporate support to a national health system. However, given the long-term abandonment of inner-city areas by most corporations, the location of industry in non-urban sites may be seen as a fair way to compete.

Ultimately, the creation of an enlarged economic region poses questions of the harmonization of social policies that have an appeal to notions of fairness. The fact that attachment to these notions is likely to differ among countries and is open to manipulation by economic interests is cause for both outrage and cynicism. However, the belief that an economic solution will follow from the outcome of this larger consensus is certainly mistaken. Indeed, if recent European experience is at all relevant, a rapid move toward harmonization in economic policy, especially regarding monetary and currency targets, can shift the adjustment onto the labour market through competitive pressures on wages and dismissals. No matter how difficult, consensus on fair play regarding fundamental values should precede a fuller economic harmonization.

Each of the above considerations poses a set of extremely complex issues. In lieu of an overall solution, two observations can be made. First, it is obvious that the location decisions of firms in the post-NAFTA environment will be influenced by the policies governments choose to pursue. For the purpose of creating coherent policies, it is desirable to view the occurrence of the NAFTA as nested within the challenges posed by the structural changes in the traditional practices of firms and the increased pressures of international competition that these changes have generated for North American industry.

The OTA report is essentially correct in framing the NAFTA as an element related to the overall policy questions regarding worker training, fiscal incentives for investment, and regional development. However, the role for private initiative should not be underestimated. Indeed, governments can play an instrumental role simply by disseminating information and providing a forum for discussion and comparison. The implication of the above analysis is that the process of adjustment, once it has crossed a threshold, is largely self-organizing. The incentives for worker training and the adoption of new practices derive from both the efforts of industry seeking higher productivity and the efforts of workers seeking higher wages.

The second observation is that the decisions made at this time will have, due to the particular juncture of history, long-lasting and irreversible consequences. It is difficult to make a case for positive government policy in the economics tradition in which most policy makers are trained. For those who would like to have a proactive policy, a consideration of the externalities in the long-term dynamics of creating regionally-based industrial networks will have to suffice.

There remains, of course, the possibility that firms, because they are rule-based organizations, do not always know what is best. We leave the sagacity of this conclusion to another forum, except for an elliptic surmise, somewhat along Pascal's wager: if doubt is entertained over the foresight of enterprises, it may be worthwhile for a government (with sufficient foresight) to entertain policies which firms do not have the luxury of time to consider.

ENDNOTES

1 Office of Technology Assessment, 1992:6-7.

2 Raymond Vernon estimated that during the 1960s the top 180 U.S. multi-national corporations were establishing, on average, six subsidiaries each year. See his *Sovereignty at Bay*. For a study on the impact of American national organizing principles on direct investment, see Kogut, 1992.

3 Data are from balance of payments, compiled by Investment Canada (now Industry Canada). Of course, there are two important distortions here: exchange rate movements and the neglect of reinvested earnings (especially large for the United States, due to its large stock of overseas investment). However, other data show similar trends.

4 See Hounshell (1984) for a study of the origins and diffusion of American mass production. This material, and its diffusion to service industries, is also described in Kogut (1992).

5 For a compendium of country studies discussing this trend, see the contributions to Kogut (1993).

6 The data are given and discussed in the introduction to Bowman & Kogut (forthcoming), which is a compilation of multi-disciplinary studies on the redesigning of the corporation.

7 A thorough discussion of these two principles can be found in Coriat (1991).

8 These data were collected by Jaeyong Song from unpublished data gathered from the Bureau of Economic Analysis and its Japanese equivalent.

9 See Wolf and Globerman (1992).

10 The data are given in Commissariat General du Plan (1992). See also Graham & Krugman (1989).

11 See Commissariat General du Plan (1992) and Industry Canada.

12 See, for example, the studies by Prais & Wagner (1985, for an example) on U.K. and German plant level productivity comparisons in which the primary explanation for the German superiority is found in the skill levels of workers.

13 For a discussion of the reforms introduced in the United States, see the OTA (1992).

14 See Ittner (1992).

15 This figure, with a formalization of the argument, is given in Kogut & Kulatilaka (1992).

16 See Nelson & Winter (1982) for a discussion; Berry (1982) has described these rules as the "invisible technology" of a firm.

17 See Kern & Schuman (1993).

18 See the data in Eden, this volume.

19 See Bowman & Kogut (forthcoming).

20 See Herrigel (1993) for a discussion of the role of Bosch in the industrial district of Baden Wuerttemberg and the effect of the relocation of some of its activities on the politics and economics of the region.

21 See Kogut, Walker, Shan & Kim (forthcoming).

ACKNOWLEDGEMENTS

I WOULD LIKE TO THANK Jaideep Anand and Jaeyong Song for their assistance. Lorraine Eden, Rachel McCulloch, and Roderick White provided valuable comments.

BIBLIOGRAPHY

Aoki, Masahiko. *Information, Incentives, and Bargaining in the Japanese Economy.* Cambridge, U.K.: Cambridge University Press, 1988.

Berry, Michel. *Une Technologie Invisible.* Paris: Centre de Recherche en Gestion, Ecole Polytechnique, 1982.

Blomstrom, Magnus and Edward Wolff. "Multinational Corporations and Productivity Convergence in Mexico." In *International Convergence of Productivity.* New York: Oxford University Press, (forthcoming).

Bowman, Edward and Bruce Kogut (eds.). *Redesigning the Firm.* New York: Oxford University Press (forthcoming).

Burenstam Linder, Staffan. *An Essay on Trade and Transformation.* New York: Wiley, 1961.

Chandler, Alfred. *The Visible Hand: The Managerial Revolution in American Business.* Cambridge, MA: Harvard University Press, 1977.

Commissariat Général du Plan. Investir en France, un espace attractif, (rapport du groupe localisation des investissements transnationaux). Paris: La Documentation Française, 1992.

Coriat, Benjamin. *Penser à l'Envers: Travail et Organisation dans l'entreprise japonaise.* Paris: Christian Bourgois Editeur, 1991.

Fruin, Mark. *Japanese Enterprise System.* New York: Oxford University Press, 1993.

Graham, Edward M. and Paul Krugman. *Foreign Direct Investment in the United States.* Washington D.C.: Institute for International Economics, 1989.

Herrigel, Gary. "The Political Ordering of an Industrial District: The Case of Baden Wuerttemberg." In *Country Competitiveness: Technology and the Organizing of Work.* Edited by Bruce Kogut. New York: Oxford University Press, 1993.

Hounshell, David. *From the American System to Mass Production, 1800-1932.* Baltimore: Johns Hopkins University Press, 1984.

Ittner, Christopher. "The Economics and Measurement of Quality Costs: An Empirical Investigation." unpublished doctoral thesis, Harvard Business School, 1992.

Jaffe, Adam, et al. "Geographic Localization of Knowledge Spillovers, as Evidenced by Patent Citations." *Quarterly Journal of Economics*, (forthcoming).

Katz, Lawrence, et al. "A Comparison of Changes in the Structure of Wages in Four OECD Countries," Harvard University, mimeo, 1993.

Kern, Horst and Michael Schumann. "New Reflections on the End of Flexibility." In *Country Competitiveness: Technology and the Organizing of Work.* Edited by Bruce Kogut. New York: Oxford University Press, 1993.

Kogut, Bruce. "The Permeability of Borders and the Speed of Learning Among Countries." in Holger Crafoord Lectures, Globalization of Firms and the Competitiveness of Nations. Lund: University of Lund, 1990.

_____. "National Organizing Principles of Work and the Erstwhile Dominance of the American Multinational Corporation." *Industrial and Corporate Change*, 1 (1992): 285-317.

Kogut, Bruce (ed.). *Country Competitiveness: Technology and the Organizing of Work*. New York: Oxford University Press, 1993.

Kogut, Bruce and Sea Jin Chang. "Technological Capability and Japanese Foreign Direct Investment in the United States." *Review of Economics and Statistics*, 73, (1991): 401-13.
_____. "Platform Investments and Japanese Entry in the United States Electronic Industry." mimeo, 1993.

Kogut, Bruce and Nalin Kulatilaka. "What is a Critical Capability." mimeo, 1992.

Kogut, Bruce, et al. "Platform Technologies and National Industrial Networks." In *Technology Strategies for International Competition*. Edited by J. Hagedoorn. London: Edgar Elgar, (forthcoming).

March, James and Johannes Olsen. *Ambiguity and Choice in Organizations* (second edition). New York: Oxford University Press, 1980.

Nelson, Richard R. "The Role of Knowledge in R&D Efficiency." *Quarterly Journal of Economics*, 96, (1982): 453-70.

Nelson, Richard and Sidney Winter. *An Evolutionary Theory of Economic Change*. Cambridge, Mass.: Harvard University Press, 1982.

Nishiguchi, Toshi. *Japanese Interfirm Networks*. New York: Oxford University Press, 1993.

Ohno, Taiichi. *Toyota Production System. Beyond Large Scale Production*. Cambridge, Mass: Productivity Press, 1978.

Office of Technology Assessment. *US-Mexico Trade: Pulling Together or Pulling Apart?* Washington, D.C.: U.S. Government Printing Office, 1992.

Piore, Michael and Charles Sabel. *The Second Industrial Divide*. New York: Basic Books, 1982.

Prais, Sig, and Karen Wagner. "Schooling Standards in Britain and Germany." *National Institute of Economics Review*, 1985.

Shan, Weijian. "Strategic Direct Investment in the Biotechnology Industry." mimeo, Wharton School, 1991.

Sokoloff, Kenneth. "Inventive Activity in Early Industrial America: Evidence from Patent Records, 1790-1846." *Journal of Economic History*, 48, (1988): 813-50.

United Nations Centre of Transnational Corporations. "The Triad in Foreign Direct Investment." *World Investment Report, 1991*. New York: United Nations, 1992.

Vernon, Raymond. "International Investment and International Trade in the Product Life Cycle." *Quarterly Journal of Economics*. 80, (1966): 190-207.

Vernon, Raymond. *Sovereignity at Bay: The Multinational Spread of U.S. Enterprise*. New York: Basic Books, 1971.

Whittaker, Hugh. "The Use of Computer Numerically-Controlled Machinery in the U.K. and Japan." *Country Competitiveness: Technology and the Organizing of Work*. Edited by Bruce Kogut. New York: Oxford University Press, 1993.

Wolf, Bernard and Steven Globerman. "Strategic Alliances in the Automotive Industry: Motives and Implications." Ontario Centre for International Business, Working Paper #62, 1992.

Yamawaki, Hideki. "Location Decisions of Japanese Multinational Firms in European Manufacturing Industries." In *European Competitiveness*. Edited by K. Hughes. Cambridge: Cambridge University, (forthcoming).

Yamawaki, Hideki. "Patterns of Entry by Japanese Multinationals into the U.S. and European Manufacturing Industries." In *Japanese Direct Investment in a Unifying Europe*. Edited by D. Encarnation and M. Mason. Oxford: Oxford University Press, (forthcoming).

Part II Evidence

John Knubley, Marc Legault & Someshwar Rao
Industry and Science Policy
Industry Canada

7

Multinationals and Foreign Direct Investment in North America

INTRODUCTION

ALL OF THE STUDIES IN THIS VOLUME examine from one perspective or another the implications of economic integration in North America and the changing role of multinational enterprises (MNEs)[1]. Whether the issue is location, sovereignty, lessons from other countries in the TRIAD (i.e. North America, European Community and Japan), national security or competition policy, economic integration and MNEs lie at the heart of analysis in this volume.

This study serves as background to the other studies, and from this perspective its objective is two-fold. First, it provides background information on trends in foreign direct investment (FDI) and trade which contribute to North American economic integration. Second, it identifies and discusses the structure, performance, and characteristics of the top 1,000 North America-based firms.

During the post-war period, economic integration among the world economies increased dramatically. The rapid growth of world trade, direct investment stock and the recent explosion of direct investments and of various co-operative arrangements among MNEs are both the cause and the result of increased economic interdependence among firms and nations. Along with global economic integration and the changing role of MNEs, there has been a significant increase in intra-regional trade and direct investment flows in the TRIAD countries. The increased trade and investment linkages complement one another and create a cycle of increased economic interdependence among the trading partners.[2] The MNEs are the main instruments carrying out this trade and investment.

Through trade and direct investments large firms have directly contributed to the integration of the three North American economies and increased their linkages with the overseas economies. They command huge amounts of productive resources and play a critical role in the creation and dissemination of new processes and product innovations which are fundamental to the improvements in living standards. They provide benefits in the form of technology transfer, marketing or distribution networks, and management skills (in more technical terms, "positive spillovers"). In short, large firms shape the pattern of trade and direct investment flows and the competitive position of the three countries.

The first part of this study analyzes the trade and investment linkages among the three North American countries and their commercial relations with Japan and Europe. Briefly it also examines the recent trends in Canadian inward and outward direct investment stock. Finally, it discusses the industrial structure of trade and outward direct investment of the three countries.

The second part examines in detail the structure, performance and characteristics of the top North American firms. It identifies the significance of the top firms in each of the three economies and reviews the industrial distribution of the top firms' activities. This distribution is then used to create an index of revealed comparative advantage to identify the relative strengths and weaknesses of each country's economy. It then turns to a detailed examination of the productivity performance (capital and labour) of the top firms as well as its determinants (growth, and research and development [R&D]). Finally, it concludes with a description of the characteristics (average size and outward orientation) of the top firms. The last part of this study summarizes the main findings of the paper and examines their policy implications.

The focus of analysis is the productivity performance of the top firms, with the purpose of reaching a better understanding of the competitive position of the three North American economies. The productivity performance of the top North American firms is crucial for the longer-term international competitive position and profitability of the three nations. Firm size, outward orientation, R&D intensity, and the type of activity are some of the key determinants of productivity and growth performance.

Total factor productivity (TFP) — the efficiency with which all productive resources are used in the production process — is the fundamental, long-term determinant of living standards. In addition, a country's relative productivity performance determines its international competitive position over the longer term. This involves a nation's ability to compete in international markets in terms of price, quality, variety and service, while maintaining and improving its real, per-capita income.

Total factor productivity at the aggregate level is mainly determined by two key factors: the productive efficiency of individual firms and the allocation of productive resources across firms and industries. As for nations, the relative productivity performance of firms determines their long-term competitive position internationally. Superior productivity performance enables a firm to compete with other firms internationally on the basis of price, quality, product choice and service, while paying high wages to its employees and earning adequate return on its investments.

This study concludes that the top firms, through foreign direct investment and trade, have played crucial roles in determining the comparative advantages and the competitive positions of the three countries. On the assumption that further specialization will result from increased economic integration among the three North American Free Trade Agreement (NAFTA) countries, the study suggests that:

- The United States will become more specialized in technology-intensive manufacturing and commercial services industries.

- Canada will likely become increasingly active in resources, resource-intensive manufacturing and the financial services industry.[3]

- Mexican firms will concentrate in the low to middle parts of the value-added chain in the manufacturing sector.

These results are not surprising. Rather, they confirm — with reference to aggregate and firm-specific data — the traditional economic patterns and structures in place in the three countries. They also underline the scope of economic integration in North America and the changing, but nonetheless essential, role of MNEs.

NORTH AMERICAN INTEGRATION AND TRENDS IN FDI

THIS PART OF OUR STUDY sets out the facts behind the integration of industrialized countries, particularly through foreign direct investments and their corresponding trade linkages. Global integration is described through the examination of the recent growth of the world's stock of foreign direct investment. Similarly, the regional integration of trade and investment within North America is examined, as are North American linkages with other industrialized countries, notably the TRIAD economies.

This part also considers the industrial structure of the Canadian, U.S. and Mexican economies, and identifies the strengths of each region in relation to the North American economy. Finally, Canada's inward and outward investment performance is summarized, taking into account the implications of the Canada-U.S. Free Trade Agreement.

FDI AND MULTINATIONALS

OVER THE LAST DECADE, a marked rise in foreign direct investment (FDI) by multinational enterprises has demonstrated the central role these business organizations play in the international economy. The emergence of MNEs and the significant growth of FDI are the products of globalization.

The rapid growth in world foreign direct investment enhances trade linkages among nations. Direct investments by MNEs have become the main engines of trade among nations through their positive impact on intra-firm trade. For instance, much of the trade in manufactured goods between Canada and the United States is of the intra-firm type, especially the automotive industry. Similarly, the considerable increase in trade within the European Community can be attributed to the rise in intra-firm trade, resulting primarily from the greater investment linkages among the member countries.[4]

Among other factors, the significant liberalization of foreign investment in both developed and developing economies has played an important role in increasing international capital flows. The worldwide trend toward more liberal foreign investment regimes reflects a growing consensus among policy makers that MNEs, as major vehicles for transferring capital, technology and management skills across borders, and for stimulating competition, make important contributions to economic growth and rising standards of living in both home and host countries.

The importance of multinationals in relation to international economic activity can be gauged from the following estimates by the United Nations:[5]

- By the early 1990s, the total number of multinational corporations exceeded 37,000, with more than 170,000 foreign affiliates;

- The proliferation in the number of MNEs since the mid-1980s was accompanied by a sizable expansion of FDI flows. Global outflows of FDI reached a high of US$ 234 billion in 1990. World wide outflows grew at an average annual rate of 34 per-cent from 1985 to 1990, exceeding the growth of global merchandise exports (13 per cent) and global output (12 per cent), as shown in Figure 1.

- By the end of the 1980s, the value of goods and services sold by foreign affiliates totalled an estimated US$ 4.4 trillion, far greater than world exports, estimated at only $2.5 trillion (including a substantial volume of intra-firm trade). In other words, production by foreign affiliates is of greater importance than exports in delivering goods and services to markets world wide.

The growth of intra-firm cross-border trade resulting from MNE investments has significantly contributed to the integration of the industrialized and newly industrialized economies. These factors have also strengthened the regional economic linkages within each of the TRIAD communities.

This increased economic integration is necessitated and facilitated by several interrelated developments in the world economy. These include: rapid shifts in the comparative advantage position of firms and nations; dramatic reductions in transportation and communication costs; shorter product cycles, the result of rapid changes in technology; the reduction of barriers to trade,

FIGURE 1

GROWTH OF WORLD GDP, WORLD MERCHANDISE EXPORTS & WORLD FOREIGN
DIRECT INVESTMENT OUTFLOWS, AVERAGE ANNUAL GROWTH RATE, 1985-90 (%)

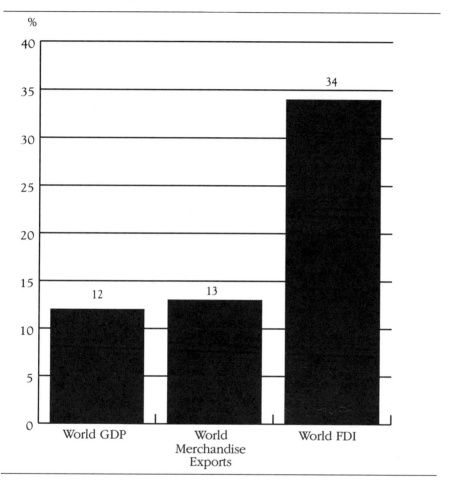

Source: World Investment Report, UNCTC (1992)

investment and financial flows; the formation of regional trading blocks; convergence
of real incomes and tastes around the world; and fierce and growing competition
among firms and nations for markets, technology, skilled labour and capital.

WORLD STOCK OF FOREIGN DIRECT INVESTMENT

THE LAST DECADE WITNESSED an explosion in the growth of foreign direct
investment activity among industrialized countries. The stock of world direct

FIGURE 2

WORLD STOCK OF DIRECT INVESTMENT ABROAD (OUTWARD)
PERCENT DISTRIBUTION BY SOURCE COUNTRIES 1980 AND 1990

1980 Total = US$ 518.5 billion

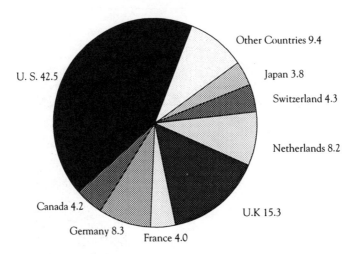

1990 Total = US$ 1,644.2 billion

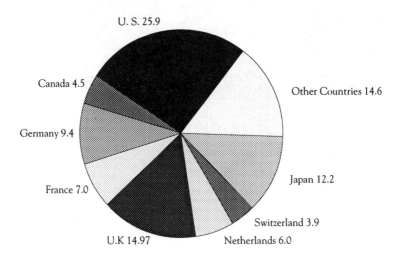

Source: Estimates based on data from U.S. Department of Commerce

FIGURE 3

WORLD STOCK OF DIRECT INVESTMENT ABROAD (INWARD)
PERCENT DISTRIBUTION BY RECIPIENT COUNTRIES 1980 AND 1990

1980 Total = US$ 505.3 billion

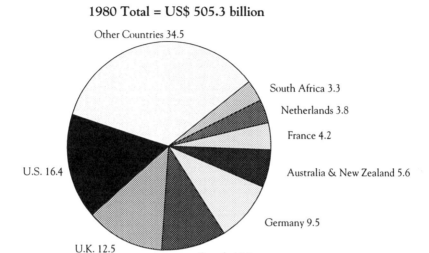

1990 Total = US$ 1,638.9 billion

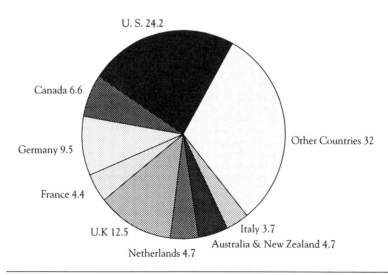

Source: Estimates based on data from U.S. Department of Commerce.

investment abroad increased threefold from US$ 518 bilion in 1980 to US$ 1,644 billion in 1990 (Figure 2). This growth of FDI activity was accompanied by a significant realignment of the distribution of international direct investment among home and host countries.

The most notable development was the transformation of the United States from the traditional source country of worldwide direct investment to a major recipient country of international FDI. In 1980, the United States accounted for 42.5 percent of world's outward direct investment stock and 16.4 percent of inward direct investment stock. By 1990, however, the U.S. share of outward direct investment stock had fallen to 25.9 percent while its share of inward world direct investment stock rose to 24.2 percent (Figures 2 and 3).

A second trend over the past decade has been the significant increase in Japan's share of outward direct investment stock. By 1990, Japan's outward investments accounted for 12.2 percent of total world direct investments abroad — a three-fold increase of its 1980 share of 3.8 percent. Similarly, Germany, France, and the category "other countries" increased their outward share of the world's direct outward investments over the same period by 1.1 percent, 3.0 percent and 5.2 percent respectively.

NORTH AMERICA AND THE WORLD ECONOMY

THE TRIAD COUNTRIES ACCOUNT for between 70 percent and 80 percent of total world output, trade and direct investment stock. In 1991 the North American share of world output (GDP) and direct investment stock was just below 30 percent (Table 1). This makes North America the largest trade and investment block in the TRIAD. Although the role of the Pacific Rim in the world economy is considerably smaller than that of the European Community and North America, its importance has been growing rapidly and this trend is

TABLE 1

SHARES OF AND TOTAL WORLD GDP, TRADE AND INVESTMENT, 1991

INDICATOR	NORTH AMERICA (%)	EUROPEAN COMMUNITY (%)	ASIA PACIFIC (%)	REST OF WORLD (%)	TOTAL WORLD (US$ BILLION)
GDP	29	23	17	31	22,300
Trade (Exports plus Imports)	18	38	18	26	7,000
FDI Stock (Outward plus Inward)	28	41	10	21	3,800

Source: Estimates based on data from UNCTC (1993) and U.S. Department of Commerce

expected to continue. The economies of the Pacific Rim are anticipated to grow at a much faster pace than those of Europe and North America.[6]

Although the NAFTA countries accounted for only about 18 percent of world trade in 1991, they accounted for 28 percent of world direct investment. In the 1980s, there was a dramatic increase in foreign direct investment in the United States, largely from Japan, Canada and Europe (particularly the United Kingdom). The new investment linkages will likely lead to more North American intra-firm trade with the other two trading blocks, thereby raising its share of world trade.

The United States accounts for the lion's share of North American GDP at 88 percent. Canada at 9 percent and Mexico at 3 percent contribute the rest. Both Canada and the United States are developed economies and members of the G-7. In contrast, Mexico is a newly industrializing economy, positioned to achieve rapid growth if it can integrate fully into the United States and Canadian industrialized economies.

The trade and investment linkages among the three countries are strong and growing. This is shown by changes in both intra-regional trade and intra-regional investment. In 1991 intra-regional trade among the three countries accounted for 19 percent of total North American trade (US$ 1,260 billion). The investment linkages are not as strong as the trade linkages, with intra-regional direct investment being 11 percent of the total North American foreign direct investment stock (US$ 1,064 billion). However, these linkages are becoming stronger. For instance, Canadian direct investment in the United States has increased substantially in the last 20 years, while it has grown significantly in Mexico (but) from a small base. At the same time, U.S. direct investment in Mexico and Canada continues to grow from a very solid foundation.

The United States is the largest commercial partner of both Canada and Mexico. In the case of Canada, 75 percent of total Canadian merchandise exports in 1991 went to the United States and imports from the United States accounted for almost two-thirds of Canada's total merchandise imports. Similarly, Canada's investment linkages with the United States are very strong and growing. Sixty-four percent of the stock of foreign investment in Canada is from the United States and 58 percent of Canadian direct investment abroad (CDIA) is located in the United States. On the other hand, its trade and investment linkages with Mexico are relatively weak (Figure 4).

Canadian investment relations with Europe are much stronger than its trade linkages. Europe (mostly the U.K., Netherlands and Germany) accounts for between 25 percent and 30 percent of Canada's total direct investment stock, but its share in total Canadian merchandise trade is only about 10 percent. The large amount of intra-regional trade within the European Community (at almost 60 percent of all trade) likely explains this weak correspondence between Canada's trade and investment linkages with Europe.

Canada's commercial relations with Japan, the economic leader of the Asia Pacific Rim, are significant and growing.[7] With respect to trade, the

FIGURE 4

GEOGRAPHIC DISTRIBUTION OF CANADIAN TRADE AND DIRECT INVESTMENT STOCK
(% OF TOTAL AND US$ BILLION, 1991)

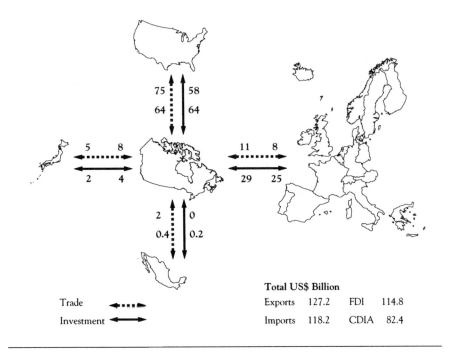

		Total US$ Billion			
Trade		Exports	127.2	FDI	114.8
Investment		Imports	118.2	CDIA	82.4

Source: Estimates based on data from Statistics Canada

relationship is balanced, with Japan shipping manufactured goods to Canada and Canada shipping natural resources to Japan. In the case of investment, the relationship is one-sided with Canadian investment in Japan relatively small. However, during the late 1980s and early 1990s, both Canadian investments in Japan and Japanese investment in Canada have grown substantially.

Europe (mainly Germany, France and the U.K.), Canada and Japan are the most important commercial partners of the United States. Canada accounted for about 20 percent of total U.S. merchandise trade in 1991 and between 7 percent and 15 percent of its total direct investment (inward plus outward) stock. Like Canada's, the U.S. investment linkages with Europe are considerably stronger than its trade linkages (Figure 5).

The trade and investment relations between the U.S. and Mexico are fairly sizeable and have been growing steadily. Since Mexico is expected to grow much

FIGURE 5

GEOGRAPHIC DISTRIBUTION OF U.S. TRADE AND DIRECT INVESTMENT STOCK
(% OF TOTAL AND US$ BILLION, 1991)

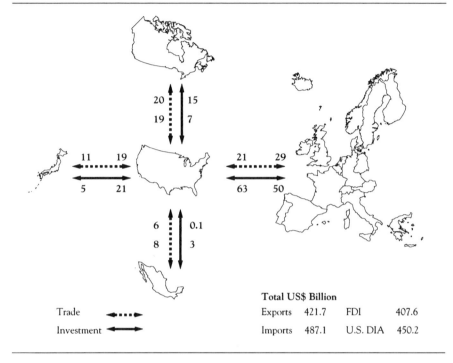

Total US$ Billion			
Exports	421.7	FDI	407.6
Imports	487.1	U.S. DIA	450.2

Trade

Investment

Source: Estimates based on data from U.S. Department of Commerce.

faster than Canada and the United States, due to the catch-up process of a newly industrializing economy, Mexico's future shares in the North American economy, and in total U.S. trade and direct investment, are expected to increase significantly.

Mexico's largest and most important commercial partner is the United States: two-thirds of all its trade and direct investment is with the United States (Figure 6). It also has important commercial relations with Europe and Japan. On the other hand, Canada does not currently play a significant role in Mexican trade and foreign direct investment.

In sum, North America plays a major role in the world economy. Intra-regional movements within the three countries account for a significant share of total North American trade and investment stock, and these linkages are growing and expected to strengthen in the post-NAFTA period. The three North American economies also have important commercial relations with Europe and Japan. This implies that the locational and organizational decisions of intra- and extra-

FIGURE 6

GEOGRAPHIC DISTRIBUTION OF MEXICAN TRADE AND DIRECT INVESTMENT STOCK
(% OF TOTAL AND US$ BILLION, 1991)

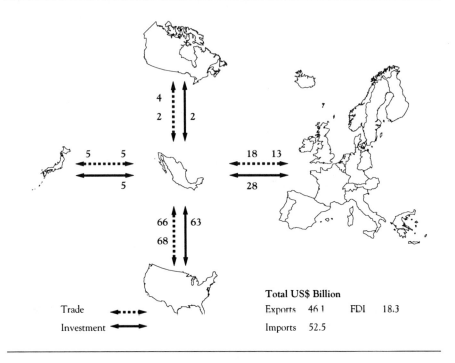

Source: Estimates based on data from Banco de Mexico (1992) and U.S. Department of Commerce.

regional MNEs could play an even larger role in the future restructuring of the North American economies.

CANADA'S INVESTMENT PERFORMANCE

THE FOLLOWING SECTION examines in some detail the recent trends in Canada's inward and outward direct investment stocks.

Foreign Direct Investment

In the late 1980s, Canada embarked upon a policy of trade and investment liberalization with the United States which included dismantling the National Energy Program and changing the Foreign Investment Review Agency to Investment Canada, and which culminated in the Free Trade Agreement (FTA)

FIGURE 7

GROSS AND NET FOREIGN DIRECT INVESTMENT FLOWS TO CANADA, 1980 TO 1992
($ BILLION)

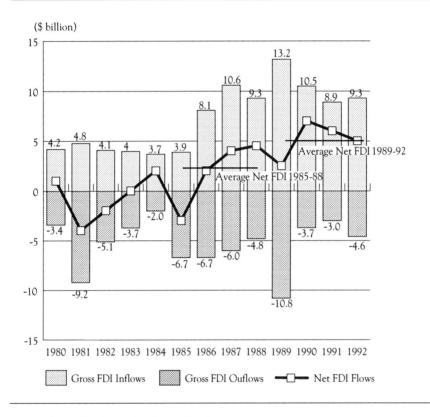

Source: Estimates based on data from Statistics Canada.

between Canada and the United States. Since the inception of the FTA in 1989, foreign investors have shown a significant interest in Canada as reflected in a sharp rise in cross-border capital flows. Underlying this development is the confidence in the business opportunities that have been created in both Canada and the United States by the FTA and the security of U.S. market access that has been provided to foreign investors locating production in Canada.

From 1989 to 1992, Canada attracted a total of $19.8 billion of net FDI flows, or on average about $5.0 billion a year. This compares with cumulative FDI of $7.6 billion in the four preceding years (1985-1988), or on average roughly $2.0 billion a year (Figure 7). Almost 40 percent of these flows in the post-FTA years originated in the United States.

At year-end 1992, the stock or book value of FDI in Canada stood at $136.6 billion, up from $131.6 billion in the previous year. Globalization has led to a diversification in the origins of FDI. While the United States continues to account for the bulk of FDI assets in Canada, its relative share of FDI stock has diminished since the early 1980s, from a high of 77.8 percent in 1980 to 66.7 percent in 1988. Strong capital inflows from the United States since the FTA have slowed the decline in the U.S. share of FDI stock, even showing a slight upturn in 1992 (Figure 8).

In the interim, members of the European Community raised their stake in FDI in Canada, from 16.9 percent in 1980 to 23.5 percent in 1992. The most impressive gains, however, were made by Japan, which more than quadrupled its relative share of FDI stock, from 0.9 percent in 1980 to 4.1 percent in 1992. The Pacific Rim, including Japan, has emerged as a significant source of foreign capital with 7.0 percent of FDI assets in 1991.

Canadian Direct Investment Abroad

Attracting investment to Canada is only part of Canada's total investment effort. For Canadian companies to remain competitive, they must invest abroad. They need the benefits of economies of scale, access to new markets, and the alliances that international investment brings. Particularly in light of Canada's relatively small domestic economy, Canadian outward direct investment is an important strategy for Canadian MNEs who intend to compete globally.

At the end of 1992, the stock of Canadian direct investment abroad stood at $99.0 billion, up 4.8 percent from the previous year (Figure 9). Over the past decade, faster growth of CDIA relative to FDI stock has resulted in bringing about a better balance between Canada's inward and outward direct investment activity. CDIA stock accounted for over 70 percent of Canadian FDI stock in 1992, compared to about 50 percent in 1982.

Since the mid-1980s, CDIA has gradually diversified, moving away from the traditional U.S. market and into Europe. While the United States has continued to account for the bulk of CDIA in 1992 (58.4 percent), its relative share of these assets has dropped about 10 percentage points since 1985. During this period, much of Canada's overseas direct investment was destined for the European Community, whose share of CDIA rose by 7.5 percent. In 1992 the U.K. (which in the past has served Canadian investors as a springboard to Europe) accounted for only one-half of that gain.

In 1991, Canada's direct investment in Japan rose almost 125 percent to reach $1.7 billion or 1.8 percent of total CDIA stock. In 1980, less than one-half of one percent of CDIA was located in Japan. Today Japan and France are tied as the seventh-largest destination(s) of CDIA.

FIGURE 8

COMPOSITION OF FDI STOCK, BY HOME COUNTRY, 1980-92 (% OF TOTAL)

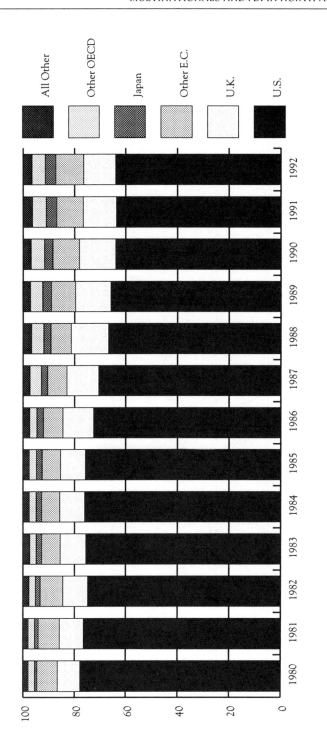

Source: Estimates based on data from Statistics Canada.

FIGURE 9

COMPOSITION OF CDIA STOCK, BY HOST COUNTRY, 1980-92 (% OF TOTAL)

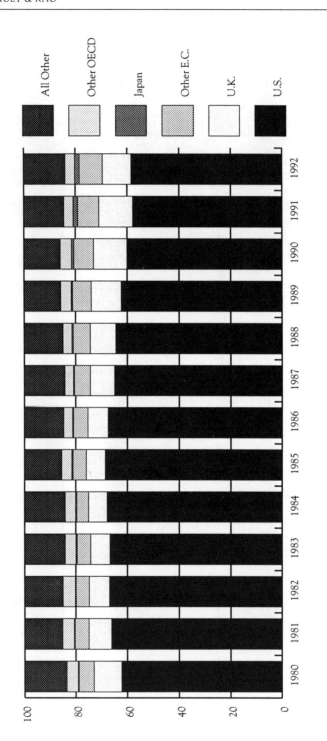

Source: Estimates based on data from Statistics Canada.

NORTH AMERICA AND ITS INDUSTRIAL STRUCTURE

AN IMPORTANT OBJECTIVE of this study is to relate the industrial composition of trade flows and direct investment stock among the three countries to the structure, performance and characteristics of the top North America-based firms. Toward this goal, we examine the industrial distribution of trade and investment linkages among the three NAFTA countries. First, the Canada-U.S. linkages are considered, followed by the Mexican trade and investment relations.

Canada and the United States

Between Canada and the United States, the industrial distribution of merchandise exports to and imports from each country is very similar, implying large intra-industry and intra-firm trade between the two countries. This also underscores the fact that they are both industrialized economies. The convergence is particularly strong in chemicals, and machinery and equipment manufacturing industries, a reflection of a substantial amount of intra-firm trade, especially in the transportation equipment industry (Table 2).

TABLE 2

INDUSTRIAL DISTRIBUTION OF CANADIAN MERCHANDISE EXPORTS TO AND IMPORTS FROM THE UNITED STATES, 1989 (% OF TOTAL)

INDUSTRY	EXPORTS	IMPORTS
Primary Industries	15.6	16.0
Manufacturing	84.4	84.0
DISTRIBUTION OF MANUFACTURING EXPORTS AND IMPORTS		
Food, Beverages & Tobacco	2.6	2.2
Paper and Publishing	12.5	3.8
Lumber and Furniture	6.6	1.8
Primary Metals	7.4	3.3
Fabricated Metals	2.0	2.6
Non-metallic Mineral products	1.0	1.2
Rubber and Plastic Products	1.8	2.4
Petroleum Refining	2.0	1.1
Textiles, Leather & Clothing	1.1	2.2
Chemical Products	5.4	7.3
Non-electric Machinery	9.5	16.5
Electric Machinery	7.3	17.1
Transportation Equipment	39.0	32.7
Miscellaneous Manufacturing	1.9	5.8

Source: Estimates by Rao and Lemprière (1992)

However, Canadian exports to the United States are more concentrated in resources, resource-based manufacturing, and transportation equipment. U.S. exports to Canada, on the other hand, are more in chemicals and chemical products, electrical and non-electrical machinery and transportation equipment industries (Table 2).

The industrial distribution of Canadian direct investment stock in the United States and the distribution of U.S. direct investment stock in Canada are similar to the distribution of trade flows between the two countries. Canadian direct investment in the United States is, however, more concentrated in resource and resource-based manufacturing and in financial service industries [banking, finance, insurance and real estate] (Table 3). In contrast, the U.S. direct investment stock is found more in chemicals and chemical products, petroleum, transportation equipment, wholesale trade and finance industries.

The complementarity of the industrial composition of trade flows and direct investment stock between the two countries, especially in manufacturing, strongly suggests that Canadian and U.S. firms are exploiting their respective positions of comparative advantage through both trade and also

TABLE 3

INDUSTRIAL DISTRIBUTION OF THE STOCK OF U.S. DIRECT INVESTMENT IN CANADA AND CANADIAN DIRECT INVESTMENT IN THE UNITED STATES, 1991 (% OF TOTAL)

INDUSTRY	U.S. DIA IN CANADA	CDIA IN THE U.S.
Petroleum	15.8	3.0
Primary Industries	8.0	14.7
Total Manufacturing	47.2	32.2
Food	3.3	3.2
Chemicals	9.8	2.2
Metals	4.9	6.1
Machinery	4.0	6.4
Other Manufacturing	3.5	14.4
Trade	9.3	0.9
Banking	12.2	6.6
Finance	6.4	8.2
Insurance	1.5	17.7
Real Estate	17.8	13.6
Services	3.2	3.0
Total	100.0	100.0

Source: Estimates based on data from U.S. Department of Commerce

direct production in each other's countries. (The comparative advantage of the two countries is discussed in some detail later.)

Mexico

Primary industries accounted for over 38 percent of total Mexican merchandise exports in 1991; the rest were in manufactured products. Surprisingly, chemicals and chemical products and machinery and equipment industries, usually classified as technology-intensive manufacturing industries, accounted for almost two-thirds of Mexico's total manufactured exports. Autos and auto parts contributed about 60 percent of all of its machinery and equipment exports (Table 4).

The large share of technology-intensive exports are mainly the result of large intra-firm exports of foreign subsidiaries, especially the U.S. affiliates. The foreign subsidiaries are taking advantage of the low labour costs and are producing the low value-added and low skill-intensive components of technology-intensive industries in Mexico. In turn, much of the output of

TABLE 4

INDUSTRIAL DISTRIBUTION OF MEXICAN EXPORTS, IMPORTS AND U.S. DIRECT INVESTMENT (STOCK) IN MEXICO, 1991 (% OF TOTAL)

INDUSTRY	TOTAL EXPORTS	TOTAL IMPORTS	U.S. DIA IN MEXICO
Petroleum	38.1	7.1	0.0
Other Industries			14.2
Total Manufacturing	61.9	92.9	73.4
Food and Beverages	7.2	7.3	8.1
Chemicals & Chemical Products	11.7	9.5	17.1
Primary Metals	10.7	7.6 }	2.9
Fabricated Metal Products }		}	
Machinery & Equipment }	53.1	58.1	3.7
Electrical Products }			4.8
Transportation Equipment }			20.2
Other Manufacturing	17.9	17.5	16.7
Wholesale Trade			7.2
Banking			0.0
Finance			3.4
Services			1.6

Note: Blanks indicate data not available.
Source: Estimates based on data from Banco de Mexico (1992), Unger (1993) and U.S. Department of Commerce.

these industries is exported back to their parents and other countries. The industrial distribution of U.S. direct investment stock in Mexico and the composition of sales and employment of top Mexican firms by industry and by foreign control, presented in the next part, support this view.

Not surprisingly, manufactured products account for almost 93 percent of total Mexican merchandise imports. Like exports, machinery and equipment and chemicals and chemical products contributed over two-thirds of Mexico's total manufactured imports (Table 4). The similarity of industrial distribution of Mexican manufactured exports and imports, again, strongly indicates the important role of intra-firm trade in its merchandise trade.

The manufacturing sector's share in U.S. direct investment stock in Mexico was 75 percent in 1991. Furthermore, chemicals and chemical products, transportation equipment and light machinery industries largely accounted for the U.S. direct investment stock in manufacturing at about 60 percent (Table 4). As mentioned above, the industrial distribution of U.S. direct investment stock strongly suggests that intra-firm trade has played a major role in the determination of the industrial composition of Mexican trade flows.

STRUCTURE, PERFORMANCE AND CHARACTERISTICS OF THE TOP NORTH AMERICAN FIRMS

THE OBJECTIVE OF THIS PART of our study is to identify and provide an overview of the structure, performance and characteristics of the top North America-based enterprises. The activities of these large firms are related to aggregate data bearing on the country-specific features of the three signators to the NAFTA. Simply put, this part aims to set out how the main economic strengths and weaknesses of the United States, Canada and Mexico are shaped by their largest firms.

The selection process identifying the top 1,000 North America-based firms is neither straightforward nor easy. Selection could be based on any one of a number of criteria, including total sales, total assets, employment, profits, growth of sales, etc. Applying each criterion independently leads to a different list of top firms.

The process used to select the top 1,000 North America-based firms for this study uses the sales criterion. This method introduces less bias toward any particular industrial grouping, thereby permitting the sample of firms to be distributed across all industries. For instance, the asset criterion results in the selection of a disproportionately larger share of firms from capital-intensive and financial industries, whereas the sales criterion ensures that the sample of firms more appropriately reflects the industrial strength of the three economies.

The sample of the 1,000 largest North American firms consists of 823 U.S.-based companies, 158 Canada-based enterprises and 19 Mexico-based firms. The sample is taken for 1991 only, so it represents a snapshot of one point in time. Data related to the firms' growth are available for a five-year period, from 1986 to 1991.

The firms were selected from the Disclosure/Worldscope Global Database. The information on Canadian and U.S. firms was verified and, as required, supplemented with information from Compact Disclosure Canada, Financial Post 500, the Fortune 500 and Moody's International. These sources did not, however, capture all of the top Mexican firms. To correct this, eight additional Mexican firms were identified and added to the list based upon information from Expansión. As a result the sample is extended to 1,008 firms.[8]

In the sections following, the structure of the top firms is first considered in geographic and sectoral terms; then, the performance of the top firms is examined in terms of productivity, growth and R&D. Finally, the characteristics of the top North American firms are analyzed, including such factors as average firm size and degree of globalization.

STRUCTURE

The Top North American Firms

Virtually all the top firms play a major role in the North American economy. Total sales of the top firms varied between US$ 0.74 and US$ 122 billion. Their combined total assets and sales in 1991 were US$ 9.2 and US$ 4.4 trillion respectively. They employed over 30 million people.

The distribution of the top 1,008 firms by country corresponds to the relative contribution of each country to the North American economy. There are 823 American companies, 82 percent of the sample, which is similar to the 88 percent U.S. share of North American GDP.

One hundred and fifty-eight Canada-based companies, or 15.7 percent of the sample, exceeds Canada's 9 percent share of North American GDP. Their 10 percent sales and 14 percent asset shares also exceed the 9 percent contribution of Canada's share in North American GDP (Figure 10).

Of the 158 Canada-based companies listed, 39 are foreign controlled. Ergo, 119 of the top North American firms in Canada, or 11.8 percent of the total number, are domestically controlled.

There are 27 Mexican companies listed, representing 2.7 percent of the sample, or slightly less than its 3 percent share of GDP. Many of them are American subsidiaries. Moreover, the UNCTC data shows that in 1992 there were no Mexican MNEs, compared to over 1,300 Canadian and almost 3,000 U.S. MNEs.

Not all of the top North American firms are necessarily MNEs. However, 400 firms reported assets and sales in more than one country. In addition, as will be discussed later in more detail, foreign assets account for

TABLE 5

SUMMARY OF CHARACTERISTICS OF SAMPLE OF TOP FIRMS (%)

COUNTRY	TOP FIRMS' SALES AS A % OF TOTAL GROSS OUTPUT	TOP FIRMS' EMPLOYMENT AS A % OF TOTAL EMPLOYMENT
Canada	52	19
United States	50	25
Mexico	19	2

Source: Estimates based on data from Disclosure Inc. Statistics Canada, and Expansión.

over 25 percent of the total assets of 217 of the top 1,008 corporations. The status of the remainder is not known.

The shares of the top U.S. firms in total U.S. gross output (value-added plus intermediate inputs) and employment were 50 percent and 25 percent respectively (Table 5). The top 158 Canada-based firms accounted for 52 percent of total Canadian gross output and 19 percent of employment. These results in turn suggest that the top U.S. and Canadian firms account for at least 25 percent of GDP of the two countries, because the share of GDP in the aggregate gross output is over 50 percent.

In contrast, the top 27 Mexican firms account for only 19 percent of Mexico's total gross output and 2 percent of its total employment. This distribution of the sales and assets of the top North American firms by

FIGURE 10

DISTRIBUTION OF TOP FIRMS - NUMBER OF FIRMS, SALES AND ASSETS (% OF TOTAL)

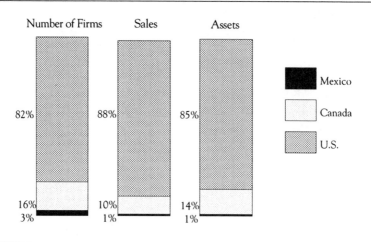

Source: Estimates based on data from Disclosure Inc. and Expansión.

country further underlines the limited representation Mexico has in the sample (Figure 10). This limited role of the top Mexican firms in the Mexican economy strongly suggests that the main characteristics of the Mexican economy are largely shaped by its small and medium-sized firms.

TABLE 6

TOP 20 U.S. FIRMS

RANK BY SALES	RANK BY ASSETS	COMPANY NAME	INDUSTRY	SALES (US$ MILLION)
1	2	General Motors Corporation	Motor Vehicles & Equipment	122,081
2	19	Exxon Corporation	Mining	102,847
3	3	Ford Motor Company	Motor Vehicles & Equipment	88,286
4	16	International Business Machines	Computer & Office	64,792
5	31	American Telephone & Telegraph	Communications	63,089
6	4	General Electric Company	Electrical Products	59,379
7	12	Sears, Roebuck & Co.	Retail Trade	57,242
8	46	Mobil Corporation	Mining	56,042
9	35	Philip Morris Companies Inc.	Tobacco	48,064
10	130	Wal-Mart Stores, Inc.	Retail Trade	43,886
11	54	Du Pont (E.I.) de Nemours	Petroleum Refining	38,695
12	82	Texaco Inc.	Mining	37,271
13	58	Chevron Corporation	Mining	36,461
14	125	K Mart Corporation	Retail Trade	34,580
15	1	Citicorp	Depository Institution	31,839
16	41	Chrysler Corporation	Motor Vehicles & Equipment	29,370
17	90	Procter & Gamble Company (The)	Chemicals & Allied	29,362
18	128	Boeing Company (The)	Aircraft & Parts	29,314
19	6	American Express Company	Securities & Brokers	25,763
20	72	Amoco Corporation	Mining	25,325

Source: Estimates based on data from Disclosure Inc.

Tables 6, 7 and 8 set out the names of the largest 20 U.S., Canadian and Mexican firms from the database. The top 20 U.S. firms are very large in terms of sales, assets and employment. Their combined assets were almost US$ 1.6 trillion in 1991. Their sales (US$ 1 trillion) accounted for over 23 percent of the total sales of all top American firms and 13 percent of all U.S. gross output. They employed more than 4 million people or approximately 4 percent of the U.S. workforce.

The sales of the top 20 Canadian firms vary between US$ 5.8 billion for Manufacturers Life Insurance Company to US$ 17.2 billion for BCE Inc. The sales of the top 20 Canadian firms accounted for 40 percent of the sales of all 158 top Canada-based firms. This corresponds to 21 percent of total gross output in Canada. Similarly, they commanded over 50 percent of total assets and more than

TABLE 7

TOP 20 CANADIAN FIRMS

RANK BY SALES	RANK BY ASSETS	COMPANY NAME	INDUSTRY	SALES (US$ MILLION)
36	48	BCE Inc	Communications	17,200
38	327	General Motors of Canada Inc.	Motor Vehicles & Equipment	16,847
60	8	Royal Bank of Canada	Depositary Institution	12,414
84	462	Ford Motor Co. of Canada Ltd.	Motor Vehicles & Equipment	10,531
101	433	George Weston Ltd.	Wholesale Trade	9,316
105	11	Canadian Imperial Bank of Commerce	Depositary Institution	9,176
111	18	Bank of Montreal	Depositary Institution	8,861
114	116	Canadian Pacific Ltd.	Transportation	8,711
123	21	The Bank of Nova Scotia	Depositary Institution	8,287
124	231	Northern Telecom Ltd.	Communications Equipment	8,182
126	175	Imperial Oil Ltd.	Mining	7,994
127	362	Brascan Ltd.	Mining	7,979
132	198	Alcan Aluminium Ltd.	Primary Metals	7,748
141	584	Loblaw Companies Ltd.	Retail Trade	7,381
143	492	Chrysler Canada Ltd.	Motor Vehicles & Equipment	7,157
144	160	Noranda Inc.	Lumber & Wood	7,118
152	70	Sun Life Assurance Co. of Canada	Insurance	6,856
171	176	Seagram Co. Ltd.	Food & Products	6,242
174	52	Ontario Hydro	Utilities	6,179
185	78	Manufacturers Life Insurance Co.	Insurance	5,845

Source: Estimates based on data from Disclosure Inc.

one-third of total employment (2 million) of all the top Canada-based firms. The top 20 firms also accounted for over 6 percent of Canadian employment.

Total sales of the top 20 Mexican firms varied from a low of US$ .85 billion for Hylsa (primary metals) to a high of US$ 18.9 billion for Petroleos Mexicanos (petroleum refining). The combined assets and sales of the top 20 Mexican firms were over US$ 118 billion and US$ 56 billion respectively. They employed about 507,000 people.

Industrial Distribution of the Top Firms

The following describes the industrial distribution of the top North American firms. Using the four-digit SIC code, the top North American firms were grouped according to their primary activity into about 40 major industries. Of these, 25 are manufacturing industries. The individual manufacturing industries have been further arranged into three major groupings: labour-intensive, resource-intensive and technology-intensive industries, which are defined in Table 9.[9]

One-third of all top Canadian firms are in mining (13 percent) and resource-intensive manufacturing (20 percent) industries. These firms account

TABLE 8

TOP 20 MEXICAN FIRMS

RANK BY SALES	RANK BY ASSETS	COMPANY NAME	INDUSTRY	SALES (US$ MILLION)
30	37	Petroleos Mexicanos	Petroleum Refining	18,884
206	168	Telefonos de Mexico	Communications	5,268
280	127	Banca Serfin	Depositary Institution	3,796
351	372	Vitro Sociedad Anomina	Non-metallic Minerals	3,004
380	655	CIFRA	Retail Trade	2,754
417	609	General Motors de Mexico	Motor Vehicles & Equipment	2,502
432	408	Grupo Industrial ALFA	Primary Metals	2,435
451	747	Chrysler de Mexico	Motor Vehicles & Equipment	2,322
532	521	Fomento Economico Mexicano	Food & Products	1,785
535	761	Volkswagen de Mexico	Motor Vehicles & Equipment	1,777
554	398	CEMEX	Non-metallic Minerals	1,704
576	527	Valores Industriales	Food & Products	1,652
637	643	DESC Sociedad de Fomento Industrial	Other Financial Services	1,467
699	555	Empresas ICA Sociedad Controladora	Construction	1,263
718	806	Grupo Industrial Bimbo	Food & Products	1,224
841	741	Corporacion Mexicana de Aviaci	Transportation	978
855	734	Celanese Mexicana	Chemicals & Allied	939
880	232	Ferrocarriles Nacionales de Mexico	Other Transportation Equipment	914
910	457	Grupo Industrial Minera Mexico	Mining	869
923	756	Hylsa	Primary Metals	852

Source: Estimates based on data from Disclosure Inc. and Expansión.

for over 25 percent of the total sales of all top Canadian firms. Similarly, the American top firms in these industries account for about 24 percent of sales of the top U.S. firms. Furthermore, over half of the sales of the Mexican top firms are in the resource-intensive manufacturing and mining industries (Table 10).

On the other hand, over 28 percent of the sales of U.S. top firms are in the technology-intensive manufacturing industries, compared to only 15 percent in Canada. In addition, 13 of the 17 top technology-intensive manufacturing firms in Canada are foreign controlled. Similarly, the activity of foreign-controlled firms is also prevalent in the mining sector. Of the 20 Canada-based mining firms, 10 are foreign controlled (Table 11). In Mexico, 16 percent of the sales of the top firms are in the technology-intensive manufacturing industries. The large share of technology-intensive industries in Mexico is mainly a reflection of the activities of foreign-controlled firms, particularly in the motor vehicle and equipment industry.

The service industries account for a larger share of the activities of top firms in Canada than in the United States and Mexico. Within the service industries, the top firms' sales, employment and assets are more concentrated in financial services and transportation in Canada than in the United States.

TABLE 9

COMPONENTS OF MAJOR INDUSTRY GROUPINGS

GROUPING	INDUSTRY
Agriculture & Fishing	
Mining	
Construction	
Labour-intensive Manufacturing	Textiles Clothing Furniture & Fixtures Printing & Publishing Leather & Products Miscellaneous Manufactured Goods
Resource-intensive Manufacturing	Food & Products Tobacco Lumber & Wood Paper & Allied Petroleum Refining Non-metallic Minerals Primary Metals Fabricated Metals
Technology-intensive Manufacturing	Chemicals & Allied Rubber & Products Machinery excluding Electrical Computer & Office Electrical Products Communications Equipment Miscellaneous Electrical Products Motor Vehicles & Equipment Aircraft & Parts Other Transportation Equipment Light Machinery
Transportation	
Communications	
Utilities	
Trade	Wholesale Trade Retail Trade
Finance	Depositary Institution Non-depositary Institution Securities & Brokers Insurance Other Financial Services
Services	Commercial Services Health Services Other Services

TABLE 10

INDUSTRIAL DISTRIBUTION OF THE TOP U.S., CANADIAN AND MEXICAN FIRMS (% OF TOTAL)

INDUSTRY	UNITED STATES				CANADA				MEXICO			
	NO. OF FIRMS	ASSETS	SALES	EMPLOYEES	NO. OF FIRMS	ASSETS	SALES	EMPLOYEES	NO. OF FIRMS	ASSETS	SALES	EMPLOYEES
Agriculture & Fishing	3	0.07	0.21	0.27	0				0			
Mining	25	4.06	8.52	2.07	20	5.05	10.55	6.17	1	2.42	1.40	3.63
Construction	9	0.32	0.76	0.58	2	0.10	0.56	0.50	1	1.75	2.04	
Labour-intensive Manufacturing	44	1.18	2.23	2.35	7	1.39	3.15	5.20	0			
Resource-intensive Manufacturing	109	5.95	13.09	8.96	31	7.07	14.78	18.34	10	53.85	53.50	35.13
Technology-intensive Manufacturing	193	17.55	28.45	24.21	17	3.08	14.71	10.89	7	12.88	16.22	35.86
Transportation	23	1.59	2.81	3.07	9	3.27	5.88	10.45	1	0.91	1.58	2.32
Communications	19	4.30	5.19	4.34	5	4.18	4.95	6.55	2	10.97	9.86	12.22
Utilities	86	6.81	6.00	2.89	12	8.71	5.54	3.42	0			
Trade	119	4.76	15.41	41.18	30	3.46	16.51	24.86	3	3.17	6.92	6.57
Finance	145	51.99	15.00	6.94	25	63.69	23.37	13.61	2	14.04	8.48	4.27
Services	48	1.42	2.32	3.15	0				0			
Total*	823	7,806	3,874	27,329	158	1,241	457	2,382	27	125	62	520

Notes: Blanks indicate data is not available.
        * Sales and assets are denominated in US$ billion and employment in thousands.

Source: Estimates based on data from Disclosure Inc. and Expansión.

In contrast, the top American service firms are more concentrated in the communications industry (Table 10).

In short, the industrial distribution of the top firms in all three countries included in this analysis, especially in Canada and the United States, is consistent with the aggregate industrial distribution of their trade flows and outward direct investment stock. These broad trends underline the relative strengths and weaknesses of the three economies, which are examined further in the next section.

Revealed Comparative Advantage

This section considers the revealed comparative advantage of Canada and the United States only, with reference to aggregate industry data and firm-specific data. The limitations of Mexican data, particularly for the top firms, make this type of analysis difficult, and therefore, analysis of the revealed comparative advantage of Mexico has not been included in this study.

Over the long term, firms and nations tend to specialize in products and services that they produce relatively more efficiently than their competitors and trading partners. Similarly, they buy those products and services which their trading partners produce relatively more efficiently. Thus, the commodity/industry composition of exports (sales) and imports (purchases) of firms and nations should reveal their comparative advantage position, provided there is a strong competition in international markets and relatively little government intervention in the marketplace.[10]

In the past, economists have computed the comparative advantage indicator of countries based on either commodity or industrial distribution of their merchandise exports. Using similar methods, three indicators of the comparative advantage position of Canada vis-à-vis the United States were estimated: trade, direct investment stocks, and the sales of the top firms. The first two measures are based on aggregate industry data. The last indicator was developed using individual firm data.

The trade-based measure for a particular industry is calculated as the ratio of that industry's share in total Canadian merchandise exports to the United States to its share in total merchandise imports from the United States. If the ratio is greater than 1, it indicates a comparative advantage for Canada vis-à-vis the United States in that industry. On the other hand, a ratio of less than 1 implies a comparative advantage for the United States. Using similar procedures, indicators of comparative advantage were computed for investment and firm sales.

All three indicators of specialization demonstrate that Canada has a revealed comparative advantage in resources, resource-based manufacturing and financial services vis-à-vis the United States. The comparative advantages shown through the trade statistics indicate that Canada has a significant advantage in paper and publishing, lumber and furniture and primary metals industries. Similarly, the direct investment statistics and the sales of top firms

TABLE 11

INDUSTRIAL DISTRIBUTION OF DOMESTIC- AND FOREIGN-CONTROLLED CANADIAN FIRMS (% OF TOTAL)

INDUSTRY	DOMESTIC-CONTROLLED				FOREIGN-CONTROLLED			
	NO. OF FIRMS	ASSETS	SALES	EMPLOYEES	NO. OF FIRMS	ASSETS	SALES	EMPLOYEES
Mining	10	2.42	6.00	5.15	10	41.83	23.38	8.51
Construction	2	0.10	0.66	0.59	0			
Labour-intensive Manufacturing	7	1.43	3.69	6.05	0			
Resource-intensive Manufacturing	26	10.79	26.25	27.78	5	5.04	4.33	4.53
Technology-intensive Manufacturing	4	1.19	3.44	5.30	13	29.75	50.69	30.83
Transportation	8	3.25	6.47	12.08	1	1.69	1.52	0.35
Communications	5	4.29	5.79	7.63	0			
Utilities	11	8.77	6.13	3.81	1	2.71	1.30	0.73
Trade	22	2.32	14.50	15.82	8	18.57	17.77	54.81
Finance	24	65.44	27.08	15.79	1	0.41	1.00	0.24
Total	119	100.00	100.00	100.00	39	100.00	100.00	100.00

Note: Blanks indicate data not available.
Source: Estimates based on data from Disclosure Inc.

exhibit advantages in Canadian resource based-manufacturing. These last two indicators also show significant comparative advantages for Canada in banking, finance, insurance and real estate industries (Table 12).

The United States, on the other hand, has a comparative advantage in technology-intensive manufacturing, trade, and service industries. The trade statistics also demonstrate the U.S. advantages in labour-intensive manufacturing industries — specifically, textiles, leather, clothing, and miscellaneous manufacturing industries. Direct investments and sales of top firms confirm the U.S. advantages in technology-intensive industries such as chemicals and chemical products and machinery and equipment manufacturing industries.

The trade and sales statistics demonstrate clearly that the Canadian and U.S. economies have minimal advantages with respect to each other in primary industries and transportation equipment industries. In the case of transportation, the indices of revealed comparative advantage may be less significant, given the large amounts of intra-firm trade (Table 12).[11]

The similarity of all three indicators of revealed comparative advantage suggest that the structure and activities of the top firms in the two countries

TABLE 12

CANADA'S REVEALED COMPARATIVE ADVANTAGE VIS-À-VIS THE UNITED STATES, 1991

INDUSTRY	TRADE	DIRECT INVESTMENT	SALES OF TOP FIRMS
Primary Industry	1.0		1.2
Food, Beverages & Tobacco	1.2	1.0	1.0
Paper & Publishing	3.3 }	1.2	1.6
Lumber & Furniture	1.7 }		
Primary Metals	2.2 }		
Fabricated Metals	0.8 }	1.2	1.7
Non-metal Mineral Products	0.8 }		
Rubber & Plastic Products	0.8		
Textiles, Leather & Clothing	0.5		
Chemical Products	0.7	0.2	0.1
Non-electrical Machinery	0.6 }		0.5
Electrical Machinery	0.4 }	0.4	0.5
Transportation Equipment	1.2 }		0.9
Miscellaneous Manufacturing	0.3		0.1
Trade		0.1	1.1
Banking		4.4	2.0
Finance, Insurance & Real Estate		2.2	1.6
Services		0.9	

Note. Blanks indicate data are not available.
Source: Estimates based on data from U.S. Department of Commerce, Statistics Canada and Disclosure Inc.

play a major role in shaping the patterns of aggregate direct investment stock and trade flows between the two countries. These results also imply that firms in the two countries generally use direct investment as an additional vehicle, in conjunction with exports, to exploit their broad areas of comparative advantage to the fullest, rather than to specialize in new areas. It is important to note, however, that factors other than comparative advantage contribute to a firm's use of direct investments. These factors include problems with market access, risk diversification, product specialization, and relative conditions in product and factor markets of the two countries.

Fastest Growing Canadian Companies   A number of industry observers in Canada have suggested that many small- and medium-size domestic companies have found niches in the technology-intensive and knowledge-intensive areas, and are experiencing rapid sales and export growth. This might appear to be inconsistent with the results of the revealed comparative advantage analysis. To capture the dynamism of these companies, and their possible effect on future comparative advantage position of Canada, we analyzed the characteristics of the 100 fastest-growing Canadian firms listed in the Profit survey (June 1992).

According to this survey, the fastest-growing companies are relatively small and new. Most were established in the first half of the 1980s. In 1991 their revenue ranged between $1 million and $70 million, and a majority of them had sales under $10 million. Their employment varied between 500 and 600 people. A large number of these firms are engaged in technology and knowledge-intensive activities such as software development and marketing, software and computer consulting, CAD/CAM services, industrial and telecommunication equipment manufacturing, cellular phone sales and service, environmental and engineering consulting, and so forth.

Between 1986 and 1991, revenue of the 100 fastest-growing Canadian companies increased from a low of 229 percent to a high of 9,738 percent. Similarly, the employment of these firms increased by between 44 percent and 6,500 percent. In addition, exports accounted for a significant share (between 10 percent and 99 percent) for 30 of the 100 firms. Furthermore, more than half of the fastest-growing firms invested between 1 percent and 25 percent of their total revenues in R&D.

While there is no doubt that these dynamic small- and medium-size firms in Canada are of significance, the fact remains that the larger firms, because of their size and dominance, define the composition of industry in each country.

PERFORMANCE

Productivity Performance

At the outset, as background to the findings of this study, it is useful to recall a report on Canada's competitive position published by the Economic Council of Canada in 1992. *Pulling Together* compared Canada's aggregate trade, productivity and innovation performance with the performance of other G-7 countries. Some of its major findings concerning Canada's productivity record include the following:

- Along with other industrialized countries, Canada has experienced a deep and pervasive decline in productivity growth since the oil-price shock of 1973.

- The longstanding aggregate U.S./Canada manufacturing labour productivity gap narrowed substantially between 1950 and 1985. The decline was from 85 percent in 1950 to 23 percent in 1985.

- However, the gap widened again between 1985 and 1990 — falling back to 41 percent in 1990. In addition, Canada lost considerable ground to other G-7 countries during this period.

- Canadian problems with respect to manufacturing productivity are not confined to just a few industries; they are rather more broadly based.

- Better labour productivity performance (level as well as growth) in the non-manufacturing industries more than offset the weak manufacturing performance, thereby closing the gaps between aggregate U.S./Canada labour productivity and real income in the post-war period, especially in the 1980s.

In general, the relative productivity performance of the top Canadian and American firms, reported below, reflects these findings.

Productivity Levels of the Top North American Firms   For purposes of assessing the productivity performance of the top firms, two indicators of productivity for each of the top firms were computed: sales per employee, and the sales/assets ratio. Sales and assets in the countries are expressed in a common currency, the U.S. dollar. These indicators are proxies for labour and capital productivity measures, respectively.

The productivity of only the top domestically controlled Canadian firms is compared with the productivity of U.S. firms, disaggregated by industry because the use of sales as a proxy for output can bias upward the estimates of labour and capital productivity of firms and industries with a significant amount of intra-firm sales. This problem is particularly acute when the productivity levels of domestically controlled firms are compared with those of foreign-controlled firms — the sales figures of foreign-controlled firms often include large amounts of imports from their parents. Much of the intra-firm import activity of foreign affiliates is therefore not related to their production activities. Instead, they are acting mainly as distribution networks for their parent companies. Consequently, since foreign-controlled firms account for over 20 percent of the top Canada-based firms, the productivity measures considerably bias upward the productivity estimates for the top Canadian firms in relation to their U.S. counterparts.

Findings   Labour productivity of the top Canadian-controlled firms in the manufacturing sector is on average 20 percent to 30 percent below the productivity levels of U.S. firms, but the productivity of the top Canadian-controlled firms is well above the U.S. levels in the construction, utilities, trade and financial services industries. These measures more than offset the Canadian disadvantage in manufacturing and certain other industries. Consequently, the labour productivity of the top Canadian-controlled firms in all industries exceeds American productivity by 23 percent.

Labour productivity (sales per employee, measured in US$) of the top U.S. manufacturing firms is, on average, about 20 percent higher than the productivity of the top domestically controlled Canadian firms (Table 13). The table clearly shows labour productivity to be lower in Canada in the three manufacturing sub-sectors. In terms of the purchasing power parity (PPP) exchange rate used in the Economic Council's recent productivity research, the productivity of top U.S. firms is about 30 percent higher than the productivity of Canadian firms.

Labour productivity of the top domestically controlled Canadian firms in the resource-intensive manufacturing industries is on average 14 percent below that of the top American firms. In the technology-intensive manufacturing industries, labour productivity of the top domestically controlled Canadian firms is almost 35 percent below the level of top U.S. firms. Like manufacturing, labour productivity of the top American firms is considerably above the productivity of the Canadian-controlled firms in mining, transportation and communications industries.

In contrast, labour productivity of the top Canadian-controlled firms in the construction, utilities, trade and financial services industries are well above the American productivity levels. Note that the average size of the top Canada-based firms also compares favourably with the average size of the American firms in the utilities, trade and financial services industries. These findings are consistent with the conclusions of the Economic Council's recent work on aggregate industrial productivity.

The relative performance of capital productivity of the top Canadian-controlled firms *vis-à-vis* the U.S. firms is the opposite of the findings on labour productivity (Table 13). Unlike the case of labour productivity, the capital productivity of domestically controlled Canadian manufacturing firms is superior to the performance of the American firms. On the other hand, the capital productivity of the top U.S. firms in utilities is higher than the productivity of the Canadian-controlled firms. On average, the capital productivity of U.S. firms is well above the Canadian level, at 56 percent.

In sum, labour productivity of the top Canadian-controlled firms in all industries exceeds, on average, the productivity of the top American firms by 23 percent. However, their capital productivity is 56 percent below the productivity of American firms. These divergent results imply that the productivity of both labour and capital inputs — total productivity (TP) — of the Canadian firms is about 3 percent to 5 percent below the productivity of American firms.

In contrast, labour productivity of the top Canadian-controlled manufacturing firms is on average 20 percent to 30 percent below the productivity of U.S. firms. However, capital productivity of the Canadian firms is 20 percent to 50 percent above the productivity of U.S. manufacturing firms. These results in turn suggest that the productivity of both labour and capital inputs — (TP) of the Canadian-controlled manufacturing firms — is, on average, only 5 percent to 10 percent below the U.S. productivity in manufacturing. (Note that the labour share in gross output is about twice the capital share.)

TABLE 13

PRODUCTIVITY PERFORMANCE OF TOP U.S., DOMESTICALLY CONTROLLED CANADIAN, AND MEXICAN FIRMS

INDUSTRY	UNITED STATES			DOMESTICALLY CONTROLLED CANADIAN			MEXICAN	
	NO. OF FIRMS	SALES/ EMPLOYMENT RATIO	SALES/ ASSET RATIO	NO. OF FIRMS	SALES/ EMPLOYMENT RATIO	SALES/ ASSET RATIO	NO. OF FIRMS	SALES/ EMPLOYMENT RATIO
Agriculture & Fishing	3	110.72	1.49	0			0	
Mining	25	537.19	1.04	10	222.25	0.80	1	46.05
Construction	9	186.29	1.17	2	215.17	2.15	1	
Labour-intensive Manufacturing	44	134.65	0.94	7	116.27	0.83	0	
Resource-intensive Manufacturing	109	207.16	1.09	26	180.22	1.59	10	68.55
Technology-intensive Manufacturing	193	166.64	0.80	4	123.72	0.93	7	49.79
Transportation	23	129.70	0.88	8	102.20	0.64	1	81.06
Communications	19	160.56	0.60	5	144.80	0.44	2	82.86
Utilities	86	276.68	0.44	11	306.78	0.23	0	
Trade	119	53.06	1.61	22	174.85	2.02	3	80.59
Finance	145	306.68	0.14	24	327.15	0.13	2	170.99
Services	48	104.69	0.81	0			0	$\int$
Total	823	141.77	0.50	119	190.77	0.32	27	68.21

Note: Blanks indicate data not available.
Source: Estimates based on data from Disclosure Inc. and Expansión.

The labour productivity level of the top Mexican firms is considerably lower than the productivity levels of the top U.S. and the domestically controlled Canadian firms in all industries. For instance, labour productivity of the top Mexican firms varies from 20 percent to 80 percent of the top Canadian controlled firms' productivity levels.

The Mexican manufacturing wages, however, are only 20 percent to 25 percent of the Canadian wages, implying substantial unit labour cost advantage for the top Mexican firms. But competition from the Mexican firms for the top Canadian and American companies will likely be very limited in the medium to long term for two reasons. First, labour costs account for less than 20 percent of the total costs in manufacturing and their importance has been steadily declining. Second, as discussed earlier, the top Mexican firms account for a very small share of total Mexican employment.

Growth Performance

Given that the growth of sales, employment and capital are important determinants of productivity growth, this section examines the growth of the top Canadian and U.S. firms over a five-year period. Detailed data for Mexican firms were not available from the database.

Between 1986 and 1991, the sales of top American firms increased at a considerably faster pace than those of their Canadian counterparts in all the major industries, except the financial services industry (Table 14). For instance, the sales of the top American firms in the resource-intensive manufacturing industries grew by 9.3 percent per year, compared to only 5.4 percent growth for the Canadian firms. Similarly, in the technology-intensive industries, the growth of the top American firms exceeded the Canadian sales growth by 4.5 percentage points per year.

The relatively weak performance of the top Canadian manufacturing firms could be due largely to two important developments: the deterioration of the cost performance of Canadian manufacturers in relation to the American firms during the period; and the increased competitive position of U.S. firms vis-à-vis their overseas competitors. In turn, the weak growth performance of the Canadian manufacturing sector likely spilled over to the Canadian service industries because of the strong interdependence between the two sectors.

Despite the strong growth performance in sales, employment of the top American firms experienced slower growth in the manufacturing industries between 1986 and 1991. These two developments imply a considerable improvement in U.S. manufacturing labour productivity during the period. For example, in the technology-intensive manufacturing industries, employment of the top U.S. firms increased by a mere 1.2 percent per year, compared to 8.3 percent sales growth.

The employment of the top Canadian firms in the technology-intensive industries increased by 1.3 percent per year, compared to 1.2 percent in the United

States. Employment by Canadian firms in labour-intensive manufacturing increased by 6.4 percent compared to 2.4 percent in U.S. industries. However, in resource-intensive manufacturing, Canadian firms' employment declined by 1.8 percent per year, compared to 2.3 percent growth of the top American firms.[12]

The stronger American sales growth in combination with similar employment growth in the two countries implies a significantly faster labour productivity growth for the top U.S. manufacturing firms relative to their Canadian counterparts. These results are consistent with the narrowing of the aggregate U.S.-Canada manufacturing productivity gap between 1986 and 1991, which is discussed in more detail later.[13]

As with sales, the top American manufacturing firms generally experienced faster growth in assets than their Canadian counterparts (Table 14). For example, the assets of American technology-intensive manufacturing firms increased by 19.3 percent per year during the 1986-91 period, compared to 11.5 percent in Canada. In contrast, Canadian firms recorded faster growth in assets in the mining, labour-intensive manufacturing, transportation, utilities, communications and financial services industries.

In Mexico, there was a increase of between 60 percent and 100 percent in the sales and between 43 percent and 90 percent in the assets of the top 27 Mexican firms between 1986 and 1991. However, this rapid growth could be due largely to the marked rise in Mexican prices and high levels of inflation during this

TABLE 14

FIVE-YEAR GROWTH PERFORMANCE, AVERAGE ANNUAL GROWTH (%)

INDUSTRY	SALES GROWTH		ASSET GROWTH		EMPLOYMENT GROWTH	
	U.S.	CANADA	U.S.	CANADA	U.S.	CANADA
Agriculture & Fishing	5.27		15.99		1.85	
Mining	6.59	5.04	2.17	5.37	(0.14)	(2.62)
Construction	10.66	0.80	21.08	(8.42)	2.24	(0.19)
Labour-intensive Manufacturing	12.96	11.73	20.26	20.53	2.36	6.39
Resource-intensive Manufacturing	9.31	5.35	12.15	9.91	2.33	(1.84)
Technology-intensive Manufacturing	8.34	3.75	19.26	11.45	1.19	1.29
Transportation	9.85	5.93	6.28	6.53	6.76	1.69
Communications	9.14	7.45	6.64	12.85	0.94	1.79
Utilities	6.06	4.10	5.35	5.79	3.83	0.80
Trade	11.52	3.22	12.92	5.35	0.39	(0.30)
Finance	4.73	17.63	5.03	15.73	0.93	0.54
Services	17.15		19.62		4.06	

Note: Blanks indicate data not available.
        Brackets indicate negative growth.
Source: Estimates based on data from Disclosure Inc.

period, factors that were not as prevalent in the United States and Canada.

R&D Performance

Numerous studies have documented the importance of R&D for productivity performance at the firm and industry level.[14] Ergo, R&D expenditure is an important determinant of inter-firm, inter-industry and inter-country differences in productivity levels; and R&D plays a significant role in the determination of the productivity growth of firms, industries and countries.

The R&D performance of the top Canadian and American firms, measured by the R&D-sales ratio, is set out in Table 15. The average R&D intensity of the top firms in the technology-intensive manufacturing industries is considerably higher than that for firms in other manufacturing industries in both Canada and the United States. For instance, the average R&D/sales ratio in the U.S. resource-intensive manufacturing industries is only 1.34 percent, compared to 5.13 percent in the technology-intensive manufacturing industries.

It is notable, however, that the top U.S. non-manufacturing firms invest significantly in R&D. For instance, the average R&D intensity of the top American firms in the commercial services (8.3 percent) and agriculture, forestry and fishing (7.3 percent) industries is considerably higher than that of the top American firms in the technology-intensive manufacturing industries (5.1 percent).

TABLE 15

R&D PERFORMANCE OF CANADIAN AND U.S. FIRMS
R&D EXPENDITURES AS A % OF SALES

INDUSTRY	CANADA	UNITED STATES
Agriculture & Fishing		7.30
Mining	1.54	0.90
Construction		4.57
Labour-intensive Manufacturing	1.38	1.01
Resource-intensive Manufacturing	0.56	1.34
Technology-intensive Manufacturing	2.21	5.13
Transportation		
Communications		
Utilities		1.68
Trade		1.03
Finance		0.98
Services		8.26

Note: Blanks indicate data not available.
Source: Estimates based on data from Disclosure Inc.

In general, the R&D intensity of the top Canada-based firms is considerably lower than the top American firms. For instance, in the technology-intensive manufacturing industries, the R&D intensity of the top Canadian firms averages 2.2 percent, compared to 5.1 percent of the American firms. Nevertheless, in mining and labour-intensive manufacturing industries, the R&D performance level of Canadian firms is significantly better than that of their U.S. counterparts.

Many have speculated on why Canada's R&D performance generally lags behind the U.S. (and other industrialized partners). One explanation is that the small size of the Canadian market plays an important role in the decisions of firms to concentrate on applied R&D compared to basic R&D. Thus, it can be argued that Canadian firms invest in R&D primarily for the purpose of adopting new advanced technologies developed in the United States and other countries.

CHARACTERISTICS

Average Size

Another determinant of the productivity of top firms is the average size of their sales, assets and employment. The larger the size of these elements, other things being equal, the more opportunity a firm has to take advantage of scale economies in production, R&D and marketing, and to improve its productivity and cost performance. The firm size also plays an important role in the determination of a firm's R&D performance and in the adoption of new and state-of-the-art product and process technologies.

Past research has indicated that about one-third of the gap between the U.S. and Canadian manufacturing productivity levels is attributable to the difference in the average size of firms in the two countries.[15] To shed further light on this important policy issue, the average size of top firms in the three NAFTA countries was computed in terms of assets, sales and employment, disaggregated by sector. These results are summarized in Table 16.

The average sales of all the top U.S. firms is US$ 4.7 billion, compared to the average asset size of US$ 9.5 billion. However, the average size varies substantially across individual industries. For instance, average sales range from a low of US$ 1.88 billion in the service industry to a high of US $13.2 billion in the mining industry. The average sales of top firms in the mining, technology-intensive manufacturing, transportation and trade industries is considerably higher than the aggregate firm size.

In contrast, the average firm size is substantially smaller in the labour-intensive manufacturing and services industries. However, the average asset size of top firms in the mining, financial services, and communications industries is substantially larger than the average of all the top U.S. firms.

The average size of top American firms is over twice the Canadian level in most of the industries. In addition, the size disadvantage is acute in the mining, construction, technology-intensive manufacturing and communications industries. On the other hand, the average size of top Canadian firms in general compares favourably with their U.S. counterparts in the labour-intensive manufacturing, utilities and financial services industries.

The average size of the top Mexican firms is high by the standards of developing countries. By sales, the average size of Mexican firms is less than the average Canadian firm size. This is due mainly to the large-scale disadvantage of the top Mexican firms in the transportation, communication and finance industries. On the other hand, the average firm size of the top Mexican firms compares favourably with the Canadian firm size in resource-intensive manufacturing and construction industries.

In short, the average size of top Canadian and Mexican firms is well below the size of top American firms. This supports the view that the North American Free Trade Agreement will enable the top Canadian and Mexican firms to obtain freer and more secure access to the large U.S. market. This should help Canada and Mexico to grow and overcome their size disadvantages and should also improve their competitive position relative to their U.S. and overseas competitors.

Globalization and Outward Orientation

A number of factors have contributed to a borderless world for consumers as well as for producers — the rapid tempo of product and process technologies, the communications revolution, the rapid, world-wide diffusion of new technologies, the liberalization of trade, direct investment and financial flows across countries and the convergence of consumer tastes around the globe. These trends, in conjunction with the emergence of the Asia Pacific Rim as a major player in the world economy, have intensified competition among firms and nations for markets and technology. In addition, shorter product cycles and the increased scope for imitation which is, in turn, the result of rapid changes in technology, have substantially reduced the pay-offs from new innovations. But the fixed R&D costs of developing, commercializing and marketing new product and process technologies are very high and rising rapidly. Moreover, the uncertainty associated with the creation and commercialization of new technologies has been increasing steadily.

These developments have necessitated global sourcing of all factor inputs and a speedier entry of business into all major markets of the OECD. Toward this end, firms are becoming increasingly global in their outlook and are establishing production, sourcing, research and marketing facilities in all the important international markets either on their own or by undertaking various types of joint ventures with firms from other countries. This trend applies to both MNEs as well as to domestically based enterprises.

In short, due to the rapidly changing patterns of comparative advantage and fierce and growing international competition, firms (especially MNEs) are

TABLE 16

AVERAGE FIRM SIZE FOR TOP U.S., CANADIAN AND MEXICAN FIRMS

	UNITED STATES			
INDUSTRY	NO. OF FIRMS	ASSETS (US$ MILLION)	SALES (US$ MILLION)	EMPLOYEES ('000)
Agriculture & Fishing	3	1,812	2,695	24
Mining	25	12,662	13,198	25
Construction	9	2,811	3,290	18
Labour-Intensive Manufacturing	44	2,099	1,966	15
Resource-Intensive Manufacturing	109	4,261	4,653	22
Technology Intensive Manufacturing	193	7,099	5,712	34
Transportation	23	5,394	4,727	36
Communications	19	17,671	10,578	66
Utilities	86	6,183	2,701	10
Trade	119	3,121	5,018	95
Finance	145	27,986	4,009	13
Services	48	2,316	1,876	18
Total	823	9,485	4,708	33

Note: Blanks indicate data not available.
Source: Estimates based on data from Disclosure Inc. and Expansión.

increasingly becoming global or footloose in their outlook, activities and strategies. This internationalization of business has important implications for national market framework laws and policies as well as for international co-operation and co-ordination.[16]

In this part of our study, the degree of internationalization of the top Canadian and U.S. firms is examined, disaggregating results by industry. The limitations of the available data on top firms again preclude analysis of Mexico. Globalization of the top firms is measured against two variables: the share of foreign assets in relation to the total assets of the firm; and the share of foreign sales in relation to the firm's total sales.[17]

Overall, more than 400 (of the 1,008) firms reported a portion of their assets and sales as foreign located. Furthermore, the analysis of the characteristics of these firms indicates that the degree of outward orientation is not correlated with any definition of the size of the firm.

The share of foreign assets in relation to total assets is over 25 percent for 33 of the 158 top Canadian companies. The top five Canadian global firms are: Thomson Corp. (printing and publishing), Dominion Textiles Inc. (textiles), CAE industries (light machinery), Varity Corp.[18] (non-electrical machinery) and Onex Corp. (wholesale trade). The share of foreign assets of these five companies varies between 66 percent and 90 percent.

TABLE 16 (CONT'D)

	CANADA				MEXICO		
NO. OF FIRMS	ASSETS (US$ MILLION)	SALES (US$ MILLION)	EMPLOYEES ('000)	NO. OF FIRMS	ASSETS (US$ MILLION)	SALES (US$ MILLION)	EMPLOYES ('000)
0				0			
20	3,133	2,410	7	1	3,021	870	19
2	601	1,290	6	1	2,184	1,264	
7	2,471	2,057	18	0			
31	2,830	2,179	14	10	6,716	3,320	18
17	2,249	3,953	15	7	2,294	1,438	27
9	4,510	2,985	28	1	1,141	979	12
5	10,364	4,522	31	2	6,843	3,059	32
12	9,000	2,108	7	0			
30	1,429	2,515	20	3	1,316	1,431	11
25	31,606	4,271	13	2	8,753	2,632	11
0				0			
158	7,852	2,892	15	27	4,619	2,298	19

Similarly, for 184 of the 823 top American firms, the share of foreign assets is greater than 25 percent. The top U.S. outwardly oriented firms are: Aflac Incorporated (insurance), Maxtor Corp. (computer and office equipment), Commodore International Limited (computer and office equipment), Standard Commercial Corp. (tobacco) and NL Industries (chemicals and allied products). Foreign assets account for more than 75 percent of their total assets.

The degree of internationalization or outward orientation of the top American and Canadian companies is fairly significant (over 20 percent) in most of the industries. For instance, in mining, the share of foreign assets of the top U.S. firms in relation to their total assets is 43 percent, compared to 28 percent in the resource-intensive and 25 percent in the technology-intensive manufacturing industries (Table 17). Similarly, the shares of foreign assets of the top American firms outside the goods industries are fairly large, ranging from a low of 11 percent in the communications industry to a high of 27 percent in the services industry. Foreign sales indicators give a similar picture about the foreign activities of the top U.S. firms.

In addition, the outward orientation of the top Canadian firms is substantially higher than that of their American counterparts in all major industries except mining. For instance, in the construction industry, the share of foreign assets of the top Canadian firms is almost 47 percent, compared to a mere 6 percent in the United States (see Table 17). These results are consistent with the results of earlier studies undertaken by the OECD and UNCTC — i.e., firms from smaller, more open economies generally venture abroad earlier than firms from larger economies.

The high degree of outward orientation of the top firms is consistent with the strong trade and investment linkages between the three countries and their strong and growing investment linkages with Europe, Japan and other countries, described earlier. These results in turn imply that the location decisions regarding production, R&D and innovation of the North America-based global firms will play a crucial role in determining the future competitive position of the three North American economies.

CONCLUSIONS

THIS STUDY HAS three main objectives: to provide an overview of integration among the three North American economies; to analyze formally the structure, performance and characteristics of the top North American firms; and to examine the role of the top North American firms in the North American economy. Our sample of the top 1,008 firms (based on total sales) is comprised of 823 American corporations, 158 Canada-based firms and 27 Mexican companies. Collectively, they play a crucial role in shaping the comparative advantage and competitive position of the three countries.

TABLE 17

OUTWARD ORIENTATION OF TOP U.S. AND CANADIAN FIRMS (%)

	FOREIGN ASSETS/TOTAL ASSETS		FOREIGN SALES/TOTAL SALES	
INDUSTRY	UNITED STATES	CANADA	UNITED STATES	CANADA
Agriculture & Fishing	36.41		33.27	
Mining	43.12	26.11	68.63	50.40
Construction	6.21	46.98	19.14	82.34
Labour-intensive Manufacturing	16.20	68.45	22.54	64.75
Resource intensive Manufacturing	28.33	35.97	32.61	54.90
Technology-intensive Manufacturing	25.31	43.80	34.00	27.99
Transportation	20.40	27.12	30.09	33.96
Communications	11.17	21.80	9.35	37.72
Utilities	20.69	1.43	23.44	6.15
Trade	14.18	33.41	15.69	26.93
Finance	24.47	31.35	25.54	56.55
Services	27.28		25.05	

Note: Blanks indicate data not available.
Source: Estimates based on data from Disclosure Inc.

Important findings include:

North American Integration

- Outward direct investments by multinational organizations grew at an average annual rate of 34 percent from 1985 to 1990, more than double the growth rate of world trade or world output.

- Over the last decade, the United States has been transformed from the traditional source country of worldwide investment to a major recipient country of international FDI;

- Between 1989 and 1992, Canada attracted a total of $ 19.8 billion of net FDI flows, or an average of $ 5.0 billion per year. In addition, globalization has led to a diversification in the origins of FDI.

- Faster growth in CDIA relative to FDI stock in the 1980s has resulted in a better balance between Canada's inward and outward investment activity.

- Like FDI, CDIA has gradually moved away from the traditional U.S. market and into Europe.

- The industrial distribution of trade flows, direct investment stock and the activities of the top firms suggest that Canada has a comparative advantage in resources and resource-intensive manufacturing and financial services. On the other hand, the United States specializes in technology-intensive manufacturing and commercial services. The United States and Canada are similar, however, to the extent that they are both leading industrialized economies that reflect their comparable levels of national income.

- Mexico concentrates on the production of resources and low skill-intensive and low value-added resource- and technology-intensive manufacturing. While this industrial composition reflects Mexico's status as a newly industrializing economy, it still includes a relatively high proportion of technology-intensive production. This is due to the strong linkages with the United States and intra-firm trade. Relative to Canada and the United States, Mexico's production is concentrated in low value-added goods.

Top North American Firms

- The top firms play a major role in the North American economy. Their combined total assets and sales in 1991 were US$ 9.2 and US$ 4.4 trillion, respectively. They employed over 30 million people. The top Canadian and American companies account for over 50 percent of the gross output and at least 25 percent of the GDP of Canada and the United States.

- The industrial distribution of the top firms in all industries is consistent with the aggregate industrial distribution of each country's trade flows and direct investment stock.

- The trade, outward investment and sales indicators of specialization all demonstrate that Canada has a revealed comparative advantage in resources, resource-based manufacturing and financial services *vis-à-vis* the United States. The United States, on the other hand, has a comparative advantage in technology-intensive manufacturing, trade and service industries.

- Relatively high labour productivity of the top foreign-controlled Canadian firms reflects substantial intra-firm trade in the Canadian manufacturing sector, especially in the technology-intensive industries.

- Labour productivity of Canadian-controlled firms is well above the U.S. level in construction, utilities, trade and financial services. As a result, the labour productivity of the top Canadian-controlled firms in all industries exceeds that of the American firms by 23 percent. But total productivity (TP) — i.e., the combined total of the productivity inputs of both labour and capital — of all the top Canadian firms is 3 percent to 5 percent below the productivity of the top American firms.

- However, similar to recent analysis regarding the aggregate productivity trends in the United States and Canada, labour productivity (sales per employee) of the top domestically controlled Canadian manufacturing firms is on average 20 percent to 30 percent below the productivity of the top American manufacturing firms in 1991. Stronger sales growth of the top U.S. firms during the 1986-91 period likely contributed significantly to the productivity gap.

- The combined productivity of capital and labour inputs of the top Canadian-controlled manufacturing firms is only 5 percent to 10 percent below the total productivity of top American firms.

- Labour productivity of the top Mexican firms is well below the productivity of the Canadian firms in all the industries (20 percent to 80 percent).

- Employment growth in Canadian manufacturing compared favourably with the experience of U.S. manufacturers between 1986 and1991.

- R&D intensity in the top non-manufacturing American firms compares favourably with the intensity of the technology-intensive manufacturing firms. On average, the R&D/sales ratio of the top Canadian firms is considerably lower than that of the top U.S. firms. However, the R&D performance of the top Canadian firms is significantly better than that of their U.S. counterparts in mining and labour-intensive manufacturing industries.

- The average size of the top American firms is over twice that of the Canadian firms in most of the industries. Nevertheless, the average size of top Canadian firms compares favourably with that of their American counterparts in the labour-intensive manufacturing, utilities and financial services industries. The size disadvantage for Canada-based firms is most noticeable in mining, construction, technology-intensive manufacturing and the communications industries.

- Aside from the resource-intensive manufacturing and construction industries, the average size of the top 27 Mexican firms is significantly smaller than the average Canadian firm size.

- Many of the top Canadian and American firms are global in their outlook, strategies and activities. For instance, foreign assets account for over 25 percent of the total assets of 217 of the top 1,008 corporations and over 400 firms reported foreign assets. In addition, the outward orientation of the top Canadian companies is considerably higher than that of their American counterparts, which is not surprising, given Canada's small domestic market.

Implications

These firm-specific findings strongly confirm the widely accepted conclusions of the previous aggregate analysis regarding the relative strengths and weaknesses of the three North American economies and the recent trends in productivity and profitability in the three countries. Since the top firms are dominant players in the North American economy, their decisions, strategies and activities will no doubt play critical roles in shaping the future competitive positions of the three countries.

Increased economic integration among the three NAFTA countries will likely lead to further specialization by firms and countries. Canada is expected to increase its specialization in resources, resource-intensive manufacturing and financial service industries. The United States, on the other hand, will further increase its specialization in the technology-intensive manufacturing and commercial services industries. Mexican firms will likely concentrate on the low to middle parts of the value-added chain in the manufacturing sector, and their growth could be spectacular as they catch up to their industrialized counterparts.

These results are not surprising. Nevertheless, other dynamic factors should be taken into account when interpreting them. In Canada's case, supplementary data show the fastest-growing firms to be relatively small and not in the top 1,008. They also tend to be in the technology- and knowledge-intensive areas.

It should be noted that while this study shows that the productivity gap in manufacturing between Canada and the United States remains substantial, recent data suggest room for more optimism. Canadian manufacturers have taken several measures to improve their productivity and cost performance during the last three years. The preliminary data also suggest that in 1993 Canadian manufacturing productivity grew at a significantly faster pace than American productivity. Better productivity performance, lower value of the Canadian dollar, and lower wage growth has resulted in closing some of the Canada-U.S. manufacturing cost gap, possibly by as much as 35 percent. But most of the improvement is due to the depreciation of the Canadian dollar.

Pressures on Canadian firms to rationalize and restructure their operations further and to become even more cost competitive will persist. The NAFTA can enable Canadian firms to grow and overcome the possible size disadvantages, to reap the benefits of scale and scope economies and to improve their relative productivity performance. Vertical linkages and alliances with Mexican firms could also help them to improve their relative cost and productivity performance.

ENDNOTES

1 An MNE is typically an enterprise form which entails integrated affiliates or subsidiaries in at least two national markets, functioning as part of an operationally unified global entity

2 For an excellent discussion of the role of MNEs in the rising global economic integration, see Encarnation (1992), Reich (1991) and Ohmae (1985).

3 Resource depletion, particularly in mining, may constrain the future growth of primary industries.

4 For details, see Encarnation (1992, 1993).

5 For details, see United Nations Centre for Transnational Corporations (UNCTC), *World Investment Report 1992: Transnational Corporations as Engines of Growth* and *World Investment Report 1993: Transnational Corporations and Integrated International Production.*

6 A detailed discussion of the growth and trade records of the Asia Pacific Rim countries is given in Rao (1992).

7 For a detailed description of Canada's trade and investment linkages with the Asia Pacific Rim, see Rao (1992).

8 A detailed description of the selection procedure, the data sources and the list of the top firms is provided in the longer version of the paper, Industry Canada Working Paper Number 1.

9 This industry grouping is consistent with the commonly used practices of the Economic Council of Canada and the OECD.

10 An excellent discussion of the concept of revealed comparative advantage is given in Balassa (1977).

11 These results are similar to the findings of Letourneau (1992), Magun (1992) and Eden & Molot (1992).

12 Employment growth was unavailable for most Mexican firms in the database.

13 For a detailed analysis of Canada's productivity record during the past 25 years, see Economic Council of Canada (1992) and Rao & Lemprière (1992).

14 For a detailed survey of the theoretical and empirical research on the linkages between R&D and productivity, see Griliches (1984) and Mohnen (1992).

15 For details, see Baldwin & Gorecki (1986).

16 See Reich (1991) and Ohmae (1985).

17 With the exception of Ford Canada, the assets and sales of Canadian subsidiaries of U.S. firms in the motor vehicle and equipment industries are included in the parent firms' statistics.

18 The Varity Corporation reincorporated as a U.S. company on July 31, 1991. Shareholders of the company became stockholders of the New Varity, a Delaware corporation. The new company is the holding concern of the old firm and its subsidiaries.

Acknowledgements

WE ARE GRATEFUL TO Alan Nymark, Ross Preston, Emmy Verdun and Lorraine Eden for their support and their comments on the draft paper. We would like to thank Christopher Wilkie for his conceptual help, and Viren Joshi and Gilles Mcdougall for their help at the early stages. We acknowledge Cheryl Fumerton, Corinne Nolan and Bonny Dupras for their technical assistance.

Bibliography

Banco De Mexico. *The Mexican Economy, 1992.*
Baldwin, J.R., and P.K. Gorecki. *The Role of Scale in Canada-U.S. Productivity Differences in the Manufacturing Sector, 1970-79,* A Research Study prepared for the Royal Commission on the Economic Union and Development Prospects for Canada (Macdonald Commission). Toronto: University of Toronto Press, 1986.
Balassa, B. *Revealed Comparative Advantage Revisited; an Analysis of Export Shares of the Industrial Countries: 1953-71,* The Manchester School of Economic and Social Studies 45, 1977.
Dunning, J.H. and R.D. Pearce. *The World's Largest Industrial Enterprises: 1962-83.* New York: St. Martin's Press, 1985.
Dunning, J.H., (ed.). *Multinational Enterprises, Economic Structure and International Competitiveness.* London and New York: John Wiley and Sons, 1985.
_____. "MNE Activity and Regional Integration in Europe and North America: Some Comparisons and Contrasts," mimeo, 1993.
Economic Council of Canada. *Pulling Together: Productivity, Innovation and Trade.* Ottawa: Ministry of Supply and Services, 1992.
Eden, L. "Multinationals in North America: After NAFTA," mimeo, 1993.
Eden, L. and M. A. Molot. "The North American Trade Block." *Canadian Business Economics,* 1, 1, (1992).
Encarnation, D.J. "Transforming NAFTA: Foreign Investment and Related Trade by Multinational Corporations," mimeo, 1993.
Encarnation, D.J. *Rivals Beyond Trade; America versus Japan in Global Flows.* Ithica, N.Y.: Cornell University Press, 1992.
Griliches, Z., (ed.). *R&D, Patents and Productivity.* Chicago: University of Chicago Press, 1984.
Letourneau, R. "Canada's Trade Performance: World Market Shares and its Comparative Advantage." Working Paper No. 43. Ottawa: Economic Council of Canada, 1992.
Magun, S. "The Role of Trade in North American Integration." In *The North American Free Trade Agreement: Labour, Industry and Government Perspectives.* Edited by M.F. Begnanno and K.J. Ready. Westport, Conn.: Quroum Books, 1992.
McFetridge, D., (ed.). *Foreign Investment, Technology and Economic Growth,* The Investment Canada Research Series. Calgary: University of Calgary Press, 1991.

Mohnen, P. *The Relationship between R&D and Productivity Growth in Canada and Other Industrialized Countries*, Economic Council of Canada. Ottawa: Canada Communication Group, 1992.

Ohmae, K. "TRIAD Power: The Coming Shape of Global Competition, The Free Multinational Corporations," mimeo, 1985.

Porter, M.E. *The Competitive Advantage of Nations*. New York: The Free Press, 1990.

Rao, P.S. "The Asia Pacific Rim: Opportunities and Challenges to Canada," Working Paper No. 37. Ottawa: Economic Council of Canada, 1992.

Rao, P.S., and T. Lemprière. "Linkages between Trade Flows, Productivity and Costs," Discussion Paper No. 46. Ottawa: Economic Council of Canada, 1992a.

_____. *Canada's Productivity Performance*, Economic Council of Canada, Ottawa: Canada Communication Group, 1992b.

Reich, R. *The Work of Nations*. New York: Vintage Books, 1991.

UNCTC. "Activities of the Transnational Corporations and Management Division and its Joint Units: The Universe of Transnational Corporations," mimeo, 1993.

UNCTC. *World Investment Report 1992: Transnational Corporations as Engines of Economic Growth*. New York: 1992.

Unger, K. "Foreign Direct Investment and Trade in Mexico," mimeo, 1993.

Lorraine Eden
Professor
The Norman Paterson School of International Affairs
Carleton University

8

Who Does What after NAFTA?
Location Strategies of U.S. Multinationals

Imagine a chessboard where, in addition to the chess pieces, there are immovable blocks scattered across the board. The impediments are more numerous in the middle of the board. Two players can manoeuvre the chess pieces around the blocks but clearly the game is less efficient than one without such barriers. Individuals who play regularly become skilled at taking the barriers into account in their game strategies. Some will hide behind them, others develop methods of avoiding the blocks, others use them to obstruct their opponents. Now suppose the rules of the game are changed and most of the blocks are removed. Several things happen. In the short run, some old strategies no longer work and individuals may lose games that they usually won. Costs are incurred in learning new strategies. It is possible that people who played the old game regularly may adapt more quickly to the new board, or perhaps new players without the handicap of history adapt more quickly. It is probable that flexibility and scanning ability will be key factors affecting success. In the long run, the game should be faster and the players more efficient. The question is: are we better off after removing the blocks?

INTRODUCTION

MULTINATIONAL ENTERPRISES (MNEs) are strategic actors in the world economy.[1] They are large, oligopolistic firms with foreign affiliates in several host countries. Their affiliates share common goals, have access to a common pool of financial, human and physical resources, and are under the common control of their parent firms. As Raymond Vernon has long argued, these three characteristics of common control, common goals, and common ownership of geographically spread resources create a paradox: on the one hand, they generate conflict between MNEs and nation states; on the other hand, they offer the potential for cooperative behaviour and mutual gain.

Since, by definition, MNEs span national borders, they immediately come into conflict with national governments. Multinational firms have goals that are narrower and more directed (e.g., maximization of long-run returns) than the complex goals of nation states (e.g., a high and rising standard of living, job creation, generation of tax revenues). MNEs have access to broader and more mobile resources. Being located in several countries means these firms can tap into human and physical resources in many locations, and move among locations as technology, endowments and prices dictate. Common control by the parent firm means that decisions affecting thousands of people in host countries can be made by head office staff on the other side of the world. For these reasons, it is not surprising that governments distrust the multinational enterprises in their midst. Home country multinationals are now seen no differently from foreign-based MNEs, because in today's world of interlocking webs among giant firms all MNEs, wherever headquartered, are seen as "them", exercising common control for the benefit of their shareholders, not their home country.

Common control, common goals and common ownership of geographically spread resources also create the potential for mutual gains between MNEs and nation states. Multinational firms have a strategic advantage over domestic firms since MNEs have access to a wider variety of resources and options than domestic firms. This makes multinationals attractive to governments that are interested in improving their country's economic growth and national competitiveness. In the 1980s governments substantially liberalized their economies and opened their doors to multinationals, treating these firms as partners in the growth process. Some authors, John Dunning (1993) for example, have argued that a new era of cooperation between MNEs and nation states — MNEs are "us" — has now replaced the old antagonisms of the 1970s.

This tension between the perceived benefits and costs of multinational enterprises is clearly evident in the current debate over regional free trade in North America. The Canada-U.S. Free Trade Agreement (FTA), which came into effect on January 1, 1989, is widely seen by the general public, the media and labour and social groups in Canada as having caused thousands of job losses, hundreds of plant closures, and the hollowing out of the manufacturing sector particularly in Ontario, as U.S. and Canadian multinationals shifted their operations to the United States. Similarly, both Canadians and Americans are predicting large losses in jobs and production to Mexico if the North American Free Trade Agreement (NAFTA) is ratified and takes effect on January 1, 1994. In both cases, multinationals are generally seen to be the primary beneficiaries of regional free trade, while labour groups and local communities are the losers.

On the other hand, all three governments have substantially liberalized their economies since the early 1980s, specifically in order to attract more inward foreign direct investment (FDI) and to make their own firms more globally competitive. During the FTA and NAFTA negotiations, the three governments were advised by industry groups where MNEs were well represented. Clearly, national governments see MNEs as partners in the international competitiveness process, even if their constituents see them as adversaries.[2] Economic studies of regional integration generally predict substantial gains to national economies from the location responses of multinationals.[3]

In this study, I try to shed some light on this paradox by examining the locational strategies of U.S. multinationals in North America and their likely responses to the NAFTA. Firms in North America may be loosely grouped into three different types. First, there are the veteran multinationals (see Vernon, this volume) which are well established within the North American region. These are primarily U.S.-owned firms, but some are Canadian. Second are the domestics or local firms that have no foreign plants. The domestics may be in either traded sectors (e.g. Mexican auto parts) or non-traded sectors (e.g. grocery stores, public utilities). Mexican firms tend to be primarily domestic (the largest are the Mexican *groupo* firms) as do smaller Canadian firms. Transplants make up the third group, North American subsidiaries with foreign parents, generally located in the United States. The transplants may be just importers and distributors of foreign products or they may have manufacturing capacity.

In this study, the focus will be specifically on the veterans, that is, on U.S. multinationals and their majority-owned foreign affiliates (MOFAs). U.S. MNEs have had branch plants in Canada and Mexico for a long time. In fact, trade and FDI patterns within North America look like a hub-and-spoke economic relationship, with U.S. firms controlling approximately two-thirds of the FDI stock and the merchandise trade flows in both Canada and Mexico (Eden & Molot, 1992). However, the U.S. share of FDI in Canada has been declining and there are also some signs that it may not rapidly increase in Mexico (see both Unger and Niosi, this volume). How will the FTA and the NAFTA affect the configuration of U.S. MNE plant locations in these three countries?

U.S. MNEs are the firms best placed to take advantage of the falling tariff and non-tariff barriers that the FTA and the NAFTA will bring. These firms are the bellwethers of change, leading the way in terms of business reactions to the FTA and the NAFTA. As they alter the configuration of their activities, other firms will follow. Are the labour groups right? Will there be massive job losses and plant closures as U.S. multinationals shift their operations to Mexico to take advantage of cheaper labour and weaker environmental regulations?

THE NAFTA AND PLANT LOCATION

THE NAFTA: MUCH MORE THAN A FREE TRADE AGREEMENT

THE NAFTA IS MUCH MORE than a simple free trade agreement; that is, it eliminates tariff barriers among the three parties, but it does much more than that. As Figure 1 illustrates, the NAFTA liberalizes crossborder trade in just about all product (goods and services) and factors markets in the three countries.[4]

FIGURE 1

EFFECT OF THE NAFTA ON PRODUCT AND FACTOR MARKETS

PRODUCT MARKETS

MARKETS FOR GOODS   MARKETS FOR SERVICES

Commitments to GATT Market Access annexes: autos & textiles Rules of Origin Customs Procedures Agriculture: access, sanitary Emergency Action Standards-related Measures Government Procurement CVD/AD Dispute Settlement	Crossborder Trade in Services Telecommunications Financial Services Land Transportation Reservations: business services Reservations: financial services

FACTOR MARKETS

MARKETS FOR LABOUR   MARKETS FOR CAPITAL

Temporary Entry for Business Persons Side Agreement: labour standards	Investment Competition Policy Reservations: investment

MARKETS FOR LAND   MARKETS FOR TECHNOLOGY

Energy and Basic Petrochemicals Environment Commitments Side Agreement: environment	Intellectual Property

The NAFTA is based on the General Agreement on Tariffs and Trade (GATT). Its clauses are extensions of the GATT principles of nondiscrimination, most favoured nation and reciprocity, applied not only to goods, but also to services, investment and intellectual property. The objectives of the agreement are to eliminate trade barriers, promote fair competition, increase investment opportunities, protect property rights, create effective procedures for administration and dispute resolution, and establish a framework for widening the agreement. The GATT obligations of each Party (nation) are affirmed, but where inconsistencies exist between the NAFTA and other agreements, the NAFTA prevails.[5] The objectives chapter makes it clear that the NAFTA is to be consistent with the GATT article 24 on free trade areas.

The greatest number of chapters in the NAFTA deal with liberalization of crossborder trade in goods, reflecting the GATT origin of the agreement, the more transparent nature of trade barriers in goods than in services and factor markets, and the difficulty of reducing barriers in the latter markets. The NAFTA eliminates tariffs and most non-tariff barriers among the three countries over a 15-year period. Because the agreement does not require harmonization of tariffs against nonmembers, tight rules of origin are introduced to prevent "backdoor" entry into the North American market through the country with the lowest tariffs. Separate deals were struck in textiles and apparel and in autos that are now widely perceived as protectionist, even though tariffs are eliminated, because of their strict domestic content requirements. The NAFTA is the first trade agreement to phase out tariffs and NTBs in agriculture (over 15 years for U.S.-Mexico trade). It also provides for a trilateral dispute settlement process in dumping and export subsidy cases, based on the successful FTA process.

The NAFTA also liberalizes crossborder markets for labour, capital, land and technology; opens up the Mexican economy to Canadian and U.S. investors; provides better security for FDI in North America; and makes exceptions more transparent by forcing governments to identify their exceptions (Rugman and Gestrin, 1993). The NAFTA guarantees national treatment and most-favoured-nation status to North American investors and investments, eliminates performance requirements, and opens up new sectors for investment. Cross-border movement of business persons is allowed. The NAFTA guarantees national treatment and opens up sectors in services (especially financial, telecommunication and cross-border transportation services). An intellectual property rights chapter provides longer patent and copyright protection for technology.

MEASURING THE EFFECTS OF THE NAFTA

BECAUSE THE NAFTA LIBERALIZES almost all product and factor markets in North America it should lead to deeper regional integration than simple tariff reduction exercises predict. Economists who have tried to estimate the economic effects of the NAFTA on the three economies have therefore under-estimated the likely effects of the agreement. General equilibrium economic models are designed to measure small changes in a few policy variables from existing conditions in countries that are roughly similar. However the models do not handle well large changes that involve more than one country at different levels of economic development, eliminating many tariffs and barriers to trade in goods, services and investments simultaneously over a long period. As a result, the models tend to underestimate the effects of major changes.[6]

FIGURE 2

THE PATH TOWARD A NORTH AMERICAN ECONOMY

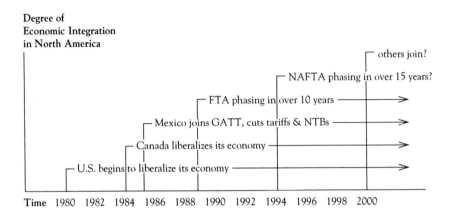

Further confounding the problem of determining the effects of the NAFTA, is the lack of clarity as to what date should be used as the benchmark for computing the effects of a free trade agreement. There are two reasons for this. First, multinationals as strategic actors are best placed to anticipate events such as the FTA and the NAFTA and to act on their beliefs. First mover advantages are important where market share is key to competitiveness; for oligopolistic MNEs this means they must be opportunistic. They are therefore more likely to invest prior to the NAFTA rather than react afterward. Thus much of the investment reaction to the FTA may have happened prior to 1989 and, for the NAFTA, prior to 1994, depending on the probability MNEs attach to the passage of the agreement and their perceptions of what would happen to such investment if the agreement were not passed. The greater the financial assets of the firm and the more importance it attaches to market share, the more likely it will be to have already reorganized its activities on a regional scale in anticipation of the free trade agreement.

Second, the NAFTA can be seen as simply another step in an ongoing process of economic integration of the North American economy. In order to measure the effects of regional free trade we need a date to use as the benchmark against which changes are to be measured. Should it be 1980 or 1984 or 1989 or 1994? As Figure 2 shows, all these dates are important, as all three countries have been liberalizing their economies since the early 1980s.

With respect to external barriers, the U.S. economy has been open to trade and foreign investment inflows since the early 1950s with tariff levels in the 1980s averaging 4 percent. However, quotas, voluntary export restraints, countervailing and anti-dumping duties have frequently been used to provide temporary protection to industries, such as autos and steel, facing serious import penetration.

Historically, Canada has had much higher tariff levels, particularly on manufactured imports, than the United States. The history of U.S. foreign investment in Canada is one of U.S. multinationals locating here to assemble and sell in the local market or to access Canadian natural resources. The main exception to this was the auto industry where the 1965 Auto Pact led to a rationalization of product lines and plant locations on a Canada-U.S. basis.

Until the mid-1980s, Mexico pursued a strategy of import substitution industrialization based on government decrees, licensing, high tariffs, domestic content regulations and restrictions on foreign ownership. As a result, FDI stocks were lower than they might otherwise have been, and they were diverted into particular sectors (e.g. the maquiladoras) where regulations were lower. Much of the FDI has been import-substituting investment designed for the local market. Foreign plants were generally small scale and inefficient.[7]

The first major impetus toward increased integration in North America began in 1980 with the domestic deregulation and privatization of the U.S. economy by President Ronald Reagan. Deregulation in the United States was soon followed by similar action in Canada after Brian Mulroney was elected Prime Minister in 1984. The Canadian and U.S. governments began negotiations for liberalizing crossborder trade through a Canada-U.S. free trade agreement in 1986. The resulting agreement, the FTA, is being phased in over 10 years, starting on January 1, 1989, and is now causing a similar rationalization in other sectors of the economy, as occurred earlier in autos.

In Mexico, the 1982 debt crisis forced President Miguel de la Madrid to reconsider, and then discard, Mexico's long-standing import substitution strategy. Mexico began by unilaterally reducing tariffs and eliminating licenses and quotas, joining the GATT in 1986, and opening the door to foreign investors. As Mexico reduced its trade barriers and liberalized its economy, the focus of FDI moved to export-oriented production. This is most visible in the explosive growth of the maquiladoras in the 1980s and in the autos and electronics industries. In June 1990, Presidents Carlos Salinas and George Bush agreed to begin negotiating a U.S.-Mexico free trade agreement, which was subsequently broadened into trilateral negotiations in 1991. The NAFTA, if it is ratified by the U.S. Congress in the autumn of 1993, will be phased in over 15 years, beginning on January 1, 1994.

Thus, measuring the effects of the NAFTA depends very much on the benchmark selected for comparison. On its own, the NAFTA is simply one event in a process of liberalization and integration of the three economies that started in autos in the 1960s. The benchmark is critical for evaluating its effects. This is illustrated below by comparing worst- and best-case scenarios for Canada if the NAFTA comes into effect in 1994.

THE WORST-CASE AND BEST-CASE SCENARIOS

IN CANADA THE VIEW is widespread that the FTA has been responsible for massive job losses and plant closures as multinationals shifted their operations to the United States. The NAFTA is also expected to cause similar moves to Mexico. In the United States this fear is also pervasive. This section sets out this worst-case scenario and compares it to the best-case scenario as generally put forward by economists and the three governments involved.

Regional Free Trade: The Worst-Case Scenario

Assume a multinational enterprise is vertically integrated with six stages of production. The stages are ranked by level of technological sophistication, with Stage 1 being the least, and Stage 6 being the most, knowledge intensive. The stages need not follow one another in production sequence. For example, in the auto industry the production of engines is technically more advanced than auto assembly, and so engines would be ranked higher than assembly. Assume the goal of the firm is cost minimization, i.e. location of each plant in the cheapest country.

Figure 3 illustrates unit costs of production if a plant were located at each of these stages in Canada, the United States or Mexico. For simplicity we assume straight line cost curves. Unit production costs, which are assumed to rise at each stage, are measured on a CIF (inclusive of insurance and freight costs and customs duties) basis, and reflect the three countries' supplies of high-skilled labour, capital and technology. We assume that Mexico, the least endowed in technology, has the lowest production costs for Stage 1 and the highest for Stage 5, and that its costs rise most rapidly. The United States, the best endowed, has the highest relative costs for Stage 1 and the lowest for Stage 5, and its costs rise most slowly. Canada's unit production costs fall in between those of the other countries.

Based on the shapes of the unit cost curves, Mexico has the lowest costs for Stage 1, Canada for Stages 2, 3 and 4, and the United States for Stage 5. The switch-over points are B and C: below B, plants in Mexico have the lowest per-unit costs, above C, U.S. plants have the lowest costs, while between points B and C, Canada is the cheapest location. Assuming the firm has the ability to site plants in the cheapest location, the MNE therefore puts Stage 1 in Mexico, Stages 2, 3, and 4 in Canada, and Stage 5 in the United States, as represented by the line A-B-C-D.

The first benchmark for comparison purposes is pre-1989. Assume the introduction of the FTA in January 1989 lowers unit production costs in both Canada and the United States because tariffs fall to zero in both countries and

FIGURE 3

EFFECTS OF THE FTA AND THE NAFTA ON THE LOCATION CHOICES OF A VERTICALLY INTEGRATED U.S. MULTINATIONAL

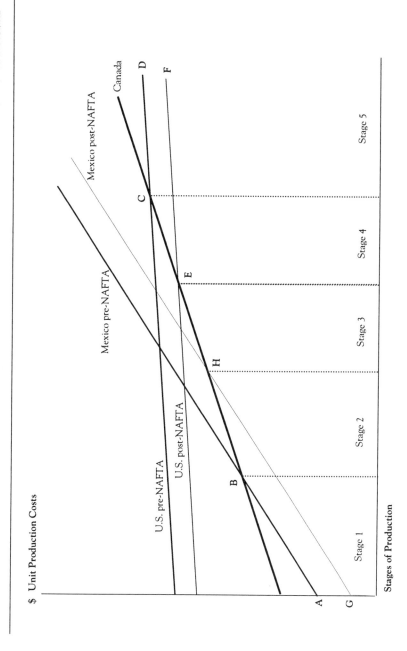

non-tariff barriers are reduced. The worst-case scenario for Canada — and the common public perception — is that with the removal of tariffs and most non-tariff barriers between the two countries, the greater size of the United States together with higher labour costs, taxes, political instability and so on in Canada will cause U.S. multinationals to close their Canadian plants and shift production back to the United States.[8] Effectively, the removal of government-imposed trade barriers means production costs fall in both locations, but the fall is greater in the United States. Instead of modelling this as both cost curves shifting downward, only the U.S. cost curve is shown as shifting downward (the net effect). The switch-over point moves from C to E. The MNE's low-cost production line is now A-B-E-F, with Stage 4 shifted from Canada to the United States. The most technically sophisticated stages of Canadian manufacturing are therefore shifted to U.S. plants.

A more complicated graph would show both the U.S. and Canadian cost curves shifting downward. As a result, Canada's competitiveness as a production location for Stage 1, vis-à-vis Mexico, improves, and there could be some investment diversion from Mexico to Canada, arising from a member country (Canada) becoming a lower cost production location vis-à-vis a non-member country (Mexico) as a result of the formation of a Canada U.S. free trade area.[9]

Now look at the effects of the proposed North American Free Trade Agreement. Like the FTA, the NAFTA reduces tariffs and NTBs, and also substantially liberalizes intra-North American transportation and investment flows. As a result, cost curves for all three countries shift downward; however, since most of the adjustment for Canada and the United States is already happening under the FTA, Mexico is the country most affected by the NAFTA. Only the net adjustment is shown; that is, the Mexican unit cost function shifts downward. The cost function for the MNE becomes G-H-E-F, making Mexico the most efficient site for locating Stages 1 and 2. Note that Stage 2 is shifted from Canada to Mexico, as Canada is assumed to have the next-lowest production costs for this stage. Again, some investment diversion could occur vis-à-vis nonmembers if, for example, U.S. multinationals shift production from plants in East Asia or the Caribbean to Mexico.

Therefore, the worst case for Canada is to be squeezed at both ends by regional free trade. The FTA causes the higher value-added stages to shift to the United States while the NAFTA causes the lower value-added stages to shift to Mexico.[10] This is the belief popularized in the Canadian press and feared by labour, social and environmental groups.

Regional Free Trade: The Best-Case Scenario

The best-case scenario for Canada is to assume that the decline in relative unit costs under the FTA favours Canada over the U.S. as a production location. Since Canada is the smaller of the two countries and had higher barriers before the FTA, instead of showing both Canadian and U.S. unit cost functions shifting downward (with the Canadian one shifting more than the U.S. one), the net shift would be shown as the Canadian cost function shifting downward. Then, as a result of the FTA, the range of activities that are cost efficient in Canada rises and Stage 5 could possibly shift to Canada. Production in Canada also becomes more efficient vis-à-vis Mexico, and Stage 1 may or may not shift to Canada. Thus Canada benefits at both ends of the production process.

As in the worst-case scenerio, the NAFTA will still benefit Mexico as a cost location relative to Canada. However, as Wonnacott and others have argued, there are three problems with seeing this as costly for Canada. First, if Canada does not take part in the NAFTA and a separate U.S.-Mexico free trade agreement is signed, Mexico still becomes a cheaper production location (so that the effect on Canada is the same), but the United States also gets preferential access to the Mexican market (which Canada would lose by not joining the NAFTA unless there were also a separate Canada-Mexico FTA). Thus, Canada loses competitiveness vis-à-vis Mexico as a production location for low-tech activities whether or not it joins the NAFTA. Second, economists argue that low-tech, low-wage production is leaving Canada in any case for locations in less developed countries; not signing the NAFTA will not prevent these (inevitable) job losses. The third argument is that Mexican products have had essentially unlimited access to U.S. and Canadian markets for several years because both countries have granted Mexico preferential tariff treatment as a developing country. Thus the costs of the NAFTA to Canada are small, whereas the benefits to Canada are large as Mexico substantially opens its economy to Canadian investors and exporters.

Some Caveats to the Analysis

There are several caveats that should be noted here. For example, there are other possible scenarios. The cost curves could have been shown as nonlinear such that one country has a cost advantage at both the low-tech and the high-tech stages. Free trade would therefore have less predictable effects, with some high- and low-tech stages shifting to the lower cost location.

Another relevant benchmark for comparison purposes would be to ask what would happen if the free trade agreement were not passed; what would be the base-case scenario? For example, if the NAFTA does not go through it is possible that the anticipatory investments in Mexico may be withdrawn, causing a crisis on the Mexican balance of payments and in the Mexican stock market. Comparing the effects of the NAFTA with the straight-line liberalization picture painted in Figure 2 gives a very different result from one where Mexico, if the NAFTA is not passed, closes its doors to trade and investment and reverts to its protectionist past. Assuming the base case is the pre-1994 situation is the same as assuming Mexico will continue unilaterally to liberalize its economy if NAFTA is not passed — an unlikely situation.

However, the real problem with the above analysis is its simplicity. Other factors also need to be considered. First, technological change will affect the ability of a high-cost location to maintain production once tariff barriers have been removed. Upgrading the labour force, improving the transportation and telecommunications infrastructure, using automation to substitute robots for labour, shifting to flexible automation techniques, and so on may have more effect on production location than changes in tariff and non-tariff barriers.[11] Second, cost is not the only determinant of production location. Production may be tied to a particular location because of the need to be close to customers or the need to use complementary but location-specific resources. Third, horizontal integration has been ignored. Most international trade is intra-industry, intra-firm trade; the FTA will encourage MNE plant rationalization with some product lines being located in U.S. plants, others in Canadian plants and increased intra-firm trade between them (as happened in the Canada-U.S. auto industry as a result of the 1965 Auto Pact).[12] To the extent this happens, free trade will not cause MNEs to shift stages of production between countries but rather to increase the specialization of product lines within stages. Fourth, Figure 3 shows only manufacturing activities. MNEs are also active in natural resources and the service industries (e.g. telecommunications, financial). To the extent that the FTA and the NAFTA increase Canada's competitive advantage as a production location in these activities, FDI in Canada should grow.

EFFECTS OF THE NAFTA ON REVENUES AND COSTS OF FIRMS

THIS DISCUSSION CAN BE made more concrete by looking at the costs of assembling cars, televisions and personal computers in Mexico and the United States, based on data in the U.S. Office of Technology Assessment (1992). In all three cases in Table 1, components are assembled in Mexico and then shipped to the United States for final sale. The table shows clearly that producing in Mexico saves on labour costs but adds transportation costs. Where labour costs are an important part of total costs, assembly is more likely to take place in Mexico. Where shipping and inventory costs are important, assembly is more likely to take place in the United States. Because these products already either enter duty free or face low U.S. tariffs, tariffs are not a consideration affecting plant location. In effect, transport costs act like a trade barrier (see Rousslang & To, 1993, for some estimates of these barriers).

Based on its analysis of several industries, the OTA (1992) argued that a U.S.-Mexico free trade agreement would lead multinationals to choose one of two strategies: a low-cost, mass production model where labour-intensive processes are shifted south to Mexico, or an upgrading strategy where flexible automation, improving labour skills, and shifting to higher value-added activities keep production in the United States. If firms follow the first strategy, U.S. wages might be forced downward toward Mexican levels.[13]

It is clear from the above that the NAFTA is likely to have a major impact on the configuration of U.S. multinational firms in North America. Table 2 shows some of the ways in which the NAFTA could affect a firm's revenues (sales, exports, income from intangibles) and costs (factor and material costs, transportation, trade costs, taxes). Based on this table, the overall effect on multinationals should be positive, that is, revenues should increase and costs should fall. This does not mean, however, that all components of the MNE, i.e. every plant, will benefit equally. In order to explore the impact of these factors on plant location decisions, I will look at the existing configuration of U.S. branch plants and then turn to an analysis of the factors affecting the location of U.S. affiliates.

TABLE 1

U.S.-MEXICO ASSEMBLY COST COMPARISONS (US$)

	MOTOR VEHICLE ASSEMBLY		TV ASSEMBLY		PERSONAL COMPUTER ASSEMBLY	
	UNITED STATES	MEXICO	UNITED STATES	MEXICO	UNITED STATES	MEXICO
Labour Costs	$ 700	$ 140	$ 90	$ 15	$ 35	$ 5
Overhead Costs	0	0	70	60	100	80
Cost of Parts and Components	7,750	8,000	225	225	865	865
Subtotal of Labour, Overhead & Materials Costs	8,450	8,140	385	300	1,000	950
Shipping Costs of Components	75	600	0	0	0	0
Shipping Costs of Finished Product	225	400	0	1.50	0	6
Inventory Costs	20	40	0	0.60	0	18
Subtotal of Shipping & Inventory Costs	320	1,040	0	2.10	0	24
Additional Duty	0	0	0	3.75	0	0
TOTAL COSTS	$ 8,770	$ 9,180	$ 385	$ 305.85	$ 1,000	$ 974
Labour Costs as a % of Total Costs	8.0	1.5	23.4	4.9	3.5	0.5
Shipping and Inventory Costs as a % of Total Costs	3.7	11.3	0.00	0.7	0.0	2.5

Source: Author's calculations based on data in U.S. Office of Technology Assessment, 1992, pp. 145, 166.

TABLE 2

POTENTIAL EFFECTS OF REGIONAL INTEGRATION ON FIRM PROFITS

COMPONENTS OF THE FIRM'S PROFIT FUNCTION	HYPOTHESIZED EFFECTS OF NORTH AMERICAN FREE TRADE ON FIRM REVENUES AND EXPENDITURES (+ RISES) (- FALLS)
REVENUES	
Domestic Sales	− As tariff and nontariff barriers fall, more firms may enter the market, reducing market share of the existing firms, especially if they are inefficient. + If the NAFTA raises incomes, this will generate more sales in the longer run.
Exports Within North America	+ Firms should have easier access to North American market + If exports and FDI are substitutes and plants are inefficient on a regional basis, MNEs may close plants and shift from FDI to exporting.
Exports Outside North America	0 No direct effect. + If the NAFTA makes domestic firms more competitive they may increase their exports outside North America.
Royalties, Licensing Fees	+ Parent MNEs should receive more revenues from intangibles due to tighter intellectual property rules on patents and copyrights.
Profit Remittances	+ The NAFTA guarantees free crossborder movement of repatriated earnings; earnings are more secure.
EXPENDITURES	
Labour Costs	− Costs will fall in sectors where unit labour costs are important since the NAFTA makes it easier to relocate plants to take advantage of lower labour costs. May be pressure to harmonize labour standards.
Borrowing and Insurance Costs	− Liberalization of FDI by North American investments and investors in banking, financial and insurance markets should make financial markets more efficient and lower borrowing costs. + Opening of the Mexican market creates new demands for these services; suppliers may raise their prices as they increase their exports and FDI in the service sector in Mexico.

TABLE 2 (CONT'D)		
Costs of Raw Materials	-	Liberalization of FDI access in North American resources should encourage exploration and development (except in Mexican oil?).
Freight and Inventory Costs	-	New rules on crossborder trucking and FDI entry should lower freight and inventory costs.
Cost of Parts	-	Should fall to extent parts were already imported within North America and tariffs are removed.
	+	May rise if necessary to source inside North America in order to meet tighter rules of origin; affects some sectors (e.g. textiles) more than others.
Telecommunications Costs	-	Should fall in Mexico with breakup of national monopoly and improvement of telecommunications infrastructure.
Pollution Abatement Costs	+	More lax enforcement of regulations means these costs are lower in Mexico. Environmental side agreement and higher Mexican incomes should eventually raise pollution abatement standards to U.S. levels, thus raising these costs.
Tariffs, Quotas, License Fees	-	The NAFTA reduces or eliminates these costs for trade within North America
	-	Tariffs remain for imports from non-member countries, but the volume of these imports is likely to fall as firms substitute imports from member countries.
Corporate Income Taxes, Value-Added Taxes	0/-	Each country keeps its own tax system. Possible increased ability to transfer price and thus avoid taxes. In the long run, should be more pressure to harmonize North American tax rates and tax bases.

PLANT LOCATION PATTERNS OF U.S. MULTINATIONALS

IN ORDER TO ASSESS the effect of the FTA and the NAFTA on U.S. multinationals, statistical data are needed to provide a picture of the role U.S. multinationals play in North America, Japan and the European Community (the Triad). This section provides such a picture, examining the majority-owned foreign affiliates (MOFAs) of U.S. non-bank MNEs located in Canada, Mexico, Japan, the European Community and world wide in terms of their balance sheets, income statements, sales, and merchandise trade with the United States. In addition, the distribution of their capital stock and sales by industry within these countries is reviewed. Finally, average employee compensation across industries is compared and a proxy for unit labour costs is calculated. This can provide some evidence as to the strength of one motivation — cost reduction — for shifting plant locations from Canada to Mexico.

WHO DOES WHAT NOW? U.S. MOFAS IN 1990

IN 1990 U.S. MULTINATIONALS owned almost 16,000 foreign affiliates, just under 2,000 of which — or 11.7 percent of the total — were located in Canada (see Table 3). Almost half were located in the European Community, while less than 1 percent were located in Mexico or Japan.

Looking first at their balance sheets, these MOFAs held $1.3 trillion of assets and $0.8 trillion of liabilities, for a net worth of $0.5 trillion, or a return of 36.7 percent on total assets. Canada, with 11.7 percent of U.S. MOFAs, held a slightly larger share of worldwide assets (14.4 percent, reflecting its much greater share of net physical assets of 22.3 percent), liabilities (14.8 percent) and owners' equity (13.8 percent) than its numbers alone would suggest. Mexico, with 0.7 percent of U.S. MOFAs, had similar percentages of assets (1.1 percent) and liabilities (0.9 percent), but a higher share of worldwide MOFA owners' equity (1.4 percent).

The Canadian and Mexican shares of worldwide MOFA income and expenses are shown in Table 4. MOFAs in Canada are larger than the average U.S. MOFA worldwide. Although they number only 11.7 percent of all U.S. MOFAs, Canadian affiliates received a larger share of gross income (14.6 percent), incurred a larger share of total expenses (15.1 percent), hired relatively more employees (16.6 percent) and paid more employee compensation (18.2 percent). They paid proportionately less corporate income taxes (8.7 percent) and other taxes (9.5 percent) but more production royalties (29.7 percent); as a result, their share of net (after tax) income was smaller (7.3 percent). In 1990, these affiliates were half as profitable as all U.S. MOFAs, whether measured by net income as a percent of sales, owners' equity or total assets (e.g. worldwide net income as a percent of sales is 6.1 percent versus 3.0 percent in Canada).

MOFAs in Mexico were also larger (1.6 percent of gross income and expenses) relative to their numbers (0.7 percent of all MOFAs), paid relatively more income taxes (2.6 percent), and were more profitable (2 percent of net income, with an income-to-sales ratio of 7.4 percent). Although they employed 7.1 percent of all MOFA employees, their share of compensation was only 1.7 percent, reflecting the much lower average compensation per employee ($671 in Mexico versus $3,122 in Canada and $2,851 worldwide). Relatively lower R&D costs were incurred by the parent firm on behalf of MOFAs in Mexico and in Canada, whether measured as a percent of total MOFA R&D or as a percent of affiliate sales or cost of goods sold.

Table 5 looks at MOFA sales of goods and services, both world wide and broken down by region (U.S., local and third countries), and in terms of the

TABLE 3

ASSETS AND LIABILITIES OF U.S. MAJORITY-OWNED FOREIGN AFFILIATES (MOFAs), US$ MILLION, 1990

	ALL COUNTRIES	CANADA	CANADA AS % OF TOTAL	MEXICO	MEXICO AS % OF TOTAL	JAPAN	JAPAN AS % OF TOTAL	EUROPEAN COMMUNITY	EC AS % OF TOTAL
Number of MOFAs	15,532	1,841	11.68	113	0.73	138	0.89	6,831	43.98
Total Assets of MOFAs	1,263,457	182,063	14.41	13,993	1.11	61,696	4.88	659,920	52.23
Total Current Assets	647,412	73,104	11.29	8,074	1.25	41,148	6.36	365,072	56.39
Total Noncurrent Assets	616,045	108,959	17.69	5,919	0.96	20,549	3.34	294,848	47.86
Net Property, Plant & Equipment	279,221	62,251	22.29	4,410	1.58	8,459	3.03	129,296	46.31
Net PPE as % of Total Assets	22.10	34.19		31.52		13.71		19.59	--
Accumulated Depreciation & Depletion	221,939	36,531	16.46	3,531	1.59	5,788	2.61	112,957	50.90
Total Liabilities of MOFAs	800,449	118,065	14.75	7,394	0.92	47,282	5.91	446,648	55.80
Current Liabilities & Long-term Debt	676,669	90,371	13.36	6,938	1.03	35,498	5.25	393,567	58.16
As a % of Total Liabilities	84.54	76.54		93.83		75.08		88.12	--
Owners' Equity	463,008	63,998	13.82	6,599	1.43	14,415	3.11	213,271	46.06
Equity as a % of Total Assets	36.65	35.15		47.16		23.36		32.32	--

Source: Author's calculations based on data in U.S. Department of Commerce, Bureau of Economic Analysis, *Operations of U.S. Parent Companies and their Foreign Affiliates*. Washington: USGPO, 1990 (as reported in the National Trade Data Base -- the Export Connection, February 1993), Tables 90-20, 90-22 Preliminary.

TABLE 4

INCOME AND EXPENSES OF U.S. MAJORITY-OWNED FOREIGN AFFILIATES (MOFAs), US$ MILLION, 1990

	ALL COUNTRIES	CANADA	CANADA AS % OF TOTAL	MEXICO	MEXICO AS % OF TOTAL	JAPAN	JAPAN AS % OF TOTAL	EUROPEAN COMMUNITY	EC AS % OF TOTAL
Number of MOFAs	15,532	1,841	11.68	113	0.73	138	0.89	6,831	43.98
Gross Income of MOFAs	1,233,496	180,637	14.64	19,717	1.60	63,055	5.11	636,683	51.62
Income from Sales of Goods & Services	1,191,832	177,200	14.87	19,330	1.62	62,117	5.21	615,192	51.62
Income from Equity Investments	19,787	983	4.97	95	0.48	72	0.36	10,915	55.16
Total Costs & Expenses of MOFAs	1,160,590	175,352	15.11	18,292	1.58	60,924	5.25	600,004	51.70
Cost of Goods Sold & General Expenses	1,067,608	164,359	15.40	16,496	1.55	55,397	5.19	556,126	52.09
Foreign Income Taxes	30,658	2,658	8.67	807	2.63	2,330	7.60	11,564	37.72
Income Taxes as a % of Total Costs	2.64	1.52		4.41		3.82		1.93	
Taxes other than Income & Payroll	89,713	8,488	9.46	704	0.78	2,922	3.26	56,658	63.15
Production Royalty Payments	3,318	985	29.69	0	0.00	1	0.03	449	13.53
Total Employee Compensation	148,353	26,962	18.17	2,489	1.68	7,165	4.83	84,435	56.91
Number of Employees	5,204	864	16.60	371	7.13	142	2.73	2,269	43.60
Average Compensation per Employee	2,851	3,122		671		5,046		3,721	
Employee Compensation as % of Total Costs	12.78	15.38		13.61		11.76		14.07	
Employee Compensation as % of PPE	53.13	43.31		56.44		84.70		65.30	
R&D Expenditures Performed by MOFAs	10,417	1,168	11.21	53	0.51	507	4.87	7,604	73.00
As % of Total Sales	0.87	0.66		0.27		0.82		1.24	
As % of Cost of Goods Sold	0.98	0.71		0.32		0.92		1.37	
Net Income of MOFAs	72,906	5,285	7.25	1,425	1.95	2,131	2.92	36,679	50.31
Net Income as % of Total Sales	6.12	2.98		7.37		3.43		5.96	
Net Income as % of Owners' Equity	15.75	8.26		21.59		14.78		17.20	
Net Income as % of Total Assets	5.77	2.90		10.18		3.45		5.56	

Source: Author's calculations based on data in U.S. Department of Commerce, Bureau of Economic Analysis, *Operations of U.S. Parent Companies and their Foreign Affiliates*. Washington: USGPO, 1990 (as reported in the National Trade Data Base -- the Export Connection, February 1993), Tables 90-20, 90-22, 90-30, 90-66 Preliminary.

TABLE 5

SALES OF GOODS AND SERVICES BY U.S. MAJORITY-OWNED FOREIGN AFFILIATES (MOFAs), US$ MILLION, 1990

	ALL COUNTRIES	CANADA	CANADA AS % OF TOTAL	MEXICO	MEXICO AS % OF TOTAL	JAPAN	JAPAN AS % OF TOTAL	EUROPEAN COMMUNITY	EC AS % OF TOTAL
Number of MOFAs	15,532	1,841	11.68	113	0.73	138	0.89	6,831	43.98
MOFA Sales of Goods & Services, all Locations	1,191,832	177,200	14.87	19,330	1.62	62,117	5.21	615,192	51.62
Sales to Affiliated Persons	286,829	36,907	12.87	6,482	2.26	9,507	3.31	154,066	53.71
Inter-affiliate Sales as % of Worldwide Sales	24.07	20.83		33.54		15.30		25.04	
MOFA Sales to the United States	123,801	41,404	33.44	5,066	4.09	3,280	2.65	22,129	17.87
U.S. Sales as % of Worldwide Sales	10.39	23.37		26.21		5.28		3.60	
Sales to U.S. Parents	98,574	33,673	34.16	4,985	5.06	3,171	3.22	17,045	17.29
Sales to U.S. Parents as % of Total U.S. Sales	79.62	81.33		98.40		96.68		77.03	
Sales to U.S. Parents as % of Worldwide Sales	8.27	19.00		25.79		5.10		2.77	
MOFA Local Sales to Host Country	795,244	129,740	16.31	13,461	1.69	55,048	6.92	412,295	51.85
Local Sales as % of Worldwide Sales	66.72	73.22		69.64		88.62		67.02	
Sales to Other Foreign Affiliates	37,875	2,188	5.78	864	2.28	3,265	8.62	20,327	53.69
Inter-affiliate Sales as % of Total Local Sales	4.76	1.69		6.42		5.93		4.93	
Intra-firm Local Sales as % of Worldwide Sales	3.18	1.23		4.47		5.26		3.30	
MOFA Sales to Third Countries	272,787	6,056	2.22	803	0.29	3,789	1.39	180,768	66.27
Third-country Sales as % of Worldwide Sales	22.89	3.42		4.15		6.10		29.38	
Sales to Other Foreign Affiliates	150,397	1,046	0.70	633	0.42	3,071	2.04	116,694	77.59
Inter-affiliate Sales as % of Third-country Sales	55.13	17.27		78.83		81.05		64.55	
Intra-firm Other Sales as % of Worldwide Sales	12.62	0.59		3.27		4.94		18.97	

Source: Author's calculations based on data in U.S. Department of Commerce, Bureau of Economic Analysis, *Operations of U.S. Parent Companies and their Foreign Affiliates*. Washington: USGPO, 1990 (as reported in the National Trade Data Base -- the Export Connection, February 1993), Tables 90-20, 90-40 Preliminary.

nature of the sales, whether arm's length or intra-firm. MOFAs in Canada sold relatively more goods and services (14.9 percent) worldwide, to the United States (33.4 percent) and locally (16.3 percent) than their numbers suggest (11.7 percent), but much less to third countries (2.2 percent). Local sales (73.2 percent) and U.S. sales (23.4 percent) together represented 97 percent of all sales by U.S. MOFAs in Canada. The affiliates sold through arm's length channels at home (only 1.7 percent of local sales were interaffiliate) but 81.3 percent of all U.S. sales were intra-firm sales to their parents. The Mexican picture is even more skewed: U.S. sales were 26.2 percent of all sales, 98 percent of which were intra-firm sales to their U.S. parents.

Table 6 provides data on U.S.-MOFA merchandise trade in 1990. Although only 11.7 percent of all U.S. MOFAs were in Canada, 36.3 percent of all U.S. merchandise exports to MOFAs world wide were shipped to MOFAs in Canada and 45.2 percent of U.S. imports from MOFAs worldwide came from Canadian affiliates, for a net U.S. deficit of $3.2 billion on this trade. Trade with U.S. parents generated 83 percent of total U.S.-MOFA trade in Canada, for both imports and exports, slightly below the worldwide MOFA intra-firm average (88 percent for exports, 85 percent for imports).

Trade between MOFAs in Mexico and the United States was also relatively large. With just 0.7 percent of U.S. MOFAs world wide, Mexican affiliates purchased 7.3 percent of U.S. merchandise worldwide exports to MOFAs and supplied 7.2 percent of U.S. worldwide imports from MOFAs, generating a small U.S. trade surplus of 0.2 billion dollars. Parent-MOFA intra-firm trade represented almost 100 percent of these flows (95.1 percent of exports, 99.0 percent of imports).[14]

An Industry Profile of U.S. MOFAs in 1990

This section examines the distribution of MOFAs by industry within countries. As proxy measures of relative importance of these foreign affiliates within their host countries, on an industry basis, Table 7 provides 1990 data on the net property, plant and equipment (PPE) by MOFA industry while Table 8 examines total sales by industry of the affiliate.[15]

Based on their net property, plant and equipment, MOFAs world wide were distributed as follows: petroleum (31 percent) and manufacturing (49 percent) are the largest, with wholesale trade, services and other industries making up the rest. MOFAs in Canada (although only 11.7 percent of U.S. affiliates world wide) held 22.3 percent of world wide PPE; thus these affiliates were on average larger than those in other host countries. As a percent of world wide PPE by industry, MOFAs in Canada were particularly concentrated in the following industries: petroleum (28.1 percent), metals (30.2 percent), other manufacturing (30.6 percent), and finance, insurance and real estate (48.1 percent). Their share was lowest in machinery (6.3 percent) and wholesale trade (9.6 percent). Comparing the Canadian numbers to Mexico, MOFAs in

TABLE 6

U.S. MERCHANDISE TRADE WITH U.S. MAJORITY-OWNED FOREIGN AFFILIATES (MOFAs), US$ MILLION, 1990

	ALL COUNTRIES	CANADA	CANADA AS % OF TOTAL	MEXICO	MEXICO AS % OF TOTAL	JAPAN	JAPAN AS % OF TOTAL	EUROPEAN COMMUNITY	EC AS % OF TOTAL
Number of MOFAs	15,532	1,841	11.68	113	0.73	138	0.89	6,831	43.98
U.S. Merchandise Exports Shipped to MOFAs	101,661	36,857	36.25	7,428	7.31	7,361	7.24	29,145	28.67
Shipped by U.S. Parents	89,649	30,599	34.13	7,062	7.88	7,098	7.92	26,598	29.67
Shipped by Unaffiliated U.S. Persons	12,012	6,259	52.11	365	3.04	263	2.19	2,547	21.20
Parent Exports as % of Total	88.18	83.02		95.07		96.43		91.26	
U.S. Merchandise Imports Shipped by MOFAs	88,607	40,017	45.16	7,239	8.17	1,859	2.10	13,442	15.17
Shipped to U.S. Parents	75,364	33,210	44.07	7,164	9.51	1,799	2.39	11,156	14.80
Shipped to Unaffiliated U.S. Persons	13,243	6,807	51.40	74	0.56	60	0.45	2,286	17.26
Parent Imports as % of Total	85.05	82.99		98.96		96.77		82.99	

Source: Author's calculations based on data in U.S. Department of Commerce, Bureau of Economic Analysis, *Operations of U.S. Parent Companies and their Foreign Affiliates.* Washington: USGPO, 1990 (as reported in the National Trade Data Base -- the Export Connection, February 1993), Tables 90-20, 90-59 Preliminary.

TABLE 7

NET PROPERTY, PLANT AND EQUIPMENT (PPE) OF U.S. MOFAS BY INDUSTRY OF AFFILIATE, US$ MILLION, 1990

	ALL COUNTRIES	CANADA	CANADA AS % OF TOTAL	MEXICO	MEXICO AS % OF TOTAL	JAPAN	JAPAN AS % OF TOTAL	EUROPEAN COMMUNITY	EC AS % OF TOTAL
Number of MOFAs	15,532	1,814	11.68	113	0.73	138	0.89	6,831	43.98
Petroleum As % of Total Industry PPE	86,637 31.03	24,377 39.16	28.14	10 0.23	0.01	1,021 12.07	1.18	31,008 23.98	35.79
Total Manufacturing As % of Total Industry PPE	137,590 49.28	25,086 40.30	18.23	3,830 86.85	2.78	5,782 68.35	4.20	76,707 59.33	55.65
Food and Kindred Products As % of Total Industry PPE	12,546 4.49	1,891 3.04	15.07	355 8.05	2.83	198 2.34	1.58	6,419 4.96	51.16
Chemicals and Allied Products As % of Total Industry PPE	31,293 11.21	3,584 5.76	11.45	615 13.95	1.97	1,022 12.08	3.27	20,085 15.53	64.18
Primary & Fabricated Metals As % of Total Industry PPE	8,052 2.88	2,435 3.91	30.24	114 2.59	1.42	115 1.36	1.43	3,045 2.36	37.82
Machinery, except Electrical As % of Total Industry PPE	19,085 6.84	1,204 1.93	6.31	na	na	2,206 26.08	11.56	12,658 9.79	66.32
Electrical & Electronic Equipment As % of Total Industry PPE	10,677 3.82	945 1.52	8.85	408 9.25	3.82	1,052 12.44	9.85	4,989 3.86	46.73
Transportation Equipment As % of Total Industry PPE	25,799 9.24	5,799 9.32	22.48	1,339 30.36	5.19	53 0.63	0.21	15,578 12.05	60.38
Other Manufacturing As % of Total Industry PPE	30,138 10.79	9,228 14.82	30.62	na	na	1,136 13.43	3.77	13,933 10.78	46.23

TABLE 7 (CONT'D)

	ALL COUNTRIES	CANADA	CANADA AS % OF TOTAL	MEXICO	MEXICO AS % OF TOTAL	JAPAN	JAPAN AS % OF TOTAL	EUROPEAN COMMUNITY	EC AS % OF TOTAL
Wholesale Trade	13,789	1,329	9.64	195	1.41	1,111	8.06	7,515	54.40
As % of Total Industry PPE	4.94	2.13		4.42		13.13		5.81	
Finance (except Banking), Insurance & Real Estate	10,215	4,911	48.08	116	1.14	286	2.80	3,620	35.44
As % of Total Industry PPE	3.66	7.89		2.63		3.38		2.80	
Services	10,165	1,952	19.20	151	1.49	219	2.15	5,379	52.92
As % of Total Industry PPE	3.64	3.14		3.42		2.59		4.16	
Other Industries	20,826	4,596	22.07	107	0.51	40	0.19	5,067	24.33
As % of Total Industry PPE	7.46	7.38		2.43		0.47		3.92	
All Industries	279,221	62,251	22.29	4,410	1.58	8,459	3.03	129,296	46.31
As % of Total Industry PPE	100.00	100.00		100.00		100.00		100.00	

Source: Author's calculations based on data in U.S. Department of Commerce, Bureau of Economic Analysis, *Operations of U.S. Parent Companies and their Foreign Affiliates*. Washington: USGPO, 1990 (as reported in the National Trade Data Base -- the Export Connection, February 1993), Tables 90-20, 90-26 Preliminary.

216

FIGURE 4

PPE BY INDUSTRY OF MOFA, 1990 (%)

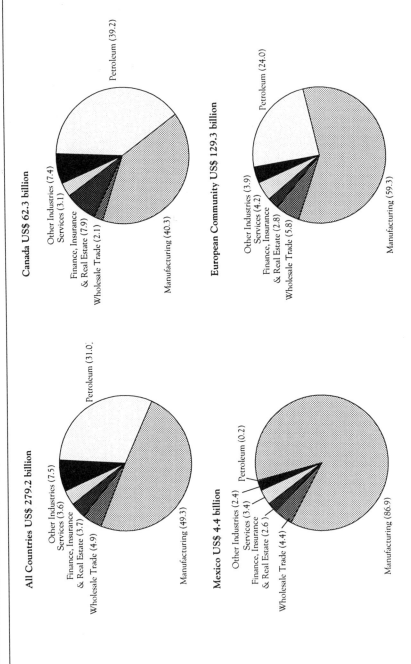

All Countries US$ 279.2 billion

Other Industries (7.5)
Services (3.6)
Finance, Insurance & Real Estate (3.7)
Wholesale Trade (4.9)
Petroleum (31.0)
Manufacturing (49.3)

Canada US$ 62.3 billion

Other Industries (7.4)
Services (3.1)
Finance, Insurance & Real Estate (7.9)
Wholesale Trade (2.1)
Petroleum (39.2)
Manufacturing (40.3)

Mexico US$ 4.4 billion

Other Industries (2.4)
Services (3.4)
Finance, Insurance & Real Estate (2.6)
Wholesale Trade (4.4)
Petroleum (0.2)
Manufacturing (86.9)

European Community US$ 129.3 billion

Other Industries (3.9)
Services (4.2)
Finance, Insurance & Real Estate (2.8)
Wholesale Trade (5.8)
Petroleum (24.0)
Manufacturing (59.3)

Mexico were largest in manufacturing (2.78 percent), particularly in the transport (5.2 percent) and electrical equipment (3.8 percent) industries. The extraordinarily low investment in petroleum (0.01 percent) is very noticeable and reflects Mexico's constitutional prohibition of foreign direct investment in petroleum.

The figures for the breakdown of industry PPE within each country are provided in Table 7 but are easier to see in Figure 4. By looking at the distribution of PPE within Canada, it may be seen that U.S. MOFAs were concentrated in manufacturing (40.3 percent) and petroleum (39.2 percent), even though manufacturing in Canada was small relative to its share for all MOFAs worldwide (49.3 percent). MOFAs in Mexico, on the other hand, were overwhelmingly in manufacturing (86.9 percent), notably in transport equipment (30.4 percent of PPE in Mexico).

Turning now to the distribution of sales by industry of MOFA, Table 8 shows that sales by MOFAs in Canada as a share of worldwide MOFA sales were highest in other industries (43 percent) and transport equipment (31.7 percent), and lowest in machinery (7 percent) and wholesale trade (8.1 percent). In Mexico, transport equipment again dominated (5.3 percent of worldwide sales) while petroleum was noticeably under-represented (0.04 percent). Figure 5 plots the sectoral distribution of MOFA sales for 1990. The dominance of manufacturing in Canada (54.5 percent) and Mexico (85.3 percent) is evident. Within manufacturing, transport equipment represented 22.3 percent of sales by MOFAs in Canada and 34 percent in Mexico.[16] Sales were lowest in services (2.5 percent), primary metals (2.6 percent) and electrical equipment (3.2 percent) in Canada, and in petroleum (0.5 percent), services (1 percent), finance, insurance and real estate (1 percent) and primary metals (1.6 percent) in Mexico.

Table 9 provides data on total MOFA employment,[17] average employment compensation and unit labour costs by industry for 1990.[18] The average wage for MOFAs in all industries varied enormously from a low of $6,700 (Mexico) to an average of $28,500 (all countries) to a high of $50,500 (Japan). The average MOFA wage in Canada was $31,200, above the overall average but below the average in Japan and the European Community. Note it was more than four times higher than the average Mexican compensation package.

The range is similar for all manufacturing; however, here the gap for Canada was more pronounced. The average MOFA wage in manufacturing in Canada was $38,000, now higher than the world average and the average EC wage, and more than six times larger than the average level in Mexico. Canada is the only country of the five cases shown where there was a substantial differential between the average wage for MOFAs in all industries and in manufacturing. This could reflect the superior productivity levels of workers in Canadian manufacturing, better negotiating by Canadian trade unions, an older age distribution in this sector, residual protection from high (but falling) Canadian tariffs on manufactured goods, the Auto Pact, or other factors. Within industries there was also significant variation in wage levels. In some

TABLE 8

Sales by U.S. Majority-Owned Foreign Affiliates (MOFAs), by Industry of Affiliate, US$ million, 1990

	All Countries	Canada	Canada as % of Total	Mexico	Mexico as % of Total	Japan	Japan as % of Total	European Community	EC as % of Total
Number of MOFAs	15,532	1,814	11.68	113	0.73	138	0.89	6,831	43.98
Petroleum	237,227	25,384	10.70	101	0.04	11,633	4.90	89,062	37.54
As % of Total Industry Sales	19.90	14.33		0.52		18.73		14.48	
Total Manufacturing	580,311	96,644	16.65	16,487	2.84	23.265	4.01	339,388	58.48
As % of Total Industry Sales	48.69	54.54		85.29		37.45		55.17	
Food and Kindred Products	60,361	7,116	11.79	1,879	3.11	1,907	3.16	34,483	57.13
As % of Total Industry Sales	5.06	4.02		9.72		3.07		5.61	
Chemicals and Allied Products	107,227	11,233	10.48	2,985	2.78	4,094	3.82	69,723	65.02
As % of Total Industry Sales	9.00	6.34		15.44		6.59		11.33	
Primary & Fabricated Metals	23,306	4,607	19.77	363	1.56	377	1.62	13,414	57.56
As % of Total Industry Sales	1.96	2.60		1.88		0.61		2.18	
Machinery, except Electrical	113,761	7,950	6.99	na	na	na	na	76,020	66.82
As % of Total Industry Sales	9.55	4.49						12.36	
Electrical & Electronic Equipment	45,979	5,613	12.21	1,406	3.06	3,118	6.78	19,128	41.60
As % of Total Industry Sales	3.86	3.17		7.27		5.02		3.11	
Transportation Equipment	124,759	39,508	31.67	6,572	5.27	159	0.13	65,964	52.87
As % of Total Industry Sales	10.47	22.30		34.00		0.26		10.72	
Other Manufacturing	104,917	20,617	19.65	na	na	na	na	60,656	57.81
As % of Total Industry Sales	8.80	11.63						9.86	

TABLE 8 (CONT'D)

	ALL COUNTRIES	CANADA	CANADA AS % OF TOTAL	MEXICO	MEXICO AS % OF TOTAL	JAPAN	JAPAN AS % OF TOTAL	EUROPEAN COMMUNITY	EC AS % OF TOTAL
Wholesale Trade	223,536	18,152	8.12	1,747	0.78	18,553	8.3	119,928	53.65
As % of Total Industry Sales	18.76	10.24		9.04		29.87		19.49	
Finance (except Banking), Insurance & Real Estate	60,035	11,833	19.71	340	0.57	6,237	10.39	24,946	41.55
As % of Total Industry Sales	5.04	6.68		1.76		10.04		4.05	
Services	42,358	4,414	10.42	197	0.47	1,749	4.13	27,823	65.69
As % of Total Industry Sales	3.55	2.49		1.02		2.82		4.52	
Other Industries	48,366	20,773	42.95	457	0.94	681	1.41	14,044	29.04
As % of Total Industry Sales	4.06	11.72		2.36		1.10		2.28	
All Industries	1,191,832	177,200	14.87	19,330	1.62	62,117	5.21	615,192	51.62
As % of Total Industry Sales	100.00	100.00		100.00		100.00		100.00	

Source: Author's calculations based on data in U.S. Department of Commerce, Bureau of Economic Analysis, *Operations of U.S. Parent Companies and their Foreign Affiliates.* Washington: USGPO, 1990 (as reported in the National Trade Data Base -- the Export Connection, February 1993), Tables 90-20, 90-32 Preliminary.

TABLE 9

EMPLOYEES, EMPLOYEE COMPENSATION AND UNIT LABOUR COSTS OF U.S. MOFAS

	ALL COUNTRIES			CANADA		
	LABOUR FORCE ('000)	AVERAGE EMPLOYEE COMP. (US $)	UNIT LABOUR COST	LABOUR FORCE ('000)	AVERAGE EMPLOYEE COMP. (US $)	UNIT LABOUR COST
	L	W =W L/L	W L/P Q	L	W =W L/L	W L/P Q
Petroleum	188	42,207	0.03	32	65,688	0.08
Manufacturing	3,358	27,772	0.16	429	38,014	0.17
Food	329	21,842	0.12	34	30,000	0.14
Chemicals	488	31,451	0.14	46	40,391	0.17
Metals	182	24,962	0.19	31	33,839	0.23
Machinery	500	36,952	0.16	34	45,824	0.20
Electrical Equipment	485	17,959	0.19	36	35,000	0.22
Transport	606	31,611	0.15	120	41,475	0.13
Other Manufacturing	767	25,870	0.19	129	35,543	0.22
Wholesale Trade	507	40,444	0.09	59	34,797	0.11
FIRE	129	44,760	0.10	31	36,355	0.10
Services	409	28,406	0.27	61	22,230	0.31
Other	613	15,108	0.19	252	15,933	0.19
All Industries	5,204	28,507	0.12	864	31,206	0.15

Source: Author's calculations based on data in U.S. Dept of Commerce, Bureau of Economic Analysis, *Operations of U.S. Parent Companies and their Foreign Affiliates*. Washington: USGPO. 1990 (National Trade Data Base – the Export Connection, Feb. 1993), Tables 90-32, 90-54, 90-56 Preliminary.

cases (e.g. petroleum in Mexico and Japan, financial, insurance and real estate [FIRE] services in Mexico) where U.S. MOFAs are significantly under-represented the numbers may well be suspect and should be treated cautiously. Figure 6 plots average compensation levels for some of these sectors.

Historically, unit labour costs have been used by economists as one pre-dictor of production costs. The general public point to the large difference in wage levels between Canada and Mexico illustrated by the $31,206 Canadian and $6,709 Mexican wages in Table 9 and use this gap to argue that the NAFTA will cause jobs to flee to Mexico. Economists, however, argue that wages generally reflect productivity levels; people are paid more because they are worth more (Watson 1993). Higher wages reflect better education, higher capital-labour ratios, newer technology and so on. A better measure of cost differential is unit labour cost defined as the wage rate divided by the average productivity of labour or, alternatively, total employee compensation per unit

TABLE 9 (CONT'D)

BY INDUSTRY OF AFFILIATE, 1990

MEXICO			JAPAN			EC		
LABOUR FORCE ('000)	AVERAGE EMPLOYEE COMP. (US $)	UNIT LABOUR COST	LABOUR FORCE ('000)	AVERAGE EMPLOYEE COMP. (US $)	UNIT LABOUR COST	LABOUR FORCE ('000)	AVERAGE EMPLOYEE COMP. (US $)	UNIT LABOUR COST
L	W=WL/L	WL/PQ	L	W=WL/L	WL/PQ	L	W=WL/L	WL/PQ
1	20,000	0.20	na	na	na	51	50,118	0.03
330	6,488	0.13	80	50,138	0.17	1,523	37,005	0.17
31	7,484	0.12	2	57,550	0.08	120	32,508	0.11
37	9,811	0.12	21	43,762	0.22	233	41,618	0.14
11	5,455	0.17	2	40,500	0.21	86	30,837	0.20
17	6,647	na	31	61,613	na	282	44,759	0.17
92	4,533	0.30	14	38,071	0.17	144	29,944	0.23
81	6,284	0.08	1	25,000	0.16	315	38,273	0.18
62	7,210	na	10	42,900	na	342	32,509	0.18
10	16,200	0.09	33	49,212	0.09	258	44,027	0.09
1	39,000	0.11	11	72,182	0.13	55	54,545	0.12
17	4,294	0.37	13	34,308	0.26	227	34,762	0.28
12	4,500	0.12	na	na	na	156	20,968	0.23
371	6,709	0.13	142	50,458	0.12	2,269	37,212	0.14

of output produced. Unfortunately data on output is not available so sales revenues must be used as a proxy (Eden & Molot, 1992). Unit labour cost figures are provided in Table 9 and illustrated in Figure 7.

The first important point to note is that the variation in unit labour costs is significantly lower than the variation in average wages. In fact, comparing MOFAs in the same industry in different countries, unit labour costs were often strikingly similar. For example, the numbers vary from a high of 0.15 (Canada) to a low of 0.12 (Japan and all countries) with Mexico at 0.13. In manufacturing, the numbers vary from 0.17 (Canada and the EC) to 0.13 (Mexico). In transportation equipment Mexico had a clear advantage (0.08) compared to all the other cases. The second point to note is that Canada was often at the high end in terms of unit labour costs, which is cause for concern assuming the 1990 figures were not a one-time event. Where the differential between Canada and Mexico is significantly large (e.g. transport equipment) there may be reason to be concerned about plant shifts to Mexico.[19] The third point to note is that in some industries unit labour costs were higher in Mexico than in Canada (e.g. services, electrical equipment, FIRE, petroleum). In such cases the NAFTA could cause plants to move northward.[20]

FIGURE 5

SALES BY INDUSTRY OF MOFA, 1990 (%)

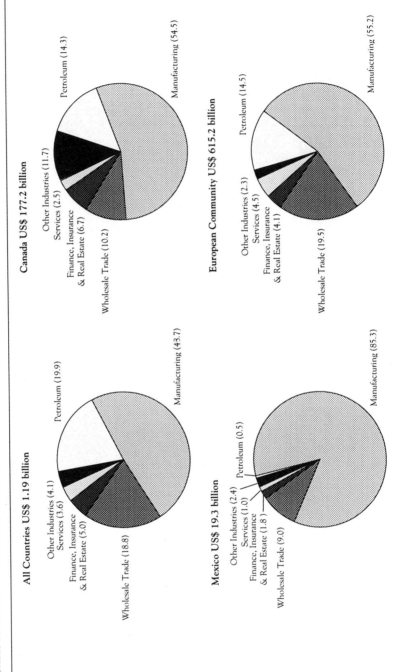

All Countries US$ 1.19 billion

Manufacturing (43.7)

Petroleum (19.9)

Other Industries (4.1)
Services (3.6)

Finance, Insurance
& Real Estate (5.0)

Wholesale Trade (18.8)

Canada US$ 177.2 billion

Manufacturing (54.5)

Petroleum (14.3)

Other Industries (11.7)
Services (2.5)

Finance, Insurance
& Real Estate (6.7)

Wholesale Trade (10.2)

Mexico US$ 19.3 billion

Manufacturing (85.3)

Petroleum (0.5)

Other Industries (2.4)
Services (1.0)

Finance, Insurance
& Real Estate (1.8)

Wholesale Trade (9.0)

European Community US$ 615.2 billion

Manufacturing (55.2)

Petroleum (14.5)

Other Industries (2.3)
Services (4.5)

Finance, Insurance
& Real Estate (4.1)

Wholesale Trade (19.5)

FIGURE 6

AVERAGE EMPLOYEE COMPENSATION, 1990

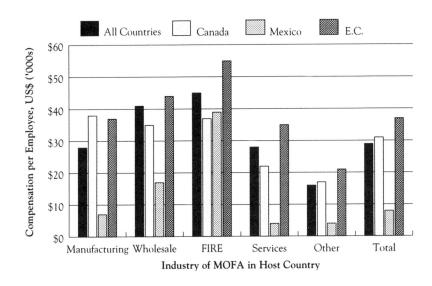

FIGURE 7

UNIT LABOUR COSTS, 1990

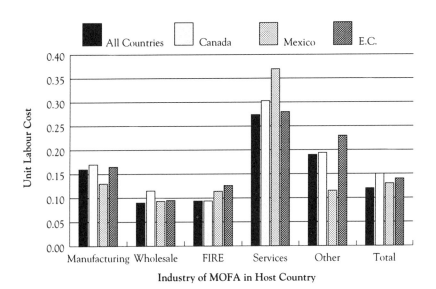

Who Does What Now?

In summary, the key information about the relative roles of U.S. MOFAs in Canada and Mexico, based on 1990 data, is as follows:

Canada has 12 percent of all U.S. MOFAs world wide. MOFAs in Canada are large in terms of their shares of world wide MOFA assets (especially PPE), gross income, expenses and employees. Their shares of world wide PPE are highest in petroleum, other manufacturing, and finance, insurance and real estate. MOFAs in Canada pay relatively higher royalties and lower corporate taxes, but receive less net income. They also sell relatively more goods and services. Of these sales, just under three-quarters are arm's-length local sales, with almost all the rest intra-firm sales to their U.S. parents. Their shares of world wide sales of goods and services are highest in other industries and transport equipment. Over one-third of all U.S. merchandise exports to MOFAs go to Canada and almost one-half of U.S. imports from MOFAs come from Canada. Average employee compensation is higher in Canada compared to MOFAs in all countries, as are unit labour costs in many industries.

Mexico has just under 1 percent of all U.S. MOFAs world wide. MOFAs in Mexico are also large in terms of gross income, expenses, income taxes paid, net income earned, and labour compensation. They stand out in terms of their labour intensity; over 7 percent of MOFA employees world wide work in Mexico. They are also distinctive by their absence from the petroleum sector, measured either by PPE or sales, and by their dominance in manufacturing, particularly in transportation equipment. Almost 30 percent of total sales are to the United States (almost entirely intra-firm), the rest are local and mostly at arm's length. MOFAs in Mexico are heavily involved in two-way merchandise trade with the United States, almost all of which is with their U.S. parent firms. Average employee compensation is significantly lower compared to MOFAs in all countries, but unit labour costs are roughly comparable.

In this section we have provided a statistical "snapshot" of the activities of majority-owned foreign affiliates of U.S. multinationals in 1990. The question we want to address, however, is not the current pattern, but who will do what after NAFTA? In order to answer this question, we need to develop a theory of international production that explains the current pattern of MOFA activities, and then use this theory to predict likely reactions of U.S. multinationals to the NAFTA.

Multinationals and the Theory of International Production

Why do Multinationals set up Foreign Plants?

In order to explain the locational strategies of multinational enterprises, it is necessary to examine their value chains, that is, the products and processes that take place within the firm. As Figure 8 shows, the range of value-adding activities in which a firm can engage include: primary activities (extraction and processing of raw materials, fabrication of parts and sub-assemblies, final assembly, sales and customer service) and support activities (head office functions, support services and technology development). Another way to view this is sectoral: resources, manufacturing and services. When a firm engages in two or more of these activities in a linked fashion (e.g. parts, assembly and sales) the firm is said to be vertically integrated; when a firm has two or more plants at one of these stages (e.g. several assembly plants in different locations), the firm is horizontally integrated.

This concept of the value chain may be used to explain why firms set up plants in foreign countries. The reasons may be internally driven (either by product requirements or the nature of overall firm requirements) or externally motivated (by strategic interactions with rival firms or by government regulations) or both. I hypothesize that there are six general motivations behind the establishment of a subsidiary or branch plant in a foreign country: the search for raw materials, the search for new markets, the search for low-cost production locations, the need to provide support services to other parts of the MNE, financial reasons, and strategic motivations for offshore location.[21]

The Search for Raw Materials

First, MNEs establish foreign plants in order to access natural resources not available at home. This type of resource-seeking international production was typical of MNEs in the early part of the 20th century. The so-called Old International Division of Labour (OIDL) linking developed and developing countries was based on vertically integrated trade in raw materials.

In the stereotypical case, natural-resource seeking MNEs go into resource-rich countries to set up natural resource (e.g. mining, oil) extraction plants. The MNE brings in a package of capital goods, engineers, and technology, and uses domestic labour and energy inputs to extract the raw materials. The raw materials are either exported directly to the parent or other affiliates in unprocessed form or processed in an adjacent plant and then exported in semi-processed form. The latter case provides some upgrading of technology inflows and local capability. Economies of scale relative to the size of downstream demand determine the size of plant. The raw material flows are intra-firm so that transfer prices are used to price the products as they are sold from one plant to another. However, since the products are commodities, arm's length market prices are likely to exist for comparison. Transport and energy costs are important for determining upgrading possibilities; so too are tariff and NTBs in downstream countries, as these tend to discourage host country upgrading. Typically most developed countries have had a cascading tariff structure (higher tariffs the higher the degree of processing) and cascading tends to discourage upgrading in the host country.

FIGURE 8

THE TYPICAL VALUE CHAIN OF A MULTINATIONAL ENTERPRISE

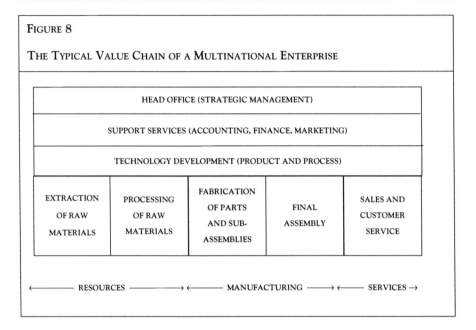

The Search for Market Access

The second motive for setting up a foreign plant is to secure access for products in foreign markets. This type of market-seeking international production replaces exports to a country with production inside that country. The product may be either a final good (e.g. autos) or an intermediate good (e.g. auto parts) or business services (a financial affiliate). There are several motivations for wanting market access:

- **Tariff jumping or defensive FDI** If a country has high tariffs and/or non-tariff barriers designed to keep out foreign goods, exporting firms that consider this market to be important are likely to incur the costs of setting up inside the tariff walls. Such inward FDI is an efficient (for the firm) response to internalizing market imperfections caused by government policy, but inefficient from the viewpoint of world welfare. An additional problem occurs if excessive entry results as MNEs compete strategically to enter new markets. The term 'miniature replica effect' was coined to describe the high cost production based on excessive numbers of product lines supplying too small a market that occurred in Canadian manufacturing in the 1950s and 1960s as a result of high Canadian trade barriers.

- **New or expanded market entry**   When a previously closed market opens up to foreign firms, particularly if the market is of large size or strategic importance, firms will enter to supply that market. The opening of China and Eastern Europe to foreign investment and the (expected) removal of U.S. prohibitions against U.S. firms doing business in Vietnam are examples. Related to this is the formation of free trade areas and customs unions which induce entry by new MNEs seeing the possibilities of a larger market with reduced intra-regional barriers (and possibly higher barriers against imports so that tariff jumping may also be a factor).

- **Following customers abroad**   This is a common motivation for firms that provide intermediate goods and services to down-stream businesses. When Japanese automotive assembly plants moved into North America in the mid-1980s, auto parts suppliers from Japan followed a few years later. Hotel chains provide similar services to their international customers, regardless of their location. Banks set up branches in foreign countries to supply their manufacturing customers with the same services they have at home.

- **Rationalizing the production of existing plants**   When a free trade area is formed, some MNEs will already have plants within the market, each of which may have been primarily oriented to its own domestic market. When the interregional barriers come down, there is a new possibility for the firm to rationalize production among existing plants. The MNE may rationalize vertically (i.e. change plant functions so that the plants become vertically integrated) or horizontally (i.e. change product lines so that each plant specializes in a different product line and then intra-firm trades with the others).

Recently some multinationals have begun developing regional core networks of affiliates. These "regionally integrated, independently sustainable networks of overseas investments [are] centered on a Triad member", according to the UN Centre for Transnational Corporations (UNCTC 1991, p. 42). Each network tends to have a lead plant in a member of the Triad plus affiliates located in regional spoke countries (e.g. lead plants in the United States with cluster plants in Canada and Mexico). By setting up a core network the multi-national ensures that it has access to, and that its affiliates become regional insiders in, each of the three Triadic regions. The UNCTC argues that regional core networks have economic (comparative advantage, economies of scale) and political (avoidance of tariff and non-tariff barriers) motivations. In practice, what may become more important if the trading blocs do become protectionist is the potential for these foreign affiliates to be seen as insiders within each bloc and thus be spared the entry barriers facing outside firms that attempt to trade with or invest in the bloc.

The Search for Low-Cost Production Sites

Third, MNEs set up foreign plants in locations where inputs into the production process are cheaper than at home; this is primarily a search for cheaper labour inputs, but it could also be a search for cheaper energy or materials. While the resource-seeking stage is tied to the location of natural resources and the market-access stage is tied to the location of markets, the cost-reducing stages are more footloose and can move from country to country in search of lower production costs.

Developing countries set up export-processing zones to encourage MNEs to assemble and manufacture low-technology products for final assembly and sales in the Triad countries. Such world wide sourcing has been called the New International Division of Labour (NIDL), because it links developing country labour-intensive manufacturing to Triadic high-tech assembly and sales, creating enormous flows of intermediate goods trade in parts and partly assembled products.

Providing Support to Other Affiliates

Fourth, provision of business services to support other parts of the MNE may be shifted to offshore locations. These include the sales, producer service, technology and head office stages. The sales distributor is often the first move a firm makes into a new market, while other producer services follow at a much later date when the MNE has established a more diversified subsidiary base. Services affiliates are the fastest-growing category of FDI according to the UNCTC; their purpose is to supply accounting, finance, marketing, and so on in support of the MNE's manufacturing and resource-based affiliates. With respect to technology development, historically little R&D was decentralized from the parent firm's location; however, with new products and processes being developed throughout the Triad, it is now more important that MNEs have access to the latest technology, wherever developed. As a result, R&D affiliates are being set up outside the home country (e.g. U.S. labs in Europe, Japanese labs in the United States).

Financial Motivations

Fifth, there may be financial motivations for setting up foreign plants. Fluctuations in exchange rates may affect the price of foreign assets; if firms treat FDI as a long-run decision such changes are unlikely to affect the plant location decision. They may, however, affect the timing of the investment. Exchange rates can also affect the costs of production between countries, causing footloose firms to move to lower-cost locations. For example, Japanese MNEs, faced with the sharp rise in the yen and the subsequent increase in wage rates, have shifted labour-intensive stages offshore to ASEAN countries.

Setting up a plant in a tax haven, primarily designed as a conduit for evading national taxes on financial flows, was and still is a common MNE strategy. Competition among U.S. states to attract FDI inflows through subsidies and tax holidays may have shifted such investment from other countries (e.g. Canada) or simply from one state to another.

Strategic Risk-Reduction Motivations

Finally, there may be strategic motivations for setting up a foreign plant. Some authors (Vernon, for example) have argued that MNEs follow risk avoidance strategies that focus on increasing their share of global markets. Large MNEs are international oligopolists, engaged in strategic games with their rivals, fighting over global market shares. In addition, they face opportunistic governments and trade unions bent on securing their "fair" (read "larger") share of the global pie of rents created by these firms. Thus business strategy may dictate plant location if other reasons (such as market access or cost reduction) are unimportant. Some examples of strategic motivations are:

- **International diversification of assets** Setting up competing plants in several locations allows for international diversification of risk. MNEs can reduce the political risks of being held hostage or expropriated by governments, the economic risks of fluctuating exchange rates, and the geographic risks of disruptions in upstream supplies (e.g. crude oil for refineries). As Vernon (1983) shows, risk avoidance can lead to vertical integration. In fact, in an industry where some firms are vertically integrated and others are not, the independents can reduce the risk of opportunistic behaviour from the integrated MNEs (affecting supplies and/or markets) by becoming integrated themselves. Risk avoidance can also lead to horizontal integration as a way of, for example, avoiding the risk of government barriers by becoming an "insider" in the market. (Eden and Molot, 1993).

- **Oligopolistic competition for market share** There are several possible oligopolistic strategies that can increase market share. For example, market pre-emption may be a motivation for setting up a new plant since the first firm into a new market has a first mover advantage over follower firms; in addition the firm may be able to pre-empt the competition. Opportunistic retaliation may be a rationale; i.e. one firm may retaliate against second firm's entry into its market by a tit-for-tat strategy that involves entering the second firm's market. This results in both firms having hostages in each other's markets and should reduce opportunistic behaviour. A third motivation is following the leader since in an uncertain world following the leader may be the most efficient long-run strategy in a loose oligopoly. This induces bunching of foreign investment. In high-tech sectors such as computers foreign firms may set up windows on the competition. Another possible motivation is to co-opt the competition by becoming an insider in a regional market through mergers, acquisitions or joint ventures with a domestic partner.

U.S. Multinationals and Plant Location in North America

Based on the motivations for foreign plants outlined above, I conclude that plants have specific purposes within the MNE hierarchy. These are: market access, resource seeking, cost reduction, support services, financial and/or strategic motivations. Where (in which specific country or region) these plants will be located will depend on their plant function, whether or not they need to be close to other plants within the MNE, what locational factors they need, and which locations offer the most attractive sites. That is, the choice of plant location will depend on the specific characteristics of the products, firms, industries and countries involved. Table 10 outlines some possible effects each can have on the plant location decision.

This table is developed from Dubois, Toyne and Oliff (1993) who examine product-, firm- and industry-specific factors affecting the international manufacturing strategies of multinationals. My analysis broadens theirs to encompass all stages of production, but focuses specifically on plant location decisions within North America. I examine the four factors in detail below and use them to develop hypotheses about the impact of NAFTA on MNE plant location.

Product-Specific Characteristics

The type of product is important. Product is defined as the total package of benefits offered to the customer, not just the physical entity but also intangibles such as security of supply, technical assistance, and finetuning. If the good or service is distinctive and needs to be tailored for a segmented market or if customer involvement with the product is important, then the MNE maximizes its local responsiveness through locating plants near major customers. On the other hand, if the product is a mass-market, standardized good, the MNE is more likely to locate production in the lowest cost location. The type of consumer also matters. Industrial customers tend to work with a small number of upstream suppliers with product lines in order to minimize transaction costs.

Hypothesis 1:   The production of mass produced, standardized goods is more likely to be footloose and move to Mexico. Where local responsiveness to the consumer is important, production will stay close to the final market.

The value-to-weight ratio also affects the likelihood of producing the product off shore. Since transportation costs are often tied to weight, the lower this ratio, the more likely the product is to be manufactured close to the market.

Hypothesis 2:   The higher the value-to-weight ratio, the more likely production is to shift to the lowest-cost production site.

TABLE 10

FACTORS AFFECTING THE PLANT LOCATION CHOICE

PRODUCT-SPECIFIC CHARACTERISTICS	FIRM-SPECIFIC CHARACTERISTICS	INDUSTRY-SPECIFIC CHARACTERISTICS	COUNTRY-SPECIFIC CHARACTERISTICS
Type of product (consumer good, capital good, business service, intangible)	How firm competes in market (price, market share, customer service)	Number of competitors, size and degree of market concentration	Economic (area and population size, income, factor costs, transportation and communications costs)
Stage in product life cycle (new, mature)	Amount of international experience (trade, investment, international alliances)	Age and rate of growth of industry, rate of technological change in industry	Social/cultural (language, culture, psychic distance)
Weight-to-value ratio (high, low)	Size and profitability of firm (economies of scale and scope, resource base, excess capacity)	Degree of globalization of firms in industry (local, regional)	Political/legal (tariff & non-tariff barriers to trade, FDI regulations, taxes, legal system)
Degree of product differentiation (commodity, brand name)	Nature of the value chain of the firm (in-house, sub-contracting), number, location and functions of existing plants	Type, importance and strength of related and supporting industries	General role played by government in economy (attitude toward competition, FDI, public infrastructure)

The stage in the product life cycle can affect the location decision. As products become more mature, location becomes more footloose and cost reduction becomes more important so that MNEs are more likely to shift manufacturing offshore as the product matures. Related to this is the technological intensity of the product. The higher the technology level, the more likely the product itself is to be produced close to the R&D affiliate (generally in the home country).

> **Hypothesis 3:** Mature products are more likely to be produced in Mexico; new and high-tech products in Canada and the United States.

Just-in-time (JIT) production requires upstream suppliers to locate close to their major industrial customers (e.g. auto parts plants near assembly plants). Undifferentiated products with high labour content can be either produced in highly automated home country plants or dispersed to low-cost labour sites in developing countries.

> **Hypothesis 4:** JIT production requires location near downstream firms. Generally this means location closer to final markets, i.e., the United States. Thus JIT discourages production in Mexico.

Firm-Specific Characteristics

Dubois et al. (1993) show that the goals of the firm affect the international manufacturing decision. Firms tend to place differing emphases on cost/efficiency (lowest production cost), quality (product performance), flexibility (the ability to make range of different products and/or adjust output volume rapidly) and dependability (providing dependable products, delivery and price). A focus on the first strategy, cost minimization, is more likely to lead to world wide sourcing of inputs and global manufacturing than are the other strategies.

> **Hypothesis 5:** Firms located in mature, mass production industries, industries where import penetration is high and/or where managers have short-run time horizons, are the ones most likely to use cost-minimization strategies based on cheap labour costs. Such firms are most likely to shift production to Mexico (see Kogut, this volume).

The level of international experience also matters: the greater the experience, the more likely is offshore production. The motivation for a firm going abroad the first time (a new MNE) may be very different from subsequent investment decisions (a veteran or established MNE). For veteran MNEs, expansion may be into new areas or locating new plants in existing areas of penetration. New plants may involve either new product lines, either vertically or horizontally related to existing plants, or be a way to rationalize production with existing plants, or involve the closure of old, obsolete plants and their replacement by more modern facilities. Further, in each case expansion may be either greenfield (a new investment) or brownfield (through mergers and/or acquisitions). Related to this is the size of the firm. Large firms have the economies of scale and scope and the resource base to support production offshore.

> **Hypothesis 6:**   The largest U.S. multinationals with plants scattered throughout the Triad are the firms best placed to reconfigure their activities so as to take advantage of the FTA and the NAFTA. They should therefore be more footloose than domestic firms.

The nature of the firm's value chain (that is, its historical configuration of activities) also affects the plant location decision. The number, location and functions of existing plants will affect the decision on where to locate a new plant.

> **Hypothesis 7:**   Decisions on plant location are made within the context of the MNE's overall strategy and structure, and are therefore firm-specific.

Industry-Specific Characteristics

The largest MNEs are international oligopolists, faced with rivals that they know in various markets around the world. Every action is therefore taken with some presumption as to how the rival firms will react. At the industry level, the number of competitors in the industry, their size, profitability, how they compete, how international they are, the degree of market concentration, will all affect the firm's plant location decision because MNEs are international oligopolists. Therefore their actions will depend upon the anticipated reactions of their competitors, and *vice versa*.

> **Hypothesis 8:**   The more internationalized the industry, the more footloose will be U.S. multinationals.

Country-Specific Characteristics

The firm must use some foreign factors in connection with its domestic firm-specific advantages (FSAs) in order to earn full rents on these FSAs. Therefore the locational advantages of various countries are key in determining which will become host countries for the MNE. Clearly the relative attractiveness of different locations will change over time. The country-specific advantages that influence where an MNE will invest can be broken into three categories: economic, social/cultural and political/legal. Economic advantages include the quantities and qualities of the factors of production, size and scope of the market, transport and telecommunications costs, and so on. Social advantages include psychic distance between the home and host country, general attitude toward foreigners, and overall stance toward free enterprise. Political CSAs include the general and specific policies that affect inward FDI flows, international production and intra-firm trade.[22]

> **Hypothesis 9:** Economic, social/cultural and political/legal factors all influence the plant location choice. As regional integration reduces trade barriers, economic and social CSAs will have more impact on plant location.

Table 11 provides a broad-brush, general comparison of country-specific advantages of Canada, Mexico and the United States in 1990.[23] The table is subdivided into comparisons of economic CSAs (grouped according to Michael Porter's "diamond" of competitive advantage, i.e., factor conditions, demand conditions, structure of firms and industry rivalry, and related and supporting industries), and social/cultural and political/legal CSAs. The table argues that Canada and the United States are much closer to each other than to Mexico, reflecting Mexico's economic position as a developing country with a historically closed economy.

In terms of economic CSAs, the table argues that Canada is relatively well endowed in natural resources and high-skilled labour, the United States in capital, technology and high-skilled labour, and Mexico in low-skilled labour (see also Knubley, Legault and Rao, this volume). Canada's market is small, urban and high-income; the U.S. market is large, urban and high-income; while Mexico's market is split between a relatively large, mostly rural, low-income segment and a small, urbanized, high-income segment. Competition is oligopolistic in most industries, with U.S. MNEs dominating in all three countries, as U.S. multinationals do in technology generation. In related/supporting industries, Canada's strengths lie in the financial sector and public infrastructure; U.S. strengths are in transport and communications, business services, and agglomeration economies; Mexico is weak in these industries.

In terms of social/cultural CSAs, language differences are important; differences in labour and environmental standards are primarily due to weaker enforcement in Mexico (see Mayer, this volume). Finally, in terms of political/legal CSAs, the historical role of Mexico and Canada as host countries to U.S. FDI is reflected in their FDI regulatory policies; the traditional home country role of the United States in its more relaxed regulation of MNEs (see Kudrle, this volume).

TABLE 11

A BROAD-BRUSH COMPARISON OF COUNTRY-SPECIFIC ADVANTAGES WITHIN NORTH AMERICA, 1990

COUNTRY-SPECIFIC ADVANTAGE	CANADA	UNITED STATES	MEXICO
	COUNTRY-SPECIFIC ECONOMIC ADVANTAGES		
FACTOR CONDITIONS			
Quantity and Quality of Primary Factors (endowment of land, labour, capital, energy)	Natural-resource abundant, energy-rich, small and ageing labour force, high rate of unionization.	Capital and land abundant; large and ageing labour force; high wages and low rate of unionization.	Rich in petroleum reserves; abundant young & unskilled labour force; low wages; low education levels; high rate of unionization; low labour participation rate.
Advanced Factor Creation (educated, high-skilled labour)	Small and well-educated labour force; most R&D through government.	Large, high-skilled labour force; global competitive advantage.	High-skilled, educated labour is very small percent of total labour force.
Creation and Adaptation of New Technologies	Most product technology imported through licensing and/or FDI; adaptation of existing rather than creation of new technology; competitive strengths in resource-based technologies; some adoption of lean production techniques.	Innovation center; globally competitive; world leader in product but not process technology creation; some diffusion of lean production techniques.	Product technology imported through licensing and/or IFDI; generally slow adaptation of existing technologies; most sectors have technology gap; some competitive plants in auto sector.

TABLE 11 (CONT'D)

A BROAD-BRUSH COMPARISON OF COUNTRY-SPECIFIC ADVANTAGES WITHIN NORTH AMERICA, 1990

COUNTRY-SPECIFIC ADVANTAGE	CANADA	UNITED STATES	MEXICO
	COUNTRY-SPECIFIC ECONOMIC ADVANTAGES		
DEMAND CONDITIONS			
Market Size and Characteristics (income levels, urbanization, age distribution, discriminating consumers)	Small but very high income market; primarily urban; population 27 million and ageing; slow growing domestic market too small to achieve economies of scale in mass production industries.	Large, very high income market; primarily urban; population of 253 million, slow growing and ageing; market sufficient to achieve economies of scale in mass production industries customers very demanding; high-income/high-taste market; Triad economy.	Medium-sized but low-income market; large disparities in income distribution; large informal sector; primarily rural population of 83 million, rapidly growing and young; current market too small to achieve economies of scale in mass production industries.
STRUCTURE OF FIRMS AND RIVALRY			
Degree of rivalry among firms; presence of joint corporate linkages; industry concentration levels	Tight, interlocking group of families own shares in largest businesses; concentration ratios high in capital-intensive sectors due to small market size; manufacturing, resources, finance and retail sectors oligopolistic.	Competition among firms high but most industries oligopolistic; biggest firms are world leaders and compete globally for market share.	Tight, interlocking group of families own most local, large-scale businesses; joint ventures with foreign firms; high degree of nationalized firms.
Size of firms and degree of multinationality	Largest firms still small by global standards; some multinationals mostly in natural resource sector; high foreign ownership; especially by U.S. MNEs, of resource and manufacturing sectors.	Largest firms globally in many sectors; largest number of head-quarters for multinationals; MNEs especially prevalent in manufacturing and services; rapid growth in inward FDI with Asian and European transplants.	Domestic firms small; few multi-nationals headquartered in Mexico; high degree of foreign ownership, especially U.S., in nonrestricted sectors; joint ventures in restricted sectors.

TABLE 11 (CONT'D)

Openness of firms to innovation and adaptation of new technologies.	Primarily follower firms; innovative firms in resource, transport and telecommunications; generally slow adaptation of new technologies.	Leaders in product innovation; some difficulty in moving from innovative to market stages; problems with process innovation.	Primarily follower firms; generally slow adaptation of existing technologies imported through licensing and FDI.
RELATED AND SUPPORTING INDUSTRIES			
Transportation and communications (T&C)	Good T&C infrastructure, but long distances from east to west (population spread out along the 49th parallel); high transport costs act as barrier to interprovincial trade; Ontario "golden triangle" close to U.S. northeast and midwest, so costs lowest here.	Producers in northeast and mid-west "core" have costs effectively zero; low costs for producers in other regions.	Poor T&C infrastructure plus most cities are long distance from North American "core" so T&C costs high; Major investments needed to offset distance to U.S. central markets.
Presence of strong business services sector	Financial sector strong historically, business services hampered by small market size.	Strong, weakened by collapse of thrifts, competitive advantages in engineering, advertising, accounting services, and so on.	Small and inefficient; many sectors historically nationalized are now being privatized.
Competitive machine tool and capital goods industries	Small and inefficient except in public infrastructure projects.	Regionally large and competitive, but facing substantial import competition from Asia.	Small and inefficient.
Public goods infrastructure: commercial, legal, educational, public health	Very good, financed by general taxes.	Good in general but decaying inner cities, health costs borne primarily by large firms.	Poor, traditionally provided through nationalized firms.

TABLE 11 (CONT'D)

A BROAD-BRUSH COMPARISON OF COUNTRY-SPECIFIC ADVANTAGES WITHIN NORTH AMERICA, 1990

COUNTRY-SPECIFIC ADVANTAGE	CANADA	UNITED STATES	MEXICO
		COUNTRY-SPECIFIC ECONOMIC ADVANTAGES (CONT'D)	
RELATED AND SUPPORTING INDUSTRIES (CONT'D)			
Agglomeration economies from locating in same place	Clusters of firms in regional centres, especially "golden triangle" around Toronto; natural resource-based clusters in Western and Eastern Canada.	Clusters of manufacturing firms, historically in Northeast-Midwest; some now rust belt areas as businesses move to southern U.S.; high-tech clusters in California; "hub" of North America remains central U.S.	Clusters in Mexico City (population 20 million) and around Monterrey; clusters of maquiladoras along Mexico-U.S. border.
		COUNTRY-SPECIFIC SOCIAL/CULTURAL ADVANTAGES	
General public attitude towards foreigners and foreign goods	Traditionally open to investment inflows; worries over levels of U.S. foreign investment and loss of cultural sovereignty especially in the 1970s.	Traditionally open to investment inflows; some concerns over national security; desire for "level playing field" with foreigners; recent "Japan bashing".	Traditionally anti-U.S. attitude, suspicious of U.S. foreign investment, particularly in petroleum; worries over loss of cultural sovereignty.
Psychic distance: language, culture, customs	English with some French primarily in Quebec; bilingual country.	English with some Spanish.	Spanish with some English.

TABLE 11 (CONT'D)

Labour standards	High union membership in manufacturing and government services; resistance to introduction of flexible automation; high strike rates historically.	Low union membership; confrontational relations between labour and business; headquarters of many international unions.	High union membership outside maquiladoras; company unions in many plants; labour laws give unions considerable power in principle.
Environmental standards	Federal environmental regulations; Canada-U.S. border committee.	CAFE rules in autos; federal environmental standards.	Tight environmental laws but weak enforcement; U.S.-Mexico border committee.
COUNTRY-SPECIFIC POLITICAL/LEGAL ADVANTAGES			
Role of government in the economy	Heavy in public infrastructure; sizeable government deficit and national debt; substantial privatization and downsizing since 1980; heavy involvement in education and health; legal and administrative system well developed common law; Parliamentary democracy.	Laissez-faire; defense spending largest government role; large government deficit and national debt; legal and administrative system well developed, common law; democratic republic.	Government intrusive role in economy through regulation and public ownership; substantial divestment since 1986; government budget in surplus but debt still large; legal and administrative system less developed, based on Napoleonic code, subject to corruption; democratic republic with historical political élites.
Government attitude toward MNEs	General open door to FDI; some screening of very large acquisitions or culturally sensitive sectors; long-standing foreign firms seen as insiders in Canadian market.	Supportive of domestic MNEs and outward FDI; fear of Asian competition and transplant contributions to economy, foreign transplants seen as outsiders.	Historical negative attitude to inward FDI, especially from the U.S.; foreign firms seen as outsiders.

TABLE 11 (CONT'D)

A BROAD-BRUSH COMPARISON OF COUNTRY-SPECIFIC ADVANTAGES WITHIN NORTH AMERICA, 1990

COUNTRY-SPECIFIC ADVANTAGE	CANADA	UNITED STATES	MEXICO
	COUNTRY-SPECIFIC POLITICAL/LEGAL ADVANTAGES		
General government trade & investment strategy	Historically high tariffs against imports, falling since Tokyo Round; strong commitment to participation in multilateral organizations such as the GATT; perception of nation as small, open economy reliant on access to U.S. and world markets for trade and FDI.	Generally low U.S. tariffs against imports, Congress traditionally protectionist while Executive pro free trade; long time participant in multilateral organizations such as the GATT; perception of nation as hegemony responsible for ensuring liberal world trading order.	General import-substituting industrialization until 1980s; move to export-oriented industrialization since joining GATT in 1986; unilateral reduction in tariffs and NTBs especially licensing; perception of nation as developmental state, dependent on United States.
Specific policies affecting intra-North American trade and investment	Auto Pact; countervailing and anti-dumping duty legislation; screening of inward FDI; vestiges of the National Energy Policy; restrictions on foreign ownership particularly in banking and culture; compulsory licensing of pharmaceuticals; preferential tariffs for developing countries; national treatment under the FTA.	Various non-tariff barriers including voluntary export restraints, quotas under the MultiFibre Arrangement and subsidies to agriculture exports; Auto Pact; Section and Super 301; preferential tariffs for developing countries and 806/807; heavier use recently of countervailing and anti-dumping legislation; Exon-Florio on national security; limits to foreign ownership in key sectors; national treatment under the FTA.	Constitutional limits on FDI in petroleum; the autos and FDI decrees; regime of high tariffs, licenses and NTBs now being unilaterally dismantled; key sectors closed to inward FDI; maquiladoras program.

The next section predicts the effects of the NAFTA on plant location strategies of U.S. multinationals within North America, based on their current configuration of activities, and on an analysis of the factors likely to influence these location decisions.

WHO DOES WHAT AFTER NAFTA?

CANADA HAS ABOUT 12 percent of U.S. MOFAs world wide. MOFAs in Canada are relatively large, with strong representation in the petroleum, other manufacturing, and the finance, insurance and real estate industries. Three-quarters of Canadian MOFA sales are arm's length local sales, with most of the rest intra-firm sales to their U.S. parents; by industry, world wide sales are highest in other industries and transport equipment. Canadian MOFAs are heavily engaged in intra-firm export and import trade with their U.S. parents. Average employee compensation of MOFAs in Canada is high compared to U.S. MOFAs world wide, as are unit labour costs in many industries.

Mexico, on the other hand, has just under one percent of all U.S. MOFAs world wide; they are relatively large affiliates and very labour intensive. They dominate in manufacturing, particularly in transport equipment, and are absent from the petroleum industry. Almost 30 percent of total sales go to the United States (almost all intra-firm); the rest are local and mostly at arm's length. MOFAs in Mexico are also heavily involved in two-way merchandise trade with their U.S. parent firms. Average employee compensation is well below world wide MOFA levels, but unit labour costs are roughly comparable.

Given this existing configuration of MNE activities in Canada and Mexico, how can we expect the NAFTA to affect plant location decisions? Table 12 attempts to answer this question by looking at the roles Canadian and Mexican plants play within MNE affiliate groups and examining how the NAFTA is likely to affect these roles. Table 12 outlines the six basic motivations for setting up foreign plants: the search for natural resources, new markets, and cheap production locations, the need to provide support and financial services to the MNE family, and strategic risk-reduction motivations. In each case, the Table identifies country-specific advantages likely to attract such plants, and then uses this information to predict how the NAFTA will influence the existing locational configurations of U.S. multinationals in North America.

THE SEARCH FOR RAW MATERIALS

THE NAFTA SHOULD CAUSE U.S. MNES to rationalize their resource-based plants within North America. There should be more investment in endowment-rich areas in Mexico where inward FDI has previously been restricted. FDI should flow into the Mexican petrochemical sector, but not directly into petroleum

TABLE 12

EFFECTS OF THE NAFTA ON PLANT LOCATION STRATEGIES OF U.S. MULTINATIONALS

MOTIVATION	COUNTRY-SPECIFIC ADVANTAGES	EFFECT ON PLANT LOCATION
Search for Raw Materials	- abundant, cheap natural resources - low energy and capital costs - low transport costs	Rationalization of production within the NAFTA. More investment in endowment-rich areas where inward FDI previously restricted, especially in Mexico. Possible upgrading of plants from simple extraction to processing as downstream tariff barriers fall.
The Need for Market Access	- size, income level and characteristics of market - local content rules, tariffs and NTBs - economies of scale in final assembly - cost of capital and highly-skilled labour - transportation and communications infrastructure	Where markets are important, rationalization of existing plants in terms of products and/or processes. Agglomeration effects and economies of scale encourage shift of production to largest market (U.S.). Closure of inefficient plants in small markets and replacement with local distributors. Rapid growth in Mexico of FDI in previously closed sectors.
Search for Cheap Production Locations	- low-cost labour and capital - geographic proximity to downstream firms - trade preferences encouraging offshore production - subsidies to local production	Rationalization of parts plants and sub-assemblies based on lowest cost location (including subsidies). Set up new plants in most cost-effective locations. Possible closure of inefficient plants.
Providing Support Services and Financial Services within MNE Family	- entrepôt functions (e.g. good telecommunications and transportation infrastructure) - tax haven country	For existing MNEs, rationalization of existing subsidiary support functions; shift to centralizing support functions within the U.S. parent. For new MNEs, increased probability of establishing sales and distribution offices in other member countries. Centralization of R&D in parent likely to continue. Shift to marketing for North America as one market.
Strategic Risk-Reduction Motivations	- large and growing market - oligopolistic industries with rent-yielding potential - sectors previously closed to FDI	The NAFTA reduces risk so FDI increases. MNEs' desire for first mover advantages generates waves of FDI into Mexico before and immediately after NAFTA signed, particularly into previously closed sectors.

extraction, due to Mexican constitutional restrictions. In addition, as downstream tariff and non-tariff barriers fall, general upgrading of resource-based plants from simple extraction to processing activities can be expected. While resource-based industries like the mining and petrochemical industries are pollution intensive, the environmental side agreement to the NAFTA should tighten the application of these rules in Mexico, reducing its attractiveness as a haven for polluting activities (see Mayer, this volume).

THE NEED FOR MARKET ACCESS

WHEN TRADE BARRIERS such as tariffs and government procurement policies have been important in influencing market access, MNEs are likely to have set up plants inside national markets to secure such access. The NAFTA reduces these barriers within North America, thereby reducing the need for MNEs to be located in a specific national market. Rationalization of existing plants in terms of products and/or processes is therefore likely, thus increasing both the degree of horizontal and vertical integration within the MNE and the amount of intra-firm trade flows within North America.

Where agglomeration effects and economies of scale are important, these will favour the location of production within the largest market, the U.S. hub, rather than the Canadian or Mexican spokes (see Vernon, and Eaton, Lipsey & Safarian, "Agglomeration Effects", this volume). In such cases, we expect closure of inefficient plants in small markets and their replacement with local distributors. For example, U.S. and Canadian auto exports to Mexico should rise rapidly as Mexico dismantles the trade-balancing requirements of the 1989 Auto Decree; some closures of inefficient plants in Mexico may occur. Related to this, where the MNE is using lean production technologies based on just-in-time delivery and production, parts plants are likely to follow downstream firms. Thus, the first-round location decisions of market-driven assembly plants are likely to be followed by a second round of parts plants investments (e.g. auto parts are likely to follow assemblers, see McCarthy, 1993). On the other hand, where a local presence is important for local sale (e.g. distribution, consumer services) or consumer tastes vary widely between national markets, the activities are not footloose, so the NAFTA should not shift such activities.

Where sectors have been closed to inward FDI prior to the NAFTA, there should be increased inward FDI into these sectors, particularly if strong market growth is expected. For example, consumer services such as finance, insurance and telecommunications should expand in Mexico after the NAFTA.[24] Retailing is another sector expected to expand rapidly; retail floor space in Mexico City is extraordinarily low for a city of 20 million. For example, the Mexican affiliates of Sears, Wendy's, Wal-Mart and Pepsi Cola are among the most profitable affiliates of these U.S. multinationals; all these firms are investing heavily in Mexico in anticipation of the NAFTA (*The New York Times*, July 21, 1993).

THE SEARCH FOR LOW-COST PRODUCTION SITES

REDUCTION OF TRADE BARRIERS under the NAFTA should increase the importance of economic factors such as unit labour costs as influences on the location of cost-driven plants. MNEs with labour-intensive parts plants located in the ASEAN and Caribbean countries may close those plants and shift production within North America. Tight rules of origin, particularly in the autos and textile sectors, should also encourage more onshore sourcing of parts and components. Rationalization of parts plants and sub-assemblies based on lowest cost location (including subsidies) is likely as MNEs move to set up new plants in the most cost-effective location. This should lead to increased vertical integration, and the possible closure of inefficient plants both inside and outside North America.

Two factors will be key to this decision for cost-reducing plants, in terms of comparing location in Mexico rather than in Canada or the United States. First, MNEs must trade off lower unit labour costs (as determined by wage rates and labour productivity) in Mexico against higher transport and infrastructure costs. Since the NAFTA improves crossborder transportation, we expect the natural insulation of transport barriers to decrease, increasing the probably vertical integration of Mexican plants into the MNE hierarchy (see also Unger, this volume). In addition, Mexican workers, when placed with world class plants and technology, are as productive as workers in Canada and the United States (as documented, for example, in the Ford Hermosillo plant). This should lead to increased parts and components production in labour-intensive, medium-technology activities such as consumer electronics, textiles and auto parts, as predicted by the Office of Technology Assessment (1992).

The second factor is the rate at which the MNE adopts lean production technologies, as opposed to continuing the 1970s strategy of mass production accompanied by world wide sourcing of parts and components. Lean production strategies encourage clustering of parts plants near the parent firm (lead plant) and downstream assembly and R&D plants. If agglomeration encourages plant location in the U.S. hub after the NAFTA, then lean production should discourage the erection of cost-reducing plants in low-wage locations (see Kogut, this volume). This may have more impact on U.S. outward FDI in plants in export-processing zones in Asia than in Mexico.

PROVIDING SUPPORT AND FINANCIAL SERVICES

WITH NATIONAL BORDERS BEING ERODED, the necessity for U.S. MNEs to have regional head offices in Mexico and Canada should be reduced. Some rationalization of existing subsidiary support functions (e.g. finance, government relations) is expected as the parent firm centralizes its head office support functions within the U.S. parent. U.S. MNEs should shift to treating North America as one integrated market for advertising purposes.

Centralization of R&D in the parent firm is likely to continue since the NAFTA prohibits the use of non-tariff barriers such as local content rules and performance requirements (see Eaton, Lipsey & Safarian, "Agglomeration", this volume).

STRATEGIC RISK-REDUCTION MOTIVATIONS

NAFTA REDUCES THE RISK for firms investing within North America so that intra-North American FDI flows should increase (see Vernon, and Eaton, Lipsey & Safarian, this volume). This desire of the largest U.S. multinationals for first-mover advantages in the Mexican market has already generated waves of inward FDI into Mexico. These should continue immediately after the NAFTA is signed into law, particularly into previously closed sectors, so that bunching should be visible.

SUMMARY

IN SUMMARY, IT IS EXPECTED THAT the NAFTA will induce substantial rationalization and possibly some downsizing of U.S. majority-owned foreign affiliates both inside and outside North America. As a result, the degree of horizontal and vertical integration of these MNEs should increase, creating more intra-firm trade and investment flows within North America, and perhaps smaller trade and investment flows between North America and Europe and Asia. Substantial investments in Mexico are anticipated, primarily in market access and resource-seeking investments in sectors where FDI has been restricted. However, given that: 1) differentials in unit labour costs in the three countries, while favouring Mexico, are currently not large, 2) Canadian and U.S. tariffs on Mexican exports are already low, and 3) labour costs are a small and declining share of total production costs for most stages of production, wholesale migration of plants from Canada or the United States to Mexico is not expected. In fact, relocation to the United States, both by foot-loose stages of production and by regional head office functions where economies of scale and agglomeration are important, is more probably for U.S. MOFAs in Canada than relocation to Mexico.

CONCLUSIONS

THE QUESTION, "Will NAFTA cause U.S. multinationals to shift their branch plants to Mexico?" requires both a simple answer and a complex one. The simple answer is "no", the NAFTA will not cause a massive exodus of plants from Canada and the United States to Mexico. As the statistics on U.S. MOFAs show, wide differentials exist in average employee compensation within the same industry but in different countries. However, unit labour costs are much more homogeneous, reflecting the fact that highly productive workers are better paid, and in some industries unit labour costs are higher in Mexico. Therefore widespread closures of U.S. branch plants in Canada are not predicted, even for firms where labour costs are a large proportion of total costs.

The complex answer to the question is that there will be both closures and changes. These are likely to be much greater than simple econometric trade models predict because the NAFTA is much broader than a simple tariff-removal exercise. As government regulatory and trade barriers fall, liberalization will lead to reorganization and rationalization of MNE activities within each country and between countries.

U.S. MNEs are the firms best placed to take advantage of the falling tariff and non-tariff barriers that the FTA and the NAFTA will bring because they are already located in all three countries. The configuration of their plants was historically based on the "blocks" governments had positioned on the North American "chessboard". With governments now removing these blocks, the underlying economic factors will have more impact on location decisions. Because MNEs are international oligopolists, concerned about their shares of global markets, they will change the configuration of their activities in order to increase their international competitiveness.

U.S. MNEs are expected to locate, close and/or expand their plants with the whole North American market in mind. This should lead to reduced numbers of product lines in various plants and increasing horizontal trade among plants. MNEs are also likely to segment their production process among plants so that more vertical intra-firm trade takes place. As a result there should be more cross-border vertical and horizontal intra-firm trade. Certain product lines, industry segments, and plant functions will shift among the three countries and these will cause job losses and plant closures in certain locations. Precisely which plants and/or locations will depend on a complicated array of factors, some of which are exogenous to the firms involved (such as factor prices and transportation costs) and others which are firm-specific (such as the nature of the products produced and the ingenuity and entrepreneurship of the individuals involved). In each case, decisions will be taken at the level of the firm and we can but identify the factors that will be important in the decision making, without knowing the final outcome.

It may be concluded that the NAFTA will cause a variety of responses by U.S. multinationals, depending on their particular configurations of product-, firm-, industry- and country-specific characteristics. The strategic role each plant plays within the MNE, the types of locational factors the plant needs, and the country-specific advantages of various locations within North America will all affect the outcome. For most U.S. multinationals, low wages are a minor consideration in these location decisions. Rationalization of plant functions, either in terms of horizontal specialization in particular product lines, or vertical specialization in particular processes, is much more likely than plant flight to Mexico.

ENDNOTES

1 See Chesnais (1992), Dunning (1993), and the *Economist* (1993).

2 On the labour, social and environmental arguments concerning the NAFTA, see *The New York Times* (1993), *Business Week* (1993), Globerman and Walker (1993), Lemco and Robson (1993), Morici (1991), Prestowitz et al. (1991), Randall et al. (1992), OTA (1992), UNA-USA (1992), and Reifman (1992).

3 See Dunning (1993), Emerson et al. (1988), Investment Canada (1991), Rugman (1990) and UNCTC (1990).

4 For good summaries of the NAFTA see Government of Canada (1992), Globerman and Walker (1993), and Hufbauer and Schott (1993).

5 The only exception to this is global environmental accords such as the Ozone Accord and the Basel Convention on hazardous wastes, where the environmental accord takes precedence over the NAFTA.

6 Good analyses of the FTA and the NAFTA can be found in Cushing et al. (1993), Eden & Molot (1992), Fry & Radebaugh (1991), Globerman (1991), Globerman & Walker (1993), Hufbauer & Schott (1992, 1993), Lustig et al. (1992), Morici (1991), Prestowitz et al. (1991), Randall et al. (1992), Reynolds et al. (1991), Rugman (1990), UNCTC (1990), ITC (1991) and Watson (1991, 1992, 1993).

7 For a detailed history of FDI and industrial restructuring in Mexico see UNCTC (1992).

8 This hypothesis is discussed in Niosi's study in this volume.

9 Such investment diversion would be one reason for Mexico's desire to join the FTA.

10 Womack et al. (1990) predict this pattern for the North American auto industry, with the smaller, lower value-added autos being produced in Mexico and the larger, higher value-added ones in Canada and the United States.

11 While technological change will have pervasive effects on U.S. multinationals and their configuration of plants in North America, in this study we concentrate primarily on regional integration. See Eden (1991) and Morton (1991) for detailed analyses of the impacts of flexible automation on MNEs.

12 A long-running debate in Canada has focused on the role the Auto Pact safeguards, which effectively requires one car to be assembled here for each one sold here, have played a part in maintaining assembly functions in Canada, with some authors maintaining that the safeguards have not been binding since the mid-1980s and could therefore be dropped. The Canadian government, however, was successful in both the FTA and the NAFTA negotiations in keeping the Auto Pact in place in spite of U.S. pressures to eliminate it, see Eden & Molot (1993).

13 Leamer (1992), using a Heckscher-Ohlin three-factor model, reached similar predictions concerning the wage gap.

14 This table also illustrates the points made in the Encarnation study in this volume concerning U.S. MOFAs in Japan. Note the large trade surplus ($5.5 billion) and the higher proportion of U.S. exports (7.2 percent) relative to imports (2.1 percent) compared to the share of U.S. MOFAs in Japan (0.9 percent).

15 We do not have data on the output or value added by industry, so PPE (a measure of the net physical capital stock) and sales are proxies for the relative size of MOFAs by industry in the host country.

16 Note that MOFAs in Canada, in the transport equipment industry, had 31.7 percent of world wide sales but only 22.5 percent of world wide PPE. This probably reflects the less capital-intensive nature of the primary activity in Canada (vehicle assembly) compared to parts and components production. Mexico, on the other hand, had 5.3 percent of world wide sales and 5.2 percent of world wide PPE in this industry.

17 While we do not discuss this in detail here, one can compare the labour force data among countries and across industries as another proxy for the relative size of MOFAs in particular countries and sectors. For example, 16.6 percent of the 5.2 million workers employed in U.S. MOFAs in 1990 were in Canada, 7 percent were in Mexico. Some other shares are: manufacturing (Canada 12.8 percent, Mexico 9.8 percent), transport equipment (Canada 19.8 percent, Mexico 13.4 percent), electrical equipment (Canada 7.4 percent, Mexico 19 percent).

18 Average compensation was calculated as total employee compensation (not provided) divided by the number of MOFA employees. Unit labour costs were calculated as total employee compensation divided by total MOFA sales (from Table 8).

19 Clearly, in order to make predictions as to the likelihood of plant shifts due to differences in unit labour costs, we would need data at a much finer level than the two-digit SIC code.

20 Unfortunately, the U.S. data do not provide the same information for U.S. parents, so that we cannot perform unit labour cost comparisons for the parent firms. However, Table 1 does provide such numbers for three assembly operations; unit labour costs are much higher in these plants than in the U.S. plants.

21 Dunning (1993) and UNCTC (1990) provide somewhat differently organized lists, although similar factors are discussed.

22 See McCarthy (1993) for an interesting discussion of the regional CSAs that have led German MNEs to locate in the Carolinas.

23 The table of country-specific advantages developed here is an amalgamation of Dunning's basic OLI model (see Dunning, 1993) and Michael Porter's diamond model of competitive advantage (see Porter, 1991). Porter's diamond consists of economic factors influencing plant location, and thus appropriately belongs within the group of country-specific economic advantages.

24 For example, per capita consumption of insurance in Mexico is $30 per year; in Canada it is $1,200 and in the United States it is $1,900. The market in Mexico for insurance is predicted to grow from $4.5 billion today to $50 billion, with Mexico moving from 27th to the 7th largest market in the world. See *Business Week*, August 9, 1993.

ACKNOWLEDGEMENT

I WOULD LIKE TO THANK, without implication, Investment Canada (now Industry Canada), Ivan Feltham, Chuck Hermann, Christopher Maule, Maureen Molot, Subi Rangan and Ray Vernon for helpful comments and discussions. The paper was presented at the 1993 International Studies Association annual meetings in Acapulco and at the Maxwell School, Syracuse University, and I thank the participants in those sessions for their comments. The bulk of this research was undertaken while I was on sabbatical leave from Carleton University, on a 1992-93 Canada-U.S. Fulbright Award as Visiting Professor at the Kennedy School of Government, Harvard University, and the Department of Finance, The Ohio State University. Research support was also provided by Industry Canada and the Social Sciences and Humanities Research Council of Canada. I would like to thank these institutions for their support.

BIBLIOGRAPHY

"America's Newest Industrial Belt." *The New York Times*, Business Section, (March 21, 1993): 1,14.

"America's Back Door." *Far Eastern Economic Review* , (July 11, 1991): 44, 46.

"Everybody's Favourite Monsters: A Survey of Multinationals." *The Economist*, (March 27, 1993): 1-20.

"The Mexican Worker." *Business Week*, (April 19, 1993): 84-92.

"Mexico: A Market that is Ready for Services." *The New York Times*, (July 21, 1993): C10-11.

"Why Insurers are Splashing Across the Rio Grande." *Business Week*, (August 9, 1993): 68.

Canada, Government of. *North American Free Trade Agreement: An Overview and Description*. Ottawa: Government of Canada, August 1992.

Chesnais, Francois. "An Approach to a Unified Analysis of Foreign Direct Investment, International Trade, Technology and Competitiveness in the Context of Globalization." Presented at the conference Maastricht Revisited: Convergence and Divergence in Economic Growth and Technical Change, University of Limburg, The Netherlands, December 10-12, 1992.

Cushing, Robert, et al. (eds). *The Challenge of NAFTA: North America, Australia, New Zealand, and the World Trade Regime*. Austin, Texas: University of Texas, 1993.

Dubois, Frank, et al. "International Manufacturing Strategies of U.S. Multinationals: A Conceptual Framework Based on a Four-Industry Study." *Journal of International Business Studies*, 24, 2, (Second Quarter 1993): 307-33.

Dunning, John. *Multinational Enterprises and the Global Economy*. Workingham, UK and Reading, Massachusetts: Addison-Wesley Publishing Company, 1993.

Eden, Lorraine. "Multinational Responses to Trade and Technology Changes: Implications for Canada." In *Multinationals, Technology and Economic Growth*. Edited by Donald McFetridge. Investment Canada Research Series. Calgary: University of Calgary Press, 1991.

Eden, Lorraine and Maureen Appel Molot. "Comparative and Competitive Advantage in the North American Trade Bloc." *Canadian Business Economics*. 1, 1, (Fall 1992): 45-59.

_____. "Insiders and Outsiders: Auto Industry Policy Choices in the NAFTA Debate." In *The Challenge of NAFTA: North America, Australia, New Zealand and the World Trade Regime*. Edited by Robert G. Cushing et al. Austin, Texas: University of Texas, 1993.

Emerson, Michael, et al. *The Economics of 1992: The E.C. Commission's Assessment of the Economic Effects of Completing the Internal Market*. Commission of the European Communities. Oxford: Oxford University Press, 1988.

Fry, Earl H. and Lee H. Radebaugh (eds). *Investment in the North American Free Trade Area: Opportunities and Challenges*. Provo, Utah: Brigham Young University and Toronto: Ontario Centre for International Business, University of Toronto, 1991.

Globerman, Steven (ed). *Continental Accord: North American Economic Integration*. Vancouver: The Fraser Institute, 1991.

Globerman, Steven and Michael Walker (eds). *Assessing NAFTA: A Trinational Analysis*. Vancouver: The Fraser Institute, 1993.

Hart, Michael. *A North American Free Trade Agreement: The Strategic Implications for Canada*. Halifax: Institute for Research on Public Policy and the Centre for Trade Policy and Law, 1991.

Hufbauer, Gary Clyde and Jeffrey J. Schott. *NAFTA: An Assessment*. Washington, D.C.: Institute for International Economics, 1993.

_____. *North American Free Trade: Issues and Recommendations*. Washington, D.C.: Institute for International Economics, 1992.

Investment Canada. *Canada-U.S.-Mexico Free Trade Negotiations: The Rationale and the Investment Dimension*, Ottawa, Investment Canada, August 1990.

_____. *The Opportunities and Challenges of North American Free Trade: A Canadian Perspective*, Working Paper No. 7. Ottawa: Investment Canada, April 1991.

Kahle, Egbert. "Europe 1992: Issues and Implications." In *The Business of Europe: Managing Change*. Edited by Roland Calori and Peter Lawrence. New York: Sage Publications, 1991.

Leamer, Edward. "Wage Effects of a U.S.-Mexican Free Trade Agreement." NBER Working Paper No. 3991. Cambridge, Mass.: National Bureau of Economic Research, February 1992.

Lemco, Jonathan and William Robson (eds). *Ties Beyond Trade: Labor and Environmental Issues under the NAFTA*. Canadian-American Committee, Toronto: C.D. Howe Institute and Washington, D.C.: National Planning Association, 1993.

Lustig, Nora, Barry Bosworth and Robert Lawrence (eds). *North American Free Trade: Assessing the Impact*. Washington, D.C.: The Brookings Institution, 1992.

McCarthy, Michael. "Why German Firms Choose the Carolinas to Build U.S. Plants." *The Wall Street Journal*, (May 4, 1993): A1, A12.

Morici, Peter. *Trade Talks with Mexico: A Time for Realism*. Washington, D.C.: National Planning Association, 1991.

Morton, Michael. *The Corporation of the 1990s: Information Technology and Organizational Transformation*. New York and Oxford: Oxford University Press, 1991.

Porter, Michael. *The Competitive Advantage of Nations*. New York: The Free Press, 1990.

Prestowitz, Clyde, Jr., and Robert Cohen with Peter Morici and Alan Tonelson. *The New North American Order: A Win-Win Strategy for U.S.-Mexico Trade*. Washington: Economic Strategy Institute, 1991.

Randall, Stephen et al. (eds). *North America Without Borders? Integrating Canada, the United States and Mexico*. Calgary: University of Calgary Press, 1992.

Reifman, Alfred. *NAFTA and Jobs: An Overview*. CRS Report for Congress. Washington, D.C.: Library of Congress Congressional Research Service, December 21, 1992.

Reynolds, Clark, et al. (eds). *The Dynamics of North American Trade and Investment*. Stanford: Stanford University Press, 1991.

Rousslang, Donald and Theodore To. "Domestic Trade and Transportation Costs as Barriers to International Trade." *The Canadian Journal of Economics*. 26, 1, (February 1993): 208-21.

Rugman, Alan. *Multinationals and the Canada-United States Free Trade Agreement*. Columbia, South Carolina: University of South Carolina Press, 1990.

Rugman, Alan and Michael Gestrin. "The Investment Provisions of NAFTA." In *Assessing NAFTA: A Trinational Analysis*. Edited by Steven Globerman and Michael Walker. Vancouver: The Fraser Institute, 1993.

United Nations Association of the USA (UNA-USA). *The Social Implications of a North American Free Trade Agreement*. Report of the Economic Policy Council of the United Nations Association of the USA. New York: United Nations Association of the USA.

United Nations Centre on Transnational Corporations (UNCTC). *Regional Economic Integration and Transnational Corporations in the 1990s: Europe 1992, North America, and Developing Countries*. UNCTC Current Studies Series A, No.15. New York: United Nations, 1990.

United Nations Centre on Transnational Corporations (UNCTC). *World Investment Report 1991: The Triad in Foreign Direct Investment*. New York: United Nations, 1991.

_____. *Foreign Direct Investment and Industrial Restructuring in Mexico: Government Policy, Corporate Strategies and Regional Integration*. UNCTC Current Studies Series A, No.18. New York: United Nations, 1992.

United States General Accounting Office (GAO). *North American Free Trade Agreement: U.S.-Mexican Trade and Investment Data: Report to the Honorable Richard A. Gephart, Majority Leader and to the Honorable Sander Levin, House of Representatives*. Washington, D.C.: U.S. Government Printing Office, September 1992.

United States International Trade Commission (ITC). *The Likely Impact of a Free Trade Agreement with Mexico*. Report No. 2352, Washington, D.C.: U.S. Printing Office, February 1991.

United States Office of Technology Assessment (OTA). *U.S.-Mexico Trade: Pulling Together or Pulling Apart?* Washington, D.C.: U.S. Government Printing Office, 1992.

Watson, William. *Policy Forum on the North American Free Trade Area*. Kingston, Ontario: John Deutsch Institute for the Study of Public Policy, 1991.

Watson, William. "North American Free Trade: Lessons from the Trade Data." *Canadian Public Policy*, XVIII, 1, (1992): 1-12.

Watson, William. "The Economic Effect of NAFTA." *C.D. Howe Commentary*, 50, (June 1993).

Womack, James P., et al. *The Machine That Changed The World*. New York: Rawson Associates, 1990.

D. Eleanor Westney
Associate Professor of Management
Sloan School of Management
Massachusets Institute of Technology

Japanese Multinationals in North America

INTRODUCTION

JAPAN IS A RELATIVE NEWCOMER to the ranks of major foreign direct investors in North America and, indeed, to foreign direct investment (FDI) generally. During the 1980s Japan's total FDI rose dramatically, taking Japanese shares of the world's FDI flow from about 6 percent in the late 1970s to nearly 30 percent in 1989 (Froot, 1989). During this period, North America became the primary target for Japanese investment in both manufacturing and non-manufacturing sectors. However, in 1990 the torrent of Japanese investment overseas slowed considerably, and continued to slow over the following two years. Economic factors — the combination of the recession in North America and the collapse of the "bubble economy" in Japan — were largely responsible for the cutbacks, but the changes in both the local and home country economies also accelerated a process that had already begun in many leading Japanese firms: a re-examination of internationalization strategies and organization, triggered in part by the increasingly strident criticisms of the growing Japanese presence in the United States.

The surge in Japanese investment in manufacturing sectors in North America during the 1980s was largely defensive in nature, intended to protect and maintain the prospects for expanding markets won by exports but threatened by actual or anticipated protectionism and by the sudden rise in the value of the yen in 1985-86. In the United States, however, the very rapidity of the Japanese response to demands by U.S. policy-makers — that Japanese firms serve the U.S. market by local production rather than by export — created a backlash of criticism alleging that Japanese FDI was "taking over" North American industry and eroding local manufacturing capabilities (Komiya & Wakasugi, 1989; Yamamura, 1989).

Popular criticism of Japanese investment in North America contained strong elements of xenophobia, as both Japanese spokesmen and North American free market economists were quick to note. However, the popular media debates, like those among policymakers and academic analysts, hinged

253

largely on the more complex issue of whether the Japanese multinational enterprises (MNEs), which had so suddenly become an important part of the North American landscape, differed significantly from Western MNEs in their organization and management and therefore in their impact on the local business environment and, if so, why. The differences most often noted, both in the popular press and in academic analyses, are the higher proportion of home country managers in key positions in offshore subsidiaries, the greater propensity to supplement local production with home-based components and exports, and the greater reliance on an "organization-set" (the supporting infrastructure of suppliers, service providers, and even construction firms) brought over from Japan and reconstructed in the new environment.

While most observers agree with this characterization of Japanese MNEs, they have disagreed profoundly over whether these features are a result of: the relative newness of North American subsidiaries (life cycle effects); the timing of the internationalization of Japanese firms in an era of cheap transport and efficient telecommunications that have allowed greater centralization (period effects); the general nature of Japanese companies that has influenced the strategy and structure of offshore operations (country effects); or the product of the particular industries or sectors in which Japanese FDI has been concentrated (organizational field effects).

The issue of the nature and origin of the structure and behaviour of Japanese MNEs is of much more than academic interest; it is an essential element in coming to grips with the issues of how the NAFTA is likely to affect Japanese FDI and with the implications of Japanese FDI for the competitiveness of the three countries in the region. This study begins with a brief look at the macro patterns of Japanese investment in North America and attempts to understand more clearly the firm-level factors that have shaped those investments and that will affect the nature and impact of investment in the future.

THE MACRO PATTERNS OF JAPANESE INVESTMENT IN NORTH AMERICA

FROM THE LATE 1970S North America, Japan's largest offshore market, has been the major target of Japanese foreign direct investment. Throughout the 1980s its share of Japan's growing outflow of foreign direct investment increased. By the end of the decade, North America was the destination of half of Japan's FDI outflows. Asia, which had accounted for approximately one-quarter of the 1980 outflow, attracted only 12.2 percent in 1989 — although of course the absolute amount of investment was considerably higher in 1989 (Table 1).

Japanese analysts attribute the growth in FDI during the 1980s to two factors (Ishii, 1992). The first was the imposition (or threat of imposition) of

TABLE 1

JAPAN'S FOREIGN DIRECT INVESTMENT IN THE 1980S, BY REGION
(% OF FDI OUTFLOW)

REGION	1980	1985	1989
North America	34.0	45.0	50.2
Western Europe	12.3	15.8	21.9
Asia	25.3	11.7	12.2
Oceania	9.5	4.3	6.8
Central/South America	12.5	21.4	7.8
Other	6.4	1.8	1.1
Total ($ million)	4,693	12,217	67,540

Source: Japanese Ministry of Finance data.

trade barriers in the United States and the European Community (EC), which began in the early 1980s (and accounted for the first major rise in FDI into North America in 1981) and which continued through the decade. The second and more important was the sudden rise in the value of the yen that began in September of 1985, when the exchange rate was about 238 yen to the U.S. dollar, to the present rate of about 106 yen to the U.S. dollar. The increased value of the yen had a strong effect on manufacturing firms, which found their costs rising rapidly, relative to their offshore revenues, and which responded by moving substantial amounts of lower value-added production to Asia and higher value-added production into their major markets, primarily the United States and the EC. But the high yen also prompted service firms and investors in real estate to seek higher return on investments outside their home market as their stronger currency gave them advantages over local investors (Froot, 1989). According to some accounts (e.g. Ishii, 1992), the so-called bubble economy of the late 1980s led to a rapid increase in the salience of non-manufacturing FDI. In fact, however, the ready availability of investment capital during the bubble contributed to the ease with which manufacturing firms could finance offshore operations in response to the shifts in exchange rates. Consequently the balance between manufacturing and non-manufacturing sectors remained fairly steady over the decade (Table 2).

Some analysts have noted that a relatively high proportion of Japanese FDI is from non-manufacturing sectors. Over two-thirds of U.S. and U.K. FDI has been in manufacturing, whereas Japanese manufacturing accounted for a considerably lower percentage during the 1980s (Komiya & Wakasugi, 1991). As we shall see below, this is partly a reflection of the different structure of the Japanese MNE, which often separates sales and distribution and production into individual subsidiaries instead of as a single country subsidiary, thereby lowering the investment that is tallied as manufacturing.

TABLE 2

JAPAN'S FOREIGN DIRECT INVESTMENT BY YEAR, 1980-90 (US$ MILLION)

YEAR	TOTAL	MANUFACTURING	MANUFACTURING AS % OF TOTAL
1980	4,693	1,706	36.3
1981	8,932	2,305	25.8
1982	7,703	2,076	26.9
1983	8,145	2,588	31.8
1984	10,155	2,505	24.7
1985	12,217	2,352	19.2
1986	22,320	3,806	17.0
1987	33,364	7,832	23.5
1988	47,022	13,805	29.3
1989	67,540	16,284	24.1
1990	56,911	15,486	27.2

The most distinctive feature of Japanese FDI, however, has been its extraordinary compression in time. Of cumulative Japanese FDI from 1951 through 1989, two-thirds occurred between 1986 and 1989. The peak year, 1989, accounted for 28.6 percent of the total cumulative Japanese investment in manufacturing in North America and 59.6 percent of the cumulative investment in services (*Business International*, August 13, 1990, p. 270). This surge drew great attention from the public and from policy makers, and made inward FDI a salient political issue in the United States, even though, as economists pointed out, Japan still lagged behind the United Kingdom as an investor in North America.

This scale of FDI was not sustained. In 1990, Japanese FDI dropped by 15.7 percent from the previous year, and investment in North America dropped even more precipitately, by 19.4 percent. The scale of the 1990 reduction was somewhat disguised by the largest single investment to date by a Japanese firm: the $6.1 billion acquisition of MCI by Matsushita (which accounted for 23 percent of total Japanese investment in North America in that year). In 1991 and 1992, Japanese investment dropped further.

"Softer" information from the level of individual firms indicates that this slowdown in FDI is not a temporary phenomenon. A survey of managers by Japan's Ministry of Finance in 1991 found four reasons for the 1990 decline in FDI: 1) many enterprises felt that they had already established their overseas base; 2) companies had difficulty raising capital abroad; 3) companies had difficulty raising investment capital in Japan; and 4) global recession had affected their assessment of overseas market potential (*Japan Economic Almanac* 1992, p. 30)

In that same year, the Export-Import Bank of Japan conducted a survey of 551 manufacturing companies with three or more overseas production subsidiaries and found that 55 percent planned to reduce their investment abroad in the medium term (1992 through 1994), while 12 percent planned to hold it at 1991 levels and 34 percent planned an increase. Firms in the chemicals and electrical machinery industries were the most aggressive in their planning; firms in the auto, steel, and general machinery industries were most negative, focusing on strengthening their current offshore bases and perhaps adding R&D, but not expanding production significantly (Ishii, 1992:10-12).

The data from the Export-Import Bank survey also suggest that while North America remains an important focus of activity for Japanese firms, the main target of Japanese FDI may be shifting to Asia. While slightly less than half of the firms surveyed planned to increase their investment in the U.S. and Canada over the long term, more than two-thirds anticipated expanding in the ASEAN countries and over 70 percent planned investments in the People's Republic of China (Ishii, 1991:10-12). Asia's growing role as both a production base for Japanese firms and a market has been emphasized over the past year by the Japanese press. In contrast, press attention to North America has focused on the prospects for exacerbated U.S.-Japan tensions rather than on the NAFTA and its implications for regional economic growth. In MITI's 1991 White Paper, for example, the section providing a regional survey of the world economy includes a chapter on Europe, concentrating on the relationship between the changes in Russia and Eastern Europe and the continued progress towards economic unification; a chapter on Asia, which emphasizes the promise of growth and expansion in the region, and a chapter on the United States, centred on the continuing economic stagnation and including in its 38 pages only two paragraphs on the NAFTA.

The apparent lack of Japanese interest in the NAFTA, especially when compared to the intense interest in the integration processes in the EC, can be understood in terms of the regional dominance of the United States. Japanese policy makers and businessmen apparently believe that the United States will set the NAFTA terms relevant to Japanese investment, and therefore their strong focus on understanding and influencing U.S. policy need not be modified significantly to take account of regional rather than national politics.

Despite the changing scale and direction of Japanese FDI, the geographic distribution within North America has remained steady. Throughout the 1980s, the United States was the major target of Japanese investment in this region (Table 3). Japanese investments in Canada have remained under 5 percent of the North American total, about half the level that might be expected given the relative size of the Canadian economy (Rugman, 1990). And, as Rugman's 1990 study found, they have been concentrated in the resource-based industries and in trade and distribution rather than in manufacturing.

The Free Trade Agreement (FTA) between Canada and the United States had no discernible effect on the Japanese propensity to invest in Canada. While Japanese investments in Canada rose in 1989, the rise was proportional to the increase in investment in the United States. Mexico has had even less prominence in Japanese FDI (it is worthy of note that throughout

TABLE 3

JAPAN'S FOREIGN DIRECT INVESTMENT IN NORTH AMERICA
FISCAL 1987 - FISCAL 1991 (US$ MILLION)

YEAR	UNITED STATES	CANADA	MEXICO
1987	14,704	653	28
1988	21,701	626	87
1989	32,540	1,362	36
1990	26,128	1,064	168
1991	18,026	797	193
Cumulative as of			
March 31, 1992	148,554	6,454	2,067

JAPANESE FDI IN CANADA AND MEXICO AS A RATIO OF JAPANESE FDI IN THE
UNITED STATES 1987-91

YEAR	CANADA	MEXICO
1987	.044	.002
1988	.029	.004
1989	.042	.001
1990	.041	.006
1991	.044	.011

the decade Japanese government data defined "North America" as the United States and Canada and put Mexico into the regional category of Central and South America). Japanese investment in Mexico was negligible until the mid-1980s. Since then, however, investment in production facilities in the maquiladoras has increased, and now accounts for about 15 percent of employment in these border regions (Beechler & Taylor, 1993). Japanese FDI in Mexico, however, may be understated by the official data, since several of the maquiladora plants are owned by the U.S. subsidiaries of Japanese firms rather than directly by the parent.

The data on Japanese FDI may also underestimate the scale of Japanese involvement in the region's industrial structure in another way. Japanese investment in the United States has been changing in mode: more firms have been resorting to acquisitions rather than greenfield operations, and firms have been making non-equity alliances or investments below the 10 percent level required to meet the official definition of FDI (and inclusion in official U.S. tallies of Japanese FDI). Both strategies are partly in response to U.S. criticisms of Japanese investments and partly a way to leverage existing investments.

This discussion has concentrated so far on the aggregate data on investment patterns, rather than on the firm-level configuration of those investments. But some interesting firm-level data have been provided by Ishii's 1988 study (reported in Ishii, 1992) of 21 Japanese MNEs with production operations offshore. Of these 21 firms, 20 had production subsidiaries in the

United States; 13 of those companies had more than one separately incorporated subsidiary, for a total of seventy-three. Nine had manufacturing subsidiaries in Mexico, of which three companies had two subsidiaries, for a total of twelve. Only five companies had manufacturing subsidiaries in Canada, and each of these had only one, for a total of five (and, of these, one company's Canadian subsidiary was acquired when its U.S. parent company was purchased in 1985, and so does not represent a strategic decision to invest in Canada). It is worth noting the contrast with Asia, where these 21 companies had a total of 181 manufacturing subsidiaries. These firm-level data reinforce the implication of the macro data of the strong U.S. focus of Japanese FDI in North America and the importance of Asia in the global production networks of the leading Japanese firms.

But much of the attention devoted to Japanese FDI in North America has focused not on its scale but on its nature: that is, on the features of Japanese MNEs that differ from patterns established by Western MNEs. The following sections outline those differences and assess their implications for future patterns of Japanese FDI and for policy makers in the host countries.

ARE JAPANESE MNES DIFFERENT?

A NUMBER OF STUDIES HAVE FOUND that in the 1980s Japanese MNEs exhibited features that distinguished them from their Western counterparts, features that seemed to characterize Japanese firms in virtually all sectors of manufacturing and commercial activity. One of the most studied is a relatively high proportion of home country managers in key positions (Trevor, 1983; Bartlett & Yoshihara, 1988; Pucik et al., 1989). A survey of Japanese manufacturing firms conducted at the end of the decade by the Export-Import Bank found that more than half of the U.S. subsidiaries had Japanese nationals in the post of CEO, head of technology, head of production, and head of accounting. Only in human resource management and business management were the top positions held by locals in more than half of the firms (Table 4).

Subsidiaries in the EC, the NICs of Asia (Korea, Taiwan, Singapore and Hong Kong), and the ASEAN countries were also likely to have a high proportion of Japanese in the key positions in technology, production, and accounting.

The high ratio of Japanese managers does not mean, however, that the home country organization delegates decision making to its expatriates in the subsidiary, as was so frequently the case in the "mother-daughter" structures of European multinationals (Franko, 1976). In fact, a second widely observed feature of Japanese offshore subsidiaries is a propensity to depend on the home country organization for support activities in technology development, components and inputs, and decision making in general. A recent MITI survey of decision making in Japanese subsidiaries overseas and U.S. subsidiaries in Japan found that on every one of eleven types of planning and

TABLE 4

LOCAL MANAGERS IN JAPANESE SUBSIDIARIES (%)

| | SUBSIDIARIES LOCATED IN: | | | |
POSITION	UNITED STATES (n = 268)	EC (n = 199)	NICs (n = 253)	ASEAN COUNTRIES (n = 231)
CEO	44.8	54.3	54.9	53.7
Business Manager	40.3	36.7	44.7	33.8
Head of Technology	44.8	41.7	41.9	35.5
Head of HRM	65.3	57.8	65.2	69.3
Head of Accounting	48.9	50.3	50.2	48.9

Source: Survey of Japanese manufacturing firms conducted by Export-Import Bank of Japan, data published in 1990, reported in Ishii (1992), p. 28.

decision-making about which the questionnaire inquired (from planning capital investments to decisions about production volumes and warehousing volumes), U.S. subsidiaries in Japan had higher levels of responsibility than did their Japanese offshore counterparts (Tsusho Hakusho [MITI White Paper] 1991, p. 225). These data reinforce a widely held impression that Japanese subsidiaries overseas remain dependent on their parents for key support activities, especially in technology.

A third feature of Japanese investment in North America that has drawn both popular and scholarly attention is the low level of internalization of value adding (the tendency to "screwdriver" assembly, and the related tendency to recreate the home country organization set in North America, including suppliers, financial institutions, and even general contractors (Wassman & Yamamura, 1989; Gerlach, 1989). This has been most evident in the auto industry, where the investments in ten North American plants by the seven major Japanese auto firms have been accompanied by a wave of Japanese auto parts firms investing, sometimes reluctantly, in North American plants to provide parts of a kind and quality and on a delivery cycle that the auto firms have come to expect in their home plants. The major Japanese steel firms also made substantial investments in North America (in joint ventures and acquisitions) largely to serve the Japanese auto firms.

A fourth feature of Japanese MNEs that has only recently received widespread attention is their relatively low profitability (DeNero, 1990; Komiya & Wakasugi, 1991). Systematic data are difficult to obtain, since few of the wholly owned Japanese subsidiaries in the United States provide separate information on the profitability of their offshore subsidiaries. But a McKinsey study (reported in 1990) found that for the Japanese firms on which data were available, U.S. return on sales in 1987-1990 averaged 4 percent, compared with a return in Japan of 17 percent. This is in marked contrast to U.S.

subsidiaries in Japan, which not only have a higher profit level than their Japanese counterparts, but often have the highest profits of any subsidiaries in their MNE network.

Finally, a fifth feature of Japanese MNEs that has been relatively neglected in the literature is the propensity to create multiple subsidiaries within a major market, each linked more closely with its counterpart in Japan than with other local subsidiaries. The data from the Export-Import Bank cited earlier, in which 20 firms have 73 subsidiaries in the United States, provide an illustration of this trait. The multiple-subsidiary pattern is particularly marked in the large diversified electronics firms such as NEC, which had 11 wholly owned subsidiaries in the United States by the end of the 1980s (Kobayashi, 1989, pp. 312-20), or Fujitsu, which by 1992 had 13 U.S. subsidiaries (not including Amdahl, in which it had a 42 percent equity share). Even an automobile firm such as Honda has seven subsidiaries in the United States (Ishii, 1992, p. 144). In several companies the subsidiaries are in different businesses, which are divisions of the parent company in Japan but separate companies off shore. These subsidiaries are also differentiated by function in many cases. Japanese MNEs had an early tendency to separate their sales subsidiaries from their manufacturing subsidiaries, a tendency that several companies have maintained. Recently, as they have added R&D to their offshore activities, leading Japanese MNEs have incorporated their R&D centres independently, often setting up separate subsidiaries in each technology sector (Westney, 1993). The single "country subsidiary" is, therefore, not the basic geographic unit of most leading Japanese MNEs, as it had been for most Western MNEs. This multiple subsidiary structure makes it difficult for the individual subsidiaries even in the largest markets to develop an autonomy and a strategic momentum of their own, and underlies the dependence of the subsidiary on the parent organization for resources and strategic direction.

How likely are these differences from Western MNEs to persist? The first four — the high proportion of expatriate managers, high subsidiary dependence on the parent, the low level of subsidiary value-adding, and the low level of profitability — can plausibly be explained by the relative recency of Japanese FDI. The fifth, the multiple subsidiary structure, is more difficult to classify as a life cycle effect. If the main explanation for differences lies in life cycle effects, then the clear implication is that Japanese MNEs will, over time, come to resemble their Western counterparts. Komiya and Wakasugi, in a 1991 article, adopt this perspective explicitly:

> Japanese enterprises in the manufacturing industry are generally in the early stages of their overseas operations....There is as yet no Japanese enterprise that can truly be called multinational such as BASF, Exxon, General Electric, Hoechist (sic), General Motors, IBM, IT&T, Shell, and Unilever, which are engaged in production, marketing, export, and research and development in many countries of the world. Recently, Japanese companies such as Honda,

Sony, Matsushita, and Nissan have been developing into multinational enterprises, but the activities of their subsidiaries still center around production and
marketing within each host country, and their exports are to neighbouring
countries.... It is to be expected, however, that if the Japanese subsidiaries,
especially those in developed countries, continue to develop at more or less
the same pace as in recent years, they will be run more and more as part of the
global strategies of their parents, and many of the latter will develop into full-
fledged multinational corporations. (1991, p. 60-61)

The widespread assumption that Western MNEs constitute a normative
model for Japanese firms may in fact contribute to the validation over time of
the life cycle explanation. It has been a truism of sociology since the days of
C.H. Cooley that what is perceived to be real is real in its consequences, and
today's institutional theory argues that normative and mimetic isomorphism
(the pull to emulating organizational patterns valued by key groups within and
outside the organization or patterns perceived to be effective and conducive to
better performance) is a powerful influence on organizational evolution
(DiMaggio and Powell, 1983).

Yet, even if one believes that Western MNEs are likely to be models for
the evolution of Japanese MNEs, it is necessary to recognize that the base from
which the latter are evolving, as Bartlett has pointed out, differs significantly
from that of many of the Western MNEs to which they are compared (Bartlett,
1986). Transportation and communications technology allowed a far greater
level of concentration of activities in an MNE's home country in the 1970s
and 1980s, when most Japanese firms were stepping up their expansion abroad,
than in earlier decades. But certain country factors made Japanese companies
eager to exploit those technologies to develop MNEs that were more home-
country centred than many of their Western counterparts.

The earliest studies of Japanese multinationals recognized that the
patterns of internationalization of Japanese firms were strongly influenced by
the distinctive features of the Japanese firm (Yoshino, 1976; Trevor, 1983).
But both Japanese and Western models of the essential features of the
Japanese firm have changed over the past three decades. Much of the early
work on Japanese organization concentrated on the factory rather than the
firm, and centred on the intra-firm structural features that most strikingly
differed from the model of the Western firm — such as the seniority wage
system, the enterprise union, and so-called lifetime employment. By the mid-
1980s, attention was shifting to the strategic behaviour of the firm and its
broader institutional context (see for example Kagono, et al., 1985; Aoki, 1987;
Nonaka, 1989, 1990; Fruin, 1992; Aoki and Dore, 1993). These features include:

- The much smaller size of the "core" Japanese firm, which centres
  its activities on the high value-added activities of technology
  development and final assembly.

- A "network structure" whereby this core firm augments its internal capabilities through a "pyramid" of subsidiaries, some of which specialize in other parts of the value chains of the core firm (components and sub-assemblies, sales and distribution) and some of which are engaged in businesses spun off by the parent because they require a different wage structure from that of the parent, or because they are not closely related to the core capabilities of the parent.

- A pervasive approach to the generation and use of information that emphasizes creating new information rather than processing existing information and adding value through dense information flows. Much of this dense information flow appears to be socially but not formally structured and relies heavily on interpersonal communications. Aoki (1988), who views information structure as central to his model of the Japanese firm, emphasizes the dense horizontal communications within and across the subunits of the firm, which he sees as conducive to continuous improvement and learning. Nonaka, another theorist who sees information as the key to understanding the Japanese firm, emphasizes "information creation" — adding value to information by amplification and expansion — as the distinguishing feature of the Japanese approaches to managing information, as opposed to the "information processing" approach of Western managers, which reduces and condenses information (Nonaka, 1990). The common elements among the information-focused models of the Japanese firm are that information flows in Japanese firms are denser, less constricted by formal channels, more dependent on interpersonal interactions, and more oriented to learning and improvement than in the model of the Western firm.

Matushishita Electric Industrial Company, Japan's largest consumer electronics company, provides one example of the basic structure of the Japanese firm: a core or parent firm, whose activities focus on technology development and final assembly, supported by a network of subsidiaries. In 1990 Matushishita had just over 42,000 employees (Asahi, 1989). Within this parent company were R&D and manufacturing for the major businesses associated with the Matsushita/Panasonic brand name: appliances, audio-visual equipment and home electronics, office equipment (such as fax machines and personal computers), semiconductors, electronic systems for autos, refrigeration and environmental systems. Much of the sales and distribution within Japan was carried out by separately incorporated regional sales companies, which constituted one part of the Matsushita group of companies.

The group companies employed about 135,000 people, in more than 100 subsidiaries, ranging from regional sales companies to subsidiaries that produce components (such as refrigeration units and compressors for appliances and electrical devices such as high-volume semiconductors) and to subsidiaries in quasi-related businesses like National Homes, a company manufacturing prefabricated housing.

The group is held together only in part by shareholding (the shares of the major subsidiaries are traded on the Japanese stock markets, and the parent company usually owns a substantial number but not necessarily a majority of the shares). The more important integration mechanism is a flow of people from the parent company to the subsidiaries, on both temporary and permanent transfers. This has two effects: it allows the parent company to select and bring back those employees with the greatest ability and strongest commitment, and it fosters the dense sharing of information along the value chain, which in all of Matsushita's businesses stretches across the formal, legal boundaries of the parent firm. In these so-called vertical *keiretsu*, the flow of people across companies is vertical rather than horizontal and is shaped by the parent firm; most cross-company transfers of any duration are *from* the parent *to* the subsidiaries. Managers are dispatched from the parent company to occupy key management positions in the affiliated companies, and the resentment this causes within the affiliates' management ranks is balanced by the access to parent company information networks that these transfers allow. This vertical *keiretsu* structure is most strongly marked in the auto and electronics industries, but to some degree characterizes most of Japanese industry, including service firms.

The relatively small size and the technological focus of the core firm means that the development of new technology frequently involves cooperation with other firms, some of which are within the group and some of which are outside suppliers or major customers (Westney, forthcoming). The oft-noted higher propensity of Japanese firms to engage in joint R&D can be ascribed as much or more to the structure of the firm as to any cultural propensity for co-operation, as much as many Japanese may favour the cultural explanation.

There are several explanations for this structural pattern. The most common is the wage factor: as a key part of the postwar labour settlement, Japanese managers agreed to standardize wages and salaries within the boundaries of the firm, using seniority and education as the key determinants rather than the job or function. This has proved an advantage in many respects, such as intra-firm mobility across functions (for example, engineers move from R&D into manufacturing with none of the problems experienced in the U.S. firm in moving from a high-salaried to a low-salaried environment). But in consequence, Japanese firms have been severely limited in the extent to which they can differentiate wages across functions or businesses. Therefore the high value-adding activities in all major businesses are concentrated in the parent firm, and activities in which value-adding is lower (or in some cases, higher, as in specialized software facilities) are put into separate companies, governed internally by the same homogenization principle, which works within but not across *keiretsu* firms.

Two additional explanations concern information. One is that the creation of separate companies renders the parameters of costs and value adding much more transparent. The second concerns management control systems. Japan, in this view, never really experienced the first office revolution caused by the typewriter that made possible the creation of impersonal control systems based on standardized written communications (the first Japanese typewriter was not produced until 1920, and it was a cumbersome affair that could only be operated by a highly trained expert, at the expense of a great deal of time and effort). As a result, Japanese organizations have continued to rely more heavily than their Western counterparts on face-to-face, personal communication in their control systems, and they encounter limits to scale sooner (Itami, 1982).

The Japanese MNE can be viewed as an extension of the vertical group structure of the Japanese firm. To return to Matsushita, for example, the United States, where it established a sales and distribution company in 1959, had seven manufacturing subsidiaries by the end of the 1980s and had begun to add R&D to its value chain. The eight laboratories that Matsushita had established in the United States by 1993, however, were each incorporated as separate companies, each closely linked to a parent laboratory in Japan. The laboratories were coordinated by yet another U.S. incorporated company, Panasonic Technologies, which had only one American on its board of directors (see Westney, 1993 for a detailed discussion of the patterns of internationalization of R&D in Japanese companies). Such a structure allows a parent company to engage in carefully targeted "selective tapping" (to use Michael Porter's apt phrase) to gain access to a specific set of regionally concentrated resources, such as a certain kind of labour market or access to a key customer or cluster of customers.

The complexities of the structure of Japanese MNEs, which creates, in effect, a group of companies rather than a single offshore subsidiary, are clearly shaped by the group structure of the home country and, in turn, strongly affect the other features of Japanese MNEs so often noted by their critics. The specific configurations of the individual companies do not mirror those of individual companies in the home country; that is, the offshore "group" is not a "miniature replica" of the parent group, as I pointed out above. But the structural principle — the firm as a "group" structure — shapes both home and international organization As in the domestic Japanese case, a critical component of integration across the group firms is the transfer of parent company personnel to the subsidiaries, a largely one-way flow of people, mirrored in the heavy reliance on expatriate managers in the Japanese subsidiaries overseas. Japanese expatriates also play a key role in maintaining across borders the dense horizontal information flows on which Japanese firms rely so heavily.

Furthermore, the domestic structure of the Japanese firm shapes both the scope of the offshore subsidiaries and the high propensity of those subsidiaries to rely on their parent's Japanese suppliers. The offshore subsidiary of a Japanese manufacturing firm engages only in high value-added assembly because its parent firm engages in high value-added assembly. Its close information links with key supplier firms, especially in terms of the flows of information and people involved in shared development of new products and new technologies, differ substantially from those hitherto common elsewhere in the world, especially in North America, and Japanese firms have tended to press their suppliers to move offshore to sustain those relationships in the new setting. Ironically, it is in precisely those industries (notably the auto industry) where the "mass movement" of leading Japanese firms has been greatest and therefore the movement of suppliers the most marked and the most threatening to local suppliers, that the strong demonstration effect of the Japanese patterns has created the greatest change in local firms, increasing their ability to penetrate the supplier networks.

These features of the Japanese firm support the argument that there is a strong "country effect" on the structure and behaviour of Japanese MNEs that may change but will not disappear over time (see Kogut's discussion of the persistence of country-based patterns over time in this volume). But there may well be factors at work that are linked to the industry within the country, rather than simply the country — that is, an organizational field effect produced by the institutional structure of the particular sector or industry. There is reason to believe that organizational field effects may be particularly strong for Japan's MNEs, given that two industries, automobiles and electronics, account for most of Japan's FDI in manufacturing, and have strongly influenced the model of the Japanese firm.

Both the auto and electronics industries have complex value chains for which the combination of disaggregation into separate firms and integration through dense information linkages is both possible and advantageous. (This is in contrast to the chemicals or pharmaceuticals industries, for example, in which Western MNEs continue to dominate world markets.) Also, it has been in these industries that the complex vertical groups (keiretsu) have been most strongly institutionalized. It is therefore quite possible that country effects and organizational field effects have been confounded in the analysis of Japan's MNEs. It may well be difficult to separate them at present. Some analysts have pointed out (see the Japan Economic Institute, 1992) that comparisons between Japanese and Western MNEs rarely, if ever, control for industry, partly because differences in global competitiveness make systematic industry comparisons virtually impossible (for example, all of the foreign auto plants and most of the consumer electronics plants in the United States are currently Japanese owned).

The key distinction, however, is between those who view the differences between Japanese and Western MNEs as a result of life cycle effects and those who view them as produced by fundamental differences in the structure of the

Japanese MNE, either attributable to period effects or to country (or organizational field) effects. The distinction has important practical implications both for policy makers and for managers of Japan's MNEs.

THE IMPLICATIONS OF THE DIFFERENCES

WESTERN DISCUSSIONS of the differences between Japanese and Western MNEs have, quite naturally, tended to focus on the implications for Western host countries. These discussions have moved from an early interest in blue collar workers (reflecting the long-standing focus of the theories of the Japanese firm on the factory) to the implications for managers and the effects on the local economy. At issue are not only the implications themselves, but also two further considerations: whether they are attributable to life cycle effects and therefore likely to change naturally over time, or whether they are attributable to period or country effects and therefore unlikely to change significantly without major policy interventions by host governments.

The implications for local managerial employees are not controversial. There is general agreement that the high proportion of expatriate managers in Japanese subsidiaries and the virtually negligible movement of local managers into positions in the home country organization creates a "bamboo ceiling", a limit on the upward mobility of local managers in Japanese subsidiaries (Pucik, et al., 1989; Trevor, 1991). Moreover, the multiple subsidiary structure that Japanese MNEs have constructed in major markets (such as the United States) makes even the top positions in any one subsidiary less influential and more dependent on the parent company than comparable positions in a more locally integrated subsidiary. While the efforts currently under way by Japanese companies to develop more local managers for top positions in their subsidiaries may go some way toward addressing the "bamboo ceiling" problem, the effect of the multiple subsidiary structure on local management will be more resistant to amelioration over time. But it is unlikely that the mobility opportunities for a handful of highly paid professional managers will become a focus of major policy intervention by host governments, unless those opportunities are linked to the second issue, the effect on the local economy.

Given that Japanese MNEs in North America tend to have lower levels of local value adding and a greater propensity to draw on their home country for components and subassemblies than their Western counterparts, Western policy makers have some concerns that they have fewer multiplier effects on the local economy. There are three schools of thought on the issue:

1) The lower contribution to the local economy is simply a matter of the early stage of Japanese investment, and will change naturally over time as the subsidiaries mature and become more firmly established in their local environment (Komiya & Wakasugi, 1991).

2) Japanese MNEs have used the new communications and transport technologies to good effect, and the absence of strong country subsidiaries makes it much easier for Japanese to integrate across borders without facing the stronger resistance that can come from national subsidiaries in longer-established Western MNEs. In addition, their firm structure increases the likelihood of continued centralization of high value-added activities in Japan. These period and country effects mean that Japanese MNEs are unlikely to increase their local value adding substantially without strong policy interventions from host governments and concerted pressures from competitors and potential customers and employees. Robert Reich seems to be leaning to this position in his comments on Japanese MNEs in his 1991 article, "Who is Them?", when he suggests that if Japanese MNEs do not follow the pattern of the increasingly global MNE, competitors, host governments, and labour markets will combine to force them to conform.

3) The lower immediate economic multiplier is more than offset by the stimulus to change and improvement that the Japanese subsidiaries provide to the local environment. In the industries where active Japanese investment (as opposed to portfolio investment) has been concentrated, Japanese firms are transferring technology and organizational capabilities abroad and increasing, in Michael Porter's words, the dynamism of the local environment. The changes in the nature of competition have often been painful for local firms, but many analysts argue that they have a net positive effect on the national competitiveness of host countries through FDI in such industries as the auto industry, electronics, and steel (Dunning comes close to making this argument in his 1986 study of Japanese investment in Britain).

In Europe, this debate has tended to follow national lines: British analysts and executives are more likely to adopt the third position and French commentators the second (Ishikawa, 1990, pp. 95-117). In the United States, the debate has taken second place to an analogous discussion over the use of policy instruments versus natural evolution (through exchange rates and market forces) in improving the position of Western firms in the Japanese market, although there have been signs recently that the nature and activities of Japanese MNEs in the United States may become a more salient political issue in the near future (this past year Congress has authorized an inquiry into investments in R&D and high value-added manufacturing by foreign firms in the United States). For countries that have tended to rely heavily on FDI in their industrial systems, such as Canada (and, increasingly, Mexico), whether to control Japanese direct investment is a matter of much less interest than how to attract such investment.

But the most powerful influence on the amount and location of future Japanese investment offshore is the viewpoint of the top managers of Japan's MNEs, and for them the issue of why Japanese MNEs differ from their Western counterparts and in what directions they should evolve has an urgency well beyond that accorded it by Western policy makers. Even if the Japanese managers personally believe unreservedly in life cycle explanations of the features of their firms of which host countries complain, they know that what-ever host country policy makers may choose to do, they themselves cannot leave the evolution of their firms to the natural course of events. Japanese managers are intensely conscious of the fact that there will inevitably be differences across firms in the extent to which they are able to draw competitive advantages from their international operations, and that the future of their own company depends heavily on the rapidity and the effectiveness with which they manage the internationalization process, compared to their Japanese competitors.

In the 1980s Japanese writings and speeches on internationalization strategies were framed largely in terms of *genchika* — "localization". In the 1990s this was joined by the term *insaida-ka* — "insiderization", the process of becoming a true insider in the local system. While *genchika* can focus on clear parameters such as the ratio of local to expatriate managers and the proportion of local value adding, "insiderization" hinges on much more subjective factors: acceptability and legitimacy. Furthermore, because it is subjective, its parameters can shift over time. This creates problems for Japanese managers, because being accepted as a local insider may require a degree of isomorphism (structural similarity) with local firms that is at odds with the current structure of the Japanese multinational enterprise.

The problems are not new. Studies of Japanese MNEs have long recognized that the internationalization strategies of Japanese managers are strongly affected by their fear that, in the words of Yoshino in the mid-1970s, "In order to undertake major expansion internationally, Japanese companies must bring about changes in their management system.... And in the process, they may well sacrifice those elements that have made the system so effective internally" (cited in Trevor, 1989, p. 92). Nearly two decades later, Ishii's study of Japanese MNEs opens on the same note: to adopt completely local patterns means to lose the source of the firm's competitiveness, and to become the same as local firms in quality and productivity (Ishii, 1992:2, 11-12). The fear that adaptation to local environments in major markets such as North America may require changes not only in the organizational systems of subsidiaries but even in the parent company in Japan has, if anything, grown stronger with "insiderization". Henry DeNero, of the international consulting firm McKinsey, whose 1990 article on Japanese MNEs, was based on his own and his colleagues' consulting experience with "more than half of Japan's 100 leading multinationals" (p. 158), concluded that Japanese MNEs must make fundamental changes in their home country systems — not only their centralized decision-making processes but also their strong functional orientation and their upstream focus (both integrally linked to the group structure of the Japanese firm), their "consensus orientation" (one aspect of their information systems), and their human resource management systems. DeNero clearly subscribes to the "country effects" view of the differences between Japanese and Western multinational enterprises.

Japanese MNE managers are therefore facing three related challenges. They must deal with accelerating economic pressures as the yen continues to strengthen (its value is apparently approaching the unprecedented level of 100 yen to one U.S. dollar), thus pushing more of their activities off shore. They are facing political and social pressures for change in their offshore subsidiaries and in their headquarters-subsidiary relationships in order to become accepted as "insiders" in their major markets. In addition, they face increasing pressures to change their home country organizations to make them more open to interdependent relationships with their subsidiaries. Ironically, this last pressure for change at home comes after a decade that has witnessed a growing body of writing identifying Japanese manufacturing firms as proto-types of the lean, flexible, high-commitment, information-centred, networked organization of the future (see, for example, Dore, 1987; Nonaka, 1989; Itami, 1990; Shimada, 1988, 1989; Florida & Kenney, 1993). Much of this literature regards Japanese firms as having been able to develop and apply advanced material and organizational technologies to their organizational systems, partly because they developed later than the Western firms that were often their models. But even in the 1980s, Japanese scholars even more than their Western counterparts believed that the inevitable internationalization of Japanese firms was a process that would test the validity of the model of the Japanese firm as more than a distinctive national variant of the modern corporation and stretch the model as it moved to accommodate a range of diverse foreign environments.

One route toward internationalization taken by several of Japan's leading corporations in the 1950s was to identify "leading edge" management tech-nologies and then adopt and adapt them in the domestic context. In MNE organization, many of Japan's leading MNEs, like some of their Western counterparts but with greater ease, have seized on the prospects for region rather than country becoming the key geographical dimension of the MNE of the future. They are therefore moving toward a regional rather than a country-centred structure, with regional headquarters in Asia (usually in Singapore), North America (invariably in the United States), and Europe (where the choice of location is less clear cut). These regional headquarters, in turn, integrate across the various sub-units within their geographical area and are densely linked with the home country headquarters. NEC, for example, calls its model "mesh globalization" (Nakamura, 1991). Its model involves four major businesses — consumer electronics, computers, electronic devices, and telecommunications systems — centred on Japan and networked across production and development bases in three regions: the U.S., Europe, and the Asian NIES. (Note that, at least as of 1991, NEC defined the United States as a region, rather than North America.) Yazaki, the automotive parts supplier, has a regional strategy that involves three regions: Asia, centred on Japan; North America, centred on Detroit but involving subsidiaries in Ontario and in Latin America; and Europe, centred on Cologne and involving subsidiaries in the United Kingdom, Sweden, Spain and Switzerland. Honda and Nissan have both announced that they are building regional structures, with European and North American headquarters (*honbu*) to parallel the Japan headquarters. The electronics firms Sony and Matsushita have also announced Asian headquarters outside Japan, both centred in Singapore, where the provision of inducements to MNEs to make Singapore a regional headquarters is a key element of government policy.

Many Japanese MNEs either have already adopted the regional structure or are planning to follow these long-time bellwethers of Japanese industry. But exactly what a "regional headquarters" means in concrete terms remains somewhat vague. This apparent vagueness can be explained by Ikujiro Nonaka's exposition of Japanese management as essentially neither "top-down" nor "bottom-up", but rather something he calls "middle-up-down": top management articulates a very general and inspiring "vision" of the company's direction and identity, and charters middle management to work with the lower ranks of the organization to translate the vision into operational terms. Middle managers then take these operational terms to top management as part of a process of evolving and expanding the vision (Nonaka, 1989). The process of building an effective regional headquarters, however, in which middle managers are responsible for putting concrete form to the regional headquarters concept, is somewhat unclear in many companies: should the responsibility be taken by Japanese managers assigned to the regional headquarters? by local managers? by Japanese managers in Japan? (without whose cooperation the enlargement of the capabilities of regional subsidiaries will be extremely difficult). The obvious answer is that some mix of all three is essential. But what constitutes an effective mix (and in whose eyes) is still problematic in many firms.

Moreover, as an articulation of what is supposed to be an inspiring vision of the future, the concept of the regional headquarters can raise expectations abroad beyond what the company can quickly deliver. When the President of Hitachi Ltd. sets the strategic policy in the United States as "Establish a miniature Hitachi in the U.S., which is the largest market for us" (quoted in Noanaka, 1990:85), or when Honda sees the aim of establishing a regional headquarters in the United States as generating social recognition that "Honda is one of the American firms managed by Americans" (a quotation, ironically, from the Japanese director of Honda America, cited by Nonaka, 1990:86), locals may feel that they have been promised a level of autonomy and activity that corporate headquarters feels cannot be granted quickly or, perhaps, even granted at all. Not many corporations have sufficient resources to duplicate their entire value chain in each of the major regions of the world. Especially in R&D and process engineering, scale economies and the huge "sunk costs" of R&D in the home country mean that while local production for the regional market may be feasible in the long run (and necessary if trade blocs emerge), the "top end" of the value chain, which is increasingly prized by governments and regarded as the most important element of local value adding, will not likely be dispersed geographically in proportion to offshore sales or even to offshore production.

Partly in response to these dilemmas, the form of MNE proposed in the middle and late 1980s by international management researchers such as Hedlune (1986), Prahalad and Doz (1987), and Bartlett and Ghoshal (1989), as the model for the future (the "transnational", multi-focus firm, heterarchy, "network MNE") stressed interdependence among the various units of the MNE, including the home country organization, rather than local autonomy. In this model, individual subsidiaries specialize in certain technologies or product lines, and draw others from elsewhere in the MNE network. Given the distinctive pressures on the Japanese MNEs created by their highly visible competitiveness in certain key industries (especially autos and consumer electronics), and the high levels of concentration of activities in their home country, it is not surprising that the more traditional ideals of localization and local autonomy should hold such appeal for Japanese MNE top managers as solutions to the growing criticisms aimed at their "Japanese-ness". It remains to be seen whether by anchoring those ideals in a regional (rather than a country) organization, Japanese MNEs are following a trajectory of evolution that was traced earlier by European and U.S. MNEs at a similar point in their life cycle, or whether they are taking another step on the road they are so clearly pursuing in technology: moving from followers and adapters to leaders and innovators.

THE ROLE OF CANADA IN A NORTH AMERICAN REGIONAL STRUCTURE

WHILE MANY JAPANESE MNEs have a genuinely regional distribution of their activities in Asia and in Europe, their strategy in North America tends to be a country (rather than a regional) strategy. As the data presented earlier on the number of subsidiaries located in North America indicated, Japanese firms have tended to centre their activities in the United States. There are several reasons for this. Japanese firms lack the long-standing and substantial investments many leading U.S. MNEs have made in Canada over the years. Therefore, while U.S. MNEs may, as Bartlett and Ghoshal (1989) suggest, react to the declining strategic importance of the Canadian national market by defining a role for their Canadian subsidiaries as "contributors" — subsidiaries whose capabilities are put to work in the MNE in clearly-defined niches — most Japanese MNEs face the prior issue of whether to build capabilities in Canada at all. Furthermore, Japanese do not feel the attraction that Canada has for European companies, for whom Canada provides a culturally congenial bridge to the United States.

As we saw earlier, the need to reduce costs by moving production out of Japan is only one of the challenges facing Japan's MNE managers. The organizational challenges of building the "new" regional MNE, the political and social dilemmas of "insiderization", and the reassessment of the firm's domestic organization in comparison to "global best practice" all have great salience for Japanese managers.

The pessimist could argue that Canada has little to offer. Few Canadian firms can be portrayed as exemplars of the "new" lean, networked, flexible firm of the future, and therefore the effort to portray Canada as the heartland of the organizational revolution in the West is bound to be unconvincing. Additionally, the case of Honda in Canada, where the Canadian government was unable to prevent the U.S. customs authorities from ruling that Canadian-made Accords did not meet North American local content requirements, make it difficult to argue that locating in Canada can lower the political risk to which Japanese firms are so sensitive. Clearly, many Japanese managers will feel that locating within the borders of the United States is politically and socially the lowest-risk strategy for them at a time when continuing friction over trade is likely.

Under the circumstances, what arguments for Japanese investment (outside the resource industries, which have their own locational logic) can Canada present? The challenge lies in articulating a role for itself in a North American regional strategy for Japanese firms. One argument is that Canada offers a credible alternative production site, so that Japanese production centres in the United States will be less likely to become hostage to arbitrary actions by governments or other stakeholders, and more able to gain concessions on operating conditions and work organization (Toyota, for example, has apparently decided to expand its production in Ontario, in preference to its plants in California or Kentucky. Having three plants dispersed within North America allows a firm far greater leverage than production within a single country).

In addition, a case can be made that a genuinely regional strategy should involve regionally distributed activities. The benefits include generation of greater internal variety and a richer reservoir of potential international management talent. The vision of the regionally distributed MNE cannot fully be realized if one of the regions is a single country. Perhaps, given the strong orientation of the leading Japanese firms to a vision of what the MNE of the future should be, this may be a more convincing argument than all the elaborate calculations of differential operating costs that a more conventional approach to influencing location strategies would suggest.

BIBLIOGRAPHY

Aoki, Masahiko. *Information, Incentives, and Bargaining in the Japanese Economy.* Cambridge: Cambridge University Press, 1989.

Aoki, Masahiko and Ronald Dore, (eds.). *The Japanese Firm: The Source of Competitive Strength.* New York: Oxford University Press, (forthcoming).

Asahi Tetsuro. *Matsushita Denki no Kigyonai Kakumei* [Matsushita Electric's Internal Revolution]. Tokyo: KK Nihon Sofutobanku, 1989.

Bartlett, Christopher A. "Building and Managing the Transnational: The New Organizational Challenge." In *Competition in Global Industries.* Edited by Michael E. Porter. Boston: Harvard Business School Press, 1986.

Bartlett, Christopher A. and H. Yoshihara. "New Challenge for Japanese Multinationals: Is Organization Adaptation their Achilles Heel?" *Human Resource Management.* 27-1 (Spring 1988):19-43.

Bartlett, Christopher A. and Sumantra Ghoshal. *Managing Across Borders: The Transnational Solution.* Boston: Harvard Business School Press, 1989.

Beechler, Schon and Sully Taylor. "The Transfer of Human Resource Management Systems Overseas: An Exploratory Study of Japanese and American Maquiladoras." In *Japanese Multinationals: Strategies and Management in the Global Kaisha.* Edited by Nigel Campbell and Nigel Holden. London: Routledge, 1993.

Business Week. "Shaking Up Detroit: How Japanese Auto Plants in the U.S. are Changing the Big Three." Cover story, August 14, 1989.

Clark, Rodney. *The Japanese Company.* New Haven, Connecticut: Yale University Press, 1979.

DeNero, Henry. "Creating the 'Hyphenated' Corporation." *McKinsey Quarterly.* 4, (1990).

Dore, Ronald P. *British Factory Japanese Factory.* Berkeley: University of California Press, 1973.

Dunning, John H. *Japanese Participation in British Industry.* London: Croom Helm, 1986.

Edgington, David W. *Japanese Direct Investment in Canada: Recent Trends and Prospects.* B.C. Geographical series, Number 49. Vancouver: University of British Columbia, 1992.

Franko, Lawrence G. *The European Multinationals.* Greenwich, Connecticut: Greylock, 1976.

Froot, Kenneth A. "Japanese Foreign Direct Investment." NBER Working Paper No. 3737, June, 1989.

Gerlach, Michael. *Alliance Capitalism: The Social Organization of Japanese Business.* Berkeley: University of California Press, 1992.

Graham, E.M. and P.R. Krugman. *Foreign Direct Investment in the United States.* Washington, D.C.: Institute for International Economics, 1991.

Ishii Masahi. *Nihon Kigyo no Kaigai Jigyo Tenkai* [The Development of Overseas Business by Japanese Firms]. Tokyo: Chuo Koronsha, 1992.

Ishikawa, Kenjiro. *Japan and the Challenge of Europe 1992.* London: Pinter Publishers, 1990.

Itami Hiroyuki. *Nihonteki Keiei o koete* [Beyond Japanese-style Management]. Tokyo: Nihon Keizai Shimbunsha, 1982.

Japan Economic Almanac 1992. Tokyo: Nihon Keizai Shimbunsha, 1992.

Japan Economic Institute. "Japan's Multinational Corporations at a Turning Point." *JEI Report,* March 6, 1992.

Kagono, T., I. Nonaka, K. Sakakibara and A. Okamura. *Strategic vs. Evolutionary Management.* Amsterdam: North-Holland, 1985.

Kenney, Martin and Richard Florida. *Beyond Mass Production: The Japanese System and its Transfer to the U.S.* New York: Oxford University Press, 1993.

Nakamura Genichi. *NEC Su-pa-21 Keiei* [NEC Super-21 Management]. Tokyo: Daiyamondo-sha, 1991.

Nonaka, Ikujiro. "Toward Middle-Up-Down Management: Accelerating Information Creation." *Sloan Management Review,* 29, 3 (1989):9-18.

_____. "Managing Globalization as a Self-renewing Process: Experiences of Japanese MNEs." In *Managing the Global Firm.* Edited by Christopher A. Bartlett et al. London: Routledge, 1990, pp. 69-94.

Porter, Michael E. *The Competitiveness of Nations.* New York: Free Press, 1990.

Pucik, Vladimir, Mitsuo Haneda and George Fifield. *Management Culture and the Effectiveness of Local Executives in Japanese-Owned U.S. Corporations.* Tokyo: Egon Zander International, 1989.

Reich, Robert. "Who is Them?" *Harvard Business Review,* 69, 2 (March-April 1991):77-88.

Rugman, Alan M. *Japanese Direct Investment in Canada.* Ottawa: Canada-Japan Trade Council, 1990.

Trevor, Malcolm. *Japan's Reluctant Multinationals: Japanese Management at Home and Abroad.* London: Pinter, 1983.

_____. "The Overseas Strategies of Japanese Corporations." *The Annals of the American Academy of Political and Social Science,* 513, (January 1991):90-101.

Tsusho Sangyo Sho. *(MITI) Tsusho Hakusho* [MITI White Paper]. Tokyo: Okurasho Insatsusho, 1991.

Voisey, Christopher J. "The International Organizational Network as Core Capability: Global Product Development in Fujitsu Limited." MIT-Japan Program Working Paper, 1993.

Wassman, Ulrike and Kozo Yamamura. "Do Japanese Firms Behave Differently? The Effects of Keiretsu in the United States" In *Japanese Investments in the United States: Should We Be Concerned?.* Edited by Kozo Yamamura. Seattle: Society for Japanese Studies, 1989.

Westney, D. Eleanor. "Cross-Pacific Internationalisation of R&D by U.S. and Japanese Firms." *R&D Management,* 23, 2, pp. 171-81.

_____. "The Evolution of Japan's Industrial R&D." In *The Japanese Firm: the Source of Competitive Strength.* Edited by Masahiko Aoki and Ronald Dore. New York: Oxford University Press, (forthcoming).

Wolf, Bernard M. and Glen Taylor. "Employee and Supplier Learning in the Canadian Automobile Industry: Implications for Competitiveness." In *Foreign Investment, Technology, and Economic Growth,* The Investment Canada Research Series. Edited by D. McFetridge. Calgary: University of Calgary Press, 1991.

Yamamura, Kozo, (ed.). *Japanese Investment in the United States: Should We be Concerned?* Seattle: Society for Japanese Studies, 1989.

Yoshino, Michael Y. *Japan's Multinational Enterprises.* Cambridge, Mass.: Harvard University Press, 1976.

Yoshino, Michael Y. and Thomas B. Lifson. *The Invisible Link: Japan's Sogo Shosha and the Organization of Trade.* Cambridge, Mass.: M.I.T. Press, 1986.

John H. Dunning
Emeritus Professor of International Business
University of Reading

10

MNE Activity: Comparing the NAFTA and the European Community

INTRODUCTION

T HE PURPOSE OF THIS STUDY is to review the effects of regional integration on the organization and structure of multinational enterprise (MNE) activity into and out of the European Economic Community (EC); and to compare and contrast these effects to those which might be expected to arise from a NAFTA. The first part of this study briefly outlines the similarities and differences between the kinds of economic integration forged by the two trading blocs. Part two theorizes on the likely consequences for foreign direct investment (FDI) arising from these interdependencies. Part three considers the role played by the changing regulatory environment in the European Community (EC) for the intra-EC organization of MNE activity. Part four examines the evidence of the consequences of Mark I and Mark II European integration for the level, composition and organization of both EC and non-EC owned MNE operations. Finally, with this evidence in mind, Part five speculates on the possible effects of a NAFTA both within the free trade area and between the participating countries and the rest of the world.

FORMS OF ECONOMIC INTERDEPENDENCE

T HE CONSIDERABLE LITERATURE on regional economic integration identifies a spectrum of economic interaction between sovereign Nation States which varies from complete isolation at the one extreme to complete political and economic union at the other. In between, the stages of economic interaction may be grouped first, according to the degree of formality of the regime governing the behaviour of the member countries and, second, according to the areas of decision- making over which national sovereignty is replaced, in whole or in part by regional sovereignty.

Table 1 summarizes some of the characteristics of the member states comprising the EC and the NAFTA in the post-World War II era; while Table 2 compares and contrasts some of the features of the NAFTA with those

TABLE 1

CHARACTERISTICS OF MEMBER STATES IN THE EC AND THE NAFTA

EC

- 12 (at first 6, later 9 and 10) member states; no dominant country until 1992.

Countries broadly comparable in economic structure (apart from Ireland) until the accession of Southern European countries in 1980s.

Central core of EC now industrial Rhineland; but distance between main industrial areas in leading EC countries tolerable.

Exchange rate instability, not withstanding introduction of exchange rate mechanism (ERM).

- A mixture of widely different languages, history, legal and political systems.

Long history of inter-European strife.

Clear distinction between Anglophile and Francophile cultures, work ethic and attitudes toward authority.

Broadly comparable population paths.

- Broadly similar economic systems, but degrees of control exercised on trade and FDI varied considerably. Also system and role of government perceived to be very different in France and Italy, cf. (e.g.) UK and Germany.

- Both inter- and intra-MNE activity were largely confined to market-seeking (import substituting) activities prior to formation of the EC. There were few intra-European special trading arrangements, except in particular products, e.g. steel.

FDI in the 1950s was strongly concentrated in the larger industrialized countries, with the UK receiving the bulk of non-EC investment.

Within the EC, the UK was the leading outward foreign direct investor.

NAFTA

- 3 member states, dominated in population and GNP by the United States.

The economic asymmetry between the United States and Canada and Mexico is much greater than (economic) distances between core and periphery.

Land mass nine times greater than the EC.

Greater income differences between poorest and richest country.

Externally greater stability in exchange rates, at least in past 5 - 10 years.

- Fewer non-economic differences between Canada and the United States (although some noticeable intra-country regional differences).

Ethnic and cultural differences greater between the main body of the United States and Mexico, but less pronounced in the border territories.

Noticeably higher rate of population growth of Mexico, the United States and Canada.

- Extensive government intervention in Mexico until mid-1980s.

Canada and US have pursued largely liberal trade and FDI policies since early 1980s.

Canadian and U.S. tariffs generally lower than their Mexican equivalents.

- Due to the special trading relationships, e.g. between the United States and Mexico and the United States and Canada, there was more efficiency-seeking FDI, particularly between the United States and Mexico; although in the 1960s and 1970s tariff barriers led to much defensive market seeking, e.g. U.S. FDI in Canadian manufacturing industry.

There was also more natural resource -based FDI in each of these countries: in Canada and Mexico, largely by U.S. or UK firms; in the United States, mainly by European MNEs.

of the European Community in 1992.[1] As the tables show, the NAFTA (like the earlier Canada-U.S. Free Trade Agreement) embraces some attributes of both a free trade area and a customs union. In many respects it is a less intensive or shallower form of integration than either the post-1957 (Mark I) EC (which comprised a customs union, but one in which there were substantial intra-EC non-tariff barriers), or post-1992 (Mark II) EC integration (which is intended to remove all obstacles to the intra-EC movement of people, capital, goods and services). At the same time, the NAFTA does embrace several issues, e.g. with respect to government procurement, technical barriers to trade, and values of origin and dispute settlements not addressed by EC Mark I integration. Over the current decade — as spelled out by the Maastricht Treaty — it is the intention of (most of) the EC to move towards more complete monetary and fiscal union, including the formation of a European Central Bank, but such (Mark III) EC integration will not be considered in this study, as the issues it involves are of little relevance to the NAFTA partners.

SOME THEORETICAL ISSUES

THE INTERFACE BETWEEN MNE activity and regional integration juxtaposes the theories of economic integration and international production. In brief, regional integration affects the level and composition of economic activity of the participating countries through its impact on both the locational decisions of firms and their ownership and organization structures. In the absence of trans-border FDI, the issue becomes solely one of the location of production, and of trade patterns arising from such production.

As the literature suggests, integration — whether shallow or deep — may cause a relocation of activity through the diversion or creation of trade, both within the integrated area, and between the member countries and the rest of the world. Thus, a lowering of tariffs by reducing the costs of transfer of goods and services from country A to country B, is likely to redirect value-added activity from the previously protected country to the exporting country. At the same time, restructuring the natural resource or created asset advantages of the two nations, may give rise to new opportunities for trade, and hence raise the level and/or change the composition of economic activity in both of them. Depending on the extent to which the external tariff between the integrated countries and the rest of the world is higher or lower than that prior to integration, there may be a diversion or creation of extra-integrated area trade. Depending on the size and economic strengths and weaknesses of the participating countries, and their respective responses to integration, the geographical concentration of value-added activities within the region may be intensified or lessened; and intra-regional economic relationships be more or less stabilized.[2]

Economists also find it helpful to distinguish between the *primary* or *initial* effects of integration and the *secondary* or *consequential* effects. The

TABLE 2

THE EUROPEAN COMMUNITY (AS OF 1993) AND NAFTA: SOME COMPARISONS AND CONTRASTS

	EUROPEAN COMMUNITY	NAFTA
1. TRADE AND PRODUCTION		
(a) Informal cooperation		
(b) Complementation agreements		
(c) Removal of tariff barriers	• All intra-EC barriers eliminated. Common external tariff adopted.	• All to be eliminated or phased out over 5, 10 or 15 years. Special provisions for agricultural products, energy and basic petrochemicals. No common external tariff, e.g. Mexico will be allowed to maintain relatively high tariff levels on imports from the rest of the world.
(d) Removal of non-tariff barriers	• Most to be removed by the end of the 1990s.	• Some degree of liberalization is occurring, e.g. with respect to safeguarding government procurement. The elimination of NTBs, e.g. technical standards, trucking and port service, may take longer to achieve. Immediate goal is national treatment and intra-NAFTA compatibility in standard-related measures. Sets up a new regime in intellectual property.
(e) Rules of origin	• The question of what constitutes an "EC made" good (i.e. a good with a substantial EC content) is still a matter of controversy, but the EC is gradually establishing the rules of the game.	• Involves preferential tariff treatment for goods considered to be North American. Local content percentages beginning to be identified, e.g. in automotive products. Within NAFTA, rules of origin are replacing intra-North American tariffs and NTBs.
(f) Services	• Inter-EC regulations on trade and rights of establishment to be largely eliminated. Principle of mutual reciprocity established.	• Principle of equal treatment to be established. Gradual liberalization of financial services up to 2000.
(g) Dispute settlements	• Harmonized by European Commission	• Trilateralizes the Canadian-FTA process.

	EC	NAFTA
(h) Special provisions	• For agriculture and a limited number of strategically-sensitive manufacturing and service sectors.	• Economic coordination and transfers found in EC unlikely to be part of NAFTA. For example, each nation will operate separate agricultural programs.
2. FREE MOVEMENT OF PEOPLE	• Gradually being accomplished by the introduction of the EC passport and the harmonization of labour laws and employment conditions.	• A truly liberal movement of labour is not part of NAFTA. *De facto*, there are likely to be many obstacles to the free movement of people, especially between Mexico and the United States. Treaty specifically allows for cross-border movement of business persons.
3. FREE MOVEMENT OF ASSETS	• Largely activated. Most financial markets are already deregulated. There are currently few restrictions on the sourcing of capital or on currency movements. Concept (but not practice) of European Monetary Union is accepted by most of the 12 member states.	• Free movement of currency. Expropriation of assets forbidden. Concept of national treatment established. Some control permitted of intra-NAFTA corporate acquisitions, e.g. by Mexican authorities.
4. MONETARY AND FISCAL UNION	• A goal (of most of the EC) yet to be achieved. Some fiscal harmonization is being achieved in the EC 92 program.	• Not immediately envisaged. Only a limited amount of fiscal harmonization is currently in operation (especially between Mexico and the United States and Mexico and Canada).
5. SOCIAL PROGRAMS	• Extensive social policies and fiscal transfer mechanisms; EC developing its own environment policies.	• Little coordination of social programs; no clear policy on the environment.
6. POLICIES OF NATION STATES TOWARD FDI	• Attempts to move toward harmonization, but a recent study of the OECD shows considerable latitude among member countries remains, e.g. toward liberalization of FDI in services.	• No formal coordinative system envisaged.
7. POLITICAL UNION	• Not currently envisaged.	• Not currently envisaged.

former embrace the immediate consequences of integration for the costs of supplying goods and services from various locations. Take, for example, the removal of tariff barriers, as a result of Mark I EC integration in 1958 and the conclusion of the Canada-U.S. Free Trade Agreement in 1989. The primary consequence of this kind of integration is to increase the competitiveness of goods exported from (say) France to (say) Italy or from Canada to the United States, relative to those produced by domestic firms in Italy and the United States. Clearly, the extent to which exports will increase will depend on the relative importance of the transfer costs saved, any effect the extra sales of the exporting companies may have on its production costs, and the elasticity of demand for the final products traded. As far as firms from countries outside the integrated market are concerned, the locational effects will depend upon the value of the common external tariff and/or level and structure of non-tariff barriers relative to those previously imposed by individual countries; although, like the companies producing within the integrated area, they, too, should benefit from the removal of intra-country trade barriers.[3]

To some degree, the primary or initial effects of integration — whatever its form — will be country, sector and firm specific. Certainly, the income and employment consequences from Mark I EC integration have not been equally spread among the six founding member states; any more than those of the NAFTA are likely to be symmetrically distributed between the United States, Canada and Mexico. Economic theory suggests that the countries most likely to gain from freer trade are those whose pre-integration tariff barriers most impeded the efficient allocation of their domestic resources. Also, insofar as small countries are likely to be more trade-intensive than large countries, it might be supposed that they will especially benefit from integration — particularly if the supply and demand elasticities for their traded products are high. At the same time large countries which are sheltered from foreign imports may find that the additional competitive import competition may help raise the technical efficiency and widen the marketing networks of their domestic firms.

Clearly too, the impact of the elimination of tariff barriers will vary according to how important they are in relation to the total costs of supply. In part this will depend on country-specific characteristics, such as the pre-integration tariff levels and the economic or psychic distance involved between the trading partners.[4] Product-specific factors are also likely to influence the effects of regional integration inasmuch as the level and relative significance of tariff reductions and the response of consumer demand and producer supply will vary according to the nature of the goods and services supplied.

Finally, the locational consequences of an economic integration are likely to be firm specific. Consider, for example, the removal of non-tariff barriers consequent upon Mark II EC integration (i.e. EC 1992). The elimination of border controls, which represent a fixed cost to firms, is likely to benefit small (relative to large) firms. The cessation of favoured treatment in the procurement policies by governments towards firms located in their own country will clearly not be welcomed by uncompetitive firms in that country. Firms which already have a network of value-added activities, or marketing contacts and distribution outlets within the integrated region, are particularly well placed to benefit from the harmonization of technical standards. MNEs, and particularly those that are already pursuing a polycentric or regiocen⁻ ic organizational strategy, are among those most likely to gain (Chakravarthy & Perlmutter, 1985).

It is, however, the secondary effects of integration that are most likely to be of the greatest long-term significance for the regional allocation of economic activity. These arise mainly from the geographical and industrial restructuring of production and markets by firms within and outside the integrated area, and from the new opportunities for 'insider' firms to increase their technical and scale efficiencies by reducing their production and transaction costs. As observed in the studies by Kogut and by Eaton, Lipsey & Safarian in this volume, economic integration may also be expected to spur innovation and technological progress; and to refashion organizational structures. Such effects are dynamic and are likely to be a major force in the restructuring and growth potential of the participating economies.

Such gains may be substantial. The European Commission has estimated that the completion of the internal market will raise the GNP of the EC by up to 6.5 percent per annum (Cecchini, Catinat & Jacquemin, 1988). This is expected to be achieved by both an improvement in industrial productivity and a reduction in unemployment. On average, too, consumer prices are expected to fall by 6.0 percent. About two-fifths of this reduction is expected to be brought about by the elimination of non-tariff barriers; another one-third from the better exploitation by firms of the economies of scale and scope, and the balance from a reduction in business inefficiencies and monopoly profits, arising from more intensive competition.

For the NAFTA, estimates of the economic effects indicate small gains for both the U.S. and Canada and larger gains for Mexico.[5] Estimates of the increase in real GDP for the U.S. range from 0.02 percent to 0.50 percent and for Canada they range from 0.1 percent to 0.4 percent. Real GDP in Mexico is estimated to increase by 0.1 percent to 11.4 percent. Similarly, real wages are estimated to increase by 0.1 percent to 0.3 percent in the U.S. and by 0.04 percent to 0.05 percent in Canada; in Mexico, real wages are estimated to increase by 0.7 percent to 16.2 percent.

There are other consequences of regional integration as well, which, although less quantifiable, may be no less important for the ownership and location of economic activity. Foremost among these are the policies adopted by the supervising body of the integrated region (compare those of the individual member countries) toward competition and restrictive practices, industrial relations and work practices, social affairs, the migration of labour, employment legislation, regional inequities, environmental protection, accounting and auditing procedures, deregulation or privatization of financial services, and toward trade and investment negotiations with non-member countries.

One further point: not only are the consequences of regional economic integration likely to effect the distribution of economic activity within the region, but it will also affect the relationship between these units and those outside the integrated area. Currently, the perceived effects of EC 1992 are encouraging EC owned firms to conclude alliances with Japanese and North American firms to protect or advance, not just their European, but their global competitive positions. This is particularly the case in high-technology sectors where the fixed costs of innovation, production and marketing are becoming so huge that firms can only survive by capturing regional or global markets, or by sharing these costs with other firms. In the last resort, then, the firm-specific effects of regional integration must be evaluated in terms of the costs and benefits of the coordination of global economic activity and not just that which takes place within the integrated area.

Insofar as the substantive difference between the content of post-1992 EC integration and NAFTA integration lies in the more comprehensive elimination of non-tariff barriers in the former scheme, the primary and secondary effects of the two forms might be expected to be different. Exactly *how* different, however, will depend on the economic structure of the participating regions and especially on the relative sensitivity of intra-regional trade in goods and services to the removal of non-tariff barriers as compared to tariff barriers. Mark I EC integration, for example, had little impact on intra-EC trade in services, as most obstacles to such trade consisted of government related non-tariff barriers rather than an *ad valorem* tariff or quantitative duties. It may then be reasonably expected that the benefits of the NAFTA will be similarly directed to tariff sensitive activities.[6]

Before further considering NAFTA/EC differences which arise from geography, economic structure, political and culture-specific variables, rather than the content of integration, let us now consider the role played by MNEs in affecting the consequences of integration.

How MNEs may Affect Integration

Intra-regional FDI

In the absence of MNE activity, the transaction of goods and services across national boundaries is confined to arm's length trade. FDI introduces a new mode of delivery and also affects the pattern of ownership of producing and trading firms. The distinctive feature of MNE activity is that it internalizes cross-border markets in intermediate products — notably producer services — and enables the economies of scale and scope to be better exploited. As a consequence, inter-firm trade is partially replaced by intra-firm trade; while the common ownership of production brings with it more plant specialization, closer cross-border value-added linkages, and also restructures both the industrial and geographical composition of trade.

The literature distinguishes between four main kinds of MNE activity: *market seeking, resource seeking, efficiency seeking* and *strategic asset seeking* (Dunning, 1993a). In the European Community, most MNE activity is of the first, third and fourth sorts. In the NAFTA, especially in Canada as the background paper to this volume shows, there is more resource seeking FDI, while strategic asset seeking investment is mainly confined to Canadian MNE activity in the United States.

The effects of integration on each of these types of MNE activity are very different; as are the subsequent consequences of such activity on the location and ownership and organization of international production. It is also important to distinguish between the impact of integration on *intra*-regional FDI and *extra*-regional FDI. Inasmuch as defensive market seeking investment is partially driven by tariff or non-tariff barriers, an elimination of these may be expected to lead to a substitution of intra-regional investment by intra-regional exports. By contrast, regional integration is likely to induce an increase in aggressive intra-regional *market seeking* and *efficiency seeking* FDI. This is because reduction in *structurally distorting* market failure, coupled with the particular ability of MNEs to capitalize on *endemic* market failure[7] is likely to promote a more efficient territorial and industrial allocation of economic activity.

The literature identifies two kinds of efficiency seeking FDI. The first is designed to take advantage of differences in the geographical disposition of natural or created factor endowments. Much MNE activity in export oriented manufacturing production in the Far East and in Mexico is of this kind. Sometimes this leads to the vertical specialization of particular *processes* along the value-added chain, and sometimes it leads to the horizontal specialization of products across value chains. Where such specialization reflects differences in natural resources or labour costs, it tends to be between countries at different stages of economic development; although there is a good deal of U.S. direct investment in Canadian natural resources. Within the EC, there is some MNE specialization of resource-seeking MNE activity between the Southern European countries and the more industrialized nations.[8] While the geographical distribution of Japanese investment in high-skill and technology-intensive sectors suggests the availability and quality of critical created assets (e.g. R&D facilities), skilled manpower and a supportive transport and communications infrastructure are the key determinants (Dunning, 1993b).

Efficiency-seeking FDI may also lead to a restructuring of intra-regional investment better to exploit the economies of scale and scope. It also helps promote Linder type trade, based on cross-border differences in consumer tastes. Once again, MNEs (especially those already operating in the integrated region) are in a privileged position to coordinate the required division of labour in their various production units, the location of which will be determined both by the ease of market access and by the availability of the appropriate supply capabilities.[9]

Insofar as competition among firms in the integrating countries switches from being national to regional — or even global,[10] it is likely that, in addition to the reorganization of intra-firm activities, some restructuring of product markets and some strategic regrouping of firms will occur. In the first two decades of the European Common Market, such efficiency seeking FDI was limited by very high inter-country transaction costs, including legal, cultural and language barriers. Some, at least, of these obstacles will be removed as a result of EC 1992; and in anticipation of this the number of mergers and strategic alliances between EC firms — especially EC MNEs — has increased sharply in the last five years or so.[11] Most of these associations fall under the category of strategic asset-seeking FDI, which is defined as investment prompted primarily by the need to acquire foreign assets to protect or advance a regional or global marketing position of the acquiring company (or merging companies), vis-à-vis that (those) of its competitors.

Much of this latter kind of MNE activity has been in high-technology or information intensive sectors, and has been between firms in the larger and most advanced industrial countries. Although some such intra-North American FDI — especially by Canadian and Mexican firms seeking to align themselves with U.S. companies — might be expected, the removal of non-tariff barriers would not likely be as significant an incentive for such investment as it is proving to be in the European Community.

Finally, the extent to which intra-regional MNE activity will increase as a result of integration will depend on the competitiveness of MNEs vis-à-vis uninational firms. In the EC, for example, the contribution of EC owned subsidiaries to the output and trade of the Community has risen considerably over the past decade, especially in sectors which are technology and trade intensive. Data assembled and published by EUROSTAT and the UN Transnational Corporations and Management Division (TCMD)[12] confirm that FDI has been one of the main vehicles by which EC firms have gained from regional integration. As a result, their stake in EC output — particularly manufacturing output — has increased. Similarly, there is reason to suppose that home based NAFTA MNEs will increase their share of the output of the three participating countries over the next decade or more.[13]

Extra-regional FDI

The effect of regional integration on direct investment by corporations with headquarters outside the region (i.e. extra-regional MNEs) will depend first on the extent, level and structure of the trade barriers between the region and the rest of the world; second, on the global competitive or ownership advantages of these MNEs vis-à-vis those originating from the region, or of unilateral firms; and third, on the extent to which regional integration *per se* is likely to favour extra-, relative to intra-regional, MNE activity.

Once again, the response of firms producing outside the integrated area (outsider firms) will essentially rest on two things: the extent to which outsider firms are treated differently by the regulating authorities, relative to firms producing inside the area (insider firms); and the ability of the former to reorganize or restructure their value adding activities both within the integrated area and between the area and the rest of the world. The evidence from the EC strongly suggests that, prior to the late 1990s, U.S. owned firms were more successful in rationalizing their European activities to meet the challenges of the customs union than EC owned firms (Cantwell, 1992). This success may be due to the U.S. firms' experience of operating multiple plants in their home countries; or because U.S. firms have found it easier to exploit non-economic intra-EC market failures[14] than have their European counterparts; or because, being insiders, EC firms have tended to service other EC markets by way of exports more than have non-EC firms.

The completion of the internal market has given further impetus to non-EC firms to become insiders. Japanese and non-EC European MNEs have joined U.S. firms in stepping up their direct investments in the EC to safeguard markets that might otherwise be lost to EC based firms, following the removal of such non-tariff barriers as discriminating procurement policies by national governments and the harmonization of technical standards.[15] The main thrust of Japanese FDI in the EC only dates back to the mid-1970s;[16] but from the start, Japanese firms have treated the EC (and, indeed, Western Europe as a whole) as a unified market and have organized their production, procurement and marketing strategies accordingly.

Indeed, in some sectors, notably, motor vehicles, electronics, rubber tires and investment banking, the organization of the European activities of Japanese MNEs is part of a long-term strategy directed towards increasing their penetration of global markets. So far, except, perhaps, in the auto industry, the Japanese have not viewed North American integration in quite the same way. This may be because the United States dominates its NAFTA partners as a production base in most of the sectors in which their MNEs have strong ownership advantages. At the same time, one might expect more Japanese investment in Mexico in the more labour-intensive component supplying sectors in the 1990s.

Earlier in this study, I suggested that the consequences for regional integration are likely to vary between sectors and countries. Since the level and structure of MNE involvement is also sector and country specific, it follows that the effects of integration on FDI in, and between, the member countries will be highly selective. The removal of intra-EC tariff barriers in the 1960s, for example, led to the most dramatic increase in intra-EC trade in products that possessed four attributes. First, the tariffs to which they were previously subjected accounted for a relatively significant component of total costs; second, their price supply and demand elasticities were high; third, their production was subject to scale economies; and fourth, they were faced with relatively few non-tariff barriers. Such products included motor vehicles, most domestic electrical appliances, pharmaceuticals, office equipment, rubber tires, some kinds of mass-produced machinery and industrial instruments. In most of these sectors, non-EC MNEs (of mostly U.S. origin) not only had a significant investment stake prior to the formation of the EC, but have either maintained or increased that stake since the mid-1960s.[17]

The completion of the internal market is likely to affect a rather different group of sectors. These are set out in Table 3, alongside the degree of MNE involvement in these sectors, and our estimate of the kind of MNEs (by country of origin) most likely to gain following the removal of non-tariff barriers. As the table shows, the leading service sectors in countries in which there is a medium to high MNE involvement, together with some manufacturing industries which were relatively unaffected by Mark I integration, are among the most likely to be affected by EC 1992. The table also suggests that while the Japanese MNEs may be among the main gainers in the electronics, office equipment and financial services sectors, European (especially EC) foreign investors are well poised to increase their market share of products in which MNE involvement is relatively low; and especially those that are dependent on public authorities for their procurement.

As has been argued elsewhere (Dunning 1988a), there are two contrasting views of the effects of Mark II integration on the ownership of economic activity. First, since the European owned firms failed to take advantage of Mark I integration because of their relative inability to overcome intra-EC non-tariff barriers, the removal of these barriers will be particularly beneficial to them. Among the expected gainers are most services and manufactured products where the idiosyncratic requirements of customers are especially important, e.g., white goods and telecommunication equipment. It is further believed that, in the technologically more advanced countries, the completion of the internal market will help EC owned firms to become more globally competitive.

The second and opposing view is that extra-regional (especially Japanese) MNEs that currently enjoy substantial competitive advantages over their U.S. and EC counterparts will build on these advantages; and that, even in those international sectors in which they do not currently possess such advantages, (e.g. food processing, pharmaceuticals, etc.), they will seek to use their financial strength and marketing opportunism to acquire European based rivals.

However, there is little doubt that Europe 1992 is providing a new catalyst to MNE activity. In contrast to the situation in the 1960s and 1970s, it is European and Japanese MNEs that are currently the most aggressive foreign investors, and the most prone to engage in cross-border asset restructuring. In the three years ending December 31, 1990, (1988 - 1990) intra-European merger and corporate transactions averaged $91.9 billion a year, three and one-half times those of the previous three years (1985 - 1987).

TABLE 3

SECTORS MOST LIKELY TO BE AFFECTED BY EC 1992 AND MNE INVOLVEMENT

IMPACT	SECTOR	MNE INVOLVEMENT	LIKELY GAINERS
1. Reduction in protection Increased competition	a. Financial services	High	E & J*
	b. Pharmaceuticals	High	E & U.S.
	c. Telecommunication services	Medium	E
2. Shift from fragmented local to integrated EC-wide market	a. Distribution	Low	E
	b. Food processing	Medium	?
	c. Transport (trucking)	Low	E
3. Gain of technical economies of scale through sale of standardized goods and services	a. Electronics	High	J
	b. Packing	Medium	E & U.S.
	c. White and other comsumer goods	Medium	E & J
4. Dependence on public procurement	a. Computer equipment and services	High	E & J
	b. Defence contractors	Low	E & U.S.
	c. Telecommunication equipment	Medium	E & U.S.
5. Industries where the single market leads to import substitution (EC goods instead of imports)	a. Chemicals	Medium	E & U.S.
	b. Electrical components	High	J
	c. Office equipment	High	J
6. Industries where price differential exists between countries with different indirect taxation (e.g. VAT) levels.			

Note: E - European firms
       J - Japanese firms
       U.S. - U.S. firms

Source: Adapted from *Business International* (1989): *Gaining a Competitive Edge in the New Europe* and originally published in Dunning (1993a).

Taking the six-year period as a whole, the French and Italian companies had the greatest increases in their European transactions, even though about 58 percent of all intra-European M&As have involved British firms (Walter, 1992).[18] From the early 1980s, the Japanese have treated Western Europe as a single market; but, most certainly, EC 1992 is encouraging them to engage in more high value activities — including some research and development — and to transfer their unique system of pyramidal and multi-layered networking to an EC environment (Dunning 1986, Ozawa 1991).

There is also some suggestion that EC 1992 has led to an acceleration of intra-EC product and process specialization — and, with it, intra-EC trade.[19] Thus, new clusters of auto production are being developed around the Nissan assembly plant in North East England and around the Toyota plant in the Midlands. The Rhine Valley, on the other hand, is the favored location of Japanese firms for high precision mechanical and electrical engineering activities. To some extent, the emerging pattern of Japanese MNE activity in the EC is replicating that which has already occurred in the United States[20] but the Japanese investors' vision of a "Fortress Europe", together with their concern over the future level of voluntary export restraints (VERs) — not to mention the continued appreciation of the yen in relation to most EC currencies — is speeding up the transplant of downstream activities in sectors like autos and electronics. At the same time, several Japanese MNEs are hedging their bets by increasing their exports to EC markets from their offshore Asian subsidiaries, which are not currently subject to VERs by the EC.

THE REGULATORY FRAMEWORK

FOR MANY YEARS THE regulatory framework affecting both intra-regional and extra-regional FDI in the European Community has been very different from that likely to be established by the NAFTA. A review of the 293 directives issued by the EC Commission to eliminate most intra-EC non-tariff barriers suggests that relatively few are significant obstacles to intra-North American trade and commerce.[21] Exceptions include those which relate to the cross-border marketing of services and the public procurement of sensitive manufactured goods (e.g. defense equipment). Examples include the exports of Canadian telecommunication equipment to the U.S. and the setting up of U.S. owned insurance companies in Mexico.

Since the establishment of the EC, both national and community policy towards inbound MNE direct investment activity has gradually become more liberal. There are currently (July 1993) few exchange controls on either extra- or intra-EC investment flows; restrictions on the raising of local finance by foreign affiliates are largely nonexistent; many sectors previously denied to foreign investors have now been opened up — at least to EC MNEs[22] — while most EC countries have replaced fairly detailed and multifaceted authorization procedures by simple notification or verification devices (OECD, 1991).

At the same time, several EC countries still impose a variety of performance conditions on the subsidiaries of extra-EC MNEs. Often the adherence to these is the price extracted by host governments for tax concessions and other fiscal incentives offered to foreign investors. Two requirements are most widely imposed — even by the most liberal administrations: first, that over a stipulated period of time, a certain proportion of the output of a foreign subsidiary in an EC country will be actually produced in the EC (the local content requirement); and second (and this is linked to the first), that a foreign investor will, by some agreed date, undertake at least some of its higher value activities in its European subsidiaries. Both these provisions — together with the encouragement of VER — are particularly addressed to Japanese investors. Certainly, the most serious concern — and one which is echoed by some U.S. authorities in respect of Japanese FDI and by some Canadian authorities in respect of U.S. inward investment — is that Europe might become a low value-added base serving the higher-value activities of Japanese MNEs undertaken in their home country.

In contrast to most of its constituent countries, the European Commission does not have a policy toward either outbound or inbound FDI activity. Indeed, its philosophy, as revealed in various of its published reports, is that nationality of ownership does not matter as a factor influencing the efficiency of intra-EC resource organization and utilization.[23] But through its various economic and social programs, as agreed by the member countries, there is no question that nationality can, and does, influence the level and structure of MNE activity.

There has already been considerable research on the impact of the first phase of European integration on both the volume and direction of MNE activity, and the ownership and organization of such activity.[24] Much less work has been done on the consequences of pre-1992 EC integration for the policies of individual member states towards inward or outward investment. In a recent study, the OECD (1991) identified European integration as one of the factors making for a more liberalized climate towards MNE activity, although it would seem that the main changes in policy have occurred only in the last quarter of the Community's existence (that is, over the last eight years or so). However, although regional integration has dramatically changed the FDI policies of national governments, it has affected both the costs and benefits of different kinds of MNE activity, and the opportunity costs of those activities. This has forced national governments to be more competitive in their bidding for inbound investment, and to reshape their general economic strategies (Panic, 1991).

The completion of the internal market is likely to be reinforced by EC 1992 which liberalizes even further both markets and the opportunities open to MNEs. Since EC directives and regulations have also led to a harmonization of many national policy instruments and measures which might otherwise have affected the locational decisions of firms, it follows that purely commercial considerations will be of even greater importance — particularly those concerning the underlying supply capabilities offered by individual countries, many of which are strongly government influenced (Porter, 1990).

It is, then, the way in which countries respond to regional integration in their resource organization and utilization policies, as much as regional integration *per se*, that will determine their success or failure in both attracting new inward investment and providing the opportunities and incentives for competitive-enhancing outward investment.

However, there are other aspects of European integration which have affected the intra-EC distribution of MNE activity. One is the social program of the European Commission which, in the 1960s and 1970s, helped shape the attitudes of foreign MNEs towards investing in the EC (Robinson, 1983). Another is the current attempt by the Commission to help the poorer parts of the Community to develop their resource potential, and to assist the restructuring of other regions suffering from above-average unemployment. To promote these latter two objectives, the Community provides grants or loans, known as *fiscal transfers*, which are financed by the more prosperous member states.

Such fiscal transfers are, quite intentionally, discriminatory in their consequences. They may be deployed by the recipient countries in various ways, some of which affect their relative attractiveness to foreign investors. Structural adjustment funds, for example, may be used to upgrade the infrastructure of less-prosperous economies in such a way as to redirect *efficiency-seeking* MNE activity away from the wealthier EC countries. Or fiscal transfers might be used to assist domestic firms in the upgrading of their technological capabilities, which may in turn help to improve their competitiveness *vis-à-vis* other European firms in the markets in which they both compete.

Thus, by a number of means designed to help the poorer regions of the EC become more productive, the Commission has affected the level and geographical composition of both inward and outward direct investment. But other policies (such as those aimed to stimulating the innovatory capacity of EC-based firms in cutting-edge technologies) are more likely to favour the wealthier countries, as it is from these that MNEs in advanced-technology sectors tend to originate. A study of the membership of government-funded research-based consortia and of the recipients of grants from the various EC-funded science and technology initiatives reveals that these are mainly located in the high-income EC nations (Mytelka & Delapierre, 1987). Such subsidies, then, will enhance the ability of countries to be outward investors, and, by improving their domestic resource capabilities, make them more attractive to inward investors.

Generally, the completion of the internal market will affect the relative competitiveness of EC firms *vis-à-vis* non-EC firms, and the attractions of a European location for production by all kinds of firms. Because some of the main beneficiaries of the deeper integration are likely to be in the service sectors, one would expect an increase in *efficiency-seeking* and *strategic-asset-seeking* MNE investment in the years to come. Also, through an increase in intra-European competition, one might also expect to see the emergence of a leaner and fitter group of European MNEs, better equipped than their predecessors to penetrate global markets.

At the same time, the future policy of the Community towards the importation of products from non-EC countries is not yet clear. The outcome will certainly affect the amount of EC *market-seeking* investment, particularly that of products currently subject to VERs. The future stance of the

Community is intimately tied up with the progress of the GATT negotiations, but it is precisely this area of international economic activity which the European Community — by virtue of *being* the EC — is most likely to influence.

At a micro-organizational level, the European Commission can and does affect the actions of both domestic and foreign-based MNEs through the provisions of the Rome Treaty. Foremost among these provisions is a wide range of regulations designed to reduce monopolistic practices and encourage competition in the Community.[25] Examples include those laid down in Article 85 of the Treaty, which is especially directed to advancing employment protection and worker participation; the harmonization of aids to inward investment (Articles 92-94 of the Treaty); and a variety of directives and rulings on environmental, safety and health matters. One particularly pertinent example of a regional ruling directly affecting inward investment is that made by the Commission in July 1991 about the local content of a 'European-made' car produced in the Community by Japanese-owned firms. Cars with the prescribed amount of local (EC-made) content can then be traded freely in the EC without any barriers. At the same time, the Community pegged the level of imports of Japanese cars at the 1990 level until 1998, when all quotas are to be abolished. It is by decrees or directive measures such as these that the EC may have a direct impact on the level and direction of MNE activity and on the policies of individual member states.

In summary, although the European Commission does not have a policy towards MNE activity *per se*, many of its macro-organizational actions affect, for better or worse, both the total amount of FDI in the EC and its distribution among the member states. Take, for example, environmental standards and regulations. If these are kept at too high a level, they will not only divert MNE activity to non-EC countries (because an EC location will become less competitive), but within the EC, they will redirect it from low-wage, low-productivity countries to high-wage, high-productivity countries. These latter countries are also those tending to have high tax rates and social expenditures along with more stringent environmental standards (Sweeney, 1991). By contrast, a reduction in domestic content requirements, or of other non-tariff barriers, is likely to lead to more foreign investment in the EC — from which all EC countries should benefit, to a greater or lesser extent.

Stated simply, the EC can opt for two rather different mixes of policies. One is to force poorer EC members to adopt a social charter that would, for example, force the poorer members to adjust their wages, welfare and environmental standards closer to the levels of the higher-income members. This would tend to put the poorer countries at a distinct disadvantage and divert the flow of inbound direct investment from them to their wealthier neighbours. It would also have the probable effect of reducing the total amount of FDI in the EC. At the other extreme, the EC might choose to implement policies that do not attempt to keep investment from being diverted from high-income to low-income member states. The likely outcome of this strategy would be that high-income countries would unilaterally reduce their tax rates and/or lower their social transaction costs so as to make themselves more competitive with the rest of the EC — and, indeed, the rest of the world. In this event, the net result would be an increase in both domestic and foreign investment and a reduction in structural unemployment (Sweeney, 1991).

Under the NAFTA, the Free Trade Commission is responsible for overseeing the entire Agreement. Cabinet-level officers from all three countries, supported by their officials, are responsible for its implementation and further elaboration. Ultimately, they will also manage all disputes. In addition to the Commission, the NAFTA establishes eight Committees and six Working Groups. Although the NAFTA establishes these administrative organizations and determines their specific functions, collectively they fall far short of an EC-type supranational body. The NAFTA dispute settlement provisions come closest to establishing such a body.

The NAFTA provides detailed mechanisms for the resolution of both state-to-state and investor-state disputes. The NAFTA provides for binding arbitration of investor-state disputes under the Investment Chapter, and, in the case of Panels, resoultion of disputes on anti-dumping and countervailing duty matters. In the case of state-to-state disputes on all other matters, the NAFTA dispute resolution provisions are non-binding.

The NAFTA will have little authority to standardize or to harmonize national policy instruments in any meaningful way. For this reason integration of the NAFTA is likely to be much shallower than either Mark I or Mark II EC integration, and its effect on both intra- and extra-MNE activities will be confined largely to those arising from trade diversion, the creation effects of the removal of tariff barriers, and those stemming from the changing competitive positions of "insider" and "outsider" MNEs, *vis-à-vis* uninational firms.

EMPIRICAL RESEARCH ON THE EFFECT OF INTEGRATION ON MNE ACTIVITY

THE LITERATURE

USING SOME OF THE CONCEPTS introduced earlier, I now turn to a review of some empirical studies of the consequence of (regional) economic integration on FDI and MNE activity. Broadly speaking, these fall into three main groups. The first comprise those that attempt to examine the relationship between integration and the level and pattern of inward or outward direct investment. Several cross-sectional studies undertaken in the 1960s (as described in UN [TCMD] 1993) pointed to a structural shift of U.S. outward direct investment towards EC countries in the decade or so after the formation of the Community. Later work showed that Ireland's accession to the EC led to a substantial increase in FDI from both the United States and other Community members to that country, while the U.K.'s share of new U.S. investment in the

EC increased sharply in the years immediately before and after its accession. Shelburne (1991) has argued persuasively that the rate of growth in the GNP of both Spain and Portugal has been increased as a direct result of their accession to the EC in 1986; by contrast, the decade after accession was one of anaemic growth and increasing unemployment for Greece. Other data suggest that, in the 1960s, U.S. firms were substituting EC production for exports from the United States (Dunning, 1993b), while their share of EC production and exports relative to that of EC owned firms also rose. Finally, according to EUROSTAT, the annual flow of intra-EEC FDI rose five times between the announcement of EC 1992 and the end of 1989. This was more than twice as fast as extra-EC and FDI.

A second group of empirical studies has focussed on the link between the discriminatory tariff effects of economic integration and the extent to which U.S. investment in the EC is replaced by U.S. exports to the EC. The findings from these studies are mixed, and often contradictory. This is due partly to the difficulty of researchers in separating the tariff from other variables which might affect U.S. investment in the EC; partly to the different measures used by researchers to identify the tariff changes; and partly to the differences in the specifications of the models used. However, even those studies which seem to suggest that the level of tariffs is a statistically significant variable influencing U.S. direct investment have acknowledged that much of the more important "pulling in" was the growth of the EC market. Indeed, one economist (Goldberg, 1972) has calculated that about 80 percent of the new investment of U.S. firms in the EC during the period 1958 to 1970 could be explained by the market growth and broadening hypothesis. Of course, part of this growth and broadening was, itself, due to removal of the intra-EC tariff barriers.

A third group of studies has sought to examine the factors affecting the distribution of U.S. investment within the EC. Since 1958, the role of inbound direct investment (vis-à-vis domestic investment) in each of the member states has increased; most dramatically so in some of the smaller nations, like Belgium, the Netherlands and Ireland. It is these latter nations which have attracted the largest share of efficiency seeking export oriented FDI relative to their national outputs, with MNEs in the heavy chemicals and metal using sectors especially favouring Belgium and the Netherlands; and those in food, drinks, textiles and light chemicals preferring an Irish location. Unfortunately, none of the relevant empirical studies has attempted to evaluate the extent to which the changing geographical disposition of FDI is due to economic integration per se.

In the last decade, the factors influencing the location of foreign affiliates in the European Community have changed. Increasingly, it is the availability of educated and well-trained manpower, technological capacity and a good transportation and communications network which have become the main driving force. Size of country is no longer an important demand related variable; rather it is the country's geographical position in relation to the major industrial markets of the European Community. Exceptions include FDI in natural resource-based and more labour-intensive manufacturing and service activities. Here, the peripheral countries of the EC, e.g. Spain, Portugal, Ireland and Denmark, and the more outlying regions of the core industrialized countries, continue to attract both Japanese and U.S. FDI. A classic example is the proportion — probably around one-third — of Japanese owned manufacturing activity currently directed to the less prosperous countries (e.g. Spain) or regions (e.g. South Wales) of the European Community.

Surveys conducted on the factors influencing the location of FDI within the EC all point to the increasing role played by transaction costs of business activity, that is, those costs associated with market failure, especially those influenced by government policy, at both national and regional levels (Dunning, 1993b). Such government policies (those being pursued by the Clinton administration, for example) are also likely to become more (rather than less) significant in influencing the location or relocation of MNE activity in the NAFTA and within particular NAFTA countries — notably the United States and Canada. At the same time, the much greater asymmetries and distances between the member countries might be expected to work towards rather more geographical concentration of FDI in the three NAFTA countries than in most of the 12 European Community nations.

Let us now look at one or two examples from the experience of MNEs operating in the EC. Broadly speaking, the literature (Doz, 1986, Cantwell, 1992, Dunning, 1993a) records three kinds of corporate response to European integration. First there are companies like SKF, 3M, Scott Paper, Philips of Eindhoven, and Toshiba and Nissan which adopted a pattern of more intensive product (i.e. horizontal) specialization among their European plants. Sometimes, but not always, this rationalization has been accompanied by a Pan European marketing strategy. GM concentrates its Nova production in Spain. 3M produces scotch tape in its German factory and its 'Post-it' notes in its U.K. factory. Previously, these companies manufactured a fairly wide range of products in each country for sale mainly to consumers of that country.

Second, there are the MNEs which have chosen to focus their activities along a particular value-added chain, i.e. vertical specialization. The Ford Motor Company now concentrates its European production of engines in Valencia (Spain), gear boxes and differentials in Bordeaux (France), and the major body processing components in Saarlouis and Valencia. Like Ford, IBM, while practicing dual or multiple sourcing, concentrates its European output of different parts and components for its computers in one or more of its EC facilities. Though fairly diversified at their final stages of production, most non-European pharmaceutical MNEs tend to limit the production of their active ingredients, as well as their R&D activities, to a few EC locations, notably the U.K., France, West Germany and Ireland.

Third, the pattern of intra-EC economic activity may be changed by the type of *inter*-firm competition promoted by regional integration. Thus, the removal of restrictions on government procurement, and the encouragement of the harmonization of cross-border technical standards may open possibilities for more inter-firm specialization of similar products. In the European (and indeed global) paint industry, for example, the German firm BASF specializes in automobile paints, and the U.K. firms Courtaulds and ICI specialize in marine, decorative and industrial paints.

It should be noted, however, that not all MNEs have adopted a strategy of product or process specialization as a result of regional integration. Those which have to meet the needs of idiosyncratic markets may find any benefits from economies of scale are outweighed by the reduced demand or additional costs of product or process adaptation. The excellent documentation of the white goods sector in the EC by Baden-Fuller and Stopford (1991) shows that, although there has been an increase in industrial concentration, there is little evidence of any trend towards the globalization of products or markets. The authors show that, even within Europe, there are significant differences in cross-border consumer tastes, distribution channels, production, promotion and development methods which, taken as a whole, seriously inhibit European MNEs from exploiting the benefits of regional integration.[26] Other examples of the need to take account of country-specific consumer tastes outweighing the advantages of production economies include carpets and some kinds of textiles. In these cases, integration is likely to make little difference to corporate strategies; neither will it do so where transport costs are an important component of the total costs of production, or where products are strongly location bound.

In several respects, the response of MNEs to Mark I integration in the EC can be expected to be repeated in the NAFTA. However, there is likely to be relatively more vertical rationalization of U.S.-Mexico manufacturing FDI than U.S.-Canadian manufacturing FDI, due primarily to more substantial differences in labour costs between the U.S. and Mexico. By contrast, defensive import substituting investment by U.S. firms in Canada will probably fall; while horizontal efficiency seeking investment, particularly in Southern Ontario, is likely to increase. It is also probable that there will be more strategic asset-seeking investment by the large Canadian MNEs in the United States as they seek to build up their global competitive positions.

Earlier research by Doz (1986) and Doz & Prahalad (1987) also emphasized the importance of national governments in influencing the strategies of MNEs. Using the percentage of the sales of particular sectors to government (i.e. the degree of public procurement) as a proxy for government influence, Doz (1986) concluded that in sectors (military aircraft and electricity generating equipment, for example) where this ratio was the highest in the early 1980s, MNEs were most likely to adopt nationally responsive strategies. By contrast, in those sectors where the ratio of government purchases was the lowest (CTV tubes, agri-tractors and autos, for example), they tended to practice regionally or globally integrated strategies.

Since EC 1992 will reduce barriers to government procurements, along with the privatization and deregulation of national markets, it is highly likely that there will be a further reappraisal of the organization of transnational activities, and especially of those MNEs currently pursuing nationally responsive strategies.

There are, of course, other factors which have discouraged cross-border corporate integration for many years. These include cross-border controls, differential technical standards and fiscal policies. Others are more "natural" barriers, e.g. transport, costs and differences in buying cultures. While most of the former will disappear with EC 1992, the latter may not. As a result, at least some MNEs will continue to adopt nationally, rather than regionally, oriented strategies. According to Doz and Prahalad (1987), a successful locational strategy is one that balances the global advantages of exploiting the advantages of the governance of related assets and proprietary knowledge, while continuing to recognize the importance of adapting its products and production methods to the specific needs of local markets. However, such a reorganization of activities is unlikely to be undertaken by MNEs in the NAFTA because many of the 1992 EC-type barriers either do not exist or are unaffected by the free trade agreement.

Finally, the U.S. Department of Commerce regularly provides macro-statistical data on the extent to which product or process specialization is practiced among U.S. multinationals in the EC and LAFTA, and how this has changed over time. *Inter alia*, these reveal, first, that the proportion of sales of U.S. manufacturing affiliates in the EC exported to other parts of Europe rose from 14.1 percent in 1957 to 30.5 percent in 1989. Second, they show that the export propensity of U.S. affiliates in the EC and, to a lesser extent, in the major LAFTA countries (e.g. Brazil and Mexico), is considerably greater than that in other parts of the world. However, as a result of the NAFTA it might be reasonable to expect an increase in trade between U.S. firms and their affiliates north and south of the U.S. border.

A Recent Survey

A RECENT SURVEY of 56 of the largest U.S., European and Japanese MNEs, carried out by Tom Gladwin, Teretumo Ozawa and myself for the UN (TCMD) in 1992, reveals a wide diversity of strategic responses by senior executives to EC 1992. The full results of this survey will be published by UNCTAD later in 1993 but, in the following paragraphs and in Table 4, we highlight [with the permission of the UN (TCMD)] some of our findings and the extent to which we believe they may have relevance to the strategic thinking of MNEs now producing or contemplating producing in the NAFTA.

- EC 1992 will trigger an acceleration of market growth in the EC relative to that in other parts of the world. However, most non-EC based MNEs anticipate playing only a limited role. We

TABLE 4	
PERCEIVED EFFECTS OF EC 1992 AND NAFTA ON MNE ACTIVITY	
(– PERCEIVED LEAST ++ PERCEIVED GREATEST)	

EC	NAFTA
MARKET GROWTH	
• 0 → + Noticeably industry-specific: service firms recorded + → ++, while most market growth is expected to come from pan-European customer segmented growth, increased EC importance in strategic planning and expected growth in EC.	• + → ++ Again, strongly industry- and country-specific. Growth prospects probably most favourable for FDI in trade-related activities in which member states enjoy a comparative advantage.
COMPETITIVE STRATEGY	
• 0 → ++ Very marked in some sectors; with response of MNEs tending to favour a product differentiation rather than a low cost strategy. Also more co-ordination of value chain activities among EC affiliates, particularly those of U.S. origin. EC 1992 effects most likely to be experienced by large and service-intensive firms.	• 0 → + Most pronounced effect likely to be felt in certain regions in the United States and Canada and in sectors exposed to additional competitive pressures (e.g. the more mature, but labour intensive, U.S. industrial sectors.
COST REDUCTION	
• + 0 → + EC 1992 has induced a massive wave of corporate restructuring in the EC. Increased cross-border M&A activity envisaged as well as a streamlining of organizational structures. Effect most marked in intra-EC investment in services.	• 0 → ++ More selective impact which directly arises from economies of specialization. Could be quite significant in case of market oriented Mexican and/or Canadian firms wishing to penetrate the United States or Latin American countries.
TECHNOLOGICAL INNOVATION	
• - → ++ Economic integration thought to aid MNE partici-pation in high cost R&D projects by enlarging markets and easing conditions for strategic alliances. But not all sectors (e.g. services) considered this effect to be of importance.	• - → + Again, more likely to be selective in view of overwhelming predominance of the United States in innovating activities. But some technological clusters in the NAFTA may evolve (sometimes with support of MNEs) in Canada and Mexico, e.g. especially those in more (natural) resource-intensive sectors.
LOCATION OF ECONOMIC ACTIVITY	
• 0 → ++ Most firms agreed that EC 1992 would markedly affect the modality by which they serviced EC markets, and that there would be a shift in value-added activity toward the EC away from other regions.	• - → + Possibly less significant, except around national border of the United States with Canada. But likely to encourage more clustering of economic activities within member states.

cont'd.

TABLE 4 (CONT'D.)

PERCEIVED EFFECTS OF EC 1992 AND NAFTA ON MNE ACTIVITY

EC	NAFTA
SOURCING AND TRADE	
• + → ++	• - → +
One of most important perceived effects on MNE activity of EC 1992. FDI generally thought likely to supplant some exports and increase (through intra-firm intermediate product trade) others. Effect on concentration and relocation of value-added activity is likely to be highly industry-specific, e.g. services thought less likely to be affected than telecommunications and consumer electronics.	More vertical specialization of MNE activity likely to occur between Mexico and United States (and Canada); more horizontal specialization between Canada and the United States.
FUTURE PROTECTIONISM	
• 0 → +++	• 0 → +
Perceived by firms – especially those in strategic sectors or those in which intra-Triad competition is especially fierce – to be most important. In particular, auto, textile fibres, consumer electronics and banking MNEs (especially those of Japanese origin) are viewed as a major likely influence for their investment strategies. Concern over reciprocity arrangements was most generally voiced by Japanese firms, but also U.S. MNEs in some strategically sensitive and service sectors. Generally, the fear of "Fortress Europe" was regarded by non-EC firms as the single most potent force leading to more defensive seeking FDI in EC. Insider/outsider distinction was less marked in reciprocity requirements of Japanese and U.S. firms, rights of establishment in public procurement policy, and in the recognition of technical standards.	Probably much less significant as impact of NAFTA per se on intra-Triad trade and investment is likely to be comparatively small. However, the exact effects are difficult to assess, as the proposed NAFTA agreement currently makes no immediate provision for a common external tariff and there are few reciprocity arrangements with extra-NAFTA nations.

Source: Study on effect of EC on the activities of TNCs, to be published by UN (TCMD) in 1993; and author's own speculations.

believe this conclusion can be generalized to apply equally to the NAFTA situation.

- EC 1992 will intensify intra-European competition. Most MNEs plan to cope with this by pursuing product differentiating rather than cost-reducing strategies. We believe that this conclusion is more applicable in the case of U.S.-Canada than U.S.-Mexico trading and FDI relationships.

- EC 1992 is inducing only a small percentage of MNEs to exploit scale and scope economies, or to rationalize their supplier networks, manufacturing and distribution systems, in order to reduce their production or transaction costs. We believe that a rather larger proportion of U.S. and non-NAFTA MNEs may seek to invest in Mexico to exploit such advantages.

- EC 1992 does and will continue to encourage a wave of corporate restructuring. However, this is unlikely to involve much backward integration. We believe that there will be more intra-NAFTA vertical integration between U.S. and Mexican firms, but that otherwise the pattern of industrial consolidations will be broadly similar.

- EC 1992 is having a significant effect on reallocating the locus and focus of corporate R&D intended to serve the needs of a unified EC market. We believe a similar relocation of such activities will occur in the NAFTA.

- EC 1992 is likely to attract FDI into the EC that will be export substituting, but little locational shifting (either inside or outside of the EC) is anticipated given the declining importance of labour costs. Specifically, the completion of the internal market appears to be providing little incentive for market seeking investments by developing nations. In the NAFTA, we expect rather more locational shifting to take place, thus reducing labour costs, although this is unlikely to be the main effect of the Agreement.

- EC 1992 is likely to induce net trade creation for developing nation suppliers of primary goods but net trade diversion for developing nation suppliers of manufactured goods, with intra-EC trade rising in importance. We anticipate that the NAFTA will have only a marginally adverse affect on the primary exports of outsider developing countries; except, perhaps, in the case of Caribbean textiles.

- EC 1992, as it interacts with the liberalization of Central and Eastern European markets, is likely to result in a relocation of some export-oriented FDI from developing nations to such countries as Hungary, Poland and Czechoslovakia, especially in selected sectors such as automobiles, consumer electronics and chemicals. By contrast, these developments are likely to have only a peripheral effect on MNE activity in the NAFTA.

- EC 1992 is perceived as providing the foundation for a "Fortress Europe", especially by Japanese and developing nation enterprises which anticipate continuing discriminatory quotas, local content requirements, public procurement barriers and EC/member state subsidies to key industries. These concerns could well be paralleled by a "Fortress North America". Much will depend on the future of GATT and bilateral U.S.-Japanese and U.S.-EC trade negotiations.

CONCLUSIONS

THERE ARE BOTH similarities and differences between the content of Mark I and Mark II EC integration and the NAFTA. The similarities are mostly shown in their expected effects on trade and FDI following the removal of tariff barriers, although the form, content and distribution of the effects will vary according to industry, country and firm-specific characteristics. In the case of the NAFTA, the failure to agree on a common external tariff with the rest of the world may also bring with it distinctive consequences.

The differences arise from the more extensive removal of non-tariff barriers between EC countries compared with those currently envisaged by the NAFTA countries; and from the greater attention paid by the former area to social issues, and the intra-regional distribution of costs and benefits. The experience of European integration suggests that the four kinds of FDI and MNE activity described in the text are affected differently by the removal of tariff barriers and other obstacles to the freedom of movement of assets, goods and people. Setting aside the important differences in the size, geography and economic structure of the countries comprising the NAFTA and the EC (and in particular the greater asymmetry in the economic relationship between the U.S. and its northern neighbour than that between any pair of countries in the EC), the consequences for FDI are likely to be similar, and follow the predictions set out earlier in this study. But, as in the case of the EC, the distribution of FDI between the member countries of the NAFTA is likely to be uneven, with the greatest gains being recorded by those countries (and regions within countries) offering the most cost-effective locations for exploiting the integrated market.

To some extent, the industrial hinterland of the United States and Southern Ontario in Canada may be compared with the core industrial countries in the EC, with most of Mexico and most of the rest of Canada being likened to the outer ring of European countries and regions (Spain and Portugal in Mexico's case; Denmark and parts of the U.K., Germany and Italy in Canada's case). Insofar as distance seems likely to be negatively correlated with the ripple effects of integration, it might be supposed that, apart from (natural) resource-intensive FDI, the regions of Mexico and Canada furthest removed from the major markets of the NAFTA will benefit least from new MNE activity, and could indeed be net losers from integration. Furthermore, as a reduction in trade and investment barriers between two countries with very different factor endowments may lead to a substantial relocation of economic activity, the economies of the regions adjacent to the Mexican-U.S. border are likely to incur significant adjustment costs.

However, although primarily a trading agreement, the NAFTA does embrace some of the ingredients of a customs union, and goes considerably further in its attempt to lower non-tariff barriers and harmonize trade and investment relationships than did Mark I EC integration. To this extent, the effect of the NAFTA on some sectors — including service sectors — unaffected by pre-1992 European integration may be quite pronounced; particularly in the later 1990s.

Table 5 summarizes some of the main responses of the intra and extra EC MNEs to European integration described in the previous sections; and some possible reactions of intra- and extra-NAFTA MNEs to North America's integration.

In conclusion, I have two final, and possibly controversial, thoughts. The first is that I find it difficult to perceive that the kind of economic gains enjoyed by the member states of the EC over the past 35 years are likely to be repeated in the NAFTA. This is because in 1957, the political, cultural and social framework of Europe was far more divisive and damaging to its economic health than the contemporary situation in Canada, Mexico and the United States. If the United States itself consisted of several countries, each with its own language, political and legal systems and cultures, then the gains of economic integration might be expected to be much greater — even though much of this would probably be of an intra-U.S. nature. One suspects, then, that the effects of the NAFTA on the combined GNP of the three participating countries will be less pronounced and considerably more geographically concentrated. It may also be that FDI (and other trans-border associations, e.g. strategic alliances) will play a more important role in affecting the level and distribution of intra-NAFTA value added activity than it did — at least in the early days of European integration — within the European Community.

The second thought is that, whereas regional integration in the 1960s and 1970s was best seen in the context of a politically and economically fragmented world in which cross-border corporate integration was the exception rather than the rule, the scenario in the early 1990s is totally different. We now live in a globally integrated economy and, increasingly, both corporations and governments are viewing their economic strategies towards regional integration in that light. In their reactions to the NAFTA — far more than in their response to Mark I EC (but not Mark II EC) — both sets of actors are looking at its implications for their international competitiveness. The extent to which the NAFTA leads to more Japanese FDI in Mexico or more Canadian MNE activity in the United States will then rest on the extent to which companies perceive their global goals to be better advanced by this strategy. Similarly, the U.S., Mexican and Canadian governments are likely to view any extension of the NAFTA in terms of how it may further affect the competitive position of their resources and firms, vis-à-vis those of their main trading rivals. To this extent, the objectives and evaluation of regional

TABLE 5

EC AND NAFTA: SUMMARY OF ACTUAL OR LIKELY RESPONSES OF MNEs

EC	NAFTA

INTRA-EC MNE ACTIVITY

• Prior to the mid-1980s this was limited due largely to intra-EC non-tariff barriers and relative ease of exporting goods (but not services) within EC. There has been a substantial increase in this kind of MNE activity and EC related strategic alliances over the past 5 - 8 years. Predominantly, this has been of an efficiency or strategic asset-seeking kind, except that in the less developed countries (or regions within countries of the EC), there has been some natural resource-(including low cost labour) seeking FDI. Such limited data as are available suggest that some of the smaller EC countries, e.g. Belgium and the Netherlands, have gained a relatively larger share of efficiency-seeking (import subsituting) FDI since 1958.

• A considerable increase in all kinds of intra-North American FDI, except defensive market-seeking investment, is anticipated. However, the types of composition are likely to be country-specific; and also related to the extent of non-tariff barriers that remain. The future of peripheral areas in Canada and Mexico is less secure, unless they can evolve "clusters" of economic activity. Infrastructure and the availability of human and physical capital are likely to become more important determinants of the location of intra-North American FDI.

EXTRA-EC MNE ACTIVITY

• **Inward** This has been largely of an import substituting or strategic asset acquiring kind when viewing the EC as a single market; but its location within the EC has primarily been driven by resource or efficiency-seeking criteria. (This applies equally to de novo and to sequential FDI.)

• **Inward** The effect on inward efficiency-seeking investment is unlikely to be as substantial as in the EC; although both Mexico and Canada are expected to attract some non-EC investment (in rather different sectors) in order to gain access to U.S. markets. Especially in Mexico there is also likely to be an increase in market-seeking investment, including that destined for Latin American countries with whom Mexico has, or is likely to have, agreement. Strategic acquiring FDI is unlikely to be greatly affected by the NAFTA.

• **Outward** While the competitiveness of European firms has improved over the past 30 years, it is difficult to pinpoint how much of this is due to the EC initiative. One hypothesis is that prior to 1992, by its competitive enhancing effects, U.S. FDI in the EC has helped European firms to upgrade their capability to become MNEs or increase their foreign investments. The removal of tariff barriers in post-1992 integration is likely to improve European competitiveness as a result of intra-European or Japanese FDI.

• **Outward** The competitive position of the United States is likely to be only marginally affected by the NAFTA. Mexico's ability to become an outward direct investor is likely to be enhanced. The impact of the NAFTA on Canadian competitiveness will depend on its effect on Canada's high value activities in each of the main industrial sectors.

integration are now very different from those embraced in earlier times, and these differences are likely to become even more pronounced as we move toward the 21st Century.

ENDNOTES

1 For a review of some of the major regional integrative schemes of recent years, see Jovanovic (1992), UN (TCMD, 1993) and Robson (1993).

2 This point is taken up more fully by Raymond Vernon in his study in this volume. In particular, one might conceive of two kinds of intra-regional economic relationships emerging from integration. One is best described as a "hub and spoke" relationship in which a core country dominates economic activity in the region, but there is another relationship as well — an asymmetric relationship between it and the other nations. The other is a "spider's web" relationship in which there is no dominant member state, but rather an intricate interpenetration of resource flows and markets by firms of the participating nations.

3 This point and others related to the effects of regional integration on the location of economic activity are taken up in more detail in the Eaton, Lipsey & Saffarian papers in this volume.

4 Thus, ceteris paribus, the greater the cross-border marketing costs (which reflect psychic or economic distance), the lower the proportional effect of any tariff reduction.

5 See Table 2-1 of USITC 1993.

6 The NAFTA agreement is unclear as to the extent to which non-tariff barriers between the participating countries will be removed. Some government-induced barriers, e.g. restrictive procurement policies, are mentioned in the treaty, but others, e.g. with respect to fiscal harmonization are not. (See Table 2.)

7 For an analysis of the differences between structurally distorting and endemic market failure, see Chapter 4 of Dunning (1993a).

8 For an examination of the patterns of FDI in these countries and how these are related to the revealed comparative advantages of natural resources and created assets, see Chapters by Juhl, Dunning and Simoes in Dunning (1985).

9. The role of government in affecting the location of FDI in a global economy is discussed in Dunning (1993b).

10 Indeed, the primary rationale behind EC 1992 was to provide a more favourable economic environment for European firms in their bid to sustain their global market positions vis-à-vis their U.S. and Japanese competitors.

11 Some details are given by Hagedoorn and Schakenraad (1990).

12 Formerly the UNCTC.

13 At the same time, through sub-contracting and other networking

arrangements, they may stimulate the output of smaller non-MNEs in Mexico, Canada and the U.S.

14 Especially those to do with cross-border culturally related transaction costs.

15 As detailed at length in Cecchini, Catinat & Jacquemin (1988).

16 For further details, see a forthcoming volume edited by Mason & Encarnation (1993).

17 This was in spite of the dramatic recovery of the German economy in the 1960s and 1970s. For further details of the shares of European exports accounted for by the affiliates of U.S. MNEs and other (mainly European) companies in the EC, see Dunning (1988) Chapter 5.

18 Of course, not all of the recent growth of intra-European M&As is attributable to European integration. Among other reasons noted by Walter (1992) for the M&A boom in Europe are: a) an overdue need for industrial restructuring in Europe, b) the availability of financial resources, c) the transfer to Europe of much of the M&A know-how that accumulated in the United States during the 1980s and, d) the increasing liberalization of capital markets in Europe (itself being part and parcel of European integration).

19 For further details, see Encarnation in this volume.

20 See also Westney in this volume.

21 For example, the cost of intra-American border controls is less than their pre-1992 intra-EC equivalents, while U.S. and Canadian technical standards are broadly comparable.

22 For non-EC investors, several EC countries still limit or regulate the conditions of entry into the finance, insurance, telecommunications, publishing, airlines, maritime transport, nuclear power and armament sectors. For further details see OECD (1991).

23 For example, hardly any mention is made of the likely impact of EC 1992 on foreign investment into or out of the Community by the Cecchini report.

24 See especially UN (1993) and Dunning (1992, 1993a). In particular, it is possible that countries like the United Kingdom, Germany and Italy would have adopted less liberal policies towards inward investment in the absence of the EC. This is simply because MNEs would have had less opportunity to engage in efficiency-seeking investment. In other words, their affiliates would most likely have been more responsive.

25 For further details and an analysis of these issues, see Graham & Warner in this volume.

26 For example, Italian housewives traditionally prefer top-loading machines while German and U.K. housewives prefer front-loading machines.

ACKNOWLEDGEMENT

I WISH TO THANK Lorraine Eden and Alan Rugman for their comments on an earlier draft of this study; and Wendy Dobson, who acted as a most constructive discussant of the paper when it was presented at the conference organized by Investment Canada.

BIBLIOGRAPHY

Baden-Fuller, C. W. F. and J. M. Stopford. "Globalization Frustrated: TheCase of White Goods." *Strategic Management Journal*, 12, (1991): 493-507.

Business International. "Gaining a Competitive Edge in the New Europe." Geneva and New York: Business International,1989.

Cantwell, J. A. "The Effects of Integration on theStructure of Multinational Corporation Activity in the EC." In *Multinationals in the New Europe and Global Trade*. Edited by M. W. Klein and P. J. Welfens. Berlin and New York: Springer-Verlag, 1992.

Cecchini, P., et al. *The European Challenge 1992. The Benefits of a Single Market*. Aldershot Hants: Wildwood House, 1988.

Chakravarthy, B. S. and H. V. Perlmutter. "Strategic Planning for a Global Business." *Columbia Journal of World Business*, 20, (1985): 3-10.

Doz, Y. *Strategic Management in Multinational Companies*. Oxford: Pergamon, 1986.

Doz, Y., and C. K. Prahalad. "A Process Model of Strategic Redirection in Large Complex Firms: the Case of Multinational Corporations." In *The Management of Strategic Change*. Edited by A. Pettigrew. Oxford: Basil Blackwell, 1987, pp. 63-83.

Dunning, J. H. "The United Kingdom." In *Multinational Enterprises, Economic Structure and International Competitiveness*. Edited by J. H. Dunning. Chichester and New York: John Wiley and Sons, 1985.

_____. *Japanese Participation in British Industry*. London: Croom Helm, 1986.

_____. *Explaining International Production*. London and Boston: Unwin Hyman. 1988a.

_____. *Multinationals, Technology and Competitiveness*. London: Allen and Unwin, 1988b.

_____. "The Global Economy, Domestic Governance Strategies and Transnational Corporations: Interactions and Policy Implications." *Transnational Corporations*, 1, 3, (1992): 7-46.

_____. *Multinational Enterprises and the Global Economy*. Wokingham, England and Reading, Mass.: Addison Wesley, 1993a.

_____. *The Globalization of Business: The Challenge of the 1990s*. London and New York: Routledge, 1993b.

Goldberg, M. A. "The Determinants of U.S. Direct Investment in the EEC: A Comment." *American Economic Review*, 62, (September 1972): 692-99.

Hagedoorn, J. and J. Schakenraad. "Strategic Partnering and Technological Cooperation." In *Perspectives in Industrial Economics*. Edited by B. J. Dankbaar et al. Holland: Kluwer, 1990.

Jovanovic, M. N. *International Economic Integration*. London and New York: Routledge, 1992.

Juhl, P. "The Federal Republic of Germany." In *Multinational Enterprises, Economic Structure and International Competitiveness.* Edited by J. H. Dunning. Chichester and New York: John Wiley and Sons, 1985.

Mason, M., and Encarnation, D. J. (eds). *Japanese Foreign Investment in a Unified Europe: Impacts on Japan and the European Community.* Oxford University Press (forthcoming, 1993).

Mytelka, L. K., and M. Delapierre. "The Alliance Strategies of European Firms and the Role of ESPRIT." *Journal of Common Market Studies,* 26, (1987): 231-255.

OECD, *Measures Affecting Direct Investment in OECD Countries.* Paris, OECD, 1991c.

Ozawa, T. "Japanese Multinationals and 1992." In *Multinationals and Europe 1992.* Edited by B. Burgenmeier and J. L. Mucchielli. London and New York: Routledge, 1991.

Panic, M. "The Impact of Multinationals on National Economic Policies." In Multinationals and Europe 1992. Edited by B Burgenmeier and J. L. Mucchielli. London and New York: Routledge, 1991.

Porter, M. E. *The Competitive Advantage of Nations.* New York: The Free Press, 1990.

Robinson, J. *Multinationals and Political Control.* Aldershot: Gower, 1983.

Robson, P. (ed.). *Transnational Corporations and Economic Integration.* United Nations Library on Transnational Corporations, London, Routledge, 1993.

Shelburne, R. C. *The North American Free Trade Agreement: Comparisons With and Lessons from Southern EC Enlargement.* Washington: U.S. Department of Labor, Economic Discussion Paper No. 39, 1991.

Simoes, V. C. "Portugal." In *Multinational Enterprises, Economic Structure and International Competitiveness.* Edited by J. H. Dunning. Chichester and New York: John Wiley and Sons, 1985.

Sweeney, R. J. "The Competition for Foreign Direct Investment." In *The Global Race for Foreign Direct Investment in the 1990s.* Edited by L. Oxelheim. New York: Springer-Verlag, 1992.

United Nations (TCMD). *From the Common Market to EC 1992.* New York: United Nations, 1993.

UNCTC. *Regional Economic Integration and Transnational Corporations in the 1990s: Europe 1992, North America and Developing Countries.* New York: U.N. Sales No. E90 II A 16, 1990.

Walter, I. "Patterns of Mergers and Acquisitions, 1985-90". In *The Global Race for Foreign Direct Investment in the 1990s.* Edited by L. Oxelheim. Berlin and New York: Springer-Verlag, 1992.

Yannopoulos, G. N. "Multinational Corporations and the Single European Market." In *Multinational Investment in Modern Europe: Strategic Interaction in the Integrated Community.* Edited by J. C. Cantwell. Aldershot, Hants and Brookfield, Vermont: Edward Elgar, 1992.

Dennis J. Encarnation
Professor of International Business
Harvard Business School

11

Intra-firm Trade in North America and the European Community

A CROSS NORTH AMERICA AND THE European Community, multinational corporations are increasingly securing market access through foreign direct investment (FDI).[1] Such investment enables multinationals to exert sizeable influence over international trade — indeed, in some cases, FDI even leads trade, as intra-company shipments link multinational parents with their majority-owned subsidiaries abroad. These subsidiaries, moreover, actually record more foreign sales directly through offshore production and overseas distribution in North America and the European Community (EC) than is generated there through imports. When combined, such production and distribution either supply the local market expressly hosting that particular foreign investment, or is exported both to nearby countries and back home. In these ways the foreign investment and related trade strategies of multinational corporations operating in North America and the European Community have followed a common evolutionary path.[2]

Promoting that common evolution, regional integration joins a broad array of interrelated factors which have long been recognized in the academic literature, and which are examined in greater detail below.[3] In this literature, a market's sheer size and its location in the product cycle are often cited. So, too, are a variety of industry characteristics, such as the pressures exerted by oligopolistic competitors or powerful buyers. Upstream, for example, these competitors may exploit scale economies and related cost advantages that must be matched by other contenders; while downstream buyers seeking greater service may, for instance, force the creation of proprietary distribution systems and related marketing assets. Both tangible and intangible, such assets may be so specific to a particular firm that their use incurs especially high transaction costs that can best be overcome through intra-company transfers — as distinct from arm's-length exchanges among unaffiliated buyers and suppliers. Finally, in recent years, even government policies have encouraged a common evolution in North America and the European Community. Gone are the trade restrictions and capital controls imposed at various times by both host and home governments; in their place are bilateral and multilateral agreements designed expressly to accelerate foreign investment and international trade flows. When totalled, these several interrelated, often competing, factors shape the foreign investment and related trade strategies pursued by multinationals.

Understanding both the degree and the source of variation in those multinational strategies are the main subjects of this study. My contention is that such variation, while still apparent, has, over time, diminished considerably — between countries, within industries, and among nationalities — all because multinationals have followed a common evolutionary path. Along that path, multinationals have confronted numerous strategic trade-offs, which I have simplified and present below as binary choices, beginning with decisions over equity ownership.

Majority Subsidiaries vs. Minority Affiliates

MULTINATIONAL CORPORATIONS CREATE and sustain competitive advantage through their skillful management of tangible and intangible assets in product and process technologies, as well as through their marketing skills and organizational structures.[4] Such assets are specific to each individual firm, and are often best exploited when that firm owns a majority (up to and including all) of the equity shareholdings in its foreign subsidiaries. Compared to minority shareholdings, a majority position tends to ensure that the multinational parent holds a higher degree of managerial control over the foreign use of that multinational's firm-specific assets. Such managerial control, in turn, often helps to reduce the high costs that can plague more arm's-length transactions between foreign suppliers of firm-specific assets and unaffiliated buyers overseas.[5] Instead of using such arm's-length transactions, these foreign suppliers transfer their tangible and intangible assets internally — directly to their majority-owned subsidiaries abroad. Later, reverse transfers also take place, as foreign subsidiaries begin to ship goods and services back to their multinational parent, as well as to other related affiliates overseas. In the end, this circular flow enhances the total pool of technological, marketing, and organizational assets available to both the multinational parent and its majority subsidiaries.

Since the Second World War, U.S.-based multinationals have consistently invested in majority-owned subsidiaries, rather than in minority-owned affiliates. Indeed, as early as 1957, U.S. multinationals reported to the U.S. Commerce Department (in its first postwar census of foreign operations of U.S. companies) that they owned upwards of three-quarters of the equity invested in their subsidiaries abroad.[6] For the Americans, this strong preference for majority (including 100 percent) shareholdings remained phenomenally stable over the next three decades,[7] even as fresh outflows of FDI from the United States reached their post-war high (during the late 1960s and early 1970s) and then subsequently fell off, to be replaced by reinvested earnings in existing subsidiaries.[8] As a result of these investments, U.S. multinationals consistently reported that their majority-owned subsidiaries contributed an ever-larger share of total foreign sales recorded overseas by all U.S. multinationals operating abroad: reaching three-quarters by 1966 (in the Commerce Department's first "benchmark" survey of U.S. FDI),[9] and climbing to four-fifths by 1990 (in the Department's most recent annual survey).[10] What little remained was dispersed across equal-partnership joint ventures and minority U.S.-owned affiliates. Thus today, for American multinationals, majority ownership of foreign subsidiaries remains a prominent characteristic of their foreign-investment strategies.

That ownership strategy has enjoyed its greatest success in other industrialized countries. Specifically, in Canada and across EC member-states, majority U.S.-owned subsidiaries clearly prevail. In fact, within these countries, U.S. multinationals continue to boast that they own, on average, over four-fifths of the total shareholders' equity invested in all their foreign affiliates (Table 1). Their shareholdings do, however, vary along the value-added chain: Those subsidiaries engaged principally in overseas distribution, for example, generally evidence a larger proportion of U.S. shareholdings than do those subsidiaries engaged principally in offshore manufacturing, which in turn evidence a larger proportion of U.S. shareholdings than do those subsidiaries directly tied to natural-resource extraction abroad. As a result, in Canada, U.S. oil companies report below-average shareholdings in their subsidiaries, while U.S. automakers and U.S. retailers boast above-average shareholdings in their Canadian subsidiaries. Such variation reflects, in part, differences in financial (and other operational) risks, especially since average investments are typically lower in downstream retailing than, say, in upstream oil refining, where greater risks may be shared with joint-venture partners.

Such variation in U.S. shareholdings also reflects wide differences in government policies, which vary not only across industries and along the value-added chain, but also across countries. Within North America, for example, just compare the incidence of majority U.S. shareholdings in Canada and Mexico. In marked contrast to U.S. multinationals in Canada, those same corporations in Mexico report that they own, on average, less than one-half of the total shareholders' equity invested in all their foreign affiliates (Table 1). Yet, despite such obvious differences, in both Canada and Mexico the incidence of majority shareholdings increases as we move down the value-added chain. Specifically, in Mexico, U.S. natural resource and (especially petro-) chemical companies have principally invested upstream in minority-owned joint ventures, while U.S. automakers have concentrated their down-stream investments in majority U.S.-owned subsidiaries. In Mexico today (as in Canada not long ago), government policies restrict foreign ownership in petroleum and other natural-resource based industries, while encouraging majority shareholdings in export-oriented manufacturing.

When comparing Canada and Mexico, however, wide variation in majority U.S. shareholdings does not simply reflect obvious differences in

---

TABLE 1

FOREIGN OWNERSHIP BY MULTINATIONALS INVESTING IN NORTH AMERICA AND WESTERN EUROPE, LATE 1980S [a]

U. S. MULTINATIONALS (MNEs) ABROAD				
EQUITY	IN CANADA	IN THE EC	IN JAPAN	IN MEXICO
US$ Value (billion)	$68.7	$196.3	$35.6	$10.7
of which:				
% U.S.	92.3	86.6	36.5	48.6
% Local	7.7	13.4	63.5	51.4

FOREIGN MULTINATIONALS (MNEs) IN THE UNITED STATES			
EQUITY	CANADIAN MNEs	EUROPEAN MNES [b]	JAPANESE MNES
US$ Value (billion)	$27.1	$76.5	$21.0
of which:			
% Foreign	73.4	89.8	74.3
% Local	26.6	10.2	25.7

Notes: [a] Data on US MNCs for 1989; data on foreign MNCs in the US for 1987.
   [b] Data for European MNCs in the US available only for investors based in France, Germany, the Netherlands, and the United Kingdom.
Sources: U. S. Commerce Department, Bureau of Economic Analysis, *U.S. Direct Investment Abroad: 1989 Benchmark Survey, Final Results* (Washington, DC: USGPO, October 1992), Tables II.B.11 and III.B.11, pp. 56, 154; and *Foreign Direct Investment in the United States: 1987 Benchmark Survey, Final Results* (Washington, DC: USGPO, August 1990), Tables C-3, C-4, C-5, C-7, and C-9, pp. 34-40.

---

national levels of economic development. To the contrary, when measuring the incidence of majority U.S. ownership, Japan has far more in common with developing Mexico than it has with its G-7 partners. Indeed, in marked contrast to either Canada or the EC, Japan continues to evidence the strong legacy of capital controls that limited both the value of FDI inflows and the level of foreign ownership in earlier times.[11] Consequently, as recently as 1990, a decade after formal liberalization, those limited U.S. investments in majority U.S.-owned subsidiaries still generate a relatively small proportion ($62 billion out of $103 billion) of the total sales recorded by all U.S. multinationals in Japan — in fact, a smaller proportion than that generated in Mexico by majority U.S. subsidiaries there.[12] Nevertheless, in industry after industry, the incidence of major U.S. shareholdings in Japan has risen dramatically since 1980, especially with the abolition of formal capital controls. This lower incidence of majority foreign subsidiaries in Japan (and in Mexico) has worked to deny

U.S. multinationals the same market access that they enjoyed in Canada and the EC — or that foreign multinationals enjoyed in the United States.

Indeed, foreign ownership patterns in the United States look much like U.S. ownership patterns in Canada and the EC, but not those in Japan. As a result, Canadian, European, and Japanese multinationals all evidence a high incidence of majority ownership in their U.S. subsidiaries. For the Europeans, at least, such a high incidence mirrors that recorded by the Americans in Europe (Table 1), with limited variation across industries. The Canadians and Japanese, by contrast, seem more inclined to invest in minority foreign-owned joint ventures, but the differences remain quite small. Few of these minority Canadian or Japanese joint ventures are found in the U.S. distribution system, where their sizeable investments are actually concentrated in majority foreign-owned subsidiaries. Rather, most of their minority joint ventures are engaged principally in U.S. manufacturing, albeit in widely different industries (for example, autos and electronics for the Japanese; food and metals for the Canadians). Despite such variations across these several industries, however, majority Canadian or Japanese ownership still prevails. Moreover, the slightly higher incidence of minority foreign-owned joint ventures by Canadian and Japanese multinationals can be explained partly as a mere "vintage effect". While their earlier and smaller investments across a broad range of industries were concentrated in minority joint ventures, the recent and sizeable surge of Canadian and Japanese FDI into the United States has largely entered majority subsidiaries. With this surge, the ownership strategies of multinational corporations of different national origins have begun to converge, as majority-owned subsidiaries have become the preferred means to gain and maintain market access.

FOREIGN SALES VS. INTERNATIONAL TRADE

AFTER SECURING MAJORITY OWNERSHIP and managerial control, multinationals typically employ their foreign subsidiaries to sell far more in overseas markets than they and other exporters back home ship to these same markets. In general, foreign sales come from three sources: the host-country market of the foreign subsidiary; the home-country market of that subsidiary's parent; and third-country markets that are typically in close geographic proximity to the host country. To supply these several markets, multinationals may decide to invest in overseas distribution channels consisting of dedicated sales and service networks, or they may decide to invest directly in offshore production. But before considering the actual sources and final destinations of foreign sales by multinational subsidiaries, it is in order first to compare the total value of those foreign sales (the numerator in Table 2) to the total value of bilateral trade (the denominator). Such a comparison establishes the primacy of FDI as the principal means for gaining access both to downstream markets for products and to upstream sources of supply.

For the Americans, the predominance of foreign sales over international trade is *not new*, although some analysts have only recently discovered it. For example, as recently as 1991 Susan Strange asserted that in the "evolution of international business . . . the mid-1980s were a milestone as the volume of international production for the *first time* exceeded the volume of international trade" (emphasis mine).[13] On the contrary, at least for the Americans, as early as 1957 the foreign (largely majority U.S.-owned) subsidiaries of U.S. multinationals reported total overseas sales at twice the value of total U.S. exports.[14] By 1966, the combined foreign sales of these majority U.S. subsidiaries had risen to represent three times the value of all U.S. exports.[15] Subsequently, that 3:1 ratio of foreign sales to U.S. exports has remained largely unaltered. In fact, during 1990, U.S. multinationals continued to sell just over three times as much overseas through their majority subsidiaries than the United States exported to the world[16] — further testimony to the fact that U.S. FDI continues to carry international competition well beyond cross-border trade.

For the Americans, however, the relative mix of overseas sales generated either by foreign investment or international trade varies widely across regions. At one extreme is the European Community where during 1990 majority U.S.-owned subsidiaries sold well over six times more than did all U.S.-based exporters (Table 2) — a ratio that has remained quite stable since the mid-1960s.[17] By then, several factors combined to attract U.S. multinationals to invest in Europe: the growth in EC demand for sophisticated products already available in the United States, the erection of common EC barriers to U.S. exports of these products, the reduction of comparable barriers to internal EC trade, and the exertion of formidable pressures by both strong EC buyers and powerful EC competitors. These pressures proved especially irresistible in oligopolistic industries where scale economies upstream and after-sales service downstream remain critical. In autos, for example, during 1990 U.S. automakers and component suppliers sold over 20 times more through their majority-owned subsidiaries operating in the EC than they did through U.S. exports to the EC.[18] In this instance regional integration has served as an important stimulus, encouraging the growth of sales by U.S. subsidiaries to the European Community.

At the opposite extreme from Europe is Mexico, where U.S.-based exporters during 1990 sold nearly twice as many goods and services as did majority U.S. subsidiaries operating there (Table 2). Of course, compared to the EC, Mexico constitutes a much smaller (national) market, where product cycles still show significant lags. Given these market constraints, plus the strict implementation of capital controls, what little U.S. FDI did enter Mexico was limited in value and concentrated in minority joint ventures, all as a result of stiff capital controls. Instead, U.S. corporations supplied the Mexican market principally through cross-border trade, which itself faced stiff import restrictions. However, the recent liberalization of Mexico's trade and investment policies promises to reverse many of these earlier patterns,

TABLE 2

THE RATIO OF FOREIGN SALES BY MULTINATIONAL SUBSIDIARIES TO U.S. TRADE, 1990 (US$ BILLION)

THE RATIO OF U.S. SUBSIDIARIES' SALES ABROAD TO U.S. EXPORTS

LOCATION OF SUBSIDIARIES	FOREIGN SALES BY MAJORITY U.S. SUBSIDIARIES (A)	U.S. EXPORTS (B)	RATIO OF SALES TO EXPORTS (A/B)
All Countries	1,191.8	393.6	3.03
of which:			
The EC	615.2	98.1	6.27
Canada	177.2	83.7	2.12
Japan	62.1	48.6	1.28
Mexico	19.3	28.3	0.68

THE RATIO OF FOREIGN SUBSIDIARIES' SALES IN THE UNITED STATES TO U.S. IMPORTS

NATIONAL ORIGIN OF SUBSIDIARIES	U.S. SALES BY FOREIGN SUBSIDIARIES (A)	U.S. IMPORTS (B)	RATIO OF SALES TO IMPORTS (A/B)
All Countries	1,168.5	495.3	2.36
of which:			
The EC	494.9	91.9	5.39
Canada	127.1	91.4	1.39
Canada (adjusted)[a]	127.1	51.4	2.47
Japan	313.1	89.7	3.49

Note: [a] Adjusted by subtracting from all U.S. imports shipped from Canada those imports shipped by U.S. subsidiaries operating in Canada.

Sources: U.S. Commerce Department, Bureau of Economic Analysis, U.S. Direct Investment Abroad: Operations of U.S. Parent Companies and their Foreign Affiliates, Preliminary 1990 Estimates (Washington: USGPO, September 1992), Table III.E.3, n.p.; and Foreign Direct Investment in the United States: Operations of U.S. Affiliates of Foreign Companies, Preliminary 1990 Estimates (Washington: USGPO, August 1992), Table E-4, n.p.; and International Trade Administration, Office of Trade and Investment Analysis, U.S. Foreign Trade Highlights: 1991 (Washington: USGPO, May 1992), Table 2, p. 11.

especially for multinationals seeking lower labour costs. U.S. automakers and component manufacturers are illustrative of future trends. During 1990, their majority subsidiaries in Mexico sold over twice as much as they exported to Mexico.[19] Such trends are likely to continue as U.S. FDI in Mexico continues to grow in response to the NAFTA.

The recent strategy of U.S. automakers in Mexico closely follows their long-standing operations in Canada. Just as we saw in Mexico, U.S. automakers and component manufacturers in Canada reported during 1990 that their majority subsidiaries sold over twice as much as they exported across the border.[20] (In both countries, auto parts and components were the largest category of U.S. exports, and in both countries these parts and components accounted for roughly 10 percent of all U.S. exports.)[21] Yet in Canada, but not in Mexico, that 2:1 ratio of subsidiaries' sales to U.S. exports actually represented the average for all U.S. corporations operating across different industries. Certainly, this figure remained well below the 6:1 ratio enjoyed by U.S. subsidiaries in the EC (Table 2). Nevertheless, U.S. corporations invested in Canada — as they had in the EC — to gain access to a sophisticated (and long-protected) domestic market, where foreign investors often faced stiff performance requirements in exchange for market access. But unlike the EC, Canada (along with Mexico) offered geographic proximity to the United States to foreign investors eager to reduce transport and transaction costs. The result, therefore, was a hybrid multinational strategy that mixed high levels of foreign investment and related trade.

Like U.S. corporations in Canada, Canadian corporations in the United States appear, at first glance, to have also adopted a hybrid strategy that mixes trade and investment. By 1990, Canadian subsidiaries recorded U.S. sales with one-and-a-half times the value of Canadian exports to the United States (Table 2). But this Table is deceptive because U.S. subsidiaries in Canada contribute exceptionally high levels of Canadian exports to the United States. These should be subtracted from Canada's total exports to the United States to obtain a more accurate measure of the relative importance of FDI to (largely) Canadian-owned corporations seeking access to the U.S. market. Indeed, when this correction is made, we find that Canadian subsidiaries in the United States sold two-and-a half times more than Canadian-owned corporations exported to the United States.[22] Moreover, regardless of the measure employed, we can safely say that these ratios have increased significantly over the last two decades. For example, figures for 1974 suggest that, by either of these measures, Canadian exports exceeded the U.S. sales of Canadian subsidiaries in the United States. But with the subsequent growth of Canadian FDI in the United States, especially during the 1980s, U.S. sales by Canadian-owned subsidiaries surely outstripped all Canadian exports to the United States — as Canadian multinationals followed the same evolutionary path charted earlier by the Americans.

Further along that evolutionary path are the Europeans. But for them, too, such progress is a recent phenomenon. By 1974, for example, European subsidiaries sold three times more in the United States than did European-based exporters; this 3:1 ratio for the Europeans fell far short of the 6:1 ratio of foreign sales to international trade enjoyed at that time by the Americans in Europe.[23] However, over the next two decades, the Europeans erased this difference, so that by 1990 EC subsidiaries in America actually reported U.S. sales five to six times larger than U.S. imports from Europe (Table 2). Thus, quite recently, the Europeans in the United States and the Americans in the European Community have achieved a rough parity in the strategic mix of both foreign investment and international trade they employ to secure access to each other's market.

Like American, European, and Canadian multinationals before them, Japanese corporations have also come to generate more of their overseas sales through foreign investment rather than through international trade. But compared to any of these multinationals, especially the Americans, this evolution is of very recent origin, reflecting the prolonged status of the Japanese as traders rather than investors. In fact, as late as 1977, Japanese subsidiaries reported total foreign sales to be roughly equivalent to Japanese exports worldwide.[24] But by 1990, following a decade of rapid growth in Japanese FDI abroad, Japanese subsidiaries (most of which were majority Japanese-owned) reported foreign sales two-and-a-half times larger than all Japanese exports worldwide.[25] This ratio proved even larger in both the United States and the European Community, where during 1990 Japanese subsidiaries sold four times more than did Japanese exporters (Table 2). Thus, in both the United States and the European Community, the Japanese have come to pursue the same foreign-investment strategies that have continued to elude the Americans (and Europeans) in Japan — strategies that have proved so successful elsewhere in the world first for American, European, Canadian, and now for Japanese multinationals.

LOCAL VS. EXPORT MARKETS

TO GENERATE FOREIGN SALES, multinational corporations focus principally on the local market hosting their majority subsidiaries. Nowhere is this more apparent than in the United States where, during 1990, Canadian, European, and Japanese multinationals all reported that the local U.S. market consumed well over 85 percent of their subsidiaries' total U.S. sales.[26] Consequently, export sales back home and to third countries remained negligible. Especially for the Canadians, neither a reduction in (transportation and transaction) costs resulting from geographic proximity, nor related gains from the regional integration of production and sales operations has exercised much influence on the final destination of their subsidiaries' sales. As a result, exports back to Canada by Canadian subsidiaries in the United States are still negligible. Similarly, European multinationals exported an equally small proportion of their subsidiaries' U.S. sales back to the EC. By comparison, Japanese subsidiaries operating in the United States had much larger exports back to their home market, but again these U.S. exports (principally food and raw materials) paled in comparison to local U.S. sales. In short, the sheer size of the local U.S. market continues to exert a powerful influence on the investment strategies of major foreign investors in the United States.

Of course the relative importance of the local market may vary over time, as it has for U.S. multinationals. First measured in 1957, and continuing for at least another decade, local markets in host countries accounted for three-quarters of all foreign sales generated abroad by majority U.S. subsidiaries.[27] However, beginning in the late 1970s and continuing through the 1980s, the contribution of host markets to the worldwide revenues of majority U.S. subsidiaries has gradually

TABLE 3

THE DESTINATION OF SALES BY MAJORITY U.S. SUBSIDIARIES IN CANADA, MEXICO, AND THE EUROPEAN COMMUNITY, 1990

ALL INDUSTRIES			
SALES	CANADA	MEXICO	THE EC
Total (US$ billion) of which:	177.2	19.3	615.2
% Local	73.2	69.6	67.0
% Back to the U.S.	23.4	26.2	3.6
% To 3rd Countries	3.4	4.2	29.4

AUTOMOBILE INDUSTRY ONLY			
SALES	CANADA	MEXICO	THE EC
Total (US$ billion) of which:	39.5	6.6	66.0
% Local	36.5	50.0	53.9
% Back to the U.S.	60.0	45.0	3.5
% To 3rd Countries	3.5	5.0	42.6

Source: U.S. Commerce Department, Bureau of Economic Analysis, *U.S. Direct Investment Abroad: Operations of U.S. Parent Companies and their Foreign Affiliates, Preliminary 1990 Estimates* (Washington: USGPO, September 1992), Table III.F.2, n.p.

declined, so that by 1990 this contribution reached two-thirds of total foreign sales.[28] That 1990 contribution, moreover, varied little across host countries in North America and Western Europe (Table 3).

What does vary for U.S. multinationals is the actual destination of subsidiaries' sales generated outside the local host-country market. Again at one extreme is the European Community, where exports to third countries, mostly other EC member-states, represented nearly 30 percent of the total sales recorded by U.S. subsidiaries (Table 3). Worldwide, by comparison, American subsidiaries sold just over 20 percent of total foreign sales in third-country markets.[29] What remains of foreign sales, after subtracting those destined for host- and third-country markets, is largely shipped back home. Over the postwar period, at least for the Americans, exports back home have doubled their relative contribution to total sales by U.S. subsidiaries, reaching one-tenth of total foreign sales worldwide during 1990.[30] Such increases result less from large changes in the industrial composition of U.S. FDI, and more from growing differences in corporate strategy within the same industry and across different regions.[31] Here, U.S. operations in Canada and Mexico both contrasted sharply with comparable operations in the EC. In both countries, despite their obvious differences, majority U.S.-owned subsidiaries generated a large and comparable share — fully 25 percent — of their total sales by exporting goods and services back to the United States. So, while the final destination of their subsidiaries' sales may differ, North American trade by U.S. multinationals closely parallels their intra-EC trade, as they move to integrate their regional operations.

Leading the way in regional integration, both in North America and in Western Europe, are U.S. automakers pressured to realize scale economies in the management of cross-border, multiplant operations (Table 3). In both Canada and Mexico, as well as across the EC, the majority-owned subsidiaries of U.S. automakers and related suppliers consistently rely on export markets for more than one-half of their total sales. That export share is largest in Canada, where Ford, GM, and Chrysler have tightly integrated their Canadian subsidiaries with their parent operations just across the border in the United States. In this case, U.S. automakers have been aided by bilateral treaties (most notably the 1965 Auto Pact), as well as a variety of U.S. and Canadian laws, all of which have eventually reduced trade barriers and encouraged foreign investment. Many of these same U.S. laws (e.g., 9801 and 9802),[12] plus the recent expansion of export processing zones in Mexico (continuing the Maquiladora program initiated in 1965) have also helped to make Mexico an attractive location for U.S. automakers and their suppliers looking to invest directly in inexpensive sources of supply. Finally, in the EC, Ford and GM employ their production sites — principally in the United Kingdom, Germany, and Spain — to supply the rest of the European market. (Japanese automakers, located principally in the U.K., show a similar EC pattern.[13]) Across the European Community, as well as in Canada and Mexico, the pressures of regional integration on U.S. automakers greatly exceed the pull of national markets.

OFFSHORE PRODUCTION VS. OVERSEAS DISTRIBUTION

TO GENERATE THEIR FOREIGN SALES, multinational corporations often invest in majority-owned subsidiaries producing offshore goods and services that are then supplied to markets both abroad and back home. As a practical matter, pressures to increase such offshore production greatly increase when any of several conditions arise: when national governments severely constrain, or credibly threaten to limit, imports;[14] when global competitors derive significant cost and related advantages from their overseas location;[15] when indigenous buyers in large markets demand closer relations with their foreign suppliers;[16] and when foreign exporters fear the increased risks of exchange-rate fluctuations.[17] Otherwise, multinationals will continue to supply offshore markets through international trade, at times supplemented by direct investment in overseas distribution. Such distribution is especially important in industries requiring dedicated sales channels and after-sales service.

The Americans have been quick to respond to the pressures for offshore production. At least as early as 1957, and continuing for more than three decades thereafter, the value of offshore production by U.S. multinationals was twice the value of U.S. manufactured exports.[38] The Americans concentrated most of their foreign manufacturing in advanced markets, especially in the European Community where, during 1990, majority U.S.-owned manufacturing subsidiaries generated sales nearly five times larger than U.S.-based manufacturers exported to the EC (Table 4). To illustrate an extreme case, consider how U.S. automakers and parts suppliers generate their European sales. During 1990, U.S. auto exports (including parts and components) to the EC totalled roughly US$ 2.5 billion.[39] Compare this sum to the sales generated both in local host markets (US$ 36 billion, reported above in Table 3) and in nearby regional markets (US$ 28 billion) by the EC plants of U.S. automakers. For U.S. corporations, then, direct investment in offshore production has become their principal strategy for gaining and maintaining market access in the EC.

By contrast, in Mexico, international trade still remains as important as offshore production to U.S. corporations. In fact, U.S. subsidiaries manufacturing in Mexico reported 1990 sales as roughly equal to the value of all U.S. manufactured exports to Mexico (Table 4). Such a ratio is actually quite common across developing economies,[40] where few incentives push multinationals to invest in offshore production. But in Mexico, recent increases in U.S. FDI have begun to reverse earlier trends. Again, consider the auto industry: By 1990, the total Mexican production (one-half for sale in the local market, and one-half for sale in the United States, according to Table 3 above) of U.S. automakers was more than double the value of all U.S. auto exports to Mexico (principally parts and components for reexport).[41] As a result, U.S. automakers have come to account for fully one-third of the 1990 sales reported by all U.S. subsidiaries manufacturing in Mexico. With the

TABLE 4

OFFSHORE PRODUCTION, MANUFACTURED EXPORTS, AND OVERSEAS DISTRIBUTION BY U.S. CORPORATIONS, 1990 (US$ BILLION)

LOCATION OF SALES	SALES BY MAJORITY U.S. SUBSIDIARIES ENGAGED PRINCIPALLY IN MANUFACTURING	U.S. EXPORTS OF MANUFACTURED GOODS	SALES BY MAJORITY U.S. SUBSIDIARIES ENGAGED PRINCIPALLY IN WHOLESALING
Canada	96.6	73.9	18.2
Mexico	16.5	25.0	1.7
The EC	339.4	81.3	119.9

Sources: U.S. Commerce Department, Bureau of Economic Analysis, U.S. Direct Investment Abroad: *Operations of U.S. Parent Companies and their Foreign Affiliates, Preliminary 1990 Estimates* (Washington: USGPO, September 1990), Table III.E.3, n.p.; and International Trade Administration, Office of Trade and Investment Analysis, U.S. *Foreign Trade Highlights:1991* (Washington, DC: USGPO, May 1992), Tables 10 and 11, pp. 28, 32.

NAFTA such trends are likely to continue, even with the simultaneous relaxation of Mexican import restrictions (on, say, fully made-up autos), as Ford, GM, and other U.S. manufacturers continue their pursuit of low cost production sites.

By comparison, Canada lies between the extremes represented today by Mexico and the EC. For in Canada, U.S. subsidiaries engaged in offshore production reported 1990 sales as having a dollar value one-and-one-half times that of U.S. manufactured exports to Canada (Table 4). This ratio can be explained by looking at the Canadian plants operated by U.S. automakers, who account for fully one-third of the Canadian production undertaken by all U.S. multinationals (roughly the same share of combined sales also contributed by U.S. auto plants in Mexico). During 1990, U.S. auto exports to Canada totalled roughly US$ 17 billion,[42] slightly above sales generated in the Canadian market (US$ 14 billion, reported above in Table 3) and exported to the U.S. market (US$ 24 billion) by U.S. automakers manufacturing in Canada. Such large sums reflect the simple fact that U.S. automakers on both sides of the U.S.-Canada border have sought to exploit scale economies as they manage their multiplant operations.

So large, in fact, is the Canadian production of U.S. auto and component makers that during 1990 it equalled roughly two-thirds of the combined sales of all Canadian multinationals engaged in U.S. manufacturing (compare Table 3 with Table 5). Indeed, the value of that U.S. production actually fell below the total value of all Canadian exports of manufactured goods to the United States. However, when we subtract from these Canadian exports the value of those exports to the United States shipped by U.S.-owned subsidiaries in

TABLE 5

U.S. PRODUCTION, MANUFACTURED IMPORTS, AND U.S. DISTRIBUTION BY FOREIGN CORPORATIONS, 1990 (US$ BILLION)

NATIONAL ORIGIN OF SUBSIDIARIES OR SOURCE OF IMPORTS	SALES BY FOREIGN SUBSIDIARIES ENGAGED PRINCIPALLY IN U.S. MANUFACTURING	U.S. IMPORTS OF MANUFACTURED GOODS	SALES BY FOREIGN SUBSIDIARIES ENGAGED PRINCIPALLY IN U.S. WHOLESALING
The EC	195.4	81.2	111.5
Canada	58.2	69.6	28.4
Japan	59.3	89.1	219.4

Sources: U.S. Commerce Department, Bureau of Economic Analysis, *Foreign Direct Investment in the United States: Operations of U.S. Affiliates of Foreign Companies, Preliminary 1990 Estimates* (Washington: USGPO, August 1992), Table E-4, n.p.; and International Trade Administration, Office of Trade and Investment Analysis, *U.S. Foreign Trade Highlights: 1991* Washington, DC: USGPO, May 1992, Tables 10 and 11, pp. 28, 32.

Canada, a different conclusion emerges. With this correction, the value of (truly) Canadian production in the United States is greater than (largely) Canadian-owned manufacturers exported to the United States (compare Table 2 and Table 5). Of even greater importance is the fact that the U.S. production of Canadian multinationals grew during the 1980s at a rate at least twice that recorded by Canadian-manufactured exports to the United States.[43] With such growth, Canadian multinationals in the United States are following the same evolutionary path charted long ago by the Americans in Canada.

The Europeans, whose movement is also of recent origin, were quick to follow that U.S. path. As early as 1974, the value of U.S. production by European multinationals roughly equalled U.S. imports of European manufactured goods.[44] If we add to this figure the estimated value of additional assembly operations by European subsidiaries engaged principally in U.S. wholesaling, the total value of local production may well exceed the value of all U.S. imports from Europe. Still, in the early and mid-70s such offshore manufacturing remained well below comparable production by U.S. multinationals in Europe. However, over the next two decades the Europeans moved to cut this difference in half, so that by 1990 their manufacturing subsidiaries in the United States actually reported U.S. sales nearly three times larger than U.S. imports of European manufactured goods (Table 5). As a result, both American and European multinationals have generally managed to produce and sell many more manufactured goods in each other's home market than they and other national exporters shipped across the Atlantic.

In contrast, the Japanese have pursued a very different offshore-manufacturing strategy — one that still lags Japanese exports of manufactured goods. As recently as 1990, for example, foreign sales resulting from the offshore production by Japanese subsidiaries in the United States (or the EC)[45] were two-thirds the total value of Japanese manufactured exports to these markets (Table 5). Even when the value of assembly operations of Japanese subsidiaries engaged principally in overseas distribution are added to these local sales figures, the total value of Japanese production in America and Europe still barely equals U.S. (and European)[46] imports of manufactured goods from Japan. For the Japanese, however, this low ratio of foreign production to international trade actually represented a significant *increase* in offshore manufacturing. Indeed, just a decade earlier (in 1977), Japanese manufacturers and (to a lesser extent) Japanese trading companies reported exports from home four times larger than the worldwide production recorded by Japanese subsidiaries abroad.[47] Yet, even after such growth, these Japanese subsidiaries had little in common with U.S. multinationals in Europe or European Community multinationals in the United States.

Far more central to the foreign-investment strategies of Japanese multinationals has been the establishment of majority-owned subsidiaries engaged in overseas distribution (Table 5). During 1990, for example, such intra-company shipments accounted for over three-fifths of all Japanese exports to the

United States.[48] Much of this trade consisted of autos, nearly all of which were shipped intra-company, by Japanese automakers (with very little involvement by Japanese trading companies) to their majority subsidiaries engaged in U.S. wholesaling. Here, the Japanese did not act alone. On the contrary, nearly all EC auto exports to the United States are also shipped by EC automakers to their wholesaling subsidiaries in the United States.[49] From this perspective, EC and Japanese automakers differ only in the value of total exports they ship to the United States. Otherwise, both have established dedicated sales channels and after-sales service networks for shipments between their parents and their U.S.-based distributors.[50]

In addition to downstream marketing of home-country exports, wholesaling subsidiaries also increase foreign sales by serving as upstream sources of overseas supplies. Specifically, these subsidiaries often serve as purchasing agents, both for their parents back home and for affiliated subsidiaries in third countries. Of particular significance to American multinationals have been those U.S. wholesaling subsidiaries that supply third-country markets — especially those in Europe, where affiliated subsidiaries were among their major buyers.[51] Otherwise, for the Americans, wholesaling subsidiaries have proved to be of little value as purchasing agents for shipments back home, supplying less than 2 percent of all U.S. imports during 1990.[52] However, for the Japanese, wholesaling subsidiaries represent much more important sources of shipments back home. These Japanese subsidiaries reported to MITI during 1990 that they had supplied nearly one-half of all Japanese imports worldwide — and the figure was higher still (roughly four-fifths) for Japanese imports from the United States.[53] These imports consisted largely of agricultural products, metals, and other raw materials — all of which remained in short supply in Japan but were plentiful in America. So, in marked contrast to the Americans, the Japanese (beginning with Japanese trading companies, but increasingly including Japanese manufacturers) invested far more aggressively in wholesaling subsidiaries in order to exploit the lower transaction and information costs they enjoy back in Japan, where they tightly control their own proprietary distribution systems.[54]

INTRA-COMPANY SHIPMENTS VS. ARM'S-LENGTH TRADE

MUCH OF THE TRADE CONDUCTED by multinational corporations is shipped intra-company, among and between parents and their subsidiaries — a fact that has recently attracted the renewed attention of scholars.[55] For multinationals, such trade ensures greater control over both upstream supplies and downstream markets that do more than engage in arm's-length transactions with unaffiliated buyers and suppliers. Intra-company trade also substantially lowers the high costs which these arm's-length transactions normally impose on those cross-border exchanges of the technological, marketing, and organizational assets necessary to compete successfully through foreign production and overseas distribution. Only with majority ownership do multinationals exercise sufficient managerial control to dictate their subsidiaries' decisions regarding these exchanges; such control is far more circumscribed in minority affiliates. Empirically, intra-company trade seems especially prominent in auto and other industries where significant economies can be achieved through the integration and coordination of multiplant operations; or where additional advantages can be gained through after-sales service.

Consider U.S.-Canada trade. During 1990, nearly all U.S. auto exports to Canada were shipped by Chrysler, Ford, and GM directly to their majority-owned subsidiaries across the border. Similarly, over 80 percent of all U.S. auto imports from Canada were shipped by these same U.S. subsidiaries back to their U.S. parents. This two-way auto trade has important implications for total bilateral trade, since autos represent the largest single class of goods traded between the United States and Canada (accounting for over one-fifth of all U.S. exports to Canada, and over one-quarter of all U.S. imports from Canada).[56] As a result, when totalled across all industries, intra-company shipments between U.S. parents and their Canadian subsidiaries during 1990 contributed nearly 40 percent of all U.S. trade — both imports and exports — with Canada (Table 6). By contrast, Canadian multinationals contributed little of the remainder, given their more limited investments in the United States. Indeed, most U.S.-Canada trade not shipped intra-company by U.S. multinationals was shipped at arm's length by unaffiliated buyers and suppliers with no direct investments in either of the two countries. In this instance, low transaction and transportation costs, both resulting from geographic proximity, plus limited government impediments to market access, together aided cross-border trade independent of foreign investment.

As in Canada, so too in Mexico, auto trade principally entails intra-company shipments between the parent operations of the U.S. big-3 and their majority subsidiaries across the border. Indeed, during 1990, such shipments accounted for nearly 100 percent of all U.S. auto exports to — and all U.S. auto imports from — Mexico. But unlike U.S.-Canada trade, U.S. commerce with Mexico is not nearly as dependent on autos (which, during 1990, accounted for just over one-tenth of all two-way trade south of the border).[57] Moreover, as discussed above, Mexico — in sharp contrast to Canada — has attracted little U.S. FDI in the face of stiff capital controls, which then forced that limited investment into minority U.S.-owned joint ventures. Such minority ventures are typically poor markets for U.S. exports. Given these several factors, then, a much smaller proportion (roughly 25 percent) of the two-way flow of U.S.-Mexico trade is conducted intra-company. Instead, roughly 75 percent of U.S.-Mexico trade is shipped among unaffiliated buyers and suppliers with no direct investments in either of the two countries (Table 6). Yet, such arm's-length shipments are likely to diminish in the future, at least as a proportion of total U.S.-Mexico trade. Instead, intra-company shipments are likely to grow in response to the NAFTA, for as the dollar value of U.S. FDI in

TABLE 6

U.S. BILATERAL TRADE WITH AMERICA'S TOP FOUR TRADING PARTNERS: INTRA-COMPANY VS. ARM'S LENGTH SHIPMENTS, 1990[a]

TRADE WITH CANADA (US$ BILLION)

DIRECTION OF TRADE	U.S. PARENTS TO/FROM MAJORITY U.S. SUBSIDIARIES IN CANADA	CANADIAN AFFILIATES IN U.S. TO/FROM CANADIAN PARENTS	U.S. PARENTS TO/FROM UNAFFILIATED FIRMS IN CANADA	CANADIAN AFFILIATES IN U.S. TO/FROM UNAFFILIATED FIRMS IN CANADA	ALL OTHER TRADE
U.S. Exports	30.6	1.1	14.7	1.0	36.3
U.S. Imports	33.2	6.8	11.4	0.7	39.3

TRADE WITH MEXICO (US$ BILLION)

DIRECTION OF TRADE	U.S. PARENTS TO/FROM MAJORITY U.S. SUBSIDIARIES IN MEXICO	MEXICAN AFFILIATES IN U.S. TO/FROM MEXICAN PARENTS	U.S. PARENTS TO/FROM UNAFFILIATED FIRMS IN MEXICO	MEXICAN AFFILIATES IN U.S. TO/FROM UNAFFILIATED FIRMS IN MEXICO	ALL OTHER TRADE
U.S. Exports	7.1	0.1	4.7	0.1	16.3
U.S. Imports	7.2	0.6	3.6	1.6	17.2

TRADE WITH THE EUROPEAN COMMUNITY (US$ BILLION)

DIRECTION OF TRADE	U.S. PARENTS TO/FROM MAJORITY U.S. SUBSIDIARIES IN THE EC	EC AFFILIATES IN U.S. TO/FROM EC PARENTS	U.S. PARENTS TO/FROM UNAFFILIATED FIRMS IN THE EC	EC AFFILIATES IN U.S. TO/FROM UNAFFILIATED FIRMS IN THE EC	ALL OTHER TRADE
U.S. Exports	26.6	8.7	33.6	7.5	21.6
U.S. Imports	11.2	31.8	17.8	3.7	31.0

TRADE WITH JAPAN (US$ BILLION)

DIRECTION OF TRADE	U.S. PARENTS TO/FROM MAJORITY U.S. SUBSIDIARIES IN JAPAN	JAPANESE AFFILIATES IN U.S. TO/FROM JAPANESE PARENTS	U.S. PARENTS TO/FROM UNAFFILIATED FIRMS IN JAPAN	ALL OTHER TRADE
U.S. Exports	7.1	22.5	6.8	12.2
U.S. Imports	1.3	73.2	12.5	2.2

Note: [a]MNE-related arm's length trade estimated for 1990 using data from 1989 (for U.S. MNEs) and 1987 (for Canadian, EC, Japanese, and Mexican MNEs).

Sources: U.S. Commerce Department, Bureau of Economic Analysis, *U.S. Direct Investment Abroad: Operations of U.S. Parent Companies and their Foreign Affiliates, Preliminary 1990 Estimates* (Washington: USGPO, September 1992), Table III.H.1, n.p.; and *Foreign Direct Investment in the United States: Operations of U.S. Affiliates of Foreign Companies, Preliminary 1990 Estimates* (Washington: USGPO, August 1992), Table G-2, n.p.; and *U.S. Direct Investment Abroad: 1989 Benchmark Survey, Final Results* (Washington, DC: USGPO, October 1992), Tables II.Q.2 and II.Q.5, pp. 113, 116; and *Foreign Direct Investment in the United States: 1987 Benchmark Survey, Final Results* (Washington, DC: USGPO, August 1990), Tables G-24, G-28, G-30, G-34, pp. 142-152; and International Trade Administration, Office of Trade and Investment Analysis, *US Foreign Trade Highlights: 1991* (Washington, DC: USGPO, May 1992), Tables 2 and 3, pp. 11, 15.

Mexico rises along with the incidence of majority U.S. ownership, so too will the dollar value of U.S.-Mexico trade in fully made-up cars and other U.S. goods previously restricted by Mexican import barriers.

While U.S.-Mexico trade continues to represent an extreme case of arm's-length commerce, U.S.-Japan trade illustrates the growing predominance of intra-company shipments. In this case, Japanese multinationals exercise unrivalled control over the two-way flow (Table 6). In fact, by 1990, over 60 percent of all U.S. imports from Japan were shipped intra-company, largely by the parents of Japanese multinationals to their (principally majority) subsidiaries in the United States. Here again, the auto trade figures prominently, with automobiles accounting for over one-third of all U.S. imports from Japan, most of which (over 80 percent) are shipped by Japanese automakers directly to their U.S. subsidiaries.[58] In contrast, however, autos contribute little to U.S. exports to Japan. Yet, once more, intra-company trade predominates, with shipments from Japanese subsidiaries in the United States back to their Japanese parents accounting for upwards of two-thirds of all U.S. exports to Japan. Largely raw materials and agricultural products, these U.S. exports are then channelled by Japanese multinationals into their proprietary distribution channels back home. There, Japanese trading companies and manufacturers often enjoy lower information and transaction costs, as well as related advantages, than do more arm's-length U.S. exporters. For the Japanese, then, foreign direct investment has created the *principal* channels for two-way trade flows with the United States.

In contrast, U.S. multinationals exercise no appreciable influence over U.S. bilateral trade with Japan. Here, limited U.S. FDI, and the concentration of that FDI in minority foreign-owned affiliates serves as an especially high barrier in Japan to U.S. exports. Indeed, minority affiliates typically represent poor markets for national exports, even in those host countries where affiliates' sales are relatively large. For example, during 1990, U.S. exports to minority U.S. affiliates world wide remained negligible — accounting for only 6 percent of all U.S. exports to U.S. multinationals abroad — even though minority affiliates contributed just under 20 percent of all U.S. multinational sales.[59] In Japan, U.S. exports to minority U.S. affiliates during 1990 barely totalled US$ 2.5 billion, considerably less than the US $7 billion of U.S. exports shipped in the same year to majority U.S. subsidiaries in Japan.[60] Yet, as noted above, these majority subsidiaries accounted for barely US $62 billion of sales in Japan, well below the US$ 103 billion in Japanese sales recorded by minority U.S. affiliates. In short, because Japan has long hosted a disproportionately large share of minority affiliates, and because these affiliates generally refrain from purchasing U.S. exports, U.S. multinationals in Japan have contributed a relatively small share of this bilateral trade. By contrast, for the Japanese, the higher incidence of majority subsidiaries in the United States actually has granted to Japanese exports far greater access to the U.S. market than the Americans have been able to secure in Japan through their limited investments concentrated in minority affiliates.

In marked contrast to U.S.-Japan trade, U.S.-EC trade remains far more symmetrical (Table 6), as do U.S.-EC investment flows. As a result of that investment, in fact, intra-company trade contributed over one-half of all U.S. imports from the EC. Here again, autos figure prominently. Automobiles comprise the largest class of traded goods (accounting for 16 percent of U.S. imports from the EC), of which nearly 90 percent are shipped intra-company, by BMW and other EC automakers to their majority-owned subsidiaries in the United States.[61] Indeed, as a general rule, the parents of EC multinationals are the largest suppliers of U.S. imports from Europe. Conversely, looking at U.S. exports to the EC, the parents of U.S. multinationals are the largest contributors, often through intra-company shipments to their majority subsidiaries in the EC. Here, U.S. automakers are not active, since U.S. auto exports remain small; indeed, in the absence of much auto trade, intra-company shipments to the EC accounted for just one-third of all U.S. exports to the EC. Finally, what remains of U.S.-EC trade is shipped at arm's-length between unaffiliated exporters and importers. Here again, foreign direct investment plays a major role, with the U.S. parents of American multinationals serving both as major exporters to unaffiliated EC buyers, and as major importers from unaffiliated EC suppliers. This has left all other U.S.-owned enterprises to ship, again through arm's-length trade, roughly one-fifth of America's exports to the EC, and roughly one-third of U.S. imports from the EC. Thus, neither American nor European multinationals singularly dominate bilateral U.S.-EC trade.

IMPLICATIONS FOR GOVERNMENT POLICY

THE CORPORATE BEHAVIOUR analyzed in this study has not only been shaped by public policy, but also has important implications for future government actions. This is especially true as Canada, Mexico, and the United States together move to ratify and then implement the NAFTA. Yet, at the risk of oversimplification, the NAFTA (as well as the earlier bilateral accord between Canada and the United States) can be viewed as the formal codification and timely acceleration of an ongoing process of regional integration already well under way, thanks to the foreign investment and related trade strategies of multinational corporations. Thus, multinationals have led the way toward regional integration, and this fact alone has important implications for government policy.

Beginning with Mexico, the recently accelerated liberalization of national policies has already begun to accomplish many of the economic goals pursued by both Mexico and the United States, goals otherwise embodied in the NAFTA. Specifically, the eradication of most foreign capital controls and the pursuit of export-oriented trade strategies have already done much to attract increased levels of U.S. FDI inflows and, correspondingly, to increase Mexico's trade with the United States. Should such liberalization be reversed, however, Mexico's recent gains could prove to be ephemeral. Indeed, prior to liberalization, the high incidence of minority foreign-owned subsidiaries and the limited value of their FDI kept Mexico well outside the evolutionary path otherwise followed by multinationals elsewhere in North America and Western Europe. But with liberalization, that path now passes through Mexico, even in the absence of a formalized NAFTA. Indeed, because of domestic policy changes, Mexico is already a major beneficiary of regional integration, thanks in large part to the foreign investment and related trade strategies of multinational corporations.

With more emphasis, the same may be said for Canada, where the regional integration strategies of multinationals find their earliest origins (at least in North America), and where these strategies enjoy their greatest success — so great, in fact, that Canada now faces ongoing asymmetries in trade and investment with the United States that are surprisingly akin to the asymmetries encountered by the United States in its relations with Japan. In both instances, multinationals from one country (U.S. multinationals in Canada; Japanese multinationals in the United States) account for most bilateral investment flows and control a sizeable proportion of bilateral trade. While such asymmetries inevitably feed public fears, they need not influence public policies — and certainly not policies designed to redress asymmetries through the imposition of trade and investment restrictions. Rather, one of the strong policy implications flowing from this study is that increased FDI outflows (from Canada to the United States; from the United States to Japan) offer the prospect not only of increasing the foreign sales of multinationals, but also of positively influencing national exports. This seems especially true, for example, when those exports benefit from proprietary sales channels and after-sales service. In short, rather than view the outflow of Canadian FDI to the United States as an indicator of national economic decline — as Canadian officials are known to do — an alternative interpretation holds that FDI outflow can also be a sign of maturing national economic resurgence.

The same can be said of U.S. FDI outflows, although in the United States, FDI attracts much less policy attention than does international trade. Witness President Clinton's recent efforts to "talk down the dollar". Hardly a U.S. investment strategy (since it increases the dollar cost of foreign assets), the decline of the dollar is ostensibly focused on reversing U.S. trade deficits. Yet, these pages document the tight interrelationship between trade and investment. For example, investment in offshore production creates new demands for U.S. machinery exports; similarly, investment in overseas distribution supplies after-sales service demanded by foreign importers. In response, government policy should not be to manipulate the value of the dollar upward, to reverse earlier trends. Rather, as a bare minimum, governments should elevate FDI to the same policy level afforded trade, so that the consequences of each on the other can be better assessed.

What has attracted greater attention in the United States has been the sizeable and sudden inflow of FDI into the country, especially during the 1980s. In this connection, the decline of the U.S. dollar can now be viewed as part of a national investment strategy, albeit one designed to entice foreigners to buy lower-priced U.S. assets. As in Canada, so too in the United States, these inflows have fed public fears. But once again, they need not prompt public policies designed to restrict trade and investment, noting especially that one of the major policy implications flowing from this paper is that FDI inflows are positively associated with the creation and distribution of national wealth — not just through increased investments in local production and distribution, but also through the strong influence these foreign investments exert over international trade.

ENDNOTES

1. For an earlier analysis of comparable trends across the Pacific Basin, see Dennis J. Encarnation, *Rivals beyond Trade: America versus Japan in Global Competition*, (Cornell: Cornell University Press, 1992), esp. pp. 1-31, 183-202.

2. For an earlier comparison of the evolutionary path followed by American and Japanese multinationals, see Dennis J. Encarnation "A Common Evolution? A Comparison of United States and Japanese Transnational Corporations," *Transnational Corporations* (February 1993): 7-31.

3. For a review of these factors, see Richard E. Caves, *Multinational Enterprise and Economic Analysis*, (Cambridge: Cambridge University Press, 1982).

4. For a survey of these assets, see Caves, *Multinational Enterprise and Economic Analysis*, esp. pp. 1-30, 195-211.

5. For a description of the infirmities afflicting the efficient allocation of intangible assets through conventional markets, see Oliver E. Williamson, "Markets and Hierarchies: Some Elementary Considerations," *American Economic Review* (May 1973): 316-325.

6. U.S. Commerce Department, Office of Business Economics, *U.S. Business Investments in Foreign Countries: A Supplement to the Survey of Current Business*, (Washington: USGPO, 1960), Table 20, p. 108; hereafter cited as Commerce Department, *U.S. FDI, 1957 Survey*.

7. For example, during 1977, American multinationals reported to the Commerce Department that over 80 percent of their "owners' equity" resided in majority U.S.-owned subsidiaries; see U.S. Commerce Department, Bureau of Economic Analysis, *U.S. Direct Investment Abroad, 1977*, (Washington: USGPO, 1981), Table II.A.18, p. 123, and Table III.A.18, p. 242; hereafter cited as Commerce Department, *U.S. FDI, 1977 Benchmark*.

8 Robert E. Lipsey, "Changing Patterns of International Investment in and by the United States," in Martin Feldstein, ed., *The United States in the World Economy*, (Chicago: University of Chicago Press for the National Bureau of Economic Research, 1988), pp. 488-92; David J. Goldsbrough, "Investment Trends and Prospects: The Link with Bank Lending," in Theodore H. Moran, ed., *Investing in Development: New Roles for Private Capital?*, (Washington, D.C.: Overseas Development Council, 1986).

9 U.S. Commerce Department, Bureau of Economic Analysis, *U.S. Direct Investment Abroad, 1966: Final Data*, (Washington: USGPO, 1975), esp. Table J-4, p. 167, and Table L-1, p. 197; hereafter cited as Commerce Department, *U.S. FDI, 1966 Benchmark*.

10 U.S. Commerce Department, Bureau of Economic Analysis, *U.S. Direct Investment Abroad: Operations of U.S. Parent Companies and their Foreign Affiliates, Preliminary 1990 Estimates*, (Washington: USGPO, November 1992), Tables II.E.3 and III.E.3, n.p.; hereafter cited as Commerce Department, *U.S. FDI, 1990 Survey*.

11 Encarnation, *Rivals*, esp. pp. 209-12; also see Dennis J. Encarnation and Mark Mason, "Neither MITI nor America: The Political Economy of Capital Liberalization in Japan," *International Organization* (Winter 1990): 25-54.

12 Commerce Department, *U.S. FDI, 1990 Survey*, Tables II.E.3 and III.E.3, n.p.

13 Susan Strange, "The Name of the Game," in Nicholas X. Rizopoulos, ed., *Sea-Changes: American Foreign Policy in a World Transformed*, (New York: Council on Foreign Relations Press, 1991), p. 242.

14 For sales data, see Commerce Department, *U.S. FDI, 1957 Survey*, Table 22, p. 110; for trade data, see U.S. Commerce Department, Bureau of International Commerce, "United States Trade with Major World Areas, 1955 and 1956," *Overseas Business Reports* (May 1957): 2, 8.

15 For sales data, see Commerce Department, *U.S. FDI, 1966 Benchmark*, Table L-2, p. 198; for trade data, see U.S. Commerce Department, Bureau of International Commerce, "United States Trade with Major World Areas, 1965 and 1966," *Overseas Business Reports* (May 1967): 3, 12.

16 For sales data, see Commerce Department, *U.S. FDI, 1990 Survey*, Table III.E.3, n.p.; for trade data, see U.S. Commerce Department, International Trade Administration, *U.S. Foreign Trade Highlights: 1991*, (Washington, DC: USGPO, May, 1992), Table 2, p. 11.

17 For data, see note 15 above.

18 Commerce Department, *U.S. Direct Investment Abroad: Preliminary 1990 Estimates*, Table III.E.3; Commerce Department, *U.S. Foreign Trade Highlights: 1991*, p. 88.

19 Commerce Department, *U.S. Direct Investment Abroad: Preliminary 1990 Estimates*, Table III.E.3; Commerce Department, *U.S. Foreign Trade Highlights: 1991*, p. 128.

20 Commerce Department, *U.S. Direct Investment Abroad: Preliminary 1990 Estimates*, Table III.E.3; Commerce Department, *U.S. Foreign Trade*

Highlights: 1991, p. 76.

21 Commerce Department, *Foreign Trade Highlights: 1991*, pp. 11, 76, 128. In Canada, the second largest category of U.S. exports consisted of fully made-up cars and trucks, U.S. products largely excluded from Mexico as a result of high import tariffs.

22 For sales data, U.S. Commerce Department, Bureau of Economic Analysis, *Foreign Direct Investment in the United States, Volume 2, Report of the Secretary of Commerce, Benchmark Survey, 1974,* (Washington, DC: USGPO, April 1976), Table K-5, p. 139; for trade data, see U.S. Department of Commerce, International Trade Administration, Office of Trade and Investment Analysis, *U.S. Foreign Trade Highlights,* (Washington, DC: USGPO, various years).

23 Ibid.

24 During 1977, when Japanese exports to the world totaled US$ 85 billion, Japanese affiliates abroad reported foreign sales of roughly US$ 85 billion (or 22.8 trillion yen). For sales data see Japan, Ministry of International Trade and Industry, Industrial Policy Bureau, *The 8th Survey of the Overseas Business Activities of Japanese Enterprises [Dai hachi-kai wagakuni kigyo no kaigai jigyo katsudou]* (Tokyo: MITI, 1979), Table 51, p. 54; hereafter cited as MITI, *Japanese FDI, 8th Survey.* For trade data, see International Monetary Fund, *International Trade Statistics Yearbook: 1980,* (Washington, DC: IMF, 1981), p. 243.

25 For sales data, see MITI, *Japanese FDI, 21st Survey,* Table 2-12, pp. 88-89; for trade data, see International Monetary Fund, *Direction of Trade Statistics Yearbook: 1992,* (Washington, DC: IMF, 1992), p. 158.

26 U.S. Commerce Department, Bureau of Economic Analysis, *Foreign Direct Investment in the United States: 1987 Benchmark Survey, Final Results,* (Washington, DC: USGPO, August 1990), Tables G-2 and G-24, pp. 120, 142.

27 Commerce Department, *U.S. FDI, 1957 Survey,* Table 22, p. 110; Commerce Department, *U.S. FDI, 1966 Benchmark,* Table L-1, p. 197.

28 Commerce Department, *U.S. FDI, 1977 Benchmark,* Table II.H.1, p. 318; Commerce Department, *U.S. FDI, 1988 Survey,* Table 34, n.p.; Commerce Department, *U.S. FDI, 1990 Survey,* Table III.F.2, n.p.

29 MITI, *21st Overseas Survey,* pp. 78-79, 88-89; Commerce Department, *U.S. FDI: 1990 Annual Survey,* Table III.F.2, n.p.

30 Commerce Department, *U.S. FDI, 1990 Survey,* Table III.F.2, n.p.

31 For supporting data, see Raymond Vernon and Subramanian Rangan, "Foreign Direct Investment in the Adjustment Process," in Ippei Yamazawa and Akira Hirata, eds., *Industrial Adjustment in Developed Countries and Its Implications for Developing Countries,* (Tokyo: Institute of Developing Economies, 1991), pp. 167-81.

32 According to one estimate, generously supplied by Subramanian Rangan, roughly 26 percent of total U.S. merchandise exports to Mexico during 1988 were covered under section 9802. For Canada, the comparable share is less than 10 percent of U.S. exports there.

33 Dennis J. Encarnation, "Investment and Trade by America, European, and Japanese Multinationals Across the Triad," in Mark Mason and Dennis J. Encarnation, eds., *Does Ownership Matter? Japanese Multinationals in Europe*, (London: Oxford University Press, forthcoming, 1994), Chapter 6.

34 For an early analysis of the relationship between trade policies and foreign direct investment, see Grant L. Reuber et al., *Foreign Private Investment in Development*, (Oxford: Oxford University Press for the Organization of Economic Cooperation and Development, 1973), especially pp. 120-32; for a more recent analysis, see Stephen E. Guisinger et al., *Investment Incentives and Performance Requirements: Patterns of International Trade, Production and Investment*, (New York: Praeger, 1985), especially pp. 48-54.

35 For a recent study of location-specific advantages, see Michael E. Porter, *The Competitive Advantage of Nations*, (New York: The Free Press, 1990).

36 For the impact of such "buyer power" see Michael E. Porter, *Competitive Strategy: Techniques for Analyzing Industries and Competitors*, (New York: The Free Press, 1980).

37 DeAnne Julius, *Global Companies and Public Policy: The Growing Challenge of Foreign Direct Investment*, (London: Royal Institute of International Affairs, 1990, pp. 88-91).

38 For sales data, see the following Commerce Department publications: *1957 Survey*, Table 22, p. 110; *U.S. FDI, 1966 Benchmark*, Table L-3, p. 199; *1977 Benchmark*, Table II.H.1, p. 318; *U.S. FDI, 1988 Survey*, Table 34, n.p.; *U.S. FDI, 1990 Survey*, Table III.F.2, n.p. For trade data, see Commerce Department, "International Business Indicators," *Overseas Business Reports* (January 1973), Table 5, p. 14; *U.S. Foreign Trade Highlights* (various years).

39 Commerce Department, *U.S. Foreign Trade Highlights: 1991*, p. 88.

40 For Japan, see Figure 2 above. For LDCs, see Commerce Department, *U.S. FDI, 1990 Survey*, Tables II.E.3 and III.E.3, n.p.; and *U.S. Foreign Trade Highlights: 1991*, Table 10, p. 28.

41 For U.S. subsidiaries' sales, see Table 3; for U.S. exports, see Commerce Department, *U.S. Foreign Trade Highlights: 1991*, p. 128.

42 Commerce Department, *U.S. Foreign Trade Highlights: 1991*, p. 88.

43 Compare the data presented in Table 5 with the following: U.S. Commerce Department, Bureau of Economic Analysis, *Foreign Direct Investment in the United States, 1980*, (Washington, DC: USGPO, October 1983), Table E-6, p. 104; and U.S. Commerce Department, International Trade Administration, *U.S. Foreign Trade Highlights, 1980*, (Washington, DC: USGPO, July 1989), Table V.2A, p. 87.

44 For data, see note 22 above.

45 Encarnation, "Investment and Trade by America, European, and Japanese Multinationals," forthcoming.

46 Ibid.

47 For sales data see, MITI, *Japanese FDI, 8th Survey*, Table 51, p. 54; for trade data see, IMF, *Direction of Trade Statistics Yearbook: 1980*, p. 242. Specifically, in the United States, 1974 estimates of Japanese manufactured exports ranged as high as ten times the value of local production.

48 For trade data, see Commerce Department, U.S. *Foreign Trade Highlights: 1991*, Table 11, p. 32. For sales data, see U.S. Commerce Department, Bureau of Economic Analysis, *Foreign Direct Investment in the United States: Operations of U.S. Affiliates of Foreign Companies, Preliminary 1990 Estimates*, (Washington: USGPO, August 1992), Tables E-4, G-2, n.p.; hereafter cited as Commerce Department, *FDI in U.S., 1990 Survey*.

49 U.S. Commerce Department, Bureau of Economic Analysis, *Foreign Direct Investment in the United States: 1987 Benchmark Survey, Final Results*, (Washington, DC: USGPO, August 1990), Table G-31, p. 149; Commerce Department, U.S. *Foreign Trade Highlights, 1991*, p. 89.

50 For evidence, see Dennis J. Encarnation, "Cross-Investment," in Thomas K. McCraw, *America versus Japan*, (Boston: Harvard Business School Press, 1986), Tables 4-2 and 4-3, pp. 120, 126; and "American-Japanese Cross-Investment," in Stephan Haggard and Chung-in Moon, eds., *Pacific Dynamics: The International Politics of Industrial Change*, (Boulder, Colorado: Westview Press, 1989), Tables 8.2 and 8.4, pp. 212, 232. Also see Yamawaki Hiroyuki, "Exports and Direct Investment in Distribution: Evidence on Japanese Firms in the United States," Discussion Paper FS 111, Wissenschaftszentrum, Berlin, n.d.

51 For intra-company trade within Europe, the most recent data are for 1989; see U.S. Commerce Department, Bureau of Economic Analysis, *U.S. Direct Investment Abroad: 1989 Benchmark Survey, Final Results*, (Washington, DC: USGPO, October 1992), Tables III.F.10 and III.F.11, pp. 198-199. For third-country sales during 1990, see Commerce Department, U.S. *FDI: 1990 Annual Survey*, Tables III.F.8, n.p.

52 For sales data, see Commerce Department, U.S. *FDI, 1990 Survey*, Table II.H.22, n.p.; for trade data, see Commerce Department, U.S. *Foreign Trade Highlights: 1991*, Table 3, p. 15.

53 For sales data, see MITI, *21st Overseas Survey*, Table 2-12, pp. 78-79, 88-89; for trade data, see IMF, *Direction of Trade Statistics: 1992*, Table 158, p. 240.

54 For an early survey of these barriers see, Michael Yoshino, *The Japanese Marketing System: Adaptations and Innovations*, (Cambridge, Mass.: MIT Press, 1971); for more recent surveys, see the following chapters in Paul Krugman, ed., *The U.S. and Japan: Trade and Investment*, (Cambridge, Mass.: MIT Press for the National Bureau of Economic Research, 1991): Itoh Motoshige, "The Japanese Distribution System and Access to the Japanese Market," and Ito Takahashi and Maruyama Masayoshi, "Is the Japanese Distribution System Really Inefficient?"

55 See, for example, Encarnation, *Rivals beyond Trade*, esp. pp. 26-31, 190-197; Leo Sleuwaegen and Yamawaki Hideki, "Foreign Direct Investment

and Intra-Firm Trade: Evidence from Japan," Discussion Paper #9002/G, Institute for Economic Research, Erasmus University (Rotterdam), n.d.

56 Commerce Department, *U.S. Foreign Trade Highlights: 1991*, pp. 11, 15, 76-77.

57 Ibid., pp. 11, 15, 128-129.

58 Ibid., pp. 11, 15, 79; U.S. Commerce Department, Bureau of Economic Analysis, *Foreign Direct Investment in the United States: 1987 Benchmark Survey, Final Results,* (Washington, DC: USGPO, August 1990), Table G-31, p. 149; hereafter cited as Commerce Department, *FDI in U.S.: 1987 Benchmark.*

59 For U.S. exports to U.S. affiliates abroad, and overall sales data, see Commerce Department, *U.S. FDI, 1990 Survey*, Tables II.E.3, II.H.5, II.H.22, III.E.3, III.H.2, n.p.; for overall U.S. exports, see Commerce Department, *U.S. Foreign Trade Highlights: 1991*, Table 2, p. 11.

60 Ibid.

61 Commerce Department, *U.S. Foreign Trade Highlights: 1991*, pp. 15, 89; Commerce Department, *FDI in U.S.: 1987 Benchmark*, Table G-31, p. 149.

ACNKOWLEDGEMENT

I WANT TO EXTEND my special thanks to Subramanian Rangan for his extensive and constructive comments.

Kurt Unger
Director, Academic Affairs
Centro de Investigación y Docencia Económicas

12

Foreign Direct Investment in Mexico

INTRODUCTION

THE PERFORMANCE OF THE Mexican economy in the 1990s is still uncertain; this is despite the promising results of 1990 and 1991, which were accompanied by some worrisome signs, particularly with respect to the trade deficit. The stagnation that began in 1982 and continued throughout the rest of the 1980s was a consequence of the adjustments required to correct the major macroeconomic imbalances inherited from decades of import-substitution industrialization. These imbalances produced a highly indebted economy with virtually no potential to pay back the debt, or to sustain the previous pattern of growth.

1982 was the last full year of the import-substitution era initiated in the 1940s. During the 1960s and 1970s, the last two decades of this period, there was ample evidence to show the structural nature of the problem: industrial growth continued to depend on increasing deficits in the balance of trade. The very high growth experienced in 1980 and 1981 triggered the long-term trend of the trade deficit and made it impossible for international lenders to sustain the deficit's financing which, in turn, led to the 1982 debt moratorium and all the effects that followed. Internally, the main effects were an inflation rate of 98.9 percent for 1982, and the virtual collapse of new private and public investment.[1]

Since 1982 economic policy has been conducted in two stages. The first stage centered very successfully on monetary and fiscal policy to control inflation and reduce the public sector deficits. This was necessary in order to restore minimum acceptable conditions for the country's external debt to be negotiated. The second stage, after 1986, opened the economy in order to re-establish Mexico's economic base and to direct its growth along the lines of a more competitive international economy. The last, and probably most substantive, move in this respect is the initiative for the NAFTA.

However promising and successful the results may be to date — judged either by the way inflation has been controlled or by the restoration of financial health both externally and internally — there are still major uncertainties about the long-term competitive conditions of the Mexican economy. The most important uncertainties stem from the limited investment that has taken place since 1982,[2] and from the acute dependence on imports that develops immediately after any sign of recovery. In this regard the NAFTA's anticipated effects on trade may be more limited than originally estimated. First, because imports are already at a high level and, second, because exports cannot be increased due to reduced production capacity resulting from the limited investment that occurred during the 1980s.[3]

This worrying mix of recent results may be best illustrated by the fact that since 1990 the GNP has been highly vulnerable to the balance-of-trade effect, even after inflation was under control. The deficit of the current account, particularly the growing trade deficit of 1990-92, has applied a sudden brake to further growth.

The deficit on the balance of trade illustrates the two sides of the structural problems that derive from events in Mexico in the 1980s. During that decade there was very little new investment in production facilities, so there was little growth in exports. On the other hand, more and more imports were needed, both to satisfy replacement needs and to accommodate the increasing demands for imports that resulted from the opening of the economy.

The other expected benefit of the NAFTA apart from trade gains, expected increased inflow of foreign investment, is also in doubt. Despite official claims that large inflows of foreign capital will accompany the liberalization process, there is evidence of three weakening trends. First, the inflow of foreign investment in the recent past has consisted only in part of direct investment capital. A major destination of foreign capital has been the stock market and *not* fixed investment that would add directly to productive capacity. Second, new foreign investment has been concentrated in services rather than in manufacturing. Third, the import content of Mexican production, both for exports and for domestic consumption, has increased dramatically and will continue at very high levels for the foreseeable future. The latter trend is most clear in major trading sectors dominated by transnational corporations (TNCs) that are struggling to restructure their international competitiveness.

In short, the three major issues of current concern with foreign investment addressed in this study are:

- new foreign direct investment (FDI) has been more limited than is generally perceived;

- FDI is now targeting services in place of manufacturing; and

- the FDI which has taken place has been associated with increased *imports* into Mexico from plants with excess capacity elsewhere, rather than with the movement into Mexico of entire lines of production.

This study is organized into two parts. The first describes the recent evolution of FDI in Mexico and the institutional changes implemented in the effort to attract more FDI. The second part examines Mexico's trade performance and the role of FDI. This also includes a discussion of Mexico's balance of trade and a look at the dominant role of foreign firms in exports. Finally, there are some scenarios for firms' actions followed by the conclusion that measures to reduce imports may become a key policy for the future.

THE EVOLUTION OF FDI IN MEXICO: 1980-92

A FTER ACHIEVING the highest-ever level of GNP (both total and per capita) in 1981, the Mexican economy collapsed in 1982 (Table 1). The economy remained very depressed and experienced drastic reductions in GNP in 1982, 1983 and 1986. In 1987, even after the very short recovery of 1985, total GNP was still lower than the 1981 level (at constant prices). The first signs of sustained recovery were to come very late in the decade, between 1989 and 1991, when the rate of growth rose above 3 percent each year.

New FDI followed a pattern similar to that of the GNP, surging only during the last years of the decade after registering only low levels during most of the 1980s. In this respect, FDI was not different from other sources of private or public investment, which remained at very depressed levels between

TABLE 1

PUBLIC AND PRIVATE INVESTMENT (DOMESTIC AND FOREIGN) AS A SHARE OF MEXICO'S GDP (US$ MILLION)

YEAR	GDP	INVESTMENT			PERCENTAGE OF GDP		
		PUBLIC	PRIVATE		PUBLIC	PRIVATE	
			DOMESTIC	FOREIGN		DOMESTIC	FOREIGN
1981	249.96	30.23	34.04	1.70	12.1	13.6	0.7
1982	170.57	17.36	21.17	0.63	10.2	12.4	0.4
1983	148.78	9.79	15.63	0.68	6.6	10.5	0.5
1984	175.67	11.60	18.47	1.44	6.6	10.5	0.8
1985	184.43	12.25	21.09	1.87	6.6	11.4	1.0
1986	130.10	8.47	14.32	2.42	6.5	11.0	1.9
1987	141.07	7.37	14.85	3.88	5.2	10.5	2.8
1988	172.98	8.76	21.50	3.16	5.1	12.4	1.8
1989	205.31	9.98	24.67	2.91	4.9	12.0	1.4
1990	241.84	11.95	28.64	4.98	4.9	11.8	2.1
1991	283.62	12.36	33.11	9.90	4.4	11.7	3.5

Source: CIEMEX-WEFA *Perspectivas Económicas de México*, various issues, and NAFINSA *El Mercado de Valores*, no. 18, September 15, 1992.

1982 and 1989. The significant response of new FDI came during the period between 1990 and 1992, in reaction to the relaxation of long-standing legal restrictions on foreign investment in many areas of activity, and to measures liberalizing technology transfers, improving property rights, and reducing tariffs on imports (see Appendix A and Kudrle's comparative account of changes in this volume).

However, two features of recent foreign investment inflows deserve close examination. First, a growing proportion of new foreign capital has gone into the stock market. Most of this capital was used to acquire shares in a few recently privatized companies, such as Telmex (the telephone company), and did not directly create new productive capacity. Furthermore, funds invested in the stock market can be extremely volatile, as was shown recently after the news that the NAFTA will be delayed until "parallel" negotiations on labour and the environment are completed.[4] Table 2 shows that whereas total foreign capital inflows have increased considerably, foreign direct investment has risen only modestly.

TABLE 2

ANNUAL FLOWS OF FOREIGN DIRECT INVESTMENT IN MEXICO, 1980-92
(US$ MILLION)

YEAR	(1) NEW FDI	(2) INVESTMENT IN STOCK MARKET $	(3) % CHANGE	(4) STOCK OF FDI $	(5) % CHANGE
1980	1,622.8			8,458.8	
1981	1,701.1			10,159.9	20.1
1982	626.5			10,786.4	6.2
1983	683.7			11,470.1	6.3
1984	1,429.8			12,899.9	12.5
1985	1,729.0			14,628.9	13.4
1986	2,424.2			17,053.1	16.6
1987	3,877.2			2,930.3	22.7
1988	3,157.1			24,087.4	15.1
1989	2,499.7	414.0		26,587.1	10.4
1990	3,722.4	1,256.0	203.4	30,309.5	14.0
1991	3,565.0	2,881.8	129.4	33,874.5	23.1
1992	5,700.0[a]	2629.7	- 8.7	42,000.0[a]	15.3

Note: [a] Rounded preliminary figures.
Source: NAFINSA, El Mercado de Valores, no. 18, Sept. 15, 1992. U.S. Department of Commerce, Business Statistics 1961 - 1988. Survey of Current Business, June 1992 and SECOFI.

Second, since 1988 most FDI has been in services, overtaking by far investment in manufacturing, which previously accounted for more than three-quarters of the total but now accounts for only 50 percent (Tables 3 and 4). Also, many service activities are non-tradeables, such as banking, fast food franchises (McDonalds and the like), retail distribution (including imported goods), and restricted telephone services (cellulars), etc. In these activities the purpose of FDI is to control the Mexican market, since export markets are restricted to the parent company. Investment in manufacturing industries, on the other hand, remained very modest, including that directed toward relatively dynamic industries such as automobiles, chemicals and electronics. In this respect, the future growth of industrial exports from foreign firms in these sectors cannot be expected to proceed as successfully as it did during most of the 1980s. (I shall return to this point later.)

Furthermore, although recent annual data suggest a large increase in FDI inflows, actual investment is, in fact, likely to have been significantly less. These figures represent *approvals* by the National Commission for Foreign Investment of new FDI or expansions, not actual inflows. It is not unreasonable to expect foreign firms to seek removal of legal and bureaucratic barriers in advance of the actual undertaking of projects. It follows, therefore, that it cannot be assumed that these approvals were actually realized during 1991 and 1992. Many foreign investors are still awaiting approval of the NAFTA. The delay associated with U.S. approval of the NAFTA has led the Mexican government to slow the progress of its new

---

TABLE 3

ANNUAL FLOWS OF FOREIGN DIRECT INVESTMENT IN MEXICO BY ECONOMIC SECTOR, 1980-92 (US$ MILLION AND % OF TOTAL FDI)

YEAR	TOTAL FDI	MANUFACTURING[a]	SERVICES	TRADE	MINING	AGRICULTURE
	$	%	%	%	%	%
1980	1,622.8	79.2	8.1	7.3	5.3	0.1
1981	1,701.1	82.6	18.8	10.0	(11.1)	(0.3)
1982	626.5	60.9	37.6	0.2	1.1	0.3
1983	683.7	87.3	1.9	8.6	2.2	0.0
1984	1,429.8	88.8	8.5	2.2	0.4	0.1
1985	1,729.0	67.4	25.2	6.3	1.0	0.0
1986	2,424.2	79.2	13.3	6.2	1.3	0.0
1987	3,877.2	61.9	37.0	- 0.5	1.3	0.4
1988	3,157.1	32.3	59.5	7.8	0.8	(0.4)
1989	2,499.7	39.3	44.1	15.5	0.4	0.8
1990	3,722.4	32.0	59.2	4.6	2.5	1.6
1991	7,015.2	18.9	73.8	6.2	0.4	0.6
1992	5,705.1	27.4	57.6	14.2	0.2	0.7

Note: [a] Includes maquiladoras.
Source: Own calculations with data from NAFINSA *El Mercado de Valores* no. 18, September 15, 1992.

TABLE 4

CUMULATIVE FOREIGN DIRECT INVESTMENT IN MEXICO BY ECONOMIC SECTOR,
1980-92 (US$ MILLION AND % OF TOTAL FDI)

YEAR	TOTAL	MANUFACTURING[a]	SERVICES	TRADE	MINING	AGRICULTURE
	$	%	%	%	%	%
1980	8,458.8	77.6	8.5	8.9	5.0	0.1
1981	10,159.9	78.4	10.2	9.1	2.3	0.0
1982	10,786.4	77.4	11.8	8.6	2.2	0.0
1983	11,470.1	78.0	11.2	8.6	2.2	0.0
1984	12,899.9	79.2	10.9	7.9	2.0	0.0
1985	14,628.9	77.8	12.6	7.7	1.9	0.0
1986	17,053.1	78.0	12.7	7.5	1.8	0.0
1987	20,930.3	75.0	17.2	6.0	1.7	0.1
1988	24,087.4	69.4	22.7	6.2	1.6	0.0
1989	26,587.1	66.6	24.7	7.1	1.5	0.1
1990	30,309.5	62.3	29.0	6.8	1.6	0.3
1991	37,324.7	54.2	37.4	6.7	1.4	0.4
1992	43,029.8	50.6	40.1	7.7	1.2	0.4

Note: [a] Includes maquiladoras
Source: Own calculations with data from NAFINSA El Mercado de Valores no. 18, September 15, 1992.

law on foreign investment already before the Mexican Congress. Consequently, authorization for private business to invest in other lines of production, such as those previously reserved to the state (e.g., petrochemicals, energy, etc.), has been slow.

There have been no major changes in the sources of new FDI relative to previous investment patterns. The United States continues to account for more than 60 percent of the cumulative FDI approvals,[5] as well as for a high proportion of the yearly figures, as shown in Tables 5 and 6. The rest is shared in similar proportions, not exceeding 6 percent each, by Great Britain, Germany, Japan, Switzerland, France, and some others. Canada has lately increased its FDI in Mexico, returning to its previous share of between 2 percent and 3 percent of total foreign direct investment.

MEXICO'S TRADE PERFORMANCE AND THE ROLE OF FDI

MEXICAN BALANCE OF TRADE: FROM SURPLUS (1982-88) TO GROWING DEFICIT (1989-92)

EXPORTS HAVE PLAYED a very important role in Mexico's trade performance over the last decade in two respects. First, exports reacted rather quickly after the collapse of domestic demand between 1982 and 1984, limiting the extent

TABLE 5

ANNUAL FLOWS OF FOREIGN DIRECT INVESTMENT IN MEXICO BY COUNTRY OF ORIGIN (US$ MILLION AND %)

YEAR	ANNUAL TOTAL FDI $	USA %	GREAT BRITAIN %	GERMANY %	JAPAN %	SWITZERLAND %	FRANCE %	SPAIN %	SWEDEN %	CANADA %	NETHERLANDS %	ITALY %	OTHER COUNTRIES %
1980	1,622.8	66.5	3.0	10.5	7.6	6.9	1.2	4.9	0.7	1.1	0.0	-1.8	-0.5
1981	1,701.1	63.0	2.4	8.6	12.5	4.4	0.6	6.0	0.9	0.3	0.0	0.3	1.0
1982	626.5	68.0	1.2	6.4	10.4	3.7	1.1	6.4	-0.3	1.3	0.0	0.3	1.5
1983	683.7	39.0	7.2	16.1	0.6	2.4	16.1	1.9	4.3	3.2	0.0	0.1	9.2
1984	1,429.8	63.8	3.1	10.7	2.5	4.2	0.6	0.8	4.3	2.3	0.0	0.0	7.8
1985	1,729.0	76.7	3.3	3.2	4.6	8.2	0.6	0.8	0.3	2.0	0.0	0.0	0.2
1986	2,424.2	49.8	4.3	9.0	5.9	1.4	13.1	3.9	1.0	1.7	0.0	0.2	9.9
1987	3,877.2	68.9	11.1	1.2	3.4	2.5	0.8	3.2	0.9	0.5	0.0	0.1	7.4
1988	3,157.1	39.3	24.3	4.3	4.7	2.7	4.8	1.1	1.0	1.1	0.0	0.0	16.6
1989	2,499.7	72.6	1.8	3.4	0.6	7.8	0.7	1.8	0.3	1.5	1.9	0.3	7.5
1990	3,722.4	62.0	3.1	7.7	3.2	4.0	4.9	0.3	0.4	1.5	3.4	0.1	9.4
1991[a]	3,565.0	66.9	2.1	2.4	2.1	1.9	14.0	1.2	0.4	2.1	3.4	0.1	3.5
1992[a]	3,599.6	45.9	11.9	2.4	2.4	8.8	1.9	1.0	0.1	2.5	2.3	0.2	20.8

Note: [a] Totals for 1991 and 1992 here are lower than those in Tables 2 and 3 as they do not include authorized expansions of stock capital to firms previously registered at the Mexican stock market.

Source: SECOFI. Direccion General de Inversion Extranjera.

TABLE 6

CUMULATIVE FOREIGN DIRECT INVESTMENT IN MEXICO BY COUNTRY OF ORIGIN (US$ MILLION AND %)

YEAR	CUMULATIVE FDI TOTAL $	USA %	GREAT BRITAIN %	GERMANY %	JAPAN %	SWITZERLAND %	FRANCE %	SPAIN %	SWEDEN %	CANADA %	NETHERLANDS %	ITALY %	OTHER COUNTRIES %
1980	8,458.8	69.0	3.0	8.0	5.9	5.6	1.2	2.4	1.5	1.5	0.0	0.3	1.6
1981	10,159.9	68.0	2.9	8.1	7.0	5.4	1.1	3.0	1.4	1.3	0.0	0.3	1.5
1982	10,786.4	68.0	2.8	8.0	7.2	5.3	1.1	3.2	1.3	1.3	0.0	0.3	1.5
1983	11,470.1	66.3	3.1	8.5	6.8	5.1	2.0	3.1	1.5	1.4	0.0	0.3	2.0
1984	12,899.9	66.0	3.1	8.7	6.3	5.0	1.8	2.9	1.8	1.5	0.0	0.3	2.6
1985	14,628.9	67.3	3.1	8.1	6.1	5.4	1.7	2.6	1.6	1.6	0.0	0.2	2.3
1986	17,053.1	64.8	3.3	8.2	6.1	4.8	3.3	2.8	1.5	1.6	0.0	0.2	3.4
1987	20,930.3	65.5	4.7	6.9	5.6	4.4	2.8	2.9	1.4	1.4	0.0	0.2	4.1
1988	24,087.4	62.1	7.3	6.6	5.5	4.2	3.1	2.6	1.4	1.3	0.9	0.2	4.9
1989	26,587.1	63.1	6.8	6.3	5.0	4.5	2.9	2.6	1.3	1.4	1.0	0.2	5.1
1990	30,309.5	62.9	6.3	6.5	4.8	4.4	3.1	2.3	1.2	1.4	1.3	0.2	5.6
1991a	33,874.5	63.4	5.9	6.0	4.5	4.2	4.3	2.2	1.1	1.5	1.5	0.2	5.4
1992a	37,474.1	61.7	6.4	5.7	4.3	4.6	4.0	2.1	1.0	1.5	1.6	0.2	6.9

Note: [a]Totals for 1991 and 1992 here are lower than those in Tables 2 and 4 as they do not include authorized expansions of stock capital to firms previously registered at the Mexican stock market.

Source: SECOFI. Direccion General de Inversion Extranjera.

TABLE 7

MEXICO'S MERCHANDISE EXPORTS, 1981-91 (US$ BILLION)

	1981	1982	1983	1984	1985	1986	1987	1988	1989	1990	1991
Total	19,429.9	21,229.6	22,312.0	24,196.0	21,952.5	15,756.8	20,656.4	20,656.1	22,764.9	26,950.3	27,175.0
Crude Oil	13,305.3	15,622.7	14,793.1	14,967.5	13,308.8	5,580.2	7,877.0	5,883.4	7,291.8	8,920.7	7,264.2
Agriculture and Fishing	1,482.4	1,233.3	1,188.5	1,460.8	1,408.8	2,098.4	1,543.0	1,670.3	1,753.9	2,162.4	2,372.6
Mining Industries	1,210.4	979.6	873.7	767.9	510.3	509.7	575.9	660.3	604.8	616.9	546.6
Manufacturing	3,427.3	3,386.0	5,447.9	6,985.7	6,720.6	7,566.2	10,588.4	12,381.3	13,014.1	14,966.3	16,808.3
Food & Beverages	679.2	707.4	724.6	821.9	747.1	954.9	1,313.7	1,369.3	1,268.1	1,095.2	1,215.6
Textiles & Clothing	181.3	150.3	191.3	275.3	207.1	341.5	566.2	626.4	622.8	632.2	763.9
Wood & Wood Products	59.3	52.0	81.9	98.1	91.4	106.6	134.5	181.8	197.8	167.5	190.0
Paper and Printing	81.4	78.4	75.1	96.9	99.1	139.1	222.3	323.9	268.9	202.9	234.4
Oil Derivatives	610.9	260.8	737.8	1,244.2	1,351.1	639.6	632.0	617.8	423.7	892.3	642.7
Petrochemical	132.7	115.6	136.1	160.7	106.9	87.4	120.8	207.9	160.4	290.7	258.9
Chemical	457.3	441.6	627.8	755.9	676.3	820.1	1,093.1	1,397.5	1,537.0	1,678.8	1,974.8
Plastic Products & Rubber	22.6	26.1	44.1	64.8	50.3	80.0	112.4	156.2	178.8	126.9	173.2
Nonmetalic Minerals	124.7	139.6	210.2	288.5	315.3	375.6	446.8	526.8	566.7	524.6	647.6
Steel & Steel Products	64.0	112.4	318.6	377.7	246.0	446.7	629.6	759.0	866.7	973.6	1,034.2
Base Metals	70.3	377.7	562.3	510.3	403.2	474.2	630.2	818.0	1,033.2	963.2	750.7
Metal Products, Machinery & Equipment	893.9	888.0	1,663.0	2,216.6	2,335.7	3,016.9	4,618.4	5,300.4	5,782.1	7,418.5	8,924.2
Other	49.8	36.0	75.0	74.7	91.2	83.7	68.3	96.3	108.3		
Other Industries	4.4	8.0	8.8	14.1	4.0	2.3	72.1	60.8	100.3	283.9	183.3

Source: Banco Nacional de Comercio Exterior, *Comercio Exterior*, various issues.

TABLE 8

MANUFACTURED EXPORTS FROM MEXICO: 25 MAIN PRODUCTS 1980-91 (% OF ALL MANUFACTURED GOODS)

25 MAIN PRODUCTS	1980	1981	1982	1983	1984	1985	1986	1987	1988	1989	1990	1991
	39.8	39.0	49.6	52.8	49.8	52.5	59.9	60.2	58.4	58.9	61.4	61.3
1 Automobiles	2.9	2.0	2.0	2.0	1.7	1.7	8.3	11.9	11.5	12.5	16.8	21.7
2 Automobile Engines	0.9	1.8	6.3	11.1	14.1	15.5	15.4	11.7	11.0	10.2	10.1	7.1
3 Auto Parts	6.2	4.8	3.9	3.3	3.9	3.6	3.7	3.9	3.7	3.0	2.8	2.7
4 Machinery Parts	0.8	1.0	0.7	0.8	0.7	1.5	1.2	1.2	1.6	2.1	2.0	2.4
5 Information Processing Equipment	0.2	0.1	0.1	0.3	0.7	1.0	1.2	2.1	2.8	2.9	2.4	2.3
6 Iron Bars and Ingots	0.2	0.0	1.3	1.6	1.2	0.5	1.6	1.7	1.6	1.8	2.2	1.9
7 Glass and Glass Products	1.6	1.4	2.0	1.9	1.9	2.3	2.3	2.0	1.9	1.8	1.7	1.8
8 Tubes & Pipes of Iron & Steel	0.8	0.8	0.8	1.4	1.7	1.3	1.0	1.6	1.7	1.9	1.5	1.6
9 Other Electrical Machinery & Apparatus	0.6	0.2	0.3	0.5	0.5	0.5	0.5	0.6	0.7	1.1	1.7	1.5
10 Plastic Materials & Artificial Resins	0.2	0.5	0.9	0.9	1.1	1.0	1.1	1.7	1.8	1.7	1.7	1.4
11 Silver Bars	0.0	0.0	8.8	7.3	4.8	3.9	3.9	3.5	2.6	2.6	2.0	1.4
12 Iron/Steel Manufactures	0.9	0.8	0.8	2.1	2.0	1.5	2.7	2.4	2.3	1.9	1.7	1.4
13 Polycarboxylic Acids	0.8	1.5	1.8	2.0	1.8	2.2	1.8	1.5	1.6	1.7	1.4	1.4
14 Frozen Shrimp	11.3	10.1	10.9	7.0	5.8	4.9	4.5	4.2	3.0	2.6	1.4	1.3
15 Synthetic and Regenerated Fibres	0.5	0.9	1.3	1.5	1.7	1.3	1.9	2.2	1.8	1.7	1.2	1.2
16 Copper Bars	0.0	0.0	0.2	0.1	0.0	0.1	0.1	0.4	1.2	1.6	1.1	1.2
17 Gas-Oil	0.4	2.7	0.6	4.1	1.4	3.2	2.7	0.9	0.4	0.7	2.1	1.2
18 Gas - Butane and Propane	5.2	4.2	1.2	0.9	0.8	2.0	0.8	0.8	1.0	0.7	1.7	1.2
19 Fruits and Vegetables, Preserved	1.9	1.7	2.1	1.1	1.1	1.2	1.0	1.0	0.9	1.2	1.1	1.1
20 Trucks	0.9	1.2	0.4	0.3	0.4	0.4	0.4	0.2	0.3	0.2	0.3	1.0
21 Beer	0.7	0.8	0.8	0.5	0.5	1.0	1.5	2.1	1.5	1.2	1.1	1.0
22 Insulated Electrical Wires	1.1	0.6	0.7	0.9	0.8	0.5	0.5	1.2	1.6	1.4	1.0	1.0
23 Magnetic Tapes/Phono	0.3	0.2	0.2	0.1	0.1	0.2	0.4	0.2	0.5	0.6	1.2	0.8
24 Plastic & Resin Manufactures	0.4	0.4	0.5	0.4	0.4	0.5	0.7	0.6	0.6	0.7	0.5	0.8
25 Dyes and Varnish	0.9	1.1	1.0	0.7	0.7	0.8	0.8	0.8	0.9	0.9	0.8	0.8

Source: Own calculations with data from Banco de México, Indicadores del Sector Externo.

of deterioration of the economy. Second, exports have contributed substantially to the more recent recovery. Probably most important of all is that manufactured exports have taken the lead — even exceeding oil exports since the collapse of oil prices in 1986 (Table 7). Manufactured exports now account for about 60 percent of Mexico's total exports.

The most important and dynamic manufactured exports are in a few TNC-dominated sectors, notably the automotive industry, computing equipment, and chemicals/petrochemicals. There are also a few other sectors where the dominant actors are large conglomerates of national ownership (mostly private but some state-owned), such as food and beverages, steel, glass, cement and oil derivatives, but exports from TNCs are by far the more important.

Even more important (as indicated in Table 8) is the very high concentration of Mexican exports in a few products and the small number of firms in each product, as already noted in other works (Unger, 1990; Peres, 1989). Recent evidence points to no more than 50 products (and probably not more than 100 firms) accounting for about three-quarters of all Mexican manufactured exports. The top 25 products represent 61.3 percent of total manufactured exports in 1991.

Although data at the firm level are difficult to obtain, one recent attempt estimated 76 percent of total exports (i.e. including oil exports) for 1991 were made by only 30 firms.[6] Among the leading exporters, after PEMEX the state oil company, were GM, Ford, Chrysler, Telmex (the telephone company), VW, Industrial Minera, Alfa, IBM, Mexicana de Aviación, Met-Mex Peñoles, Gruma, Vitro, Renault, Tamsa, Aeroméxico*, Celanese Mexicana, Cydsa, DuPont, Motorola, Spicer, Kodak, Transportación Marítima*, Condumex, Frisco, Televisa*, IMSA, GISSA, Novum, and Irsa. Given the predominance of U.S. TNCs among these firms and the overwhelming importance of the United States as the destination of manufactured exports (between 82 percent and 85 percent in recent years), a high proportion of these exports are likely to be intra-company exports (see Encarnation's estimates, this volume).[7]

In spite of some official supporters that interpret export growth as due to changes in relative factor prices, particularly in response to the decline of real wages (estimated to have fallen by 50 percent between 1982 and 1991), there are other explanations stemming more from the logic of what firms perceive as short- and medium-term actions to improve their profitability. These alternative arguments seem to favour the hypothesis of corporate strategic behaviour when confronted with sunk investment in depressed domestic markets. Such was the Mexican situation for many firms after 1982. For the future as well, we may expect the behaviour of TNCs to be even more uncertain and determined less by individual plants, factors or prices. Firms' rationalization plans are more likely to be based on estimates of capacity utilization of the three countries together.[8]

To understand the growth of Mexican exports requires an understanding of more than relative prices. In fact, most manufactured exports are in relatively capital-intensive activities. This measure applies both across industries and within each exporting industry. The leading sectors in exports, such as automotive, chemicals and petrochemicals, steel and computers, are much more capital intensive than most other industries. Also, in most cases the plants oriented to exports are more capital intensive than plants in the same industry devoted to the domestic market.

The latter case is well documented for the Mexican auto industry. According to Lamming (1989, p.8):

> Mexican assembly plants fall readily into two categories — plants designed primarily to serve the domestic and Latin American markets, and plants designed to supply the North American market. Some plants perform a little of both, others are changing over time, but for now this division is easy to make on a plant-by-plant basis. Not surprisingly, we have found that those Mexican plants with North American export capabilities are indeed more productive, more capital intensive, operate with leaner production systems, and produce fewer defects.

The North American export-oriented plants are concentrated in the north of Mexico and when compared with plants in the centre of the country, show considerably greater automation and higher levels of technical skill in their labour force (Wong-Gonzalez 1989, cited in Ramírez 1993).

There were two major reasons for the recent Mexican ability to supply export markets: first, the favourable exchange rate that prevailed during most of the 1980s as a consequence of major devaluations of the peso; second, the investment in new plants that took place around 1978-82 when the domestic market was booming. These new investments were very important in the sectors now leading exports (automotive, chemicals, computers, steel, etc.).

In the late 1970s and early 1980s, the most important export sectors, dominated by TNCs, were investing to gain a solid base in the domestic market. Some of the new plants were designed to serve external markets so that they could pay for their imports. In the automotive industry, for instance, the auto decrees of the 1970s and 1980s required trade balancing. Since firms expected large increases in their domestic sales, they had to anticipate how to balance the increases in imported content. Most firms responded by investing in new plants to produce auto parts and components (notably engines for all firms) and some lines of finished vehicles (such as the Ford-Mazda Tracer model at the Hermosillo plant) for export.

The same basic principles also apply to the restructuring of the computer industry during the mid-1980s, and to the export performance of typewriters and photocopying equipment, as documented previously (Unger, 1990). Although the growth patterns do not necessarily yield the same results year by year, all these products suffer from an export capacity limited by a shortage of production facilities in Mexico. In these sectors, as much as in the automobile industry, the TNCs were prodded into export production by the Mexican government, which demanded trade balancing with the required degree of balancing varying by industry. Firms like IBM, Hewlett Packard, Xerox, Olympia and Olivetti were not likely to export more than is required by the government, particularly since they have positioned themselves as solid competitors in the Mexican domestic market.

Clear indications of this were given during interviews at the U.S. head-quarters of some of these firms.[9] In the 1980s exports were either from plants recently installed to export, or from other plants facing a depressed domestic market. In any case, these were exports due to past decisions and there is not much reason to expect them to continue to grow unless new investments are in place. In fact, a reduction in the rate of expansion of these exports can be seen after 1988, when the use of installed capacity in those plants neared its limits. As noted earlier, private investment, both from foreign and domestic sources remained at very low levels throughout the 1980s. The U.S. recession may have had an influence on the limited performance of Mexican exports in 1991 and 1992, but I would argue that the effect of capacity limitations predominates.

Public investment was constrained even more than private investment as a result of the debt-adjustment programs. The import intensity of both types of investment is high, imports comprising most of the capital goods and a proportion of the intermediate goods. The limit to both public and private investment caused a reduction in imports of capital and intermediate goods related to investment projects.

TABLE 9

BALANCE OF MERCHANDISE TRADE WITH MEXICO[a] (US$ BILLION)

YEAR	EXPORTS		IMPORTS		TRADE BALANCE	
	$	% CHANGE	$	% CHANGE	$	% OF GDP
1981	19.42		23.95		- 4.53	- 1.8
1982	21.23	9.3	14.44	- 39.7	6.79	4.0
1983	22.31	5.1	8.55	- 40.8	13.76	9.2
1984	24.19	8.4	11.25	31.6	12.94	7.4
1985	21.95	- 9.3	13.21	17.4	8.74	4.7
1986	15.75	- 28.2	11.43	- 13.5	4.32	3.3
1987	20.65	31.1	12.22	6.9	8.43	6.0
1988	20.65	0.0	18.9	54.7	1.75	1.0
1989	22.76	10.2	23.41	23.9	- 0.65	- 0.3
1990	26.95	18.4	31.09	32.8	- 4.14	- 1.7
1991	27.17	0.8	38.36	23.4	- 11.19	- 3.9

Note: [a] These figures do not include maquiladoras' trade, which is included in the Services Account of Mexico's balance of payments.
Source: Bancomext, *Comercio Exterior*, various issues.

Higher exports and lower imports yielded a positive trade balance between 1982 and 1988 for the first time in many years (Table 9), although this ended after the 1989 recovery in domestic demand. In fact, in 1991 and 1992 there was no growth in exports. By contrast imports began to rise dramatically in 1988, following the opening of the economy, and continue to increase sharply. The deficit in the balance of trade became substantial in 1991, reaching US$ 11.19 billion or 3.9 percent of GDP.

FOREIGN FIRMS' PARTICIPATION IN EXPORTS AND IMPORTS

The Import Content of Dynamic Exports (Key Sectors)

The successful growth in exports has been accompanied by an even more dramatic rise in imports (Table 10). In 1988 imports grew by 54.7 percent, and from 1989 to1991 the average annual growth was 26.7 percent. Most imports are manufactured goods (about 93 percent in 1991), and the most important goods are imported by the same industries that lead exports: automobiles, electronic equipment and chemicals (Table 11). Strongly rising imports of consumer goods — such as food and beverages and textiles and clothing — became important as of 1988.

Imports can be subdivided into three categories: consumer, intermediate and capital goods.[10] It is the growth of the latter that is usually associated with

---

TABLE 10

DISTRIBUTION AND ANNUAL GROWTH RATES OF MERCHANDISE IMPORTS TO MEXICO BY PRODUCT TYPE

| | TOTAL | | COMPONENTS | | | | | |
| | | | % DISTRIBUTION | | | % ANNUAL CHANGE | | |
YEAR	US$ BILLION	% ANNUAL CHANGE	C	I	K	C	I	K
1980	18.9		13	60	27			
1981	23.95	26.7	12	57	32	14.7	20.4	46.4
1982	14.44	- 39.7	11	58	31	- 45.9	- 38.0	- 40.6
1983	8.55	- 40.8	7	67	26	- 59.9	- 31.8	- 51.1
1984	11.25	31.6	8	70	23	39.3	36.4	16.8
1985	13.21	17.4	8	68	24	27.1	14.6	23.0
1986	11.43	- 13.5	7	67	26	- 21.3	- 14.9	- 6.6
1987	12.22	6.9	6	72	22	- 9.4	15.6	- 10.8
1988	18.90	54.7	10	69	21	149.4	46.8	53.2
1989	23.41	23.9	15	65	20	82.3	16.9	18.4
1990	31.09	32.8	16	62	22	44.6	26.9	43.0
1991	38.36	23.4	15	63	23	12.1	25.1	26.8

Notes: C   Consumer Goods
      I   Intermediate Goods
      K   Capital Goods
Source: Own calculation with data from BANCOMEXT, *Comercio Exterior*, various issues.

TABLE 11

COMPOSITION AND GROWTH RATES OF MANUFACTURED IMPORTS TO MEXICO BY SECTOR OF ORIGIN AT CONSTANT 1982 PRICES (%)

	ANNUAL AVERAGE GROWTH RATE			COMPOSITION			
	1983 - 1985	1986 - 1987	1988 - 1991	1980	1985	1988	1991
Total	3.8	- 3.5	30.1	100.0	100.0	100.0	100.0
All Manufactured Goods	5.4	- 3.3	31.5	86.6	85.7	88.6	92.9
Food & Beverages	- 6.7	2.4	55.5	6.4	3.8	6.5	6.8
Textiles & Clothing	27.5	6.0	69.5	1.4	1.1	2.4	3.7
Wood & Wood Products	22.0	- 14.0	56.8	0.4	0.4	0.4	0.7
Paper & Printing	2.9	19.6	16.9	3.4	3.2	4.2	3.3
Oil Derivatives	33.1	- 12.3	24.4	1.6	4.8	2.7	3.3
Petrochemicals	20.0	- 10.6	0.6	2.9	5.1	3.5	1.2
Chemicals	8.2	0.7	21.7	8.0	10.2	10.0	8.8
Plastic Products & Rubber	19.9	3.5	37.6	1.3	1.9	2.5	2.9
Nonmetallic Minerals	19.6	2.3	34.9	0.9	0.8	0.9	1.1
Steel & Steel Products	5.3	- 8.5	34.0	9.9	5.6	5.8	5.7
Base Metals	39.8	- 15.8	22.6	2.1	2.8	2.2	1.4
Metal Products & Machinery Equipment	2.5	- 3.4	33.6	45.1	43.5	45.3	51.4
1. For Agriculture & Cattle	50.4	- 34.9	14.0	2.1	2.4	1.0	0.5
2. For Transport & Communications	- 7.2	6.8	41.1	14.5	11.4	13.6	20.2
2.1 Automotive Industry	- 1.9	18.7	49.9	10.2	7.4	10.3	17.5
a. Automobiles	7.1	- 11.1	33.6	2.2	1.7	1.4	1.1
b. Autoparts	6.5	25.9	54.4	7.9	5.7	8.9	16.4
2.2 Other Transport Equipment	- 10.4	- 2.4	23.6	4.3	4.0	3.3	2.7
3. Special Machinery & Equipment for Divers Industries	0.6	- 3.2	28.9	22.7	19.2	19.1	18.5
4. Precision and Professional Equipment	15.8	- 4.6	26.8	1.6	2.6	2.1	2.2
5. Electrical & Electronic Machinery	18.4	- 5.5	37.6	5.9	8.9	10.4	10.4
Other Industries[a]	16.2	- 1.7	43.7	1.5	1.4	1.6	2.2

Note: [a] Including photographic, cinematographic, optical goods and clocks.
Source: Banco de México. Indicadores del sector externo, 1981 - 1992.

TABLE 12

MANUFACTURED IMPORTS BY MEXICO: 25 MAIN PRODUCTS, 1980-91 (% OF ALL MANUFACTURED IMPORTS)

	1980	1981	1982	1983	1984	1985	1986	1987	1988	1989	1990	1991
25 Main Products	**37.6**	**35.9**	**38.3**	**34.7**	**36.0**	**38.2**	**40.6**	**45.5**	**42.6**	**49.1**	**48.6**	**49.7**
1. Autoparts	5.9	4.8	4.5	3.0	2.9	2.9	2.8	7.0	5.8	13.0	13.7	14.7
2. Information Processing Machinery (& Parts)	1.4	1.2	1.2	1.8	2.2	2.9	3.1	4.4	3.9	3.2	3.1	3.1
3. Spare Parts & Engines for Autos	3.2	3.5	3.1	2.5	3.5	3.8	3.5	3.2	4.2	3.6	2.5	3.0
4. Radio-TV Transmitters and Parts	1.0	1.2	1.1	0.7	0.9	1.7	2.2	1.6	2.8	3.1	2.6	2.8
5. Electric Parts Fittings	1.7	1.9	2.2	2.3	2.8	3.2	3.5	2.6	2.8	2.3	2.3	2.3
6. Natural/Synthetic Resins & Appl	1.2	1.3	1.5	2.3	2.3	2.5	2.8	3.0	2.9	2.5	2.2	2.0
7. Radiotelephone & Telegraph Equipment	0.8	0.6	1.2	1.0	1.4	1.8	2.3	1.8	1.8	1.6	2.1	2.0
8. Gasoline	0.1	0.0	0.5	0.2	0.2	0.0	0.0	0.2	0.1	1.0	1.4	1.9
9. Fresh and Frozen Meat	0.2	0.3	0.4	0.3	0.5	0.8	0.5	0.4	1.5	1.3	1.1	1.7
10. Medical & Analysis Instruments	1.6	1.7	2.1	1.6	2.1	2.5	3.0	2.6	1.8	1.3	1.4	1.6
11. Plates & Sheets of Iron or Steel	3.5	2.4	2.3	1.4	1.7	1.2	1.3	1.4	1.8	1.8	1.6	1.6
12. Mixtures for Industrial Uses	1.4	1.3	1.6	2.4	2.2	2.0	2.1	2.4	1.9	1.6	1.5	1.3
13. Aircraft (& Parts)	1.7	1.5	1.3	1.2	0.6	0.8	1.2	1.7	1.1	0.9	1.5	1.1
14. Metal Work Machinery	2.6	3.4	4.7	3.9	2.8	1.8	2.2	1.6	1.9	1.4	1.3	1.1
15. Prepared Paper & Cardboard	1.3	0.9	1.0	0.9	0.8	0.8	0.6	0.8	1.0	1.1	1.0	1.0
16. Pumps, Motorpumps & Turbopumps	1.9	2.3	2.2	2.9	1.6	2.2	1.6	1.7	1.4	1.1	1.0	1.0
17. Ball Bearings, Sweepback & Pulley	0.7	0.7	0.7	0.8	1.2	1.2	1.0	1.0	1.0	0.9	1.1	1.0
18. Synthetic or Artificial Textile Yarns	0.3	0.2	0.3	0.1	0.2	0.3	0.4	0.5	0.7	0.8	0.9	1.0
19. Garments & Leather Footwear	0.0	0.0	0.1	0.0	0.1	0.1	0.1	0.1	0.2	0.7	0.9	0.9
20. Textile Machinery (& Parts)	2.1	2.0	1.9	0.5	0.8	1.1	1.4	1.1	1.6	1.4	1.3	0.9
21. Pulp & Waste Paper	1.2	0.6	0.9	2.1	2.1	1.6	1.9	3.3	2.4	1.8	1.3	0.9
22. Automobiles	1.0	0.9	0.7	0.2	0.2	0.4	0.4	0.4	0.4	0.4	0.9	0.8
23. Loading & Lifting Machinery	1.5	1.9	1.6	1.1	1.2	0.9	1.1	0.8	0.8	0.9	0.7	0.8
24. Cameras (Mainly Industrial)	0.6	0.7	0.6	0.4	0.6	0.7	0.8	0.7	0.6	0.5	0.7	0.7
25. Prepared Mixtures/Pharmaceutical Products	0.7	0.5	0.7	1.2	1.1	1.1	1.0	1.2	1.1	0.9	0.7	0.7

Source: Own calculations with data from Banco de México, *Indicadores del Sector Externo*.

a healthy process of modernization. However, in the recent Mexican case, the growth of consumer imports has been more than proportional, resulting in a significant change in the structure of imports, as noted in Table 10. The share of consumer goods in total imports increased 10 percentage points between 1987 and 1991, accounting for 15 percent of the import basket in 1991. Some intermediate goods (industrial materials, mainly parts and components), used in assembling products for export markets, also increased after the reduction of Mexican domestic content requirements. The overall share of imported intermediate goods has, however, remained around two-thirds of total imports. Capital goods (machinery, equipment and parts), on the other hand, have not exceeded a modest 23 percent of total imports in recent years, compared to an average 30 percent between 1980 and 1982, the period of intensive investment.[11]

Fifty products accounted for slightly more than 60 percent of total imports in 1991. The top 25 products accounted for 49.7 percent (Table 12). The most important of these were imports of autos,[12] autoparts,[13] computers, components for information equipment, chemicals, and others of the same kind that are also important as exports. Their importance and recent growth, however, have become more substantial on the import side than on the export side.

The changing structure of traded goods reveals a correspondence between imported and exported goods. Imports are increasingly concentrated in a smaller number of products and in intermediate inputs of the same industries' leading exports (Table 13). Part of the explanation, especially for imports of some finished goods, may rest in the limits that domestic capacity constraints have put on local responses to the growth of domestic demand. But for the most part, the pattern of imports and exports within each industry suggests that there is an active process of international restructuring in the production of both finished goods and parts/components.

The need for Mexican firms to adjust their production in response to changes in domestic demand and to the competitive pressures of freer international trade has led most of them to concentrate their activity in certain products or components. Most industries have become more dependent on a new mix of imported products and inputs, both in their production for local consumption and for export. The ratio of imports to production in manufacturing nearly doubled during the late 1980s, rising from an annual average of 7.3 percent between 1982 and 1986 to 13.2 percent in 1990. The ratio of imports to production in the leading export industries increased substantially (Table 13). Also, some firms have become distributors of imported products and have given up most of their local production.

This trend toward increasing import sourcing was corroborated recently in studies at the firm level for the chemical/petrochemical and machine tools industries (see Unger, 1993). In these industries, some of the successful exporters or major domestic players (both TNCs and national firms alike), are consolidating in Mexican plants those product lines or stages of the production chain which are both less technologically demanding and, in the short and

TABLE 13

THE RATIO OF IMPORTS TO DOMESTIC PRODUCTION FOR SELECTED INDUSTRIES,
1982 AND 1990

	1982	1990
Autoparts	49.2	120.7
Electrical Machines	15.4	31.0
Non-electrical Machines	48.6	57.6
Chemicals	15.2	17.3

Source: Author's estimates based on Banco de Mexico data.

medium runs, more profitable. Other more sophisticated lines of production are served through imports. This reasoning could also explain, at least partly, the restructuring taking place within the Mexican automotive industry (Ramírez, 1993). The vehicles exported to the United States, for instance, usually contain 85 percent to 90 percent imported components, due mainly to U.S. requirements. By contrast, the import content of units produced by General Motors in 1989 for sale in the Mexican market was estimated at between 50 percent and 60 percent (based on author's interviews in Detroit, 1989). Although empirical proof is pending, it can be argued that such increases/adjustments in the import content in Mexican operations of TNCs may deprive Mexican industry of valuable technological spillovers that would otherwise have been associated with forgone foreign direct investment. (See Harris, 1991, p.11-16, for a similar discussion of Canada and the technology transfer debate.)

The Growth of Maquiladora Exports

The rate of growth of maquiladora exports in dollars has exceeded that of manufactured exports and total exports and has remained much more dynamic than the others. In the years since 1985 annual growth has been around 25 percent (Table 14). This pattern of growth has brought the value of maquila exports equal to that of manufacture exports, which have lagged behind (column 5 in Table 15).

However impressive this performance may appear, one must bear in mind the nature of maquiladora operations, i.e. the assembly of imported inputs. It is consequently more appropiate to look at value-added in maquila operations than at gross figures of total exports. Domestic value-added of maquila exports remains around 25 percent.[14] This figure, after fluctuations between 1983 and 1987, has risen steadily since 1987. However, it is still far below the highest 30 percent average achieved between 1981 and 1982 (column 9 in Table 15).

TABLE 14

MAQUILADORA INDUSTRY IN MEXICO - GROWTH RATES OF EXPORT VALUE BY TYPE
OF PRODUCT EXPORTED CONSTANT 1982 PRICES (% CHANGE)

	1986	1987	1988	1989	1990	1991[a]
Total	19.1	22.2	48.0	36.6	18.7	12.6
Food Products	- 7.5	- 12.9	22.7	22.9	20.1	
Textiles	2.8	2.8	34.0	9.3	16.9	
Footwear &Leather Products	- 8.4	- 6.5	41.2	25.1	52.3	
Wood & Metal Furniture	41.7	61.0	155.6	55.5	33.2	
Chemicals	168.6	195.4	1,383.2	103.6	38.2	
Transport Equipment	21.1	27.2	43.9	30.7	14.7	
Non-Electrical Machinery & Equipment	28.6	27.0	117.8	39.5	5.3	
Electrical & Electronic Machinery & Equipment	18.0	17.4	19.1	23.9	19.3	
Electrical & Electronic Materials	20.2	26.1	54.7	49.0	17.0	
Toys & Sporting Goods	- 12.1	- 19.2	46.3	65.9	22.8	
Other Manufacturer Industries	44.1	44.5	85.4	52.6	21.5	
Services	18.2	60.0	196.9	10.1	54.0	

Note: [a] Excelsior, *Financial section*, March 8, 1993.
Source: Banco de México *Indicadores del Sector Externo*, various issues.

The changes in value-added follow changes in the sectoral composition
of these exports. Three sectors continue to account for a very large proportion
of maquila operations: electrical-electronic materials, transport equipment
(auto parts) and electrical equipment. They account for 71.2 percent of export
value and 73.0 percent of imported inputs (Tables 16 and 17). The major
change in their participation is the increase of electronics and the reduction of
electrical equipment. The latter might be interpreted as an indication of the
final phasing out of mature lines of equipment that have lost markets. Other
traditional maquila sectors, such as textile products, footwear and leather, and
toys and sporting goods, have eroded during the 1980s, partly as a result of
competition for location elsewhere.

The majority of maquila operations is still conducted in U.S.-controlled
plants (Table 18). In 1988 there were 834 such U.S. plants in Mexico,
accounting for 56 percent of the total 1,490 plants. But more revealing is that
these U.S. plants are much larger than the others, since they represented 78
percent of total fixed investment that year. Some of these purportedly U.S.
plants may in fact be owned by subsidiaries of Japanese firms already
established in the United States, but this cannot be verified from official
statistics. A large and growing number of rather small plants is also owned by
Mexicans (e.g. in the clothing, food and toys sectors), including many

TABLE 15

EXPORTS FROM MAQUILADORA INDUSTRY AS SHARES OF TOTAL EXPORTS AND MANUFACTURED EXPORTS (US$ MILLION AND %)

	(1) EXPORTS	(2) EXPORTS	(3) MAQUILADORAS	(4) MAQUILADORAS	(5) PERCENTAGES	(6) PERCENTAGES	(7) PERCENTAGES	(8) PERCENTAGES	(9) PERCENTAGES
YEAR	TOTAL	MANUFACTURED	TOTAL EXPORTS	VALUE ADDED	(3/2)	(3/1)	(4/2)	(4/1)	(4/3)
1981	19,419.6	3,427.3	3,207.8	977.3	93.6	16.5	28.5	5.0	30.5
1982	21,229.7	3,366.0	2,707.3	811.0	80.4	12.8	24.1	3.8	30.0
1983	22,312.0	5,447.9	3,697.4	828.2	67.9	16.6	15.2	3.7	22.4
1984	24,196.0	6,985.7	4,911.9	1,160.9	70.3	20.3	16.6	4.8	23.6
1985	21,866.4	6,720.6	5,093.2	1,267.2	75.8	23.3	18.9	5.8	24.9
1986	15,775.0	7,576.2	5,645.8	1,294.5	74.5	35.8	17.1	8.2	22.9
1987	20,656.2	10,588.4	7,105.1	1,598.1	67.1	34.4	15.1	7.7	22.5
1988	20,657.6	12,381.3	10,145.7	2,337.4	81.9	49.1	18.9	11.3	23.0
1989	22,764.9	13,014.1	12,495.1	3,047.3	96.0	54.9	23.4	13.4	24.4
1990	26,838.4	14,861.0	14,095.2	3,606.5	94.8	52.5	24.3	13.4	25.6
1991	27,120.3	16,750.6	15,828.2	4,133.9	94.5	58.4	24.7	15.2	26.1

Note: [a] The value of maquiladoras exports is not included in total exports in Column (1).
Source: Own calculations with data from Banco de México, *Indicadores del Sector Externo* and INEGI.

TABLE 16

MAQUILADORA INDUSTRY
DISTRIBUTION OF EXPORT VALUE BY TYPE OF PRODUCT EXPORTED (%)

	1985	1986	1987	1988	1989	1990
Total	100.0	100.0	100.0	100.0	100.0	100.0
Food Products	1.0	0.8	0.6	0.6	0.6	1.1
Textiles	7.4	6.4	5.8	4.6	4.5	4.7
Footwear & Leather Products	1.5	1.2	1.1	1.0	1.3	0.9
Wood & Metal Furtniture	2.2	2.6	3.6	4.1	4.6	4.7
Chemicals	0.0	0.1	0.3	0.4	0.4	1.1
Transport Equipment	28.3	28.7	29.4	28.1	27.1	27.7
Non-electrical Machinery & Equipment	1.2	1.3	1.6	1.7	1.5	1.4
Electrical & Electronic Machinery & Equipment	22.6	22.4	18.4	16.7	16.8	13.7
Electrical & Electronic Materials	24.5	24.7	26.0	28.4	23.1	29.8
Toys & Sporting Goods	3.2	2.4	2.1	2.6	2.7	2.0
Other Manufacturer Industries	6.6	8.0	9.6	10.7	11.0	11.2
Services	1.5	1.5	1.6	1.3	1.6	1.8

Source: Banco de Mexico, *Indicadores del Sector Externo*, various issues.

TABLE 17

MAQUILADORA INDUSTRY
DISTRIBUTION OF IMPORTED INPUTS BY TYPE OF PRODUCT IMPORTED (%)

	1985	1986	1987	1988	1989	1990
Total	100.0	100.0	100.0	100.0	100.0	100.0
Food Products	1.0	0.7	0.5	0.4	0.4	0.5
Textiles	7.6	6.4	5.6	4.4	4.1	4.4
Footwear & Leather Products	1.5	1.1	1.1	0.9	1.2	0.8
Wood & Metal Furtniture	1.6	2.1	3.2	3.7	4.4	4.4
Chemicals	0.0	0.0	0.1	0.3	0.3	0.9
Transport Equipment	29.0	30.2	31.0	28.9	29.2	28.5
Non-electrical Machinery & Equipment	1.1	1.1	1.6	1.7	1.5	1.5
Electrical & Electronic Machinery & Equipment	23.8	22.9	18.6	16.8	17.1	14.4
Electrical & Electronic Materials	24.1	24.9	26.4	29.3	22.5	31.1
Toys & Sporting Goods	3.3	2.2	2.0	2.5	2.5	1.8
Other Manufacturer Industries	6.5	7.7	8.9	10.3	10.2	10.3
Services	0.6	0.8	1.1	0.8	1.2	1.4

Source: Banco de Mexico, *Indicadores del Sector Externo*, various issues.

TABLE 18

FOREIGN DIRECT INVESTMENT IN THE MAQUILADORA INDUSTRY IN MEXICO (1988)

INVESTMENT ORIGIN	NUMBER OF PLANTS	(%)	FIXED INVESTMENT[a]	(%)
United States[b]	843	56.0	7,645	78.0
Mexico	566	38.0	1,470	15.0
Japan[b]	48	3.2	385	3.9
Co-investments[c]	21	1.4	130	1.3
Other[d]	21	1.4	170	1.8
Total	1,490	100.0	9,800	100.0

Notes: [a] Value in US$ million.
[b] Major stockholders.
[c] Mexican capital is more than 50%.
[d] Includes enterprises from Korea, Taiwan, Great Britain, France, Netherlands, Spain, Sweden, Germany, Finland, Czechoslovakia and Brazil.
Source: Expansión, October, 1992, with information from SECOFI, COLEF, CIEMEX-WEFA and Asociación Mexicana de Parques Industriales Privados.

industrial plants that have recently migrated from the domestic to the maquila sector.[15]

CONCLUSIONS

ON THE WHOLE, the recent record of foreign investment shows the following:

- New FDI in Mexico has been considerably more limited than total foreign investment.

- Recent foreign investment has moved into the service sector and the stock market rather than into the manufacturing sector.

- FDI has led to increased imports of goods, parts/components and other inputs into Mexico from plants with excess capacity in other parts of the world.

The recourse to imports is a direct result of exposing the relatively inefficient Mexican industry to international competition through the liberalization of imports. But it may also have to do with the relocation of world wide capacity for reasons other than Mexican efficiency. In any case, competitive pressures have led to the consolidation of certain segments within Mexican industries.

The activities in Mexico that are likely to survive international competition are mature products or components of industries that have become more dependent on imported inputs, be they for local consumption or for export production. Also, the TNCs oriented to the assembly of finished goods and/or to the production of parts and components for export markets are becoming more like assembly maquiladora-type production, with little domestic integration even though the assembly is now more sophisticated. Insofar as the recent period of liberalization has incorporated free trade and investment elements that the NAFTA will formalize and expand, major changes should not be expected in the near future if the Agreement does come into force.

Beyond the general trends, some differences can be noted in the way changes are taking place. There are substantial differences between sectors and some differences between firms within sectors in the way they have adjusted to recent liberalizing measures, but most sectors have generated larger imports than before. Some industries combine imported inputs with other sources of domestic competitiveness. This applies to some of the successful exporters of resource-based products such as petrochemicals, steel products and other non-ferrous metals. In these industries, TNCs and national firms alike see their future in consolidating the basic and intermediate production chains which are both less demanding technologically and more profitable in the short run. The rules of international competition can be expected to apply in the domestic market of the future as well, and these rules are set out by large highly-integrated international conglomerates that may use transfer pricing in order to obtain a profitable return for vertically integrated operations.

Other promising areas for TNCs may involve increasing their vertical integration, using imported inputs from their parent companies for consumer goods that may be less subject to cost competition and more prone to product differentiation in the Mexican market. At the extreme, this option may include the import of finished goods from other plants of the same TNC, which are usually goods of larger profit margins demanded by the higher income brackets (luxury vehicles, domestic appliances, latest-generation electronic devices and the like). Other more promising new ventures for TNCs in the near future may relate not so much to the development of new products as to down-to-earth environmental concerns: recycling of plastics, sewage and water treatment, biotechnology applications to chemical pollution, etc.

Perhaps the most damaging effect of the adjustment policies of the 1980s has been to reduce the concern of firms, both TNCs and domestically owned, with the development of longer-term technological capabilities. Short-term opportunities appear to be much more profitable, including distribution rather than manufacturing, and most of all, financial ventures. The long run becomes more risky under these conditions.

Another conclusion that seems inevitable is that growth in the economy will continue to be constrained by the balance of trade. Given that the capacity to develop more exports does not currently exist for the most part, it will become necessary to introduce far-sighted policies to promote new avenues for the development of new exports or for efficient new substitutes for imports. New foreign investment to contribute toward these goals will be most welcome in the near future.

The arguments developed here can be summarized in response to the question "What are the issues that have influenced and will influence TNCs' decisions about Mexico?" My response is that not much new investment will take place in the sectors in which most FDI has occurred in the past (i.e., auto, chemical/petrochemicals, pharmaceuticals, steel). Most of these products in North America (and the world for the most part) are experiencing *over-capacity* and therefore the leading force will be *rationalization* rather than new plants. Mexican plants achieved near full capacity utilization through exports when domestic demand was depressed in the mid-1980s, with the result that rationalization has already advanced substantially. Nonetheless, the TNCs may sacrifice certain less efficient Mexican lines to the benefit of other locations that are in better shape on the basis of scale economies, technology, or other factors. This translates into higher *intrafirm imports* into Mexico — which is already taking place. The limits to this process are defined by the size of the trade *deficit* that will continue to grow in relation to the growth of the economy. One obvious step in coming to grips with the deficit could be devaluation but, given its effects on inflation (and the very high weight attached to the control of inflation in the current administration), it does not seem viable to expect a devaluation in the near future. Instead, we may soon have the typical conditions that require governments to play a more active role and impose controls on trade and investment, no matter how reluctant the Mexican government may be to reverse recent liberalization.

ENDNOTES

1 For more detailed estimates on inflation and investment for the period 1980-1991 see Tables I.3 and II.6 in Unger, 1993 (forthcoming).

2 Both public and private investment were severely cut after 1982; public investment continued at only one-third of its 1981 peak of U.S.$30 billion between 1983 and 1991. Private investment also fell to between 50 percent and 70 percent of the highest level in 1981 for all the years between 1982 and 1989. Not until 1990 was the 1981 level regained. See Table I.3 in Unger, 1993 (forthcoming).

3 In fact, most estimates of Mexican trade gains associated with the NAFTA are rather modest, even when they are based on the most optimistic scenarios aimed at supporting the Agreement. See the collection of papers in Bosworth, et al., 1993.

4 During February 1993, foreign investment in the stock market declined 11.3 percent, from $28.5 billion to $25.3 billion. Although 80 percent of that investment is in American Depository Receipts (ADRs) that are traded in New York and thus do not involve a direct outflow of foreign exchange, their signs are eventually transmitted to the rest of the market (see *El Financiero-Análisis*, 4 Marzo 1993, p.1A).

5 The statistics on origin, as do others on new FDI, refer to proposals from firms to official authorities to undertake FDI projects, *before* these are actually carried out. Given that these data from the National Commission on Foreign Investment (CNIE) refers to FDI approvals and not to actual inflows of foreign capital that will necessarily occur along a more extended time horizon, we must be even more cautious in the interpretation of FDI. Estimates of value are shown in Table 5.

6 The concentration of exports in very few firms applies in Mexico as it does in other countries. It is, however, more acute and of a different nature for Mexico as compared, for instance, with other Latin American countries. A close view of the 200 major exporters of the region (*America Economia*, Sept. 1992, no. 65), shows three differences. First, there is a higher degree of concentration in Mexican exports with fewer firms accounting for a larger proportion of total exports (30 leading firms account for 76 percent of exports); this proportion is greater compared to Brazil's (95 firms accounting for 54.1 percent), to Argentina's (33 firms for 41.5 percent) and to others. Second, the dominant sectors in Mexico, besides oil, are automotive and electronics, whereas in the other countries resource-based exports predominate. Third, Mexico has a much clearer predominance of TNCs within the group of major exporters; in Brazil and Argentina, state-owned and domestic private enterprises play the leading role.

7 With few exceptions, notably those of firms in services identified with an asterisk (*), most are well known TNCs in manufacturing listed among the 1008 most important industrial firms in North America (see Industry

Canada, Working Paper No. 1). It is difficult to be convinced that these exports are not traded intra-company on the basis of TNCs' participating with 49 percent of capital (or a little less) in joint ventures, as Encarnation suggests. In most firms, a foreign share above 25 percent is enough to secure control, and the more so if access to the U.S. market is the aim.

8 One indication in that direction is the recent announcement that GM will relocate all production of Cavaliers from Mexico (see *El Financiero*, 22 June, p. 14) to Lansing, Michigan, in search of economies of scale not only for assembly, but also in the sourcing of components used in common with other models. This is a clear example of Vernon's concern with economies of scale (see Vernon, this volume). As for GM Mexico, its role in the search for specialization gains in the short run will be in the production of pick-ups and trucks, both for export and for the domestic market, a result that is somewhat different from that anticipated by Womack (1991).

9 In Unger (1990) we reported some first-hand evidence from interviews at the head offices of TNCs that were leaders in Mexican exports in 1989. For the most part, they were not contemplating further significant increases in new investment in Mexico. In a sense, they felt that they had done their share for Mexican operations, notwithstanding that they also under-stood that Mexican policy was becoming more liberal.

10 This breakdown of imported goods is provided by the Mexican Government classification of imports by industry or activity, which is based on the UN standard classifications of trade and industry. A product is classified as consumer, intermediate or capital good at the point where it is produced.

11 These percentages contradict what has so far been the main official defense of raising imports, i.e. that capital goods for new investment were the major component of imports. According to data presented in Table 12, the capital goods share of total imports shrank from an average of 30 per-cent in 1980-82 to 25 percent in 1983-86 and to 22 percent in 1987-91.

12 The importation of vehicles was introduced in the 1989 decree, allowing firms with trade surpluses to import finished vehicles not produced in Mexico.

13 According to one very recent study still being conducted for the motor industry in Mexico, a new pattern of specialization has been developing within Mexican industry during the 1980s. Plants in the north produce basically for export, while those in the centre of Mexico produce mostly for the domestic market. These two types of plants have very different degrees of integration with their parent companies: plants in the north rely much more on imported parts than those in the centre (Ramírez, 1993, p. 59).

14 This is the ratio of Value Added in Maquila Exports divided by the Total Value of Maquila Exports in the Mexican statistics (for 1990: $3,606.5/$14,095.2 = 25.6 percent). These numbers differ substantially from the U.S. calculation for duty purposes. In the same year, the ratio

of the Dutiable Value Added of U.S. imports to total U.S. imports in category 9802.00.80 was 50.1 percent ($6,424/$12,814). The main difference is in the numerators, i.e., what Mexican authorities define as value-added (VA) in Mexico is different from what the United States classifies as dutiable VA.

15 These plants may explain, to a large extent, the increase in the number of maquiladora plants in recent years — from 1,467 in 1989 to 1,925 in 1991 (see U.S. General Accounting Office 1992, p. 84).

APPENDIX

RECENT LEGAL AND INSTITUTIONAL CHANGES IN THE FDI REGIME IN MEXICO

IN RECENT TIMES Mexico's authorities have taken important steps toward a more flexible regulatory framework concerning direct foreign investment (see Kudrle's comparative account in this volume). This new *Regulation to the Law to Promote Mexican Investment and Regulate Foreign Investment* was published in May 1989. The new Regulation (Reglamento) permits FDI equity participation of up to 100 percent in 58 sectors of Mexican economic activity; in an additional 36 sectors where FDI was not previously permitted at all, the maximum level of FDI was restricted to 49 percent. These include such traditionally sensitive sectors as petrochemicals and fishing.

Some other important changes are shortly expected to follow the April 1993 initiative to the Mexican Congress that proposes to extend the 100 percent foreign equity to secondary petrochemicals and others (see Kudrle this volume). The Mexican government has oficially recognized the need to relax foreign ownership restrictions in order to attract substantial amounts of new foreign capital to finance the expected deficit on the current account and to supplement shortages in domestic savings for several years to come.[1]

The new rules were also designed to ease the registry of firms with foreign capital. One of the most important simplifying changes allows for automatic participation (Regimen de Inversión Automática) without the requisite of official authorization from the national commission (CNIE). A total 90 percent of the 7,203 foreign investments were registered through this automatic mechanism between 1989 and 1991.[2]

Another newly instituted change is the Neutral Investment Regime, which has been used extensively to invest in the stock market. This important mechanism allows firms to issue "neutral" shares that do not carry corporate rights.

Some other important policies that accompanied the liberalizing measures on FDI described above are related to import liberalization and to the relaxation of the rules for technology transfer. Policy in these areas now represents a major change with respect to the more interventionist policies in vogue during the decades of import-substitution industrialization.

The main expression of the new policy favouring more liberal technology transfer is the *Law for the Development and Protection of Industrial Property* of June 27, 1991, which includes the abrogation of the Law for the Control and Registry of Technology Transfer introduced in 1972. It is now generally accepted in Mexico that, in the new context of intensified competition in the domestic market following the liberalization of international trade since the mid-1980s, "it is no longer necessary that the government in Mexico regulate the private contracting of technology or the private conveyance of industrial property rights". (Villareal, 1991, p.122).

The spirit of change is in giving firms more freedom to contract technology transfer, either with respect to sources or the terms contracted (payment, period, restrictions, renewal conditions, etc.). The underlying assumption has two bases: first, that firms are more capable than governments in determining what is to their benefit to acquire; and, second, that the government is incapable of putting the interventionist agenda into practice. Given the more competitive environment in which firms operate, competitive pressures can be left to guide their decisions. Regulation is then moved to the sanctioning of anti-competitive practices through standard (although difficult to enforce) anti-trust legislation.

Property rights and patenting have also been changed in the direction of guaranteeing longer and more generous protection to innovators, as if the length and ease of obtaining protection would decide firms' innovation choices. Firms in a few sectors, notably the pharmaceutical industry,[3] were influential in setting the new, more flexible rules.There are four salient features to the new rules. They: 1) extend the protection of patents to 20 years from the date of application (previously protection was granted for patented inventions for 14 years, counting from the date on which the patent was granted); 2) extend the protection of commercial trademarks from five to ten years, offering the possibility of renewing registrations; 3) include access to patenting to areas previously excluded, notably for inventions in biotechnology (biotechnological procedures and their resulting products, genetic procedures, vegetable varieties, micro-organisms, chemical products, and alloys); and, 4) introduce economic penalties and prison terms for those who violate industrial or commercial secrets.

As for the reduction of tariffs on imported goods, most existing rates were cut by one-half. The average tariff rate was reduced from 22.7 percent to 11.8 percent (weighted average) between June and December 1987. Rates for most capital goods industries were left at levels slightly above the overall average, although transport equipment (other than automotive) and iron and steel reduced their tariff levels to between 6 percent and 7 percent. Tariffs on engines, auto bodies and other major automobile parts were reduced from 27.7 percent to 12.5 percent. Only electronics and domestic electrical appliances retained average rates around the 20 percent level.[4]

ENDNOTES

1 According to José Cordoba (Chief of the Coordinating Office of the President), new foreign capital of $15,000 million per year will be required over the next 10 years. (During 1992 the figure remained short at $8,000 million). His estimate is based on a 6 percent GNP growth rate, the ratio of investment/GNP growing from 20 percent to 23 percent, and domestic savings/GNP rising 3 points to 19 percent (*El Financiero*, 30/4/92, p. 6).

2 Even though the other 10 percent of operations accounted for a larger sum of dollars invested (see *El Mercado de Valores*, no. 18, 9/15/92).

3 It should be evident that the arguments of one industry cannot be extrapolated elsewhere, as it is implicit in generalizing the rules. It is also evident that different sectors have different constraints on advantages in innovation, as suggested by the Schumpeterian/evolutionary writings of Freeman, Pavitt, Scherer, Nelson and others. Unfortunately, it seems that these theories have not come to the knowledge of officers in charge of Mexican policy.

4 See A. Ten Kate and F. de Mateo, 1989, p. 327.

BIBLIOGRAPHY

America Economía. 65. New York: Nanbei Ltd. (Septiembre 1992).

El Financiero-Análisis. El Financiero S.A. de C.V., Mexico, (4 Marzo 1993): 1A.

Harris, Richard. "Strategic Trade Policy, Technology Spillovers and Foreign Investment." In *Foreign Investment, Technology and Economic Growth*, The Investment Canada Research Series. Edited by D.McFetridge. Calgary: University of Calgary Press, 1991.

Investment Canada. 1993. An Outline of Investment Canada Papers to the MNE Conference, mimeo (Draft outline and tables).

Lamming, Richard. "Research and Development in the Automotive Components Suppliers of New Entrant Countries: the Prospects for Mexico." mimeo. Cambridge: IMVP International Policy Forum, 1989.

Peres, Wilson. *Foreign Direct Investment and Industrial Development in Mexico*. Paris: OECD-Development Centre, 1989.

Ramírez, Jose C. "Recent Transformations in the Mexican Motor Industry." *IDS Bulletin* (Institute of Development Studies). Brighton: University of Sussex, 1993.

SECOFI. Evolución de la Inversión Extranjera en México en 1992. Dirección General de Inversión Extranjera. Enero, México, 1993.

Ten Kate, Adriaan and Fernando de Mateo. "Apertura comercial y estructura de la protección en México: Estimaciones cuantitativas de los ochenta." *Comercio Exterior*, 39, 4, (Abril 1989). México.

Unger, Kurt. Mexican Manufactured Exports and U.S. Transnational Corporations. U.S. Senate Commission for the Study of International Migration and Cooperative Economic Development. Working Paper 22, March 1990.

_____. "Productividad, Desarrollo Tecnológico y Competitividad Exportadora en la Industria Mexicana." *Economía Mexicana. Nueva Epoca*, no. 3, México, 1989.

_____. *Ajuste Estructural y Estrategias Empresariales en las Industrias Petroquímica y Maquinas Herramientas de México*. México: Centro de Investigación y Docencia Económicas, (forthcoming), 1993.

Villarreal, Roberto. "Mexico's New Intellectual Property Legislation." In BANAMEX, *Inversión Extranjera Directa-Direct Foreign Investment*, Mexico, October 1991.

Womack, James. "A Positive Sum Solution: Free Trade in the North American Motor Vehicle Sector." In *Strategic Sectors in Mexican-U.S. Free Trade*. Edited by M.Delal Baer and Guy F. Erb. Washington: The Center for Strategic and International Studies, p.31-65. 1991.

Jorge Niosi
Professor
Department of Administrative Sciences
Université du Québec à Montréal

13

Foreign Direct Investment in Canada

N O SINGLE THEORY CAN EXPLAIN all the effects of regional economic integration on the location of productive activities of multinational enterprises (MNEs). It has been argued that regional integration — such as that experienced by the EC in 1957 and its growth up to 1992, and the FTA in 1989 and its subsequent expansion into the NAFTA in 1993 — will attract foreign corporations, or at least corporations from outside the target area, that are willing to abandon their previous exporting practices and establish production facilities in the area. Part of the motivation of such corporations is the desire to take advantage of the new scale economies and/or the fear of discrimination against non-regional corporations in the target area. A recent UN study termed this strategy *defensive export-substituting investment* (UNCTC, 1990).

MNE investments from other areas can also increase. This strategy has been termed *rationalized foreign direct investment*. Additionally, MNEs can begin to make direct investment in the new trading zone, where they had not previously exported, in what is termed *offensive export-substituting investment*.

MNEs based in the expanded region may also rationalize their activities in the market by closing foreign subsidiaries within the area. In this context local production is replaced by domestic production and exports to partners' markets. The opposite can also apply: new investment may be de-localized in favour of the new partner(s) if resource, fiscal or other considerations make it more economical to produce abroad than in the home market.

Most of these strategies imply some increased levels of trade among the partners in the region, and decreasing trade levels between each partner, the region, and non-regional countries. They also suggest that foreign, non-regional MNEs will invest, or increase their investment, within the region.

Since its inception in 1957, the European Economic Community (EC) has attracted massive amounts of U.S. direct investment, especially in manufacturing. It is noteworthy that these investments were not matched by other EC corporations (UNCTC, 1990). Although trade increased mostly among EC countries, non-EC countries were responsible for the most significant portions of direct investment.

The UNCTC study predicted an increasing direct investment flow between the United States and Canada, through a "positive-sum" rationalization strategy, with Canada winning more U.S. FDI than the opposite. In Canada, abundant natural resources, cheap energy, excellent infrastructure, relatively inexpensive labour, and geographical proximity to the United States were seen to operate in support of that trend. Several Canadian authors (Safarian, 1985; Burgess, 1985) have also argued that free trade would increase both trade and investment between Canada and the United States.

Other views of the FTA have been less enthusiastic. Wilkinson (1991) suggested that the Canada-U.S. Trade Agreement would increase U.S. foreign direct investment in Canadian natural resources and primary transformation, and reduce U.S. investment in Canadian manufacturing. He also suggested that the FTA included no provisions to protect Canada from increasing U.S. trade protectionist actions. Other authors have been more cautious, arguing that Canada may attract more U.S. direct investment because of better quality control and a cheaper dollar, but currency uncertainties and the high cost of capital could also deter American firms from investing in Canada (Crookell, 1989).

From another perspective, several authors have focused on the evolution of U.S. trade policy towards an undeclared structure of managed trade (Zysman & Tyson, 1983). The adoption of managed trade follows the relative decline of U.S. competitiveness in global industry. The steadily increasing use of voluntary export restrictions (VERs), anti-dumping suits, voluntary restraint agreements (VRAs), orderly marketing agreements (OMAs) quotas and other forms of managed trade since the 1960s put the FTA and the NAFTA negotiations under a different light. The combined effect of these measures toward more managed trade raises the question of how free trade agreements will affect the evolution of American foreign trade negotiations and restrictive agreements. Also, will Canada receive more favourable treatment under the FTA or the NAFTA, or will it be forced to negotiate special clauses like any other U.S. trading partner?

Finally, penetration of foreign markets can also be achieved through technology transfers, and technological alliances (long-term agreements between independent corporations with the aim of producing new or improved products and processes). Canadian and American firms have conducted both types of technical arrangements for decades, and they both constitute alternatives to trade and FDI. Exports in an increasingly liberalized market are another alternative. These options also raise the question of what set of preferences will Canadian, U.S. and Mexican firms adopt under the NAFTA?

As technological alliances develop parallel to FDI among firms of different countries, one wonders whether Canadian firms would give preference to their American neighbours over Western European, Japanese or other foreign firms. This question must also be considered in the light of EC experience, where firms have tended to link among themselves through a dense network of collaborations (Woods, 1987; Delapierre, 1992). Are North American firms building a similar network within the FTA?

With this array of hypotheses and questions, I decided to test some of them against available evidence. Specifically, I wanted to determine whether the FTA has had an effect on inward and outward direct investments into and from Canada, by examining closely the flows and stocks of FDI originating both inside Canada and outside Canada (with its main trading partners).

CANADA AS A HOST COUNTRY FOR FOREIGN DIRECT INVESTMENT IN THE 1980S

FOREIGN DIRECT INVESTMENT IN CANADA only partially reflects the general post-war trends of world direct investment abroad. Since the Second World War, the United States has been the largest single source of direct investment capital abroad. Nevertheless, its dominant position has eroded steadily since 1960, as the rates of European and Japanese investment abroad grew and eventually surpassed the American rate (Franko, 1978; UNCTC, 1988). Between 1960 and 1985, the share of U.S. FDI in the world stock of FDI declined from 47 percent to 35 percent (UNCTC, 1988). During the same period Japanese, Swiss, Swedish, Italian and Canadian MNEs grew at a faster rate. British MNEs kept their second place, but also lost some share of world direct investment abroad, from 18 percent to 14 percent during the same period. By 1988, the EC was at parity with the United States in terms of stock of FDI (not including intra-EC FDI) and Japan had overtaken the United States in terms of flows (UNCTC, 1991). The relative decline of U.S. and U.K. multinationals was accompanied by the relative decline of American (and British) industry in the global economy during the post-war period (Niosi, 1984, Bellon & Niosi, 1987, Coates & Hillard, 1986, Dertouzos et al., 1989).[1]

By the end of the Second World War, U.S. sources represented the overwhelming majority of FDI in Canada and by 1950 U.S. FDI in Canada still constituted more than 86 percent of the total. At that time, the United Kingdom was practically the only other major source of FDI in Canada, with almost 12 percent (Tables 1A and 1B). The economic recovery of Western Europe over the course of the 1950s and 1960s brought German, French and other EC direct investment to Canada. By 1965 EC corporations already owned 17 percent of the total FDI in Canada and the American share had declined to 82 percent. The shares of Japanese and other countries' FDI in Canada were almost negligible. By the early eighties, however, U.S. FDI in Canada had declined to approximately 75 percent, EC direct investment had stabilized around 17 percent, and Japanese and other Western European MNEs (mainly Swiss and Scandinavian) were investing in Canada.

TABLE 1A

TOTAL FOREIGN DIRECT INVESTMENT IN CANADA, 1950-91 (C$ MILLION, SELECTED YEARS)

YEAR	UNITED STATES	EC	JAPAN	OTHER[a]	TOTALS
1950	3,549	468[b]		81	4,098
1965	14,408	3,075	10	371	17,864
1983	58,446	13,454	1,611	3,902	77,413
1984	63,355	14,118	1,790	4,122	83,385
1985	66,013	14,860	1,925	4,428	87,226
1986	67,025	18,164	2,291	4,921	92,401
1987	71,806	20,485	2,479	7,073	101,843
1988	73,710	24,963	3,149	8,723	110,545
1989	78,217	27,488	4,104	9,149	118,958
1990	80,931	31,094	4,138	10,425	126,588
1991	83,775	30,786	5,345	11,724	131,630
Increase 1983-8					
(%)	25	88	106	131	43
Annual average ($)	2,943	2,380	340	1,019	6,681
Increase 1988-91					
(%)	14	23	70	34	19
Annual average ($)	3,355	1,941	732	1,000	7,028

Notes: [a] Other includes Mexico; by the end of 1991 the total stock of Mexican direct investment in Canada was C$1 million.
[b] Figure for the U.K. only.
Source: Statistics Canada, *Canada's International Investment Position, Historical Statistics 1926-1991*, Cat. 67-202, Ottawa, 1993.

TABLE 1B

TOTAL FOREIGN DIRECT INVESTMENT IN CANADA, 1950-91 (%, SELECTED YEARS)

YEAR	UNITED STATES	EC	JAPAN	OTHER	TOTAL (%)
1950	86.6	11.4[a]		2.0	100
1965	81.5	17.2		1.3	100
1983	75.4	17.4	2.1	5.1	100
1984	76.0	16.9	2.1	5.0	100
1985	75.7	17.0	2.2	5.1	100
1986	72.5	19.7	2.5	5.3	100
1987	70.5	20.1	2.4	7.0	100
1988	66.7	22.6	2.8	7.9	100
1989	65.8	23.1	3.4	7.7	100
1990	63.9	24.6	3.3	8.2	100
1991	63.6	23.4	4.1	8.9	100

Note: [a] Figure for the U.K. only.
Source: Statistics Canada, *Canada's International Investment Position, Historical Statistics 1926-1991*, Cat. 67-202, Ottawa, 1993.

TABLE 2A

FDI in Canadian Manufacturing Industry, 1950-91
(C$ million, selected years)

YEAR	UNITED STATES	EC	JAPAN	OTHER[a]	TOTAL
1950	2,125	288[b]		19	2,432
1965	6,435	1,091		122	7,648
1983	25,773	3,852	225	1,216	31,066
1984	27,930	4,081	209	1,219	33,439
1985	31,233	4,383	200	1,353	37,169
1986	33,330	6,142	342	1,461	41,275
1987	34,440	6,072	579	2,766	43,857
1988	35,419	8,198	1,393	2,877	47,887
1989	39,781	8,747	1,834	2,864	53,226
1990	41,674	10,558	1,823	2,955	57,010
1991	43,625	10,877	2,662	3,422	60,586
Increase 1983-88					
(%)	37	113	467	137	54
Annual average ($)	1,929	869	234	332	3,364
Increase 1988-91					
(%)	23	33	91	19	27
Annual average ($)	2,735	893	423	182	4,233

Notes: [a] Other includes Mexico; by the end of 1991 the total stock of Mexican direct investment in Canada was C$1 million.

[b] Figure for the U.K. only.

Source: Statistics Canada, *Canada's International Investment Position, Historical Statistics 1926-1991*, Cat. 67-202, Ottawa, 1993.

TABLE 2B

FDI in Canadian Manufacturing Industry, 1950-91 (%, selected years)

YEAR	UNITED STATES	EC	JAPAN	OTHER	TOTAL (%)
1950	87.3	11.8[a]		0.9	100
1965	84.1	14.3		1.6	100
1983	83.0	12.4	0.7	3.9	100
1984	83.5	12.2	0.6	3.6	100
1985	84.0	11.8	0.5	3.6	100
1986	80.8	14.9	0.8	3.5	100
1987	78.5	13.8	1.3	6.3	100
1988	74.0	17.1	2.9	6.0	100
1989	74.7	16.4	3.4	5.4	100
1990	73.1	18.5	3.2	5.1	100
1991	72.0	18.0	4.4	5.6	100

Note: [a] Figure for the UK only.

Source: Statistics Canada, *Canada's International Investment Position, Historical Statistics 1926-1991*, Cat. 67-202, Ottawa, 1993.

During the 1980s, Japanese, EC and other (mainly other Western European) direct investments in Canada grew at a faster rate than U.S. FDI. By 1991, at 64 percent, U.S. corporations represented less than two-thirds of the total FDI in Canada, with increasing investment coming from the EC, Japan and other Western countries. Mexican FDI in Canada was negligible.

The pattern was similar in the manufacturing area: non-American sources were generally winning ground. In this specific sector, however, American FDI held its dominant position more easily than elsewhere. By 1991, U.S. corporations still represented 72 percent of FDI in Canadian manufacturing, against 18 percent held by EC corporations, 4 percent by Japanese and 6 percent by other sources (Tables 2A and 2B). Many American companies consider the Canadian market to be simply an extension of their own home market and, consequently, their manufacturing investments in this country tend to follow suit.

CANADA AS A RECIPIENT OF U.S. FDI

UNTIL THE EARLY 1950S, Canada followed Latin America as the most important destination of U.S. FDI (Tables 3A and 3B). Between 1950 and the mid-1960s, however, Canada became the primary host country of American multinationals. Nationalization of utilities, petroleum and other industries by Latin American governments, reduced both the presence of U.S. corporations and the attraction of that region for future U.S. investments. Canada, on the contrary, remained open to American and other foreign businesses.

In 1966, however, there was a shift; Western Europe became, and has since remained, the single most important destination of U.S. investment abroad (Tables 3A and 3B). Since then, Canada's position as a host of American capital has declined — from 31 percent of total U.S. FDI in 1965, to 21 percent in 1980, and 15 percent in 1991. Neither the nationalistic policies of the Trudeau era (1968-1984) nor the free-trade attitude of the Conservatives (1984-1993) has altered that long-term trend. The nationalizations and restrictions imposed by the Liberal government produced a strategy of U.S. net disinvestment from Canada. The free trade course adopted by the Conservatives did not, however, change Canada's position as a less desirable destination of American FDI (Tables 3A and 3B). As a host country, Canada represents a declining share of U.S. direct investment abroad. In fact, between 1988 and 1991, during the first three years of the FTA, Mexico has attracted more U.S. FDI than Canada, and this applies to U.S. FDI in manufacturing as well as to total U.S. FDI (Tables 4A and 4B).

Since the early 1980s, U.S. corporations have used trade more and investment less to penetrate their partner's market. In the 1980s, trade in manufactured goods between both countries soared, as both U.S. and Canadian companies followed their "preferred" course — exporting from their domestic facilities. In the last ten years, measuring on the basis of two three-year periods — 1981 to 1984 and 1989 to 1991 — Canadian exports of manufactured goods

TABLE 3A

U.S. DIRECT INVESTMENT ABROAD ON A HISTORICAL COST BASIS AT YEAR END, 1950-91 (US$ MILLION, SELECTED YEARS)

YEAR	CANADA	EC	JAPAN	MEXICO	OTHER	TOTAL
1950	3,579	1,179[a]	n	415	5,917	11,788
1965	15,319	6,304	675	1,177	42,495	49,478
1983	44,339	70,210	7,661	4,381	80,612	207,203
1984	46,830	69,688	7,920	4,597	83,959	212,994
1985	46,909	81,380	9,235	5,088	87,708	230,250
1986	50,629	95,629	11,472	4,750	97,320	259,800
1987	57,783	123,999	15,684	4,913	111,928	314,307
1988	62,656	131,069	18,009	5,712	118,807	335,893
1989	63,919	149,465	18,800	7,341	132,894	372,419
1990	67,033	177,642	20,997	9,398	149,016	424,086
1991	69,510	188,710	22,918	11,570	158,488	450,196
Increase 1983-88						
(%)	41	87	135	30	46	62
Annual average ($)	3,663	12,171	2,070	266	7,833	25,738
Increase 1988-91						
(%)	9	44	27	103	37	34
Annual average($)	1,951	19,213	1,636	1,953	15,300	38,101

Notes: [a] Six countries of the original EC.

n = Negligible

Source: U.S. Dept. of Commerce, *Survey of Current Business*, various issues.

TABLE 3B

U.S. DIRECT INVESTMENT ABROAD ON A HISTORICAL COST BASIS AT YEAR END, 1950-91 (%, SELECTED YEARS)

YEAR	CANADA	EC	JAPAN	MEXICO	OTHER	TOTAL (%)
1950	30.4	10.0[a]	n	3.5	50.2	100
1965	31.0	12.7	1.4	2.3	54.9	100
1983	21.3	33.9	3.7	2.1	39.0	100
1984	22.0	32.7	3.7	2.2	39.4	100
1985	20.4	35.3	4.0	2.2	38.1	100
1986	19.5	36.8	4.4	1.8	37.5	100
1987	18.4	39.4	5.0	1.6	35.6	100
1988	18.7	39.0	5.4	1.7	35.3	100
1989	17.2	40.1	5.0	2.0	35.7	100
1990	15.8	41.9	5.0	2.2	35.2	100
1991	15.2	41.9	5.1	2.6	35.2	100

Notes: [a] Six countries of the original EC.

n = Negligible

Source: U.S. Dept. of Commerce, *Survey of Current Business*, various issues.

TABLE 4A

U.S. DIRECT INVESTMENT ABROAD IN MANUFACTURING ON A HISTORICAL COST
BASIS AT YEAR END, 1983-91 (US$ MILLION)

YEAR	CANADA	EC	JAPAN	MEXICO	OTHER	TOTAL
1983	19,209	34,525	3,915	3,687	21,571	82,907
1984	20,879	34,040	3,942	3,988	22,404	85,253
1985	21,831	41,885	4,584	4,053	22,347	94,700
1986	23,406	50,082	5,443	3,776	22,170	104,877
1987	25,800	64,914	7,073	3,959	24,894	126,640
1988	28,884	67,749	8,929	4,976	28,407	138,725
1989	30,213	70,258	9,092	5,861	29,255	144,679
1990	31,790	80,508	9,910	7,196	35,062	164,466
1991	32,360	85,664	10,437	8,493	38,459	175,413
Increase 1983-88						
(%)	50	96	128	35	31	67
Annual average ($)	1,935	6,645	1,003	258	1,367	11,164
Increase 1988-91						
(%)	12	26	17	71	35	26
Annual average($)	1,159	5,972	507	1,172	3,351	12,229

Source: U.S. Dept. of Commerce, *Survey of Current Business*, various issues.

TABLE 4B

U.S. DIRECT INVESTMENT ABROAD IN MANUFACTURING ON A HISTORICAL COST
BASIS AT YEAR END, 1983-91 (%)

YEAR	CANADA	EC	JAPAN	MEXICO	OTHER	TOTAL (%)
1983	23.2	41.6	4.7	4.4	26.1	100
1984	24.5	39.9	4.6	4.7	36.3	100
1985	23.1	44.2	4.8	4.3	23.6	100
1986	22.3	47.8	5.2	3.6	21.1	100
1987	20.4	51.3	5.5	3.1	19.7	100
1988	20.8	48.9	6.4	3.6	20.3	100
1989	20.9	48.6	6.3	4.1	20.1	100
1990	19.3	49.0	6.0	4.4	21.3	100
1991	18.4	48.8	5.9	4.8	22.1	100

Source: U.S. Dept. of Commerce, *Survey of Current Business*, various issues.

to the United States, taken as a percentage of all Canadian exports of manufactured goods, increased from 76 percent to 78 percent. The U.S. propensity to export to Canada has also increased from 19 percent to more than 21
percent. Over the decade, both countries also increased their propensities to
import from one another (Statistics Canada, Cat. 65-504).

CANADA AS A HOST OF JAPANESE FDI

SINCE ITS EARLY BEGINNINGS IN 1951, Japanese FDI has gone through three different stages. In the first, until 1974, traditional Japanese manufacturing industries (such as textiles, shoes, leather and garments) went abroad looking for cheap labour to compensate for rising Japanese wages. In the second stage, between 1975 and 1984, capital-intensive industries, such as automobiles, and consumer electronics, invested heavily in developed countries with a goal to reduce trade frictions and penetrate markets. Since 1985, which marked the beginning of the third stage, these same industries have tried to position themselves as global manufacturers, while more technology-intensive companies (such as semi-conductor and biotechnology firms) invest in highly developed countries with a view to obtaining strategic knowledge (Ozawa, 1979 and forthcoming). Developing countries in South-east Asia were the main host countries of Japanese FDI during the first stage. In the second and third stages, developed countries, mainly the United States, then the European Community, became the primary hosts of Japanese FDI.

The first large Japanese direct investments in Canada were in timber and pulp production, and in mining. By 1973, these two areas accounted for more than three quarters of total Japanese FDI in this country. In the late 1980s the automobile manufacturers and some autoparts transplants began to arrive, along with additional investments from the large Japanese trading houses.

Today, Japanese direct investment in Canada is concentrated primarily in commerce. As of 1988, two-thirds of all large Japanese enterprises in Canada were active in wholesale trade. These also represented 79 percent of the sales and 47 percent of the assets of Japanese subsidiaries in Canada. By the end of 1988, according to Statistics Canada, only 27 of 130 large Japanese subsidiaries were engaged in Canadian manufacturing (Table 5A). Using the Japanese External Trade Organization data, there were, in 1991, 290 Japanese corporate subsidiaries in Canada, of which 45 were in manufacturing (JETRO, 1991). Prominent among these were the three Japanese automobile manufacturers (Honda, Toyota and a GM-Suzuki joint-venture) and nearly 20 autoparts transplants located in Ontario. Manufacturing, nevertheless, concentrates most Japanese FDI in Canada (Table 5B). In the meantime, the North American, and then the world, recession significantly reduced Japanese investment flows abroad, both in Canada and elsewhere, from $67.5 billion in 1989 to less than $40 billion in 1991.

Canada represents a small and declining share of Japanese investment abroad (Table 6). Japanese FDI in Canada declined from 3 percent in 1976 to 2.2 percent in 1984 and to 1.8 percent in 1987. Also, as a percentage of Japanese FDI in the United States, Canada declined from 14.3 percent in 1976 to 7.9 percent in 1984 and to 5.5 percent in 1987 (see also Westney in this volume).

A few words of explanation are in order concerning the trends suggested by these data. First, Canadian trade frictions with Japan never attained the

TABLE 5A

JAPANESE DIRECT INVESTMENT IN CANADA BY INDUSTRY, 1958-91 (C$ MILLION, SELECTED YEARS)

YEAR	MANUFACTURING	FINANCIAL	MINING & SMELTING	COMMERCE	OTHER	TOTAL
1958	43	56	2	23	4	128
1963	66	91	3	29	6	195
1968	91	157	6	61	6	321
1973	423	245	33	68	37	806
1978	617	363	26	112	95	1,213
1983	858	629	13	205	151	1,870
1988	2,530	1,458	526	219	333	5,065
1991	3,161	2,099	857	261	413	6,792

Source: Statistics Canada, *Canada's International Investment Position, Historical Statistics 1926-1991*, Cat. 67-202, Ottawa, 1993.

TABLE 5B

COUNTRY OF CONTROL, NUMBER OF ENTERPRISES AND MAIN INDUSTRY OF FOREIGN CORPORATIONS IN CANADA, 1988 (SELECTED COUNTRIES)

VARIABLE	UNITED STATES	U.K.	FRANCE	GERMANY	NETHERLANDS	JAPAN
Number of Enterprises						
Manufacturing	984	127	34	68	15	27
Wholesale Trade	702	160	36	81	15	86
Mining	179	20	15	10	5	16
Other Industries	241	14	10	26	11	1
Total, non-financial industries	2,106	321	95	185	46	130
Sales (C$ billion)						
Manufacturing	127	14	3	3	6	3
Wholesale Trade	28	7	4	4	1	13
Mining	11	2				
Other Industries	27	3	1	3		1
Total, non-financial industries	193	26	8	9	7	16
Assets (C$ billion)						
Manufacturing	78	16	3	2	10	4
Wholesale Trade	16	3	2	2	1	4
Mining	45	4	1	1		
Other Industries	21	2	3	1		1
Total, non-financial industries	160	27	7	5	11	8

Source: Statistics Canada, CALURA, various issues.

same levels as the U.S.-Japan disputes because the Canadian trade deficit with Japan has always been relatively smaller than the American trade deficit. Also, by 1991, Japan's share represented 66.2 percent of the total U.S. trade deficit. Thus, the Japanese perceived the need to placate Canada's grievances with Japanese FDI to be less than acute.[2] Second, the Canadian market is smaller and less stable politically, and is thus less attractive to Japanese FDI. Finally, the present wave of Japanese overseas investment is linked to knowledge-intensive industries (such as electronics, biotechnology, and advanced materials development) industries that are not predominant in Canada. Because FDI in high technology tends to be attracted more by prospective acquisitions than greenfield investment, Canada is a much less attractive place for Japanese investors than the United States.

The FTA (and the promise of the NAFTA) have not been important inducements for Japanese manufacturing companies to locate in Canada, and Japanese investment in this country remains — except for the large trading companies — a marginal element. In this respect, the more cautious approaches concerning the future of Japanese direct investment in Canada have proved to be the more accurate (Wright, 1989; Morris, 1991).

CANADA AS A HOST OF EC INVESTMENT

BY THE END OF 1989, multinationals from the European Economic Community had advanced their relative global position, leading even the United States as foreign direct investors. These MNEs are not only integrating the EC through their intraregional foreign direct investment, they are also rapidly increasing their North American FDI. By 1990, overseas investment in North America by EC MNEs was larger by far than North American (U.S. and Canadian) FDI in the EC .

By the late 1980s, Canada had become as attactive a destination for European investment as the United States. Between 1985 and 1990, the EC's stock of foreign direct investment in Canada increased by 110 percent, from C$ 14.916 billion to C$ 30.314 billion (Statistics Canada, Cat. 67-202). In the same period, the EC's stocks of FDI in the United States also increased by 110 percent, from US$ 107,105 million to US$ 224,500 million (U.S. Dept. of Commerce).

However, the larger EC investors in both countries (UK corporations) increased their U.S. investments by 136 percent, while they increased their Canadian investments by only 104 percent. Canada was also less attractive for French corporations (an increase of 130 percent in Canada compared to an increase of 180 percent in the United States), but it lured more German capital (an increase of 106 percent in Canada, compared to an increase of 91 percent in the United States).[3]

All in all, *Canada is a declining host of world direct investment.* Between 1967 and 1987, its share of the world stock of inward direct investment has

TABLE 6

JAPANESE INVESTMENT ABROAD (SELECTED YEARS AND COUNTRIES, US$ MILLION)

COUNTRY	1976	1984	1987	1992
United States	4,080	19,894	35,455	148,554
Canada	585	1,575	1,951	6,454
Other	14,740	49,962	68,564	162,167
Total	19,405	71,431	105,970	317,175
Canada as % of Total	3.0	2.2	1.8	2.0
Canada as % of U.S.	14.3	7.9	5.5	4.3

Source: Japan, Ministry of Finance. Data for 1976 and 1984 as elaborated by J. Dunning and J. Cantwell,
   IRM *Directory of Statistics of International Investment and Production*, Basingstoke, UK: Macmillan, 1987.

shrunk from 18.2 percent to 8.5 percent — more than the percentage share loss registered by developing countries (from 30.6 percent to 22.1 percent). During the same period the American and British shares increased from 9.4 percent to 25.2 percent and from 7.5 percent to 9.3 percent respectively. (Investment Canada, 1991).

CANADA AS A SOURCE OF FOREIGN DIRECT INVESTMENT

THE UNITED STATES HAS ALWAYS BEEN the most important destination for Canadian direct investment abroad (CDIA). The overall trend, however, changed slightly in the 1980s (Tables 7 to 9). Between 1980 and 1984, the United States represented a rising share of CDIA, reaching almost 71.7 percent in 1984. At the same time, the EC lost ground as a destination of CDIA, falling to a low of 8.9 percent. Pull factors (from the larger U.S. market size and diversity, increasing non-tariff barriers in the United States, greater American productivity, and others) and push factors (from higher political risks in Canada, heavier government regulations, more expensive labour and taxes) are generally conceded as explaining this early 1980s trend (Rugman, 1987 and 1990).

However, 1984 represents a point of inflection in the geographical structure of CDIA, since in that year the United States reduced its share of Canadian foreign direct investment to a level of 57.9 percent in 1991, while the EC more than doubled its share, to 21.2 percent (Table 7). Between 1985 and 1991, Japan also doubled its share of total CDIA, from 0.4 percent to 0.9 percent. Since 1985, and despite the FTA, the EC has attracted relatively more CDIA than the United States. Also, Mexico remains marginal as a destination of Canadian direct investment abroad. Nevertheless, the flow of Canadian direct investment into the United States remained impressive even in this period of European luring. In the seven calendar years from 1985 to 1991, Canadian corporations invested more in the United States than those from any

TABLE 7

RELATIVE DISTRIBUTION OF CANADIAN DIRECT INVESTMENT ABROAD BY
GEOGRAPHICAL AREA, 1951-91 (SELECTED YEAR ENDS, %)

YEAR	UNITED STATES	EC	MEXICO	OTHER	TOTAL (%)
1951	78.2	6.9	0.5	14.4	100
1961	66.4	13.2	0.4	20.0	100
1971	52.0	14.3	0.8	32.9	100
1981	66.1	14.3	0.7	18.9	100
1984	71.7	8.9	0.6	18.8	100
1988	64.4	16.5	0.2	18.9	100
1991	57.9	21.2	0.2	2.7	100

Source: Statistics Canada, *Canada's International Investment Position, Historical Statistics 1926-1991*, Cat 67-202, Ottawa, 1993.

TABLE 8A

FDI IN THE UNITED STATES ON A HISTORICAL COST BASIS, 1985-91
(US$ BILLION)

YEAR	U.K.	OTHER EC	JAPAN	CANADA	MEXICO	OTHER	TOTAL
1985	43.6	63.5	19.3	17.1	0.5	40.6	184.6
1986	51.4	73.4	23.4	18.3	0.8	42.0	209.3
1987	75.5	85.5	34.4	24.7	0.2	43.1	263.4
1988	95.7	92.5	51.1	26.6	0.2	48.7	314.8
1989	103.5	108.8	67.3	30.4	0.4	58.5	368.9
1990	102.8	121.6	81.8	30.0	0.6	59.9	396.7
1991	106.0	125.9	86.7	30.0	0.6	58.8	407.6

Source: U.S. Dept. of Commerce, *U.S. Survey of Current Business*, various issues.

other country except the United Kingdom and Japan (Tables 8A and 8B). During those years, Canadian investment in the United States totalled more than US$ 32.5 billion, preceding French, German and Dutch multinationals in investment outlays in the United States. Nevertheless, Canada's share of U.S. inward FDI has fallen from 9.3 percent in 1985 to 7.4 percent in 1991.

The Canadian industries that were attracted to the United States market during the second half of the 1980s and early 1990s were primarily resource-intensive (wood and paper, mining and smelting) and services, such as finance and real estate (Table 10). These sectors concentrated 86 percent of Canadian direct investment in the United States. The two industries that experienced actual reductions in the value of their investments were merchandising and petroleum and natural gas.

TABLE 8B

FDI IN THE UNITED STATES ON A HISTORICAL COST BASIS, 1985-91 (%)

YEAR	U.K.	OTHER EC	JAPAN	CANADA	MEXICO	OTHER	TOTAL
1985	23.6	34.3	10.5	9.3	0.3	22.0	100
1986	24.6	35.1	11.2	8.7	0.3	20.1	100
1987	28.7	32.5	13.1	9.4	0.1	16.4	100
1988	30.4	29.4	16.2	8.4	0.1	15.5	100
1989	28.1	29.5	18.2	8.2	0.1	15.9	100
1990	25.9	30.7	20.6	7.6	0.2	15.1	100
1991	26.0	30.9	21.3	7.4	0.1	14.3	100

Source: U.S. Dept. of Commerce, *U.S. Survey of Current Business*, various issues.

TABLE 9

CANADIAN DIRECT INVESTMENT ABROAD, 1980-91, BY AREA OF DESTINATION (C$ MILLION)

YEAR	UNITED STATES	EC	JAPAN	MEXICO	OTHER	TOTAL
1980	16,781	4,440	109	165	5,472	26,967
1981	22,356	4,827	99	223	6,342	33,847
1982	23,781	4,612	110	217	6,838	35,558
1983	26,576	4,076	200	251	7,756	39,859
1984	32,151	5,573	231	270	9,197	47,422
1985	37,074	6,803	232	209	9,805	54,123
1986	39,424	7,849	225	207	10,787	58,492
1987	43,365	10,395	242	183	12,609	66,794
1988	46,497	11,880	354	178	13,237	72,146
1989	50,341	15,200	395	222	14,621	80,779
1990	52,800	18,046	770	230	16,040	87,886
1991	54,639	19,988	1,721	188	17,899	94,435
Increase 1983-88						
(%)	80	134	77	- 29	71	81
Annual av'ge ($)	3,984	1,361	51	- 15	1,096	6,457
Increase 1988-91						
(%)	18	68	386	6	35	31
Annual av'ge($)	2,714	2,702	456	3	1,554	7,429

Source: Statistics Canada, *Canada's International Investment Position, Historical Statistics 1926-1991*, Cat 67-202, Ottawa, March 1993.

As for Canadian investment in the EC, trends were somewhat different (Table 11). Manufacturing was more important than in the United States, with wood and paper, beverages, iron and its products, and other manufacturing (mainly transportation and telecommunications equipment), being the most

TABLE 10

CANADIAN DIRECT INVESTMENT IN THE UNITED STATES, 1985-90
(C$ MILLION AND % INCREASE)

INDUSTRY	YEAR			INCREASE (%)	
	1985	1988	1991	1985-88	1988-91
Beverages	2,393	1,779	2,692	- 26	51
Non-ferrous metals	5,132	6,118	6,178	19	1
Wood and paper products	3,427	4,951	7,872	44	59
Iron and iron products	1,308	1,992	2,085	52	5
Chemical and allied products	4,196	4,781	5,835	14	22
Other manufacturing	1,466	1,711	1,933	17	13
Manufacturing subtotal	17,921	21,333	26,596	19	25
Merchandising	1,814	3,560	2,539	96	- 29
Mining and smelting	1,095	2,236	4,027	104	80
Petroleum and natural gas	5,637	3,447	3,560	- 39	3
Utilities	845	1,417	1,079	68	- 24
Financial	8,080	10,875	12,596	35	16
Other enterprises	1,681	3,723	4,242	121	14
Total	37,074	46,497	54,639	25	18

Source: Statistics Canada, *Canada's International Investment Position, Historical Statistics 1926-1991*, Cat 67-202, Ottawa, 1992.

important industries along with finance and real estate services. Primary industries were less important in Europe than they were in the United States. We can hypothesize that at least some of the same pull factors that lure Canadian companies to invest in the United States, are also at work in the case of the EC — larger and more diversified markets, government non-tariff barriers, and so forth.

However, smaller Canadian firms preferred to invest in and/or to transfer technology to the United States rather than to the EC, probably because of their more limited resources and knowledge of the European markets (Niosi & Rivard, 1990).

FOREIGN TECHNICAL ALLIANCES OF CANADIAN FIRMS

FROM 1990 THROUGH 1991, Canadian firms concluded more foreign technical alliances with Western European than with American partners. Table 12 shows the distribution of the international technological alliances entered into by Canadian firms operating in electronics, transportation equipment, advanced materials and biotechnology. Alliances with EC partners constitute almost half the total foreign alliances of Canadian firms. American alliances were less numerous (than EC alliances) across the board, except in

TABLE 11

CANADIAN DIRECT INVESTMENT IN THE EC, 1985-91
(C$ MILLION AND % INCREASE)

INDUSTRY	YEAR			INCREASE (%)	
	1985	1988	1991	1985-88	1988-91
Beverages	1,424	2,431	2,789	71	15
Non-ferrous metals	1,784	2,109	3,292	18	56
Wood and paper products	721	1,716	2,608	138	52
Iron and iron products	187	553	801	196	133
Chemical and allied products	254	257	495	1	93
Other manufacturing	130	318	548	145	72
Manufacturing subtotal	4,499	7,384	10,531	64	43
Merchandising	201	387	451	93	17
Mining and smelting	130	73	151	- 44	107
Petroleum and natural gas	655	856	1,055	31	23
Utilities	166	30	164	- 82	447
Financial	1,054	2,617	1,474	148	- 44
Other enterprises	98	534	1,230	445	130
Total	6,803	11,880	19,998	75	68

Source: Statistics Canada, *Canada's International Investment Position, Historical Statistics 1926-1991*, Cat 67-202, Ottawa, 1992.

TABLE 12

INTERNATIONAL TECHNOLOGICAL ALLIANCES OF CANADIAN FIRMS, 1990-91

SECTOR	UNITED STATES	EC	JAPAN	OTHER[a]	TOTAL	% DISTRIBUTION
Advanced materials	10	10	2	2	24	15
Biotechnology	16	27	3	2	48	30
Electronics	16	30	10	10	66	41
Transportation equipment	9	8	4	1	22	14
Total	51	75	19	15	160	100
Total (%)	32	47	12	9	100	--

Note: [a] Mostly Korean firms; there were no Mexican firm among the "other".
Source: J. Niosi, *CREDIT Survey on Canadian Technological Alliances*.

transportation equipment. International technical alliances were most often conducted by large and medium-size Canadian owned and controlled corporations with significant FDI. If anything, these figures complement and corroborate FDI findings. In recent years, Canadian MNEs began to move abroad but, despite the FTA, Canadian investors consider the EC to be at least as good a destination as the United States. Mexican firms have not appeared even once as partners in alliances with Canadian firms, confirming their relative marginality in terms of FDI, both in Canada and the United States.

These specific findings on alliances can be explained by the complementarity of European and Canadian industries, and by the more widespread use of strategic alliances in the EC than in the United States through the many inter-European programs launched since 1984, of which at least one of the largest, EUREKA, admits foreign partners (Niosi, 1992; Niosi & Bergeron, 1992; Niosi, 1993). The many alliances of the BCE/Northern Telecom group in Europe (with Matra in France and Mercury in Britain), Bombardier (with the Transmanche consortium and Aérospatiale in France), and the lure of small Canadian biotechnology firms attracting large European pharmaceutical firms (like Allelix, and Biochem Pharma) are all examples of this trend.

CONCLUSIONS

REGIONAL TRADING BLOCKS (the expanded EC, and Canada and the United States under the FTA) have indeed attracted foreign direct investment from non-member trading partners. In addition, defensive export-substituting investment and rationalized foreign direct investment have been made by both EC and Japanese firms. In addition, offensive export-substituting investment has also been drawn from a marginal group of newly industrialized countries (NICs) including Korea and (to a lesser extent) Mexico. Investment in the Canadian auto industry by the Hyundai Corporation is the most prominent example. There is, however, no Mexican equivalent to Hyundai.

Some American and Canadian corporations have reorganized their investments and strategies, often for the purpose of increasing their investments in the larger U.S. economy. This was certainly the case with the Canadian steel firms, but also with some Canadian building materials companies, including Jannock, McMillan Bloedel and Norbord. Also, several American companies decided to close their Canadian subsidiaries, in order to serve the Canadian market from the United States. These cases included Gillette and, more recently, Beloit.

The United States and Canada have both increased their investment in the EC over the last decade following the 1986 expansion and preceding the EC 1992 new rules. Japanese MNEs have continued to invest in the United States, but less so in Canada, probably to counter American trade complaints. EC corporations have also invested at similar rates in both the United States and Canada to take advantage of the 1989 FTA and the coming NAFTA.

Canadian corporations have increased their direct investment in the United States, but in relative terms their capital investment grew much faster in the EC, and even in Japan (although from a smaller base) than in the United States. In North America this part of the "trade versus direct investment" equation has evolved much in the way Safarian, Burgess and others predicted: both Canadian exports and investments in the United States have increased.

Conversely, the FTA has not increased the attraction of Canada as a destination for FDI or alliances for American corporations. Although we may be witnessing the birth of a "fortress Europe" through intra-EC direct investment, trade and alliances, there is nothing similar taking place in North America.

The main conclusion that emerges from our figures is that cross-investment in North America has fallen during the 1980s and that the FTA has not — at least up to now — reversed the trend. Different factors may explain this. First, since 1990, recessions in both Canada and the United States may have reduced the availability of capital required by North American companies to invest in each other's country. Second, during the late 1980s and early 1990s, Japanese and EC investment in both Canada and the United States grew rapidly, crowding out Canadian investment in the United States and American investment in Canada. Third, EC-1992 is more interesting for both Canadian and American MNEs than is the FTA. Also, one must bear in mind that the EC has implemented many of its policies in order to build intra-community trade, investment and technological co-operation. Conversely, the FTA is simply a free trade agreement, and does not include anything comparable to the billion-dollar ESPRIT, RACE, BRITE, EURAM, or other EC programs. Lacking public inducement either to invest or to cooperate with their FTA partners, North American companies evaluate market opportunities differently. Fourth, the more open FTA and Canadian policies allow U.S. multinationals simply to pull out of Canada and to export in, so some U.S. subsidiaries in Canada are closing down and U.S. exports are being substituted for U.S. FDI. Also, American corporations are facing strong competition in their own domestic market in key areas like automobiles, consumer electronics, chemicals, cement and machinery. Much of that competition is coming from Japanese and European transplants in the United States as well as from the direct manufacturing exports from Japan and Europe. The need to consolidate their domestic operations may dictate the U.S. strategy of exporting instead of investing in order to penetrate the Canadian market. In the circumstances, U.S. FDI in Canada should be expected to fall and to stabilize at a lower level.

Other factors explaining reduced U.S. FDI in Canada may include higher costs (taxes, capital), a less extended scientific and technological infrastructure, currency risks, and Canadian political uncertainties. High costs and particularly high taxes and interest rates may also be important factors restraining American business from investing in Canada.[4]

Although Canada has liberalized its foreign direct investment policies since the early 1980s, the United States has been moving slowly, but consistently, in the opposite direction, toward increased protectionism through managed trade. Under the new Democratic administration, managed trade may well become the explicit philosophy of the American government. This change in policy constitutes an extra inducement for Canadian — and probably for some Mexican — firms to locate in the United States, in order to keep access open to the larger market. The foreseeable future may witness the continuance of both opposite developments in Canada and the United States, thus reinforcing the trend towards increased CFDI in the United States, without any significant American counterpart.

ENDNOTES

1 See Vernon (1986) for the conditions under which American corporations could stop their relative decline.

2 On several occasions in 1993, Canadian Industry Minister Michael Wilson suggested that U.S.-Japan trade disputes were attracting Japan's commerce and investments to the United States instead of Canada. See the Industrial Bank of Japan *Quarterly Survey* (1993, 1) for a list of U.S.-Japan trade frictions and the way they were solved.

3 Foreign investment figures produced in the United States and Canada are not strictly comparable, as definitions are slightly different. Growth rates, conversely, may be compared.

4 Some of these factors may also explain the recent rush of Canadian direct investment in the United States as Canadian corporations seek efficiency gains, reduced uncertainties and costs through direct access to a larger and more stable market.

BIBLIOGRAPHY

Bellon, B. and J. Niosi. *L'industrie américaine. Fin de siècle*. Paris: Seuil, 1987 (English translation, Black Rose, Montreal, 1988).

Burgess, D.F. "The Impact of Trade Liberalization on Foreign Direct Investment Flows." In *Canada-U.S. Free Trade*. Edited by J. Waley and R. Hill. Toronto: University of Toronto Press, 1985, pp. 193-99.

Cline, W. *Trade Policy in the 1980s.*Washington D.C.: Institute for International Economics, 1983.

Coates, D. and J. Hillard (eds). *The Economic Decline of Modern Britain*. Sussex, UK: Harvester Press, 1986.

Crookell, H. "Managing Canadian Subsidiaries in A Free Trade Environment." In *International Business in Canada*. Edited by A. M. Rugman. Toronto: Prentice Hall Inc., 1989, Ch. 12.

Delapierre, M. "Towards a New Europeanism: French Firms in Strategic Partnerships." In *Strategic Partnerships in the World Economy*. Edited by L. K. Mytelka. Rutherford, NJ: Fairleigh Dickinson University Press, 1992.

Dertouzos, M.L., et al. *Made in America. Regaining the Productive Edge*. New York: Harper.

Dunning, J. and J. Cantwell. *IRM Directory of Statistics of International Investment and Production*. Basingstoke, UK: Macmillan, 1987.

Franko, L. "Multinationals: The End of U.S. Dominance." *Harvard Business Review*, (Nov.-Dec. 1978): 93-101.

Halperin, A. and M. Teubal. "Government Policy and Capability- Creating Resources in Economic Growth." *Journal of Development Economics*, 35, (1991): 219-41.

Investment Canada *International Investment: Canadian Development in A Global Context*, Working Paper Series, Ottawa, 1991.

Jenkins, B. *The Paradox of Continental Production*. Ithaca and London: Cornell University Press, 1992.

JETRO. *Third Survey of Japanese-Affiliates Firms in Canada*. Toronto, 1991.

Justman, M. and M. Teubal. "A Structuralist Perspective on the Role of Technology in Economic Growth and Development." *World Development*, 19, 9, (1991): 1167-83.

Keohane, R.O. *After Hegemony*. Princeton, NJ: Princeton University Press, (1984).

Morris, J. "A Japanization of Canadian Industry?" In *The New Era of Global Competition*. Edited by D. Drache and M. Gertler. Montreal and Kingston: McGill-Queen's University Press, 1991, pp. 206-28.

Niosi, J. "Le déclin de l'industrie américaine." *Revue d'économie industrielle*. Paris: N° 30, (1984):9-25.

_____. "Strategic Partnerships in Canadian Advanced Materials." *R&D Management*, 23, 1, (1993): 17-27.

_____. *Canadian-American Free Trade and Technological Development of Canadian Firms*. A Report presented to the Science Council of Canada, Ottawa, 1992.

Niosi, J. and M. Bergeron. "Technical Alliances in the Canadian Electronics Industry: An Empirical Analysis." *Technovation*, 12, 5, (1992): 309-22.

Niosi, J. and J. Rivard. "Canadian Technology Transfer to Developing Through Small and Medium-Size Enterprises." *World Development*, 18, 11, (1990):1529-42.

Ozawa, T. *Multinationalism, Japanese Style*. Princeton, NJ: Princeton University Press, 1979.

Ozawa, T. "Technical Alliances of Japanese Firms: an Industrial Restructuring Account of the Latest Phase of Capitalist Development." In *New Technology Policy and Social*

Innovation in the Firm. Edited by J. Niosi. London: Pinter (forthcoming).

Reich, R. *The Work of Nations.* New York: Random House, 1991.

Rugman, A. M. *Outward Bound: Canadian Direct Investment in the United States.* Toronto: C.D. Howe Institute, 1987.

Rugman, A.M. *Multinationals and Canada-U.S. Free Trade.* Columbia, SC: University of South Carolina Press, 1990.

Safarian, A. E. "The Relationship Between Trade Agreements and International Direct Investments." In *Canadian Trade at the Crossroads.* Edited by D. W. Conklin and T. Courchesne. Toronto: Ontario Economic Council, 1985, pp. 206-21.

Statistics Canada. *Canada's International Investment Position,* Cat.N° 67-202, Ottawa, Annual.

_____. *Corporations and Labour Unions Return Act* (CALURA), Cat. N° 61-210, Ottawa, Annual.

_____. *Trade Patterns: Canada-United States.* The Manufacturing Industries 1981-91, Cat. N° 65-504, Ottawa, March 1993.

Thurow, L.B. *Head to Head. The Coming Economic Battle Among Japan, Europe and America.* New York: Morrow and Co., 1992.

U.S. Department of Commerce. *Survey of Current Business.* Washington DC, Monthly.

United Nations Center for Transnational Corporations (UNCTC). *Transnational Corporations in World Development, Trends and Perspectives.* New York: UNCTC, 1988.

_____. *Regional Economic Integration and TNCs in the 1990s: Europe 1992, North America and Developing Countries.* New York, 1990.

_____. *The Triad in Foreign Direct Investment.* New York: UNCTC, 1991.

Vernon, R. "Gone are the Cash Cows of Yesteryear. In *The Multinational Enterprise in Transition.* Edited by P. D. Grub et al. Princeton: The Darwin Press, 1986, pp. 3-12.

Wilkinson, B. "Regional Trade Blocks: Fortress Europe vs Fortress North America." In *The New Era of Global Competition.* Edited by D. Drache and M. Gertler. Montreal and Kingston: McGill-Queen's University Press, 1991, p. 51-82.

Woods, S. *Western Europe: Technology and the Future.* London: Croom Helm, 1987.

Wright, R.W. "Japanese Investment in Canada." In *International Business in Canada.* Edited by A. M. Rugman. Toronto: Prentice Hall, 1989, Ch. 4.

Zysman, J. and L. Tyson. *American Industry in International Competition.* Ithaca, NY: Cornell University Press, 1983.

Part III Policy

C. Fred Bergsten
Director
Institute for International Economics

14

New Rules for International Investment

ALMOST TWENTY YEARS AGO, I wrote an article in *Foreign Affairs* titled "Coming Investment Wars?"[1] My cardinal example was Canada. Canada had just passed the Foreign Investment Review Act (FIRA) and had begun applying, at least in principle, tough performance requirements on foreign investors to make sure they would provide significant benefit to the Canadian economy.

In my article, I conjured up a scenario of conflict in the investment area not unlike the conflict we have, unfortunately, experienced in the trade area. In my scenario, the host country sets up several performance requirements. The home country retaliates. The host country reacts again, and both countries are caught in a spiral with firms trapped in the middle. This image of a possible evolution of investment wars was extremely relevant because Canada was only one of many countries that, at the time, were mandating performance requirements or incentives.

At the time, I debated with Raymond Vernon and others as to whether nations had surrendered their sovereignty to multinational firms. I contended that national sovereignty was not at bay at all; it had simply shifted to the host countries, which were increasingly able to harness multinational firms to their national interests. I then called for what all good classical, international economists would: a new international regime — a GATT for investment. Its purpose was to put rules in place that would preempt full-blown investment wars and institute an international regime in the one major area of world economic affairs where none existed.

Fortunately for the world, there have not been any investment wars — at least not so far. Yet, the need for an investment regime is stronger than ever. Such a regime could be part of the existing global trade regime because trade and investment decisions are inextricably linked. Although it may not yet be time for a GATT for investment, it is clear that we cannot solve our trade problems without also dealing with investment issues.

In the last 20 years, the world *has* seen the development of a regime of sorts in the investment area. This quasi-regime is not a grandiose, comprehensive, all-encompassing GATT for investment but is nonetheless apparent on several levels: multilateral, bilateral, regional, and national. There is an OECD Code on Capital Movements, which has, to some extent, been strengthened in the last decade. The Multilateral Investment Guarantee Agency (MIGA) at the World Bank deals with one aspect of those problems. There are bilateral investment treaties and a network of tax treaties. In addition, we have regional decisions to govern investment — most notably the Canada-United States Free Trade Agreement (FTA) and now the North American Free Trade Agreement (NAFTA), which pushed the envelope substantially in the creation of very constructive international agreements in investment.

The European Community has moved ahead in this area, as it has in many others. The EC does not have a comprehensive investment agreement; rather it has functional components such as competition policy agreements and subsidy denial agreements that represent an important step toward international cooperation in governing investment and limiting the possibility of conflict between countries.

Some efforts have failed, including the long-winded and abortive United Nations effort to negotiate codes for multinational firms. The Uruguay Round encompasses efforts to negotiate trade-related investment measures (TRIMs) but I am afraid it (the Uruguay Round) will not get very far.

Unilateral liberalization of investment regimes has also occurred over the last decade. The United States, however, has moved in the opposite direction. By adopting the Exon-Florio amendment to the *Omnibus Trade and Competitiveness Act* of 1988, the United States has for the first time put in place a regime that can restrict the inflow of foreign investment. Exon-Florio is a comprehensive notification requirement that could, if desired, become a comprehensive screening requirement. To date, it has not. In one sense, Exon-Florio may only represent the United States' moving closer to the practice of the rest of the world, while other countries that have been most restrictive have liberalized. But the United States has moved in the direction of restrictions and that is at least a modestly worrisome sign on the investment policy front.

The investment regime, in other words, consists of bits and pieces. As Murray Smith mentioned, globalization has been extremely rapid. Whole sets of new issues have arisen in which investment policy is front and centre on the international agenda. This raises the question: what kind of investment regime should the world have?

The evolution of an investment regime, as well as attempts to address the whole nexus of investment policy issues, is linked inextricably to the course of the international trade regime for two major reasons.

First, for all its problems, we do have a world trade regime: the GATT, the European Community, and the growing network of regional arrangements. Regional efforts to deal with investment have probably been the most active and most important components of this process over the last couple of decades. The regional arrangements between our countries, in the NAFTA and the Canada-U.S. FTA, have moved further toward a truly comprehensive arrangement than any of their predecessors. The TRIMs exercise, now part of the Uruguay Round, would be the most comprehensive international agreement on key parts of the investment equation if it succeeded even modestly.

Perhaps even more importantly, trade and investment are themselves inextricably linked and have become inseparable in international economic terms. The clearest example of the linkage between trade and investment, and the consequent need for new international arrangements to deal with investment issues, is the case of Japan. If I were writing an article today on the risk of coming investment wars, Japan would be my starting point.

The Japan problem is at the core of the international trade problem. Indeed, it is that concern about Japan that heightens the risk of managed trade, protectionist reactions, and a variety of deviant trade policy behaviours that few economists would support.

In terms of the current global imbalances, Japan is now the world's only major surplus country; every other country in the G7 is in deficit. That is a dramatic change from eight to ten years ago, when the United States was alone with a big deficit and other nations were in surplus. That was clearly an American problem of dollar overvaluation and soaring budget deficits that required an American adjustment. Now the shoe is on the other foot; Japan is the problem and its surplus sticks out very pointedly.

The core of the Japan problem today, going beyond the macroeconomic side (to which I return later) to the trade dimension, lies not primarily with government policies but with corporate practices — particularly collusive behaviour among Japanese firms that make up the *keiretsu* system. This is the conclusion I and a colleague draw in a new, comprehensive Institute study on the U.S.-Japan problem and what ought to be done about it.[2] My analysis certainly does not suggest that all components of *keiretsu* behaviour are bad in economic terms. Many elements of *keiretsu* practices are efficiency enhancing and deserve not to be damned but emulated. Many American companies are in fact incorporating practices such as cross-shareholding, to foster patient capital, or just-in-time delivery systems and design-in techniques with suppliers. Such practices demonstrably enhance efficiency and help explain Japanese economic success both domestically and in international competition.

But there are important parts of the *keiretsu* system that do violate both norms of economic efficiency and, certainly, norms of international comity. The vertical integration techniques through which suppliers outside the corporate family are excluded, for example, are clearly anti-competitive. The capture of parts of the distribution system and the exclusion of products from firms outside the family run counter to norms of international competition and efficiency.

Keiretsu behaviour is, of course, not aimed primarily at foreigners — it is aimed at any firm outside the family group. The *keiretsu* do not discriminate against foreigners; they discriminate against anybody outside the group. That is not much comfort to excluded foreigners, but it is an indication of the depth of the practice and the pervasiveness of the system.

It is clear that one cannot get at these collusive Japanese business practices and *keiretsu* arrangements through traditional trade policy measures. The obvious policy response — obvious at least for those trained in the Western tradition — is anti-trust policy.

The U.S. government tried to broach the subject of anti-trust policy quite extensively in the Structural Impediment Initiative (SII) talks in 1989-90. U.S. officials at those talks made a little progress, but I think it is fair to say not very much. There has yet to be a *keiretsu*-busting case by the Fair Trade Commission of Japan.

A year ago, the Bush administration made a new attempt to apply U.S. anti-trust policy to Japan. To do so, the administration resurrected a U.S. anti-trust policy doctrine that allowed the United States to investigate anti-competitive behaviour in a foreign country as long as it affected the U.S. market. In other words, a Japanese practice that discourages U.S. exports to Japan is fair game. You can imagine the reception the head of the Anti-trust Division of the U.S. Justice Department received when he went to Tokyo, marched into the Japan Fair Trade Commission, and announced that this is what the United States had in mind. Understandably, no one likes the idea of the extraterritorial application of U.S. law.

The next possibility is to work bilaterally to reach an investment agreement that covers anti-trust and competition policy. If the Japanese government itself is serious about response to *keiretsu* practices and collusive behaviour by Japanese companies, as it said it was during the SII talks, why can't U.S. and Japanese anti-trust authorities jointly launch actions to curtail these practices simultaneously in the Japanese and U.S. markets? Such action would be much more likely to succeed than any conceivable unilateral moves by a single government against Japan. It is, however, most unlikely that Japan will act on its own without this sort of *gaiatsu*.

In addition, success in joint anti-trust action would be much more likely if there were international norms, rules, and practices for competition policy. Two colleagues at the Institute, J. David Richardson and Edward M. Graham, are working on a comprehensive study of international competition policy and recommendations for improving it.[3] New norms and new international arrangements in this area might help crack what is one of the toughest problems today, and one of the most threatening to an open and successful collaborative international economic system.

Competition policy must therefore be on the negotiating agenda. It probably will be on the U.S.-Japan bilateral agenda as those negotiations get under way again. It ought, however, to be dealt with internationally in the first instance. In subsequent global trade negotiations after the Uruguay Round (a "Clinton Round"?), competition policy in particular, and investment policy generally, have to be near the top of the agenda.

A broader aspect of the Japan problem is its relatively low levels of imports. Much debate has centered on whether Japan is an outlier in this regard — that is, whether it imports less than would be expected of a country of its size, wealth, and industry composition, and whether it imports fewer manufactured products in particular. There is no question that Japan is the outlier when it comes to inward foreign direct investment. The share of value added by foreign firms in most of the European economies runs somewhere on the order of 20 percent. In the relatively closed U.S. economy, the share is at least 10 percent, but is growing fast. The share of value-added by foreign firms in Japan is 1 percent; this figure has long remained unchanged.

This difference is important to firms attempting to do business in Japan because they believe (correctly) that they must invest there if they are to be able to sell there. Japan itself clearly suffers, not only from its failure to import from foreign investors but also because it has no hostages in the political debate when it faces pressure from the United States or other countries. One key reason the United States is so prone to bash Japan and not Europe or Canada is the presence, in those other countries, of U.S. companies with a stake in protecting the host country from bashing by their own government. Japan has few foreign firms to go to bat for it in Washington (or any other country capital) to try to call off the attack. In this respect, it is very much in Japan's interest to expand its role as a host to foreign investment.

This points out another gap in our international systemic framework and the need to strengthen the investment regime. There would be a much greater prospect of foreign investors getting into Japan if Japan signed an international agreement that ensured the right of establishment, national treatment, non-restrictive business practices, and agreed tax policies, including transfer pricing regimes. Many American companies in Japan face difficulties daily in their negotiations with the tax and financial authorities in that country. So, using Japan as an illustration of today's toughest international economic problem, there is clearly a case for a much more systematic international investment regime.

As I suggested earlier, however, the prospects for progress on investment issues will be heavily affected by what happens in trade policy. In the trade arena, there are three major interrelated issues at the moment. First, will the multilateral GATT system regain credibility, or will it even survive? Second, will regionalism continue to grow? Will it supersede the global network in importance and in the degree to which countries rely on regional arrangements? What effects would the ascendance of regionalism have? Third, are we headed toward managed trade with Japan and other countries, especially with the Clinton administration talking tough in the United States?

The central, underlying question is whether the Uruguay Round will succeed. Its failure clearly would lead to a renewed outbreak of protectionism, regionalism, and unilateral initiatives launched against trading partners. In the United States, the entire GATT system would be discredited if the round failed. The GATT would still be in place but it would be badly wounded. The Uruguay Round is thus the overriding issue.

There is no doubt that the Clinton administration strongly and unequivocally supports a rapid, substantial, and successful conclusion of the Uruguay Round. Its efforts to obtain fast-track authority through the end of the year demonstrate this commitment. Administration officials did waffle at first because they were not sure how to deal with what they regarded as "the inherited Bush trade policy agenda". Their initial reaction was to try to change what they had inherited but they now understand that the only sensible course for getting on to a new "Clinton trade agenda" is to finish the inherited, uncompleted tasks first, and as quickly and as successfully as possible. They now understand that and are doing so. The President and the rest of the administration have now voiced unequivocal support both for the Uruguay Round and the North American Free Trade Agreement (NAFTA).

In addition, the fundamental impact of Clinton's economic policy on world trade policy and America's trading partners is unambiguously positive because the Clinton program at long last starts coming to grips with America's underlying domestic economic problems. I would like to see a much bigger budget reduction program, but the Clinton program will at least cut it almost in half over the next four years — and the Congress may actually up the ante, as they have done recently. The Clinton program also attacks our human capital problems, low investment rates, inadequate technology commercialization, crumbling infrastructure in public investment — the whole range of issues underlying the competitive position and economic problems of the United States.

The United States has displayed, and it may again in the future, display protectionist or isolationist tendencies, lashing out at the rest of the world, because it lacks confidence in its ability to compete effectively. Until we deal with our underlying domestic problems, we are going to be an unreliable trading partner. However, if the Clinton structural reform program is faithfully carried through, if it is supported by the Congress, and if the American public has the patience to stick with it over the years, it will be unambiguously good for America's international economic posture and therefore good for America's trading partners.

As well as being committed to reforming many parts of the economy, the Clinton administration is also very activist in a social sense. But the budget deficit has to be cut, not increased, as part of that program. Consequently, there is not much money with which to fund new social initiatives. The administration is thus faced with two choices: give up the social initiatives, or make the companies pay for them.

The latter option is the direction in which much of the Clinton program is going. Whether it is health care reform, new environmental regulations, or social (or in some cases economic) policy objectives, additional costs will be levied on U.S. companies. At least in some cases, the companies will demand a *quid pro quo* for the administration's making a tough competitive situation tougher by adding to the costs of doing business. In some sectors the companies will seek trade protection. There has already been discussion of such measures in the automobile and the aircraft industries (the latter is, fortunately, an exporter and therefore unlikely to resort to protectionism). But there may be cases in this interim period — during which the United States will be trying to achieve that new and healthier position I mentioned earlier — where the demands of U.S. industry will be hard to ignore. Those who do not like that approach must watch closely for signs of protectionism, because it is a genuine risk in this context.

Although the United States will push for completion of the Uruguay Round, it cannot guarantee its success. The United States is but one leader in a tripolar world economy, now without the clout that its role in maintaining world security during the Cold War gave it. I still would not give the Uruguay Round better than a fifty-fifty chance of success because of the problems on the European side of the equation. The French view and the inability of German leadership to forge a joint, constructive position in Europe continue to put a big question mark over the possible outcome.

Even with a successful Uruguay Round, the multilateral system is not out of the woods. Since the Uruguay Round started seven years ago, additional problems have cropped up, including many of the investment-related issues discussed here. So Uruguay Round or no, there is a danger of backsliding and a likelihood that regional arrangements will proliferate. Consequently, even with a successful Uruguay Round, we must avoid a long hiatus before international negotiations begin again. Remember that after the Kennedy Round and the Tokyo Round, there were long periods of delay before the international bicycle started moving forward again toward liberalization. During those periods there was, in fact, much protectionist backsliding. This time, a new group of eminent persons should be set up to start thinking immediately about the next round — the same way that the Leutweiler Commission did in 1985. Such a round could take up issues such as trade and the environment, and competition policy.

Regardless of what happens on the multilateral front, there will be additional regional developments. I also think that the NAFTA will eventually pass the Congress. The administration will declare victory once the side agreements are negotiated and will strongly support passage of the NAFTA in Congress. The Democrats in the Congress have an overwhelming stake in the success of this administration and cannot afford to break with it on such issues lest it undermine their chance to pass health care reform, the economic program, and the budget. So the NAFTA is likely to go through without too much trouble.

Once passed, the NAFTA will probably be extended to other countries in the Western hemisphere. President Clinton has repeated President Bush's offer to other countries of the hemisphere: when you are ready, and when you have liberalized sufficiently, we are ready to talk to you.

Note the interesting lack of reciprocity in these North-South trade negotiations. In discussions concerning the prospect for North-South trade negotiations, scholars have traditionally suggested that such talks should be non-reciprocal — that is, the developing countries should get better access to developed-country markets and longer timetables in which to open their markets to the rest of the world. The NAFTA and the Western hemisphere trade liberalization idea moves in the opposite direction. It is certainly non-reciprocal: the developing countries must liberalize first — bring down tariffs, open up trade and investment regimes, and get their economic houses in order — before the United States will enter into negotiations with them. At that point, they must still bring down their much higher duties to a reciprocal level, and so the United States benefits.

Ross Perot has not looked at the numbers. The great sucking sound he has mentioned from the north to Mexico is the sound of a vast flood of exports from the United States into Mexico in the last three years — not a flood of jobs from the United States to Mexico. We shifted from a $2 billion deficit with Mexico in 1990 to an $8 billion trade surplus last year. This swing created a quarter of a million jobs in the United States, and the number will continue to rise as long as President Carlos Salinas' reforms are locked in by the NAFTA and the trade liberalization spelled out in that agreement takes place as projected.

The big regional issue now, however, is not the Western hemisphere. It is another region of the world, with which both Canada and the United States are intimately involved: the Pacific Basin. At its ministerial meeting last year, the Asia Pacific Economic Cooperation group decided to set up a Group of Eminent Persons (which I chair) to suggest what the future course of Pacific Basin economic relations should be. The United States will host this year's APEC ministerial in Seattle in mid-November. Again, as the Clinton administration seeks to form a new agenda in trade policy, there is enormous interest in coming up with new initiatives in the Pacific Basin and the ministerial meeting is an ideal platform from which to launch such initiatives.

The members of the APEC Eminent Persons Group, which has been preparing its recommendations for the Seattle meeting, do not speak for their governments, although they are appointed by them. They are all outstanding people, including the Canadian representative John MacDonald. All members of the group have expressed a desire to achieve Pacific free trade. From the Asian perspective, there are three compelling reasons for wanting such an arrangement. First, they are not sure the GATT system is going to be sustained; its role in settling international economic disputes is therefore uncertain. And although they strongly support the Uruguay Round, they are not sure of its successful conclusion.

Second, they hate the NAFTA. Here in Canada you may not realize the tremendous passions that it stirs in countries outside North America; they think they are being badly hurt by it. The Asians dislike it, partly for traditional trade-diversion reasons but perhaps more for attention-diversion reasons; they worry that the United States and Canada are focusing on this hemisphere rather than across the Pacific.

The third and related point is that they are afraid that the United States may withdraw from the Pacific. The Asian countries are haunted by the fear, not of Japan, but of China. They are unsure how this newly emerging giant, already the world's third- or fourth-largest economy, will affect (their) regional security as it modernizes, as its economy booms, and as its leadership looks to new horizons in the region without a Soviet threat to counter them. Those countries are terrified that North America, and particularly the United States, might withdraw from the Pacific. They therefore want to forge new institutional arrangements, as the Europeans have done for the last fifty years, to bind North America more closely to the Pacific. A Pacific free trade agreement would be one way to accomplish this. Our group has not yet decided what it will recommend, but I am confident that significant new initiatives will come out of the November 1993 ministerial.

One of the initiatives that the Australians are promoting in this context is a fairly extensive investment code for the Pacific. This initiative constitutes a recognition that the investment problems I mentioned earlier ought to be dealt with at the international level by an intergovernmental agreement. The Australian initiative will likely be part of any set of initiatives that emerge from our Eminent Persons Group.

The third question I raised was whether the Clinton administration is headed down the road toward managed trade, a question that plagues Japan and a number of other countries but that plagues Canada in particular. President Clinton and the Japanese Prime Minister agreed to create a new framework for U.S.-Japan economic relations at their July 1993 meeting. One of the administration's goals in these negotiations is to find a way to manage, with quantitative indicators, the macroeconomic balances between their two countries. The United States suggested that the Japanese accept a quantitative target for reducing their current account surplus, which is headed toward 4 percent of GNP — as high as it was at its peak in the mid-1980s. This surplus stands out because all other major industrialized nations are in deficit. Although the Japanese have not accepted the proposed target of 1.5 percent to 2 percent, it represents a new type of managed trade effort — at the macroeconomic level.

The term 'managed trade' usually refers to sectoral measures rather than to this type of macroeconomic target. One means that has been discussed for managing trade in specific sectors is a voluntary import expansion (VIE). To its credit, the administration has moved away from the old voluntary export restraints (VERs), which are trade-restrictive, to the VIE, which is trade-expanding and seeks to increase competition over time in markets rather than reduce it. The semiconductor agreement is widely seen as a success, and our independent analysis supports this conclusion.[4] The increase not only in U.S. sales, but also in sales from other countries into the Japanese semiconductor market, would not have occurred without that particular VIE. Although we raise many practical questions about VIEs and would not want to see them applied too extensively, there may be times when they are appropriate in the case of the Japanese market.

In sectors where there is a clear non-market outcome but no barrier can be pinpointed as a focus for traditional negotiating, there are only two options. One is to encourage Japanese cartels to co-opt the foreign firms. This way, a few foreign firms can gain a share of the rents. It is the second- or third-best outcome, but it may be the most politically feasible and may make the most sense if there are few foreign firms that can compete in the market.

If a large number of foreign firms in the sector stand to benefit from greater opening of the market, then a VIE (as in the case of semiconductors) is better because it sharply increases the number of participants in the market and increases competition in that Japanese sector. If an increase in imports results, as it did in semiconductors, in the development of close ties between the consuming firms and the suppliers through design-in and other techniques, then a VIE may well be market expanding as well as internationalizing over time.

Managed trade is nothing new. At least 15 percent to 20 percent of U.S.-Japan trade is now managed. Most of that was installed by the Reagan and Bush administrations. The Reagan administration got the Japanese to agree to quantitative limits on auto sales to the United States, quantitative limits on steel sales to the United States, and quantitative limits on machine tool sales to the United States. The Bush administration negotiated quantitative targets on Japanese imports of semiconductors, Japanese imports of autos, and Japanese imports of auto parts. This managed trade has been occurring for years in sector after sector. I do not endorse this trend but I would note that it has been occurring for years, and is likely to continue as we deal with the Japanese problem over the foreseeable future.

In sum, the world trading system is characterized by even more uncertainty than usual. Despite some hopeful signs, the outcome of the Uruguay Round is far from certain. There is the prospect for more regionalism, probably extending into the Pacific area, with its compatibility with the global regime dependent on a successful agreement of that regime. There will probably be more managed trade which, if managed unskillfully, could leave trade policy open to political capture.

What do these developments in the world trading system mean for the investment regime? It is clear that a number of the key international trade issues require investment-oriented approaches. The *keiretsu* problem, for instance, involves restrictive business practices and antitrust issues. This problem underscores the need to enter the Japanese market through investment as well as trade, and it goes to the heart of the question of global competition policy, which should encompass a means for dealing rationally with anti-dumping statutes around the world. The Japanese case also raises issues of state intervention, such as incentives and performance requirements for foreign investors. Global competition policy should limit further the distortions that those interventions cause in the international economy.

Assuming the Uruguay Round succeeds and we are then ready to move constructively, both on new regional arrangements and to a new Clinton Round (or whatever one calls it) in the GATT, investment issues should now move front and centre. The time is not right, nor is there a need, for a separate GATT for investment. But a new investment regime, negotiated in the trade regime context, will and should be a top priority for global economic negotiations in the years ahead.

Comment

Sylvia Ostry
Chairman, Centre for International Studies
University of Toronto

I WANT TO TALK A LITTLE bit about some of the problems on the investment side that I think are going to be more difficult to come to grips with than the kind of proposals that Fred Bergsten and Monty Graham have spelt out so clearly. I think these problems are particularly relevant in the light of what we have heard and what one can anticipate from the Clinton administration. I also think that these difficult problems would continue to create serious frictions, even if there were convergence of competition policy and the kinds of investment rules that have been laid out in various places.

First of all, I want to say that the issue of getting rules for international investment is of paramount importance. By that I mean multilateral rules developed by the OECD (as opposed to the GATT) because, for the foreseeable future, the OECD is better staffed and has already undertaken a great deal of analysis of both investment issues and related matters such as trade and competition policy. If desired, the OECD codes could be deposited later in the GATT as part of a new post-Uruguay agenda, which must obviously include investment policy and competition policy as priority issues.

Please note that I speak of a *post*-Uruguay agenda and *not* of another GATT round (whether or not blessed with President Clinton's name). I would hope that when this round is over there will be a commitment for continuing negotiations. If that is not the case, there is a danger of GATT negotiations becoming more and more irrelevant. The pace of change today is such that the issues troubling governments are "settled" by other means. By the time another round is agreed to, the agenda spelt out, and the fifteen or so working groups organized, whatever was on the agenda is past history.

I have often said that the Uruguay Round could be described as "too much, too late". For example, the issue of the trade-related investment measures (TRIMs) reflects the attitude of the developing countries of the 1970s; it is an attempt to eliminate or minimize the conditions that govern inward investment. Now there is a total reversal in policy ambience. The UN publication on investment last year pointed out that there were 85 unilateral investment-liberalizing measures taken by developing countries. The problem now is not TRIMs; the problem is the *competition for investment*. TRIMs are simply a reflection of the global dialogue of the 1970s. Efforts to launch the round began in the early 1980s and simply carried forward the conditions of the 1970s. TRIMs became part of the agenda at the 1986 meeting in Punta del Este. This is but one example of the slippage that takes place in organizing large decennial rounds of negotiations.

Another issue which has developed since the Uruguay Round was launched is the use of trade policy as investment policy in the 1980s. The European Community (EC) was most effective in using trade policy as investment policy. The use of anti-dumping measures plus negotiations behind the scenes, changes in rules of origin, etc., was, in effect, investment policy. The American voluntary export restraints (VERs) on Japanese autos turned out to be investment policy. So, what should now be on the agenda are investment-related trade measures (IRTMs).

Another issue that emerged in the 1980s is the relationship or the linkage between investment and industrial policy in the high-tech area. We could label it IRIPs, for investment related industrial policy measures. Again, this first became evident in the EC in the high-tech sectors. In the EC science and technology programmes, which started in the early 1980s, and were given a big push in the *Single European Act*, a major thrust was the creation of pre-competitive generic research consortia which are jointly funded by government and industry. The issue of whether a foreign subsidiary was eligible to be part of the consortium depended on whether that subsidiary would undertake the first commercial use of the technology developed by the consortia in Europe. Thus, a form of domestic content governs participation — although the term is never used.

This is clearly an investment-related industrial policy mechanism. This new concept of domestic content implies that a foreign firm must establish a research and development presence in order to be able (eligible) to participate in consortia. Moreover, the foreign subsidiary must have not only an R&D capacity to participate, it must also have the requisite facilities in place in Europe to ensure the first commercial exploitation of the technology subsequently developed.

In the upcoming EC Fourth Framework program on science and technology (which I have not seen in detail), the likely debate will not be whether to get rid of these conditions for participation, but to raise the perfectly logical question as to whether foreign firm participation should also be conditional on reciprocal access to such consortia for EC subsidiaries in the foreign subsidiary's home country. The Europeans are concerned that when the Americans moved for the first time to create a similar consortium called Sematech, they forbade entry to *any* foreign subsidiary. Siemens applied and was denied entry, although IBM Europe is a participant in a similar European program. The American argument is that Sematech is funded under their defence program and therefore foreign members are precluded under the terms of the funding.

But the national security issue will not settle the debate over reciprocity. The Clinton administration has said on various occasions that Sematech, or the consortia model, will form an important part of the new administration's competitiveness agenda. Further, a new amendment to the antitrust legislation proposes to move beyond what the Europeans allow (i.e. joint research) and also to permit joint *production* consortia to be exempt from triple damages and to be judged by rule of reason on a case-by-case basis. Included in this bill are two clear "reciprocity" conditions: the principal facilities for production must be located in the United States (which means that IBM Canada could not participate, for example), and a foreign subsidiary must come from a country with anti-trust legislation no less favourable to American subsidiaries.

The debate on the American HDTV standard also links industrial policy and foreign investment. One issue raised in the final determination of the standard is: "How many high wage jobs will be produced on the soil of the United States?" This is part of a larger ongoing debate about "Who is Us?" However that debate is eventually settled, industrial policy and investment policy will be linked. Hence, we shall have to think about international rules for investment-related industrial policies (IRIPs).

In a way, both IRTMs and IRIPs are the opposite of TRIMs. A competition for investment is taking place not only in the third world, but also in the OECD countries, and not just for investment but for *a particular kind* of investment. I think one has to look at that and ask, how can we have rules that are not self-defeating rules? That will not be easy.

Let me also say that apart from the issue of protectionist pressures, which arise because of the added tax burden on American industry (protection is cheaper than subsidies), another source of protectionism will stem from growing concern about jobless growth and, in the United States especially, growing income disparity between skilled and unskilled workers. This will also create competition for investment, especially "good investment" which yields high-wage jobs.

Another source of friction in the area of investment is the asymmetry of investment access as between Japan and other industrialized countries. While I am not a competition policy expert, I have been at many meetings where this issue has been raised and the usual consensus seems to be that the problem of asymmetry of investment access will not be solved by the harmonization of competition policy. The problem is rooted in the nature of corporate governance (the horizontal *keiretsu* in Japan; the role of banks in Germany, etc.). Harmonization of corporate governance systems along Anglo-Saxon lines seems highly unlikely to me. So there is no obvious or easy answer to this problem either.

Yet, trade and investment are complementary routes to effective market access for multinational corporations, and the easiest way to enter a market is through merger or acquisition. Anglo-Saxon markets are structurally porous because the stock market is a market for corporate control. But this is not the case in most of Europe and certainly not in Japan.

Finally, let me say that all these issues are now on the table in discussions between the United States and Japan. The United States seems to have rejected the multilateral route, even though the OECD is actively discussing and analysing structural impediments, competition policy, investment access and so on. It is quite true that there are problems of effective market access and presence, and that some countries are structurally more impenetrable than others. The structural impediments arise largely from different systems, and different models of capitalism. As globalization has accelerated, system friction has arisen because of system divergence. But I strongly believe that these issues should be tackled multilaterally. My fear is that the United States and Japan will try to settle the complex problems that arise from system friction through bilateral negotiations which could well result in mutually agreed, market-sharing arrangements. Then the European Community will say "Me too", and the logical outcome will be Triad cartels in sector after sector.

Cartels are inherently unstable. They exclude the less powerful. I come from a non-powerful country. Cartels are a rotten deal for middle-sized countries. A transparent, multilateral, rules-based system is a much better bulwark against economic friction and political instability.

ENDNOTES

1 C. Fred Bergsten, "Coming Investment Wars?", *Foreign Affairs*, (October 1974): 135-52.
2 C. Fred Bergsten and Marcus Noland, *Reconcilable Differences? United States-Japan Economic Conflict*, (Washington: Institute for International Economics, 1993).
3 Edward M. Graham and J. David Richardson, *Global Competition Policy*, (Washington: Institute for International Economics, forthcoming).
4 Bergsten and Noland, Ibid, pp. 132-42.

Robert Thomas Kudrle
Associate Dean for Research
Hubert Humphrey Institute of Public Affairs

Regulating Multinational Enterprises in North America

THE REGULATION OF multinational enterprise (MNE) activity in North America has changed as much since 1980 as any other aspect of foreign economic policy. This study examines the main features of those changes for Canada, Mexico and the United States. Relatively little attention is paid to the resulting impact of those changes on the closely associated stocks and flows of incoming foreign direct investment (IFDI). A sufficient reason for focusing attention on regulatory changes can be found in the complexity of change — one study could scarcely treat both regulatory shifts and their effects. Moreover, isolating the impact of changing MNE and IFDI regulation from other developments in the context of rapidly changing economic policy would pose an enormous challenge.[1]

Separate consideration of the three North American countries certainly confirms the complexity of the relationship between MNE activity and policy. Many analysts attribute a large part of increased MNE participation in the U.S. economy during the 1980s to a fear of impending trade protection, while the sharp increase in MNE activity in Mexico in recent years was triggered by dramatic liberalization both in the domestic economic environment and in trade and foreign investment policy.[2] On the other hand, Canada's Foreign Investment Review Agency (FIRA), widely regarded as a deterrent to MNEs, appears to have had little impact on aggregate flows of IFDI during its existence between 1974 and 1984 (Kudrle, 1991a).

The connection between changing patterns of MNE activity and recent regulatory changes in North America is, perhaps, best viewed as a set of policy responses to powerful changes in the direction of international business.[3] After slow growth in the early 1980s, global IFDI tripled between 1984 and 1987. From 1985 to 1990, global production increased by only 12 percent and merchandise exports by 13 percent, but IFDI increased by 34 percent (United Nations, 1992:1). One reason underlying Canada's motive in seeking free trade with the United States was Canada's shrinking share of the world's direct investment. Increasingly, Canadians understood that MNEs bring both unique resources and competitive stimulation to the domestic economy as well as an opportunity to integrate Canadian activity with worldwide development, production, and sales in many global industries. Similar motivations, compounded by a debt crisis and economic instability, impelled the Mexican unilateral trade and investment liberalizations about the same time. Changing MNE activity and global flows of IFDI affected U.S. policy in quite a different way: surging investment, which sharply increased the share of foreign-owned assets, generated some increased regulation and calls for still tighter controls.

This study traces the history of MNE policy and closely related regulations for the three North American countries since 1980. After a brief introduction, the general policies are examined, followed by a detailed look at specific sectors of the three economies where MNE and IFDI policy is restrictive in most industrial countries. This is followed by a discussion of other relevant regulations in North America and an evaluation of policy developments. The closing section considers prospects for future liberalization, North American development in a global context, and immediate policy prospects.

AN OVERVIEW

ALL COUNTRIES PLACE SOME RESTRICTIONS on MNE activity and IFDI. The restrictions are either general — historically, the most common practice has been some kind of approval or screening process — or specifically applicable to certain sectors of the economy. These controls have usually been justified on the grounds that they conform to widely accepted national goals such as prosperity, security and autonomy (Kudrle, 1992). However, during the 1980s most developed countries shifted their major attention away from what MNEs might do *to* a nation-state toward what they can do *for* it. Increasingly, this has meant not just trying to get the best deal from firms wanting to operate within a national boundary but more ambitious attempts to attract MNE attention in the first place — striking recognition that MNEs are indeed the spearheads of economic globalism (Ostry, 1992). The North American experience since 1980 traces one instance of the regional interplay of two powerful forces: residual economic nationalism in MNE policy pitted against a growing recognition by the state that imposing constraints on MNEs' struggle for global competitiveness may cause national economic welfare to suffer. This study traces the policy results of the changing balance of these forces in three very different economies and argues that, with few exceptions, the remaining restrictions on MNE activity within North America are likely to harm the welfare of all three states.[4]

U.S. POLICY

AMERICAN POLICY HAS CHANGED LEAST over time and its story is the easiest to tell. A few sectors at the federal level are either closed to foreigners or restricted in various ways. Individual states also impose various restrictions, mainly with respect to banking, insurance and agricultural land. Otherwise, the United States has been relatively open to MNEs and IFDI during most of its history. The Federal government was persuaded of the need to monitor IFDI more closely after the 1973 oil crisis — when oil prices increased suddenly and a large investment influx from the Middle East joined a growing flow from Europe and Canada. Federal attention was quickly focused through the Committee on Foreign Investment in the United States (CFIUS) comprised of the secretaries of several cabinet departments. However, CFIUS did little but keep its eyes open for many years. It was given its first really important assignment as part of the major federal IFDI policy change in the post-war period: screening acquisitions and mergers for possible detriment to "national security" in the Exon-Florio Amendment of 1988.

CANADIAN POLICY

CANADA'S ECONOMIC POLICY TOWARD MNEs has gone through several phases — each closely linked to general economic relations with the United States. Although the United States made its greatest IFDI penetration into Canada in the interwar period, most political activity focused on their trade relations. This had been the case ever since Canada's protectionist "National Policy" of 1879 attempted to modify the economically compelling North-South flows across the border and to forge strong east-west linkages within Canada. Nonetheless, free trade was discussed intermittently, and after the Second World War the United States replaced Britain as Canada's largest export market. By 1960 the United States was absorbing 56 percent of all Canadian exports. But American dominance was even greater in IFDI than it was in trade, and by 1973 foreign-controlled corporations accounted for 58 percent of Canadian manufacturing, 75 percent of petroleum and natural gas, 46 percent of other mining and smelting, and 26 percent of all other industries outside of agriculture and finance. This was the highest incidence of foreign ownership of any major industrial country; the United States accounted for over 80 percent of the total (Safarian, 1983:14).

Canadian public opinion polls showed increasingly greater skepticism toward MNEs and IFDI during the sixties (Rugman, 1980:127) following the Gordon Commission's 1957 warnings of possible foreign domination and Finance Minister Gordon's proposed restrictions on IFDI in his 1963 budget. Subsequently, three major studies critical of foreign MNEs and IFDI appeared: the Watkins (1968), Wahn (1971) and Gray (1972) Reports all registered concerns over the volume of foreign investment in Canada, and the Gray Report explicitly recommended a foreign investment screening agency. Enabling legislation was passed in 1973; the Foreign Investment Review Agency (FIRA) began reviewing acquisitions of Canadian firms in 1974 and of new businesses late in 1975. About the same time, the Trudeau government announced that it was exploring the possibility of a "third option" for Canada's international posture: greater diversity in economic partnerships.

This was distinguished from both the prevailing policy and attempts to link Canada still more closely with the United States.

Although causal relations are still disputed, the late 1970s and early 1980s saw lagging Canadian productivity growth (Morici, 1991:52) coupled with apparently futile Canadian efforts to find plausible alternatives to increasing trade with the United States. Indeed, by 1985 the U.S. share of Canada's exports had grown to 76 percent (Lipsey & Smith, 1985:47).

Many factors contributed to the decision by Prime Minister Mulroney to propose free trade to the United States in 1985. A large segment of elite opinion was catalyzed by the Royal Commission on the Economic Union and Development Prospects for Canada (Macdonald Commission) which openly criticized a broad range of Canadian internal and external economic policies in its 1985 Report.[5] But another factor impelled a more urgent approach to the Americans. The soaring U.S. dollar in the early eighties, and a sudden almost universal American perception that many of its trading partners were being "unfair", caused Congressional unease. This led to a substantial increase in the use of "contingent protection" laws, which made life less certain and less profitable for exporters to the U.S. (Lipsey and Smith, 1985:5; Rugman and Anderson, 1987). Consequently, Canadians began to fear losing what they already had.

On the American side, business complained about FIRA as a symbol of excessive Canadian economic *dirigisme* affecting U.S. interests. In fact, by the early 1980s the Trudeau government had already decided that flagging IFDI might be a factor in declining productivity growth and therefore began to look more favourably on foreign MNEs. The Progressive Conservative government elected in late 1984 went even further: it changed the name of the screening agency to Investment Canada and publicly promoted IFDI rather than its screening function.

The Free Trade Agreement (FTA) signed on January 2, 1988 contained several assurances for the Americans: no screening for start-up investments, a substantially increased floor below which IFDI would not be screened, a fixed set of exempt sectors, and a number of other assurances against a range of potentially unfavorable changes in future IFDI policy. The FTA gave Canadians some relief from the caprices of U.S.-administered protection while locking in Canadian IFDI access to the U.S. market (Raby, 1990). Foreign IFDI policy became increasingly important to Canada during the eighties; while Canada's outgoing foreign direct investment (OFDI) was only about half of its IFDI in 1983, this ratio had grown to 70 percent by 1991.

MEXICAN POLICY

LIKE CANADA, MEXICO EXHIBITS conscious and continuous reaction to the United States in its foreign economic policy (Hansen, 1971; Whiting, 1992). Unlike Canada, Mexico has not historically vacillated about free trade with the United States. The Mexican Revolution of 1917 saw the beginning of a series of governments vigilant against excessive dependence on its northern neighbour. This is not to say that this dependence could be avoided: the lion's share of Mexico's trade has always been with the United States (Hansen, 1971:65-66, 169). Nonetheless, Mexico pursued an aggressive import-substitution policy from the 1930s onwards, and the U.S.-dominated stock of IFDI shrank from 30 percent of GDP in 1940 to 4 percent in 1981 (Whiting, 1992:31).

The Mexican constitution of 1917 adopts a tone of general apprehension about foreign ownership, and declares natural resources off-limits to foreigners. Moreover, Article 28 contains a number of sectors reserved for the Mexican government. Although foreign firms immediately began using a number of ingenious legal devices to participate in the supposedly closed oil, railroad, and agriculture industries in the 1920s and 1930s, nationalizations followed that chilled the investment climate until well after the Second World War. Rapid growth of the Mexican economy thereafter found foreign investors again seeking participation. IFDI regulation was codified in 1973 by the Law on Foreign Investment (LFI), which limited most foreign participation to a maximum of 49 percent ownership and restricted certain sectors more severely. The LFI also created an administering agency that issued detailed regulations and conducted screening.

The developments leading to the recent Mexican trade and investment liberalization are familiar, although causal interpretations differ sharply (Lustig, 1992:1-13). High oil export prices in the early 1970s precipitated spending assumptions that were dashed by price collapse. The debt crisis forced a policy change which became more thoroughgoing as partial measures failed to improve the economy. IFDI restrictions were eased in the late seventies and early eighties. More loosening occurred in 1988, and in May 1989 entire sectors of the economy were freed from maximum ownership restrictions (Hufbauer and Schott, 1992:76-77). These developments were part of a general turnaround in economic policy: "the tendency is for the market to replace regulation, private ownership to replace public ownership, and competition, including that from foreign goods and investors, to replace protection" (Lustig, 1992:1).

Export dependence on the United States grew substantially during the eighties: from 53 percent in 1982 to 71 percent in 1990, while the share of intra-firm exports by U.S. MNE affiliates nearly quadrupled, accounting for over one-quarter of the total by 1989 (United Nations, 1992:40-41). Nonetheless, the failure of the Brady plan of early 1989 to lure back flight capital and to attract new foreign investment drove decision-makers in ever greater numbers to the option of free trade with the U.S. (and eventually with Canada).[6]

This study concentrates on the regulation of foreign MNEs by North American governments, but much IFDI within North America is also outgoing foreign direct investment (OFDI) from one of the three countries. According to Investment Canada data, the accumulated stock of IFDI as a ratio of GDP in 1991 was 7.2 percent in the United States, 19.4 percent in Canada and 17.3 percent in Mexico. In that year, U.S. investors owned 65 percent of the Canadian stock and 63 percent of the Mexican stock while Canadian investors held 7.4 percent of the U.S. stock and about 1.5 percent of the Mexican stock. Mexican investors owned less than 0.2 percent of the U.S. stock and a negligible share of Canada's. These figures seriously understate the role of MNEs in each country because a large part of their activity is financed from local sources (see Vernon, this volume).

Since 1980 neither Canada nor the United States has raised barriers to its own firms' foreign operations; Mexico restricted the outward flow of capital only briefly beginning in late 1982 as part of an attempt to deal with its balance of payments crisis (Weintraub, 1990:141).

GENERAL RESTRICTIONS

UNLIKE THE UNITED STATES, both Canada and Mexico have imposed general as well as sectoral restrictions since 1980.

CANADA

FROM ITS INCEPTION, FIRA distinguished between takeovers of established firms and business startups. Reviews of takeovers began in 1974; reviews of new startups began late in 1975. In both cases, the fundamental criterion was "significant benefit" for Canada. Little evidence was made public about how the process actually worked, and a large number of applications that were initially viewed with skepticism by FIRA were modified and successfully resubmitted. Acceptance rates varied considerably over time (Globerman, 1984). Acquisitions in manufacturing, for example, had an approval rate of only 60 percent during the first review period; during FIRA's last years approximately 90 percent of manufacturing acquisitions were approved. Investment Canada has approved 100 percent of all reviewed investments since its inception in 1985. According to Investment Canada, however, some 11 percent of all approvals through 1990 involved specified performance requirements (Husband, et al., 1991:44).

The Investment Canada regime changed several elements of the process by which foreign investments were reviewed: the threshold for direct purchase of a Canadian business was placed at C$5 million; the criterion underlying review became "net benefit to Canada"; reviews of new businesses were discontinued; and reviews of indirect acquisitions — resulting from the foreign purchase of a parent firm — were made considerably less stringent. Under the previous regime the threshold for unimpeded transfer of ownership between foreigners was found to be onerous (Safarian, 1993:126-140).

With the exception of the more tightly controlled sectors (discussed in the following sections), the Canadian posture liberalized considerably even before the FTA talks. But the Americans wanted more. At one of the early hearings convened to authorize the United States to pursue the FTA, U.S. Trade Representative Clayton Yeutter told the Senate Finance Committee that his objective was to obtain "a Canadian policy environment as open to inflows of foreign direct investment as is our own" (Raby, 1990:422). In fact, the modification of Canadian policy was far more modest than that. For U.S. investors, the screening floor for most investments was raised from C\$ 5 million to C\$ 150 million at the beginning of 1992 (indexed subsequently for inflation). The threshold for review still covers the assets of the top 600 Canadian companies; the average size of an acquired firm in 1988 was \$400 million (Raby, 1990:422).

Some performance requirements were also bargained away. Minimum equity and all direct trade-related provisions were abandoned, leaving room to bargain with entering firms about research and development, training and employment levels, technology transfer, and product mandates (Raby, 1990:424). The latter two were scrapped subsequently as part of the NAFTA's version of national treatment, although it is still permissible to phase out such restrictions over a 10-year term (Hufbauer & Schott, 1993:80).

MEXICO

MEXICAN INVESTMENT RESTRICTIONS reached their zenith immediately after the LFI of 1973 and the establishment of its administering agency, the Comisión Nacional de Inversión Extranjera (CNIE). Subsequently, many sectoral restrictions were relaxed, and the general 49 percent control over parts of the economy was waived during the presidencies of Lopez Portillo (1976-1982) and de la Madrid (1982-1988). New guidelines were issued in 1984 to promote MNE activity in certain sectors; later, screening was lifted from *maquiladoras* investments,[7] and from most investment stakes (up to 49 percent) in 1988. In May 1989 regulations and guidelines defined "classified" and "unclassified" activities. Several classified sectors continued to be excluded to foreigners or subject to screening. They were either 1) activities reserved for the state, 2) activities reserved for Mexican nationals, 3) activities subject to maximum percentage ownership shares, or 4) activities requiring CNIE approval for majority foreign ownership. In the remaining unclassified sectors (representing about two-thirds of the economy), foreign investments up to \$100 million received automatic approval and could be 100 percent foreign-owned provided certain financing, trade-balance, and locational requirements were met (Hufbauer & Schott, 1992:77).

The NAFTA extends sectoral liberalization for Mexico's North American partners while retaining various sectoral restrictions explained in the following section. Moreover, Mexico retains the right to screen acquisitions above US\$ 25 million when the NAFTA goes into effect. This will rise to an inflation-corrected US\$ 150 million in 10 years. Taken alone, this covers much less of the economy than the C\$ 150 million for Canada, not only because of the value differential between the U.S. and Canadian dollars, but also because Mexican firms are generally considerably smaller.

The NAFTA extends liberalization further by banning most performance requirements as violations of national treatment; by outlawing expropriation except for the internationally generous compensation principle long favoured by the United States; and by disallowing nationality restrictions for managers, but not for corporate board majorities (Hufbauer & Schott, 1992:80-81).

Looking at the evolution of general rule-making for Canada and Mexico, there was a clear liberalization period prior to the NAFTA following a partial movement towards national treatment of the United States by Canada under the FTA. The NAFTA comes close to national treatment over a large part of all three economies. Some sectors may be closed, but if foreign ownership from within North America is legal, most special treatment based on that fact alone is disallowed.[8]

SECTORAL RESTRICTIONS

SOME INDUSTRIES ARE CLOSED to IFDI in all countries, and the affected sectors tend to be similar in most industrial states. Partly in order to put this exploration into a broader comparative context, sectoral categories for IFDI based on OECD surveys are employed.

BANKING, FINANCE, AND INSURANCE[9]

RESTRICTIONS ON BANKING AND FINANCE are among the most universal and long-standing controls imposed on foreigners, perhaps because of widespread fear of a largely invisible threat to national well-being. Only five of the 23 countries that responded to an OECD survey in the mid-eighties (OECD, 1987) reported allowing foreigners unimpeded access. Nonetheless, in recent years most countries have used access to their domestic market as a bargaining chip in negotiating reciprocal rights elsewhere (Ryan, 1990), an indication that the pursuit of national advantage rather than security or autonomy concerns lie behind most restrictions today.

In the United States, this policy area is controlled mostly by the states (Bale, 1983:40). Nonetheless, the federal *McFadden Act* bans interstate branch banking — hence all banking requirements must be satisfied on a state-by-state basis[10] — and the *Glass-Steagall Act* largely separates commercial and investment banking, a distinction not found in Canada or, since 1990, in Mexico (Hufbauer and Schott, 1992:307).

Historically, Canadian banking regulation has combined high concentration with a determination to avoid foreign control. Prior to legislation of 1980, banks could be chartered only by an Act of Parliament. To increase competition, a new category of banks was then introduced which allowed for sole ownership by either a foreign or a domestic entity (Bartholomew, 1989:20). Nonetheless, the entrenched major banks continued to dominate the market. No more than 25 percent of the assets of a major bank could be owned abroad, and total domestic assets held by the subsidiaries of foreign banks were capped. The FTA introduced national treatment for the United States which included a maximum 10 percent share of assets of the major banks for any one owner, foreign or domestic (Safarian, 1991:70; Canadian Response, 1993:24-25).

The United States has presented few barriers to brokerage activities, and Canadian brokerage restrictions have varied over time. Ontario restrictions on foreigners were lifted in 1986, and (Canadian) federal restrictions were removed in 1988 (Schott and Smith, 1988:142-143). Insurance interpenetration between the two countries was already high before the FTA (Schott & Smith, 1988:139). Overall, the FTA considerably increased the advantages of U.S. financial firms in the Canadian market (Canadian Response, 1993:25).

In common with nearly all post-war developing countries, Mexico developed a tightly controlled banking sector. The nationalization of the Mexican banks in 1982, which was part of an attempt to deal with the international credit crisis, generated profound distrust throughout the domestic business sector, and many politicians immediately regretted it. Nonetheless, governments throughout the eighties saw political danger in reprivatization during a period of austerity and controversial market-oriented reforms. A third of the banking system was eventually privatized in 1987, however, and business confidence in the permanence of economic reform soared in May 1990, when complete privatization was announced (Lustig, 1992:25,107).

Citibank was the sole foreign bank presence in Mexico at the time of nationalization. It was untouched partly because the government did not want to remind foreign investors of the nationalizations of the 1930s.[11] Citibank's foreign monopoly continued until the signing of the NAFTA, by which time its five branches held 6 percent of total Mexican bank assets (Hufbauer & Schott, 1992:306).[12] Brokerage firm ownership before the NAFTA was limited to 10 percent by one foreign owner and 30 percent total (Hufbauer & Schott, 1992:319). Insurance participation was limited to 49 percent.

The NAFTA agreement changes access to all three markets — gradually but greatly. At present, U.S. and Canadian banks can hold up to 8 percent market share when the agreement begins; this will rise to 15 percent by 1999, with individual banks restricted to 1.5 percent of the total market capitalization. Most restrictions will then end in 2000 with some further protection.[13] In brokerage, there are parallel restrictions along with more liberal market shares.

Insurance follows a path similar to banking and brokerage with even more liberal shares and short-run growth caps that distinguish among U.S. and Canadian firms that now hold partial ownership, new joint ventures, and new wholly-owned subsidiaries. All restrictions on the NAFTA partners will end with the turn of the century (Hufbauer & Schott, 1993:6-64).

The financial sector illustrates two complications concerning investment in a free trade area. The first turns on the distinction between reciprocity and national treatment. American banking restrictions are generally more onerous than those elsewhere in the world, so reciprocity without a change in U.S. policy would tend to disadvantage U.S. banks abroad (Fry, 1991:10). The Canadians and Mexicans agreed to national treatment (by subsidiaries only) in the hope that both interstate banking and closer combinations of invest- ment and commercial banking will soon be legal in the United States. The second issue involves rules of origin, which lie at the heart of free trade agree- ments. The United States and Mexico assign nationality in banking by looking at the place (country) of incorporation — the usual international standard — while Canada insists on 50 percent ownership by nationals.

BROADCASTING AND CULTURAL INDUSTRIES

THE ORIGINAL U.S. RESTRICTIONS ON FOREIGN participation in broadcasting were aimed at protecting national security (Seitzinger, 1989). It is difficult to believe that they provide any such service today; nonetheless, no U.S. broadcast entity can be more than 20 percent directly owned by foreigners, and greater than 25 percent indirect ownership can be granted only by the Federal Communications Commission. Virtually all other developed countries combine some direct government role with some sort of discrimination in favour of national ownership of private broadcasting stations (Kudrle, 1992:17-19).

Some Canadians may consider national security to be ample reason for limiting foreign investment in broadcasting, but the national autonomy motive stands out. Today, broadcasting is protected as part of Canada's general posture toward "cultural industries", which also includes newspapers and periodicals, book publishing, printed music, film, video, and sound recording products. When Investment Canada replaced FIRA, provisions calling for the careful screening of both new businesses and acquisitions relevant to "Canada's cultural heritage or national identity" remained (Investment Canada, 1992:38). Also, foreign ownership of both broadcasting and cable are capped at 20 percent (Canadian Response, 1993:24). The Americans came to the FTA talks intending to remove or greatly modify such protection (Raby, 1990: 404), but they came away empty-handed; these industries still lie out- side the agreement.

Mexico harbours similar autonomy concerns. In its 1989 investment liberalizations, private broadcasting was reserved for Mexican nationals, and publishing and associated industries were among those for which CNIE approval had to be granted in order for foreign investors to assume a majority interest (Hufbauer & Schott, 1992:77). The NAFTA fails to remove broadcasting restrictions and limits foreign participation in cable television to minority holdings.

One aspect of the NAFTA closely related to the cultural industries has to do with the protection of intellectual property. Mexico has introduced substantial reforms that bring such protection more closely in line with

Canadian and U.S. practice. Nonetheless, disputes between the United States and Canada may loom in the future because the NAFTA (building upon the FTA exemption) fails to provide even minimum copyright protection for cultural industries (Hufbauer and Schott, 1993:86-87).

The FTA allows for cultural industry retaliation against further restrictions with "measures of equivalent commercial effect". These are grandfathered under the NAFTA, while any new Mexican restrictions can be confronted by retaliation with the "same discriminatory rules or procedures" — a potentially far more damaging response because the U.S. market is so much larger (Article 2106 and Annex 2106).[14] Important parts of the U.S. entertainment industry have never accepted Canadian cultural protection and are not pleased that similar variances have been granted to Mexico. They can be expected to voice their objections at every opportunity.

TELEPHONE AND TELECOMMUNICATIONS SERVICES[15]

HISTORICALLY, THIS SECTOR HAS OPERATED as a government monopoly in most countries; in recent years a few countries have privatized their telephone systems. The reticence of others is often based in part on the power over equipment purchasing that governments can exercise to favour domestic suppliers. The increasing interdependence of telecommunications and computer technology cannot be ignored by most countries pursuing any kind of industrial policy. This has greatly complicated telecommunications agreement in the Uruguay Round of the ongoing GATT negotiations (Roseman, 1988).

Telephone companies in the United States may be owned by foreigners, but microwave transmission, widely used in this industry, is controlled as broadcasting. Enhanced (or value-added) services are provided extensively by foreign firms (Cowhey, 1990:173).

Bell Canada was for many years controlled by AT&T, which provided the Canadian firm with hardware from Western Electric. When AT&T's interest was sold to Canadians in the late fifties, Bell Canada established Northern Telecom, its own hardware producer, which became a successful international competitor (Litvak & Maule, 1981:75-79; Dewhirst, 1983:56-57) and an important player in the U.S. market after the breakup of AT&T (Cowhey, 1990:180). Canadians accepted some enhanced U.S.-owned services before the FTA, and although basic telephone services are not covered by that agreement, enhanced services are (Annex to Chapter 14). Foreign ownership of Canadian common carriers cannot exceed 20 percent (Canadian Response, 1993:26).

Mexico's low-technology monopoly telephone system, Teléfonos de Mexico, was privatized in 1989 through the sale of a controlling 20.4 percent of its stock to a consortium including Southwestern Bell and France Telcom (up to 49 percent foreign ownership was legal at the time) with an additional 14 percent placed on the New York Stock Exchange (Hufbauer & Schott,

1992:79). The system was then opened for private competition in ancillary and enhanced services (Lustig, 1992:111). The NAFTA agreement eliminates the 49 percent maximum foreign share for most enhanced services immediately and the rest by July 1995. Although basic telecommunications are not covered by the agreement, the three countries have agreed to discuss liberalization in that segment in the future (Article 1309:2).

ENERGY PRODUCTION AND OTHER PUBLIC UTILITIES

IN MOST COUNTRIES THE OPPORTUNITY FOR foreign investment in this sector is limited by the government's role. In electricity generation, the largest single segment, the government almost always either owns facilities directly or regulates rates of return. The latter practice means that the usual motive for foreign investment through acquisition, a substantial reconfiguration of acquired assets for increased profits, must be of limited appeal.

In both the United States and Canada public and private utilities are surrounded by both national and subnational regulation. Foreign investment restrictions unconnected with natural resources persist mainly at the subnational level (hydroelectric power — an important source of energy in Canada — blurs the distinction between public utility and resource issues). The FTA affected public utilities mainly by sorting out the myriad rules on trading in electricity between the two countries (Hufbauer & Schott, 1992:201-202).

In Mexico, the Federal Commission on Electricity (CFE) was created in 1937 and became Mexico's sole producer in 1984 (Lustig, 1992:104). The NAFTA liberalizes the previous regime only by allowing firms to generate electricity for their own use. No intra-firm cross-border transmission is allowed, and all surplus must be sold to CFE (Hufbauer & Schott, 1993:35).

LAND AND NATURAL RESOURCES

ALL COUNTRIES CONTROL FOREIGN OWNERSHIP of natural resources to some extent. In the United States, foreigners are either banned altogether or subject to certain legal forms in mining, hydroelectric power, and the use of federal lands. Nuclear power facilities cannot be acquired by foreigners. Many states have additional restrictions on the ownership of real property, especially farmland (Seitzinger, 1989:18-19). Canada has somewhat similar restrictions (see for example, Safarian, 1983:15), but there are noteworthy differences with respect to energy.

In 1980 the Trudeau government introduced a National Energy Policy (NEP) that aimed to increase Canadian control of oil and gas production, nearly 70 percent of which was held by foreigners at the time. The scheme provided incentive grants to Canadian-owned firms for exploration on federal land; eligibility for these grants turned on a Canadian ownership percentage that would rise over time. The nationally owned oil company, Petro-Canada, was given a retroactive 25 percent share in the free leases that had previously been granted to others (Fry, 1983:14-15). In the years following, investment plummeted — the result of a combination of lower world energy prices, official discouragement of foreign investment, investor doubts about the future policy environment, and the investment capacity of Canadian firms, some of which became over-burdened with debt, taking over U.S. assets (Verleger, 1988:124-25).

Trade with the United States was greatly facilitated after the NEP, a program which included controlling oil and natural gas exploration and production and oil prices was scrapped in 1985. The FTA simplified energy trade, and it removed aspects of the incentive scheme that systematically discriminated on the basis of nationality of ownership. However, the requirement of 50 percent Canadian ownership for frontier activity and the policy of rejecting foreign acquisitions of healthy Canadian oil firms were retained (Raby, 1990:416; Safarian, 1991:80).

The Mexican Constitution's special concern with natural resources has profoundly affected policy. Oil and gas exploration in Mexico has been controlled by the state monopoly, PEMEX, since the foreign oil concessions were nationalized in 1938 (Lustig, 1992:104). PEMEX was completely reorganized in 1992. Nonetheless, the NAFTA allows foreigners to compete within only a small part of its activity: a selected set of basic and secondary petrochemicals. Most of the industry — from exploration through to gasoline stations — remains closed (Hufbauer & Schott, 1993:34-35).[16]

Transportation

Historically, governments have kept a sharp regulatory eye on transportation for national security reasons. The natural monopoly characteristics of early railroads provided an additional incentive.

The U.S. government controls intra-territorial water traffic very tightly in a web of controls and subsidies ostensibly related to national security. The government also restricts the foreign ownership of an airline operating within the United States to 25 percent (Seitzinger, 1989:12-17)[17] and restricts only Mexicans from the ownership of trucking firms in an obvious attempt to force liberalization of Mexican law. In Canada, air and water restrictions are similar, but the provinces play a larger role in transportation policy. Some provinces employ a "public interest test" that allows incumbent firms essentially to veto new entry. Ontario abandoned this practise in 1988.

Although the possibility of liberalizing restrictions related to water transportation was considered in the FTA talks, resistance from the U.S. maritime industry was so strong that the entire agreement was put in jeopardy (Schott, 1990:29). Hence, transportation was left out of the agreement altogether. U.S. transportation investment in Canada can thus be reviewed (where it is not explicitly prohibited) without regard to the more liberal screening otherwise accorded U.S. investment under the FTA (Fry, 1991:15; Kazanjian, 1991:89-90).

The relatively undeveloped Mexican railway system has always operated as a state monopoly, although under the NAFTA investors can build spur lines and market their services. Prior to 1989 trucking, which handles over 80 percent of all Mexican freight, was highly regulated through the control of licenses. In 1989, when entry and routes were freed, the trucking industry became quite competitive (Lustig, 1992:109). Under the NAFTA Canadian and U.S. investors are permitted to acquire 49 percent of Mexican bus and truck companies that operate internationally; this will increase to 100 percent by 2004. Purely domestic bus and truck transport will remain closed to foreigners. The agreement also liberalizes foreign investment in Mexican port facilities, but otherwise maritime activity is largely ignored. Mexico also removes the ban on foreign investment in air transport, matching the 25 percent cap long held by its partners (Hufbauer and Schott, 1993:68-70). The NAFTA advances transportation relations between Canada and the United States by including this sector in its dispute settlement provisions (Gestrin and Rugman, 1993:9).

THE AUTOMOBILE INDUSTRY

THE SHEER SIZE OF THE AUTOMOBILE INDUSTRY ensures that any regulatory change that potentially affects its location will command immediate attention.[18] In the early 1960s a dispute over Canadian auto tariffs led to the *Autopact* in which both the U.S. government and the major automakers agreed with the Canadian government that a certain amount of existing and future industry sales in Canada would involve Canadian production (for details of the agreement, see Wonnacott, 1988). In fact, the required amount of Canadian content has been greatly exceeded for many years. The FTA retained the *Autopact's* essential protections; it also introduced other adjustments which, in terms of Canadian policy, make Canada a less attractive source of North American production for non-U.S. firms.[19]

The NAFTA revised substantially the methodology used to measure North American content (previously U.S. and Canadian content) necessary to satisfy rules of origin. Minimum content requirements were also raised from 50 percent to 62.5 percent after eight years, which implies some net increase in protection. The NAFTA's major innovation, however, was to remove all Mexican trade balancing restrictions in automobiles and to allow the achievement of an essentially integrated North American market for the Big Three manufacturers (which already dominate Mexican car manufacturing and sales) by 2004. This will have a substantial effect on the structure of IFDI among the three states, and North America may emerge as the world's low cost auto producer (Hufbauer & Schott, 1993:37-43).

OTHER REGULATORY ISSUES

SOME FORMS OF REGULATION ARISE necessarily from the simple fact that foreign direct investors are *foreigners*; tax policy is among these. Two major tax differences can distort investment decisions away from the underlying productivity of capital worldwide: different effective corporate tax rates among countries — which is not a major issue among the three countries of North America — and the special tax treatment of foreign earnings by home and host countries.

The FTA did not deal with MNE taxes between the United States and Canada because a satisfactory tax treaty already existed between them, although the reciprocal withholding tax rates on royalties, interest and dividends are higher than agreed rates in most U.S. treaties with other industrial countries (Hufbauer & Schott, 1992:89). Mexico, generally, had much higher withholding tax rates; a bilateral treaty with the United States of September 1992 reduced these to 10 percent on portfolio dividends (after five years), 5 percent on IFDI dividends, and 10 percent on royalties. An earlier Canada-Mexico tax treaty established generally comparable reductions (Hufbauer & Schott, 1992:89). This policy change may be very important for Mexico because tax experts believe that Mexican IFDI is quite sensitive to tax levels (Ugarte, 1991; Shah & Slemrod, 1991).

The increasing investment integration of the North American economy that NAFTA is meant to facilitate will necessarily lead to increased conflicts over appropriate prices for international intra-firm transactions ("transfer prices") (see Vernon, this volume). One or more of three innovations could ease the ensuing difficulties: 1) the NAFTA partners could evolve a formula to allocate liability based on a weighting system derived from the international distribution of sales, payroll and assets (as practised by most of the American states) to be used exclusively by, or when elected by, a firm; 2) national tax authorities could co-operate on advance pricing agreements (APAs) to cover transfer price practices for individual firms; or 3) special arbitration procedures could be established to resolve disagreements between authorities as is the practice in the EC (for a discussion of these ideas in a global context, see Hufbauer, 1992:149-151).

The NAFTA assures unrestricted capital movements and profit remittances. Also, the scope of the NAFTA applies to a much broader range of investments than simply those involving "control"— the main criterion of the FTA. Curiously, however, the NAFTA does not recognize networks among independent producers, perhaps the fastest growing category of international connection (Gestrin & Rugman, 1993:3).[20]

The FTA grandfathered discriminatory legislation that the agreement did not explicitly modify, including laws at the state and provincial levels. The NAFTA takes an alternative approach: all laws that fail to conform to national treatment must be enumerated in one of the annexes. Subnational governments generally have two years to file. Nothing was done, however, to override existing subnational prerogatives.[21] In the U.S. case, this leaves as a possible entry barrier the anti-takeover legislation now in place in 42 states (Husband, et al., 1991:41). In Canada, interprovincial barriers have made trade among them even less free than within the European Community and may be costing the country 1 percent of national income. Such barriers deter MNE activity by balkanizing the national market in many sectors, particularly in those sectors dependent upon discriminatory government procurement (*International Trade Reporter*, 1991:1469).

The NAFTA does not apply to restrictions on foreign investment for national security reasons. This leaves the United States free to apply the Exon-Florio Amendment to the *Trade Act* of 1988, which allows the President to deny a foreign acquisition on "national security" grounds without appeal. The Bush Administration exercised its authority sparingly (for a review through mid-1991, see Liebeler, 1991:53-55), and no Canadian or Mexican firm yet appears to have been so disadvantaged. Moreover, Canada and Mexico are considering parallel surveillance which could employ their existing screening agencies and provide them with a mandate to consider security issues in all acquisitions irrespective of size (see Frost & Graham, this volume).

Another form of discrimination against foreign investors practised by the United States is embodied in Sematech, the semiconductor research and development consortium. Antitrust exemption and Department of Defense (DOD) subsidies have been given to support the R&D efforts of the consortium, which bars subsidiaries of foreign firms (Graham & Krugman, 1991:150). Some commentators (Gestrin & Rugman, 1993; Rugman & Gestrin, 1993) have expressed concern that the NAFTA does nothing to prevent increased discrimination of this kind.

DISPUTE RESOLUTION

IFDI DISPUTES IN NORTH AMERICA have seriously affected relations among the three countries over several decades. The nationalization of the Mexican oil industry in 1938 soured relations with the United States for many years thereafter, and the United States successfully attacked Canadian import substitution elements of FIRA performance requirements in the GATT (Leyton-Brown, 1985).

The FTA treated investment disputes under a broad mechanism called "Institutional Provisions" within which one country notified the other of any measure affecting the other's interest, and consultation followed. If the dispute could not be resolved, it was referred to the Canada-U.S. Trade Commission composed of high-ranking officials from each country. The Commission, which operated by consensus, then chose either binding arbitration or advice from a panel of selected experts. The former course rendered a decision which, if not followed, could result in retaliation by the offended country; the latter course, although more complex, could lead to essentially the same outcome (Schott and Smith, 1988:66-67).

The NAFTA takes an even bolder approach to investment disputes by allowing panels to render decisions under rules established by the International Center for the Settlement of Investment Disputes of the World

Bank, or the United Nations Commission on International Trade Law. Binding opinions can be brought to courts of a NAFTA country for enforcement (Articles 1120-1136).

EVALUATION

THE THREE COUNTRIES SHARING the North American continent have pursued policies to cement trade and investment links that would have seemed almost impossible in 1980. This convergence has been based on a profound change in the fundamental economic strategies of the two smaller players. Canada's approach to the United States with the FTA aimed essentially at escaping U.S. administered protection, but a basic revision of Canadian thinking on MNEs and IFDI had already taken place. Generally, those in charge of Canadian policy had concluded that a small developed country, however successful it may have been in the past, could not maintain growing prosperity without embracing market-driven interdependence; the intermittent use of government power to dampen market forces slowed growth. Canada was not alone. The studies of the Macdonald Commission, dealing with the internal workings of the Canadian economy and its external connections, paralleled similar evaluations and conclusions concerning the relative role of markets and government action undertaken by other OECD countries during the 1980s. Canada's rethinking in many ways resembles that of other small, rich countries such as Australia, New Zealand and Sweden. This new perspective was, in turn, part of a broader preoccupation with markets that dominated the attention of policy makers in the richer countries during this period.

Mexico's policy shift was far more dramatic than Canada's. Until the reforms of the 1980s, Mexican policy epitomized comprehensive state discretion supposedly aimed at development. The debt crisis narrowed the range of national possibilities so severely that liberalization and increased openness could be sold even to very skeptical members of the country's political and economic elite. Initially, this strategy was both risky and discouraging for many of its proponents. Mexico could find something of a model in post-Allende Chile, but this merely highlights the political complexities of the new departure. Moreover, it must be remembered that *sustained* Mexican per capita growth did not actually begin until 1989 — several years after the succession of policy changes began. In fact, uncertainty about the permanence of Mexican policy changes continued to be an issue during most of the 1980s, and much liberalization was accomplished by decree rather than through formal revision of the law. In this environment, the willingness of Mexico to conclude a treaty commitment like the NAFTA became particularly important as grounds for business confidence. More IFDI entered Mexico in the three years after the NAFTA negotiations were announced than had been invested over the previous 20 years (*Wall Street Journal*, 1993b).

Many economic commentators — while full of praise for most of the content of the NAFTA — are unhappy about the time period over which the major Mexican reforms are to be introduced. They are well aware that the present value of $1 in ten years, discounted at 5 percent, is only $0.61. They should also keep in mind that only ten years ago Mexico was still in the grip of semi-autarky.

THE INCOMPLETE COMMUNITY

CHANGES IN BOTH the Canadian and Mexican postures towards MNEs were part of a general rethinking about state policy towards prosperity. Recent theoretical developments in trade theory do not overturn the presumption that states — especially small ones — achieve maximum prosperity through trade based on market-driven comparative advantage. IFDI can be favoured both as the handmaiden of trade (Graham & Krugman, 1992:57-59) and as a package of resources to augment the productivity of the recipient workforce (Reich, 1992). Any national location will be attractive to the MNE, other things equal, as long as production from that location can reach the largest possible market.

Although the search for prosperity drove Canadian and Mexican policy reforms, economists sometimes ignore or minimize other goals. Officials charged with advancing national welfare through foreign policy must also consider the security of the state and its autonomy. These goals too must underlie IFDI policy.

SECURITY

THE TERM 'NATIONAL SECURITY', as used here, refers strictly to the physical defense of a national territory.[22] Canada and the United States identified the same major national security threats over most of the post-war period and have worked together effectively to face them; this common enterprise has taken the form of both strategic alignments and production cooperation (Legault, 1985). Between Canada and the United States few barriers to MNE activity — now or earlier in the post-war period — can plausibly be based on immediate security concerns in either country. Nonetheless, effective policy tools are in place in both countries: assets can be commandeered in times of emergency, and well-tested techniques can be applied to protect both states against espionage (for an extended discussion of contingencies, see Bobrow & Kudrle, 1991).

Technologically sophisticated activity on national territory may build defense-relevant competence.[23] This line of reasoning has led some U.S. commentators to recommend that the U.S. government require onshore production by some foreign defense suppliers (Graham & Krugman, 1992:149-155). But whatever the wisdom of this prescription may be for the United Sates, Canada's security cannot plausibly rest on its own autonomous, comprehensive technological superiority. Most Canadian defense objectives can be achieved in the post-Cold War world by using the same basic strategy that has always proved satisfactory in the past: co-operation with allies — particularly the United States — while seeking legitimate special treatment as a U.S. defense supplier.

Historically, the security situation in Mexico has been very different from that of its NAFTA partners. Mexico's overall foreign policy changed dramatically during the eighties. Whereas it was once a leading voice for a rhetorically unified Third World, it now pursues a new path — abandoning a cause that scarcely still exists. Mexico's principal security concern is not global but regional — notably the potential threat from the unstable neighbours to the south, and Guatemala in particular (Weintraub, 1990:37). Despite these considerations it is difficult to make a case for substantial restriction of IFDI on grounds of national security.

AUTONOMY

IF THE USUAL NATIONAL SECURITY arguments for controlling foreign invest-ment lack credibility in all three countries, autonomy must necessarily remain a continuing concern for both Canada and Mexico. Autonomy, as used in this study, means being *maître chez nous*.[24] That goal can be considered in two dimensions: autonomy of action and autonomy of thought. For two countries that are similar in so many ways, the United States and Canada stand virtually at opposite ends of the autonomy spectrum in both dimensions,[25] and Mexico shares many of Canada's concerns.[26]

Autonomy of national action has been reduced simply as a consequence of general interdependence. For example, the efficacy of national macroeconomic policy has diminished everywhere, but the change for smaller countries came earlier and was more forceful than was the case for larger ones. One of the motives underlying Canadian and Mexican economic nationalism in trade and investment policy has stemmed from a resistance to this loss of autonomy. The recent changes in policy, however, have grown out of the recognition that such nationalism was exacting a high prosperity price for only little autonomy gain.

Autonomy of thought can be threatened by the international transmission of foreign tastes and values, and policies may be devised to resist it. Canada attempts to meet this challenge by controlling not only MNE activity but also the content of broadcasting (for a critical discussion, see Acheson, Maule & Filleul, 1989). These measures are augmented by an extensive subsidy system in support of domestic cultural and artistic production. Canada controls the mix of foreign and domestic cultural products on the basis of the nationality of producers rather than the content of the product. This approach is also reflected in Mexico's policy on broadcasting in the NAFTA. In addition to requiring domestic ownership, a majority of those producing and performing in live broadcasts must be Mexicans.[27]

Cultural protection can make good theoretical sense (mutual citizen coercion to produce a public good), but its manifestation through policy often smacks of the triumph of producing interests in rejecting more efficient and effective policy. Moreover, even when national culture is being "protected" by direct subsidization on the basis of content and the development of artistic competence, it faces an increasingly difficult challenge. The manipulation of money prices can promote approved consumption only so far; most cultural products take time and require attention to consume. Public opinion probably will not support severe restrictions on foreign products (such as banning foreign satellite programs or sharply restricted cable offerings) in favour of domestic substitutes. Therefore, even if the population enthusiastically subsidizes local output, its willingness to absorb that output tends to be quite limited.

Another policy pattern related to autonomy (often seen as somehow serving prosperity or security) is the reaction of both Canadians and Mexicans to foreign investment in natural resources. Foreign ownership restrictions on oil and gas are contained in both the FTA and the NAFTA. Canadian federal authorities defended the introduction of the National Energy Policy (NEP) in 1980 by arguing that no other developed country allowed such extensive owner-ship of "crucial non-renewable energy resources" (Fry, 1983:14). This is more of an emotional appeal than a solid argument — as is the passage in the Mexican constitution declaring that, with respect to natural resources, "the ownership of the Nation is inalienable and imprescriptible". In fact, foreign ownership of Mexican natural resources is not a closed issue; a glaring exception is the provi-sion within the NAFTA allowing for 100 percent foreign ownership of new coal mines (Hufbauer & Schott, 1993:36).[28]

A strong case can be made that foreign exploitation of natural resources can be more easily monitored, with most significant effects measured and evaluated, than perhaps any other kind of IFDI. Considering the sophistication of the domestic regulatory mechanisms in both Canada and Mexico, a scenario in which a foreign business enterprise can somehow work against the host nation's interests — undetected and undeterred — is difficult to confect and even more difficult to believe. On the other side of the argument stands the undeveloped energy production potential of both countries, which some ana-lysts contend can only be realized with unrestricted foreign equity (Verleger, 1988:123-127; Hufbauer & Schott, 1993:34-35).

Unlike the case of the cultural industries, where the goal can be cogently stated despite suspect means, the restriction of foreign investment in energy and other natural resources seems to have only an emotional connection with any national goals.

The failure of the NAFTA to liberalize the energy sector substantially may be its most glaring failure with respect to the MNE. Less important restrictions remain in many sectors, however, and few of them can be claimed to serve clear national goals effectively. Overall — even ignoring the Autopact — more than a quarter of each economy remains subject to some form of nationalistic IFDI discrimination (for rough calculations, see Kudrle, 1992); the most prevalent is in Mexico, the least in the United States. This suggests a need for considerably more policy adjustment before North America can claim to be a true investment community.

THREE DIMENSIONS OF MNE POLICY

LOOKING AT THE EXPERIENCE OF ALL THE COUNTRIES since 1980, three topics deserve special consideration: openness, discrimination, and asymmetry.

Openness

Only the United States has not significantly liberalized its IFDI regime. Of course the United States was already very open in 1980 and it had very little left to liberalize, especially at the federal level. Moreover, despite fears about the future abuse of Exon-Florio, its actual employment since 1988 has been very sparing. In Canada, there has been considerable nominal liberalization, although it remains unclear how significant screening under the FIRA or Investment Canada has ever been in most sectors. In Mexico, the liberalization has been dramatic and substantial, with much of it taking place several years before the NAFTA. Nonetheless, even after the full implementation of that agreement, Mexico will still protect much more of its economy than will Canada or the United States.

Discrimination

What of discrimination? The usual Vinerian distinction between "creation" and "diversion" cannot easily be applied to investment independent of trade. A set of new investment opportunities in one place does not necessarily reduce the amount of investment available elsewhere because of the MNE's exploitation of public goods internal to the firm. In practice, however, most MNE activity involves not just factor flows but identifiable trade flows as well.

The FTA and the NAFTA certainly discriminate on matters affecting MNEs. For example, during 1992 only U.S. investors faced the higher floor imposed by Investment Canada review. But Investment Canada's well-publicized 100 percent approval rate suggests a receptiveness not limited to the United States. The major discrimination probably lies in the greater opportunity for bilateral bargaining that Canada retains with non-U.S. investors. It must be remembered, however, that under a free trade agreement relations with non-member countries reside with each member. If Canada chooses unilaterally to extend the C$ 150 million floor to all foreign investors, the United States would have no recourse.[29]

The Mexican case is also instructive. The NAFTA gives discriminatory access to North American investors in a range of industries. But the 1989 IFDI liberalization shows the overall direction of Mexican policy, and sources close to the Mexican government report that many recent liberal practices will soon be codified in a new law. Increased foreign investment (including portfolio investment) constitutes a major Mexican objective and further unilateral liberalization can be expected. Mexico intends the NAFTA to signal a permanent change in policy for *all* foreign MNEs, not just for those from its NAFTA partners. Indeed, those NAFTA partners have been vigilant in their attempts to ensure that other foreign investors in Mexico are not allowed excessively generous access to their own domestic markets.

During the 1980s, the United States blocked a number of legislative attempts to deny foreign investment access to countries allegedly providing insufficient reciprocal benefit — most notably Japan. If there are future U.S. restrictions on IFDI, however, whether at the state or the federal level, most will affect countries outside North America while leaving Canadian and Mexican investors exempt.

Two provisions of the NAFTA apply specifically to all investors and not just to those from partner countries. The United States, Canada and Mexico have pledged (without specifics or remedies) not to encourage environmentally questionable investments from anywhere (Article 1114 and 1101.c). Also, performance requirements may not be applied to "non-Party" investors (Article 1106).[30] If this were not the case, one could imagine essentially competitive bids for an investment niche in a NAFTA country in which the host might be able to strike a more favourable bargain with a "non-Party" investor. Most NAFTA provisions apply to firms owned outside North America so long as they maintain "substantial business activities" in the territory of the country from which the intra-North American expansion takes place (Article 1113.2).

Asymmetry

Finally, the history of North American policy toward MNEs and IFDI since 1980 demonstrates enduring asymmetry. Under the FTA the Americans accepted Canadian protection of their cultural industries and some energy discrimination; under the NAFTA both Canada and the United States accepted Mexican restrictions that are far more extensive than their own practices. This is not surprising. Bargaining across trade and investment issues allowed by comprehensive agreements invites sectoral asymmetry.

PROSPECTS FOR FURTHER LIBERALIZATION

UNILATERAL LIBERALIZATION

SEVERAL DEVELOPMENTS MAY GENERATE further North American IFDI liberalization beyond that already achieved through the NAFTA negotiations. Mexico may act unilaterally to liberalize further a number of sectors simply to increase the flow of capital and associated inputs into the economy as a whole. In the United States and Canada, however, additional liberalization will turn on more specific circumstances in certain industries.

Trade liberalization, without reciprocity or broader bargaining has, historically, rested on two forces: "objective" studies of national losses resulting from protection that tend to orient relatively disinterested elite opinion towards greater openness, and political pressure from those who stand to make substantial gains from greater import availability. Both forces are muted in the case of IFDI. The case for an increase in national income based on specific infusion of capital, management and technology is frequently difficult to make persuasive, and domestic gainers from IFDI permissiveness may lack determination because of uncertainty about outcomes. Nonetheless, at least four circumstances can lead to unilateral liberalization.

First, where an industry clearly falls short of its international potential in generating national income, unilateral liberalization may be undertaken. Such an occurrence appears to have motivated the recent Canadian removal of the ban on foreign acquisition of healthy energy firms and a legislative initiative to remove the 50 percent Canadian ownership requirement for oil and gas production licenses in frontier areas (Investment Canada, 1992:38). Similar developments and motivations may yet generate a softening of the Mexican position on IFDI in the core of its energy industries.

Second, unilateral liberalization might arise from circumstances analogous to the "failing firm" defense for an otherwise impermissible takeover under competition policy. If a troubled firm in a controlled sector cannot obtain resources from the domestic market, the government faces the choice of putting up public funds, allowing foreign participation, or presiding over wasting assets and unemployment. If, for example, Air Canada's new relationship with Continental does not restore the firm's fortunes, such a situation might develop. Earlier discussions with American Airlines generated unsuccessful pressure for increasing the allowed foreign ceiling to 49 percent. In the United States, the lack of adequate capital for U.S. Air triggered permission for British Air to take a 49 percent share under a discretionary provision previously granted to the Transportation Secretary.

Third, unhappy customers can also generate pressure for liberalization. Dramatic data on the difference in cost and availability of telecommunications services between the United States and Canada has produced pressure in Canada somewhat akin to the groundswell that cost Teléfonos de Mexico its monopoly (Taylor, 1990:18-19). An attempt to develop a competitive national telecom network in Canada out of a set of poorly integrated local and regional monopolies will almost certainly be designed to maximize the role of Canadian-owned firms, but it may well permit greater U.S. participation as well.

Finally, parts of the domestic industry may rebel against the regulatory regime. Considerable evidence suggests that the essentially populist regulation of the United States has prevented some banks from growing to sufficient size to compete effectively in the international market, and all banks from performing highly profitable intermediary functions (Ryan, 1990).

Accumulating evidence spells the probable demise of both kinds of restriction — a development which Canadian banks in particular are in a legal and strategic position to exploit.

CO-OPERATIVE LIBERALIZATION

LIBERALIZATION IN THE TERMS just discussed holds obvious implications for bargaining among the three partners in the NAFTA and with others. Partners should grant small concessions where recognized domestic welfare for the liberalizing party looms large and domestic opposition is slight. On the other hand, liberalization is far less likely in sectors where the political price of change is high while the economic stakes are modest. Some state and provincial regulations fall into this category. Restrictions on agricultural land ownership, for example, while internationally offensive, cause little economic damage. Anti-takeover legislation must be treated more seriously, however. Foreign observers note with dismay the inconsistency between American attacks on performance requirements and other barriers to MNE entry in international forums and the proliferation of similar practices at the state level.[31]

A careful look at the competitive impact of subnational restrictions will inevitably be needed as the United States and Canada attempt to co-ordinate and perhaps ultimately integrate their competition policies, a development (with Mexico) envisioned in NAFTA Article 1504. The political difficulties involved in fighting subnational governments while doing battle with powerful commercial interests may explain why the FTA and the NAFTA have accomplished so little in these areas and so much remains to be done.[32]

Early efforts to co-ordinate competition policy focused on the integration of antidumping action with competition policy (Feltham, et al., 1991; Graham & Warner, this volume). This laudable ambition, however, must be contrasted with the failure of the NAFTA to move significantly beyond the FTA's implicit hope that dumping disputes will be subject to new GATT constraints. Current uncertainty holds potential importance for investment. To the extent that the United States is seen by its NAFTA partners as employing antidumping tactics on firms operating from its territory as a means of attracting investment to the United States — a device frequently used in the EC against Asian firms (English and Smith, 1993:177; Tyson, 1992:248-249) — serious new disputes could arise. Generally, the NAFTA partners should view with concern the advice of some analysts that the United States should manipulate policy to increase onshore MNE activity substantially (Gaster, 1992). Some U.S. gains might come at their expense. This possibility adds urgency to Canada's concern that the FTA's apparent promise to clarify administered protection seems to have dissolved. Canadian fears of cultural domination and concerns in the United States over national security pose special challenges to some aspects of investment liberalization.

The problem of the Canadian cultural industries cannot be treated as a single entity. Those restrictions least related to cultural identity and artistic competence — such as product distribution — will continue to be under great pressure, both within and outside Canada. Other policy modifications related to cultural industries are also likely to stem from technical change, which will reduce the value of certain kinds of discrimination and make them easier to bargain away.[33]

Despite the moderation in its use so far, Exon-Florio remains an unacceptably loose cannon that damages U.S. and foreign welfare by contributing to business uncertainty. America's NAFTA partners (and other countries) should face potential restrictions on MNE activity explicitly confined to national security, and their own use of controls on national security grounds should be similarly confined. Canadian and Mexican firms should be included in all U.S.-sanctioned industry consortia that receive R&D subsidy or antitrust exemption unless a security problem can be demonstrated, provided they accord U.S. firms the same treatment. Remaining discrimination can be reduced if sufficient agreement is obtained on security-related trade and investment controls in all three countries (See Graham & Warner, this volume).

NORTH AMERICAN MNE REGULATION IN A GLOBAL CONTEXT

THE NAFTA IS BEING CLOSELY WATCHED from abroad for its possible negative impact on outsiders just as the FTA was in earlier years. Overall, the agreement appears to be more consistent with the GATT than most regional agreements and promises economic gains for most other countries because of trade increases generated by higher North American income. In the investment area, the most serious diversion between the region and the rest of the world may come from the revised rules of origin for automobiles. Generally, non-North Americans need have really serious concerns about either trade or investment diversion only if the Uruguay Round collapses and the ensuing confusion generates strong protectionist pressures in the United States.

The basic posture of the Bush Administration's Initiative for the Americas and the nominal openness signaled by the NAFTA's accession provisions strike the right chord in a global economy uncertain about whether regional liberalization substitutes for or complements multilateralism. The long-run security, autonomy and prosperity goals of all three NAFTA countries point to a need for the continuous development of their collective regionalism as a building block rather than as a juggernaut.[34] Specifically, Canada and Mexico should exercise their influence to keep U.S. pressure on Europe and the Pacific to maintain and extend openness while stressing the receptiveness of the NAFTA to new trade and investment partners. With special regard to investment, Europe should be encouraged to moderate and make transparent all efforts to lure MNE activity (Gaster, 1992), while Japan's public efforts to encourage the entry and growth of foreign MNEs (Bergsten & Noland, 1993:79-82) should be carefully monitored and pressure maintained against Japan's public and private practices that restrict foreign participation to the detriment of Japanese consumers.

In making the case for more explicit attention to investment in multilateral discussions, the United Nations (1992:267-280) recently made much of Investment Related Trade Measures (IRTMs) — policy-induced changes in trade that inadvertently affect investment. These are distinguished from Trade Related Investment Measures (TRIMs) with their GATT-relevant effects on trade in goods. The United Nations should probably distinguish the most potentially divisive category of all (at least among developed countries) — TRIMs — that aim to entice certain activity to a country's territory, frequently in an attempt to capture rents and externalities promised by high-technology research and development, and fabrication. These measures differ from IRTMs in that the diverted investment is scarcely unintended, but they also differ from traditional TRIMs because they frequently shape future, rather than existing, trade and because of their sharply limited-sum character. Fundamental development in many industries will likely take place in only a few firms, and if such activity is lured internationally from one country to another, a significant loss or gain may be perceived by both.

If the United States were to follow some European practice and abandon its posture that only U.S. firms can participate in such consortia as Sematech, it could open the game to firms of all nationalities meeting certain local R&D and manufacturing qualifications, or it could especially favour Canada and Mexico. If it chooses the former, it may be accused of enticement; if it chooses the latter, discrimination. This is an area of MNE policy greatly in need of more international agreement and co-operation. In this as in other areas, Canada and Mexico have an important interest in encouraging a generally liberal and internationally co-operative United States, one that sets as few unilateral rules as possible. However much the United States fails to discriminate against them, if a posture of "Fortress North America" develops, Canada and Mexico will find themselves where they do not want to be: very junior partners in an international "industrial policy" that limits their autonomy for illusory prosperity gains.[35]

If the NAFTA partners, particularly the United States, which accounts for 88 percent of current North American production, follows a generally liberal path, the agreement may provide considerable global impetus for increased liberalization on investment-related matters. Three major areas of the Uruguay Round that closely affect investment are: the General Agreement on Services, the discussions on Trade-Related Investment Measures (TRIMs), and the Trade Related Intellectual Property (TRIPs). Talks related to these areas will, at best, initiate processes that will strengthen gradually over the years ahead (United Nations, 1992:66-75). Similarly, the draft Decision on TRIMs promises a possible future consideration of competition issues; the NAFTA is likely to make substantial progress first. In each of these areas, as well as with the strengthened dispute resolution mechanisms that build on FTA experience and success, the NAFTA moves forward in ways that will be carefully watched by those concerned with MNE and IFDI policy everywhere.

The NAFTA's role as a general model for broader MNE-led integration should not be exaggerated. For example, except by ensuring that the parties adhere to their own laws, the NAFTA does not progress on the "unfair trade" front. Indeed, commentators have noted that the Dunkel restrictions on subnational subsidies broach territory that the NAFTA avoids (English & Smith, 1993:177). Generally, Ostry (1992) identifies several post-Uruguay "system friction" issues: competition policy, R&D policies, foreign direct investment policy, and the corporate governance elements of financial market regulation. The development of the NAFTA will only be relevant to some issues. Because Mexico is essentially converging to U.S. and Canadian practice, the approaches of those two countries matter most, and they are typically similar by international standards. Competition policy norms and procedures are similar, as are intellectual property rights and the institutional structure that generates innovation. Unprecedented similarities in foreign investment policy have comparable economic meaning because of the similar structures of the two economies. Some corporate control issues remain outstanding, but they constitute only moderate entry barriers at most. Overall, many issues of intra-Triad relations will be given little guidance by North American integration — even over the longer term.

Both the NAFTA's processes of cooperation and its tangible economic results will be watched with special care by the developing countries. The FTA presented a bold new idea of enormous importance: relatively "deep" economic integration by two countries of greatly differing size with a minimum of political spillover. Mexican liberalization culminating in the NAFTA added an even more challenging element: a high level of economic integration between two cooperating rich countries with quite similar income levels, political cultures and legal systems, and a poorer country grounded in very different traditions. Mexico was therefore obliged to make many substantial adjustments in law and practice to achieve congruence with its partners. If Mexico enjoys great economic success under the NAFTA, along with some social and political progress, the reservations about greater agreed liberalization expressed by many developing countries during the Uruguay Round will soften in future negotiations.

IMMEDIATE PROSPECTS

THIS STUDY HAS ASSUMED the NAFTA to be a reality. In fact, its prospects vary almost daily. Although the Mexican government remains solidly committed, there are limits to how far it can go to accommodate the labour and environmental concerns raised by the Clinton administration. Difficult negotiations will continue over how much power the special trilateral commissions monitoring these issues will be given, but if the monitoring groups appear to be largely window dressing, the agreement may fail to pass Congress (*Wall Street Journal*, 1993a:A1). In Canada, concern is regularly expressed not only about possible threats to sovereignty posed by the commissions but also about the underlying agreement itself, and, indeed, both the FTA and the NAFTA are now opposed by a solid majority of the population (*Business Week*, 1992:59). More broadly, Canadians are concerned about the ultimate cohesion of their country and the cloudy economic prospects generated by doubts about that cohesion.[36]

Even if the NAFTA successfully navigates the ratification processes in all three countries, serious disputes or even withdrawal from the agreement (which formally requires only six months' notice) cannot be ignored. Opposition on MNE and IFDI grounds could come from several quarters. U.S. disagreements with Canada over some issues — perhaps in the cultural or auto industries — could bring down that part of the bargain, while high levels of MNE penetration into Mexico could generate irresistible political pressure to control it (see Vernon, this volume), particularly if overall income growth flags.

In the United States domestic politics remains an unpredictable source of breakdown because of the porous nature of the American political system and volatile attitudes Americans have toward their trading partners. While MNE activity from Canada and Mexico seems unlikely to be especially controversial, the U.S. preoccupation with "unfairness" and "foreign control" will continue to complicate relations within North America at the same time as it poses a fundamental threat to a number of extra-regional relationships — especially those with Japan and the European Community.

Recent U.S. legislative proposals connected with MNEs capture some of the flavour of contemporary unease. Among other possible modifications of U.S. law, the last two Congresses have considered bills designed to extend Exon-Florio to "economic security"; to narrow foreign political activity by disallowing Political Action Committees (PACs) formed by the U.S. employees of majority foreign-owned subsidiaries; to magnify the negative publicity given to lobbyists for foreigners by broadening the definition of those who must register; to increase the level of detail and decrease the confidentiality of foreign subsidiary data reporting requirements; to insist on greater general investment reciprocity or reciprocity in specific sectors (particularly telecommunications and financial services); to place additional barriers to foreigners in regulated industries (such as cable television); to disallow foreign-owned firms from antitrust exemptions for research and development; and to base taxes owed by foreign subsidiaries on benchmarks unrelated to their own performance (Fry, 1991:14-18; Liebeler, 1991:51-60; Graham & Krugman, 1991:141-155).

Some of these legislative forays have internal political or international strategic purposes that are quite unrelated to their enactment, but some are truly intended for passage and are widely supported. The past few years have seen the current U.S. Vice-President, Al Gore, labour as a senator to broaden Exon-Florio and the current Secretary of the Treasury, Lloyd Bentsen, lead senatorial attempts to restrict PACs of foreign subsidiaries. Ross Perot speaks routinely about "the thousands of foreign lobbyists who run Washington". And the fears are not solely focused on the Japanese. One of the most notable influence-peddling episodes of the Reagan administration involved work for Canadian interests. Massive Mexican lobbying for the NAFTA in Washington has been widely cited by the agreement's opponents.

When the present volatile U.S attitudes towards MNEs and IFDI are considered along with deep-seated concerns in Mexico and Canada of much longer standing, unpredictable political pressures may lead to illiberal policy shifts toward closure and control. MNE activity — even within the Continent — will remain an important political issue in all three North American countries well into the twenty-first century. The rational pursuit of national welfare by the three countries dictates the further development of an investment community, but all timetables are nonetheless subject to serious revision.

ENDNOTES

1 MNEs and IFDI are strongly linked, but they are obviously not the same thing. Two distinctions stand out. While most direct investment is made through business enterprises, it clearly need not be. Much land investment, for example, is made by unincorporated individuals. Second, while MNEs bring much more than capital to a new market, they frequently bring very little capital — much of the capital they control in the host market is raised locally. Logically, at least five major sets of policies determine MNE activity and IFDI flows over a significant period of time. First, policies aimed directly at MNE activity or requiring domestic production may obviously increase or decrease total activity. Second, policies may encourage or discourage the amount of direct investment capital employed by a host-country's foreign-owned firms, thus altering the relation between MNE activity and IFDI. Third, policies affecting international trade may be even more important, given the intimate connection between IFDI and trade (over 70 percent of trade across the U.S.-Canadian border, for example, takes place within MNEs, and changes in trade flows obviously affect the IFDI associated with them). A fourth set of policies aimed at increasing investment in particular regions or industries — regardless of the nationality of that investment — may also increase IFDI. Finally, changes in the relative attractiveness of a certain national market as a host for IFDI often results from general economic policy changes, especially those related to growth prospects (Weintraub: 1990:101).

2 Analysts believe that had Mexico merely eased restrictions on foreign ownership, the flows would have been much lower. The liberalization was necessary, but not sufficient, for much of the increase.

3 Chris Wilkie stressed the importance of this point to me in a private conversation.

4 The normative judgment that North Americans would benefit from a more developed investment community does not ignore the fact that market-induced shifts in investment may sometimes fail to pass a social cost-benefit test. The issue is merely whether controlling investment across national borders typically makes more sense than controlling it across state or provincial borders: i.e., what role should nationalism *per se* play in investment policy?

5 The Commission was supported by the work of many distinguished Canadian economists, most of whom had long been skeptical of protection and many other forms of state intervention. Canadians might therefore have been less surprised than they were by the endorsement of free trade with the United States by 11 of the 12 Commissioners at the conclusion of their study (Lipsey, 1986).

6 Canada joined the U.S.-Mexico discussions to gain maximum benefit from the FTA with the United States. If the two smaller countries had free

trade with the United States but not with each other, firms interested in all three markets would tend to concentrate activity at the "hub" at the expense of the "spokes".

7 *Maquiladoras* started in 1965 as firms in Mexican border zones where goods in bond could be transformed (usually just assembled) with duties into the United States payable only on the value-added (Weintraub, 1990:156-164). The scheme was extended to other parts of Mexico.

8 In fact, the rule is the more generous of national or most-favoured-nation treatment (External Affairs, 1993:62). The superiority of this standard — long established in U.S. bilateral treaties — to the simpler criterion of national treatment is subject to dispute (Bergsten and Graham, 1990:54). An example of the difference is provided by Japan's especially favorable tax treatment of foreign subsidiaries — a policy compensation for decades of exclusion (Bergsten and Noland, 1993:81).

9 These discussions, although they contain some detail, do not pretend to be complete. In particular, many of the general statements in the text admit to exceptions.

10 The 1978 *International Banking Act* removed an advantage from foreign entrants by obliging them to follow domestic restrictions on interstate banking (Graham and Krugman, 1992:145).

11 Citibank performed an important function in the Mexican economy as custodian of foreign holdings in the Mexican stock market.

12 At that time 138 foreign banks were represented in Mexico, only four of which were Canadian (Hufbauer and Schott, 1992:307).

13 If foreign banks secure more than 25 percent of the total market by the end of 2004, a three-year moratorium can be declared. Remaining restrictions would limit mergers that would increase market share above 4 percent, thus insulating the largest Mexican banks from takeovers.

14 I am grateful to Michael Gestrin for pointing out this asymmetry.

15 In the OECD data, this category includes postal services because in most countries the telephone system is an offshoot of the postal monopoly.

16 Foreigners cannot operate FCC-licensed microwave common carriers (which are controlled as broadcasting stations) without special permission.

17 Much of Mexico's agricultural land is operated by *ejidatarios* who do not have ownership. Nothing suggested a greater or more permanent change in national policy than the 1991 revision of the constitution envisioning the privatization of such land (Lustig, 1992:145), but there is no provision for foreign ownership.

18 The U.S. Secretary of Transportation is authorized to allow ownership up to 49 percent in the national interest. This discretion has recently been exercised in the British Air/U.S. Air arrangement. It may be undone if the United Kingdom fails to move quickly toward more "open skies".

19 This is not a sector tracked in the OECD data, although it commands government attention and often intervention in many countries.

20 Among other changes, the *Autopact* itself was limited to current members (excluding most Japanese firms), and Canadian duty remission practices for exporting to the United States by non-members of *Autopact* were eliminated. Tariffs on autos between the two countries were to be phased out over a period ending in 1998.

21 No reliable data have been gathered on the amount of production and trade touched by such agreements. They seem to prevail mainly in high-technology industries and opinions differ widely as to how much more important they will become (*Economist*, 1993:15-16).

22 The NAFTA may constrain state regulation of insurance (Hufbauer & Schott, 1993:63).

23 In particular, the term is not used to mean "economic security", a phrase emphasized in the Clinton campaign but abandoned early in the administration perhaps as appearing to cloak particular economic policies with the mantle of national survival (the unit originally called the Economic Security Council became the National Economic Council instead). Generally, policies pursued for the purpose of increasing economic stability internationally, and which are thus perhaps somewhat analogous to the function of some national "economic security" policies in the lives of individuals, remain here simply as elements of the prosperity goal.

24 Production capacity may not be necessary if safe sources of supply are available or stockpiling is feasible.

25 Many autonomy concerns derive from instrumental service to the prosperity and security goals, but autonomy is valued for its own sake as well (Kudrle, 1991b: 34-38).

26 Autonomy in this context does not mean "autonomy of the state" against its own society (Raymond Vernon has asked "how autonomous is the U.S. government from General Motors?"). The term here is used to refer to autonomy from non-national influence alone. As in the case of national security, the narrowness of the definition grows from a focus on the efficacy of economic nationalism in investment policy.

27 Another important distinction to be made with respect to autonomy turns on foreign intent. For example, the Canadian government might take determined action to expel U.S. cultural influence if it believed that the manipulation or destruction of Canadian self-awareness was a matter of U.S. policy rather than an incidental result of commercial opportunity.

28 The practical difficulties and questionable results of the quota practices are copiously documented in Acheson, Maule and Filleul (1989).

29 Mexico's acceptance of binding dispute resolution on investment matters suggests the abandonment of the Calvo Doctrine that all property disputes must be decided in national courts. This apostasy — after decades of robust assertion — provides another major index of the extent of Mexico's policy change.

30 The NAFTA partners cannot complain if their treatment is matched by the accommodation of others. Any attempt to give outsiders a better deal, however, would violate MFN (see endnote 8).

31 I am grateful to Dr. José Canela of the Mexican Free Trade Office in Washington for clarifying these and several other points of the NAFTA treaty.

32 Discriminatory taxation in the form of "unitary taxes" at the state level may also disadvantage foreign firms, but interstate competition (as well as federal intervention) has provided a sharp brake on their effect.

33 Greater national discipline over state and provincial policy could also assist in avoiding destructive competition for investment from outside North America (Morici, 1991:148).

34 Some have argued that the recent easing of a rule requiring indirect foreign acquirers (i.e., the shift from one foreign owner to another) of book publishers to divest within two years demonstrates Canadian flexibility on IFDI in the cultural industries. In fact, the change merely brings this aspect of policy into line with the practice in such sectors as film and sound recording and only assures that continued foreign ownership is considered (Investment Canada, 1992:38). This appears to be only a minor change.

35 The United Nations (1992:42-45) has argued for the importance of regional integration of MNE activity as a stepping stone to broader integration and contrasts it with the perils of regionalism in trade. But the same document acknowledges MNE-led regional integration influencing subsequent integration policies and explicitly notes the high local content requirements in the NAFTA advocated by the U.S.-based automakers. The strong link between trade and investment consistently stressed by the U.N. removes much of the practical meaning of the argument that regionalism in one dimension is less threatening to global liberalization than in the other.

36 Some recent schemes to entice IFDI to the United States, for example, proceed as if the GATT simply did not exist. Gaster's recent proposal (1992) involves both a 25 percent tariff on industrial imports and MNE performance requirements, including local content, enforced by manipulation of tax benefits. Canada and Mexico would be ill served by tying their economic destinies to any U.S. government that seriously entertained such proposals.

37 The declared intention of some Canadian politicians to retain FTA but reject NAFTA implicitly embraces the same "hub and spoke" outcome that prompted Canada to join the NAFTA talks to avoid (see endnote 6).

ACKNOWLEDGEMENTS

I WISH TO THANK Lorraine Eden, Geoff Nimmo, Alan Nymark, Simon Reich, Emmy Verdun, Raymond Vernon and Chris Wilkie for helpful suggestions in preparing this work. Also, my thanks to Stacey Grimes and Bob Klassen for preparing the research materials.

BIBLIOGRAPHY

Acheson, Keith, et al. "Folly of Quotas on Films and Television Programs." *The World Economy*, 12, 4, (December 1989): 515-24.

Bale, Harvey E., Jr. "The U.S. Federal Government's Policies toward Foreign Direct Investment." In *Regulation of Foreign Direct Investment in Canada and the United States.* Edited by Earl H. Fry and Lee H. Radebaugh. Provo, Utah: Brigham Young University, 1983.

Bartholomew, Philip F. "The FTA and the U.S. and Canadian Financial Systems: Regulatory Perspectives." *Canada-U.S. Outlook*, 1, 2, (October 1989).

Bergsten, C. Fred and Edward M. Graham. "Global Corporations and National Governments: Are Changes Needed In the International Economic and Political Order In Light of the Globalization of Business?" Washington: Institute for International Economics, 1990 (mimeo).

Bergsten, C. Fred and Marcus Noland. *Reconcilable Differences? United States-Japan Economic Conflict.* Washington, D.C.: Institute for International Economics, 1993.

Bobrow, Davis B. and Robert T. Kudrle. "Economic Interdependence and Security: U.S. Trade and Investment Policies for a New Era." Paper originally prepared for the World Congress of the International Political Science Association, 1991.

Business Week. "Northern Disorder." November 9, 1992, pp. 58-59.

Canadian Response to the APEC (Asia Pacific Economic Cooperation) Investment Survey (Draft) March, 1993 (mimeo).

Cowhey, Peter F. "Telecommunications." Chapter 4 in *Europe 1992: An American Perspective.* Edited by Gary Clyde Hufbauer. Washington, D.C.: The Brookings Institution, 1990.

Dewhirst, Gordon H. "The Canadian Federal Government's Policy Toward Foreign Direct Investment." In *Regulation of Foreign Direct Investment in Canada and the United States.* Edited by Earl H. Fry and Lee H. Radebaugh. Provo, Utah: Brigham Young University, 1983.

Economist. "Survey: Multinationals, Back In Fashion." March 27, 1993.

English, H. Edward and Murray G. Smith. "NAFTA and Pacific Partnership: Advancing Multilateralism." Chapter 5 in *Pacific Dynamism and the International Economic System.* Edited by C. Fred Bergsten and Marcus Noland. Washington, D.C.: Institute for International Economics, 1993.

External Affairs and International Trade. *NAFTA: What's It All About?* Ottawa: Government of Canada, 1993.

Feltham, Ivan et al. "Competition (Antitrust) and Antidumping Laws in the Context of the Canada-U.S. Free Trade Agreement: A Study for the Committee on Canada-United States Relations of the Canadian Chamber of Commerce and the Chamber of Commerce of the United States." Ottawa: Canadian Chamber of Commerce, 1991.

Fry, Earl H. "Foreign Direct Investment in North America: Political and Legal Considerations." Chapter 1 in *Investment in the North American Free Trade Area: Opportunities and Challenges.* Edited by Earl H. Fry and Lee H. Radebaugh. Provo, Utah: Brigham Young University, 1991.

_____. "Foreign Investment in the United States and Canada: The Setting." in *Regulation of Foreign Direct Investment in Canada and the United States.* Edited by Earl H. Fry and Lee H. Radebaugh. Provo, Utah: Brigham Young University, 1983.

Gaster, Robin. "Protectionism with Purpose: Guiding Foreign Investment." *Foreign Policy,* (Fall 1992): 91-106.

Gestrin, Michael and Alan M. Rugman. "The NAFTA's Impact on the North American Investment Regime." C.D. Howe Institute *Commentary.* 42, (March 1993).

Globerman, Steven. "The Consistency of Canada's Foreign Investment Review Process — A Temporal Analysis." *Journal of International Business Studies.* (Spring/Summer, 1984):119-129.

Graham, Edward M and Paul R. Krugman. *Foreign Direct Investment in the United States* Second Edition. Washington, D.C.: Institute for International Economics, 1991.

Hansen, Roger D. *The Politics of Mexican Development.* Baltimore and London: The Johns Hopkins University Press, 1971.

Hufbauer, Gary Clyde. U.S. *Taxation of International Income: Blueprint for Reform.* Washington, D.C.: Institute for International Economics, 1992.

Hufbauer, Gary Clyde and Jeffrey J. Schott. *NAFTA: An Assessment.* Washington D.C.: Institute for International Economics, 1993.

_____. *North American Free Trade: Issues and Recommendations.* Washington, D.C.: Institute for International Economics, 1992.

Husband, David, et al. "The Opportunities and Challenges of North American Free Trade: A Canadian Perspective." Investment Canada Working Paper No.7, April, 1991.

International Trade Reporter. Vol. 8, October 9, 1991.

Investment Canada. *Annual Report, 1991-92.* Ottawa, Ministry of Supply and Services Canada, 1992.

Kazanjian, John A. "The Trade and Investment Implications of the Canada-U.S. Free Trade Agreement." Chapter 5 in *Investment in the North American Free Trade Area: Opportunities and Challenges.* Edited by Earl H. Fry and Lee H. Radebaugh. Provo, Utah: Brigham Young University, 1991.

Kudrle, Robert Thomas. "The Foreign Investment Review Agency and U.S. Direct Investment In Canada." Freeman Center Working Paper No. 91-4, Humphrey Institute of Public Affairs, 1991a.

_____. "The Challenge Within: Foreign Direct Investment in Europe and the United States." Chapter 2 in *Investment in the North American Free Trade Area: Opportunities and Challenges.* Edited by Earl H. Fry and Lee H. Radebaugh. Provo, Utah: Brigham Young University, 1991b.

_____. "No Entry: Sectoral Controls on Incoming Direct Investment in the Developed Countries." Paper prepared for the 1992 Annual Convention of the International Studies

Association. A revised version will appear in *Multinationals In the Global Economy*. Edited by Lorraine Eden and Evan Potter. London: Macmillan, 1993.

Legault, Albert. "Canada and the United States: The Defense Dimension." Chapter 5 in *Canada and the United States: Enduring Friendship, Persistent Stress*. Edited by Charles F. Doran and John H. Sigler. Englewood Cliffs, N.J.: Prentice Hall, Inc., 1985.

Leyton-Brown, David. *Weathering the Storm: Canadian-U.S. Relations, 1980-1983*. Toronto: Canadian-American Committee, 1985.

Liebeler, Susan W. "Keeping the U.S. Market Open to Foreign Direct Investment." Chapter 3 in *Investment in the North American Free Trade Area: Opportunities and Challenges*. Edited by Earl H. Fry and Lee H. Radebaugh. Provo, Utah: Brigham Young University, 1991.

Lipsey, Richard G. "Will There Be a Canadian-American Free Trade Association?" *The World Economy*, 9, 3 (September 1986).

Lipsey, Richard G. and Murray G. Smith. *Taking the Initiative: Canada's Trade Options in a Turbulent World*. Toronto: C.D. Howe Institute, 1985.

Litvak, I. A. and C. J. Maule. *The Canadian Multinationals*. Toronto: Butterworth & Company (Canada) Ltd., 1981.

Lustig, Nora. *Mexico: The Remaking of an Economy*. Washington, D.C.: The Brookings Institution, 1992.

Morici, Peter. *The New Special Relationship: Free Trade and U.S.-Canada Economic Relations in the 1990s*. Ottawa: The Center for Trade Policy and Law and the Institute for Research on Public Policy, 1991.

OECD. *Controls and Impediments Affecting Inward Direct Investment in OECD Member Countries*. Paris, 1987.

Ostry, Sylvia. "The Domestic Domain: The New International Policy Arena." *Transnational Corporations*, 1, 1 (February 1992): 7-26.

Raby, Jean. "The Investment Provisions of the Canada-U.S. Free Trade Agreement: A Canadian Perspective." *American Journal of International Law*, 84, (April 1990): 394-443.

Reich, Robert B. *The Work of Nations: Preparing Ourselves for 21st Century Capitalism*. New York: Vintage Books, 1992.

Roseman, Daniel. "Toward a GATT Code on Trade in Telecommunication Equipment." *The World Economy*, 11, 1, (March 1988): 135-49.

Rugman, Alan M. *Multinationals in Canada: Their Performance and Economic Impact*. Boston: Martinus Nijhoff Publishing, 1980.

Rugman, Alan M. and Andrew D.M. Anderson. *Administered Protection In America*. London: Croom-Helm, 1987.

Rugman, Alan M. and Michael Gestrin. "The Investment Provisions of NAFTA." In *Assessing NAFTA: A Trinational Analysis*. Edited by Steven Globerman and Michael Walker. Vancouver, BC: The Fraser Institute, 1993.

Ryan, Cillian. "Trade Liberalization and Financial Services." *The World Economy*, 13, 3, (September 1990): 349-66.

Safarian, A. Edward. "Free Trade and Foreign Direct Investment: Interim Report." Chapter 4 in *Investment in the North American Free Trade Area: Opportunities and Challenges*. Edited by Earl H. Fry and Lee H. Radebaugh. Provo, Utah: Brigham Young University, Kennedy Center, 1991.

_____ . *Governments and Multinationals: Policies in the Developed Countries*. Washington, D.C.: British-North America Committee, 1983.

_____. *Multinational Enterprise and Public Policy: A Study of the Industrial Countries.* London: Edward Elgar, 1993.

Schott, Jeffrey J. and Murray G. Smith. "Services and Investment." Chapter 6 in *The Canada-U.S. Free Trade Agreement: The Global Impact.* Edited by Jeffrey J. Schott and Murray G. Smith. Washington, D.C.: Institute for International Economics, 1988.

Seitzinger, Michael V. "Foreign Investment in the United States: Major Federal Restrictions." Washington: Congressional Research Service, The Library of Congress, April 7, 1989.

Shah, Anwar and Joel Slemrod. "Do Taxes Matter for Foreign Direct Investment?" *World Bank Economic Review*, 5, 3, (1991): 473-91.

Taylor, Allan R. "Canada's Future Telecom Policy." *Transnational Data and Communications Report*, (January 1990):18-20, 28.

Tyson, Laura D'Andrea. *Who's Bashing Whom? Trade Conflict in High Technology Investment.* Washington D.C.: Institute for International Economics, 1992.

Ugarte, Fernando Sanchez. "Taxation of Foreign Investment In Mexico: The North American Perspective." in *The Dynamics of North American Trade and Investment.* Edited by Clark W. Reynolds et al. Stanford, Calif.: Stanford University Press, 1991, pp. 166-85.

United Nations, Transnational Corporations and Management Division, Department of Economic and Social Development. *World Investment Report, 1992: Transnational Corporations as Engines of Growth.* New York: United Nations, 1992.

Verleger, Philip K., Jr. "Implications of the Energy Provisions." Chapter 5 in *The Canada-U.S. Free Trade Agreement: The Global Impact.* Edited by Jeffrey J. Schott and Murray G. Smith. Washington, D.C.: Institute for International Economics, 1988.

Vernon, Raymond. *Sovereignty at Bay: The Multinational Spread of U.S. Enterprises.* Cambridge, Mass: Harvard University Press, 1971.

_____ . *The Dilemma of Mexico's Development: The Roles of the Private and Public Sectors.* Cambridge, Mass.: Harvard University Press, 1963.

Wall Street Journal. March 15, 1993(a), p. A1.

Wall Street Journal. July 2, 1993(b), p. B1.

Weintraub, Sidney. *A Marriage of Convenience: Relations between Mexico and the United States.* New York: Oxford University Press, 1990.

Whiting, Van R. *The Political Economy of Foreign Investment in Mexico: Nationalism, Liberalism and Constraints on Choice.* Baltimore and London: The John Hopkins University Press, 1992.

Wonnacott, Paul. "The Auto Sector." Chapter 4 in *The Canada-U.S. Free Trade Agreement: The Global Impact.* Edited by Jeffrey J. Schott and Murray G. Smith. Washington, D.C.: Institute for International Economics, 1988.

Ellen Frost   *&*   Edward M. Graham   **16**
Counsellor to the   Senior Fellow
U.S. Trade Representative   Institute for International Economics

Multinationals and North American Security

INTRODUCTION

THIS STUDY DESCRIBES changing concepts of "national security" and explores their impact on North American policies toward multinationals and inward foreign investment in defense-related industries. It analyzes several new trends affecting such investment — notably the globalization of industry, the growing importance of economics, and the "technology imperative". Implications are drawn for North America, with special emphasis on Canada.

Broadly speaking, national security concerns in North America (especially in the United States) are shifting in the direction of economics in the sense that, relative to foreign policy objectives and other goals usually associated with national security, economic goals have become more explicit and more pronounced. This general shift reflects a growing realization that the strength of a national economy is inseparable from its national security. The specific goals usually acknowledged in this context include the expansion of jobs and exports in the high technology sectors, and the maintenance of a healthy commercial manufacturing base.

The focus on economics forces a look at the fundamental issues of what exactly constitutes "national security" and how this relates to "economic security". Alas, this latter term is often used as a cipher for the idea that, somehow, autarky — or at least autarky in the production of defense-related goods and services, including "dual use" goods that have end uses in both military and civilian applications — is essential for national security. Hence the assertion that "national security equals economic security" is increasingly heard from protectionist constituencies. But this statement is patently false: the pursuit of autarkic policies in today's world would impoverish a nation and would not enhance its economic welfare, because both dynamic and static gains from international integration are lost if a nation pursues autarkic policies. Thus, if national economic strength is equated with national security, autarkic policies weaken the former and, presumably, lower rather than raise the latter.

The "autarky equals national security" line of reasoning is so patently false that one might also think it can be easily dismissed.[1] It is implicitly the reasoning behind the agenda of many a political constituency, however, and it is also the sort of reasoning that is easily swallowed by politicians when responding to such a constituency.

A more sophisticated version of "economic security" is that certain activities must be carried out at home, rather than imported from abroad or even carried out by local affiliates of foreign-controlled corporations, if the full benefits, including external benefits (or, as termed in contemporary economics literature, "positive externalities") are to be locally realized from these activities. Indeed, some such activities and the externalities they generate might be deemed so critical to national security that they must be "de-integrated" from the global economy — even if this implies some net reduction in economic efficiency and hence in overall economic welfare. Otherwise put, a nation might consciously decide to pay higher costs to carry out some activities at home even though it is known that the relevant goods and services can easily be acquired more economically from abroad. For example, a country might prefer to maintain full capability for producing military aircraft at home, even though overall costs of the aircraft could be reduced, (therefore enhancing economic welfare) if some or all of the aircraft were to be sourced from abroad. But this begs the question, precisely which activities *must* be carried out at home. This assessment requires detailed knowledge of the trade-off between loss of efficiency (rising costs) and loss of self-sufficiency.[2]

At a "micro" level, defense-related investment has seldom been subjected to such a trade-off because it is often implicitly assumed that autarky is the best policy for defense businesses. As a consequence, governments have typically been uncomfortable over the possibility that open trade and investment policies might render defense industries dependent upon foreign-controlled suppliers of critical products and services. Accordingly, virtually all nations pursue policies with respect to defense industries that make them relatively closed to foreign participation. As a result, industries deemed vital to national security have been sheltered from normal competitive practices. National security exemptions are sanctified in what are otherwise trade (and investment) liberalizing instruments — most notably in the "national security carveout" of the GATT, but also in the *Treaty of Rome*, the Canada-U.S. Free Trade Agreement (FTA), the North American Free Trade Agreement (NAFTA), and innumerable national laws and regulations. In most instances defense markets are heavily protected, distorted by numerous buy-national barriers, and unusually politicized. As a result, and with few exceptions, defense markets of most of the G7 nations remain heavily national in character and content. In all western nations, prime contractors are usually either state owned or heavily dependent on government procurement. In North America one result has been that (unlike the situation in the markets for civilian high-technology products) there has been no competition from Japan to spur improvements in the quality and pricing of defense-related end-goods.

Despite this companies supplying goods and services for national defense are becoming globalized at the subcontractor level. This is largely the result of technology transfer, offsets, co-production arrangements and other forms of defense collaboration that have been promoted by governments since the 1960s. But also, according to a recent OECD staff study of transnational manu- facturing in Canada, France, Germany, Japan, the United Kingdom and the United States, in the 1980s imports of intermediate inputs, including those relevant to the defense industries, rose more rapidly than domestic sourcing. Among the six industries in which this pattern is most prevalent, three have direct implications for defense: aerospace, computers, and communications equipment and semiconductors. (OECD Letter, No. 6, November 1992, p. 8.) Furthermore, in a study of three U.S. weapons systems — the HARM missile, the Mark 48 torpedo, and the Verdin Communication System — the U.S. Department of Commerce found that the number of identified foreign suppli- ers increased from 1 percent of second tier suppliers to 5 percent of third tier suppliers to about 12 percent of fourth tier suppliers. Canada accounted for 42 percent of identified foreign procurement, followed by Japan at 19 percent and the United Kingdom at 7 percent. (Department of Commerce 1992, pp. ii-iii.) Thus, to a certain extent, weapons systems and other defense-related goods have become national in form but are actually international in content.

In recent years, the structure of defense industries in the industrialized nations has been changing. The principal force driving this change has been the shrinkage of these industries in the wake of the collapse of the Soviet threat and the subsequent reduction in defense procurement budgets. The result has been a wave of mergers, acquisitions, divestitures and diversification schemes of all kinds by prime contractor defense firms. In addition, the policy framework in which the defense industries operate is itself in a state of flux. For example, many countries are opening up their industries — including defense-related industries — to foreign investment. This is part of a turn toward economic liberalization that is especially evident in Eastern Europe and parts of Latin America, but it is also occurring in France, Sweden and Japan.

In the United States, by contrast, where official policy has been open to inward investment in most sectors throughout the post-World War II era, the level of foreign participation in the U.S. economy in the last decade or so has become significant enough to attract widespread attention with one result being some pullback from open policies. The U.S. reaction is one manifestation of the fact that the globalization of the world economy can generate a backlash of fear: to some, the entry into the domestic economy of foreign-controlled multi- national firms via foreign direct investment spells a loss of national sovereignty, the export of jobs, the siphoning off of technology, and the "hollowing out" of the national industrial heritage. In response to the question "Who is us?", one answer is, "Who cares if our factories are owned by us, as long as they flourish on our soil?" But another response is likely to be, "We, not they, are 'us' and it matters that 'we' own our factories". This policy debate is especially visible in the United States, but it is going on in other countries as well (Graham & Krugman, 1991; Reich, 1991; and Tyson, 1991 and 1992).

The remainder of this study is divided into four parts. The next part examines the national security issue in the context of the new global environment, with special emphasis on policy changes now occurring in the United States with respect to national security and how these are being affected by changes occurring in the global environment. The third part examines policies of the North American nations at the intersection of foreign direct investment (FDI) and security. Again, much of the emphasis is upon what is going on in the United States in this regard. Finally, the last part looks specifically at Canada, asking particularly if, in light of the previous discussion, Canada should screen FDI on security grounds.

NATIONAL SECURITY IN THE NEW GLOBAL ENVIRONMENT

IN RETROSPECT, the end of the Cold War has spawned a number of distinct transformations. The first, as already noted, is the virtual disappearance of the Soviet threat. The probability of an all-out nuclear war between the West and the former East-block countries has shrunk so low that some would say it is effectively zero. Likewise, the risk of a massive conventional attack against Western Europe or an assault on Japan by Russia is now minimal. In fact, none of the G7 nations currently faces a serious military threat from any other country. Free at last from Cold War rivalries, the permanent members of the United Nations Security Council are finding it possible to cooperate. The number of UN peace-keeping operations is at an all-time high, albeit some have been far from successful. One unanswered issue of the times is to what extent the United Nations can function as a peacekeeper.

Another transformation resulting from the dissolution of the Soviet Union is the end of the bizarre stability associated with bipolarity. A new rash of states, some of them heavily armed (notably Ukraine), have emerged to challenge the prevailing international order. In Eastern Europe, where the chill of the Cold War drove most ethnic and religious rivalries underground, old hatreds have resurfaced and in some cases (most notably in the former Yugoslavia) these have resulted in armed conflict.

Meanwhile, and quite apart from the Cold War, new challenges to global security have arisen. These consist of diffuse, borderless threats that cannot be defeated by guns and missiles: environmental pollution, overpopulation, and the suppression of human rights, any or all of which can spur massive migration. These are amplified by the continuing proliferation of nuclear, chemical, and biological weapons know-how; by global trade in conventional weapons; by the global narcotics trade and its links with organized crime; and by terrorism.

One result is that, unlike the Cold War, regional military conflicts show no signs of withering away. At least 30 conflicts around the world have been registered since 1990, some of which are still raging as this volume goes to print. Three major regional conflicts (Iraq-Kuwait, Yugoslavia, and Rwanda) began in 1991. In 1992, Somalia dissolved into armed anarchy, prompting the United States (with the blessing of the UN Security Council) to send in troops to ensure the delivery of food shipments.

In response to the changed circumstances, new regional security arrangements are being formed and new life is being breathed into old ones. It is, however, much too early to assess their effectiveness.

IMPLICATIONS FOR DEFENSE PROCUREMENT

IN ALL COUNTRIES under discussion, projected weapons requirements are being scaled down. The shift from Cold War scenarios to localized conflict in unpredictable places puts a premium on versatility, mobility and communications. Nations are choosing smaller, multi-mission, technologically sophisticated tactical forces. Relative to acquiring new and expensive systems, the option of upgrading existing systems is now more attractive in that their upgrade is usually less costly and new systems are no longer required to counter Soviet threat.

Former U.S. Congressman Les Aspin, Secretary of Defense in the Clinton Administration, has called for a four-part "resource strategy" consisting of selective upgrading, selective low-rate procurement, "rollover plus" (prototype building and testing), and "silver bullets" (highly capable systems procured in limited quantities) (Aspin & Dickinson, 1992). Thus far Aspin has said little about procurement from abroad or about foreign investment, but his Deputy Secretary, William J. Perry, was a leading champion of international arms collaboration during the Carter Administration and will presumably fill the leadership void in this area.

With a common foreign policy remaining an unfulfilled goal, *de facto* the members of the EC find it more difficult to define common defense equipment needs in security terms. France, for example, wants to retain the option of intervening in Africa, while Germany is still wrestling with the notion of sending troops abroad for any reason. Japan is reluctant to alter its defense-only posture and still shies away from anything that smacks of force projection. In the meantime, the collapse of the Soviet Union has not by any means ended the large global market for arms. Indeed, the acceleration of regional conflicts, combined with global overcapacity in the arms industries has, if anything, added to global demand especially from arms-importing nations. At present there is no effective international mechanism to regulate or curtail the sale of non-nuclear arms.

NEW TRENDS IN THE UNITED STATES

CHANGES IN THE DEFINITION of "national security" have been more marked in the United States than in other countries rated as major defense suppliers.

The shift is more dramatic not only because the end of the Cold War arguably mattered more to the United States than to any other Western country (except perhaps Germany), but also because the American definition of "national security" had acquired an exclusively military meaning. This latter is key to understanding what is going on in Washington today.

In the early 1960s, the U.S. dominance of the global economy was near its height and in fact was so well established that the economic component of national security was taken for granted. National security came to mean providing and sustaining the military force needed to protect the territorial integrity of the United States and its allies against aggression, and it was implicitly assumed that economic constraints would not be binding upon this mission. The U.S. economy, it was assumed, could take care of itself.

These simplistic (but widely accepted) notions were severely tested by the Viet Nam war, which demonstrated if nothing else that even the United States faces a "guns or butter" trade-off. The reluctance of the Johnson and Nixon administrations to acknowledge this trade-off (and hence their failure to ask the American people to make the economic sacrifices needed to sustain the war) contributed to rising inflation, the dollar crisis of 1971, and other economic ills that have not entirely been corrected to this day.

What finally shook American leaders out of their complacency, however, was the challenge from Japan, manifest in the massive trade deficits of the 1980s and a new burst of Japanese investment in the United States. The underlying causes of the U.S. deficits were the overvalued dollar and macro-economic imbalances at home, but their effects were tangible and painful. Entire industries in which Americans had always thought of themselves as leaders, such as automobiles and electronics, appeared to be in danger of disappearing from the domestic U.S. economy. Simultaneously, the success of the Western European Airbus program presented a challenge to yet another industry in which Americans took their lead for granted: aerospace. An escalating war of words during the mid-1980s over the issue of state subsidies to this program sparked bitter conflict with the EC. In 1990, news that a government-owned corporation in Taiwan planned to buy a controlling interest in McDonnell-Douglas' commercial aircraft division aroused fears that an "Asian Airbus" would also soon be seen in the sky.

Taken together, the rash of trade disputes with Western Europe and Japan prompted charges of "unfairness" and called into question the degree of "burden sharing" within the Western alliance. Most of this criticism rained down on Japan, but to a lesser extent France and Germany were also targets of U.S. discontent. Two of the four Asian "tigers", South Korea and Taiwan, also experienced some spillover effects. But for the most part, other U.S. allies (including Canada and the United Kingdom — both major sources of direct investment in the United States) largely escaped U.S. resentment.

In Congress, the new link between economics and national security has taken a particularly negative form. The emphasis has been on stopping putatively "bad" things such as the proposed coproduction of a fighter support aircraft (FSX) with Japan and more recently Thomson CSF's effort to acquire LTV's missile division, rather than promoting "good" things, such as defense procurement reform.

Under the Bush Administration, officials in the Executive Branch engaged in what some might call "damage control" (others might call it placation of Congress) by warning allied nations that U.S. priorities were changing. In 1990, Defense Secretary Cheney warned in Tokyo that trade frictions might spill over into other concerns — an oblique way of saying that the political-security community alone could not safeguard the U.S.-Japan relationship indefinitely. In Europe, Vice President Quayle asserted that "trade is a security issue", meaning that trade disputes had been elevated to the same urgency level previously reserved for security issues. Yet, despite U.S. Trade Representative Carla Hills' vigorous and frequently successful efforts to open new foreign markets to U.S. exports, the perception grew that the Bush Administration as a whole subordinated economic concerns to traditional foreign policy priorities.

Adapting to the new mood, U.S. military leaders began to justify the presence of U.S. troops overseas in economic terms. In 1990, the Commander of the U.S. Pacific Forces told the press that his top priority was maintaining U.S. economic security rather than coping with the Soviet threat. (*Japan Times*, 6/27/90, p. 1.) The commander of U.S. Forces in Korea asserted that the presence of the U.S. force in Northeast Asia serves U.S. interests because of the trade and economic value of the region to the United States. (*Defense News*, July 20-26, 1992, p. 54.) A Defense Department report submitted to Congress in 1992, titled "A Strategic Framework for the Pacific Rim", included trade statistics as well as the statement that "roughly 2.6 million American jobs (are) dependent on our trade with the region". (Department of Defense, 1992, p. 2.) The Pentagon's annual "Net Assessment", which focussed for years on the military balance between NATO and the Warsaw Pact, will henceforth include economic factors in judging the ability of potential adversaries to develop new advanced weapons. (*Defense News*, July 27-Aug. 2, 1992, p. 4.)

The Clinton Administration is likely to formalize and intensify all of these changes. The new Secretary of Defense has a Ph.D. in economics and plans to establish an Assistant Secretary-level position to handle economic issues. President Clinton himself was elected on a largely economic platform. Fulfilling a campaign pledge, he has created a National Economic Council in the White House as a co-equal to the prestigious National Security Council. But how these players and institutions will function together remains to be seen.

Along with the new emphasis on links between defense and economics in the United States, there is a broader recognition of the importance of technology, especially "dual-use" (commercial and military application) technologies. In this context "technology" has come to mean more than advanced know-how; it also includes certain knowledge-intensive products and components such as software, precision ball bearings and advanced semi-conductors.

Experts more or less agree on the list of leading-edge technologies of vital or "critical" importance for the future: advanced materials; flexible, computer-integrated manufacturing; high-performance computing; imaging and sensing technologies; biotechnology; and new energy technologies among others. Only a handful of these technologies are uniquely military. According to the Pentagon, their priorities include high-energy density materials, hyper-velocity projectiles, pulsed power, signature control, and weapon system environment (National Critical Technologies Panel, 1991, p. 5; Mogee, 1991, pp. 16-18).

For decades, Western military planners relied on advanced technology to offset Warsaw Pact advantages in size, weight and numbers. The allied system of export controls, centred in the Coordinating Committee or CoCom, reflected this priority. What is new is a two-part phenomenon. First, technologies funded and developed for military use no longer outpace commercial technologies; in fact, the reverse has been true for some time. In 1986, the Defense Science Board, a prestigious advisory committee reporting to the Secretary of Defense, concluded that "rapid changes in the commercial world . . . offer a rich potential for Department of Defense exploitation with potential gains in performance, quality and schedule at lower costs" (U.S. Defense Science Board, 1986, p. 31).

Second, the high-technology component of a modern "smart" weapon, which is already large, continues to grow. In some weapons systems, electronics account for 25 percent to 40 percent of the value. Moreover, breakthroughs in the application of new materials and "intelligent" manufacturing to the production of weapons are already making their way to the factory floor. This is one reason why the U.S. Government, supported by industry, continues to promote the so-called "reverse flow" of technology from Japan to the United States — as opposed to the "one-way" transfer characteristic of earlier years (U.S. Defense Science Board, 1989, pp. 44-46 and A2i-ii.).

One result of these two developments is that pressures to broaden the interpretation of "national security" have been growing over the last decade. The new thinking shows up in several different policy arenas: trade policy, research and development (R&D) policy, defense procurement policy, and the debate about "strategic" industries, each of which is briefly discussed below.

Trade

Several industrial interests are hoping that President Clinton's stated concern about the industrial base will translate into protectionist trade actions. One U.S. company has revealed plans to file a "national security" trade complaint (a so-called Section 232 case) challenging Japan's near-monopoly on ceramic packaging for semiconductors. Protectionist pressures from the electronics industry are frequently justified in national security terms.

R&D

Certain U.S. members of Congress favour expanding the role of the Pentagon's Defense Advanced Research Projects Agency (DARPA) in developing dual-use technologies. Others favour a new civilian agency. There is widespread support for closer integration of commercial and military technology policy (CSIS, 1991; NAS, 1992).

Procurement

Pentagon planners have been looking for ways to capitalize on the dynamism of the commercial sector. Defense procurement policy has been inching away from military specifications in favour of commercial acquisition, but progress is slow (Gansler, 1989).

"Strategic" Industries

According to strategic trade theory, industries can be of "strategic" significance if they a) provide a higher return to factors of production than these factors could earn elsewhere in the economy, or b) provide spillover benefits for the rest of the economy (Krugman, 1986, p. 14). These industries spend above-average amounts of money on research and development and employ above-average numbers of scientists and engineers.

The appointment of Laura D'Andrea Tyson to the chairmanship of the Council of Economic Advisers has aroused concern that "strategic" high-technology industries in the United States will become candidates for subsidies and/or trade protection. Tyson, who calls herself a "cautious activist", denies that she is a protectionist and stresses that her policy prescriptions are defensive in character, arising from "targeting" policies adopted by other governments (Tyson, 1992).

AT THE INTERSECTION OF FOREIGN DIRECT INVESTMENT AND NATIONAL SECURITY POLICIES IN NORTH AMERICA

THE GOVERNMENTS OF all of the G7 countries except Canada have the authority to block or limit incoming foreign investment on national security grounds. Three of these governments (France, Japan and Canada) have the authority to screen proposed foreign investment on economic grounds. There is relatively little public information about the implementation of investment-related national security practices. Those seeking more extensive controls over incoming foreign investment in the United States have argued that the United States is less restrictive toward foreign investment than any other major Western government, although precious little evidence has been offered to back up this position (see, e.g., Spencer, 1989, p. 2). The U.S. Treasury Department, by contrast, concluded in a 1988 study that "the United States does not stand out as having a particularly more liberal investment regime than the others" (Treasury Dept., 1988, p. 1).

This section examines the policies of the two North American G7 nations in the domain of investment restrictions. The discussion here is intended primarily as a prelude to the final part of this study, dealing with the question of whether or not Canada should create a national security screening authority to complement the existing authority to screen inward investment on economic grounds.

United States

THE UNITED STATES restricts or prohibits foreign direct investment in a number of sectors and activities that historically have been deemed vital to national security interests. These include coastal shipping, broadcasting, air transport, atomic energy, oil pipelines, and a scattering of others. Today, national security rationales for these restrictions and prohibitions are arguably tenuous notwithstanding the fact that they might once have had validity and, in some sectors, that the policies related to them are undergoing *de facto* review. Most other countries maintain similar restrictions covering essentially the same sectors and activities.

In the United States, apart from these activities and sectors, routine authority to restrict foreign investment is limited to power granted to the President under the Exon-Florio amendment to the *Trade Act* of 1988, to block an acquisition or takeover of a U.S. firm on grounds that the investment threatens to impair the national security and that other measures under U.S. law cannot be brought to bear to counteract this threat. However, in times of national emergency, the President may invoke the *International Emergency Economic Powers Act* to seize the U.S. assets of foreign nationals.

Exon-Florio power is in one sense quite sweeping (unlike most other Executive measures an Exon-Florio determination cannot be challenged in court) but, offsetting this somewhat, the criterion for an Exon-Florio block is quite narrow in that a threat to the national security must be explicitly identified. This has had the effect of channelling broader political pressures for more restrictive policies regarding foreign investment in the United States into efforts (thus far largely unsuccessful) to redefine "national security" to include competitiveness, leading-edge technologies, "strategic" industries, and the like.

Foreign investment through merger or acquisition is also subject to the same antitrust review applicable to mergers and acquisitions in general. This review is conducted independently from the national security (Exon-Florio) review conducted by the Committee on Foreign Investment in the United States (CFIUS).

The CFIUS, currently chaired by the Secretary of the Treasury and including representatives from the Departments of Commerce, Defense, Justice, and State, the Office of Management and Budget, the U.S. Trade Representative, and the President's Council of Economic Advisors, actually predates Exon-Florio. The CFIUS was established by an Executive Order of the President in 1975. The immediate cause was the OPEC oil shock of 1973 and the subsequent accumulation of wealth in foreign (especially Arab) hands. At the time there was a perception in the Congress and elsewhere that Arab oil money would "buy up" key U.S. assets at "fire sale prices". (This rhetoric surfaced again in the late 1980s, only this time the buyer was Japan. See Graham & Krugman, 1991, for an analysis.)

Exon-Florio itself resulted from an amendment to the *Omnibus Trade and Competitiveness Act* of 1988 that was designed to make it easier for the President to block an incoming foreign investment on national security grounds. The amendment reflected a tug-of-war that had been ongoing between the Executive Branch and the Congress. In the end, the language did little more than formalize existing procedures, but it sent a strong signal of concern to would-be foreign investors. (Graham and Ebert, 1991, detail the history of Exon-Florio and its application during the period from 1988 to 1990.)

Because the Exon-Florio provision allows for retroactive nullification of an investment, and because "national security" is not explicitly defined by the law, companies have been routinely advised by legal counsel that the safest course of action is to notify the CFIUS in advance of a proposed investment. The irony of this development is that an Administration that prided itself on its receptive attitude toward investment and on the absence of burdensome screening procedures found itself inundated by a flurry of "prior notification" announcements. Still, Exon-Florio served to hold off more restrictive legislation and permitted the CFIUS to continue to implement a liberal investment policy. To date, only one case submitted for final review has been denied, although a number of other cases have been withdrawn where denial was almost surely expected (Graham and Ebert, 1991).

It is too early to say what the policy of the Clinton Administration will be with respect to administration of Exon-Florio. Because the new President is a former governor who actively sought foreign investment in his state and who understands the benefits of an open investment climate, it is possible that policy will not change significantly. Still, several new policy issues have crept into the Exon-Florio debate and may soon find expression in internal policy directives and implementing regulations.

For example, one influential critic of the Exon-Florio process, Georgetown University professor Theodore Moran, has called for basing foreign investment decisions not on whether the prospective owner of a U.S. defense asset is foreign or not, but rather on whether the U.S. defense acquisition community would face a resulting oligopoly. Moran believes that an investment should be blocked or subjected to performance requirements in any defense-related industry where concentration is higher than four companies or four countries supplying 50 percent of the global market (Moran, 1990, p. 82, and 1992, p. 45).

A somewhat more refined analysis makes a similar point about competition policy but calls for far-reaching procedural changes (Graham & Ebert, 1991). This would link competition (antitrust) policy with a narrower Exon-Florio process. Like Moran, Graham & Ebert believe that it is in the national security interests of the U.S. Government to seek to avoid monopoly or oligopoly, regardless of the nationality of the acquiring investor. But Graham & Ebert see no need for two independent processes, one of which channels (most) incoming foreign investment into a "national security" review, and another that subjects the same investment to a competitive effects analysis. Instead, they would combine the two processes by modifying the Hart-Scott-Rodino notification guidelines so that notice of all mergers and acquisitions (irrespective of the nationalities of the parties) with national security implications would be given to the Justice Department. They would then provide for a special review process for cases deemed to be security sensitive. This process would not be unlike the present CFIUS process. It would be conducted by an interagency committee but, unlike present procedures, this committee would review the competitive, as well as the national security implications of the case. If the case passed this screen, it would not be subject to further review on antitrust grounds by the Justice Department or the Federal Trade Commission (FTC). Cases not deemed to be security sensitive would continue to be reviewed under Justice Department and FTC procedures.

An issue fundamentally unresolved in the debate over the passage of Exon-Florio is whether or not certain sectors such as semiconductors should be subject to special trade and investment policies designed to shelter and aid U.S. firms operating in these sectors. This relates to the issue discussed earlier in the introductory section, i.e., what activities (if any) should be conducted at home under domestic ownership for national security reasons. At a time when these activities are becoming more "global", U.S. policy with respect to what these activities should be has often been characterized more by emotional appeal to nationalism than to rational analysis.

The election of President Clinton may signal a more "pro-active" (Washington jargon for the opposite of "reactive") policy toward such sectors, especially knowledge-intensive industries judged as critical to American competitiveness. Trade and investment policies are not the only, or even likely to be the main, tools selected to strengthen these industries. For example, some voices within the new administration favour policies designed to strengthen "human capital" by emphasizing education and worker retraining. Nonetheless, the trade and investment policies of the administration were not settled at the time of this writing, and one cannot rule out the possibility of these policies being directed in efforts to bolster sectors or activities deemed to be strategic.

One issue that does seem to have been settled, however, is that U.S. defense-related firms should not be sold to foreign interests controlled by foreign governments. The catalytic event in this regard was the effort, in the spring of 1992, by Thomson CSF, a French state-owned firm, to purchase the missile division of the American defense contractor LTV. What reportedly tipped the balance against the proposed acquisition in the CFIUS was not its military nature *per se*, nor even the irritation with French export policy that prevails in some policy circles, but rather the simple fact that Thomson is a majority state-owned company.

Thomson's Chairman, Alain Gomez, countered that Thomson is not subsidized. He added that government-funded R&D funds account for only 40 percent of its research budget compared to 80 percent for American defense contractors (*Defense News*, June 22-28, 1992, p. 20). Thomson officials further cited a finding from the British Monopolies and Mergers Commission that Thomson behaves, in effect, like a private company and should be treated accordingly (*Defense News*, April 20-26, 1992, p. 21).

Thomson withdrew from the case when it became clear that approval would not likely be forthcoming. Meanwhile, a government-owned corporation in Taiwan also backed away from its earlier intention to purchase a significant share of McDonnell-Douglas' commercial aircraft business. While neither case has resolved the question to what extent state ownership should constitute a decisive barrier against approval, the clear precedent is that there is *some* presumption against acquisition of a defense-sensitive firm by a foreign firm under state control.

Finally, we should note another investment-related development in the United States stemming from national security concerns: greater scrutiny of technology transfer from a competitiveness perspective. The concern is that U.S. companies seeking short-term profits might sell technology to potential foreign competitors and thus undermine America's competitive posture. This was the rationale, for example, wielded by those seeking to block the FSX transaction. A variation of this concern is that a foreign investor might acquire leading-edge U.S. technology, then transfer it out of the United States. The United States would then lose an important competitive asset.

Strictly speaking, the U.S. Government has no authority to restrict the export of technology in the name of U.S. competitiveness. Under the *Export Administration Act* of 1969, as amended, there are only three possible justifications for denial of an export license: short supply, national security, and foreign policy. Nevertheless, the Commerce Department's Industrial Resources Administration has now been assigned the task of reviewing Defense Department "Memoranda of Understanding" (MOUs) from an industrial-base perspective. This was a direct result of the controversy surrounding the proposed co-production of the FSX aircraft between General Dynamics and Mitsubishi Heavy Industries of Japan. In fact, a Deputy Assistant Secretary of Commerce now sits on the bi-national FSX Steering Committee — an unheard of possibility only ten years ago, when the Pentagon enjoyed almost complete autonomy in its international transactions (GAO, 1982). This is another area to watch.

CANADA

IN TERMS OF NATIONAL SECURITY, Canada is somewhat unusual in several respects. Canadians are rather more sensitive to the question of national "identity" than are citizens of the other G7 nations. This sensitivity results from a combination of periodic struggles with *Québecois* (French-speaking) nationalism and the desire of other Canadians to maintain certain cultural differences they perceive to exist between themselves and their neighbours to the south. As a result, the Canadian government exempts from national treatment *inter alia* foreign investment in the "cultural" industries, which include film making, publishing, and other media-related business.[3] In practice, this means that foreign ownership is restricted in these industries. Many of these industries, such as broadcasting, are the same as those in which ownership is restricted in other countries as well.

Canada does reserve the right to screen inward direct investment as per the *Investment Canada Act*. This screening is done to determine that direct investment in Canada brings economic benefits to the nation according to six specific criteria. No screening of investments is done under certain size thresholds, which are set at C$ 5 million in assets for direct acquisitions of Canadian businesses and C$ 50 million in assets for indirect acquisitions. For investment from Mexico or the United States, under the NAFTA, the thresholds are set at higher levels for most sectors, and are subject to adjustment to reflect inflation.[4] As noted earlier, the *Investment Canada Act* does not allow a direct investment to be rejected on grounds of national security.

Relevant for purposes of this study, the United States considers Canada, alone among NATO countries, to be part of a common industrial base. Industrial cooperation between the United States and Canada with respect to defense dates back to the *Hyde Park Agreement* of 1941. It was reaffirmed in an exchange of notes in 1950 and has been renewed periodically ever since. Objectives of what has become known as the Defense Development Sharing Program include promoting a strong, integrated, and more widely dispersed defense industrial base in North America; achieving the most economic use of research and development and production resources; fostering greater standardization and interoperability of military equipment; removing obstacles to the free flow of defense equipment trade; encouraging the exchange of information and technology; and according equal consideration to the business communities of both countries (U.S. Department of Defense Directive 2036.1, November 4, 1980. p. 2).

U.S. regulations recognize the uniqueness of the U.S.-Canadian relationship. Firms in the United States may export unclassified data on the U.S. Munitions list to Canada without a license, and Canadian firms may receive research and development contracts for products designed to meet purely U.S. requirements.

Like other countries, Canada is facing a decisive trade-off between national sufficiency and rising costs with respect to defense-related purchases. According to a report by the Auditor General of Canada, the Canadian government's preferences for domestically built equipment boost the cost of military procurement by as much as 20 percent (*Defense News*, November 30-December 6, 1992, p. 3). Thus far, however, there are few signs of real change either in Canadian procurement policy or in policy toward defense-related investment.

GLOBAL INDUSTRY, NATIONAL SECURITY AND CANADA

GIVEN THAT a) the globalization of defense-related industries is likely to continue, b) the nature of national security is likely to be further scrutinized and redefined, and c) the North American Free Trade Agreement is likely to be ratified by its signators, a major issue for Canada is whether or not foreign direct investment in Canada should be screened for reasons of national security. In a nutshell, the relevant question is, should Canada institute its own version of the Exon-Florio authority now extant in the United States? And, if the answer to the above question is "yes", the further issue is, how should this authority be implemented in Canada?

The case presented here is that the government of Canada should indeed have authority to screen, and to reject, foreign direct investment for reasons of national security. There are two quite straightforward reasons for this.

First, the current lack of such an authority is a breach in the national security apparatus of Canada. To stylize the situation somewhat, under existing law, Canada can, on national security grounds, block the sale of products or transfer of technology by a Canadian company to the nationals of a hostile or potentially hostile sovereign state, but it is not clear that Canada can block the sale of the company itself to those nationals on these grounds. The lack of a legal basis for blocking such a sale is exacerbated if the company is small enough to slip through the size thresholds for review under the *Investment Canada Act*. In contrast, for a larger investment, while the government of Canada does not have authority to block a transaction strictly on national security grounds *per se*, the transaction could be subject to a finding that it does not bring the mandated benefits to the Canadian economy, and hence be blocked. However, a transaction not subject to the thresholds cannot be blocked even for economic reasons.

Thus, the first reason for having authority to block foreign direct investment on national security grounds is that there could be cases where it is in Canada's interest actually to have and to use such an authority. In this regard, it should be noted that Canada has no exact equivalent to the U.S. *International Emergency Economic Powers Act*, and thus that the breach is greater in Canada than it was in the United States prior to the passage of Exon-Florio.

In the past, the breach caused by Canada having no equivalent to Exon-Florio may have been more a theoretical proposition than a practical one because direct investment in defense contractor firms was not commonplace during the Cold War period and, indeed, there was an implicit assumption that such firms were simply not acquirable by foreigners (or, at least, that large firms as such were not). But, as detailed earlier in this study, the combined effects of the end of the Cold War with the resulting opportunity to downsize defense-related activities, and the increasingly "dual" nature of modern technology has invalidated this assumption. Firms engaging in defense-related activities (or those having access to or control of technologies that are militarily useful) are increasingly as subject to foreign takeovers as are any other firms. Thus, the breach in the Canadian national defense apparatus, resulting from lack of authority to screen foreign direct investment on security grounds, could prove to be of practical importance in the coming years.[5]

A second reason for creating this authority is to bring Canada into conformity with the other signatory nations of the NAFTA. As described earlier, the United States already has such an authority. Mexico recently announced that it will create one. In the future, the three NAFTA nations might seek further to harmonize and liberalize their domestic laws and policies pertaining to direct investment including, perhaps, those laws and policies pertaining to foreign direct investment and national security. For example, it is conceivable that at some time in the future the NAFTA nations might agree not to screen direct investment originating from other NAFTA nations, including investments in areas that have heretofore been screened on national security grounds. But for such an agreement to take effect, each NAFTA nation would likely have to be satisfied that the other NAFTA nations had in place provisions to ensure that regional security interests would not be compromised by direct investment. Otherwise stated, if Canada sought to have the "Exon-Florio fence" dismantled along the Canada-U.S. border, it might be necessary to extend the "fence" so as to encircle both nations.

What benefits would accrue to Canada, other than covering its own national security breach, of having a harmonized North American policy regarding direct investment and national security? Almost surely, one benefit would be to have an input into what that policy should be. As already noted, the United States is to some extent swimming against the current on these issues, and a Canadian input could be salutary.

If Canada is to have such an authority, how should it be administered? We are wary of making specific recommendations to Canadians for two reasons: first, as Americans, we do not have a detailed knowledge of the Canadian legal and policy process; and, second, even if we did, we think it likely that few Canadians would be inclined to accept our recommendations. So, we must be satisfied to proffer some rather non-specific advice, centered on the U.S. experience with Exon-Florio.

First, the principle that the authority to block a direct investment for reasons of national security should rest at the highest level (in the case of the United States, the President; in the case of Canada, the Cabinet) is a sound one, as is the principle that the decision not be reviewable in the courts. Both principles are consistent with the notion that this authority is very powerful and is not to be used frivolously.

Second, the U.S. approach to delegation of working authority to implement Exon-Florio to specialists who recommend to the ultimate authority is also sound. In the United States, this working authority is delegated to the CFIUS, as explained earlier. In Canada, working authority would presumably be delegated to those authorities who implement the *Investment Canada Act*. The CFIUS is an interagency committee, a common (and workable) entity within the U.S. Government that brings together relevant agencies, e.g., the Defense Department (in charge of the Armed Forces and other defense functions), the Treasury Department (in charge of direct investment policy at working level), the Department of State (in charge of foreign policy at working level), and others. In Canada, working relationships among government agencies and departments tend to be less formalized than in Washington, and presumably the authorities implementing a Canadian version of Exon-Florio would make recommendations in close consultation with the Ministry of Defence, the Bureau of Competition Policy, and other relevant bodies. Whether consultations should be mandated under law, or be conducted more informally is a matter for Canada to work out; nonetheless, a Canadian version of the U.S. "interagency process" would seem to be appropriate.

In the United States, there is no formal requirement to notify the CFIUS of transactions that might be subject to Exon-Florio investigation, but neither is there any time limit beyond which the U.S. Government loses its power to conduct such an investigation.[6] On this point, the U.S. procedure has gone wrong. The finality of Exon-Florio determinations coupled with the lack of such a time limit, has caused corporate lawyers routinely to advise clients to notify CFIUS of an acquisition, takeover, or merger involving foreign investors. One result has been that the CFIUS has been deluged with notifications, most of which have been of transactions that patently have no bearing on national security. In spite of this, CFIUS is regularly subject to criticism by the U.S. Congress that it is missing important transactions.

In our view, a much better approach would be to issue detailed guidelines for notification, making it clear that cases falling within certain parameters are required to notify. The parameters could be quite broad and would serve to identify cases that potentially have national security implications for Canada so that these can, if deemed necessary, be investigated and reviewed. At the same time, the parameters could be set so as to eliminate cases that clearly have no national security implications.

Thus, these parameters surely should be set so as to capture transactions involving certain technologies or activities that are clearly within the national defense orbit. Most "high-technology" activities would almost certainly qualify but the parameters should also be designed to eliminate other categories and classes of activity, such as hotels, restaurants, toy stores, and other service subsectors, and possibly a number of major manufacturing subsectors as well. It is clear that no size thresholds would be appropriate because some security-sensitive high-technology firms are very small indeed. Overall, the parameters should be designed to catch too many rather than too few activities but, even so, many activities could be eliminated right from the start.

Under U.S. procedures, the President (or rather the CFIUS) has 30 days to decide whether or not to investigate a notified transaction, then 45 days to conduct an investigation, if one is deemed warranted, and to issue recommendations to the President. Once the recommendations have been received, the President has 15 days to decide whether to implement them. We have been told by U.S. officials engaged in the CFIUS process that these time limits have proved quite satisfactory, and Canada would be well advised to set roughly similar time limits.[7]

Exon-Florio provides for no formal definition of what constitutes the "national security" and, for reasons that have been made clear elsewhere in this study, we contend that no formal definition would be appropriate. It is as clear for Canada as it is for the United States that there should be no formal attempt to define "national security". Canada should not lock itself into any specific criteria today, knowing that tomorrow those criteria could quickly become obsolete.

The main danger of not defining "national security" is that policy makers might use a national security argument to justify actions they take against foreign investors when in fact those actions are connected remotely, if at all, to tangible defense-related criteria. In Canada, however, this risk is much smaller than it is in the United States: unlike their U.S. counterparts, Canadian officials are empowered to screen foreign direct investment on the basis of economic criteria. In the United States, the "danger" seen to be posed by Exon-Florio is that the (undefined) concept of "national security" will be expanded to include "economic security" — i.e., that Exon-Florio will be used as an economic screening tool!

Indeed, the main reason why Exon-Florio was — and continues to be — a controversial element in U.S. law and policy is that there are strong feelings on both sides with respect to whether any sort of economic screening is desirable. One side believes that no such screening is ever warranted, and persons subscribing to this view tend to fear that Exon-Florio might some day be used for the implicit purpose of such screening. The other side argues that such screening is both warranted and within the purview of Exon-Florio. But within the United States, there was virtually no opposition to a measure that would enable blockage of foreign investment on narrow national security grounds. From our standpoint the right of a government to block foreign investment for reasons of national security is almost taken for granted, and therefore any such action taken by Canada to formalize such an authority would pose problems for no one.

ENDNOTES

1 Indeed, the case can be made that much of the security and foreign policy of the defunct Soviet Union was predicated on the assumption that autarky was a self-evident need. To the extent that this was the case, surely the results speak for themselves.

2 That is, if the cost reduction enabled by sourcing (for example) an aircraft component from abroad were very high but the risk of the resulting "dependence" on foreign sources might lead to the inability of the nation to field the aircraft at a time of national emergency were low (perhaps because the component can be stockpiled, or because it can be sourced from a number of geographically dispersed suppliers), the trade-off is different from that if the cost reduction were low but the risk of dependence were high. Thus, it is easy to see that arguments such as "imports of clothing or footwear create a dependence on foreigners and this represents a grave danger to national security", border on the ludicrous (although such arguments are still made!). However, one could not so easily dismiss a similar argument pertaining to imports of, say, an advanced microprocessor needed for satellite surveillance, made by only one firm in one location in a possibly hostile nation and for which there is no substitute.

3 That is, these industries are specifically exempted from the national treatment provisions of both the U.S.-Canada Free Trade Agreement and the NAFTA.

4 Thresholds for U.S. investors are also higher under the FTA.

5 The recommendation offered here is not that Canada should adopt aggressive new policies to prevent Canadian firms from being acquired by foreign investors when these firms engage in defense-related activities. Rather, it is paramount that Canada should have the means of blocking such an acquisition if it is deemed that there are good national security reasons for doing so. In sum, Canada should have this authority even if there is no intent at present to use it!

6 Once an investigation has been formally launched, a series of time limits goes into effect by which certain determinations must be made. Once a case is concluded, it may not be reopened except on grounds of "material omission", i.e., that evidence relevant to the determination was not available to the authorities.

7 The one chink in the U.S. armour might be the 45-day limit for a full investigation. We have been told that certain cases could not be decided within this time. In these cases, however, the CFIUS sought restructuring of the deals so as to meet certain specific security requirements; the problem, essentially, was that the parties to the transaction were not able to effect these restructuring conditions within the 45-day period. The solution to the dilemma has been for the parties to cancel the original transaction and thence to restructure the deal and renotify. The impression is that while somewhat awkward, these restructurings have not really posed any special problem.

BIBLIOGRAPHY

Aspin, Rep. Les and Rep. William Dicksinson. *Defense for a New Era: Lessons of the Persian Gulf War*. Washington, DC: U.S. Government Printing Office, 1992.

Bingaman, Jeff, Jacques Gansler and Robert Kupperman. *Integrating Commercial and Military Technologies for National Strength*. Washington, DC: Center for Strategic and International Studies, March, 1991.

Defense Science Board. *Use of Commercial Components in Military Equipment*. Washington, DC: Office of the Under Secretary of Defense for Research and Engineering, July 20-August 1, 1986.

Defense Science Board. *Defense Industrial Cooperation with Pacific Rim Nations*. Washington, DC: Office of the Under Secretary of Defense for Acquisition, 1989.

Gansler, Jacques. *Affording Defense*. Cambridge, Mass.: MIT Press, 1989.

Graham, Edward M., and Michael E. Ebert. "Foreign Direct Investment and U.S. National Security: Fixing Exon Florio." *The World Economy*. 14, 3 (September 1991).

Graham, Edward M. and Paul R. Krugman. *Foreign Direct Investment in the United States*, 2nd Edition. Washington, DC: The Institute for International Economics, 1991.

Krugman, Paul R., ed. *Strategic Trade Policy and the New International Economics*. Cambridge, Mass.: MIT Press, 1986.

Mogee, Mary Ellen. *Technology Policy and Critical Technologies: A Summary of Recent Reports*. Washington, DC: *The Manufacturing Forum*, (December 1991).

Moran, Theodore H. "American Economic Policy and American National Security." Unpublished paper prepared for Task Force on Global Security, Council on Foreign Relations. April, 1992.

Moran, Theodore H. "The Globalization of America's Defense Industries." *International Security*. 15, 1 (Summer 1990).

National Academy of Science, National Academy of Engineering, and the Institute of Medicine. *The Government Role in Civilian Technology: Building a New Alliance*. Washington, DC: National Academy Press, 1992.

National Critical Technologies Panel. *Report of the National Critical Technologies Panel*. Washington, DC: Executive Office of the President. March, 1991.

Reich, Robert B. *The Work of Nations*. New York: Alfred A. Knopf, 1991.

Spencer, Linda M. Foreign *Investment Barriers: Where America Stands Among Its Competitors*. Arlington, Virginia: Congressional Economic Leadership Institute, 1989.

Tyson, Laura D'Andrea. "They Are Not Us: Why American Ownership Still Matters." *The American Prospect*. (Winter 1991).

_____. *Who's Bashing Whom? Trade Conflict in High Technology Industries*. Washington, DC: Institute for International Economics, 1992.

U.S. Government, Department of Defense. *A Strategic Framework for the Asian Pacific Rim: Report to Congress 1992*. Washington, DC: Department of Defense, 1992.

U.S. Government, Department of the Treasury. "Survey of G-7 Laws and Regulations on Foreign Direct Investment." Unpublished paper. December 7, 1988.

U.S. Government, General Accounting Office. *U.S. Military Co-production Programs Assist Japan in Developing Its Civil Aircraft Industry*. Washington, DC: General Accounting Office. ID-82-23. March 18, 1982.

U.S. Government, Department of Commerce. *National Security Assessment of the Domestic and Foreign Subcontractor Base: A Study of Three U.S. Navy Weapon Systems*. Washington, DC: Bureau of Export Administration, Department of Commerce. March, 1992.

U.S. Government, Department of Defense. *National Military Strategy of the United States*. Washington, DC: Department of Defense. January, 1992.

Edward M. Graham   &   Mark A. A. Warner
Senior Fellow   Associate
Institute for International Economics   Curtis, Mallet-Prevost, Colt & Mosle

17

Multinationals and Competition Policy in North America

INTRODUCTION

COMPETITION POLICY formally includes two domains:

1) The regulation and control or *monopolization* of a market, where monopolization is defined as domination of a market by a firm or by a cartel, even if no monopoly in the strictest sense is achieved. This includes the regulation of practices (sometimes termed "restrictive business practices") that can lead to monopolization (e.g., predatory pricing, contractual agreements that result in substantial barriers to entry, mergers and acquisitions, etc.). Exactly how market structure and/or firm conduct constitute "monopolization" — and hence what standards should be at the basis of such regulation — is subject to considerable debate by economic and legal scholars. While these debates are not the primary focus of this study, they are referred to where needed.

2) The regulation of state aids to *industry*, including direct and indirect subsidies and the granting of preferential status (including sanctioned monopoly). Industry in this context means any enterprise or institution engaged in a commercial undertaking. Thus, state-owned enterprises fall under this category.

The first domain is commonly known as "antitrust policy" in the United States and "anti-monopolies policy" (or some variation thereon) virtually everywhere else. The second domain is commonly known as "state aids policy". In North America (Canada, Mexico and the United States), national authorities charged with antitrust enforcement generally do not have enforcement powers over state aids. In Europe, by contrast, at the Community (EC) level, enforcement powers over both reside in Directorate General IV (DGIV) of the European Commission. The authority of DGIV over state aids is constrained by definitions of what constitutes such aid (e.g., instruments to restrict imports: although conceptually these are clearly a form of state aid to industry, they are not under the purview of DGIV). Also, with some exceptions, the authority of DGIV is limited to direct subsidies, including equity injections by the state into state-owned enterprise.

According to the strict definitions offered above, it is obvious that numerous policy instruments exercised by governments, which are not formally or normally considered to be "antitrust" measures, nonetheless bear frequently upon competition policy. Indeed, almost any regulatory authority of government has some such bearing. Instruments that have particular relevance include laws and policies pertaining to intellectual property (a patent, notably, confers a temporary monopoly right upon the patent holder), regulation of imports, and the right of foreign corporations to establish or acquire affiliates within a country and to operate them on an ongoing basis.

Thus defined, the relevance of competition policy to North American multinationals cannot be overstated; these policies impinge on their production, location, growth and distribution strategies. This study focuses on how a supranational North American competition policy might assist these multinationals in making efficient choices and implementing effective strategies. In particular, we focus on mergers and price predation through dumping or subsidies. Accordingly, we build on the economic arguments of multinational location strategies presented elsewhere in this volume, especially those by Eaton et al, Eden, and Encarnation. Furthermore, we extrapolate from the various studies of corporate globalization through mergers and acquisitions contained in the second volume of this Investment Canada Research Series.[1]

Although the North American Free Trade Agreement (NAFTA) contains provisions that bear implicitly on competition policy, it does not include detailed provisions regarding competition policy. Specifically, there is no provision to create a North American competition policy to be administered by a supranational entity. The NAFTA does, however, contain a short chapter (Chapter 15) titled "Competition Policy, Monopolies, and State Enterprises". Article 1501 of this chapter requires each signatory country to have a competition law "to proscribe anti-competitive business conduct and to take appropriate action thereto", and for each country to cooperate with the others in the enforcement of this law. However, the same article stipulates that no country may have recourse to any NAFTA dispute settlement mechanism for matters arising under Chapter 15. Most of the rest of the chapter is devoted to affirming the right of signatory countries to designate monopolies or to create or maintain state-owned enterprises that might or might not be monopolies. Article 1504 calls for a Working Group on Trade and Competition to be created and to report with recommendations five years after the NAFTA takes effect.

Two questions that arise naturally, then, are:

1) Should the NAFTA contain explicit competition policy provisions?

2) Is the case for including such provisions strengthened by the increasingly "multinational" character of business firms operating in the context of the NAFTA?

This study addresses both these questions and answers both in the affirmative. Indeed, we also argue that the adoption of such provisions would ease many of the most contentious "unresolved" issues of the NAFTA. For example, one such issue is Canadian and Mexican discomfort over the continued right of the U.S. authorities to use antidumping and subsidies/countervailing measures (the so-called "less than fair value" provisions of U.S. trade law) against Canadian and Mexican exports to the United States. American uneasiness over subsidies, especially in Mexico, is another example.

The remainder of this study is divided into three sections. The first builds the case for an explicit NAFTA competition policy. The second explores institutional arrangements for accomplishing this. The third section provides a few, brief concluding remarks.

THE CASE FOR AN EXPLICIT NORTH AMERICAN COMPETITION POLICY IN THE CONTEXT OF THE NAFTA

THE MAIN ARGUMENT FOR including competition policy in a free trade agreement (or, indeed, in any trade-liberalizing measure) is that in the absence of such a policy, private barriers to trade tend to replace official barriers so that the gains from an enlarged market are nullified. Thus, for example, the *Treaty of Rome* establishing a common market in Europe explicitly grants to the European Commission powers to investigate and regulate cartels and firm dominance (Articles 85 and 86) on the premise that cartels or dominant firms can negate the gains envisaged from the creation of a common market. The (never implemented) Havana Charter that would have supplanted the existing GATT likewise contained provisions to regulate restrictive business practices that might effectively offset any gains from international trade liberalization. Furthermore, just as trade barriers can have distortive effects, so can subsidies. Hence, the *Treaty of Rome* grants the European Commission some powers to limit and regulate subsidies and other state aids to industry (Articles 92 and 93).

As discussed above, the NAFTA contains provisions to liberalize trade and investment in North America, but makes no explicit provisions for anti-monopolies policy or for state aids policy. (Indeed, sectors such as state controlled monopolies which are most likely to be affected by state aid are to a large extent exempt from the NAFTA.) However, before concluding that NAFTA is totally derelict in the matter of competition policy, it must be noted that all three of the parties to the NAFTA do have national laws, policies and regulatory bodies in the antitrust domain and that the NAFTA does encourage cooperation among the parties in this area.

In the United States, the relevant laws and institutions were put into place during the last decade of the last century (the *Sherman Act*), the early part of this one (the *Clayton Act*) and, somewhat later (the *Federal Trade Commission Act* and the *Robinson-Patman* Act). All of these have been more or less actively enforced ever since, although at certain times (such as during the Reagan Administration), their enforcement has been notably lax.

In the case of Canada, anti-monopoly laws have been on the books for as long as they have been in the United States (the *Combines Investigations Act* was passed in 1889, one year before the U.S. *Sherman Act*), but only in 1985 was the *Combines Investigation Act* (subsequently renamed the *Competition Act*) amended so as so make this enforcement effective. These amendments came into effect in 1986 and changed the law by decriminalizing some practices covered under the law (related to mergers and acquisitions and abuse of dominant firm position) and by establishing a Competition Tribunal to adjudicate the law on an administrative basis. Prior to these changes, enforcement of the law was difficult because only criminal charges could be brought for violations — something the courts were loath to do.

In Mexico, Article 28 of the Mexican Constitution of 1917 prohibits monopolies and monopolistic practices. Also, Mexican law and policy gave effect to this constitutional provision with a variety of instruments. For instance, the *Antitrust Law* of 1934 was difficult to apply and politicized the development of a competition policy. The *Law on Powers of the Federal Executive on Economic Matters* of 1950 relied exclusively on direct government intervention in business decisions and conduct. In December of 1992, the Mexican Congress abrogated these laws and passed a modern basic law. This was done largely to meet the requirements of accession to the NAFTA. On paper, the Mexican law appears to promote efficiency and the competitive process — but it is simply too early to judge whether it will be effectively enforced.

The question therefore becomes, is there a need for anything like supranational law and authority, as there is in Europe (where, we should note, national competition policy laws and institutions exist contemporaneously with Community law and authority)?[2] Or, alternatively, do the existing national institutions provide all that is needed to ensure that the benefits of the NAFTA are not lost to anticompetitive behavior? We contend that there is a need for a supranational law and authority. Our arguments boil down to four:

1) Some issues of competition policy have, (using terminology borrowed in part from the jargon of the European Community), a genuinely "North American dimension". In plain language, situations exist for which a particular outcome may be judged as optimal (or at least legal) by the authorities of one country but

which, if considered in terms of the interests of all three North American countries, would lead to a different conclusion.[3]

2) The scope and standards of Canadian, Mexican, and U.S. competition law are not entirely consistent with one another. Some form of supranational law and authority would therefore enable resolution of potential conflicts created by these inconsistencies. (If, for example, a North American law on competition were to be created, this law would presumably supersede national law for cases that fell within its scope. In turn, a North American competition law could be the basis for further harmonization of Canadian, Mexican, and U.S. law and practice.

3) Supranational competition law and authority would logically supplant "trade remedy" laws — most especially antidumping and subsidies/countervailing measures laws (but also other "safeguard" laws). At present, such laws represent no more than a second-best approach to ensuring that the benefits of more liberalized trade are not lost to predation or other anticompetitive practices, as is presumably their intent. More to the point, however, by almost any test these laws act not in accordance with this presumed intent, but rather as a form of back-door protectionism.[4] It is truly difficult to reconcile such back-door protectionism with the concept of a free trade zone, but it is also hard to argue against the notion that the gains from liberalized trade can be offset by the anticompetitive actions of very large producers. An effective supranational competition policy is the optimal way to ensure against the latter without bearing the costs of the former.

4) In order to preserve the benefits of free trade, some actions that officials (responsible for competition policy) might seek to take in the name of promoting competition would be directed not toward private firms, but rather toward governments. The main area for such actions is state aids to firms. The new(ish) economic literature on strategic trade theory, for example, posits that under certain circumstances governments might be able to achieve a net welfare gain domestically by using state aids to achieve transfer of rents from foreign to domestic residents, but at the cost of welfare losses in the affected foreign countries. To the extent that such transfers might occur within North America, they would clearly be contrary to the spirit of North American free trade.

We discuss these arguments in somewhat greater detail in the remainder of this study. The discussion is divided into three parts: The North American Dimension, where we examine issue 1) above; Differences in National Laws and Policies, where we consider issue 2); and Supranationality as an Alternative to Trade Policy Remedies, where we combine the discussions of issues 3) and 4).

THE NORTH AMERICAN DIMENSION

TO BEGIN, IT CAN BE fairly asked what issues (or cases) have a "North American dimension" that extends beyond a national dimension?

One answer is that virtually any transaction that qualifies as intra-North American direct investment has such a dimension. Such transactions include, for example, (but are not limited to) the merger, acquisition or joint venture of (or between) a firm based in one North American country with (or by) a firm based in some other North American nation. For the sake of simplification, let us assume such a transaction where, prior to the merger, neither of the merging parties has operations or is generating sales outside its home country. In this example the merger would not increase the concentration of sellers in either national market, but it would nonetheless increase seller concentration within the unified North American market. Of course this last effect by itself would not necessarily be objectionable; an increase in seller concentration would be objectionable only if competition were restricted as a result. But the point is that if national authorities consider only seller concentration within their jurisdiction (even if in fact they do not act quite so parochially), then a possibly objectionable merger might not be challenged by national authorities because the span of their jurisdiction is not sufficiently wide to judge the overall effects of the merger on competition.

Perhaps another more realistic possibility is that in the absence of a supranational competition policy, such a merger might be ruled as objectionable by one national authority whereas in the broader North American context it would not be seen as objectionable. How might this situation arise? Suppose the transaction consisted of the takeover of firm X in country A by firm Y based in country B (both countries, of course, are in North America), where firm Y is seen by the authorities in country A as being much stronger than any of the remaining firms operating in the relevant market in country A. The authorities in country A might thus seek to block the merger on grounds that firm X, once acquired and under foreign control, would emerge as the dominant firm in the local market (country A). But, viewed from an overall North American perspective, it may well be that the combined entity still has effective competition within the total free trade territory and that the merger is therefore *not* objectionable.

Both of the above scenarios assume, of course, that national authorities are parochial and incapable of judging the effects of factors beyond their national boundaries. To some extent this is unfair because in both Canada and the United States, for example, law and policy explicitly attempt to take into account the effects of international factors on the situation in the domestic market. Nonetheless, it is in order to point out that a consistent complaint of international business executives directed toward competition authorities is that major decisions involve somewhat parochial considerations. These contribute to costly uncertainties that may inhibit international mergers, acquisitions and investments.[5]

But even if national authorities are capable of analyzing the effects of mergers that extend beyond their national boundaries, there are situations where they might still make decisions that are not compatible with overall North American interests. Suppose, in the example above, that the merger entails an efficiency gain, and that from an overall North American perspective it can be ascertained that this gain overrides any effect of reduced competition. However, officials in country A (the country of the smaller firm) believe that the efficiency gains will be appropriated by the larger firm via dividend payments and hence that no benefits of these gains would be realized on their soil. Under the NAFTA, these officials would have no power (except under special circumstances) to control these payments. They might thus decide to prevent the merger on the grounds that there are no benefits to residents of their country, but the merger would, nonetheless, entail benefits to North America — and so a North American competition bureau might still allow the merger.

In recent years, two proposed acquisitions of Canadian corporations have illustrated the importance of — and the need for — international harmonization, convergence and/or co-operation for competition law and policy. In 1990, the U.S. Federal Trade Commission (FTC) reviewed the acquisition of Connaught Bio Sciences, Inc. of Canada by Institut Merieux, S.A. of France. Merieux, the only firm selling rabies vaccine on a national basis in the United States, sought to acquire Connaught, which was the only vendor of inactivated polio vaccine in the United States. The FTC identified each firm as being among the few potential entrants into the other's U.S. market (potential competitors).

Although the FTC found that the proposed acquisition would likely forestall competition within the U.S. market, it was faced with a problem — there were minimal assets in the United States with which to create a viable competitive remedy. The Canadian Bureau of Competition Policy did not challenge the acquisition despite its finding that the acquisition would eliminate competition in the Canadian rabies vaccine market. Instead, the Director allowed the acquisition to proceed but indicated that he would monitor it for three years.

To the FTC, however, it appeared that a remedy would have to be implemented in Canada. Notwithstanding this fact, by a vote of 3 to 2, the FTC obtained a consent decree from the parties whereby Connaught's rabies vaccine would be licensed to an FTC-approved licensee for at least 25 years, and FTC approval would be required if Merieux sought to purchase any other such interest in another country for a ten-year period. After a formal protest from the government of Canada, the FTC gave Investment Canada the right to veto any proposed license. (However, no mention was made of the Canadian Bureau of Competition Policy.) As a practical matter, neither Merieux nor an independent trustee has been able to find an acceptable licensee and so the FTC eventually re-opened the file for public comment with a view to dropping this requirement.[6]

Interestingly, in the *Guidelines for International Operations* issued by the U.S. Department of Justice (DOJ) in 1988, the DOJ indicated in an illustrative case that it would not take jurisdiction in a case of this kind. The FTC did not feel bound to interpret international comity concerns the same way as the DOJ — so the *Connaught/Merieux* case points to several important themes. First, the bifurcated structure of antitrust enforcement at the federal level, and dual enforcement between the state and federal level in the United States, make it difficult for contentious issues to be resolved simply by bilateral consultation and co-operation. Thus, in cases like *Connaught/Merieux*, a supra-national institutional solution is of crucial importance in reducing bilateral tension. However, *Connaught/Merieux* also illustrates how difficult it may be to achieve such a supranational institution, given the institutional basis of U.S. antitrust law.

Second, although both countries analyzed the acquisition through substantially similar approaches (Appendix A), they ultimately reached different conclusions about the acquisition. This suggests that mere convergence or, for that matter, harmonization of law and policy cannot resolve the full range of potential disputes. We believe that, at the very least, a supra-national institution would deal with a common investigatory record as well as have an analytical approach, and thus would be better suited to resolving the substantive issues. From our vantage point, it seems that this conclusion would hold at the level of remedial issues. Surely a supranational body would have more credible authority in requesting a remedy in Canada than an agency of the U.S. government.

Similar concerns were raised by the proposed acquisition of de Havilland of Canada from Boeing Co. of the United States by the French-Italian consortium comprised of Aerospatiale, S.A. and Alenia SpA. Both the EC Commission and the Canadian Bureau of Competition Policy reviewed this acquisition. Although the Canadians allowed the acquisition to proceed, the EC Commission, for the first (and so far the only) time, rejected the proposed transaction. On the basis of the limited information publicly available, it appears that the two authorities had substantial disagreement over issues such as product market definition and whether efficiencies or "failing firm" concerns ought to override concern for market power effects in Canada and the EC.[7] While not in a position to comment definitively on these issues, we believe that the *de Havilland* example only underlines the case for supranational antitrust enforcement in North America, and the need to apply it, eventually, on a much wider basis.

While both of these cases involve international mergers and acquisitions, the issues raised also apply to proposed research, production or distribution joint ventures, and other forms of international strategic alliances.[8] One advantage, then, of a supranational North American competition policy is that relevant authorities would be explicitly charged with viewing the relevant (geographical) market as no less than North American. (This would be so unless, of course, there were identifiable geographical barriers to entry — as if the relevant market were a sub-region of North America. If such barriers were discovered to exist, the authorities would then be able to view the relevant regional market in its entirety, without regard to national boundary. Presumably, if the issues were limited to a region that lay entirely within one country, they would be handled competently by national authorities alone, whereas if the region crossed national boundaries, the supranational authorities would play some role.) In making its ruling, a supranational authority would be in a position to determine the effects on a North American basis, and to recommend or take action based on an assessment of what is in the net overall benefit to North America.

The case for a supranational authority can be generalized by stating simply that in a world where the operations of firms cross national boundaries, it follows that the jurisdiction of competition authorities ought to cross national boundaries as well. In one class of situations, such a jurisdiction would make it easier to identify cases where a multinational firm's conduct might seem innocuous within a national market, but where the pattern of conduct considered over a number of such markets amounts to an abuse of market power. In a second class of situations a supranational authority might also prevent action being taken against a firm (or a transaction) by a national government where that government judges the effect of its action is to increase benefits to its nationals but where, in a larger context, the action would reduce North American welfare.

Making a case for a North American competition authority at a supranational level does not mean there is to be no continuing role for national authorities. Indeed, many situations would arise that would have no effects across a national boundary. Such situations would be best left to national authorities. In this regard, the European concept of "subsidiarity" would be a useful model for North America. Translated to a North American context, this means simply that supranational authorities would handle only those cases or situations where there are clearly effects that cross national boundaries. To make such a concept operational is not easy, and Europe is still wrestling with the problem. But in the realm of competition policy, some wisdom has already emerged from the European experience. Mergers and acquisitions are vetted by DGIV only if they meet certain overall size thresholds and if the parties to the transaction have sales above other specified thresholds in more than one European nation. Transactions are vetted either by DGIV or by national authorities, but not by both. So, if a transaction falls under DGIV's purview, and DGIV does not block it, it cannot subsequently be undone by national authorities — with one exception. If there are national security issues at stake, in the name of national security, national authorities can block a merger that DGIV would otherwise allow. Subsidiarity does not apply to DGIV's authority to review and regulate state aids to industry. If national governments could override DGIV on these matters, it would be akin to putting the fox in charge of guarding the chickens.

Differences in National Laws and Policies

THERE ARE NUMEROUS specific differences in the competition laws of Canada, the United States, and Mexico.[9] Although it is not the purpose of this study to attempt to delineate or reconcile these differences in detail, Appendices A and B examine two areas — regulation of mergers and acquisitions, and regulation of predation — where the laws, policies and procedures of the three countries differ substantially, but where harmonization might be possible.

Given the main thrust of this study (that a supranational approach to competition policy makes sense for North America), the main point of this section is that such an approach could provide a basis for harmonization of national laws, policies and procedures. We believe that such harmonization is intrinsically desirable if for no other reason than that firms operating in North America be subject to reasonably consistent competition standards. It can also be argued, of course, that creation of a supranational authority is neither necessary nor sufficient to bring about harmonization although EC experience points to the fact that supranational standards can play a catalytic role in the harmonization of national standards.[10] In North America, the very process by which supranational standards would be written (presumably via a set of negotiations conducted by expert representatives of the three governments) should facilitate harmonization and, one might hope, a revamping of certain aspects of the existing law that have become somewhat frayed in some of the countries.[11]

It would be a mistake to underestimate the difficulties that are likely to be encountered in an effort to reach common standards; they are many and great, as shown in the two Appendices to this study. The magnitude of the difficulties is, perhaps, more apparent to lawyers than to economists, but both professions have a contribution to make. It is notable, however, that difficulties occur more often with respect to the correct *means* by which to achieve an end on which the differing parties fundamentally agree than on the *end* itself. This suggests that resolution, while difficult, is not impossible. For example, as Appendix A demonstrates, there is general agreement that to the extent that mergers reduce competition, they are bad, and that to the extent that mergers increase efficiency, they are good. Thus from a public policy perspective, there is general agreement that some mergers entail a trade-off between loss of competition and gain of efficiency. But there is no agreement within North America on exactly how to measure this or how ultimately to weight the two sides of the trade-off. Despite this, as argued in Appendix A, resolution of the differences should not be considered unlikely or implausible.

Overall, our sense is that harmonization of competition laws is feasible and desirable; we also acknowledge that to achieve this, it is not necessary to adopt a supranational approach. We do believe, however, that any move in this direction will facilitate harmonization and, furthermore, that harmonization is not the only reason to seek supranationality.

Supranationality as an Alternative to Trade Policy "Remedies"

The NAFTA is designed to bring about benefits resulting from freer trade within North America and to distribute these benefits among all the signatory nations. There appears to be a strong residual fear that freer trade can also bring with it harmful consequences and that these cannot be identified *ex ante*. Thus, there has been no effort in the NAFTA to reduce the powers of the signatory countries to use, against one another, the so-called "less than fair value" (LTFV) measures of trade law — specifically the anti-dumping and antisubsidies measures which are sanctified by the GATT, but which the nations of the European Community long ago agreed to abolish with respect to intra-Community trade.

As of December 31, 1991, 15 U.S. anti-dumping orders and findings of dumping by the U.S. trade authorities were in effect against Canada and three were in effect against Mexico, out of a total of 216 such orders and findings. As of the same date, there were three countervailing duty orders and findings in effect against Canada and four in effect against Mexico, out of a total of sixty-six. Thus, roughly 8.3 percent of all U.S. anti-dumping orders and findings (Canada 6.9 percent and Mexico 1.4 percent) and 10.6 percent of all countervailing duty orders and findings (Canada 4.5 percent and Mexico 6.1 percent) pertained to North American nations. In that year, these nations generated about 25 percent of all U.S. imports (Canada 19 percent and Mexico 6 percent).[12]

There is considerable evidence and analysis suggesting that the use of LTFV measures is proliferating worldwide and that the procedures by which these are carried out are biased against importers and in favour of the interests of domestic producers.[13] This bias often acts against consumers' interests, including the case where the product is an intermediate good and the "consumer" is a firm using this good to make a final product. So, in this sense, the bias can work against certain domestic producers as well. Generally, these laws are administered by agencies using procedures biased against the importer and against which a rational defense is hard to mount.

Among the problems associated with the administration of anti-dumping laws in North America are:

- Detailed information requests and short time for firms to respond.

- Lack of a causal nexus between the alleged dumping and the "material injury" to the relevant domestic industry.

473

- Invidious comparison of individual export prices with a weighted average of home country prices to determine a dumping margin, a procedure that tends to exaggerate the magnitudes of these margins.

- Frequent use of constructed cost measures of dumping that examine average total costs rather than some measure of marginal cost, as economics suggests should be used.

- Use of pre-determined fixed minimums for profits and overhead in constructed cost measures.

- Low or non-existent *de minimis* thresholds for dumping determinations.

As a result of these factors, it is often said the LTFV laws are tantamount to a growing form of "back-door protectionism".

Proponents of LTFV laws argue that they safeguard domestic producers against imports that are somehow priced too low, whether by the intent of a firm to increase its market share by pricing below cost or by virtue of a foreign government subsidizing its exports. There is considerable debate surrounding the circumstances where such practices by an exporting firm or government are rational, i.e., whether or not the firm or government can expect to garner rents from foreigners by engaging in these practices. With respect to firm underpricing (dumping), under most theoretical scenarios rents can only be realized during periods subsequent to the underpricing: that is, the firm must at some point raise its price in order to realize the rent.[14] When this occurs, competing domestic producers might reenter the market and drive the price back down — a consideration the exporting firm must take into account. In the absence of sunk entry or exit costs, it might never make sense for a firm to engage in dumping. But if these costs are present, a firm might be able to drive its competitors out of the market and, subsequently, raise its price sufficiently to garner rents high enough to justify the earlier losses but low enough to deter new entry.

Government subsidies can achieve rent transfers from residents of a foreign country to the those of the home country under a number of circumstances, including situations where firms must precommit large amounts of resources before beginning production of a product (hence laying the groundwork for a latent "natural monopoly") or situations where a domestic firm competes against a foreign firm in the context of a Cournot duopoly. In this latter case, it is generally true that if the government of the foreign firm subsidizes its sales in the domestic market, the additional rents garnered by that firm (and, presumably, transferred back to the foreign country) will exceed the costs of the subsidy. This suggests that the subsidy would be granted in perpetuity. In the former case, the subsidy is generally granted on a one-time, lump-sum basis.[15]

In most circumstances both dumping and subsidies are likely to reduce the welfare of the entire system when used as measures to extract rents from foreigners, even if they succeed in enhancing the welfare in the nation employing the measure.[16]

Whether the circumstances actually exist under which it makes economic sense for an exporting firm to sell its products below cost (dump them) into foreign markets, or for a government to subsidize such sales, the belief is strong, particularly in the United States, that domestic firms are vulnerable to such actions within the North American market and that safe-guards are necessary to counter them when they occur. It is our understanding that Canada, while negotiating both the FTA and the NAFTA, was interested in exploring means to eliminate the LTFV laws with respect to intra-North American trade and that Mexico expressed similar interests during the latter negotiations. The United States, however, reportedly was adamantly opposed to any such possibility in both cases.

We believe, however, that competition policy will play a paramount role in any future steps in this direction. Antipredation measures in the anti-monopolies laws are designed precisely to counter efforts by one firm to achieve dominance by employing measures to drive its competitors out of business; they thus serve much the same function as anti-dumping laws. If competition policy were to move into the domain of regulation of state aids to industry, as is the case in Europe but not North America (see the introduction to this study), then competition policy could also serve much the same function as subsidies/countervailing measures law.

What would be the advantages of replacing LTFV laws with equivalent measures of competition policy? The main advantage would be to remove much of the pro-domestic producer bias now generally believed to be present in the administration of LTFV law.

In order for competition policy/ predation law to supplant anti-dumping law, a tighter predation law would be required. Present law, as discussed in Appendix B, is not well defined, especially in the United States. U.S. standards in this area are largely determined by case law interpreting relevant features of the *Sherman Act*, and the Robinson Patman amendments to the *Clayton Act*; inconsistencies in court rulings are rife. As noted elsewhere in this study, however, one of the reasons for suggesting a supranational approach to competition policy is that this would contribute to better law and policy, and predation appears to be one area where there is much scope for improvement.

One of our main points of concern in this study focuses on price predation of the kind usually addressed by national predatory pricing and price discrim-ination laws and policies. However, this emphasis should not be construed to mean that we are less interested in other non-price forms of predation. Some commentators have suggested, for example, that predation can be accom-plished by means that lead to the foreclosure or exclusion of competitors from the market. These "raising rivals costs" theories involve the use of vertical restraints (tying, refusal to deal, exclusive dealing and territorial restrictions, resale price maintenance) and contracts with input suppliers in order to gain horizontal market power.[17] It would not make sense to end international price predation while permitting firms to switch to international strategies of non-price predation. While a discussion of the strengths and weaknesses of these theories is beyond the scope of this study, we believe that any supranational institution should also be able to examine anticompetitive exclusion through non-price predation that occurs on a continental (North American) scale.

If competition policy is to supplant subsidies/countervailing measures, supranationality is an absolute requirement. A condition for this would be some effective means by which subsidies that have distortive trade effects could be controlled at the source.

INSTITUTIONAL ARRANGEMENTS FOR COMPETITION POLICY IN THE CONTEXT OF THE NAFTA

A S MUCH AS WE ADMIRE many of the features of European Community competition policy, we wish to make it clear at the outset that we do not believe that DGIV is a feasible institutional model for North America — essentially for two reasons:

First, DGIV has acted *de facto* as an investigative and prosecuting agency *and* as judge and jury in cases involving decisions relating to *Treaty of Rome* articles 85 and 86. We do not believe that it would be acceptable in North America for a supranational entity to hold as much power *independently of the signatory nations* as has DGIV. To be sure, the decisions of DGIV are reviewable by the European Court of Justice, which has tended over the years to rule in favour of the powers it has claimed. Nonetheless, DGIV has exhibited a distinct lack of accountability that would not be acceptable in North America.

Second, as suggested earlier, much of the power of DGIV has derived from rulings (or, in some important cases, *obiter dicta*) of the European Court of Justice, the supranational authority of which has not been challenged by the European states. The NAFTA by contrast has no institution that is even close to having the power or stature of the European Court of Justice, and we neither advocate nor foresee the establishment of such an institution. Thus, any powers held by a North American supranational authority would have to be backed by its standing in national courts rather than in a supranational judicial body.

Before setting out our model for a North American Competition Commission (NACC), we offer a few brief comments on the existing dispute settlement mechanisms under the FTA and the proposed Agreement itself. Recall, however, that as currently drafted the NAFTA excludes competition issues from its dispute settlement mechanisms under Chapter 15 . However, the so called "Chapter 19" dispute settlement mechanism provides for the establishment of expert panels to review administrative decisions in anti-dumping and countervailing duty cases. These panels become effective only when the relevant administrative agency has reached a final decision and all other domestic appeal avenues have been exhausted. This panel mechanism was created to deal with the perceived "administered" protection by the relevant agencies which were believed to be improperly interpreting domestic law.[18] In addition, the FTA dispute settlement mechanisms have not stemmed the number of investigations initiated by the various domestic agencies.[19] In the competition law area, particularly in the United States over the last decade, policy has been considerably more liberal than the existing precedent from judicially decided cases. Hence, recourse to FTA- or NAFTA-type dispute settlements would not likely be sufficient to deal with the kind of disputes discussed earlier.

Both the FTA (Chapter 18) and the NAFTA (Chapter 20) provide for recourse to dispute settlement panels when a party believes that an actual or proposed measure initiated by another party is likely to be inconsistent with, or would nullify and impair, obligations under either agreement. However, to be effective with respect to competition policy, the parties still would have to reach a consensus on the laws and policies to be enforced. Even then, the ultimate decision whether to adopt a panel report remains political and, at most, the vindicated party only gains the right to withdraw other trade concessions. Thus, the initial competition concern is not likely to be remedied, and the withdrawal of trade concessions or other trade disciplines may create new competition concerns over cartel behaviour in either market.

What we see as a future possibility, therefore, is a NACC styled somewhat along the lines of the Federal Trade Commission: i.e., a professional body with a full-time staff headed by a panel of commissioners appointed for fixed terms by their national governments. An equal number would serve from each country, and each commissioner would have one vote. The commissioners would be responsible for initiating cases (following procedures to be described shortly), and for decisions pertaining to their termination. Independent professional and support staffs would carry out investigations and make recommendations to the commissioners.

In the realm of anti-monopolies, the powers of the NACC would be more limited but still substantial. Subject to guidelines and procedures described below, this body would be empowered to review the conduct of firms deemed to be anticompetitive (including predatory practices) and other activities with effects that cross national borders. Based upon its findings, the NACC would be empowered to enter into settlement agreements with the relevant firms, on a case-by-case basis whereby these firms would agree to cease and desist from practices identified by the commission as anticompetitive, and obtain consent decrees approved by the relevant national courts or administrative tribunals. The consent decrees would be enforceable in the courts of any of the three signatory nations.

Alternatively, in cases where the NACC and the relevant firms are unable mutually to agree to the terms of a consent decree, the Commission would have standing to bring suit against these firms in the national courts of the signatory nations.

Subject to thresholds of a generic kind (such as those adopted in Europe), the NACC would also be empowered to review transborder mergers and acquisitions within North America and to issue recommendations concerning the consummation of a proposed merger or acquisition. However, in order to enjoin such a transaction, the Commission would be required to bring an action in the relevant national courts. The private right of action in mergers and acquisition cases exists in the United States but not in Canada or Mexico. Therefore, U.S. law would have to be amended to suspend the private right of action in cases under review by the NACC.

On the matter of how this commission would determine what cases to investigate, we look to the United Kingdom's Monopolies and Mergers Commission (MMC) as an example. The MMC can review a case only if it is formally referred to it by the UK Department of Industry and Trade. Similarly, we would require that the NACC be allowed to review a case only if it is referred to it by competent national authorities such as the Canadian Bureau of Competition Policy, the Mexican Federal Competition Commission, and the U.S. Federal Trade Commission or Antitrust Division of the Department of Justice. A key element is that any of these agencies could refer a case not only where the effects were felt within its jurisdiction but also where the anti-competitive conduct took place (in whole or in part) within the jurisdiction of another signatory nation. So, if products made by a U.S. firm in the United States were deemed to be subject to predatory pricing in Mexico, the Mexican Federal Competition Commission could refer the case to the NACC.

Once the case is referred to (and accepted by) the NACC, the Commission would have the authority to request assistance from the relevant authorities in each of the national jurisdictions. This could be accomplished through procedures along the lines of those currently in effect pursuant to the various treaties on mutual Legal Assistance in Criminal Matters between Canada, Mexico and the United States and/or the *Memorandum of Understanding between Canada and the United States as to Notification, Consultation, and Cooperation in Antitrust Matters*. Assistance could also include locating persons or objects, serving documents, taking testimony, providing documents and records, and executing requests for searches and seizures. The NACC would not have independent powers of discovery but rather would rely on the existing bilateral framework of cooperation.

Would the NACC be forced to review every case referred to it? Not necessarily. A majority vote of the commissioners would be required for acceptance. In the example above, presumably, all the Mexican commissioners would vote to accept the case. If the U.S. commissioners voted against acceptance, the decision would rest with the Canadians who, in this example at least, would serve collectively as a disinterested third party. We believe that one merit of our proposal is that where a commissioners' vote on a referred case is split between two countries along lines of nationality, the deciding ballots would be cast by commissioners from the third country. The latter, presumably, would be better placed to weigh the case solely on its merits than would those from the affected countries.

Given that the ultimate standing of the NACC with respect to anti-monopoly regulation would rest upon its ability to pursue a case in a national court, its effectiveness would depend upon the courts of all the NAFTA signatory countries behaving in a fair and impartial manner. The effectiveness of the NACC would also require that there be convergence in national laws pertaining to monopolies and monopolistic practices.

On matters of subsidies, the NACC would pit itself against a NAFTA government in any review it undertakes. For this reason the NACC must have special powers in this area. The ingredients of a successful subsidy review and regulation scheme might therefore include the following:

1) A set of standards with respect to what are, and what are not, acceptable types and magnitudes of subsidy agreed to by each NAFTA country. These standards would then be "enabled" through passage into national law in each of the three NAFTA countries. This would ensure, *inter alia*, that violations of the standards be prosecutable under national law of each country and that these laws are binding on all sub-national entities.

2) Agreement among the NAFTA governments that the NACC be empowered to review the subsidy programs of any of the three nations should include the right of the Commission to question national governments. The government of any of the three nations could also request such a review and, unlike a request for an anti-monopoly review, a review in this case would be mandatory. However, unlike DGIV, the NACC would not be empowered to self-initiate such a review.

3) Findings and recommendations issued by the NACC regarding subsidies investigations. Once issued, the government against which the complaint is lodged could either accept the findings and recommendations and take appropriate action to implement the recommendations, subject to NACC monitoring or it could contest the NACC findings and recommendations by entering into dispute settlement procedures with the government that initiated the investigation. These procedures would first entail consultations to attempt to resolve the dispute. If these failed, the case would then be submitted to binding arbitration, where

the arbitration panel would decide whether or not to order implementation of the findings and recommendations.

4) Mechanisms might allow the government lodging a complaint to contest the findings and recommendations of the NACC if it chooses to do so. If it decides to follow this course, the government with the complaint would be required to enter into dispute settlement procedures with the government against which the complaint is lodged, involving, first, consultations and, these failing, arbitration. In this event, the arbitrator could order either that the case be subject to a new investigation or that the original findings and recommendations be accepted.

5) Powers assigned to the NACC, sufficient to enable it to monitor implementation of its findings and recommendations, where a government has agreed to accept these or has been ordered to do so under arbitration. If a government failed to live up to the terms of the findings and recommendations, the NACC would then have standing to seek relief in the courts of that country under the enabling legislation.

The powers of the NACC related to state subsidies would necessarily extend to sub-national governmental entities as well as to federal governments. However, only federal authorities would have the power to bring a case before the NACC.

The granting of limited powers to the NACC to regulate state subsidies is, admittedly, rather strong stuff, and we are well aware that the United States, Canada and Mexico are probably not quite ready for it at this time. Nonetheless, we believe there are a number of merits in having the NACC exercise such powers that should be considered. The first of these merits, already discussed, is that a NACC with powers to regulate state subsidies could enable the jettisoning of the LTFV trade laws, or at least the subsidies/countervailing measures parts of these laws. These laws are themselves flawed, and their replacement would be beneficial to all.

Second, the mechanism described above would go into effect only if a subsidy is deemed by one North American government to be detrimental to its national interests. Unlike DGIV, which can go after subsidies even when "no one has complained", the only subsidies that would come under NACC purview would be those having cross-border effects deemed undesirable by a signatory government of the NACC.

Note that many of these subsidies have perverse overall effects on government budgets. For example, investment subsidies (or, as they are euphemistically termed, "incentives") to attract investment by multinational corporations are prevalent in North America, largely at the state/provincial levels. Studies have consistently indicated that these incentives have little effect on the generation of net new investment.[20] Rather, such incentives affect only the precise geographical location of an investment that, otherwise, would have been made elsewhere in North America in the absence of any incentives whatsoever. It could thus be argued that all governments would be better off if none were to offer such subsidies (or, at least, the taxpayers who fund these governments would be better off). Yet, governments often argue that they must offer such incentives essentially as offsets to similar incentives offered by rival entities. If the NACC could serve as a guarantor that no state/province would offer these incentives, all states and provinces would find it in their interests to withdraw from the incentives game.[21]

Third, there might be circumstances in which a government would wish to provide a subsidy that is arguably efficiency or welfare enhancing. Subsidies to research and development might, for example, fall into this category, as do subsidies to certain worker training programs conducted by private firms. The standards referred to in item 1) above need simply be written so as to exclude these from those practices that are actionable by the NACC.

CONCLUSIONS

WE RECOGNIZE THAT SOME of our proposals made in this study are somewhat visionary; at the same time, we recognize that others have had similar visions.[22] A North American competition policy and administering agency organized along the lines spelled out here would be resisted in many quarters. Opponents would certainly object on the basis of cost, the dangers of a new bureaucracy, and possible loss of national sovereignty. We appreciate these costs and dangers, but we also believe that our proposals minimize these and that, even after allowing for them, there is still net benefit to be had from their implementation.

It is fair to ask, "what are the benefits?" and to expect an answer involving hard figures as well as words. We admit that we have not yet attempted to quantify the benefits; on the basis of the efforts of others, however, we believe them to be substantial — even if one considers only the cost savings that would accrue from reforming the present administration of LTFV laws.[23] In addition, there is significant potential for cost savings through reform of other domestic laws and policies in all three North American countries. In short, the message of this study is: "yes" to competition among North American multinationals and "yes" to co-operation among the enforcers of North American competition policy.

ENDNOTES

1 See L. Waverman (ed.) *Corporate Globalization through Mergers and Acquisitions*, (Calgary: University of Calgary Press, 1991) especially the chapters by Khemani, Knubley *et al.*, and Baldwin and Caves.

2 Unlike the NAFTA, the *Treaty of Rome* establishing the European Common Market did not require that each member country have a competition law or authority, and in fact not all did. By now, however, all of the large European Community nations do have national laws and enforcement agencies. Hence, in Europe at the time of the inauguration of the European Community, the need for a Community competition policy was arguably more compelling than in North America at the time of the inauguration of the NAFTA.

3 This is the essence of one of the principal rationales for a European competition policy authority invested in the European Commission — that there are issues that have a community dimension that cannot be adequately handled at the national level. The community dimension must be balanced against the principle of subsidiarity, i.e., that issues not having a community dimension are within the sole jurisdiction of national authorities. The 1989 EC Merger Regulation (Council Reg. 4064/89, Dec. 21, 1989) contains explicit thresholds for determining whether or not a merger within the European Community has a community dimension.

4 The sheer volume of anti-dumping and subsidies cases within North America (i. e., where both the accuser and accused were North American) suggests that there is much more going on than ensuring that markets remain competitive. See generally, A. Anderson & A. M. Rugman, "Country-Factor Bias in the Administration of Anti-dumping and Countervailing Duty Cases" in M. J. Trebilcock & R. C. York (eds.), *Fair Exchange: Reforming Trade Remedy Laws*, (Toronto: C. D. Howe Institute, 1990) and A. M. Rugman & S. D. Porteous, "Canadian and U.S. Unfair Trade Laws: A Comparison of Their Legal and Administrative Structures", *North Carolina Journal of International Law and Commercial Regulation* (March 1990).

5 See generally, C. S. Goldman, "Regulation of Mergers, Acquisitions and Investment in a Global Market" in *Proceedings of the Eighth Annual Conference of Canada and International Trade*, Centre for Trade Policy and Law, May 19, 1993.

6 *Re Institut Merieux*, S. A., F. T. C. Docket No. C-3301 3/12/93.

7 The Director of International and Economic Affairs at the Canadian Bureau of Competition Policy has publicly stated that the Bureau decided not to challenge the merger because of "efficiency gains in Canada, the limited competitive effects on the small Canadian market for commuter aircraft, and because of the potential that de Havilland was a failing firm".

See D. Ireland *et al.*, "Globalization, the Canadian Competition Act and the Future policy Agenda" in *Proceedings of the Eighth Annual Conference on Canada and International Trade*, Centre for Trade Policy and Law, Ottawa, May 18-19, 1993.

8 See generally, E. M. Graham, "Multinational Enterprise and Competition Policy" 4 *International Economic Insights*, 26, (July/ August 1993) and E. M. Graham, "Beyond Borders: On the Globalization of Business" 25 *Harvard International Review* 8 (Summer 1993). See also Rugman & D'Cruz in this volume.

9 P. L. Warner, "Canada-United States Free Trade: The Case for Replacing Antidumping with Antitrust", 23:4, *Law and Policy in International Business*, 791, (1992); I. Feltham et al., *Competition (Antitrust) and Antidumping Laws in the Context of the Canada- U.S. Free Trade Agreement* (1991); and N. Campbell & M. J. Trebilcock, "A Comparative Analysis of Merger Law: Canada, the United States, and the European Community", 15:3, *World Competition*, 1, (March 1992).

10 See e.g. Sir Leon Brittan, *European Competition Policy: Keeping the Playing Field Level*, (London: Brassey's for CEPS, 1992).

11 The reader is entitled to ask "What might these be?" The authors had in mind specifically the U.S. *Robinson-Patman Act*. But surely other laws could also be addressed.

12 U.S. International Trade Commission, *The Year in Trade: Operations of the Trade Agreements Program*, August 1992, Tables A-20 and A-22.

13 See, for example, the excellent essays on subject in Richard Boltuck & Robert Litan (eds.), *Down in the Dumps: Administration of the Unfair Trade Laws*, (Washington, D. C.: The Brookings Institution, 1991); see especially the essays by Francois, Palmeter & Anspacher, by Boltuck, Francois & Kaplan, and by Baldwin & Moore. See also the essays in a "Symposium on Unfair Imports," 61, *University of Cincinnati Law Review* 877-853 (1993). These essays bear especially on U.S. administration of the laws, but similar biases have been found in Canada; see S. D. Porteous & A. M. Rugman, "Canadian Unfair Trade Laws and Corporate Strategy" 3 *Review of International Business Law*, 237, (1989). See also J. R. Holbein *et al.*, "Comparative Analysis of Specific Elements in United States and Canadian Unfair Trade Law," 26, *The International Lawyer*, 873, (Winter 1992). With respect to Mexico, see P. F. McLaughlin, "Mexico's Antidumping and Countervailing Duty Laws: Amenable to a Free Trade Agreement?" 23, *Law and Policy in International Business* 1009 (1992).

14 If unrealized economies of scale or of learning are extant, the firm might not have to raise price in subsequent periods in order to garner a rent. A full treatment of this case is far beyond the scope of this study. The interested reader should consult Grossman & Helpman, *Innovation and Growth in the Global Economy*, (Cambridge: The MIT Press, 1991).

15 See Grossman & Helpman 1991, *Id.*

16 Exceptions to this statement can be conceived, however. For example, if dumping drives out excess entry in an industry marked by scale or learning economies, the dumping might actually enhance overall welfare. A subsidy can do likewise. However, see P. Krugman, "Does the New Trade Theory Require a New Trade Policy" 15 *The World Economy* 423 at 437-438 (July 1992) where he warns of a possible Prisoner's Dilemma if two countries try to protect a sector subject to external economies and end up fragmenting the market, leaving both worse off.

17 T. G. Krattenmaker & S. C. Salop, "Anticompetitive Exclusion: Raising Rival's Costs to Achieve Power Over Price," 96 *Yale Law Journal* 209 (1986) and S. C. Salop and D. T. Scheffman," Raising Rival's Costs", in *American Economic Association: Papers and Proceedings* 267 (May 1983).

18 See generally, *supra* note 13, Boltuck & Litan (eds.) and A. M. Rugman, "A Canadian Perspective on U.S. Administered Protection and the Free Trade Agreement," *University of Maine Law Review* 40 (1988).

19 T. M. Boddez & M. J. Trebilcock, *Unfinished Business: Reforming Trade Remedy Laws in North America*, (Toronto: The C. D. Howe Institute, 1993).

20 See generally, S. E. Guisinger, *Investment Incentives and Performance Requirements: Patterns of International Trade, Production and Investment*, (New York: Praeger Publishing, 1985).

21 However, because the NACC would investigate a subsidy only if the case were initiated by the national competition authorities in a NAFTA country, the NACC likely would miss a subsidy offered by one U.S. state that is objectionable to other U.S. states but does not affect Mexico or Canada. The mission of the NACC is not to interfere in matters that are confined to one country. If, by contrast, the subsidy of a U.S. state were to be objectionable to a Canadian or Mexican province, that case could be brought to the NACC by the Canadian or Mexican federal authorities on behalf of the province concerned.

22 See, for instance, Dunning in this volume.

23 See, e.g., Boddez & Trebilcock, *supra* note 20.

APPENDIX A

MERGER REVIEW IN THE UNITED STATES, CANADA AND MEXICO: A COMPARATIVE ANALYSIS

INTRODUCTION

THIS APPENDIX COMPARES the key provisions and approaches of North American merger guidelines. We have taken a textual approach to interpreting these guidelines which does not include any discussion as to how the courts or agencies have dealt with the guidelines or merger review, generally. Furthermore, our focus here is on the substantive merger law and policy of each country. Ultimately, any harmonization of merger review in North America would also need to address issues of merger notification and sharing of confidential information across borders.

In April 1992 the U.S. Department of Justice (the DOJ) and the Federal Trade Commission (the FTC) (collectively, the U.S. Federal Agencies) jointly released new *Horizontal Merger Guidelines* (the U.S. Federal Agencies' 1992 Guidelines).[1] The National Association of Attorneys General (the NAAG) had published its *Antitrust Enforcement: Horizontal Merger Guidelines of the National Association of Attorneys General* (the NAAG Guidelines) in March 1987, which were revised in March 1993. The NAAG Guidelines indicate how the American states' (the states') attorneys general believe mergers should be reviewed in each of their own jurisdictions. In November 1988, the DOJ had issued new *Antitrust Guidelines for International Operations* (International Guidelines) which offer several illustrative cases as a guide to the manner in which the DOJ would analyze international mergers.

In March 1991 the Canadian Bureau of Competition Policy (the Bureau) published its *Merger Enforcement Guidelines* (Canadian Guidelines). In December 1992 the Mexican Congress passed its first Federal Law of Trade Competition (Mexican Law), which went into effect on July 1, 1993. The Federal Competition Commission (FCC) is empowered to review mergers under the Mexican Law and any promulgated, related regulations.

SUMMARY

THE DIFFERENCE in substantive standards between the U.S. federal and state authorities and their Mexican and Canadian counterparts is not insurmountable. To begin with, all three federal authorities emphasize efficiency as a means of promoting consumer welfare. Mexico and Canada also emphasize international competition as a disciplining influence on domestic prices and a source for production and dynamic efficiencies. This reflects less a difference in substance with their U.S. counterparts than a recognition of the differential in their respective market size.

Mexico appears to be more concerned with the abuse of dominance than with incipient collusion, whereas concern in Canada or the United States focuses on incipient collusion (i.e., interdependent oligopoly). One reason for this is that in Mexico it is unlikely that efficiency concerns would be used to justify "national champion" mergers in the face of domestic market power effects. However, in Canada the combination of an interdependent oligopoly standard and an efficiencies exception may make the allure of industrial policy irresistible. This runs the risk of being welfare reducing from both a Canadian and a North American perspective.

From the standpoint of creating a supranational merger review authority, the differentials in market size may make it difficult to agree on a common approach to determining market concentration. However, once such thresholds are established, the analysis at the federal level in all three countries is remarkably similar. Thus, the issue may be dealt with by determining the appropriate North American dimension needed to trigger review by the supranational body. The EC experience teaches that this is difficult, but not impossible.

Perhaps the most difficult consideration in the convergence/harmonization of the substantive competition law is in the area of the general sectoral exemptions. In the EC experience, exemptions have been retained since the Merger Regulation became effective on September 21, 1990. EC Regulation 62/17 passed in 1962 provides that businesses may forestall enforcement action by the EC Commission by seeking individual exemptions or so-called *negative clearances* from the Commission. This requires a formal notification of the terms of the agreement to the Commission. Although EC law also provides for general group or block exemptions, so far, at least, none of these applies directly to mergers. In the North American context, it appears that most of the exemptions are in regulated sectors. It could thus be argued that priority should be attached to introducing competition principles into the domestic regulatory environment and institutions.

Another difficult element for achieving substantive North American convergence is the imperfect federal convergence within the United States. Although Canada and Mexico are also federal states, in these countries the relevant federal competition law for mergers is paramount over laws in sub-national jurisdictions. In the United States, by contrast, there is an uneasy tension between federal and state enforcement of antitrust laws. However, the federal agencies and the states are currently closer to one another than they have been in a decade. Furthermore, in addition to the substantive convergence in their respective guidelines, there is increasing cooperation at the level of procedural notification and information sharing.[2]

We now turn to a review of the key elements in the analysis of mergers in the United States, Canada and Mexico.

PHILOSOPHICAL APPROACH

A. The U.S. Federal Agencies

The key federal antitrust law relevant to mergers is set out in three separate statutes. Section 7 of the *Clayton Act* prohibits mergers if their effects "... may be substantially to lessen competition, or tend to create a monopoly". Section 1 of the *Sherman Act* prohibits mergers if they constitute a "... contract, combination ..., or conspiracy in restraint of trade". Section 5 of the *FTC Act* prohibits mergers if they constitute an "...unfair method of competition".

The unifying theme of the U.S. Federal Agencies' 1992 Guidelines is that mergers should not be permitted to create or enhance market power or to facilitate its exercise. Market power is defined as the ability of a seller to maintain prices above competitive levels for a significant period of time (usually two years).

B. The American States

The state attorneys general may enforce either federal antitrust laws in federal courts on behalf of its citizens or, in some states, the state's own antitrust laws based in whole or in part on the federal antitrust laws. All of the state attorneys general have agreed to the guidelines set out in *Antitrust Enforcement: Horizontal Merger Guidelines of the National Association of Attorneys General* (the NAAG Guidelines) as a guide to the exercise of their prosecutorial discretion in merger cases.

The NAAG Guidelines state that:

> The central purpose of the (antitrust) law is to prevent firms from attaining either market power or monopoly power because firms possessing such power can raise prices to consumers above competitive levels, thereby effecting a transfer of wealth from consumers to such firms.

However, the NAAG Guidelines also recognize other social and political objectives as relevant when the states exercise their prosecutorial discretion. Unlike the U.S. Federal Agencies' Guidelines, the NAAG Guidelines take the position that allocative and productive efficiency are subsidiary to the goal of preventing wealth transfers from consumers to producers. Where market power exists, the states consider it to be unlikely that cost savings will be passed on to consumers. Furthermore, the states believe that Congress manifests its concern for productive efficiency by trying to prevent high market concentration or, in other words, that high concentration is likely to lead to various X-inefficiencies. Otherwise, the states assume that any productive efficiency gains are most likely to arise in mergers between small firms, which would not, in any case, trigger the review thresholds.

C. Canada

The best statement of the underlying philosophy of the competition law of Canada is provided in the "purpose" section of the *Canadian Competition Act* which states that:

> The purpose of this Act is to maintain and encourage competition in Canada in order to *promote the efficiency and adaptability* of the Canadian economy, in order to expand opportunities for Canadian participation in world markets while at the same time recognizing the role of foreign competition in Canada, in order to ensure that small and medium sized enterprises have an equitable opportunity to participate in the Canadian economy and in order *to provide consumers with competitive prices and product choices.* [emphasis added]

Emphasis is placed both on foreign competition to discipline domestic prices and on efficiencies that will permit Canadian producers to compete effectively in international markets. Within this framework the Bureau determines whether a merger "prevents or lessens, or is likely to prevent or lessen, competition substantially". In general, a merger will be found to violate this test if, after the merger, a party to the merger would more likely be in a position to "exercise a materially greater degree of market power in a substantial part of a market for two years or more than if the merger did not proceed ...".

D. Mexico

The purpose of the Mexican law is to:

> ... protect the process of competition and free market participation, through prevention and elimination of monopolies, monopolistic practices and other restrictions on the efficient operation of goods and services markets.

Thus, Mexican law emphasizes efficiency, but does not directly express concern for consumer prices, consumer welfare or any other social or political objectives. The FCC regulates those trusts "whose purpose or effect is to diminish, impair or hamper competition and free market participation...". A merger is considered to have that effect when the merged entity gains the power to 1) fix prices unilaterally, 2) "wrongfully dislodge" or exclude rivals, and 3) substantially facilitate or attempt to engage in monopolistic practices.

MARKET DEFINITION

A. The U.S. Federal Agencies

The first step in merger analysis is market definition. The analysis begins with a "hypothetical monopolist", defined as a "hypothetical profit-maximizing firm that (is) the only present and future seller" of all the products in question. A market is defined as a product or group of products and a geographic area in which it is produced or sold such that a hypothetical monopolist would likely profitably impose at least a "small but significant and nontransitory increase in price" (SSNIP). The U.S. Federal Agencies' 1992 Guidelines indicate that a relevant market is the smallest market that satisfies this test. Elsewhere in the Guidelines are set out the factors to be considered in assessing the actual competitive consequences of the merger in question.

The U.S. Federal Agencies use a SSNIP of "5% lasting for the foreseeable future". However, the U.S. Federal Agencies indicate that it may be appropriate to use a higher or lower SSNIP depending on the nature of the industry under analysis. The 1992 Guidelines indicate, for example, that where "premerger circumstances are strongly suggestive of coordinated interaction", the U.S. Federal Agencies may use as the base price one that is "more reflective of the competitive price" than is the prevailing price.

In defining both the product and geographic markets, the U.S. Federal Agencies' 1992 Guidelines distinguish between a hypothetical monopolist who engages in price discrimination and one who does not. The U.S. Federal Agencies also recognize that the SSNIP may not be imposed by the hypothetical monopolist in a uniform manner over all products and geographic locales under its control. Both of these approaches make it considerably easier to arrive at narrower market definitions. The widening of markets leads to lower concentration ratios and is therefore often in the interest of the defendant. However, a narrow market definition can also be in the defendant's interest if it can be argued that no horizontal effects occur between the products of the merging firms and, thus, that there is no basis for an action because technically the products are not substitutable.

The U.S. Federal Agencies' 1992 Guidelines (unlike the Canadian Guidelines) indicate that market definition focuses solely on demand substitution factors. Supply substitution factors are considered in the identification of market participants and entry analysis stages of analysis of the merger. Removing supply substitution factors from the market definition analysis has the effect of reducing the size of the relevant market and thus increases the calculated market concentration results. This effect is typically mitigated somewhat by the inclusion of "uncommitted entrants" when identifying the market participants. Uncommitted entrants are defined in the U.S. Federal Agencies' 1992 Guidelines as potential entrants who would enter the relevant market within one year without incurring significant sunk costs of entry or exit. The 1992 Guidelines distinguish uncommitted entrants from "committed entrants" who would incur significant sunk costs but who would enter within a two-year period. Such entrants are considered only in the analysis of entry conditions and not in the market definition or identification of market participants.

B. The American States

The NAAG Guidelines warn of the dangers of a mis-specified market definition. Hence, the states try to ensure that markets are defined from the perspective of the classes of consumers (or suppliers) who may be adversely affected by an anticompetitive merger. In making this determination, the NAAG Guidelines point to the use of historical data to identify classes of consumers, their sources of supply, suitable substitutes, and alternative sources of the product and its substitutes. This definition stands unless rebutted by "empirical" or historical evidence (i.e., not including expert opinion, speculation or predictions from economic theory) of the likely supply response. Potential competition from current suppliers and firms outside the geographic market (both with excess capacity) that may enter within one year of the merger may be considered.

The NAAG Guidelines also specify that the product market will be expanded only to include "comparably priced substitutes ... if and only if, considered suitable by customers accounting for 75 percent of the purchases." In terms of geographic market definition, the NAAG Guidelines stipulate that the attorneys general will include all sources of supply used within the past two years that are still present in the market. In keeping with the product market definition, the geographic market is defined as the area encompassing 75 percent of the identified suppliers. Recycled and reconditioned goods may also be considered to be acceptable substitutes.

In order to facilitate federal/state coordination, the states may permit parties filing with more than one state or with the U.S. Federal Agencies to use the U.S. Federal Agencies' approach to market definition.

C. Canada

The Canadian Guidelines are similar to the U.S. Federal Agencies' 1992 Guidelines. For market definition purposes the SSNIP is in most contexts a 5 percent increase over a one-year period. However, the Canadian Guidelines offer a more exhaustive and detailed list of evaluative criteria for assessing the likely demand and supply responses to a postulated SSNIP.

Among the factors considered in the Canadian Guidelines are: views, strategies, behavior and identity of buyers; trade views, strategies and behaviour; functional interchangeability in end use; physical and technical characteristics; switching costs; price relationships and price levels; costs of adapting or constructing production processes, distribution and marketing; and availability of second hand, reconditioned or leased products. These factors are generally consistent with the framework of the U.S. Federal Agencies' 1992 Guidelines, except to the extent that they relate to supply substitutability. The Canadian Guidelines indicate that the hypothetical monopolist approach to market definition applies, in general, to "domestic and international sources of competition".

D. Mexico

The Mexican Law sets out certain criteria for determining the relevant market. These include supply substitution (foreign and domestic) and demand substitution. Like Canada, Mexico emphasizes the international aspect of market definition. As suggested earlier, this represents less a difference in substance analysis with the United States than a recognition of the size differentials of the three economies.

MARKET SHARE/MARKET CONCENTRATION

A. The U.S. Federal Agencies

Market shares are calculated using total dollar sales, total unit sales or capacity. The U.S. Federal Agencies' 1992 Guidelines recognize that for homogenous products, capacity is the best measure of competitive significance, and that unit sales or dollar sales are better measures of competitive significance where suppliers serve differentiated buyers. In general, the market shares assigned to foreign firms are to be calculated in a manner analogous to domestic firms. The U.S. Federal Agencies' 1992 Guidelines use the Herfindahl-Hirschman (HHI) measure of concentration which is calculated by summing the squares of the assigned market shares of the identified market participants. The U.S. Federal Agencies' 1992 Guidelines indicate that industries where: HHI < 1000 are considered unconcentrated, $1000 \leq HHI \leq 1800$ are moderately concentrated, and HHI > 1800 are highly concentrated. In evaluating mergers, the U.S. Federal Agencies examine the change and the level of concentration. In the unconcentrated region, the U.S. Federal Agencies consider a merger is unlikely to have adverse competitive effects and so requires no further analysis.

In the moderately concentrated region where there is an increase of less than 100 in the HHI, the U.S. Federal Agencies also require no further analysis of adverse competitive effects. However, where the HHI increase is greater than 100, the merger will "potentially raise competitive concerns", depending on the other competitive factors. The U.S. Federal Agencies will not likely challenge a merger in the concentrated region if the resulting increase in the HHI is less than 50, but they are likely to challenge one otherwise. However, the presumption of illegality can be overcome as a result of a favourable analysis of the other competitive factors.

The International Guidelines also recognize that the supply response of foreign firms may be conditioned by factors such as voluntary or involuntary import quotas, exchange rates, distribution and marketing networks, prior reputation and levels of capacity. However, the International Guidelines indicate that these do not necessarily affect the market definition, but rather they affect the assigning of market shares and their interpretation. In assigning market shares, total foreign capacity is not counted if a foreign firm lacks the specialized distribution facilities needed to supply the additional U.S. demand. If volatile exchange rates make dollar calculations of market share difficult, the DOJ will use unit volume sales.

B. The American States

The NAAG Guidelines also use the HHI to measure market concentration. However, the rebuttable presumption of anticompetitive effect is triggered at HHI increases of 100 in moderately concentrated markets and increases of 50 in highly concentrated markets. The states (and the FTC) have a sliding scale which requires more evidence to rebut the presumption of anticompetitive effect as markets become more concentrated.

In addition, the individual states believe that a merger between a dominant firm and a small firm may increase market power without triggering the HHI review thresholds. Accordingly, there is a presumption in the United States that a merger between a firm with a 35 percent or greater market share and any other firm with 1 percent will strengthen market power. A similar presumption is applied to a merger between a firm with a 20 percent or greater market share and a small innovative firm attempting to enter a moderately or highly concentrated market.

C. Canada

Because of the relatively small nature of the Canadian economy and the generally high levels of corporate concentration, the Canadian Guidelines do not use the HHI. Instead, where the merging parties are unable to "unilaterally exercise greater market power than in the absence of the merger", and the post-merger market share of the merged entity is less than 35 percent, the Bureau does not challenge a merger. Similarly, the Bureau will not challenge a merger on the basis of the "interdependent exercise of market power" where the post-merger market share of the four largest firms is less than 65 percent or the post-merger market share of the merged entity is less than 10 percent. The Bureau makes clear that "in all cases, an assessment of market share and concentration is only the starting point of the analysis".

D. Mexico

The Mexican Law provides that in determining whether a business entity has substantial power on the relevant market, its market share must be considered. Further guidelines or regulations will presumably flesh this out.

COMPETITIVE EFFECTS: GENERAL FRAMEWORK

A. The U.S. Federal Agencies

The U.S. Federal Agencies' 1992 Guidelines state that "other things being equal", market concentration affects the likelihood that one firm or a small group of firms can successfully exercise market power. However, the same 1992 Guidelines make it clear that market share and concentration data are only the starting points of the analysis. In general, the U.S. Federal Agencies recognize two types of situations resulting in "potential adverse competitive effects" of mergers — coordinated interaction and unilateral action. Unlike previous versions, the U.S. Federal Agencies' 1992 Guidelines eschew a laundry-list approach to competitive analysis, concentrating instead on the theory of co-ordinated and unilateral action.

The 1992 Guidelines recognize that a merger may diminish competition by enabling firms "more likely, more successfully, or more completely to engage in coordinated interaction that harms consumers". This behavior includes tacit or express collusion "and may or may not be lawful in and of itself". Successful coordinated interaction entails an agreement between parties and their collective ability to detect and punish deviations so that: 1) the cost of reprisal to the deviator is greater than the short-run benefits of deviation and 2) the cost of reprisal to other parties is less than the short-run costs of deviation. Accordingly, the U.S. Federal Agencies will examine the extent to which the post-merger market conditions are conducive to coordination, detection and punishment.

The 1992 Guidelines also introduce the notion of potential adverse competitive effects arising out of post-merger unilateral conduct by the merged firm. The U.S. Federal Agencies believe that such effects are likely to occur where a merger occurs between firms producing differentiated products. However, the U.S. Federal Agencies indicate that "substantial unilateral price elevation" would require: 1) that a significant share of the sales in the market be accounted for by customers who view the differentiated products to be their first and second choices and 2) there would be no supply response by other firms in the market.

B. The American States

The NAAG Guidelines set out only four factors to consider in addition to market concentration data in determining whether to challenge a merger: 1) ease of entry; 2) collusion and oligopolistic behavior; 3) efficiencies; and 4) powerful or sophisticated buyers. The NAAG Guidelines do not have the elaborate framework for considering collusion or oligopolistic behaviour as found in the U.S. Federal Agencies' 1992 Guidelines. The states' attorneys general are concerned only with past history or evidence of current collusion.

However, the NAAG Guidelines make it clear that the absence of such behaviour will not reduce the probability of a challenge outside the established thresholds for concern.

In their discussion of the policies underlying the NAAG Guidelines, the state attorneys general discuss practices by an incumbent firm that will have the effect of raising its rivals costs. The NAAG Guidelines indicate that these practices should be prohibited where the costs are passed on to consumers. The U.S. Federal Agencies' 1992 Guidelines do not raise this issue directly, however, since it is presumably covered indirectly in the competitive effects analysis. The Canadian Guidelines also address this issue, but only insofar as considering the likelihood of entry.

C. Canada

The Canadian Guidelines include the considerations of market share and concentration among the evaluative criteria to be considered after market definition. In addition to market concentration, the Canadian Guidelines specifically enumerate the following criteria: foreign competition; business failure and exit; the availability of effective substitutes; barriers to entry; effective remaining competition; removal of a vigorous and effective competitor; and change and innovation. The Canadian Guidelines do not contain any elaborate discussion of coordinated and unilateral postmerger action, although the distinction is drawn in the market concentration discussion. However, the Canadian Guidelines do discuss market transparency, transaction value and frequency as factors that can affect successful collusion.

D. Mexico

The Mexican Law enumerates five additional characteristics to be considered in determining whether a merged entity is likely to have substantial market power. These are: 1) whether the merger can fix price or restrict supply unilaterally; 2) entry barriers; 3) the existence and power of competitors; 4) access to sources of input by the merged entity and its competitors; and 5) recent conduct.

In some respects, the Mexican Law appears to be closer to the EC model which, until very recently, was concerned principally with dominance as opposed to incipient collusion. Thus, while the U.S. and Canadian Guidelines manifest a concern for unilateral and coordinated anticompetitive effects, the Mexican Law appears to be concerned only with unilateral effects. Judging from the EC experience, a hesitant approach to efficiencies can be expected, as cost savings may be seen as reinforcing dominance and not as hampering effective collusion.

EXCEPTIONS/DEFENSES: EFFICIENCIES

A. The U.S. Federal Agencies

The U.S. Federal Agencies will evaluate any claim that "significant net efficiencies" outweigh the anticompetitive effects of the merger. Cognizable efficiencies include (but are not limited to): achieving economies of scale; better integration of production facilities; plant specialization; lower transport costs; and similar efficiencies relating to manufacturing, servicing or distribution operations post-merger. The U.S. Federal Agencies' 1992 Guidelines reiterate that the burden of proof of efficiencies rests with the proponents of the merger. In addition any claimed efficiencies must not be achievable "through other means".

B. The American States

The NAAG Guidelines make it clear that efficiencies will not save a merger that has failed its market concentration test. The NAAG Guidelines require that merging parties present "clear and convincing" evidence that the merger will lead to significant efficiencies. On the other hand, the NAAG Guidelines now follow the U.S. Federal Agencies' 1992 Guidelines in stating that only those efficiencies that cannot be achieved through other means will be considered. However, the NAAG Guidelines are still somewhat more stringent than the U.S. Federal Agencies' 1992 Guidelines in stating that the efficiencies must persist over the long run.

C. Canada

The efficiency exception in the Canadian Guidelines springs from the purpose clause (quoted above) and Section 96 of the Canadian *Competition Act*. Section 96(1) of the *Competition Act* provides that efficiency gains cannot be claimed if: 1) they would likely be achieved in any case if the Competition Tribunal issued an order to remedy an anticompetitive effect in the market such as prohibiting the merger or, 2) they are only redistributive in nature. The Canadian Guidelines indicate that in determining whether efficiencies could be achieved by other means, the Bureau will examine industry practice. If reference is made to another possible merger, the Bureau will only consider third-party bids that have already been made. The Canadian *Competition Act* specifically directs the Bureau to consider whether the efficiencies will result in increased exports and import substitution.

The Canadian Guidelines indicate that both production efficiencies and dynamic efficiencies are to be considered. However, the emphasis is placed on production efficiencies because they "...can be quantifiably measured, objectively ascertained, and supported by engineering, accounting or other data".

It should be noted here that, in a recent decision, the Chair of the Canadian Competition Tribunal commented in an *obiter dictum* that efficiency gains are to be evaluated against the dead weight loss associated with a monopoly and the transfer of wealth from consumers to producers.[3] However, the Bureau has indicated that it rejects this interpretation and will continue to apply the Canadian Guidelines as currently written.[4]

D. Mexico

There does not appear to be an efficiency exception or defense in the Mexican Law.

FAILURE AND EXITING ASSETS

A. The U.S. Federal Agencies

The U.S. Federal Agencies' 1992 Guidelines provide that an otherwise anti-competitive merger can be defended if, absent the merger, one of the parties to the merger would fail or its assets would exit the market if: 1) failure of one of the parties is imminent; 2) there is an inability to reorganize in bankruptcy; 3) there is an absence of alternative purchasers after a good faith effort to find one; and 4) without the acquisition, the assets of the failing firm would exit the market.

The U.S. Federal Agencies' 1992 Guidelines stipulate that in determining a reasonable good faith offer, the highest-valued use outside the relevant market or equivalent offer to purchase the stock of the failing firm will be considered as a reasonable alternative offer. This definition seems to make it more difficult to use this defense. Furthermore, the U.S. Federal Agencies' 1992 Guidelines provide little support for a "flailing" firm defence.[5] However, it may be possible to convert a flailing firm story directly into the competitive-effects test, on the theory that collusion is more likely among firms in financial difficulty.

B. The American States

The NAAG Guidelines recognize the failing firm defense but indicate that it will be strictly construed, even if not interpreted as strictly as by the U.S. Federal Agencies. The criteria are: 1) a high probability of failure, 2) failure of the firm to find a purchaser after a good faith effort, and 3) no fewer anti-competitive alternatives.

C. Canada

The Canadian Guidelines are also similar in framework to the 1992 U.S. Guidelines on this point, but they are more strictly construed. A firm is considered to be failing when it: 1) is insolvent or likely to become insolvent; 2) has initiated voluntary bankruptcy proceedings; or 3) has or is likely to be petitioned for bankruptcy. As with the NAAG Guidelines and the 1982 Statement, the Bureau requires that there be no competitively preferable purchaser. Furthermore, searches for an alternative purchaser would have to be made by a third party. The Canadian Guidelines also examine the possible retrenchment of the failing firm so that it does not exit but rather remains in the market at a reduced size. The Bureau will determine whether this is competitively preferable to a merger. The Bureau will also consider whether failure might facilitate new entry by a competitively superior firm.

D. Mexico

There does not appear to be a failing firm defense in the Mexican Law.

OTHER EXCEPTIONS/DEFENSES

A. The U.S. Federal Agencies

Section 7 of the *Clayton Act* provides an antitrust defense for stock acquisitions by institutional investors and others made "solely for investment". Under the *Bank Merger Act* Amendments of 1966 and the *Bank Holding Company Amendments Act* 1966, there is a modified failing company defense for bank mergers and acquisitions. This "convenience and needs" defense provides that an otherwise anticompetitive bank merger may be allowed where the defendant can establish that the public interest in the merger outweighs the anticompetitive effect. In short, there appears to be a flailing firm defense for bank mergers.

Certain regulatory statutes explicitly exempt relevant mergers from the *Clayton Act* if otherwise approved by the appropriate regulatory agency. Examples of such regulated industries are: 1) telephone and telegraph companies (but not radio and television companies); 2) rail, motor, and water carriers; and 3) newspapers. The U.S. Supreme Court has held that the DOJ may, on its own initiative, challenge mergers which are approved or subject to the approval of the Federal Maritime Commission and the Federal Energy Regulatory Commission. Similarly, with respect to bank mergers, the DOJ has the power to stay any approval of a bank merger by the Federal Reserve Board, the principal banking regulator.

Although, joint ventures are not exempt from antitrust scrutiny, under the *National Cooperative Research Act* of 1984 they may be protected from private treble damage actions.

B. Canada

There are two significant statutory exemptions that are relevant to mergers: 1) the amalgamation or acquisition of banks where the Minister of Finance has certified that the transaction is in the interest of the financial system; and 2) joint ventures. In practice, the joint venture exemption has never been used because in addition to providing additional requirements, the Canadian *Competition Act* indicates that the combination must not result in the substantial lessening of competition except to the extent reasonably necessary.

Judicial precedent (but not the statute), provides a defense where the merging parties compete under strictly regulated conditions. However, since the Canadian *Competition Act* was amended in 1986, the Bureau, nonetheless has reviewed transactions in a number of seemingly regulated sectors such as dairies, breweries and commercial air transport. The Canadian *Competition Act* also explicitly permits the Bureau to intervene and provide input into proceedings before regulatory bodies. Thus, even if a regulated conduct defense were actually recognized by the Bureau, the Bureau would still have an opportunity to address the competitive effects of proposed mergers in regulated sectors.

C. Mexico

The Mexican Law provides an exemption for state monopolies in the strategic sectors enumerated in the Constitution. These include: oil exploration, oil refining and pipelines, other hydrocarbons, radioactive materials, electricity, basic petrochemicals, mail, satellite telecommunications and railways.

The Mexican Law also exempts associations or cooperatives that sell their products directly abroad. However, certain additional criteria must be met: 1) the products must be the principal source of the wealth in the region in which they are produced; 2) they must not be sold in Mexico; 3) membership is voluntary; 4) they must be approved and licensed.

CONCLUSIONS

THIS APPENDIX HAS REVIEWED THE SIMILARITIES and differences in the substantive merger law of Canada, Mexico and the United States. It is clear from this survey that at the level of economic reasoning and legal analysis, there is already a significant convergence among the three countries. Ultimately, however, the success or failure of harmonization will turn on the ability of the three countries to agree on procedural questions, exempted sectors and permitted exceptions and defenses to findings of the likely exercise of market power within a relevant market. Although the system of dual enforcement of antitrust laws in the United States at the federal and state levels may involve problems, the convergence shown in analysis is promising. At this stage further interaction among antitrust enforcers and regulators as well as among private sector economic and legal scholars and practitioners can play a useful role in driving the harmonization of merger review law and policy in North America.

ENDNOTES

1 These guidelines replaced the DOJ's earlier guidelines issued in 1984. The DOJ first issued guidelines in 1968 and replaced them in 1982. In 1982, the FTC issued a statement setting out its own approach to merger review, but indicated that it would give "substantial weight to the DOJ's 1982 guidelines.

2 See "The National Association of Attorneys General Voluntary Pre-Merger Disclosure Compact"; "Program for Federal-State Cooperation in Merger Enforcement"; and "Protocol for Coordination in Merger Investigations Between the Antitrust Division and State Attorneys General" in Appendix A of the NAAG Guidelines.

3 Director of Investigation and Research v. Hillsdown Holdings (Canada) Ltd., 41 C.P.R. (3d) 289 (Competition Tribunal, 1992).

4 Director of Investigation and Research, "Developments and Emerging Challenges in Canadian Competition Law", Notes for Address to the 1992 Fordham Corporate Law Institute: International Antitrust Law and Policy, October 22, 1992.

5 In the jargon of antitrust lawyers and economists "flailing firm" indicates that a firm is not quite ready to exit the market, but is in very bad financial shape. In the U.S. Agencies' 1992 Guidelines "failing" firm really means "failed" firm.

APPENDIX B

CONVERGENCE/HARMONIZATION OF CANADIAN AND U.S. PREDATION/PRICE DISCRIMINATION LAWS

INTRODUCTION

IN THE TEXT OF THIS STUDY, we discussed the problems of administering dumping laws in Canada and the United States in the context of the NAFTA. In this Appendix, we review the predatory pricing and price discrimination laws in both Canada and the United States to assess the prospects for the convergence and harmonization of these laws more generally if the abolition of dumping rules can be achieved in the NAFTA environment.

PREDATORY PRICING IN CANADA

PREDATORY PRICING IS DEALT WITH primarily under Section 50(1)(c) of the *Competition Act* which makes it a criminal offense for anyone in a business to engage in a policy of selling at "prices unreasonably low, having effect or tendency of substantially lessening competition or eliminating a competitor, or designed to have that effect ..." All of these elements must be proved in order to impose a criminal penalty. Also, Section 50(1)(c) is not limited to conduct occurring within Canada, rather, its concern is with the *effects on competition* within Canada, irrespective of where the "conduct" occurred. Put another way, the Canadian predatory pricing rule may be applied extra-territorially.

Canadian courts have held that if an article is sold for more than cost, the price can never be held to be unreasonably low. Furthermore, courts have held that it may not be inferred from a price-cost relationship that a price is unreasonably low. Even in instances of below cost pricing, courts have found that other competitive factors could justify such prices.[1] Courts have also found that prices between average variable cost and average total cost may be predatory.[2]

Drawing upon this limited judicial precedent, the Director of Investigation and Research (Director) issued Predatory Pricing Enforcement Guidelines (PPEG) in 1992. The Director has indicated that in examining pricing behaviour he will look for evidence:

> [that the prices] are not competitive expedients, of brief duration, that [they] are not simply defensive reactions to pricing initiatives or behavior of other firms, or that they are not randomly occurring events attributable to specific business circumstances extant in the market at any given point in time.

The jurisprudence and the PPEG make it clear that while sales above cost are never predatory, sales below cost are not always predatory. In determining whether a sale is unreasonably low, the Director first examines market characteristics that are indicative of actual or potential market power. These characteristics include market share, concentration and conditions of entry. This stage of analysis gives the Director an indication whether the pricing behaviour could have an anticompetitive effect in Canada. The Director rarely challenges a pricing practice where the firm's market share is below 35 percent. Assuming that actual or potential market power is found, the second stage of the Director's analysis involves a comparison of price and cost for the alleged predator. Market definition and entry analysis are done according to the procedures applied by the Director in merger cases.

The criterion used by the Director to recommend enforcement action by the federal Attorney General is whether the firm in question is pricing below average variable cost. The Director examines reasonably anticipated costs, not accounting costs, recognizing that the price may fall below average variable cost for unanticipated reasons. Pricing between average variable cost and average total cost is in a "grey" zone in which the Director's decision to take action will depend on other market circumstances. If the Director does find the alleged offending firm guilty of both market power and unreasonably low pricing, he then determines whether the conduct of the firm will likely or actually lessen competition substantially in Canada.

In Canada, the Director's emphasis appears to be on short-term profit maximization where price is determined in competitive and monopoly markets where marginal cost equals marginal revenue. Thus, Canada seems to conform to a modified "Areeda and Turner" test which uses average variable cost as a proxy for short run incremental costs or marginal costs. However, unlike Areeda and Turner, the Director is prepared to examine market structure within the grey zone. It is worth noting here that the average variable cost threshold has been criticized on the grounds that some predatory pricing may occur below long-run marginal or incremental costs. For instance, some new entrants may incur out-of-pocket costs not currently faced by incumbents, e.g. to build reputation or research capacity. (Our presumption is that these costs have long been sunk to the incumbent firm.)[3] However, there is an inherent danger in pushing this logic too far because over a sufficiently long run all costs are variable. Thus a standard that looks to long-run incremental costs may amount to an average total cost test if technology is constant.[4]

The Director's approach in the PPEG appears to be to read the Section 50(1)(c) predatory pricing offense together with the Section 79 abuse of dominant position provisions of the *Competition Act*. Accordingly, in determining whether pricing is predatory, emphasis is placed on market power. This model would arguably be less open to the protectionist pressures found in the application of dumping laws. However, it is potentially rich enough to capture the strategic behavior of firms that can make credible threats through the use of sunk costs, deep pockets or reputational factors to deter the entry or re-entry of rival firms after the successful exclusion of a rival through predatory pricing.[5]

The *Competition Act* provides for a private right of action for damages for the breach of the predatory pricing laws. However, unlike U.S. law, there is no treble-damage remedy and contingency fees, and class action suits are not generally available.[6] Similarly, Canada follows the English Rule with respect to legal costs, which generally requires that the loser pays the costs of the winner in a legal action. Accordingly, in any harmonization/convergence of predatory pricing law, attention would have to be paid to the procedural rules that may affect the private incentives of parties to initiate strategic legal actions or, alternatively, to settle non-meritorious claims. That said, most dumping cases in Canada now are handled at the administrative level before Revenue Canada (which determines dumping margins) and the Canadian International Trade Tribunal (which determines material injury). At present, therefore, Canadian parties involved in dumping actions that do not reach the courts are already effectively subject to the "U.S. Rule", whereby each party pays for its own costs.

PREDATORY PRICING IN THE UNITED STATES

UNDER U.S. LAW PREDATORY PRICING may be analyzed under Section 2(a) of the *Robinson Patman Act*, Section 5 of the *Federal Trade Commission Act*, or in the context of monopolization under Section 2 of the *Sherman Act*. The *Robinson Patman Act* applies to both primary- and secondary-line injury. Primary-line injury is most similar to dumping because the focus is on the injury to the rival seller as a cause of the offending seller's below-cost pricing practice. In other words, primary-line injury, like dumping law, is concerned with the effect of price discrimination on a rival seller, not the adversely affected buyer (as in secondary-line injury). Thus, a predatory pricing claim under the *Robinson Patman Act* requires proof of price discrimination and below-cost pricing. *The Robinson Patman Act* does not apply to transborder price discrimination. Thus, as now written, the *Robinson Patman Act* would not be available as a substitute vehicle in a dumping action, but Section 2 of the *Sherman Act* may be available.

In the United States, there is, at present, no uniform standard to measure anticompetitive injury arising from predatory pricing. There is some judicial support from the U.S. Supreme Court for the view that pricing below average variable cost, or between average variable cost and average total cost indicates a predatory intent.[7] However, the U.S. Supreme Court's most recent statement on the subject in *Brooke*, declined to resolve the conflict among the lower courts. However, other courts (notably the Seventh Circuit) have also focused on the structure of the market and the extent to which profits foregone in the short term may be recouped in the long term.[8] If such profits cannot be recouped, then under this theory the low prices represent a gift to consumers. This market structure approach seems closest to the approach taken by the Director in Canada.

In dumping actions, below cost pricing is usually measured against the standard of fully distributed costs or average total costs. In the United States, some courts[9] (in the Ninth Circuit) have been willing to find predatory intent where prices are above average total cost or long-run incremental cost. In these cases, the plaintiff must prove by "clear and convincing evidence" that the pricing policy is predatory or has the tendency to eliminate rivals and create a market structure which permits recoupment. However, other courts (in the First, Sixth, Seventh, Eighth and Eleventh Circuits) have rejected this standard on the grounds that the price cut is moving price in the right direction — to the competitive level.[10] However, the Seventh Circuit, in MCI was prepared to use long-run incremental cost and not average variable cost as the standard where the case involved a regulated industry with a high ratio of fixed to variable cost.

As shown, the threshold for prosecution in Canada, generally, is pricing below average variable cost. However, prosecution may occur depending on the market structure where price falls between average variable cost and average total cost. While the "Areeda and Turner" test would not find predatory pricing in the grey zone, U.S. courts, generally, have not been willing to go that far. The Second Circuit,[11] however, has accepted this standard and the Fifth Circuit[12] has accepted it with an exception for markets with high entry barriers. The Eleventh Circuit, in *Northern Propane*, held that within the grey zone, there is circumstantial evidence of predatory intent that must be supplemented by other objective or subjective evidence of predatory intent in order to secure a conviction.

Another important feature in U.S. law that is not found in Canada is a "meeting the competition" defense to a charge of predatory pricing. This defense, is perhaps most relevant in those Circuits that apply a full cost standard of predatory pricing.[13] However, so far, it is not clear how much judicial support exists for this defense. Nonetheless, this represents an improvement over the current dumping law regime where full-cost tests are used and there is no similar defense.

Two points emerge from this survey. First, the U.S. law is unsettled as to the appropriate standard or theory to apply to predatory pricing. In some respects U.S. law is similar to Canadian law, but in some U.S. jurisdictions a price at or above cost may be found to be predatory. It would be in the interest of U.S. consumers to use the occasion of harmonization/convergence to remove this possibility. Furthermore, it would not make sense to abolish dumping, only to have U.S. courts apply the same injury standard as in a predatory pricing case. Second, some U.S courts have shown greater willingness than Canadian courts to find anticompetitive injury in the grey zone.

PRICE DISCRIMINATION

IT WOULD MAKE LITTLE SENSE to set about the task of harmonization/convergence of predatory pricing laws as a replacement for dumping and to leave price discrimination laws unchanged. Price discrimination laws represent the worst elements of the populist roots of antitrust/competition law. Except for all but the most restrictive assumptions, the efficiency and aggregate welfare effects of price discrimination appear to be indeterminate. While second- or third-degree price discrimination may involve pricing above marginal costs, they may also lead to an expansion of output. If the latter effect is greater than the former, efficiency and aggregate welfare may not be impaired. Given the ubiquitousness of price discrimination, any calculus of efficiency and welfare effects must also consider the chilling effect that prosecution may have on firms determining optimal distribution patterns. A first/best solution would be to use the occasion of North American convergence as an opportunity to abandon these laws outright. However, in a second-best order of solutions these laws should be harmonized to the least obtrusive standard possible.

Canada

Non-predatory price discrimination is dealt with mainly under Section 50(1)(a) of the *Competition Act*. Section 50(1)(a) is violated when someone, wherever situated, sells in Canada to two or more competitors at price differences that are not justified by differences in quantity. Accordingly, for non-predatory price discrimination, the focus in Canada has been traditionally on secondary-line injury (to the disfavoured buyer). This is different from the *Robinson Patman Act* in the United States, which also applies to primary-line injury (to competitors of the seller) and tertiary-line injury (to customers of the disfavoured buyers). At this stage, it also appears that, contrary to the U.S. position, Canadian price discrimination law applies only to sales to purchasers at the same level of distribution. Unlike the United States, the Director's Price Discrimination Enforcement Guidelines (PDEG) issued in 1992 indicate that it is not a defense to a charge of price discrimination for a defendant to argue that the price differentials were "cost justified" or engaged in to "meet the competition".

As with predatory pricing, the focus is on the *effect in the Canadian market* and not on the source of the effect. Accordingly, a U.S. or Mexican seller who discriminates against a Canadian buyer to the benefit of buyers in either of the other nations could be liable under Canadian law. It may also be that a Canadian seller would be liable for discriminating against a foreign buyer to the benefit of a Canadian buyer. Theoretically, liability may also be found if the Canadian seller discriminated against a Canadian buyer to the detriment of a foreign seller. (This assumes that the Section 50(1)(a) reaches primary-line discrimination.)

In the evolving North American market for trade and investment, these are not purely abstract concerns. The PDEG indicate that transactions between affiliated corporations are not exempt from the price discrimination law, unless the affiliates function as a "single economic unit" or a discount represents a "concession" in return for other intra-firm services. Accordingly, if a U.S. parent is selling to Canadian customers (even if indirectly through its own subsidiary) and to its subsidiary, it may be guilty of price discrimination under Canadian law.

International volume price concession (IVPC) discounts contracted between multinational sellers and purchasers will not likely give rise to liability by a Canadian subsidiary of the purchaser, although Canadian competitors of the purchaser have been disadvantaged by the IVPC. However, The PDEG do not clarify what would happen if a foreign parent negotiated the IVPC but did not itself contract to purchase from the seller.

The United States

The *Robinson Patman Act* is unique among U.S. antitrust laws for two reasons: 1) it does not apply extraterritorially and 2) its purpose is to protect competitors and not competition.

However, as the Canadian price discrimination law does appear to apply extraterritorially, harmonization would seem to apply here as well. Furthermore, notwithstanding its populist roots, the *Robinson Patman Act*, is widely believed to harm small firms over larger chain stores. The aggressive pursuit of price discrimination tends to promote caution among manufacturers who maintain uniform price lists and buyers who do not demand extensive discounts. By discouraging promotional price discounting, the *Robinson Patman Act* may actually hinder entry and thus further entrench existing market power. Consequently, under a harmonized system, if cross-border price discrimination were abandoned, domestic consumers could be disadvantaged if price discrimination laws are prosecuted aggressively at the domestic level. It is clear, therefore, that these laws must be abandoned altogether in the North American context.

With respect to injury from primary-line discrimination (to the seller's competitors), U.S. courts and the FTC are increasingly willing to read a predation standard into the law.[14] While it is a positive development that a principle of actual injury to competition is emerging, recall that the standard for injury is still unsettled even in predation cases. Furthermore, the predation standard has not yet been imported into the standard for injury from secondary-line discrimination. The standard remains that an injury to competition is established *prima facie* by proof of substantial price discrimination over time.[15] The negative effects on efficiency are perhaps greater as consequences of the strict prosecution of secondary-line price discrimination, than from primary-line discrimination. Vertically integrated firms are prevented from passing on efficiencies to their customers in the form of lower prices.

As bad as the *Robinson Patman Act* is for competition in the United States, it does contain a number of defenses that blunt its anticompetitive effect. For instance, defenses are provided for proof by the defendant that: 1) its price was made in good faith to meet an equally low price of a competitor; 2) its price was justified by costs of manufacture and distribution; and 3) market conditions are changing.

CONCLUSIONS

WE CONTEND THAT in the context of the North American trade and investment relationship, dumping laws are inherently protectionist and anachronistic. Instead, the three countries should aim at the convergence/harmonization of domestic laws relating to predatory pricing and price discrimination. In doing so, anticompetitive tests of predation that rely on proof of injury based on above average variable cost pricing should be abandoned and replaced with tests that make economic sense. Finally, we believe that it is in the interest of consumers in the United States, Canada and Mexico that price discrimination laws be abolished at the same time. It makes no sense to remove anticompetitive laws across borders, but to continue to apply them domestically.

ENDNOTES

1 R. v. Hoffman-La-Roche, (1980), 28 O.R. (2d) 164; affirmed (1981), 33 O.R. (2d) 694 (Ont. C.A.).

2 R. v. Consumers Glass Co., (1981), 33 O.R. (2d) 228 (Ont. HCJ).

3 R. Posner, Antitrust Law: An Economic Perspective, (Chicago: University of Chicago Press, 1976) at 188.

4 P. Areeda and H. Hovenkamp, Antitrust Law: 1992 Supplement, (Boston: Little, Brown & Company, 1992) at 706.

5 D.G. McFeteridge, "Predatory and Discriminatory Pricing" in F. Mathewson et al, The Law and Economics of Competition Policy 71, 78-81, (Vancouver: The Fraser Institute, 1990).

6 The Province of Ontario has recently moved to permit expansive class action suits.

7 Utah Pie Co. v. Continental Banking Co., 386 U.S. 685 (1967) and Brooke Group v. Brown & Williamson Tobacco, 64 BNA Antitrust & Trade Regulation Report 802, (U.S. Sup. Ct., June 21, 1993).

8 A.A. Poultry Farms v. Rose Acre Farms, Inc., 881 F.2d 1396 (7th Cir., 1989); Matsushita Electric Industrial Co. v. Zenith Radio Corp., 475 U.S. 574 (1986); Cargill, Inc. v. Monfort of Colorado, Inc., 479 U.S. 104 (1986) and Brooke supra note 33.

9 William Inglis & Sons Baking Co. v. ITT Continental Baking Co., 668 F.2d 1014 (9th Cir., 1981) and Transamerica Computer Co. v. IBM, 698 F.2d 1377 (9th Cir., 1983).

10 Barry Wright Corp. v. ITT Grinnell Corp., 724 F.2d 227 (1 Cir., 1983); Arthur S. Langenderfer v. S.E. Johnson Co., 729 F.2d 1050 (6th Cir., 1984); MCI Communic. Co. v. AT & T, 708 F.2d 1081 (7th Cir.), cert. denied, 464 U.S. 891 (1983); Morgan v. Ponder, 892 F.2d 1355 (8th Cir., 1989) and McGahee v. Northern Propane Gas Co., 865 F.2d 1274 (11th Cir., 1988).

11 Northeastern Telephone Co. v. AT&T, 651 F.2d (2d Cir., 1981).

12 Adjusters Replace-A-Car, Inc. v. Agency Rent-A-Car, Inc., 735 F.2d 884 (5th Cir., 1984).

13 Memorex Corp. v. IBM, 636 F.2d 1188 (9th Cir., 1980); Xeta v. Atex, 852 F.2d 1280 (Fed. Cir., 1988); and Richter Concrete Corp. v. Hilltop Basic Resources, 691 F.2d 818 (6th Cir., 1982).

14 Re ITT Continental Baking, 104 F.T.C. 280 (1984) and Boise Cascade Corp. v. Federal Trade Commission, 837 F.2d 1127 (D.C. Cir., 1988).

15 FTC v. Morton Salt Co., 344 U.S. 37 (1948) and Falls City Indus., Inc. v. Vanco Beverage, Inc., 460 U.S. 428 (1983).

Frederick (Fritz) W. Mayer
Assistant Professor of Public Policy Studies
Terry Sanford Institute of Public Policy
Duke University

The NAFTA, Multinationals and Social Policy

INTRODUCTION

WHEN THE GOVERNMENTS of the United States, Mexico, and Canada decided in the autumn of 1990 to negotiate the creation of the North American Free Trade Area (NAFTA), the talks were expected to cover issues of commercial law: trade and investment. Few foresaw that the negotiations could not be confined to these matters and that, instead, such issues as enforcement of environmental and workplace safety standards, labour rights, and state of democracy in Mexico would be drawn into the debate. Within weeks of the governments' decision, however, a broad coalition of labour, environmental, human rights and other groups in the United States mobilized either to oppose the NAFTA or to insist that it be accompanied by measures dealing with the isues of concern to them. At first, the demand that these side issues be included in a trade negotiation was dismissed as impractical and irrelevant. But before many months had passed, Canada, the United States and Mexico found themselves in intensive negotiations about the creation of new international institutions and dispute resolution processes designed to address environment and labour issues. The side issues had become central.

The political dynamic that brought these issues to the fore was based in part on widespread popular beliefs about the behaviour of businesses, particularly large, multinational enterprises (MNEs), and about their power in relation to states. Specifically, the social critics of the NAFTA maintained that the elimination of barriers to cross-border trade and investment would encourage "big business" to exploit differences in the level of regulation by moving production where it faces the lowest regulatory cost. They alleged that with the NAFTA, mobile capital would flee the higher cost environments of Canada and the United States for the pollution and workplace hazard haven of Mexico. Alternatively, Canada and the United States, faced with the threat of losing jobs to Mexico, would be forced to lower their regulatory standards.

Whether true or not, the allegation was politically potent. Especially in the United States, but also in Canada, it was an important catalyst for a remarkable political reaction that altered the environment in which MNEs operate in North America. Under pressure, Mexico has made significant strides toward raising the level of enforcement of its labour and environmental regulations. The side agreements to the NAFTA, if ratified, will institutional-ize this pressure, and keep the trend towards stronger Mexican enforcement on an upward trajectory.

This study considers one aspect of the relationship between MNEs and states in North America, the connection between the location of economic activity and the pattern of political regimes governing environment, labour, and other social issues. It seeks to answer two questions. First, to what extent do investment location decisions by MNEs reflect differences in the regulatory regimes of the three countries? Second, in what ways are political regimes responding to actual and expected MNE behaviour, thus changing the conditions under which MNEs make their decisions?

While environment, labour and other social policies have had some effect on locational decisions in North America, those effects are, with few exceptions, quite small, and considerably smaller than opponents of the NAFTA have claimed. It is possible to hypothesize that without a change in Mexican enforcement patterns, differences in social policies would have become somewhat more important factors in the future as barriers to capital mobility continued to fall, but this hypothesis will not be tested by events. Instead, the political forces catalyzed by the decision to negotiate the NAFTA and driven by fears of job flight have worked to narrow the differences in standards and enforcement, thus altering the calculus for investment decisions. Far from increasing the likelihood that Mexico will be a haven for corporate scofflaws, the NAFTA will more likely have precisely the opposite effect.

This study focuses primarily on environment and labour regulations, partly because they are more often alleged to have locational implications and partly because they are the most studied. Obviously, there are numerous other aspects of a social regulatory regime, including education, health, and immigration policy that might affect locational decisions. These dimensions of social policy have not been linked to the NAFTA negotiation, and North America will stop well short of a sweeping social charter on the European model. This is largely a reflection of the fundamental asymmetry of a negotiation involving the United States and two much smaller partners. For example, there is little likelihood that we will see the creation of a development fund to help the Mexican economy as the Europeans have created for its poorer mem-bers. Although Mexican President Salinas at one point proposed such a fund and the idea had support in some quarters in the United States, it was a political non-starter on Capitol Hill. Similarly, policies governing the movement of labour (i. e. immigration policy) have been largely excluded from the discussion. To a great extent this is due to the fact that the initiators of this proposal, the Mexicans, are in no position to pressure the U.S. or Canada on the issue. Interestingly, the only parts of the NAFTA that govern movement of labour are designed to make it easier for American and Canadian professionals to gain temporary access to Mexico.

THE EFFECTS ON INVESTMENT LOCATION

THE EFFECT OF DIFFERENCES in the cost of environmental, workplace safety, labour rights, and other social regulations on the location of investment within North America became a central question in the political dialogue surrounding the NAFTA. Opponents of the agreement charged that lower compliance costs in Mexico, either because of lower standards or less stringent enforcement, would tempt Canadian and American manufacturers, particularly those in pollution-intensive or hazardous industries, to flee to the haven of Mexico.

On the face of it, the social critics had a plausible case. Historically, Mexican authorities had been less vigilant in their attention to environmental and workplace safety concerns than their northern neighbors. There was also a significant increase in the amount of investment going into Mexico, and some businesses that had relocated to Mexico had demonstrated a willingness to engage in practices that would not have been permitted in Canada or the United States. Taken together, these facts were sufficient for the critics of the NAFTA to conclude that investment was being lured to Mexico by the lower regulatory cost environment. However, this conclusion does not necessarily follow. First, without controlling for the effect of lower unit labour costs on locational decisions, it is extremely difficult to distinguish the effect of differences in regulatory costs, given the high degree of correlation between the two. Second, the fact that businesses take advantage of lower standards once they find themselves in a lax regulatory environment does not necessarily confirm that their choice of location was affected by the lower standards. To evaluate whether regulatory environments are determinative requires a much more careful look at both the ways in which businesses make decisions about location and the available evidence.

INVESTMENT LOCATION THEORY

THE CONSIDERABLE LITERATURE on the factors that determine locational choices suggests several things.[1] First, larger enterprises are much more mobile and more likely than smaller firms to consider locating some or all of their production outside the boundaries of their home base. In many industries, the dominant firms are virtually stateless, so far-flung are their operations. In Robert Reich's oft-quoted words, it is hard to know "who is us".[2] Second, regulatory costs are but one of many factors firms consider in making their decisions. These factors include "materials, energy sources, markets, labour supply and costs, transportation availability and costs, capital availability, the potential for economies of scale, services and infrastructure (electricity, water supply, waste disposal, and so forth), governmental actions (taxes, incentives, regulations), and site costs".[3] In addition, decisions are affected by such intangibles as personal preferences of managers, familiarity with the options and, even, simple inertia. Third, although there is general agreement on the factors, there is less agreement on their weighting. For most industries, regulatory costs are only a very small component of total costs and, therefore, would not be expected to weigh very heavily in comparison to other factors. Even in the more pollution-intensive industries, the cost of pollution control has been in the range of only 1 percent to 2.5 percent of total costs.[4] Nevertheless, for the dirtiest and most hazardous types of production processes locational decisions could very well be affected by differences in regulatory regimes. With the advent of more stringent environmental regulation in the industrialized nations many observers have predicted a flight of these industries to avoid higher compliance costs, social blockage of new plants, and restrictions on hazardous production.

A number of researchers have attempted to test the general theory empirically by demonstrating a pattern of location based on avoidance of regulatory costs. Their focus has been on environmental costs, both because they are generally higher and more easily measured than other regulatory costs, and because the sharp increase in those costs in the United States in the 1970s should have induced a response. Despite the plausibility of the hypothesis, most of the empirical analyses are either negative or inconclusive. A recent survey of these studies by the Congressional Research Service (CRS) concludes that "[d]espite a number of investigations, the conclusions of the studies have been almost uniformly negative: there is little or no aggregate evidence of industrial relocation to take advantage of environmental compliance cost differences".[5]

There are some suggestive strands in the literature not evaluated by the CRS. For example, a recent study by Hamilton on locational decisions of hazardous waste facilities shows that firms take into account the probability of social blockage when siting their facilities.[6] Hamilton, however, focuses on arguably the strongest case, social blockage, in which the implicit cost in locations with the political capacity to prevent siting is infinite.

Although it is fair to say that to date there is no conclusive empirical evidence to support the pollution haven hypothesis, the absence of such evidence does not rule out its possibility. First, as noted earlier, it is extremely difficult to distinguish between the effects of unit labour cost differences and the effects of differences in regulatory costs. Second, it is reasonable to assume that as barriers to international relocation come down, remaining differences in regulatory costs might assume greater importance. It is on this basis that there remains a plausible case for concern about relocation to Mexico, particularly given the extremely large differences in the levels of development in Canada and the United States on the one hand, and in Mexico on the other.

INVESTMENT IN MEXICO

THE CASE FOR IDENTIFYING Mexico as a potential social hazard haven rests on the fact that there have been substantial differences in the enforcement of environmental and labour laws (although there have not been significant differences in the stringency of those laws) and only anecdotal evidence of relocation to Mexico of dirty or dangerous production previously located in the United States and Canada.

The case cannot be made on the basis of significantly lower environmental or labour laws in Mexico. Mexico's environmental law is patterned after that of the United States and is very similar in the standards it sets. Also, Mexico's labour laws are in many respects more stringent than those of the United States and are comparable to those of Canada.[7] Nevertheless, it is widely conceded that there have been significant differences in the level of enforcement of environmental, labour and other social regulations in Mexico on the one hand and in the United States and Canada on the other.

The environmental differences have been most extensively studied. A 1991 EPA study concluded that while Mexico's environmental standards were comparable in many respects to those in the United States, Mexico devoted far fewer resources to monitoring and enforcement.[8] The study reported that 90 percent of all industrial facilities, mostly smaller ones, do not have environmental permits, and that until recently Mexico had only 109 inspectors country wide to enforce its regulations. There is also considerable evidence of higher levels of pollution and poorer working conditions in Mexico than would be tolerated in either the United States or Canada. Mexico City, of course, is by some measures the most polluted city in the world. (To be fair, this is to a great extent a reflection of climate and geography rather than of regulatory tolerance.)

The pollution and poor working conditions that most alarm critics of the NAFTA, however, are in the border regions, particularly in the maquiladora plants, many of which are subsidiaries of MNEs. Here there is a good deal of anecdotal evidence of air and water pollution, toxic dumping, and of poor working conditions tolerated by lax enforcement. For example, a widely cited 1992 U.S. GAO study of six U.S.-owned maquiladoras established near the border between May 1990 and July 1991 showed that none had prepared an Environmental Impact Assessment (EIA) as required by Mexican law.[9] Failure to prepare an EIA, of course, is not necessarily evidence of failure to comply with environmental standards.

Despite the prevalence of horror stories about the maquiladora program, there is evidence that many plants are operating with environmental standards and working conditions similar to those in their other North American operations. The reputation of the maquiladoras, earned by the first wave of plants, is unfair for many of the newer plants, particularly those of large MNEs, which tend to be cleaner and safer and which, for the most part, offer better working conditions and higher wages. Many MNEs operating in

Mexico apply the same environmental and workplace safety processes there as they do in the United States and Canada. The Ford Motor Company, for example, states: "Though not required by Mexican law or regulation, Ford's policy is that Ford environmental practices in the United States also be applied at our Mexican maquiladora facilities". Whether because of fear of approbation or because there are economies to adopting standard practices regardless of location, this appears to be a common response among larger MNEs operating in Mexico.

Even if it could be established conclusively that there is a less costly regulatory environment in Mexico than in the United States or Canada, it does not follow that there has been a significant relocation of industry to take advantage of the differences. On this count, although there are a few specific examples to support the contention, the evidence for widespread relocation is mixed at best.

The evidence cited by critics of the NAFTA is almost entirely anecdotal. The most widely cited example of relocation concerned the movement of between 1 percent and 3 percent of wood furniture manufacturers in the Los Angeles area to Mexico between 1988 and 1990, most to the Tijuana area. During this period, there were considerable differences in levels of environmental compliance costs between California, where there were stringent controls on paint coatings and solvents used in furniture finishing, and Mexico, where there was no established Mexican standard to regulate these compounds. In an investigation of these relocations, the U.S. General Accounting Office (GAO) concluded that, given that compliance costs are significant for this industry, the differences in environmental costs were a contributor to the relocation decisions. Indeed, 78 percent of the sample of manufacturers who relocated indicated that the California standard was a significant factor their decision.

One should be careful not to read too much into the GAO study, however, or to generalize too far from it. The difference in the cost of regulatory compliance was swamped by the difference in the basic wage rate; in Los Angeles the basic rate was about $8.92 an hour compared to only $0.77 an hour in Mexico. Given the highly labour-intensive nature of the wood furniture industry, it is difficult to evaluate the relative importance of the regulatory factors. The GAO did not attempt to control for labour costs and this appears to be an unusual case. Such high compliance costs and such marked differences in regulatory regimes are found in few other industries. It should be noted that this is a rare instance of differences in regulatory standards as opposed to levels of enforcement which, as noted earlier, is more common. It is also worth remarking here on a phenomenon that is the subject of the second half of this study: on the basis of an October 1989 agreement, Mexico and the United States are now working towards the harmonization of standards for air pollution emissions, including standards for the compounds involved in wood furniture manufacturing.

Although there is at present little conclusive evidence of systematic shifts of production to Mexico for the purpose of avoiding U.S. or Canadian social regulation, there is certainly room for further study. As part of his study of the general effects of U.S. regulation of chemicals and processed minerals, in which he found little relocation globally, Leonard concluded that there was reason to believe that there may have been some flight to Mexico of production in highly polluting industries such as the smelting of copper, lead and zinc, and the production of hydrofluoric acid. Leonard also concluded that most of the explosive growth in the maquiladora program was in such sectors as textiles and fashion-sensitive clothing, perishable food products, building materials, household items, furniture, glass and pottery products, and a wide range of simple metal products in which unit labour costs were much more important than pollution. Nonetheless, he cautions that Mexico "appears to have been used as a pollution (or workplace hazard) haven by a few of the industries participating in the maquiladora program and by some companies engaged in the production of hazardous chemical substances."[10]

Since Leonard's study, there has been a sharp increase in the level of direct investment in Mexico. Between 1985 and 1991, the cumulative U.S. direct investment in Mexico more than doubled — from $5 billion to $11.6 billion — and it appears to be accelerating. U.S. FDI in Mexico topped $1 billion in 1991, and will be considerably higher in 1992. Growth has been concentrated in transportation equipment, chemicals and allied products, food and kindred products, and non-electrical machinery. Of these industries, however, only chemicals and allied products have unusually high environmental compliance costs.

On balance, then, we cannot conclude that there has been significant relocation of production to Mexico for the purpose of avoiding regulatory costs. For most industries, the costs appear, simply, to be too small a component of overall cost structure to make relocation worthwhile. However, there is evidence to indicate that for certain industries regulatory costs may be a significant factor in locational decisions.

It is possible that there will be greater flight after the NAFTA, as factors such as trade barriers, political risk, and poor infrastructure that might be inhibiting relocation begin to diminish in importance. To the extent that the restraints on relocation are a function of Mexico's general level of development, however, eliminating these barriers implies a likely narrowing in the factor generally thought to be most significant in the decision to move production to Mexico, i.e., lower Mexican wages. But whatever the effect of differences in environment and labour regulations on location decisions has been in the past, it is likely that these factors will play an even smaller role in the future because the political processes are narrowing the differences in the regulatory regimes.[11]

THE POLITICAL RESPONSE

THE RELATIONSHIP BETWEEN business investment location and government regulation runs both ways: private actors consider regulatory costs when making economic decisions; public actors consider the potential for private relocation when making choices about levels of regulation. Usually the increasing power of private actors, particularly of MNEs, in this relationship is stressed. When capital is very mobile, it is empowered in its relations with states, since attempts to impose costly regulations can easily be evaded. If political jurisdictions want investment, they can find themselves in a beggar-thy-neighbour situation that places downward pressure on regulatory regimes.

By providing a more secure investment climate in Mexico and lowering trade barriers generally, the NAFTA will likely increase capital mobility, thus further limiting the power of states. Much of this might well have happened without the NAFTA through a process of silent integration as Mexico moved unilaterally to open itself to foreign trade and investment. But the event of the NAFTA so transformed the political context in the United States that potent countervailing political forces were mobilized to resist capital flight and the erosion of labour and environmental standards. As a result, an entirely new regulatory regime is being constructed for North America — one which will all but eliminate the potential for regulatory evasion. The account of how this happened is worth examining.

THE POLITICS OF ENVIRONMENT AND LABOUR IN THE UNITED STATES

BECAUSE THE POLITICAL RESPONSE was stronger and more organized in the United States than in Canada (and only negligible in Mexico), I focus on the remarkable and vigorous political fight that has taken place there.

To date, there have been three significant rounds in the political bout in which fears of job loss and lower labour and environmental conditions have come to the fore: the fast track fight of 1991, the battle for candidate Clinton's mind in the 1992 election, and the struggle to control the side negotiations on labour and environment. In each round, the coalition of environmentalists, labour unions and other activist groups succeeded in raising labour and environment issues to a higher priority.

When presidents Bush and Salinas first announced their intention to negotiate a U.S.-Mexico Free Trade Area (the decision to involve Canada and make it a NAFTA came later) and Bush stated that he would like an extension of "fast track" negotiating authority to conduct the negotiation, there was little to indicate how controversial the request would become. Within weeks, however, a broad coalition of environment, labour, human rights, religious and citizens' groups had formed in opposition to the proposed agreement. Central to their concerns, from the outset, were arguments about job loss and erosion of U.S. standards. At first the Bush Administration ignored the coalition, but within months allies on Capitol Hill forced Bush to promise that he would address a number of environmental and labour concerns in order to secure passage of the negotiating authority.

During the autumn of 1992, in the heat of the presidential campaign, President Bush pushed hard to complete the negotiations and present candidate Clinton with a dilemma: support the NAFTA and risk alienating important labour and environmental constituencies or reject the NAFTA and appear to back away from an earlier statement of support, thus confirming a growing public perception of indecisiveness. Clinton hesitated, arguing that he had not had time to read the agreement. While he pondered what to do, he was inundated with advice, much of it from the highly vocal environmental and labour groups. In the end, he typically rejected both extreme alternatives and found a middle ground: he supported the NAFTA, but insisted on negotiating supplemental agreements on labour and the environment before he would ask Congress to implement the agreement. Thus the side negotiations were born.

Once in office, as the new administration struggled to decide what the talking points of the campaign really meant, the interest groups mobilized again, pushing an expanded agenda that included the establishment of North American commissions on labour and the environment with sweeping powers to investigate and to sanction instances of failure to enforce standards. The social activists largely succeeded in their effort to influence the U.S. negotiating position in the discussions, and after intense negotiations with both Canada and Mexico the three parties agreed to much of the proposed agenda. Assuming the NAFTA will now be accepted by the U.S. Congress, the result will be the creation of significant new regional institutions designed to eliminate the possibility that Mexico will be a pollution and social hazard haven.

A TYPOLOGY OF POLITICAL PROCESSES

IT IS USEFUL TO DISTINGUISH among three types of political processes at work in the domestic politics of the NAFTA: reactive, strategic and symbolic. The purpose of making these distinctions is to allow me to argue that the political response was not simply an automatic corrective, and that, therefore, the effect of regional economic integration on regional regulatory regimes cannot be predicted without regard to the specific context in which economic integration takes place.

Part of the political response to the NAFTA among labour, environmental, and other social advocacy groups can be explained simply as a reaction to the effects of the NAFTA on the interests of these groups. Because their interests were, or were believed to be, threatened, special interest groups responded by seeking ways to prevent or limit those effects. The push for measures to ensure enforcement of Mexican environment and labour law can be partly explained by this type of response.

The problem with this view of politics is that it cannot account either for the scope of what labour and environmental groups sought to achieve, or for the vehemence of their stance. Much of what the interest groups demanded of the side negotiations involved problems that preceded the NAFTA and will likely not be exacerbated in any serious way by the NAFTA. The most obvious example of an issue of this kind is the demand to clean up the border region between the United States and Mexico. There is little doubt that there is a serious environmental problem on the border. But the problem, by definition, predates the NAFTA, and there is little reason to believe that the NAFTA will make the problem worse.[12] Nevertheless, the NAFTA and images of environmental degradation were commonly juxtaposed.[13] Similarly, human rights and citizens' groups concerned about the quality of Mexican democracy insist that the U.S. not enter into the NAFTA until Mexican politics is reformed, despite the fact that there was no reason to believe that the NAFTA would make these problems worse. Nonetheless, NAFTA is associated with stories about political corruption and human rights abuses.

To understand the scope and intensity of these concerns we must go beyond a simple reactive model of politics. Part of what is at work here is strategic behaviour on the part of interest groups, particularly on the part of their professional leadership. For environmental groups in particular, the NAFTA represents an opportunity to gain on a number of issues that are not causally connected to the agreement. The focus on the border is a case in point. Environmental groups have seized upon the moment of the NAFTA to try to do something about the problem. In crude terms, their strategy is quite simple: hold the NAFTA hostage for ransom to be paid on another issue of concern. In analytical terms, they have expanded the agenda of the negotiation by linking another issue — cleanup of the border region — to the bargain, and then insisting on compensation in the coin of that linked issue.[14] Privately, many leaders in the environmental movement acknowledge the essentially opportunistic nature of their position, although they justify it by arguing that they are attempting to redress the effects of a broader economic integration of which the NAFTA is but a part.

Not all interest groups have played such a strategic game — most notably, labour unions. Instead of identifying other issues of concern, linking them to the bargain, and then extracting a price for their support, labour unions have persisted largely in simple opposition to the NAFTA itself. Partly as a result of this tactical choice, it is unlikely that unions will get as much out of the NAFTA as they might have if they had been more willing to play a strategic game. Of course, to be fair, the NAFTA threatens the interests of unions in a way that it does not threaten the interests of the environmentalists, which makes it more difficult to find ways to compensate unions sufficiently to win their support.

Yet even this extended model of political behaviour, which assumes that actors are not just reactive but are also strategic, fails to account for the extent of the political reaction to the NAFTA. In both the United States and Canada, much of the response to the NAFTA, and most of the intense popular opposition to it, has less to do with the likely effects of the NAFTA or with opportunity presented by the negotiation than with what the NAFTA symbolizes.

Symbolic logic does not require causation, merely juxtaposition.[15] It matters not that the NAFTA did not cause the excesses of the maquiladora factories on the border: it has become a symbol for pollution and exploitive working conditions. It matters not that the NAFTA has not caused the loss of manufacturing jobs in the United States and Canada, or any of the other ills that plague their industrial workers: to union members the NAFTA stands for all of this. In Canada, much of the opposition to the NAFTA is based on lingering unhappiness with the the FTA, which in turn is blamed for Canada's recession and associated other ills. There is in addition a larger mythology surrounding the NAFTA — a version of the essential populist story, a conspiracy of "big business" against the people. This concept was used by Ross Perot with great effect during the 1992 presidential campaign and he continues to use it at anti-NAFTA meetings throughout the United States.

To characterize a political response as symbolic is not to denigrate it. Indeed, without some symbolic dimension, it would be difficult to get much of a response at all, either reactive or strategic. The reason for this lies in the inherent difficulty of overcoming barriers to effective collective action. Without some demonization of the NAFTA, it is difficult to see how the voluntary associations that constitute the advocacy community for the environment and human rights in particular could mobilize effectively. The situation is somewhat different for labour unions, which have lower organizing costs, but even there, given the very limited effect of the NAFTA on most union workers, there is a need to galvanize opposition through symbolic communication.

Symbolic politics, therefore, is extremely important to the balance of power between these advocacy groups and the business community. Businesses, of course, face their own collective action problem in mobilizing in support of the NAFTA, but their problem in this regard is considerably less complicated than that faced by voluntary associations. Businesses, particularly MNEs, also have the advantage of mobility, which requires no collective action. But the supporters of the NAFTA have a much less potent symbolism to work with than do its detractors. Framing the issue as "free trade" (good) versus "protectionism" (bad) has some utility, but these abstractions are far less compelling than concrete images of shuttered factories or polluted rivers.

There is a disturbing aspect to the symbolic dimension and to the populist response to the NAFTA it engenders, however. Many of the images associated with Mexico (and by extension with the NAFTA) subtly reinforce prejudices about Mexicans and feed xenophobic (and occasionally even racist) responses. Mexico and Mexicans are portrayed as dirty, corrupt, uneducated and possibly dangerous. The subtext is that they are not like us and therefore should not be admitted to the club. Care must be taken not to tar all opponents of the NAFTA with this brush, but neither should this dimension be simply ignored.

THE NEW REGULATORY REGIME

THE POLITICAL RESPONSE ON THE environment and labour concerns will result in greater enforcement of laws in Mexico and, therefore, in reduced incentives to relocate production to evade regulation. There will likely be two legacies: the first is greater Mexican capacity for enforcement; the second is the creation of new regional institutions.

In the past few years the Mexican government has taken a much more aggressive stance in its enforcement of laws relating to labour and, especially, the environment. To combat pollution in Mexico City, for example, the Salinas government has closed several major factories (including a large Pemex refinery within the city limits), instituted a very tough auto emission standard (backing it up by requiring emissions tests twice a year), and begun large scale land reclamation and reforestation programs. At the national level, the Mexican government has reorganized its ministry that deals with the environment, created a new office of Attorney General for Environmental Enforcement, and quadrupled the number of environmental inspectors. The number of enforcement actions has reached an impressive level. In the past four years, the government has temporarily shut down more than 1,000 factories, and closed several dozen permanently, for violations of environmental and workplace standards. Beyond this, Mexican environmental officials are now involved in numerous cooperative efforts with their counterparts in the United States to assess the environmental problems on the border, to train new environmental inspectors, to design auto emissions testing programs, and to undertake a variety of research projects. Taken together, this is an impressive record in a short period of time, and leaves little doubt that Mexico will be much more serious about environmental and some labour standards in the foreseeable future.

To reinforce the unilateral Mexican actions, the supplemental negotiations on labour and the environment create new regional institutions designed to ensure enforcement of national standards. In the environment area, the supplemental agreement will create a new Commission on Environmental Cooperation with a permanent and largely independent secretariat whose powers include the ability to hear complaints from interested citizens or groups, to initiate investigations (possibly including on-site inspections), to report their findings, and to make recommendations for remediation of any problems it finds. In the labour area, the agreement provides for the establishment of national bodies to hear complaints by its citizens of violations by the other governments. In the event that a pattern of repeated offenses persists, the agreements establish tri-national dispute settlement processes. Ultimate sanctions in this process vary by country and by topic. Canada refused to accept the possibility of trade sanctions and was allowed instead to use its national courts to enforce findings of dispute panels. Because Mexico refused to accept dispute settlement for some labour issues, only consultation is available for many labour rights covered by the agreeement.

Reaction to these supplemental agreements has been mixed. In the U.S. environmental community, the more mainstream groups such as the Environmental Defense Fund, the Natural Resources Defense Council, and the World Wildlife Federation reacted very positively to the agreements and announced their support. The Sierra Club, Friends of the Earth, and other more radical environmental groups panned the agreements. The labour side agreement drew predictable criticism from the labour unions, who noted, among other things, that it was weaker than the environment agreement. Despite the criticism, however, this regime will clearly have a positive effect on enforcement patterns in both areas of social policy, and will all but guarantee that Mexico will not be a haven for businesses seeking to evade regulations in Canada and the United States.

CONCLUSIONS

THE RELATIONSHIP BETWEEN government regulatory regimes and private investment locational decisions demonstrates that causality can run in both directions. Differences in costs imposed by differences in political regimes can affect private locational decisions. Conversely, the possibility of such private relocations can trigger a political response that limits the incentives to flee.

The causal links between state and private actors are not simple, however. The more extreme fears of private actors fleeing regulation underestimate the complexity of actual locational decisions. Even when regulatory costs are high, they are but one factor in a rich array of factors affecting these decisions. In North America, one can see a certain amount of sorting of types of economic activity among the three countries of the region. But very little of the sorting appears to be driven by differences in social regulation.

The effect of private locational decisions on government action appears to be even more complicated. First, in the case of the NAFTA, fear of relocation was more important than actual relocation in inducing a political response. This suggests something about the importance of the particular political context in the United States.

Second, the event of the NAFTA served as a catalyst for the political response. Had economic integration proceeded less formally, that is, had it continued along the path it was on before the NAFTA, it is likely that relocations induced by differences in national regulatory regimes would not have mobilized political forces to the same degree, and that those differences would have persisted much longer. Primarily because of its symbolic potency, the NAFTA facilitated political organization and helped social activists overcome problems of collective action that would otherwise have limited their power.

Finally, the particular political response, that is the focus on environmental and labour rights, is an artifact of the fundamental political assymetry of the region, that is, the dominance of the United States. Integration of the political regulatory regime is occurring primarily in those policy areas where it is demanded by the United States.

There is a certain inevitability in the deepening economic integration we are witnessing in North America. To be sure, it is influenced both by the unilateral action of states — Mexico's decisions to lower its barriers to trade and investment — and by collective political action in the region — the negotiation of the NAFTA. That North America will be increasingly part of one market is clear. How we will manage that market is less clear, however. Certainly, there appears to be little likelihood that a regional political infra-structure on the EC model will be created in North America. Nonetheless, the regional political responses we have seen so far are suggestive of the possibil-ities for building a deeper and broader regional political infrastructure.

In this light, the lasting effect of the NAFTA may be precisely the opposite of what its opponents charge. Rather than contributing to the further empowerment of private actors it may, in fact, be the beginning of a recapture of power by states, either by facilitating greater cooperation among them or by creating supranational institutions capable of addressing social issues on a regional basis. To the extent that economic activity — trade and investment — becomes increasingly regional, rather than national or global, what may develop is a political architecture more coincident with the economic landscape.

It is interesting to note that those who are now critical of the supplemental agreements worry that these agreements threaten to undermine national sovereignty. They are right to note the implications for sovereignty, but they may be missing the larger point. National sovereignty has been been undermined for some time: "at bay" in Vernon's words. These institutions do not represent a further reduction of state power, but rather provide an opportunity to rebalance the equation.

ENDNOTES

1 For an excellent summary of the literature relevant to the questions considered here, see H. Jeffrey Leonard, *Pollution and the Struggle for the World Product*, (Cambridge: Cambridge University Press, 1988).

2 Robert B. Reich, Todd Hixon and Branch Kimball, "Who is Us?", *Harvard Business Review*, 68, 1 (Jan.-Feb. 1990).

3 Leonard (1988), p. 21.

4 See Maureen L. Cropper and Wallace Oates, "Environment Economics: A Survey," *The Journal of Economic Literature*, XXX, (June 1992): 675-740 and Steven Globerman, "Trade Liberalization and the Environment," in *Assessing NAFTA: A Trinational Analysis* edited by Steven Globerman and Michael Walker, (Vancouver: The Fraser Institute, 1993).

5 United States Congressional Research Service, "Review of US-Mexican Environmental Issues," 1992, p. 163. The review surveyed eight studies, three of which examined location decisions within the United States, and five of which examined location decisions internationally.

6 James T. Hamilton, "Politics and Social Costs: Estimating the Impact of Collective Action on Hazardous Waste Facilities," *RAND Journal of Economics*, 24,1, (Spring 1993).

7 See Robert A. Pastor, "NAFTA as the Center of an Integration Process: The Non-Trade Issues," in *North American Free Trade*, edited by Nora Lustig et al., (Washington: The Brookings Institution, 1992).

8 "Evaluation of Mexico's Environmental Laws and Regulations: Interim Report of EPA Findings," Office of General Counsel, International Activities Division, USEPA, 1991.

9 "U.S.-Mexico Trade: Assessment of Mexico's Environmental Controls for New Companies," GAO/GDD Report 92-113, United States General Accounting Office, 1992.

10 Leonard (1988), p.146.

11 It is worth noting that the best analyses of the likely effects of NAFTA on the North American economy do not predict a significant shift in the location of production as a result of NAFTA, and certainly not for reasons of regulatory avoidance. See, in particular, "An Economic and Budgetary Analysis of the North Amerian Free Trade Agreement," U.S. Congressional Budget Office, 1993.

12 Some have claimed that NAFTA will actually improve matters, by contributing over time to a rising standard of living. See in particular Gene M. Grossman & Alan B. Kreugar, "Environmental Impacts of a North American Free Trade Agreement," Working Paper 3914, (Cambridge, Mass.: National Bureau of Economic Research, 1991).

13 Typical of the headlines appearing in the press are "Deadly Fallout at the Border: Birth Defects, Illness Plague Towns Near Mexican Plants," *Providence Journal-Bulletin*, 9/28/92 and "Mexico's Futuristic Nightmare:

Matamoros," Linda Diebel, *The Toronto Star*, D1, 13/3/93. These stories typically paint a horrific picture of the situation in Mexican border towns and then imply that NAFTA will lead to more of the same.

14 See Frederick W. Mayer, "Managing Domestic Differences in International Negotiations: The Strategic Use of Internal Side Payments," *International Organization* 46, 4, (Autumn 1992) and James K. Sebenius, "Negotiation Arithmetic," *International Organization* 37 (Spring 1983): 281-316.

15 The literature on symbolic politics is somewhat underdeveloped. See, however, Murray Edelman, *The Symbolic Uses of Politics*, (Urbana, Ill.: University of Illinois Press, 1964).

Part IV   Lessons and New Directions

Christopher J. Maule
Professor of Economics and International Affairs
Carleton University

Rapporteur's Comment

T HE TASK OF THE CONFERENCE was to assess the effect of the NAFTA on
Canada, Mexico and the United States as a result of MNEs restructuring
their operations. Lorraine Eden, in her overview paper, concludes in simple
terms that the "good news" is, "the NAFTA will not cause a massive exodus of
plants from Canada and the United States to Mexico", but the "bad news" is
"there will be major plant reorganizations throughout North America". A
review of the conference papers does not contradict this view. It does, however, reveal just how few simple answers there are and how complex the
assessment has become.

Complexity arises because of the combination of growing interdependence
between states and the use by MNEs and domestic firms of a wide array of
contractual arrangements. Neither the boundaries of states nor the jurisdictions
of firms are well defined and it has therefore become difficult to explain
precisely what they are, how they interact and what impact they have. The
interaction between firms and states acting independently, or in concert with
each other, causes the dimensions of national sovereignty to change almost
daily with different consequences for large, medium-size and small countries.
Firms, both domestic and multinational, have to anticipate and respond to
these changes and cannot wait until new international treaties are signed and
old ones revised. Analysts often find themselves playing catch up with
decisions already made by firms and, just as often, they find the information
they need to assess the outcome of trade agreements more readily in the pages
of the business press and trade papers than in official statistics.[1] In this
context, academics and policy makers can present the concepts and relationships
to be used in assessing such matters. In the pages following, the contributions
made by the conference papers and their subsequent discussion to the question
posed is examined under two main headings: the environment for decision-
making and multinational enterprises.

The Environment for Decision-Making

The evolving scene

ONE DIFFICULTY IN ASSESSING the effect of the NAFTA has to do with isolating its effect in the "path towards a North American economy" (Eden) since 1980. In addition to past policies, there is an ongoing series of institutional and technological changes that are continually affecting international economic relationships and domestic circumstances. The papers point to the current GATT negotiations, the recently implemented FTA, deregulation, privatization and reduced restrictions on foreign direct investment (FDI) in Mexico (Kudrle), as well as technological developments. Not only is the ongoing revolution in information technology causing marked reductions in transportation and communications costs,[2] a series of organizational changes leading to different degrees and types of vertical and horizontal integration is also occurring — just-in-time production, the kanban system, team production, computer-aided design, and computer-aided manufacturing systems, to name only a few. Existing plants are being restructured to produce a wider range of products more efficiently. As the minimum optimum size of plant has declined, existing plants are also being down-sized resulting in smaller plants that can survive in competition with larger plants. The Canadian curse of inefficient manufacturing plants that are too small and diversified to enjoy plant-specific and product-specific economies of scale is being lifted, or has been entirely eliminated in some industries. A few large plants may even be restructured for "mass customization" — the mass production of customised goods and services (Davenport, 1993).

MNE decision-makers must respond to these forces; they must also anticipate future changes, such as the implementation of the NAFTA, its possible expansion to include other Latin American countries, some conclusion to the GATT, as well as developments in the European Community (EC) and the Asia-Pacific region. The question put to the conference is an important one, especially for Mexico and Canada, but in the cauldron of changes occurring, the NAFTA may be a relatively unimportant consideration for corporate decision-makers. The trouble is, *we do not know* and no representatives of MNEs were present to suggest answers. This is not to say that the economic impact of the NAFTA cannot be assessed. It is to say, however, that input of corporate officials is needed to assist in interpreting official data — little of which can ever be current or reveal the motives behind the decisions made. Public debate adds further to confuse the scene as interest groups, for and against the NAFTA, concoct scenarios to promote their causes.

Unfinished Business

THE NAFTA, if and when it arrives, will be a partially cooked omelette. This is the case put forward by Vernon, who argues that the agreement fails to recognize the MNE explicitly and also fails to identify associated problems, such as transfer pricing and regional content requirements. Graham and Warner also point to the desirability of the three countries having a common competition policy that would replace existing anti-dumping and countervailing duties regimes. Add to this differing labour and environmental standards, and social policies (Mayer), as well as different views on the meaning of national security (Frost & Graham) and the future ramifications of the agreement are evident.

Because frictions in these areas are virtually inevitable, some argued that the NAFTA would, and probably should, evolve over time into a customs union with sovereignty in some areas flowing to a supranational authority along the lines of the EC. The Canadians tended to argue against this position. They observed that, for Canada, foreign policy is a function of trade policy whereas in the United States the opposite is true (Lipsey). For Canada, losing control of its trade policy would mean losing — or a lessening of control over its foreign policy. Canada would be unwilling to accept direction from some "higher authority" regarding its trading relationships. This is not a concern over loss of sovereignty, since some loss is inevitable in any international agreement. Rather, it is the extent of the loss and the areas in which the loss would be experienced. What makes the NAFTA different from the EC is the involvement of three countries — one of which is much more powerful economically than the other two combined. The largest country would simply exercise leverage with other issues to get its way in a supranational body.[3]

The NAFTA would have received little public support in Canada if a supranational authority had been proposed at the outset of the negotiations.[4] However, it is also clear that many of the problem areas outlined by the conference participants will have to be dealt with once the agreement is in place and some mode of resolution will have to be found. The Canadian and U.S. experience with dispute-resolution mechanisms under the FTA will no doubt prove useful but, inevitably, the bargaining will take place between asymmetrical parties.[5] The existence of unfinished business partly explains why the full impact of the NAFTA will be known only after such secondary effects have worked their way through the system (Dunning). By that time, however, it will be difficult to determine whether the effects were due to the NAFTA or to some of the other forces at work.

Unfinished business will also be affected by the outcome of imminent political events — the October 1993 Canadian federal election, the decision by the U.S. Congress whether or not to ratify the NAFTA and a provincial election in Quebec in 1994, followed by Mexican presidential elections. In each case there are strong vocal opponents of the NAFTA who will influence the final outcome.

Politics Large and Small

ANOTHER CONTEXTUAL FACTOR is the use of NAFTA being made by the United States in its global trade negotiations. The NAFTA is a signal to Europe and Asia that failure to complete the GATT negotiations will likely drive the United States to focus its attention on the Americas (Vernon); if others insist on forming regional trading blocs, the United States would have one as well.

At the other extreme, some local interest groups such as environmentalists have used the agreement to gain concessions from the U.S. Congress in areas unrelated to the agreement, while others such as labour unions have sought to protect their members' jobs (Mayer). In between are state and provincial (sub-federal) governments, which now play a more important role in trade negotiations and trade flows by dint of their influence over subsidies and tax concessions to foreign and domestic investors — the so-called TRIMs or trade related investment measures.[6]

TRIMS, IRTMS and All That

THE INTERCONNECTION BETWEEN investment and trade has spawned a number of acronyms:

TRIMs - trade-related investment measures, such as foreign investment screening agencies, domestic content requirements, subsidies and tax incentives to foreign investors.[7]

TRIPs - trade-related intellectual property measures, such as laws and regulations that protect or fail to protect intellectual property rights.

IRTMs - investment-related trade measures, such as voluntary export restraints, but also tariffs and non-tariff barriers.

TIRMs (Kudrle) - trade- and investment-related measures, and IRIPs (Ostry) - investment-related industrial policy measures, such as: the promotion of the Sematech consortium, which excludes foreign firms and aims to establish world leadership in a particular industry, or the operation of the EC science and technology programmes.

The fact is that almost any domestic economic policy, and many non-economic policies, can be found to have some impact on foreign investment and trade, just as they do on competition. The questions are: which ones influence the location decision of MNEs and which ones are important enough to be incorporated in a trade or investment regime? While the NAFTA deals mostly with trade, Ostry argues that the most difficult issues are likely to arise in the area of investment where different systems of corporate governance prevail — systems that are unlikely to submit easily to policy harmonization.

Multinational Enterprises

Trade and Investment

THE DATA SEEM TO SHOW that trade and foreign direct investment are complementary and that as a regional trading area expands, investment from foreign- and domestic-owned MNEs increases and restructuring occurs. But trade increases as well, not only within the region but also between regions, with much of the trade involving intrafirm transactions (Encarnation, Dunning). One question is whether all MNEs respond in the same way, or whether there are country-specific differences based on the nationality of the parent company or the host country — i.e. do Japanese MNEs behave in a certain way everywhere or most of the time, or do they behave one way in North America and differently in Europe and Asia? These questions require considerable research, some of which has been started by Westney for Japanese firms and referred to by Vernon and Dunning.

On the issue of corporate organizational structures, my own view is that there is no "best" way to organize for a given set of political and economic conditions.[8] There may be a range of possible (efficient) structures, but every structure tends to deteriorate with time as internal bureaucratic pressures build up or management fails to respond to external signals. In time, reorganizations are needed — which may involve moving from more to less centralized control, or vice versa, or engaging in more-or-less vertical integration.[9] The current popularity of Japanese management systems in North American MNEs may be a tonic that shakes up management for awhile. However, there are already reports that the system is not working well everywhere. Some even suggest that its adoption is merely a reflection of management copying practices used in the (currently) most successful economy (McFetridge).

Some organizational arrangements may well be culturally specific. For example, Japanese keiretsu may be the product of a particular cultural context that has led to a process of organizational learning having more permanence than is found in networks and alliances elsewhere. They may not be transferable to other countries. The fact that Japanese MNEs tend to employ Japanese nationals in most senior positions in their subsidiaries (Westney) may be the "least cost" way to transfer this learning. In discussing organizational learning, Chandler does not say whether it is culturally specific, but if it is, it may partly explain why it is difficult to sustain Japanese management practices in North American-based firms.[10] If organizations need to be shaken up from time to time, then *keiretsu* organizations are probably not immune.

The charge that keiretsu behaviour tends to be collusive is serious (Bergsten & Ostry), because much of it derives from the frustrations of successive U.S. administrations (and those of other countries) in dealing with Japanese firms, and because, in the absence of a global regime for antitrust, it may lead to an increasing extraterritorial application of U.S. antitrust laws.

This, in turn, is likely to encourage other countries to introduce "blocking" legislation to prevent the implementation of foreign laws in domestic jurisdictions. Only lawyers and economists stand to gain from such an outcome. For MNEs it introduces only further uncertainty.

ARE NETWORKS NEW?

TERMS SUCH AS BUSINESS CLUSTERS, networks, alliances, and vertical and horizontal *keiretsu* pervade the discussion of multinationals (Rugman, Bergsten, Westney, Eden, Niosi). The 1992 United Nations *World Investment Report* discusses alliances as does the March 1993 *Economist Survey of Multinationals*. Alongside the worldwide count of 35,000 transnational corporations and 150,000 foreign affiliates (according to the UNCTC) is an unknown number of alliances and non-equity networks between corporations. Alliances and networks are acknowledged to be of increasing importance but little is known about their number, nature or impact. Much of the discussion of multinationals therefore takes place without a clear understanding of the boundaries of the object(s) being examined. There are selective counts of alliances (Niosi) and individual case examples such as Stentor and Benetton (Rugman & D'Cruz) and a growing literature on the topic that attempts to provide a rationale for networks, but the effects of alliances and networks on employment and other economic and political variables are not well understood.[11]

The issues raised by alliances have to do with their competitive impact in each country, the extent to which they can be used to avoid taxation, and performance controls such as rules of origin and the challenge they pose to state sovereignty and the operation of regional and international regimes such as the NAFTA and the GATT. These are topics for future research and theories of MNE organization and plant location will have to be adapted to these organizational arrangements. What is probably happening is that investors and their managers are striving to reduce transaction costs associated with problems of moral hazard, adverse selection, team production and principal-agent relationships.[12] Networks and alliances are organizational techniques designed to reduce costs and increase the flexibility of MNEs in situations dominated by rapid change. The result is increasing difficulty of governments to influence the behaviour of MNEs within their territorial jurisdictions, and difficulty for analysts to assess the impact of those MNEs on factors such as employment.

Are networks new? The answer is "no". Certainly, the term was used by Vernon in earlier writings to explain the operations of MNEs.[13] Are they increasing in number and are they important for purposes of analysis? The answer to both questions is almost certainly "yes".

AGGLOMERATION AND DISAGGLOMERATION

WHY DO FIRMS CLUSTER in certain locations — such as financial services in the City of London and Wall Street, computer-communications firms in Palo Alto and Cambridge U.K., and film making in Hollywood and Bombay? Conflicting theories of location and agglomeration provide some of the answers. On the one hand, the model developed by Eaton, Lipsey & Safarian examines the interacting effects of scale and scope economies, and changing costs of communications and transportation, suggesting that disagglomeration will not occur with the passage of the NAFTA. On the other hand, others pointed to the circumstances of economic decline and unravelling that led to the North American "rustbelt" with shrinking populations, falling real estate prices and unused facilities.

The economics of agglomeration and disagglomeration is a useful way to focus on the restructuring decisions of MNEs. The analysis can include the deterrent effects on agglomeration of congestion and pollution and moves towards telecommuting, (that is, bringing work to the worker rather than the worker to the work). High cost inner-city real estate and the increasing use of part-time employees are encouraging firms to reorganize their operations so as to make a worker's home part of the plant in which work is done. Some types of work can be transmitted to the home by telephone, coaxial cable, microwave and satellite and shipped back to the plant or head office the same way. With vastly reduced costs of communication, many places throughout the world become possible locations for MNEs. Options for restructuring are also vastly increased for certain kinds of industries.

Different sorts of MNEs have markedly different requirements. Within the three main sectors of raw materials, manufacturing and service industries, most of the attention seems to be given to the first two sectors although services constitute a growing sector. The services sector is also the one that lends itself easily to decentralization, especially in areas such as financial services, telecommunications, advertising, broadcasting, news services, airlines and hotels. Applying location theory to the idiosyncratic features of these industries could be a rewarding exercise.

THE DATA

HOW MNES RESTRUCTURE should be discernable from the data, but the data used is that of direct foreign investment — which is often revealing but seldom capable of providing answers. The data used by Encarnation, Niosi and Unger show which countries are home and hosts to foreign investment, but are a blunt tool to explain the changes observed. How much of the change in Canada is due to firms anticipating the introduction of the FTA and the NAFTA? How much is due to the actual introduction of the FTA? What would have happened in the absence of these and other policy changes? How have firms actually restructured and for what reasons? The data answer none of these questions, although clues are to be found in newspaper and journal articles.

The data provided by Knubley, Legault & Rao on the top 1,008 firms in Canada, the United States and Mexico is an important start to focusing on the behaviour of individual firms. These and other industry data show the industries in which companies from each of the three countries are specializing and where comparative advantages appear to lie as integration progresses. Differences between firms may provide important clues to the restructuring process, but the next most important step will be to get inside a representative sample of the corporations themselves.

At the outset, survey questionnaires and interviews are probably the most effective way to gather the required information. These may provide leads to how published data can be analyzed. Medical research techniques already provide ample precedent for gathering and analyzing large amounts of detailed information about organizational changes to the human body from conception on. Applying similar techniques to information about financial and material flows gathered from corporations, it may be possible to monitor in real time the organizational changes taking place within these corporations. Problems of confidentiality will occur for the outside researcher, but these can no doubt be overcome with the co-operation of the individual corporations.

The Industry Canada database constitutes an important beginning to more detailed analysis of the changes taking place in MNEs and one which should be developed further. A series of case studies of selected corporations in each of the three countries would be a logical start. Over time, a longitudinal study might reveal both the changes and the reasons for them. Working directly with corporations collecting new information that is seen to be useful to both the corporate decision-makers and policy planners is an approach to consider.

CONCLUSIONS

IN KOGUT'S VIEW, a new system is being created — one in which MNEs have a major role to play. In this scenario the NAFTA is an important trade agreement dealing with matters such as intellectual property and aspects of investment, but more attention needs to be paid to issues that affect MNEs. The ongoing process of "invisible integration" (Molot) taking place in the three countries will continue with or without the NAFTA. The agreement, if ratified, will make some difference to the way in which MNEs restructure, but what that difference will be is difficult to decipher. For Canada, failure to be part of the agreement would be detrimental, leaving it only in a "hub and spoke" relationship with the United States.

The conference papers and discussions reaffirm the importance of examining secondary effects of the NAFTA, distinguishing between MNEs of different national origins, and understanding how the agreement will interact with policies dealing with competition and restrictive trade practices, industrial relations, labour migration, environmental protection, national security, and the deregulation or privatization of financial services. The empirical evidence regarding restructuring is mixed. Of course, analysts can continue working on trade and investment flows, but my own view is that researchers should concentrate here on examining individual corporations, initially on a case-by-case basis using a sample of MNEs of different nationalities operating within the three countries. The Industry Canada database provides a worthy first step in this direction, and micro-measurement of functional activity within firms may provide additional data for analysis.

POSTSCRIPT

IN 1969, ONE YEAR AFTER the Watkins Report was published (Ed Safarian was a member of the Task Force), Gilles Paquet convened a conference on The Multinational Corporation and the Nation State. In his opening remarks, Paquet referred to MNEs as LMUs (large multiterritorial units) and stated that the questions being posed at that time were not new. They could be divided into two major subsets: those that attempt to discover the reasons for the internationalization of production, (the rules of the game that brought it about, and the organizational arrangement it calls for); and those that attempt to examine the effects of this process on the pattern of economic and social development of national economies. Among the participants, John McManus argued that the essence of direct foreign investment is not a transfer of capital, "but the international extension of managerial control over certain activities; and Stephen Hymer expressed concern over the economic power of the LMU (MNE) and associated "wastes of oligopolistic anarchy" (Paquet, 1970, pp. 63-6).

Twenty-four years later it seems the same questions are being asked. Using the conference proceedings as one source, the reader is invited to assess the progress that has been made. My own view is that there is now a better understanding of the complexity of the questions being asked and some promising lines for future research.

ENDNOTES

1 I have found useful commentary in *The Financial Times* (London), *The Wall Street Journal*, *The New York Times*, *The Economist*, and various trade and regional publications depending on the industry and region of interest.

2 The impact of the information revolution is so widespread that it can probably best be compared to the introduction of the printing press in the 1400s. Looking back, a few years hence, it will be difficult to isolate the effect on corporate restructuring of policy measures such as the NAFTA from those of information technology.

3 A contrary view is that, in a supranational body, Canada would stand to be protected from U.S. domination by having equal voting power with the other members.

4 I am reluctant to state what the Mexican position would be on this issue since it was not articulated at the conference, but I suspect it would be the same as Canada's.

5 Opponents of the NAFTA argued in favour of Canada concentrating on the GATT negotiations because of the possibility of allying itself with more countries in the case of trade disputes. Continuing disputes under the FTA indicate some of the problems of dealing with large partners.

6 At the time the Automotive Agreement between Canada and the United States was signed, the Province of Ontario was merely informed about the terms of the agreement. Today each province expects to provide input into the negotiating process.

7 A wide definition of TRIMs is used here to reflect the importance of the issues raised by Ostry which stress the current competition by states for investment.

8 In discussing manufacturing technology, Goldhar states "There is no 'standard solution' to the search for the 'best' way to organize manufacturing for the international market". (Goldhar, 1989, p. 264). See also Scherer (1992) and Radner (1992).

9 Corporations in crisis provide examples. Under Harold Geneen, ITT was a highly centralized firm which was reorganized in a decentralised way after experiencing difficulties and new managers were appointed. Recent layoffs and downsizing of firms such as IBM and automotive companies reflects a process of restructuring. The so-called jobless recovery in North America is accompanied by strong productivity growth as firms have expanded production without increasing employment. In studying corporate structures, organizational learning may be a useful concept to employ.

10 Organizational learning is described as resulting "...from solving problems of scaling up the processes of production, from acquiring knowledge of customers' needs, coming to know the availability of suppliers, and becoming knowledgeable in the ways of recruiting and training managers... ." A. D. Chandler, "Organisational Capabilities and the Economic History of the Industrial Enterprise," *The Journal of Economic Perspectives*, 6, 3, (Summer 1992): 84.

11 A useful bibliography can be found in Gilroy (1993), while *The Economist*, March 27th, 1993 lists a time series of technological alliances recorded by the Maastricht Economic Research Institute in Innovation and Technology at the University of Limburg, but apparently discontinued after 1989.

12 The inability to infer accurately what has happened is at the core of transacting difficulties in the principal-agent problem (the effort of the agent cannot be measured), in adverse selection problems (characteristics

of information cannot be measured), and in team production problems (the effort of each team member cannot be isolated or measured). Moral hazard as a form of opportunism is often described in terms of shirking or appropriating ideas which are capitalised on outside the firm.
13 R. Vernon, *Sovereignty at Bay*, New York, Basic Books, 1971.

ACKNOWLEDGEMENT

I WOULD LIKE TO THANK, without implication, Keith Acheson, Lorraine Eden, Don McFetridge, John Ravenhill and Emmy Verdun for helpful comments in preparing this paper.

BIBLIOGRAPHY

Davenport, Thomas H. *Mass Customization: The New Frontier in Business Competition*. Cambridge: Harvard Business School Press, 1993.

"Everybody's Favourite Monsters: A Survey of Multinationals." *The Economist*, (March 27, 1993), pp.1-20.

Goldhar, J.D. "Implications of CIM for International Manufacturing." In *Managing International Manufacturing*. Edited by, K.Ferdows. North Holland: Elsevier Science Publishers B.V.,1989, p. 262.

Gilroy, Bernard Michael. *Networking in Multinational Enterprises: The Importance of Strategic Alliances*. Columbia, South Carolina: University of South Carolina Press, 1993.

Paquet, Gilles (ed.), *The Multinational Firm and the Nation State*. Don Mills: Collier-Macmillan Canada Ltd., 1972.

Radner, Roy. "Hierarchy: The Economics of Managing." *Journal of Economic Literature*. XXX (September 1992):1382-1415.

Scherer, F.M. "Schumpeter and Plausible Capitalism." *Journal of Economic Literature*. XXX (September 1992):1416-1433.

United Nations Centre on Transnational Corporations (UNCTC). *World Investment Report 1992: Transnational Corporations as Engines of Growth*. New York: United Nations, 1992.

Murray G. Smith
Director, Centre for Trade Policy and Law
Carleton University and the University of Ottawa

Rapporteur's Comment

T HE PAPERS IN THIS VOLUME and the conference on which it is based provide a rich array of insights and issues. Along with a number of specific observations, I pose here some broad questions about the future evolution of policy in North America and about the responses of MNEs.

Do Multinationals Matter?

A RECENT ARTICLE IN *Fortune* magazine cited a speech given by Tom Watson Jr. (then CEO of IBM) at Columbia University in 1963. Watson noted that of the 95 largest U.S. corporations operating at the turn of the century, only two still made the list in 1960. One was General Electric, the other was US Steel. Of course, everyone knows what has happened to US Steel since then. The interesting point that the Fortune article went on to make has to do with what has happened to IBM in the meantime. IBM went the strategic network approach with Intel and MicroSoft in the early 1980s, and today the combined market value of Intel and Microsoft exceeds that of IBM.

From an investment standpoint — considering the track record of the one hundred largest U.S. corporations over the past century — this begs the question of the risk (if not the wisdom) attached to investing one's pension savings in the one hundred largest corporations comprising this list today. Even if the largest corporations and multinationals are doomed eventually to be superceded by other emerging corporations and multinationals, this does not mean the existing large multinationals do not play important roles in shaping present and future industrial and economic location decisions and for fostering innovations.

Unquestionably, we now have a much better understanding of globalization than we did in the 1980s — when foreign direct investment (FDI) grew much more rapidly than world trade, which in turn grew more rapidly than world production. What is more difficult, however, (and this addresses Vernon's point about "throwing deep") has to do with what these papers tell us about the future. Uncertainty begs the questions: How will the structure and performance of MNEs evolve in the decades ahead? Are the MNEs akin to lumbering dinosaurs, which have grown in a world fragmented by trade barriers and high transport costs, but are, with North American and global integration, destined to be overtaken by more nimble, entrepreneurial players? Or, will multinationals increase their interpenetration of national economies? And, will intra-corporate trade continue to expand its share of regional and global trade?

One set of interesting issues noted in a number of the papers includes the blurring boundaries of the multinational enterprise, the proliferation of both jargon and phenomena in terms of networks and strategic alliances. The sharp distinction between hierarchy and contract in economic organization is also becoming blurred. As both Vernon and Dunning suggest, the nature of MNEs is bound to change because of: the gradual withdrawal of trade barriers among the OECD economies; the associated interpenetration of national economies through increased intra-industry trade and intra-industry investment among the OECD members; the spreading unilateral liberalization of trade and investment among Asian and Latin American economies; and the ongoing reduction of transportation, communications and coordination costs in the modern information economy.

Examining the performance of Japanese multinationals in North America, Westney suggests that as new multinationals, Japanese MNEs are influenced by both life-cycle and period effects. Yet, Japanese MNEs also appear to retain distinctive "Keiretsu" characteristics (long term contracting arrangements) in the new environment. At the same time, at least in the automotive sector, the large centrally-controlled hierarchies of the Big Three have gradually adapted to become more keiretsu-like, with just-in-time production and long-term contractual relations with key suppliers. At least in some sectors — despite the long running U.S.-Japan governmental disputes characterized as a dialogue of the deaf in which each side shouts at the other "Be like us!" — a gradual process of convergence may be occurring in terms of the structures and strategies of Japanese and U.S.-based MNEs.

Rugman & D'Cruz raise the issue of business networks and how these interact with the non-business infrastructure. They characterize this phenomenon of business networks as centered on "flagship firms" which have key supplier and customer relationships. The emergence of business networks appears to be an important empirical development and it raises a number of interesting challenges relating to the theory of internalization.

DOES POLICY MATTER?

SEVERAL OF THE PAPERS, notably those by Kogut and by Eaton, Lipsey & Safarian, argue that history (and hence both corporate strategy and public policy) "matters". The complicated post-neoclassical framework of Eaton,

Lipsey & Safarian suggests the potential for multiple equilibria, in terms of both firm strategy and industry structure as well as the public policy bundles offered by nation states. With respect to the latter, some governments might impose high tax burdens, but provide efficient infrastructure, high quality human resources, a clean environment and high amenity levels; other governments might impose lower taxes but provide fewer amenities. Of course, there is also more scope for persistent sub-optimal performance by states than by corporations, with some states imposing higher taxes and providing fewer amenities. However, none of these considerations addresses the important issues surrounding policy regimes in North America and how those regimes are likely to evolve in the future.

INTEGRATION POLICY

APPROPRIATELY, MOST OF THE CONTRIBUTIONS in the volume assume that implementation of the NAFTA will proceed on the basis of the negotiated text. Dunning, and Eaton, Lipsey & Safarian on the one hand, and Vernon on the other hand, offer different perspectives on the response of U.S.-based MNEs to the removal of intra-North American trade barriers consequent to the proposed NAFTA and the Canada-U.S. Free Trade Agreement. Dunning suggests that intra-regional MNEs may increase horizontal efficiency-seeking investments in Canada and vertical investments in Mexico for labour-intensive stages of production. Eaton, Lipsey and Safarian suggest that the effects of an FTA will be to reduce the small country disadvantage in attracting investment. Vernon is less optimistic, suggesting that U.S.-based MNEs are more likely to retrench to their large operations in the United States as trade barriers within the region are relaxed. The Dunning and Eaton, Lipsey and Safarian contributions also attach more emphasis to the dynamic responses in terms of product specialization, technical innovation and other factors.

Some evidence on these issues is contained in the volume. Encarnation documents the substantial volume of exports by U.S. subsidiaries in Canada back to the United States. The extensive analysis of the data contained in the Industry and Science Canada paper indicates that after a period of disinvestment in Canada by American MNEs between 1980 and 1985, the American MNEs switched to significant inward investment between 1986 and 1992. It is difficult to attribute policy developments precisely as the cause of these investment responses. For example, was the upsurge in inward direct investment in 1987 and 1988 a lagged response to changes in Canadian investment policy in 1985, an anticipatory response to the implementation of the FTA, or the result of a combination of both factors? Furthermore, Niosi observes that although there was a rebound in U.S. direct investment in Canada around the time of the FTA, Canada's share of the total stock of U.S. FDI has nonetheless declined, as part of a general trend that has been underway since the late 1950s to diversify U.S. FDI.

Turning to the reaction of extra-regional MNEs, Eaton, Lipsey & Safarian observe that the effects of restrictive rules of origin are to limit the extent to which the FTA removes the small country disadvantage in attracting economies-of-scale-based investment by offshore-based MNEs that lack North American supplier networks. Both Kudrle and Ostry refer to these as "IRTMs" (Investment Related Trade Measures) in contrast to "TRIMs" (Trade Related Investment Measures). Many of the subtle issues in trade policy, whether related to rules of origin in the FTA and the NAFTA or other issues such as procurement practices, do have important if subtle implications for investment.

Niosi makes the interesting observation that Canada has done at least as well as the United States in attracting European investment since implementing the FTA — for which there are two competing explanations. On the one hand, if a European MNE anticipates that Canadian production will satisfy the FTA rules of origin, then a Canadian location may offer cost advantages over U.S. locations. On the other hand, if the production process resulting from the investment will not sufficiently transform the product to qualify under the rules of origin, then the higher Canadian tariff and the interim duty-drawback provisions in the FTA may offset the market access disadvantage of the smaller economy. In both cases, however, extra-regional investment may be induced into Canada and the United States in order to remain competitive with MNEs based within the FTA trading zone.

The contributions of Bergsten, Kudrle and Mayer serve to cast some doubt on whether NAFTA will be implemented — or to suggest, at least, that if NAFTA is implemented it will be implemented grudgingly by the United States Congress. Although Canada has already passed the implementing legislation, the results of the recent election make ultimate Canadian implementation equally uncertain. The issue is whether the postwar trend — toward economic integration through multilateral and regional initiatives to reduce trade barriers among the OECD economies, along with unilateral and regional initiatives to reduce barriers to investment — will be sustained. Bergsten's contribution underlines some of these uncertainties, referring on the one hand to the commitment of the Clinton administration to implementation of the NAFTA and the completion of the Uruguay Round, and referring on the other hand to the pressures for managed trade, which are especially intense because of the asymmetries in U.S.-Japan trade and investment relations. Bergsten argues that, beyond the Uruguay Round, investment and competition policy issues have to be brought into the trade regime on a regional and multilateral basis.

The Graham-Warner study explores a broad agenda for dealing with competition policy within North America. One facet of their proposals deals with competition policy along the lines adopted by the EC, which limits the use of subsidies. The other facet of their proposals is the replacement of antidumping laws with competition laws. This is an important element, which is deepening North American integration, and one which the Uruguay Round will not address; but achieving this goal could prove to be elusive until the macroeconomic and policy climate improves. However, political as well as economic considerations at present are likely to make it very difficult to negotiate much more than a refinement of the Uruguay Round rules for subsidies and countervailing duties in a North American context.

MACROECONOMIC POLICIES AND THE POLICY ENVIRONMENT

MULTINATIONAL SPECIALISTS, regardless of their discipline, tend to focus on microeconomic factors and firm strategies as the key determinants of MNE behaviour. Macroeconomic policy is, nonetheless, relevant to multinationals and is likely to influence the evolution of MNEs within North America if for no other reason than that macroeconomic policies influence interest rates and exchange rates. In this connection, I was struck by some of the quantitative data tabled by two discussants: Subi Rangan and Richard Wright. Both tended to suggest conclusions that exchange rate movements and capital flows do have important implications for, and influences on, both patterns of intrafirm trade and the patterns of foreign direct investment.

There are some basic macroeconomic facts we should all be aware of with respect to North America. Canada, the United States and Mexico are three large debtor countries. During the last decade the North American economies have absorbed a tremendous amount of capital inflows from the rest of the world. It is unlikely that this is going to go on forever. Indeed, these capital inflows are likely to slow and even reverse in the next decade, which implies significant reversals in trade flows and even in current account flows. Unless there is a sharp compression of imports in a Latin American style debt crisis, this implies greatly increased exports of goods and services from North America to the rest of the world. This potential shift in trade flows poses some interesting challenges in terms of both access for trade and access for investment to offshore markets. Increased investment links will be needed as the conduits of this reversal of trade and current account flows.

Macroeconomic policy influences interest rates and exchange rates, which in turn influence MNE strategies. It also acts directly to influence the trade and investment policy climate. For example, if, by the mid- to late-1990s, the U.S. economy achieves a rough balance in its current account and an overall surplus in trade in goods and services, and the economy is operating at high employment levels, then its international trade policies generally, and its remaining bilateral trade deficit with Japan (specifically), will be less contentious at least in the United States. This benign scenario assumes sustained non-inflationary growth in the OECD economies after the global recession of 1990-93 and that the United States successfully reduces its budget deficit during the recovery. (Of course, the U.S. government may be even less responsive than the Big Three automobile companies were to their "window of opportunity" and fail to achieve convergence with

Japanese macroeconomic policy of higher savings and lower deficits.)
Canadian governments face similar challenges in reducing budget deficits and
improving competitiveness.

OTHER POLICIES

AT THE MARGIN THERE IS ALWAYS scope for clever targeted policies. Richard
Lipsey has made the observation that policy matters most when regulators
know least. On this note, there is wisdom in these papers to pass along to policy
makers that should be given *ex ante* rather than *ex post*.

Technology policies and national security restrictions could become
major sources of friction in the future. Frost and Graham and Kudrle address
the issues of how economic security may be perceived by the United States
and how those changing perceptions (and resulting changes in U.S.
investment policy) might influence the way in which the investment climate
evolves in the United States, Canada and Mexico. A set of closely related
issues pertains to technology policies and the treatment of investment in
policies designed to support the development of critical technologies and the
development of government-industry research consortia.

Some of the environmental issues addressed by Mayer are important (or
are perceived to be more important) in a more integrated economy. If NAFTA
proceeds, the accords on environment and labour cooperation are likely to
promote more effective cooperation among the three governments. This
laudable goal of the side agreements was diverted by opponents to the NAFTA
to put "teeth" into these agreements in the form of trade sanctions. Canada
resisted these proposals so in the end the trade sanctions apply only to Mexico
and the United States. Between Canada and the United States, the enforcement
of environmental laws still relies upon recourse to the national courts. (In this
connection it is also worth noting with respect to the activities of MNEs that
U.S. law still has a long extra-territorial reach on environmental and other
issues, under statutes ranging from the *Foreign Corrupt Practices Act* to the
liability of directors under shareholders' remedies.)

Early in this volume, Vernon suggests that MNEs may support the
deepening of integration under the NAFTA and the development of more
formal supranational institutions. Much of the populist opposition to the
NAFTA in Canada and the United States appears to be based on the fear of
economic losses from integration and loss of sovereignty to the "corporate
agenda". Both these fears may be unwarranted. Most (but not all) of the
contributors reject the fears of economic losses from integration; and Mayer
suggests that the side agreements on Labour and the Environment and the
development of supranational institutions in the NAFTA might well serve the
interests of the three states in reasserting their authority over the economic
space of North America.

SOME CLOSING OBSERVATIONS

EUROPEAN INTEGRATION HAS BEEN DESCRIBED as a process of two steps forward, one step backward. Similarly, the pace and rhythm of North American integration remains uncertain at this point. In the extreme, rejection of the NAFTA by the United States will have the greatest short-term impact on Mexico. However, outright rejection or ambivalent, half-hearted implementation by the U.S. Congress could signal a deeper populist reaction to the pressures of globalization and a resurgence of protectionism, which would bode ill for Canada-U.S. economic relations. Also, nationalist reactions by Canada and Mexico cannot be discounted as threats to the integration process. Whatever the source of difficulty, if there are setbacks in North American integration these will have an adverse effect on both Canada and Mexico by making them less attractive for investment purposes..

Of course, the attractiveness of Canada and Mexico to investment by home-grown firms, and by American and offshore MNEs, will be influenced by a wide range of national policies. Some of the populist critics of integration fear that the NAFTA will impose constraints on national policies that are contrary to the interest of the citizens. On the contrary, whether national policy is investor-friendly or not, investment as such — including outward as well as inward — is an effective indicator of whether national policy is serving the long-term welfare of the citizenry.

Alan B. Nymark
Assistant Deputy Minister
Industry and Science Policy
Industry Canada

Rapporteur's Comment

THIS SECTION OF THE Rapporteurs' comments focuses on the policy implications raised at the Conference on Multinationals in North America. Considering the role played by the investment decisions of MNEs in the economic development of Canada, the policy discussions at the Conference are of genuine importance.

Here, I address the policy issues under five headings: the general implications of globalization; the stability of the NAFTA (i.e., what is happening to regional integration); the future for international negotiations on investment issues; the implications for locational decisions; and, the direct policy implications for Canada's microeconomic agenda.

GLOBALIZATION

GLOBALIZATION DID NOT BEGIN YESTERDAY and it will not end tomorrow; it is an ongoing, incremental process. A number of the papers point out the changing nature of the globalization process. Notably, decreased transportation costs and improved communications have allowed the exchange of goods and services to be complemented to a much higher degree by the integration of production across national boundaries. Foreign direct investment (FDI) led the process of integration in the 1980s, and will probably continue to do the same for much of the 1990s.

MNEs are, obviously, the principal actors in this process. The paper by Encarnation traces a common evolutionary path that characterizes the FDI and trade strategies of MNEs. Clearly, by linking their FDI with their trade strategies, multinationals are able to exert a sizeable influence over international commerce. Many speakers at the Conference pointed out how important it is for MNEs to be located in major markets. Speakers also talked about how the issues of trade, investment and (although mentioned less often) technology are interrelated within individual firms, and the importance of those interrelationships in achieving their strategic interests. While there were clear lessons for MNEs and globalization at this Conference, responses of nation states to the new global environment were less often discussed.

In policy terms, a few general observations can be made. The first is that the trend in the 1980s, when governments consciously reduced their role in the marketplace, may continue for much of the 1990s — if for no other reason than that there is only limited fiscal room for governments to manoeuvre. However, more activist experimentation may well emerge from time to time. The paper by Rugman and D'Cruz argues that a "flagship" firm, competing in global markets, has four potential partners to assist in its endeavours. One of these partners is the government sector. While the strategic management of the business network continues to reside in the "flagship" firm, in this scenario the government essentially plays a supporting role to major MNEs. My expectations are that government institutions, like the operations of MNEs, are still evolving, and that the coming years will see much re-engineering on the part of governmental institutions.

The second implication is that while domestic policy is becoming increasingly internationalized, international policy is, increasingly, directed toward domestic policy. MNEs are leaders in the movement toward ever greater interdependence between countries. Such interdependence means that countries can no longer afford significant divergences between their domestic and international economic policies. As MNEs continue to shift their operations between countries, differences in regulatory systems will become even more important as a determinant of plant location and expansion. These divergences between countries are at the root of the call for the international convergence of microeconomic policies.

I found it interesting that a general theme at this Conference has been that governments should not play a strong role in the process of harmonization; rather, businesses, in pursuit of their own interests, may provide the appropriate impetus to harmonization. I do not want to give the impression, however, that I believe governments should simply step back and do nothing with regard to globalization. Government policy must be allowed to evolve. Fred Bergsten, I think, is right when he states that the lack of investment rules will likely move investment issues to the forefront of a post-Uruguay round agenda. The massive surge of FDI over the last decade now makes it imperative that investment rules dealing with issues such as national treatment, market access, and transparency, be formulated. Sylvia Ostry also addressed the same issue. While the GATT continues to examine limited restrictions to trade in the TRIMs (Trade Related Investment Measures) exercise, this essentially deals with past problems. To reflect properly what is happening today, the focus should be changed from the effect of investment measures on trade, to the effect of trade measures on investment (Investment Related Trade Measures, or IRTMs).

Outward direct investment constitutes another area where government policy needs to evolve. Like most other countries, Canada has traditionally had policies with regard to inward direct investment. There have, however, been few policies concerning outward direct investment. Should Canada be supporting investments by Canadian businesses in other countries? Does foreign investment in other countries promote exports and employment in the home country, or do foreign affiliates curtail Canadian exports? Just to assure you that we are thinking of these issues, the topic of the fourth volume in this Research Series is Canadian direct investment abroad.

STABILITY OF THE NAFTA

IN MY OPENING STATEMENT at this Conference, I expressed the hope that the speakers would not put too much emphasis on the NAFTA. The purpose of this Conference is much broader than the NAFTA — it is to examine the decision-making processes of MNEs in North America, and to determine how regional integration will affect the locational decisions of these businesses. Nevertheless, since the NAFTA and the FTA have been a major part of our discussions, I would like to say a few words about them.

For Canada, the Free Trade Agreement was truly an historic step forward in the evolution of Canadian policy towards globalization. It provided Canadian companies with the opportunity to compete with U.S. companies on a more level playing field. The NAFTA takes the evolution of Canadian policy a step further — a shorter step than the first, but still a very important one.

The question "how will the NAFTA evolve in the future?" has been asked several times at this Conference. While a number of important steps are still necessary before the NAFTA becomes a reality, the document itself does provide certain clues as to future directions. First, there is the accession clause, which sets out the possibility of other countries joining the NAFTA. Significantly, it does not specify what countries might join the NAFTA. While countries such as Chile are often mentioned as possible candidates, there is also the possibility that countries beyond the Western hemisphere may be included. This points up the need to answer a number of policy questions — not the least of which is whether we should attempt to engage the Asian-Pacific countries directly through the instrument of the NAFTA? With the question of country accession left open, the NAFTA raises numerous possibilities.

Second, the NAFTA includes a large number of exceptions. Any reduction of these exceptions would be of real benefit to businesses in all three countries. Nonetheless, the exceptions in the NAFTA are a clear indication of the political difficulties experienced by the member countries in agreeing to liberalization in certain sectors. While the idea of working to reduce the number of exceptions is admirable, it is unlikely that many exceptions will be removed in the near future. The probability of the United States removing its exemption for the maritime industry, or giving up its national security review mechanism, is remote — at best.

Third, it is possible that the scope of the NAFTA could be supplemented. The paper by Edward Graham and Mark Warner, dealing with competition policy, argues that what might be needed in North America is a supranational authority to issue court enforceable decrees. While I am not sure that the three North American governments are ready to consider such a major step, the present NAFTA contains only a whisper about competition policy. The important and exciting work being done in international forums on competition policy reinforce the idea that more could have been included in the NAFTA.

There has been less discussion on technology policy at this Conference than I hoped for. The emergence of "technology consortia" or cooperative research ventures, where the focus is on pre-competitive research, has disturbing possibilities. Such consortia can have positive benefits, such as the formation of a critical mass, possible synergies through interdisciplinary participants, and the visibility and long-term nature of such ventures. However, the notion of governments introducing policies to deny access to consortia by foreign companies, even foreign companies located in the host country, gives cause for concern. I believe that technology policy and technology protectionism will be critical issues in the future.

NEGOTIATION OF INTERNATIONAL INVESTMENT AGREEMENTS

THE THIRD SET OF ISSUES concerns the negotiation of future international investment agreements. This is complicated, but important. My own experience in the NAFTA suggests that we may well have reached the limits of applying general principles, such as national treatment, to the remaining barriers. Except for the slight liberalization of the *Investment Canada Act* in the FTA and the NAFTA, neither Canada nor the United States removed any significant barriers to investment in the negotiations. There is no reason to believe this will change in the near future.

Effective market access for capital will be a critical issue for future negotiations. Major limitations on effective access now come from informal barriers. Informal barriers, by definition, are less transparent and hence are less amenable to negotiated reduction or elimination. Examples of policies and practices that can be considered informal barriers include: government-business or commercial-financial linkages, which tend to make hostile take-overs difficult; and state enterprises or highly regulated monopolies, which tend to reduce greatly the proportion of a country's economic base that is effectively open to foreign, or even private domestic, investment.

Some other issues might also be on the agenda in this type of negotiation. For example, the national security restrictions now being employed by some countries are a real worry. Ellen Frost and Edward Graham, in their paper on MNEs and national security, argue that national security concerns are rapidly becoming economic security concerns. A large part of the problem is that there is, at present, no internationally agreed-upon definition for national security. In the absence of such a definition, the United States is free to define unilaterally any perceived threat to its national security.

The paper by Frost and Graham, however, raises an interesting policy issue. With all the G7 countries *except Canada* claiming the authority to block or limit FDI inflows on national security grounds, should Canada not have the same authority?

Another issue we in Canada take very seriously is extraterritoriality. The application of laws or policies by a country outside its own jurisdiction has, unfortunately, already been applied to Canada by the United States. The trend toward increasing economic interdependence between our two countries makes it essential that there be a solid foundation of international agreement on the extraterritorial application of laws.

IMPLICATIONS FOR LOCATIONAL DECISIONS

MOST OF WHAT HAS BEEN SAID at our Conference about the fourth set of issues — implications for MNE locational decisions — leads me to believe the future is very uncertain in this regard. Vernon suggests a number of factors that will influence MNEs in making their location decisions — such as economies of scale and new technologies. However, he then went on to request that we not ask him what is going to happen, or where MNEs are going to locate, because the future is unclear. That, however, was the fundamental question of the Conference: "where" will MNEs locate "what" activities?

Participating in this Conference are internationally-renowned experts on the operations of both foreign and domestic multinationals. Also, each author, in one way or another, touches on those issues that will shape the North American structure of production and its location in the foreseeable future. I think it is fair to say that more questions have been raised than answered.

One of the most topical issues raised at this Conference had to do with the possibility of companies locating in Mexico, attracted by low wages and the lack of a strict environmental regime. The likelihood of this happening was discounted by speaker after speaker. The paper by Mayer provided an illustration of what can happen when business overreacts to the perceived opportunities in Mexico. The furniture industry in California, in response to lax environmental conditions in Mexico, re-located to Mexico. However, in anticipation of the NAFTA, Mexico greatly strengthened both its environmental regulations, and its enforcement of those regulations. Most of the furniture industry has since re-located back to California.

The question of Japanese investment in North America was addressed in the paper by Westney. The question for Canada, of course, is how to carve out a recognized niche for itself in terms of location strategies of Japanese MNEs. Although the Japanese economy is currently experiencing difficulties, some of which are reflected in the down-turn in the level of Japanese investment abroad, I am among those who believe that both the Japanese economy and Japanese investment will rebound strongly within a few years.

DIRECT POLICY IMPLICATIONS FOR CANADA'S MICROECONOMIC AGENDA

INVESTMENT IS A CRITICAL FACTOR in economic growth and job creation. It should surprise no one, therefore, that we are constantly searching for microeconomic policies that have the greatest positive impact on the investment climate in Canada.

Given the kind of information that has been brought to the table at this Conference, should we now be looking at our human capital and R&D policies differently than we did before the Conference? Is there any particular relationship between public infrastructure and competitiveness because of MNEs and the way they behave? Are MNEs attracted more to certain kinds of public infrastructure than to others?

Once we have levelled the playing field for our MNEs (as we have been aggressively doing over the last decade) how do we deal with the fact that major subsidies remain in the U.S. system? Can or should the Canadian government compete with the U.S. Treasury? Obviously, we need rules between countries.

What role is there for governments to negotiate with large MNEs? Is there any need for the old concepts of a Code of Conduct for MNEs being revived? I do not necessarily mean a written government-inspired Code of Conduct, but rather a code that the private sector adopts and uses between branch plants and head offices in particular. A voluntary model already exists within the Canadian chemical industry, which has developed its own Code of Conduct for environmental self-regulation.

What role is there for Canadian subsidiaries? Forty-five percent of the Canadian manufacturing sector is foreign-owned and many of these subsidiaries are already undergoing massive restructuring. Canadian managers are searching for new roles, and working out new and effective ways to deal with their head offices. As they strive to prove their capabilities and demonstrate their competitiveness, they run into such problems as lack of access to comparative data on the competitiveness of other company plants. So, even when there is supposedly a level playing field, internal institutional barriers can still affect the ability of a subsidiary to compete.

CONCLUSIONS

IDEAS AND CIRCUMSTANCES EVOLVE. People such as Ray Vernon and Ed Safarian must marvel at the evolution of transnational corporations and the extent to which governments today are receptive to them. For the past decade, multinational enterprises have led the process of globalization. The exchange of goods and services once dominated the process of international integration. This is no longer the case. Where simple trade once dominated integration, there is now a complex network of production across boundaries, much of which is tied directly to the process of innovation.

What are the prospects for this new form of integration, and will it lead to enhanced growth? Some speakers have suggested that the financial and physical aspects of investment are the least important and that it is, rather, the accompanying ideas and human capital that are the critical components of investment. Virtually all governments, in both the developed and developing worlds, have come to recognize the value of investment. That is why the climate for investment in Canada must compete with the climate for investment in other countries. How a government goes about creating the appropriate climate to attract, retain and develop investments is the essence of an economic policy with a central focus on productivity growth.

Precisely what part does the firm — as an institution — play in this process? Are some forms of MNEs more conducive to the public interest than others? While the current mood internationally is to accept and, indeed, to welcome MNEs as principal actors in the globalization game, what is the appropriate role for governments? Are they to remain unconcerned, passive players? This question is especially important as investment-led integration can affect a government's microeconomic strategies, including competition policy, technology policy and human capital policies. Indeed, the question also bears on the country's broader national interests.

I would like to thank all the authors and participants at this Conference dealing with MNEs in North America. While there were few policy conclusions reached during the Conference, this was, perhaps, to be expected. What did emerge, however, were numerous policy ideas which should be pursued.

About the Contributors

C. Fred Bergsten is Director of the Institute for International Economics in Washington, DC.

Joe R. D'Cruz is Associate Professor of Strategic Management at the University of Toronto and Adjunct Professor at the IMEDE in Switzerland.

John H. Dunning is Emeritus Professor of International Business at the University of Reading and State of New Jersey Professor of International Business at Rutgers University.

B. Curtis Eaton is Professor of Economics at Simon Fraser University and an Associate of the Canadian Institute for Advanced Research.

Lorraine Eden is Professor of International Affairs at The Norman Paterson School of International Affairs, Carleton University.

Dennis J. Encarnation is Associate Professor at the Graduate School of Business Administration, Harvard University.

Ellen Frost is Counsellor to the U.S. Trade Representative in Washington, DC.

Edward M. Graham is Senior Fellow at the Institute for International Economics in Washington, DC.

John Knubley is Director of Strategic Investment Analysis, Micro-Economic Policy Analysis, Industry and Science Policy at Industry Canada.

Bruce Kogut is Professor of Management at the Wharton School of the University of Pennsylvania.

Robert Thomas Kudrle is Associate Dean for Research at the Hubert Humphrey Institute of Public Affairs and Director of the Orville and Jane Freeman Center in International Economic Policy.

Marc Legault is an Economist in Strategic Investment Analysis, Micro-Economic Policy Analysis, Industry and Science Policy at Industry Canada.

Richard G. Lipsey FRSC, OC is Professor of Economics at Simon Fraser University and Alcan Fellow of the Canadian Institute for Advanced Research.

Christopher J. Maule is Visiting Fellow at the Research School of Social Sciences, Economics Program, Australian National University, and Professor of Economics and International Affairs, Carleton University.

Frederick W. Mayer is Assistant Professor of Public Policy Studies at the Terry Sanford Institute of Public Policy, Duke University.

Jorge Niosi is Professor, Department of Management Science, Université du Québec à Montréal, where he is also Director of the Centre de recherche en développement industriel et technologique (CREDIT).

Alan B. Nymark is Assistant Deputy Minister, Industry and Science Policy, Industry Canada.

Sylvia Ostry FRSC, OC is Chairman of the Centre for International Studies at the University of Toronto.

Someshwar Rao is Senior Corporate Economist in Strategic Investment Analysis, Micro-Economic Policy Analysis, Industry and Science Policy at Industry Canada.

Alan M. Rugman is Professor of International Business at the University of Toronto.

A. Edward Safarian FRSC is Professor of Business Economics in the Faculty of Management, University of Toronto, Senior Fellow of the Centre for International Studies and an Associate of the Canadian Institute for Advanced Research.

Murray G. Smith is Director of the Centre for Trade Policy and Law, Carleton University and the University of Ottawa.

Kurt Unger is Director of Academic Affairs at the Centro de Investigación y Docencia Económicas (CIDE) in Mexico City.

Raymond Vernon is the Clarence Dillon Professor of International Affairs Emeritus and the Herbert F. Johnson Professor of International Business Management Emeritus of Harvard University.

Mark A. A. Warner is an Associate in the Washington DC office of the international law firm, Curtis, Mallet-Prevost, Colt & Mosle.

D. Eleanor Westney is Associate Professor of Management in the Corporate Strategy and International Management group at the M.I.T. Sloan School of Management.